Understanding Gandhi

Understanding Gandhi

A Mahatma in the Making

1869 - 1914

By

Sarva Daman Singh

Vij Books India Pvt Ltd

New Delhi (India)

Published by

Vij Books India Pvt Ltd
(Publishers, Distributors & Importers)
2/19, Ansari Road
Delhi – 110 002
Phones: 91-11-43596460, 91-11-47340674
Fax: 91-11-47340674
e-mail: vijbooks@rediffmail.com
www.vijbooks.com

Copyright © 2018, *Sarva Daman Singh*

ISBN: 978-93-86457-84-4 (Hardback)
ISBN: 978-93-86457-83-7 (Paperback)
ISBN: 978-93-86457-85-1 (ebook)

All rights reserved.

No part of this book may be reproduced, stored in a retrieval system, transmitted or utilised in any form or by any means, electronic, mechanical, photocopying, recording or otherwise, without the prior permission of the copyright owner. Application for such permission should be addressed to the publisher.

In Sacred Memory of

My Grandfather
Kunwar Hukam Singh of Angai
Great Educationist, Philanthropist and
Social Reformer

And

My Father
Kunwar Jaidev Singh of Angai
Who taught me English,
and instilled in me
Abiding respect for Gandhi

Contents

Acknowledgements		xi
Introduction		1
Chapter 1 –	Familial Heritage: Cultural Conditioning	35
Chapter 2 –	In England: New Horizons	52
Chapter 3 –	Back Home in India	75
Chapter 4 –	In South Africa	83
Chapter 5 –	The Voyage	85
Chapter 6 –	Proselytizing Push of Christianity	95
Chapter 7 –	Indians in Pretoria	98
Chapter 8 –	The Lawyer	102
Chapter 9 –	Spiritual Quickening	106
Chapter 10 –	Persuaded to Prolong His Stay in South Africa	110
Chapter 11 –	The Indian Response	113
Chapter 12 –	Gandhi Stays On	117
Chapter 13 –	The Natal Indian Congress	120
Chapter 14 –	Inhumanity of Indenture	122
Chapter 15 –	A Lesson Learned	126
Chapter 16 –	Immersion in Comparative Religion	130

Chapter 17 –	Gandhi's Household	132
Chapter 18 –	Public Service and the Practice of Law	134
Chapter 19 –	India	136
Chapter 20 –	The Roving Publicist	141
Chapter 21 –	To South Africa	145
Chapter 22 –	Gandhi Settles Down	152
Chapter 23 –	The Gṛhastha (Householder)	156
Chapter 24 –	Spirit of Public Service	162
Chapter 25 –	Brahmacarya (Sexual Abstinence)	168
Chapter 26 –	Gandhis Return Home	172
Chapter 27 –	Calcutta and the Congress	175
Chapter 28 –	Banaras	181
Chapter 29 –	In Bombay Again	183
Chapter 30 –	In South Africa Again	187
Chapter 31 –	Life in Johannesburg	190
Chapter 32 –	Statement of Faith in Human Equality	192
Chapter 33 –	Spiritual Striving	194
Chapter 34 –	Indian Opinion	199
Chapter 35 –	Earth and Water Cures	203
Chapter 36 –	European Friends	206
Chapter 37 –	Coolie Locations and the Plague	212
Chapter 38 –	Indian Opinion: Phoenix Settlement	231
Chapter 39 –	Return of Kasturba	234
Chapter 40 –	Inroads upon Indian Livelihood	240

Chapter 41 –	Evolution of Ideas	244
Chapter 42 –	The Zulu Rebellion	248
Chapter 43 –	Brahmacarya (Celibacy)	251
Chapter 44 –	Mokṣa (Salvation)	262
Chapter 45 –	Tram Cars	265
Chapter 46 –	Return to Johannesburg	267
Chapter 47 –	The Civil Rights Campaigner	269
Chapter 48 –	Kallenbach	292
Chapter 49 –	Back at Work: To Satyāgraha	296
Chapter 50 –	Fortitude of Kasturba	317
Chapter 51 –	Towards a Union of South Africa	321
Chapter 52 –	Flagging Satyāgraha	323
Chapter 53 –	London	329
Chapter 54 –	Henry Polak in India	341
Chapter 55 –	Hind Swaraj: Collision of Cultures	344
Chapter 56 –	Gandhi Returns	369
Chapter 57 –	Indentured Labour for Natal	374
Chapter 58 –	The Transvaal Satyāgraha	377
Chapter 59 –	Self-Restraint	388
Chapter 60 –	The Travails of Satyāgraha	392
Chapter 61 –	The Parting of Ways: Harilal	399
Chapter 62 –	Life on Tolstoy Farm	405
Chapter 63 –	Satyāgrahīs	411
Chapter 64 –	Gokhale's Visit	414

Chapter 65 –	Return to Phoenix	423
Chapter 66 –	Betrayal	426
Chapter 67 –	Crisis at Phoenix	436
Chapter 68 –	Death of Rev. Joseph Doke: Declaration of Passive Resistance	440
Chapter 69 –	The Scene	442
Chapter 70 –	Negotiations and the 'Final Settlement'	476
Chapter 71 –	Farewell Meetings	488
Chapter 72 –	Gandhi, the Africans and the British	498
Chapter 73 –	Ahiṁsā, Satya and Brahmacarya	506
Chapter 74 –	Steps to Sainthood: Uneasy Birth of a Mahatma	512
Chapter 75 –	Postscript: Relevance of Gandhi	527
Glossary of Indian Words		531
Select Bibliography		535
Index		543

Acknowledgements

My friend Dr. Maha Sinnathamby asked me to write this book on Mahatma Gandhi, whom we both admire as a messiah of religious amity, Hindu-Muslim unity, and the familial indivisibility of humanity. I am grateful for his constant interest, help and gentle urging, which spurred me into some sustained writing.

The second person, whose merciless goading has often jolted me out of recurring bouts of listless lassitude to reapply myself to researching and writing, is my dear wife Kumud! She even typed the 'Introduction'; and the credit for the belated completion of this book belongs to her.

I am also grateful to Professor Goolam Vahed of South Africa, who came to see me at the Indian Consulate in Brisbane; and presented me a copy of his book *Inside Indenture*. His work gave me new insights into the plight of indentured Indians in South Africa.

Thanks are due to Dr. Navras J. Aafreedi, Assistant Professor, Department of History, Presidency University, Kolkata, for helping me with some important references.

I must also put on record my gratitude to Dr. Mark Loane, who restored my vision to enable all this research and writing! My daughters-in-law, I always call them daughters, Archana and Sangeeta helped with the typing; and my grandchildren Shiromani, Anshuman and Sarvashree gladly lent me their computer skills to bring the book to its finished form. To them all, I am most grateful.

I am sincerely beholden to my brother-in-law Colonel Vijay K. Singh, VSM, for painstakingly proof-reading the text; and for introducing me to Brigadier P. K. Vij and his son Rohan, my publishers. To them both, I am grateful for bringing out the book with expeditious care.

Sarva Daman Singh

(Sarva Daman Singh)

Jaigarh,
211 Sugars Road,
Anstead, Brisbane,
Queensland, 4070
Australia

Introduction

There are countless books on Mahatma Gandhi written by his admirers and detractors; by his followers and foes; by his colleagues and contemporaries caught in the conflict for India's freedom; by politicians, statesmen, and sentinels of colonial control; by historians and self-appointed arbiters of right and wrong. And there are thousands of essays and articles on his life and work, which is indeed as it should be. But so much of British writing is vitiated by an ineradicable prejudice against the man who came to symbolize the unequivocal rejection of imperial exploitation; and a categorical refutation of its false morality. So much of the Muslim writing fails to rise above the narrowness and intolerance of those who turned a blind eye to the composite unity of Hindu-Muslim India with its enduring ethnic, linguistic and cultural links, in running after the mirage of a Muslim millennium. Happiness, however, never arises out of hatred. Nations do not derive their validity from one religion to the exclusion of others; from philosophies that divide humanity on the basis of dogmatic aversion towards people following faiths other than one's own.

Fanatical Hindu writers, disavowing the Hindu spirit of tolerance and peaceful coexistence with other faiths, call Gandhi a mad man who was bent on wrecking their world, their immediate present as well as their future. Possessed by hatred, blinded by bigotry, impelled by the suicidal fever of religious rancour, a so-called Hindu saw it fit to murder Gandhi. Gandhi was seventy-nine. Exactly at that age today, I distinctly remember the darkness of despair that engulfed India and the world; the searing grief that smote countless hearts; the tears I shed as a young school-boy; and the sense of disconsolate desolation that gripped me. Sadly, I could not attend his funeral. His memory, though, and what he stood for, forms part of my consciousness and sense of relationship with India and the world.[1]

---

1 I wrote this when I was 79, in 2013.

A vast majority of humankind pray every day. We never tire of praying. In that spirit of prayer, indeed, as its extension, we should never tire of studying the lives of great men and women whose work on earth expressed a higher will and purpose; who lived and laboured, suffered and sacrificed for the benefit of the whole world; to relieve its distress; to assuage its anxieties; to right its wrongs. So it is that I make bold to write another book on Gandhi as I see him; to restate and re-emphasize our singular obligation to translate his dream of Hindu–Muslim unity into reality. Despair is an admission of defeat. Inaction is not an option. We must never cease to try.

He lived and died in his pursuit of peaceful coexistence amongst different religions; of basic morality transcending all doctrinal divisions; of human equality and freedom from political servitude; of social and economic justice. He remained, till his last breath, an invincible exemplar of non-violence governing all human behaviour, rejecting the resolution of any disputes by recourse to violence.

Fickle memory of the world's millions only fitfully recalls his name, forgetting his struggles and willing suffering for freedom, justice and equality, and for an end to hatred, violence and tyranny. Creeping amnesia and easy bellicosity consign his message of non-violence and love for even one's enemies to a category of inconsequential irrelevance. The world trembles only temporarily in its apathetic repose; takes note, and marches on, with minimal influence on its mode of conduct. Transience rules, unless one chooses to give one's message the garb of religion; declares oneself a prophet of God; and commands obedience. When that happens, one's followers demand conformity; and the paraphernalia of religious organization and propaganda assurers the continuity and currency of one's message, though it stays confined only to one's converts. It defeats the desire for universality, given other religious persuasions and their own jealous domains, but remains nevertheless able and alive to influence its followers. Religious creeds with their exclusive claims to heaven and happiness tend to divide and seldom unite bickering humanity. But their longevity defies the secular prophets of love and peace, whose words and deeds are easily, but so sadly, always forgotten. So many amongst us sincerely strive to liberate ourselves from the shackles of constrictive religion, but we tend only to remember the prophets of religion!

Hence the recurring need to jog our memories, and remind ourselves. The dream of Gandhi corresponds with the reality of human indivisibility;

Introduction

God's love for entire creation; and the infinite capacity of humankind to advance towards perfection. His ideals inspire and invite humanity to rise to its full potential, to bring to this earth the kingdom of heaven, to enable the meek, without discrimination, to inherit this planet. He himself spoke and wrote with an indefatigable zeal, for there was so much to do; time was so short; and life was not everlasting. To understand Gandhi, we have to trudge though a hundred volumes of his own collected works including his autobiography; and thousands of others dealing with his life and thought. Monumental biographies by Tendulkar and Pyarelal, besides so many more, add to the abundance of material, from which I hope to glean the essence of Gandhi's truth.

Gandhi equates truth with God. What is truth? How do we realize it? How do we define it? How do we express it? And what is untruth? So many of our beliefs and convictions are just beliefs sustained by faith, not susceptible of proof. All religion besides morality rests on speculation. One's faith is one's truth, the other's faith an untruth. Hence the destructive inter-religious conflicts. To Richard Dawkins and many like him religion is a lie; dogma is a delusion; God is a figment of the imagination. How does one prove a truth? How does one live a truth? The only way we may constructively construe truth is to identify it with thought, word and deed to mean what they intend to convey and to achieve, to address the ills and suffering of this world and seek to heal them. There can be no absolutism, no inflexibility, no fixity about this truth, just as there can be no rigidity about what is right or wrong in varying circumstances. The only other way we may realize the truth or the reality of our existence and its meaning is to look around and then inwards to comprehend the core of our being and relate it to the world. To define it and reduce it to words is to deny it, to limit it, to distort it. All revelations are subjective and relative, if they are put into words, reduced to articles of faith or formulas for emancipation. The only acceptable idea of truth is that of the unity of all existence including that of humankind, and therefore, our identification with the needs of the world around us. In so far as we help fulfil those needs in a spirit of justice and fair play, we serve the truth of life. That was Gandhi's Truth as I understand it, shorn of its esoteric content; and that was the truth he saw in all the religions of the world.

In his own words, 'truth means existence; the existence of that we know and of that we do not know. The sum total of all existence is absolute truth or the truth... The concepts of truth may differ. But all admit and respect truth. That truth I call God.'² '.....He, who would sacrifice his life for others, has hardly time to reserve for himself a place in the sun.'³

Gandhi calls his autobiography *The story of My Experiments with Truth*. What does he mean? Does he want to state the truth or interpret it, dilute it, stretch it, add to it or reduce it, colour it, or view it in varying lights? He certainly tries to be honest and truthful, to the point at times of brutal candour. But in the middle of his exercise, he suddenly exclaims: '... I have no diary or documents on which to base the story of my experiments. I write just as the Spirit moves me at the time of writing... I understand more clearly today what I read long ago about the inadequacy of all autobiography as history. I know that I do not set down in this story all that I remember. Who can say how much I must give and how much omit in the interests of truth? And what would be the value in a court of law of the inadequate *ex parte* evidence being tendered by me of certain events in my life?'⁴ Assailed by self-doubt, he asks if he should 'stop writing these chapters',⁵ but then declares: '... so long as there is no prohibition from the voice within, I must continue the writing.'⁶

We all know that memory is fickle, failing, limited, unreliable, inadvertently and sometimes deliberately altered, expunged or added to. An autobiography would find it exceedingly hard to be objective, as the self holds centre stage. It is unnecessary and impossible to submerge the self while referring to other actors and events. Subjectivity plays a principal part in the sifting of one's memory and material; in the imposition of a sequence; and in terms of emphasis. Prejudices persist; and like a teacher or preacher, every writer has a motive and a goal. If we believe that everything an author says is indeed verifiable, we might as well ask him or her to desist from the task. Gandhi is no exception. His veracity is not in question; but his memory and omission and selection of episodes would inevitably temper the tenor of truth.

---

2   Gora, *An Atheist with Gandhi*, Navajivan, 1951, p. 48

3   Gandhi, M.K., *India of My Dreams*, Rajpal, New Delhi, 2009, p. 66

4   Gandhi, M.K., *An Autobiography or The Story of My Experiments with Truth*, Navajivan Publishing House, Ahmedabad, 1959, p.206

5   *Ibid.,* p.207

6   *Ibid.*

INTRODUCTION

Gandhi uses the word 'truth' where he should often be using the word 'honesty', which is what he always seeks to pursue. Truth is always multi-dimensional, multi-faceted; a composite of thought, speech, action, experience, feeling and fact in its many manifestations. One who writes about truth, describes it as he sees it, as he hears it, as he experiences it, in his choice of words, also inevitably subjects it to the limitations and variations of language, influencing its meaning. Conscious or unconscious manipulation is a consequence of covert, clinging, involuntary subjectivity, however much we strive not to succumb to it. Truth is primarily *darśana*, one's perception based on one's experience and understanding, conditioned by one's intent and capacity to describe it, to reveal it, and one's choice of words to do so. The only part of our thinking subject to scrutiny is its resolution and expression in language.

We are awe-struck by Gandhi's capacity to identify himself with common humanity, completely so with the meek and the poor, and to inflict incalculable punishment on himself to atone for the errors and sins of his fellow beings. We admire his supreme solicitude for equity and justice, for common welfare, for peace and goodwill amongst all religions and all humankind. We applaud his implacable opposition to untouchability and social tyranny, and to all species of discrimination based on race, class, colour and gender. And we see his singular capacity to bend any opposition to his will by embarking on his epic life-threatening fasts.

Faith, belief and convictions, however, held the *Sanātanī* Hindu in their vice-like grip in more way than one, despite his rejection of so many immoral and indefensible, unjust, useless, meaningless and harmful practices. He could not entirely free himself from the thraldom of the Brahmin, and trod very tentatively, carefully, to question his invidious practices, always taking extraordinary care not to challenge his supercilious supremacy. The caste, not the learning of the ordinary Brahmin, made him deferential. He even took up cudgels on their behalf in Maharashtra, when non-Brahmins protested against the degrading and demeaning indignities suffered at their hands.[7] In a way Gandhi was as subservient to the Brahmins as he was to the British. He rebelled against both, but accommodated both to the farthest limits of forbearance. One could equate his attitude towards the English with his stance towards the Brahmins. Their excesses, their

---

7 The Brahmins treated all non-Brahmins as śūdras. Cf. *Collected Works*, Volume 18, p.479

sins, their discrimination and exploitation of the populace, their cruel, inhuman treatment of the down-trodden untouchables, did not move him to challenge them and confront them in order to break the barriers of ugly separatism. He made statements, very strong statements! He identified himself with the untouchables. But he never made bold to lead them in any march to the portals of any temple. Persuasion by self-suffering, not even by full-fledged *satyāgraha*, excluding any help from other sections of society, was his advice and recipe for change. If mere persuasion was enough, if the expression of moral outrage was enough, if suffering could move the hearts of those feeding fat on credulity and submissive abidance of the Hindu society, untouchability would have disappeared long ago! Voices against the evils of caste and untouchability have rent the skies of India since time immemorial; but the Brahmins have not really been roused from their sleep. Softly, softly, was Gandhi's advice to the suppressed and oppressed! Suffer more, as if they had not suffered enough! Indeed, it took Gandhi a whole lifetime to liberate himself entirely from the mental prison of class and caste, *varṇa* and *jāti*, in Hindu society. We hope to see how he finally found the will to do so.

Gandhi was not born a *Mahātmā*[8], Great soul. He became a *Mahatma* in the eyes of Tagore, and all those who agreed with the poet's perception. If one looks for the *Mahatma* from the day Gandhi bursts into public view, one is bound to miss him, or look in vain. To do so is to deny his inner growth and evolution into the maturity of considered thought and action that earned him the title. The years before he was called one were an unremitting extended essay in self-analysis, self-discovery and self-expression in word and deed that revealed him as a *Mahatma*. It was a painful, protracted process of self- realization, and understanding the true relation of self to life and the world around. Even so, the title did not tickle the holder, who often felt oppressed by its baggage.

Thus we see so much in a long life full of feverish activity aimed at reforming human nature, religious attitudes and societies, empires and their rulers, as well as the ruled. We see his ceaseless struggle for justice and freedom from the tyranny of foreign rule; and for the establishment of regimes based on democracy, where small government and decentralization would empower the people to regulate their own affairs.

---

8 From now on, we shall not be adding any diacritical marks to the word Mahatma.

Introduction

No other politician ever received so much attention and acclaim in his own lifetime. Classed with Christ and Buddha, without ever seeking to make an enemy, he made it hard for many like Einstein to imagine 'that such a one as this, ever in flesh and blood, walked upon this earth.' There are those, too, who call him a mad man, a crafty crank, an intolerable impostor, a shrewd actor, a clever *bania* (his caste), a moral masochist.[9] But a palpable unease clearly colours their criticism.

Did Gandhi know himself? We are amazed by the curious display of both credulity and questioning in his speeches and writings. He was a delightful, if at times a maddening bundle of contradictions. Indeed, every person is so many selves rolled into one. So was Gandhi an amalgam of many selves, which came to the fore in ever changing contexts. He was always alive and evolving in his reaction and response to current and changing situations all around him. His self-professed inconsistency was a reflection of his malleability and capacity to adapt his attitude and stance to situations as they unfolded. Change is synonymous with relevance. Ossified, inelastic attitudes disregard the reality of life in its transition in relation to an untold variety of social, economic and political factors. New situations, new problems invite new solutions; new maladies require new remedies. Change of attitude or policy in Gandhi's case was always clearly comprehensible in the light of new developments, and justifiable in terms of possibilities, justice and fair play. Gandhi himself made a virtue of his inconsistencies: 'At the time of writing I never think of what I have said before. My aim is not to be consistent with previous statements on a given question, but to be consistent with truth as it may present itself to me at a given moment. The result has been that I have grown from truth to truth; I have saved my memory an undue strain; and what is more, whenever I have been obliged to compare my writing even of fifty years ago with the latest I have discovered no inconsistency between the two. But friends who observe inconsistency will do well to take the meaning that my latest writing may yield unless, of course, they prefer the old.'[10] But Gandhi's assertion of an 'abiding consistency between the two seeming inconsistencies' is not always true or sustainable.

---

9   cf. John Wyllie, *India at the Parting of the Ways*, Lincoln Williams, 1934, p.9; M. N. Roy, *Problem of freedom*, Renaissance, 1947, pp. 34-47

10 *Harijan*, Sep,1939

Even Gandhi's admirers and followers were often baffled, if not exasperated, by the suddenness of some of his decisions; by the reversal of some of his movements; by the mysterious content of his enigmatic pronouncements. We all know his insistence on right means to the right end, where he would never make a compromise. He has been likened to moral messiahs; to saints and prophets; and compared with philosophers and social reformers. He has been called an individualist, anarchist, socialist, communist, liberal, reactionary, revolutionary, a religious actualist, a nationalist, cosmopolitan and so on. He was all these, and more, as he had the uncanny capacity to reconcile seemingly irreconcilable points of view. Even though his ideas and concepts evolved in the rough and tumble of political and social struggles, in the context of specific problems confronting him, it would be wrong to examine them only in terms of expediency. *Satya*, *Ahiṁsā* and *Satyāgraha* were grounded in spiritual beliefs which inspired them, and forged as instruments of struggle for justice in relation to reality. Rightness of means to an end, as I have said before, was a matter for him of supreme concern; effectiveness was secondary, though he sincerely believed that *ahiṁsā* would always ultimately deliver.

He fought for human rights in South Africa with his new-fangled armour of *Satya*, *Ahiṁsā* and *Satyāgraha*, to defeat injustice and tyranny. And then, in India, he enlarged the scope of his non-violence and *satyāgraha* with the boycott of imported goods and textiles and the use of *swadeshī*, home-made cloth and products, to rouse the masses to struggle for freedom and self-government. He sought to convince India's imperial masters of the folly and moral bankruptcy of their ways, asking them to rise to their true stature of goodness, and do what honesty, humanity and justice called for. Monetary gain could not undo the uneasy realization at least amongst some Englishmen and women, and there were quite a few, that their policies and exploitative excesses did not exactly correspond with their ideals of love and justice.

How did he seek to overcome violence with non-violence, hatred with love, greed with generosity; to disarm apathy and aversion with appreciation and concern; to defeat prejudice with deference; to thwart separatism with affectionate accommodation? What were the specific tasks that he set for himself and his followers? How did he view humankind? What did he think of religion? How did he view the religions other than his own? What according to him was the function of government? What was the meaning of democracy? What did rights betoken? What was the burden of corresponding duties? What should education be like? What should the state provide? What should people do for themselves? What sort of economy should we sustain? What should be the relationship between man and machine? How should we take care of our health? What should the state do? What can we, and should do for ourselves? How should business be based on truth? How do we make the Hindu and Muslim love one another, live peacefully with one another, without letting the difference of religion poison personal relationships and understanding? How do we teach the followers of different religions that they all share aspects of the Ultimate Truth; and that all scriptures are equally valid for their followers? As Gandhi said, let us have dialogue; let us have understanding; and let us realize that morality in human behaviour is the true essence and application of religion.

We shall attempt to find answers to these questions from Gandhi himself. We know that his philosophy has been studied with sedulous care; and his ideas have been applied to the solution of social and political problems in different parts of the world. How much, if at all, do we still adhere to his message of brotherhood, service and non-violence? Do we just conjure up his name and not the content of his life's message? How much of his message, how many of his ideas are still relevant? Time changes, circumstances vary; unforeseen developments cry for ever new approaches. Some ideas are timeless in their validity for humanity, while others date with the passage of time. Reality is for ever in a state of flux; and adaptability signified by ever new approaches is the only guarantee of our common progress towards the greatest good of the greatest number. Life is not so much about personal happiness as it is about the happiness of others around us. Happiness is not exclusive; true happiness cannot be. It is always infectious as well as inclusive.

Gandhi's moral and political thought is inextricably interwoven with his religious beliefs and moral convictions. With his axiomatic acceptance of *karma* and reincarnation, he did not indulge in any other speculation in relation to the universe and man. He scoffed at the idea of 'Gandhism' as a cult, and said: '...If Gandhism is another name for sectarianism, it deserves to be destroyed... Let no one say that he is a follower of Gandhi. It is enough that I should be my own follower... You are no followers but fellow students, fellow pilgrims, fellow seekers, fellow workers.'[11]

---

11 *Harijan*, March 1940

He worried about people reducing his statements to a rigid tyranny of literal finality; and tirelessly stressed his fallibility. We want to confront and comprehend his fallibility despite his constant striving to commune with the Great Truth that is God. For, like us all, he too was made of common clay; he too was heir to many human frailties including the compulsions of the flesh, as attested by his lifelong struggle to rise above them.

Sex is the supreme truth of life, the most emphatic, positive, undeniable expression of the will to be and to live, an indefatigable challenge to our mortality. The tug of war goes on for ever. And the joy of sex mocks the pain and suffering of disease and death. As Yudhiṣṭhira observed in the *Mahābhārata*, we all know we will die; but who cares? That is doubtless the most amazing truth of life as we know it, as we love it! Sadly, the only word Gandhi knew about sex was unclean and impure 'lust'. He was unflagging in his search for truth. What and which truth? Denial of one does not lead to the discovery of another!

Sex has never been a synonym for sin in India. India's religions have explored sex as an instrument of ineffable joy and deliverance; as an exercise in the deletion of duality in oneness with the Creator and creation; as a celebration of life through love and belonging. The Hindus worship the *Liṅgaṁ* and *Yoni* in their union as the divine source of being and becoming. Tantrism translates sexual ecstasy into salvation. The exaltation of sex is an honest acceptance of life, its basic manifestation, its joyous expression! Hindu and Buddhist art alike express that truth; and reveal its unashamed fulfilment. The seers (*ṛṣis*) of ancient India were certainly not averse to approaches for *niyoga*[12] with the spouses of petitioning husbands.

The idea that sex somehow interferes with or defeats service to others does not carry conviction. The vast majority of the great men and women of the world, including the Incarnations of the Divine in India, have been married people in deep, active physical relationships with their wives and consorts; and in India they are always worshipped together. Vālmīki's *Rāmāyaṇa* provides pulsating expressions of Rāma's pent-up passion for his abducted wife, whom he misses so sorely![13] All this is, indeed, as it should be. All kind

---

12 Commission to have sexual intercourse for the limited purpose of producing progeny.

13 *Rāmāyaṇa, Araṇya,* 60. 13,18, 24; 62. 4, Paṇḍita Pustakālaya, Kāśī, 1951. Cf. My "Terracottas from Manwā-ḍīh", in Journal of the U.P. Historical Society,

and compassionate, loving and tender, charitable and merciful emotions arise from the life-force of sex coursing through our veins. Its extinction, or its cruel suppression might also emasculate altruism, which makes us higher beings than other animals. If one is to believe Freud and others, the suppression of sex may not lead to any sublimation, but only to a sense of despair, frustration and futility. Fulfilment produces a sense of quiet contentment; of tranquil repose; love and solicitude for one's world and its happiness. Gandhi's fulminations against sex run counter to life's natural flow; and pose a purposeless challenge to the order of existence. He read only parts of the existing Hindu tradition; chose what he deemed essential; and turned a blind eye to the rest that conflicted with his life-negating panacea. If we restrict or reject the fount of life, we deprive ourselves of so much that is dear, beautiful, and irreplaceable! The prophets had their spouses. They led full lives.

And Gandhi! He imposed sexual abstinence on his wife Kasturba from the age of thirty-six. Did he have her prior consent, and later, permission to tell the world? There is a species of violence of a peremptory will here; the enforcement of a code of conduct that may not attract natural or easily willing acceptance. Violence can express and exercise itself in so many subtle ways. Any fancied or real encroachment on others' will and others' desires leading to or compelling not only suppression, but the extinction thereof, may indeed be construed as a dictatorial violence of one's will over that of others. Even if the prescription and practice yield the most desirable results, do the ends justify the means?

As a husband and father, Gandhi was a dictator. In his role that was larger than life, one could understand him identifying himself with the world around, which was his family. But were his wife and children equal to the expectations and the tasks imposed on them? Did they have a choice? We may make a mistake in judging Gandhi by applying to him our current ideas and values governing marital and family relationships. His was a different world. And he was essentially a child of his Indian world despite his exposure to the West and its ideas. Every person without exception is a child of his or her times. Great human beings transcend their times, and often mould their times with the power of their example. But some of their attitudes and actions can be understood only with reference to the social milieu that shaped their sensibility and their set of values. They

---

Volume XVIII (N.S.), Parts 1-2, P. 3

were capable of change and striking out in new directions as Gandhi's life so amply demonstrated; but there were always limits, and the conditioning of the past influencing his behaviour!

Till the very end of her life, Kasturba was not simply Gandhi's wife, but his property. He completely controlled her. When she went to a temple in Puri that refused entry to untouchables, against his wishes, he was so angry that he became physically ill. During her last illness, he prohibited the administration of penicillin to save or prolong her life. Many years earlier in South Africa, he did not allow the doctor treating her to give her beef tea even when she was dangerously ill; and hovered between life and death. He took the barely alive bundle of her body with him from Durban to Phoenix and treated her with his own potions; and luckily, she survived. Religious fanaticism has so many forms, so many expressions! This was one, with Gandhi gambling with his wife's life on the altar of his blind faith and dietary interdictions. The denial of beef tea to save her life did not save the life of a single cow. Kasturba's hung in the balance, until her health was restored by kind Providence.

Are we right to surrender our freedom of action by subjecting ourselves to the tyranny of double-speaking texts! We blindly, habitually, slavishly uphold certain traditions, while dismissively discarding others. In doing so, we exercise the undeniable autonomy of our acceptance of tradition or its denial. But what really matters is the ethical propriety of our choice. If a person's life can be saved by beef tea or penicillin, how would it be ethical to refuse to have recourse to either? How can one refuse vaccinations against infectious diseases on moral grounds? How can one refuse surgical operations to relieve suffering and prolong life, except in a hide-bound state of mind? To be meaningful and relevant, morality must rise above any arbitrary fixity to correspond with the transient trials of the human predicament. Gandhi himself took medication when required, unaware of its derivative sources; and even underwent surgical operations for piles and appendicitis. Gandhi's relations with his family, wife and sons will certainly receive our attention in the pages that follow.

We do not worship or admire a *brahmacārī*. We do not believe, as Gandhi did, that love and sex in any way detract from a person's capacity, ability and will to participate in social work and *satyāgraha*, in political activism and engagement. A normal, active physical relationship between a couple does not in any way dry up their concern for the world around, or their devotion to the causes they are fighting for; or seek to serve. It does not make them callous or selfish. It does not promote apathy. It does not reduce their strength and dilute their contribution to any collective effort or public campaign. Quite on the contrary, its denial would lead to a kind of sullenness, aloofness, impatience, and an abrasive, angry outlook on life. Embers of smothered natural appetites would distract and damage one's evenness of temper, and undisturbed devotion to work. This sort of self-suppression is a painful denial of engagement with the real world around. It will not help. It will decidedly hinder. A study shows that a night of passion in the bedroom can boost people's performance at work by making their mood five per cent better the following day, despite any loss of sleep. The positive effect lingers for at least 24 hours in both men and women. The chemical dopamine released by the sexual function activates the reward-centres in the brain. Positive emotions add to the capacity to cope with work situations. The 'hug hormone' oxytocin released during sex to add to the closeness with one's partner lasts well into the morning, motivating greater concern for the people around. According to the lead author, Professor Keith Leavitt of Oregon State University, 'we make jokes about people having a 'spring in their step', but it turns out this is actually a real thing'.[14]

Gandhi was, as he said, a Hindu; and true to Hinduism, inherited its tolerance; its inclusiveness; its belief that there were many ways to God or Truth; and therefore its acceptance of the best in all religions. He was at once a *Vedāntin* monist and a seeker of God's grace: 'What I want to achieve – what I have been striving and pining to achieve...is self-realization, to see God face to face, to attain *Moksha*. I live and move and have my being in pursuit of this goal.'[15] The *Īśopaniṣad* revealed to him the essence of Hinduism as well as the spiritual basis of 'non-violent socialism'.[16] The *Gītā* became his 'dictionary of daily reference'.[17] He was a sincere and serious student of the world's religions, in which he discerned an unmistakable unity of truth. Jainism and Buddhism deeply

---

14 Reported in *Courier Mail*, Brisbane, March 9, 2017, p.14.

15 *Autobiography*, p. XIV. *Mokṣa* is synonymous with salvation.

16 Cf. *Harijan*, May, 1947

17 Cf. The *Bhagavad Gītā* according to Gandhi, translated by Mahadev Desai, Important Books, USA, 2013, p. 3

informed his thought. Christianity and its compassion touched him. The universalism of theosophy was 'Hinduism at its best.'[18]

Religion for Gandhi was inseparable from politics, in as much as it meant honest ethical action above and beyond divisive discrimination, like Emperor Aśoka's *dhamma* expressed in compassion, charity, self-control, truthfulness, good deeds and abstention from violence.[19] Social solicitude and cooperative concern, engagement and ameliorative action was the clear purpose of this Gandhian religion synonymous with basic morality.

But where does morality come from? If we are to believe Frans de Waal, morality is the progenitor of religion, not otherwise. Religion followed as an evolved version of communal concern for peace and order in society.[20] De Waal tells us that morality does not come from God, but from our evolutionary past as a social primate. Apes are our closest relatives, and like them, humankind evolved in groups that were small, cooperative and closely knit. Like them, we are always alive and sensitive to each other's needs, moods and intent. This empathy is the seed-bed of human morality. De Waal draws our attention to two levels of morality: 'one-on-one', regulating mutual conduct between two individuals; and 'community concern', which is a more abstract inclusive concept that conditions the harmony of an entire group. Chimps and bonobos definitely have the first, as they respect ownership and expect to be treated in terms of their position in the hierarchy. De Waal, though, cites examples of a chimp stepping in to stop a fight between two others, which means that they also have a rudimentary code governing their group harmony. The bonobos, he tells us, present even better examples of moral behaviour; of mutual and communal concern for one another. And in yet another book recently published, he points out that empathy and cooperative behaviour, and aversion to inequality, the moral basis for human society, are not exclusively attributable to humans alone, but are shared by capuchins and other primates, whose social systems rest on reciprocity.[21]

---

18 Iyer, Raghavan N., *The Moral and Political Thought of Mahatma Gandhi,* OUP, New York, 1973, p.20; Tendulkar, Vol. 1, p. 86; Fischer, Louis, *Life of Mahatma Gandhi*, Jonathan Cape, 1951, p. 46; *The Diary of Mahadev Desai*, Navajivan, 1953, Volume 1, translated by V.G. Desai, p. 279; cf. Iyer, op. cit., p.19

19 Cf. The Rock and Pillar Edicts of Emperor Aśoka

20 Frans de Waal, *The Bonobo and the Atheist: In Search of Humanism Among the Primates,* Norton, 2013

21 Cf. Frans de Waal, *Are We Smart Enough to Know How Smart Other Animals*

If, then, we inherited morality from our prehistoric forebears, religion would have followed as a corollary canon, spelling out the content of human ethics. Morality arises from individual empathy and concern for the group, which creates a consensus on the shape and character of human conduct, limiting individual liberty with voluntary restraint. Indeed, de Waal has been stressing this for many long years.[22]

The basis of peaceful co-existence, this self-control is the resolute refrain of Gandhi's precept and practice. It is the distilled essence of our collective spiritual evolution. In its universality, indeed, in its illimitability, human morality stands strikingly above sectarian strife, and points the only way to pervasive harmony and understanding. Thus, the religion that he would not, could not separate from politics was pure ethics in its pursuit of *satya*, *ahiṁsā* and *satyāgraha*, truth, non-violence and insistent struggle for truth, signifying justice. A 'spiritual biography'[23] of a man who saw no dividing line between religion and morality, between religion and politics, between spiritual and material, would belie his composite being and becoming; his life lived in religion; his action actuated by ethics; his politics inseparable from his religion! For him the essence of religion was morality. It is difficult to understand 'spiritual beings having a human experience.'[24]

With his all-embracing love and personal example, he sought to bridge the divide between the Hindus and Muslims, between the masses and classes, to encourage and enable them all to draw strength from one another. Gandhi insisted that the politician in him never got past the moral idealist; and the latter took all the great decisions that mattered. Principles were decidedly not for compromise!

Gandhi's attitude towards the major religions was most respectful. He saw truth in them all and in their scriptures; and upheld people's faith in their respective religions, negating the necessity for any conversion. He could

---

Are?, Granta, 2016. Cf Matthew Cobb, 'Intelligent Relations', in *The Guardian Weekly*, 28.10.16

22   Cf. Frans de Waal, *Good Natured*, Harvard University Press, 1997; *Primates and Philosophers*, Princeton, 2009. Cf. also Bob Holmes, 'The Making of Morality', *New Scientist*, 18 May, 2013, p. 48

23   Cf. Sharma, Arvind, *Gandhi A Spiritual Biography*, Hachette, India, 2013, pp.3-4. The attempt to separate or distinguish the spiritual from the temporal is at total variance with Gandhi's thought and action always illustrating the inseparability of both.

24   *Ibid.*

not however accept any precept or practice that ran counter to morality and justice. '...There is no such thing as religion overriding morality. Man, for instance, cannot be untruthful, cruel and incontinent and claim to have God on his side.'[25] Thus his faith in the Hindu scriptures was a mixture of acceptance and denial. There were prescriptions and practices advocated in some texts that he refused to accept; and chose to challenge.

Like Emperor Aśoka in the third century B. C., he raised his voice against those who spoke ill of others' faiths, while praising their own, calling it an exercise in folly charged with grievous consequences. Religions can co-exist despite their differences; and their followers can live in peace in a spirit of respectful tolerance. Adherence to one's doctrines makes no inroads upon basic human morality that knows no barriers to its practice. Through love and *ahimsā* Gandhi sought to exorcise the demons of hatred and intolerance. Terrorism is a travesty of religion in any shape or form; and Gandhi's recognition of the validity of various faiths, and promotion of respect and understanding amongst them is the only way out of divisive hatred and blind brutality bedevilling our world.

Though Gandhi called himself a Hindu, his first biographer Rev. J. J. Doke found it hard to give him a label:

'A few days ago I was told that 'he is a Buddhist'. Not long since, a Christian newspaper described him as 'a Christian Mohammedan', an extraordinary mixture indeed. Others imagine that he worships idols... I question whether any system of religion can absolutely hold him. His views are closely allied to Christianity to be entirely Hindu, and too deeply saturated with Hinduism to be called Christian, while his sympathies are so wide and catholic, that one would imagine he has reached a point where the formulae of sects are meaningless.'[26]

He read a lot; thought a lot; said a lot; and wrote a lot, always calling himself an ordinary seeker of truth, ever conscious of his limitations; ever ready to admit and apologize for his errors of omission and commission. He was curious and eager to enlarge his horizons, to imbibe wholesome ideas alike from the past and the present; always willing to learn and to accept new ways conducive to the realization of a just and fair society.

---

25 *Young India*, 24-11-'21, p. 385

26 J.J. Doke, *M.K. Gandhi: The Story of an Indian Patriot in South Africa*, The London Indian Chronicle, 1909, p. 89.

Fairly early during his stay in South Africa, even before he embarked on his crusade to court justice for the Indians and ameliorate their lot in that land, he wrote and circulated an extremely learned essay, which illustrated the range of his reading, to highlight the achievements of Indians and Indian civilization in thought and literature. He read as much as he could, in and out of jails, including the works of Carlyle, Carpenter, Nordau, Wallace, Emerson, Garrison, Tolstoy, Ruskin and Thoreau. From Tolstoy and Ruskin he learned new lessons, which he then proceeded to translate into living reality on the farms he established in South Africa. He also drew heavily on the ancient tradition of India to establish his āshrams in India aimed at the training of volunteers who would dedicate their lives to the renaissance and reformation of Indian society; who would fight for India's independence; and who would be exemplars of love and *ahiṁsā*. He always tried to practise what he deemed to be just and right in the ordering of human relationships, never leaving it simply to theoretical exposition. He learned only later that Tolstoy's practice fell far short of his precept; and Ruskin never cared to act on his ideas.

Developed in tandem with the hurly-burly of social and political movements, his ideas were expressed in his daily speeches, discussions and writings. What he said and wrote explained his life as it unfolded; as it affected the world around him; and attracts and affects us today. He was an honest yet successful lawyer; a deft draftsman of petitions, constitutions and resolutions; an indefatigable journalist; and ever generous with moral and practical advice to people spread right across the world. He wrote books and thousands of articles on a mind-boggling range of subjects; and became, in the eyes of many, a living image of human goodness and morality. He was less concerned with government than with the moral obligations of citizens. His inveterate optimism came to the fore in his lifelong endeavour to reform and re-order the basic modes of human behaviour.

Always rational in his approach, Gandhi was yet a man of faith, which transcended reason and logic. 'Logic is a matter of mere intelligence, which cannot apprehend things that are clear as crystal to the heart.'[27] The lessons learned from his parents were burnt into his soul; but the man who helped to ground him firmly in the spiritual heritage of India was Raychand Bhai, a friend, philosopher and guide, to whom Gandhi repeatedly turned

---

27 *The Diary of Mahadev Desai*, Vol 1, Ahmedabad: Navajivan, 1953, p. 109

for advice. It was largely in South Africa that Gandhi's thoughts evolved and his concepts crystallized; and were tried and tested in his campaigns as new techniques of non-violent non-cooperation; passive resistance; civil disobedience; *satyāgraha* or moral struggle for truth and justice; boycotts and personal fasts of atonement aimed at bringing about a change of heart in friends and foes alike. *Ahiṁsā* became his trade-mark, the core of his thought and action; and any considerations of practicality became subject to uncompromising morality.

He had begun his career with great attention to his appearance; and always used dress as a statement and instrument of advancement. He consciously chose clothes to progressively identify himself with the British and the Europeans; with the Pārsīs of India; with the indentured workers of South Africa; with the Gujaratis; and, finally, with the toiling peasants and workers of India. Dress and appearance became a studied, meticulous, calculated mode of action to achieve a desired goal. The ascetic in him subjected himself to so many painful vows. That of non-possession, *aparigraha*, became universally visible in his scant raiment. I have already referred to his essays in sexual abstinence. The simplicity that surprised, the directness that disarmed, or disturbed the equanimity of his contemporaries, is eloquently described by Lala Lajpat Rai:

'They suspect him of some deep design. He fears no one and frightens no one... He recognizes no conventions except such as are absolutely necessary not to remove him from the society of men and women. He recognizes no masters and no *gurus*. He claims no *chelas* though he has many... He owns no property, keeps no bank account, makes no investments, yet makes no fuss about asking for anything he needs. Such of his countrymen as have drunk deep from the fountains of European history and European politics and who have developed a deep love for European manners and European culture, neither understand nor like him. In their eyes he is a barbarian, visionary and a dreamer. He has probably something of all these qualities because he is nearest to the verities of life and can look at things with plain eyes, without the glasses of civilization and sophistry.'[28]

Gandhi was resented and spurned by the thoroughly anglicized Jinnah, who gained primacy of the Indian Muslim leadership significantly through

---

28 Quoted in *Light of India*, ed. M.S. Deshpande, p. 277; cf. Iyer, op. cit. pp. 6-7

the exaggerated attention Gandhi paid him, always calling him Qaid-e-Azam, despite the misgivings of Maulana Azad and others. Both came out of Kathiawar. Descendant of a Hindu convert to Islam, Jinnah sold his soul to his ambition; his convictions to his ego; the interests of India's Muslims to his megalomania; and the fate of India, the land of his birth and being, to the divisive patronage of the British. The irreligious Jinnah, ironically, became the founder of an intolerant Muslim Pakistan, which was torn apart by its own inner contradictions. The religious Gandhi was hailed as the Father of secular India.

Gandhi's love of simple life shorn of all ornaments helped him identify himself with the poorest of the poor; but that simplicity was at times marred by a dogmatic rigidity which made it irksome as well as extravagant. Gandhi and his goat in London are an example in point. The simplicity of clothes and of food, if it were to become universal, would sound the death-knell of all sartorial elegance and culinary refinement. The weavers and makers of fine silk and other exquisite textiles and embroidery would go out of jobs. Beautiful carpets and their weavers would disappear from the world. Painters, sculptors, architects and their fine buildings would no longer be in demand; and the pursuit of beauty for its own sake would become an act of misguided intelligence. Simplicity should not be at loggerheads with beauty, with pomp and panoply, which also satisfy a need of the human heart and soul. The craving for magnificence can certainly co-exist with simplicity, which should not degenerate into a dogmatic rigidity of attitudes. Gandhi's *Hind Swaraj* highlights his ambivalence and the vivid variance between his statements and practice. If the Western civilization was the work of the devil with nothing to commend it, as he held, he yet owed a great deal to his Western education and the study and experience of Western ideas and political institutions; Western methods of organization; Western abidance with the rule of law; and Western discipline and hygiene. In more ways than one, he came to India via the West, even though he had imbibed indelible ideals from his mother and mentors prior to his departure for England to study law. He read his scriptures in English translation before turning to their study in the original. His ideas of law, equity, justice and fair play owed not a little to his exposure to and study of the British way of life and laws. He could never evolve into the *Mahatma* we revere without the leaven of the West, its discipline, its organization, its values and secular ideologies. So many of his negative statements about the West were little more than eruptions of hyperbolic excess. On the one hand he decried the British way of life; and on the other, ever so often, he credited them with a great sense of justice and humanity, from which Indians could learn a lot to their advantage.

He denounced railways, but always used them. He denounced modern inventions; but travelled on ships from one continent to another; on motorcars from one place to another. He used the radio and the amplifier; the postal system, the telegraph and the telephone; bifocal spectacles and artificial dentures. He denounced doctors, but used doctors and their medication, as well as surgery, as and when required. He used the press and every available means of communication and propaganda. To change the world and take it back to the utopian Indian past of his imagination, he had no qualms about using its new-fangled instruments to achieve his goal. In fact, he was against the primacy of the machine, which would increase unemployment and progressively consign humankind to the scrapheap of idle existence. There is indeed something to be said for simplicity and simple life, with as little use of machines as possible, with as little travel as necessary, with only as much speed as imperative, with as little use of fuels as unavoidable, with as little destruction of vegetation as absolutely essential, if we have any desire to save our planet. We are pumping ever more greenhouse gasses into the atmosphere, melting ice-caps, destroying eco-systems, and consigning thousands of species to extinction. We contemplate with trepidation a stark bleak future, in which the heat turned up on our planet will send billions to starvation. Billions of barrels of oil are drilled each year. Billions of passenger kilometres are flown. Billions of tons of carbon are injected into the atmosphere. Harvests will fail, as the heat will go up, as water will become increasingly scarce. Gandhi had the prescience to press the need for conservation; limiting our needs and curbing our consumption. *Mātā prithivī putro'ham prithivyāḥ*: 'The earth is my mother. I am the son of the earth', says the *Atharva Veda*. It behoves us, therefore, to heed the health of our mother!

We also notice his prepossession with sanitation and hygiene, and his tireless efforts to rouse his countrymen and women to reform their habits; not to defecate in public; not to leave their faeces exposed to the elements; not to throw their rubbish outside their doors on roads and footpaths; not to clog their drains with refuse. Has anything changed? They loved him. They adored him. But they continue, without any sense of shame or responsibility, to defile India with their dirt. India's Prime Minister, Narendra Modi is trying very hard to wake Indians up to the need for greater hygiene; but they go on building new temples and places of worship, without caring to keep Mother India clean!

A seeker and practitioner of nature cure, given to constant dietary experiments which at times seriously harmed his health, the vegetarian Gandhi pleaded only for the protection of the cow from the butcher's block. His disapproval of non-vegetarian food and communal eating is supported neither by history nor human nature. Man was born a carnivore, not above cannibalism dictated by the supreme edict for survival. Progressive conquest of the environment with tools and technological advancement led to the development of agriculture. Observation and discoveries, chance and design helped the diversification of diet with cereals, vegetables and meat. Humans learned to cook in, and on fire; and to season their food with salt and spices. The mixing and heating of raw ingredients to prepare food for dinner is a universal trait of culture unique only to humankind. Cooking, according to Richard Wrangham, Professor of Biological Anthropology at Harvard, enabled our ancestors to develop bigger brains; and facilitated our evolution from advance ape to early human. 'It gave extra energy, used for evolutionary success; reduced feeding time, freeing men to hunt; lowered weaning time, creating bigger families; allowed brain size to increase; gave us our short-faced, flat-bellied anatomy; enabled the sexual division of labour.'[29] And the art of cuisine kept pace with the evolution of cultures and civilizations, always in tune with dietary needs determined by climate. The basic truth of life subsisting on life brooked no denial despite ethical and cultural concepts with their prescriptions of vegetarianism. Life would just not be possible in parts of our world without humans consuming animal or sea food. It may be possible and practicable for a vegetarian in an arable landscape to subsist on fruits and cereals produced by the back-breaking industry of the farmer, who has to use animals to provide tractive power to till the land. And the milk derived from cows and buffaloes and other animals is not really any different from meat.[30] We are amused by Gandhi's attitude towards milk, and his assertion of its quickening effect on human concupiscence; as also his acceptance of goat milk as a convenient way out of one of his many vows.

---

29 Wrangham cited in *The Guardian Weekly,* 13.04.12, pp. 32-33. A one-million-year-old fireplace has been found in the Wonderwerk Cave in the Northern Cape Province of South Africa.

30 Cf. *Collected Works,* Vol 12, p 127, where Gandhi says, 'It is but another form of meat and man has no right to take it'.

To reduce one's diet to the barest essentials, to cut out spices and all seasonings including even salt is a denial of nature, of the need not only to eat but to enjoy it, to recoup one's physical energy, to retain one's appetite without which good health and zest for life are not possible. Gluttony is bad; excess is undesirable; but appetising food and the joy of eating wholesome food remain central to human existence, to the enjoyment of normal life. Gandhi's recipes for food and good health would spell the end of the fine art of cooking, of its variety, of its presentation, and of the hearty satisfaction derived from scrumptious food. And Gandhi's advice to eat alone, in private,[31] would signal the end of the banter and bonhomie, socializing and forging of fruitful bonds, conversations and enlightening discussions among diners eating together, enjoying the finesse of cuisine suffused with the chef's creative pride. The great cooks of the world would commit suicide. A beautiful chunk of life-affirming activity would be dictatorially expunged. A basic natural instinct would be sanctimoniously, unceremoniously discredited. Would that enrich life; add to its quality and purpose; make people more honest and loving; more tolerant and giving; less violent in their daily lives, in their thought, word and deed? Who knows?

Humans produced alcohol and alcoholic beverages as early as the seventh millennium B. C.; and have been imbibing them ever since. Religious prohibitions and social disapproval have proved unavailing. There is always a difference between the use and abuse of any substance. One can consume too much alcohol. One can eat too much food of one kind and another. One may not be able to resist any number of sweets. The fault lies with the individual, not the substance. Gandhi believed in the goodness of a government that governed least; and yet wanted to impose a prohibition on the consumption of alcohol in India. He forgot that *soma* and *surā* are as old as the oldest Indian scriptures; and neither gods nor humans ever refrained from alcoholic contentment. Alcohol serves medicinal needs; and, in drinks, serves to allay human anxiety, stress and fatigue; to bring people together; to solve issues and spread good cheer. Excess cannot be controlled by prohibition, but by education and persuasion. Coercive prohibition has never succeeded; will never succeed! Alcohol is mild, compared to the many addictive drugs and substances doing the

---

31 Cf. *Collected Works*, Vol 13, p. 94; p.301: 'The process of eating is as unclean as evacuation, the only difference being that, while evacuation ends in a sense of relief, eating, if one's tongue is not held in control, brings discomfort.'

rounds of our world. Prohibition glamorizes its consumption, pushes up its price, promotes lawlessness and corruption, and leads to the production of substandard illicit liquor resulting in the tragic loss of innocent lives.

Biographies are carved out of recorded and oral history, selective recollections, subjective sifting of details, real and contrived amnesia, likes and dislikes; and religious, socio-political and racial persuasions of the biographers. Those by Tendulkar and Pyarelal are source-books of primary material, personal testimony and informed comment. Mahadev Desai's diaries and other writings help us understand Gandhi's thought. Romain Rolland,[32] Stanley Jones,[33] and John Holmes,[34] raise Gandhi to the level of a saint, with which Mahadev Desai, Tendulkar, Pyarelal and Gandhi's close associates would readily agree. While Rolland visualized the oneness of Gandhi with the 'Universal Being', Holmes called him the 'Greatest Man since Christ'.

Vincent Sheean,[35] Louis Fischer,[36] B. R. Nanda,[37] and Geoffrey Ashe,[38] look at the saint and the politician. Fischer met Gandhi in 1942, and again in 1946. He wrote four books on Gandhi. *The Life of Mahatma Gandhi* (1950) is deservedly famous for truthfully and sympathetically presenting a picture of Gandhi's great gifts and extraordinary humanity; his honesty and humility; and his steadfast non-violence highlighting the singular greatness of the human spirit.

Eleanor Morton's *Women Behind Mahatma Gandhi*[39] tries to size up the great achievements of Gandhi, and to discover how and why he was so loved by the women around him. She writes with understanding, not

32 Rolland, Romain, *Mahatma Gandhi,* Allen & Unwin, 1924
33 Jones, Stanley, *Mahatma Gandhi: An Interpretation,* Abingdon-Cokesbury Press, New York, 1948
34 Holmes, John, *My Gandhi,* Harper and Brothers, New York, 1953
35 Sheean, Vincent, *Lead Kindly Light,* Random House, New York, 1949
36 Fischer, Louis, *The Life of Mahatma Gandhi,* Harper and Brothers, New York, 1950
37 Nanda, B. R., *Mahatma Gandhi: A Biography,* Oxford University Press, Oxford, 1958
38 Ashe, Geoffrey, *Gandhi: A Study in Revolution,* Heinemann, London, 1968
39 Morton, Eleanor, *Women Behind Mahatma Gandhi,* Max Reinhardt, London, 1954

allowing her admiration to impair her truthful portrayal of the 'little man' the world looked upon with mystical awe as a great friend of humankind, as a champion of the outcasts and 'untouchables', as a man of God. William Shirer's *Gandhi A Memoir*[40] recounts Gandhi launching the Civil Disobedience Movement, that finally led to India's freedom. He won Gandhi's friendship and confidence; held long and intimate conversations with him, which provided a first-hand insight into Gandhi's greatness, as also his prejudices and peculiarities. His perceptive portrait highlights the magnificence of the Mahatma despite the distractions of his inscrutable obsessions.

Some of the most moving writing on Gandhi is to be found in *Freedom at Midnight* by Larry Collins and Dominique Lapierre.[41] Searing accounts of the blood-thirsty madness preceding and following India's partition, the role of Jinnah and his cohorts, and the trials and travails of Gandhi in Noakhali and Delhi, would melt a heart of stone to tears. We owe them a debt of gratitude for providing an authentic picture of India in the throes of vivisection; of unutterable suffering; and of Gandhi's heroic efforts to stem the tide of cruel insanity, leading to his assassination.

Erik Erikson's *Gandhi's Truth*[42] is not exactly a biography, but an incisive psycho-analytic insight into Gandhi's personality and ideas shaping his attitudes and action. He relates Gandhi's personality to the country's culture and a specific historical moment; and looks for all the clues to understand the later Gandhi in his very first Indian campaign in Ahmedabad. He discovers that the demands Gandhi made on others and himself were incredibly hard, so much so, that the lives of the followers became part of the leader's. Erikson's observation that 'Indians...live in more centuries at the same time than most other peoples'[43] may perhaps be true. The difference, however, that he tries to determine between Western and Indian truthfulness is indeed fanciful. Any attempt to distinguish between Western and Indian ideas of truth often betrays a Western prejudice upholding their concept and practice of absolute, unalloyed

---

40   Shirer, William, *Gandhi A Memoir*, Simon and Schuster, New York, 1979

41   Collins, Larry, & Lapierre, Dominque, *Freedom at Midnight*, Collins, London, 1975

42   Erikson, Erik, *Gandhi's Truth: On the Origins of Militant Nonviolence*, WW Norton & Co, USA, 1969

43   Ibid., p. 43

truth, as against Indian variations of truth. But duplicity and diplomacy, dissimulation, prevarication, equivocation, spin, are all Western words describing the reality of Western life and practice of malleable truth. There is no difference. Strict, unalterable truth was not unknown to Indians from the days of the Ṛgveda onwards. Sat[44] and Ṛta[45] express it; the Upaniṣadic satyameva jayate nānṛtam[46] reinforces it; Sanskrit literature reiterates it; the Hindi poet Tulasī Dāsa's line prāṇa jāyen par vacana na jāyī[47] is a part of India's common consciousness. Yet, hypocrisy, falsehood and false appearances are as commonplace as in the West. Distinctive description of the bisexuality of Indians and their maternal solicitude for others is also misleading. He talks of India's mother goddesses, but forgets the mother goddesses of the West dating back to prehistory; the maternal solicitude and bisexuality of Christ; the all-embracing compassion of Mother Mary and baby Christ. The bisexuality of all humankind is a fact certainly not confined to India; there is a female hidden in every man, as there was also in Gandhi, even though he was called Bāpū (father). Indians, of course, emphatically express this truth in the images of Ardhanārīśvara illustrating in the unity of Śiva and Pārvatī the deletion of duality. The Christian church likewise represents the body of Christ as their Mother protecting her flock and providing for the faithful.

Erikson points out that Gandhi's truth lay in factualness, punctuality and responsibility. He knew no respite. He was a twenty-four hour man. As he himself said: 'God never occurs to you in person but always in action.' Erikson also presents an insightful appraisal of Gandhi's relationship with

---

44 Truth

45 Cosmic Truth or Law governing the universe. In common language, it just means the truth.

46 'Truth alone triumphs, not falsehood'.

47 A famous, popular quote from Tulasī Dāsa's Rāma-carita-mānasa (Rāmāyaṇa): 'sacrifice of life itself is preferable to betrayal of one's word'. But lying is so common in both the East and West that only lying under oath is regarded a crime. In the courts of law, statements of the accused and accusers are doctored; and the judge and jury are hard pressed to sift the truth from the sedulous web of deliberately woven untruths and half-truths. Philosophy tries to explain how people believe anything. History often illustrates that they can believe everything. And the law demonstrates that they can manage to believe or disbelieve anything. If Demosthenes is to be believed, 'a man is his own easiest dupe, for what he wishes to be true he generally believes to be true.'

his wife; and makes a fine attempt to comprehend Gandhi's sexuality; his obsession with the guilt of tumescence; his *brahmacarya* and his prepossession with hygiene. He sums Gandhi up as a 'religious actualist' with an extraordinary charisma, 'effectively true in action'.

Raghavan Iyer's *The Moral and Political Thought of Mahatma Gandhi*[48] examines the central concepts of Gandhi's thought, and explores the nexus between his preconceptions and precepts. Iyer recognizes Gandhi's perspicacity to look beyond the creeds of the past and present to the latent moral strength of humankind, to lay the spiritual foundations of a happier future.

Judith Brown's *Gandhi: Prisoner of Hope*[49] is a sober, scholarly study of Gandhi in the context of his time, in which he is portrayed in all his complexity as a man who always stood on his honour; acted on his convictions; and upheld the primacy of principles in politics. Brown examines the thought of Gandhi the visionary and politician, and presents a picture that accords with Gandhi's hopes and fears, his failures and achievements. 'As a man of his time who asked the deepest questions, even though he could not answer them, he became a man for all times and all places.'[50]

Yogesh Chadha's *Rediscovering Gandhi*[51] looks at the milestones in Gandhi's spiritual journey, which coincided with important turning points in history. Chadha lauds the combination of the politician and the humanist in Gandhi, who made the love of one's own people fully compatible with the love of entire humanity.

Rajmohan Gandhi's *Gandhi The Man, His People and the Empire*[52] purports to be a definitive biography with additional insights provided by the family archives of Gandhi. The grandson writes with verve and authority. *The*

---

48 Iyer, Raghavan, *The Moral and Political Thought of Mahatma Gandhi*, Oxford University Press, New York, 1973.

49 Brown, Judith, *Gandhi Prisoner of Hope*, Yale University Press, New Haven and London, 1989.

50 Ibid., p. 394.

51 Chadha, Yogesh, *Rediscovering Gandhi*, Century, London, 1997.

52 Gandhi, Rajmohan, *Gandhi The Man, His People and the Empire*, Haus Books, London, 2007

Good Boatman: A Portrait of Gandhi:[53] that he published earlier, tried to comprehend the violence that rocked India despite Gandhi's persistent precept and practice of *ahiṁsā*. He also tried to untangle the story of India's partition despite Gandhi's opposition. The biography is a definite advance on its predecessors in terms of relevant detail and informed, candid yet understanding comment. Rajmohan discusses Gandhi's beliefs and political campaigns; and relations with his family; with the British and the Muslims; with India and the world. In its wealth of detail, in its clarity and candour, and in its sincere honesty, Rajmohan's biography is doubtless the best of all recent publications on Gandhi.

Some authors are nowadays so intent on the demolition of the Great Soul; on distrusting, disparaging and detracting from his legacy, that they spend great energy and ability to emphasize the inessential, the irrelevant and the irreverent in his life's story. They forget that a great soul also lives in the flesh; expresses and realizes itself in the flesh; and reaches out to humanity and the world in the flesh. Every attempt to transcend the flesh is yet, ineluctably, limited by the flesh. Any admiration or approbation is always grudging, halting, reluctantly forced out of a preconceived or pre-existing prejudice. One may, for instance, go to the internet to be disgusted with ugly calumnies and figments of fervid imagination paraded as facts about Gandhi, Nehru and so many others. License and mendacity know no bounds; no decency; no scruples!

Jad Adams' *Gandhi: Naked Ambition*[54] is mischievously mistitled, with commercial considerations in mind. Naked ambition has a negative connotation, signifying a selfish purpose, an unprincipled pursuit of self-aggrandizement. Describing Gandhi's life as an excursion of naked ambition totally distorts the meaning of his aspiration to rise above self and merge himself with India and the rest of the world in his quest for the unity of all humankind. The man sought nothing for himself; neither office, nor wealth. The ambition to deliver his country and the world from imperial exploitation and tyranny was as noble as his struggle and suffering for the welfare of both the oppressed and the oppressors. There was no bitterness despite the frustrations of life-long expectations blighted by the grasping selfishness and supercilious delusions of the colonial masters; despite

---

53 Gandhi, Rajmohan, *The Good Boatman: A Portrait of Gandhi,* Viking, New Delhi, 1995

54 Adams, Jad, *Gandhi: Naked Ambition,* Quercus, London, 2010

the treatment to which he and his countrymen were subjected. There was instead an inveterate, ineradicable hope and faith in the basic goodness and self-correcting capacity of the adversary. Men like Jad Evans, like many others, fail to see Gandhi's greatness and his capacity for self-immolation to raise the spiritual and ethical awareness of others. They cannot rise above their own prejudices; their mind-casts, and the sense of loss at the hands of a half-naked fakir; their own mundane values of the greedy and acquisitive world around them. A residue of resentment against the great dismantler of colonialism often, sometimes unconsciously, vitiates the British appraisal of Gandhi. He was so different, so unlike them, yet still able to meet their forebears on equal terms, to help them rise and realize their own innate sense of goodness and humanity.

One of the recent books on Gandhi by Joseph Lelyveld has received notice for the wrong reasons. His *Great Soul: Mahatma Gandhi and His Struggle with India*[55] draws heavily without adequate acknowledgement on the excellent biography of Gandhi by Rajmohan Gandhi. He talks of the 'ambiguity' of Gandhi's 'legacy', which makes no sense, whatsoever. He should instead emphasize the ambiguity of the response by his contemporaries and their successors. A predisposition to doubt and disbelief defines the entire book. He trusts nothing. He doubts every statement, every observation, except any that disparages and diminishes Gandhi. Lelyveld laces his prose with an irrepressible will to belittle even some of the greatest self-suffering and sacrificing acts of the Mahatma. The tone persists throughout his narrative, and inevitably hurts its credibility. The choice of words and phrases throughout the book has an intentional tinge of disrespect, disregard and devaluation. There is a conscious and deliberate attempt to remove Gandhi's aura, to cut him down to the author's own ordinariness, to the author's own level of quotidian aversions. He sets out to discern and discover the *Mahatma* from the first day of his arrival in South Africa. And when he inevitably fails to find him, he almost as much as calls him a liar, an impostor, a poseur, whose covert reality was at variance with his overt pronouncements. There is an unmistakable wish and will here to reduce Gandhi to levels of common human ambition, pride and prejudice, and natural self-aggrandizement. Of course, the young barrister was not a *Mahatma* when he set foot in South Africa. He was an ordinary young man before the situation around him roused his

---

55 Lelyveld, Joseph, *Great Soul: Mahatma Gandhi and His Struggle with India*, Alfred A. Knopf, New York, 2011

conscience, beginning with his own trials and bouts of humiliation. The evolution of the *Mahatma* took time. He was certainly not above a certain amount of racial prejudice to begin with; but the passage of time and the lessons of life lifted him above the attitudes of his contemporaries to the realization of the indivisibility of entire humanity. It was a journey of self-realization. It took time. It took suffering. It took interaction and struggle with those who would not rise above their narrowness, their racial bias, their material selfishness. There was no *Mahatma* to begin with. There was an ordinary young man trying to make way for himself and his family. Circumstances brought his hidden inner potential to the fore; and spurred the rise of the *Mahatma*. Any respect and recognition are forced by Gandhi posing a challenge to the author's palpable reluctance. No doubt, Gandhi teases, annoys, challenges, drives one mad at times; but that does not mean that there should never be unqualified admiration when and where it is due; where Gandhi's determination to do and die for human happiness, to defeat the demons of racial and religious hatred and violence, should compel our approbation and applause!

Lelyveld also seems to suffer from a pathological prurience which searches for Gandhi's sexual deviations, if any, from heterosexuality. He cannot understand the habitual, friendly, loving physical closeness of Indian males without any hint or thought of sex in it. They can walk hand-in-hand, hands on each other's shoulders, or even lie in the same bed without any whiff of sex, whatsoever. Gandhi and Kallenbach were very close friends. They were experimenting with diet, almost starving themselves with only one meal a day, while at the same time practising sexual abstinence. Any sexual relationship is hard to imagine; affection yes, but not sex. It is only in the last pages of the book that Lelyveld's pejorative tone turns silent. We may not agree with many of Gandhi's ideas; we may not agree with many of his practices. We may choose to scoff at many of his dietetic and curative experiments; we may lose patience with, and totally reject his precept and practice of *brahmacarya*. We may even discard his prescription of simplicity and little possession as destructive of creativity and beauty in life, arts and handicrafts. But we are still moved by his humility and sacrifice for human understanding transcending all narrowness and bigotry, to salute his resolution; as well as the vivid illustration in his life of the meaning of 'one in many, and many in one'. The whole world is one family: *vasudhaiva kuṭumbakam*!

A unique man leads a unique life dedicated to the happiness and welfare of the entire sentient world; to the preservation and conservation of our earthly environment; to the assertion of our indivisible humanity threatened and damaged by our misguided vision of the self in relation to others. He recycles unageing truths. He shows a new way. He makes the world's sufferings his own. Yet, Lelyveld shows a studied reluctance, a premeditated unwillingness to express admiration; an irreverent inability to accept others' words; a dense cloud of doubt distorting the obvious! He even finds it hard to accept that Gandhi uttered the words 'Hey Ram,' when shot. He does not know that it is the most common, involuntary cry of sudden sharp pain on countless Hindu lips. While millions adored Gandhi, there was never any dearth of those who denigrated him, insulted him, spoke ill of the man and his actions. It is so easy to find and quote people who were blinded by self-interest and intolerance, livid with hatred! A social reformer who challenges privilege and injustice, a political activist who defies repression, exploitation and tyranny, would have adversaries at every turn. They would say and do things to pull him down, to drown him in calumny, to destroy him and his campaign. If Lelyveld cannot dismantle the legend, he certainly tries to taint it, to diminish it.

Charles DiSalvo's *The Man Before the Mahatma: M.K. Gandhi, Attorney at Law*,[56] is an illuminating piece of work coming to grips with Gandhi's study and practice of law, which thrust him into the public arena in his advocacy of basic rights and freedoms for Indians residing in South Africa. He doggedly used the law and law courts to shield Indians from official assaults and oppression. The legal system failed to serve his purpose; justice was deliberately denied; he was repeatedly defeated and rebuffed. His inability to vanquish the racist laws in the courts led him to think of civil disobedience in 1904; and employ it as an instrument of correction from 1906 onwards. The seeds of *satyāgraha* (soul-force) were sown by the systemic denial of justice to Indians in the South African courts of law. Gandhi the lawyer conceived, forged and fine-tuned the techniques of *ahiṁsā* and *satyāgraha*, which he used in the painful Indian struggle for basic living room in South Africa. DiSalvo's treatment of the story leaves us in his debt.

I must also acknowledge the insights provided by Ramachandra Guha's

---

56 DiSalvo, Charles, *The Man Before the Mahatma: M.K. Gandhi, Attorney at Law*, Random House, Noida, India, 2012

Gandhi Before India[57]. It is a comprehensive, perceptive piece of work full of wide-ranging information, and rich in analysis. But we shall for ever continue to reflect on the content and relevance of Gandhi's life.

There are so many other fine works on Gandhi, which I cannot discuss here for want of space, but to which I shall gratefully turn for help during the course of my writing.

Gandhi inspires us to celebrate our common humanity, comprehend our differences and respect dissent. Truth is not static. Its growth and renewal is coterminous with the growth of human consciousness. Human life is a struggle, but that should not detract from the recognition of our common collective destiny, our common collective search for happiness. Historians and politicians have sought to establish unreal antagonisms between religions and civilizations. India, though, has always thrived on unity in diversity; and is a secular country because the majority wills it so. Gandhi's life and martyrdom gave expression to that will. But why did he acquiesce in India's partition? What forced him to give up on his dream of India's unity, which was dearest to his heart and his life's foremost goal? The sudden despondency and acceptance of defeat, succumbing to the betrayal of India's Muslims by Jinnah's Muslim League, the dashing of nationalist Muslims' hearts and hopes, is hard to understand; and cries for an explanation! The dream shattered by the blood-bespattered division of the land yet beckons; and challenges us to do and dare!

Just as Gandhi rejected the concept of a state and nation based on religion and confined to a single religion, so, also, he rejected Marx and his doctrine of class struggle with all its concomitant violence. 'Class' was invented by Hegel years before the theoretical formulations of Marx. Gandhi, instead, sought to harmonize self-interest with the community's interest; emphasized interdependence; and insisted that the ownership of capital should be held in trust by the captains of industry and commerce for redistribution and progressive equalization of the community. And his simplicity highlighted the obscenity of conspicuous consumption. *Sarvodaya*, signifying the collective happiness of the entire community, is Gandhi's alternative to both communism and capitalism. All humankind's sufferings were his own, in the ageless spirit of the *Bodhisattva*; and he

---

57 Guha, Ramachandra, *Gandhi Before India,* Allen Lane, Penguin Books, London, 2013

would not care for his own redemption until the meanest of his fellow men and women were also there with him to cross over into the happy millennium. We cannot walk alone. We have to take everyone else with us to embrace the future!

He dedicated his entire life to the regeneration of India's 700,000 villages and their economic self-sufficiency; to give them, with democratic decentralization, a measure of meaningful autonomy. He fought against race, colour, class and caste prejudice, and the abomination of untouchability. An intuitive realization of oneness of the universe and all humankind prompted him to pursue public sanitation and hygiene with a zealot's passion and purpose. A clean environment is the first prerequisite of healthy existence.

The emancipation of women from exploitation by men, and their education and participation in public life became an issue of great import to Gandhi, who drew women out of seclusion to take part in the South African Satyāgraha and the Indian national struggle for freedom.

Freedom is an urgent, undeniable need of the human heart and soul. As the great poet Tulasī Dāsa said, a person deprived of freedom cannot be happy even in a dream: *parādhīna sapanehu sukha nāhīṁ*. Empires and imperialism deprived large regions of the world of their freedom, subjecting them to unspeakable exploitation and tyranny. Gandhi made India's freedom struggle a mass movement; and demolished the distance between the educated and the illiterate, between the classes and the masses. He was indeed the first to demonstrate the dependence of domination on acquiescence and cooperation; and with his non-violent non-cooperation, *ahiṁsā* and *satyāgraha*, signalled the world-wide end of imperialism. He subjected himself to the most exacting standards of discipline; and expected no less from his followers. And he sought to raise his adversaries to a plane of understanding and justice transcending their selfishness and designs of exploitation. We have to comprehend his concepts of *satya*, *ahiṁsā, satyāgraha, sarvodaya, swarāj* and *swadeshī*[58] to fully estimate his relevance to our times. Are they absolute values, or capable of variation in relation to current reality? He lauded the dignity of manual work with his strident advocacy of labour, likening those who did no manual work to thieves of food that was produced by the crushing hard work of the farmer.

---

58 *Satya* means truth; *ahiṁsā* means non-violence; *satyāgraha* means soul-force insisting on truth; *sarvodaya* means the rise of all connoting universal happiness; *swarāj* means self-rule; and *swadeshī* means home-made.

If the *Gītā* upholds *jñāna* or knowledge as the consummation of human endeavour, the endeavour consists of *karma* or action. Hence the emphasis on *Karma Yoga*! As long as there was a single poor and hungry person around, Gandhi's work was not done. There was so much more to do!

His political thought and social philosophy, always daring yet cautious, shaped events of far-reaching consequence, and left its indelible stamp on the course of history. He embodied the trials and tribulations of his age; he voiced its woes and worries, its injustices and inequities, and sought their redressal in a new innovative, non-violent way. We have to understand the man and his ideas. We have to appreciate his approaches and techniques. We have to accept the rightness of means to a right end, the balance between the two. We have to weigh what we think, say and do in the scales of justice and fair play. That is the pursuit and fulfilment of truth. Violence taints our deeds. We must strive to diminish suffering, not add to it. 'I object to violence', he said, 'because when it appears to do good, the good is only temporary, the evil it does is permanent…'

I want to see the man behind the aura of the *Mahatma*. I want to comprehend his greatness, and also his failings. I want to grasp the ethical principles that governed his life's activities. I want to understand how those principles are still indispensable for the right ordering of human relationships; for religious dialogues and peaceful co-existence of different faiths; for goodwill among nations; for justice and equality amongst humankind. And I will highlight the tasks he helped us complete, as well as those that still cry for our attention!

I tread in step with Gandhi as he reveals himself in his *Autobiography*, changing course when I include or discuss relevant material, or when so dictated by sequential chronology. I have read and re-read the book and its chapters, pondering his words and their meaning, often agreeing with him, but sometimes not. I look at him as he grows up; as he studies; as he dabbles in law and religion; and as he wakes up to an urgent, irrepressible sense of his duty to self and society in response to an inner call impossible to ignore. He fights injustice and inequity, but without recourse to violence; with love without malice for his adversaries; with an undying hope for a change of heart on their part. I seek to understand him as he responds to the challenges that confront him. The *Autobiography* is thus my principal framework of reference, which I closely follow to chart his steady evolution into a *Mahatma*.

This book is not a panegyric; not an ode of blind adulation. It salutes him where it should; it adores him where it must; but it also confronts him and criticizes his very human failings; disputes many of his standpoints and statements; and questions many of his practices and decisions. A great and good man; a unique man; a messiah of love and peace; but not always entirely above the weakness of the flesh, notwithstanding his loudly publicized practice of abstinence! A most uncommon man, made of common clay! Repeated retelling of his life's story will go on in the years to come. This book will certainly not be the last!

Chapter 1

Familial Heritage: Cultural Conditioning

The Gandhis were *Modh*[1] *Banias*, and came from a village called Kutiyana in the state of Junagarh. They were a trading community characterized by quiet sobriety and easy forbearance helpful in their mercantile activity, and led abstemious lives, generally avoiding meat and alcohol. Six generations of this family, however, held high office in the princely states of Kathiawar. Mahatma Gandhi's grandfather Uttamchand, popularly known as Ota Bapa, was a distinguished Diwan or Prime Minister of Porbandar respected for his integrity; and applauded for his sagacity and loyalty to his ruler. On Rana Khimoji's death, he incurred the wrath of the Queen Regent Rupali Ba by offering shelter to the innocent state treasurer, who found himself unable to meet her limitless demands. The queen dispatched an armed contingent to shell the Diwan's house to chastize his temerity and force him into submission. Ghulam Mohammad, the Muslim commander of the Diwan's body-guards, died defending his master and family. The queen's irate action was brought to an abrupt end by stern British command; but a bond was established between the Gandhis and Muslims by the death-defying allegiance of the Diwan's Makrani guard.

Ota Bapa left Porbandar to live in his native village Kutiyana, under the patronage of the Nawab of Junagarh. On the death of Queen Rupali Ba, the Nawab persuaded Rana Vikmatji to restore Ota Bapa's confiscated property, and permit him to return. The old man came back home, but expressed his inability to accept anew the office of Diwan, to which his son Karamchand, already in the service of the state, was appointed in 1847.

---

1 *Modh* comes from Modhera, a little town in Gujarat, known for its beautiful Sun Temple.

The Gandhis were worshippers of Viṣṇu. Rāma was their family deity (*kula-devatā*); and a Gandhi was one of the founders of a Rāma temple in Porbandar. They also worshipped Kṛṣṇa in the *bhakti* tradition of Vallabhācārya. Ota Bapa was himself a devotee of Tulasi's Rāma; and the love of Rāma and Tulasī's *Rāmāyaṇa* clearly passed from the grandfather to the son and grandson.[2]

Karamchand Gandhi, commonly called Kaba Gandhi, was a true legatee of his father's qualities; of incorruptible honesty and singular authority. With his quick temper held in check by his studied taciturnity, he was a great administrator and an astute manager of the affairs of state. The lack of any formal education was more than made up for by his innate intelligence and worldly wisdom. He was, deep down, a kind and understanding man, a loving and forgiving father. As Prime Minister or Diwan of Porbandar for almost twenty-eight years, he earned the admiration of the Rana and the respect of his subjects. He also served as a member of the Rājasthānik court, and as *Diwan* of the states of Rajkot and Vankaner; but never cared to amass any riches.

Karamchand married as many as four times. The first marriage at the age of fourteen produced a daughter before his wife's death. Aged twenty-five then, he married again; and this union also gave him a daughter. The third marriage followed after the death of the second wife, but remained issueless; and his wife, sadly, became an incurable invalid. Kaba did not have a son; and the longing for a male heir in India was, as it is even today, often overwhelming! With his wife's permission, he married again. Gandhi states in his *Autobiography* that his father's successive marriages followed the deaths of his previous wives. But, in fact, the third wife was still alive when Kaba Gandhi married Putli Ba, his fourth spouse.[3]

In his *Experiments with Truth*, Gandhi mustered courage enough to castigate the carnality of his father, who was over forty when he married for the fourth time.[4] It was this marriage, though, that gave Kaba three sons: Lakshmidas, Karsandas, and Mohandas, if also another daughter

---

2   Cf. Pyarelal, *Mahatma Gandhi*, Vol. 1, *The Early Phase*, Navajivan Publishing House, Ahemedabad, 1986, p.179.

3   *Ibid.*, p. 186.

4   *Autobiography*, p.3: 'To a certain extent he might have been given to carnal pleasures for he married for the fourth time when he was over forty.'

named Raliat. Mohan, the youngest, was born in Porbandar on the 2nd of October, 1869. His father was forty-seven, and his mother twenty-five.

They lived in a substantial three-storeyed mansion, which housed five generations of Gandhis. It was here that the Gandhis cultivated the values of a joint family, enjoying the benefits of family solidarity, but also cheerfully coping with the constraints and irritants of life in cramped quarters. The Hindu joint family teaches one to defer to seniors; to curb one's selfishness; and to contribute to the fortunes of the family side by side with ones's own advancement: *sa jāto yena jātena yāti vaṁśaḥ samunnatiṁ*: 'a person's birth is worthwhile, only if it brings progress and prosperity to his family.'

Kaba Gandhi almost always ate in company, often of twenty or more, including members of his family, guests and officials.[5] The joint family with its discipline, restraints, obligations and traditions left an indelible imprint on Mohandas Gandhi's character. Pyarelal, his great biographer, is quite right in his statement that Gandhi learned much from the example of his father in the management of large households, which is clearly discernible 'in the time and care that he devoted...to the trivia of *Ashrama* life'.[6]

The mercurial 'Monia', as the little boy was called by his mother, was minded by his sister and other ladies of the house, and spent time watching animals, and playing with dogs. A maid-servant named Rambha was engaged to look after him; and stayed with the family till her death. Monia loved to play outdoors; enjoyed the company of his playmates including his siblings and cousins; was generally peacefully disposed; and did not respond in kind if hit by others. Once when he complained to his mother against his elder brother, she told him to hit back; but the little boy protested: the mother should instead ask the elder brother to desist!

Putli Ba was a deeply religious woman devoted to her husband and his family. It must have been hard for the young lady to spend the first few years of her married life in the same house with an invalid co-wife, whom she had superseded at the helm of the household. But she was always serene and sincere, looking after everyone, including her in-laws, with equal devotion. Her loving solicitude was all-embracing; and Pyarelal's

---

5 Gandhi later repeatedly referred to eating as something private and personal.
6 Pyarelal, *op.cit.*, p. 193.

account of her commitment to the needs of the joint family reminds one of the passage in Vālmīki's Rāmāyaṇa, in which Anusūyā lists the qualities and duties of an ideal wife.[7]

Putli Ba infused an air of great piety into her house. The food cooked and served was strictly vegetarian, though certainly not lacking in variety. As Gandhi wrote, she 'could not think of taking her meals without her daily prayers. Going to *Haveli,* the *Vaishnava* temple - was one of her daily duties....She would take the hardest vows and keep them without flinching. Illness was no excuse for relaxing them....To keep two or three consecutive fasts was nothing to her. Living on one meal a day during *Chaturmas*[8] was a habit with her....She fasted every alternate day during one *Chaturmas.* During another *Chaturmas* she vowed not to have food without seeing the sun. We children....would stand, staring at the sky, waiting to announce the appearance of the sun to our mother.'[9]

Simply dressed in Kathiawari clothes, she was ever busy with family chores and religious rituals. With no formal education, she loved to listen to religious discourses, and fervently recited the *mantra* she knew by heart: *Sri Kṛṣṇaḥ śaraṇaṁ mama: 'Śrī Kṛṣṇa* is my refuge.' Her faith and fervour had a profound impact on her youngest son, who was also influenced by her eclectic attraction to a sect known as *Praṇāmīs*. Their founder *Prāṇa Nāth* was a *kṣatriya* resident of Kathiawar in the eighteenth century, who travelled widely, and possibly also visited Mecca. He introduced aspects of Islamic practice into *Praṇāmī* worship, which did not require any images. Their temple in Porbandar visited by Putli Ba had no icons, in place of which there were writings on the wall from Hindu scriptures as well as the *Koran.*[10] The son often accompanied his mother to this and other temples, which certainly enlarged his spiritual horizons. Mohan's special, close relationship with his mother helped shape his sensibility and sympathetic understanding of different religious beliefs and practices.

---

7   *Ibid.,* p.192; cf., *Rāmāyaṇa of* Vālmīki, *Ayodhyākāṇḍa,* 117. 16-28; cf. *Mahābhārata,* Critical Edition, III. 222.19-40 ff.

8   Chaturmas signifies the four months of the rainy season.

9   *Autobiography,* p. 4.

10 Cf., Pyarelal, *op.cit.,* pp. 213-214, 'They were even looked upon as crypto-muslims' according to Gandhi. Cf., Ramachandra Guha, *Gandhi Before India,* 2013, p. 24.

Both his parents received religious teachers including *Jaina* monks at home, and listened to their discourses. An avid listener, Mohan imbibed a good deal of knowledge from their discussions. The influence of *Jainism* on Gandhi was strong and abiding. *Jaina* monks frequented his home and accepted food offered to them. He learned of *anekāntavāda* or the many-sidedness of reality from their discussions with his father, which shaped his awareness of truth that was always multi-dimensional. He, it seems, also learned about self-cleansing through the confession of sins from them, which influenced him to confess an act of theft to his father, who quietly read his note of admission and forgave his son in the commingling of their tears. *Aparigraha*, non-possession, *satya*, truth, and *ahiṁsā*, non-violence, which became the guiding principles of his life, bore the unmistakable stamp of *Jainism*, as did the importance of vows to which he subjected himself throughout his life, initially influenced by the unflagging example of his mother. Their binding sanctity must have been reinforced by his closeness to Jainism and the spiritual sustenance provided later in his life by Raychand Bhai. With its emphasis on *ahiṁsā* and aversion to war and violence, *Jainism* proffered a congenial creed for the mercantile community. Peace is a pre-requisite of undisturbed trading activity; and *Jainism* became the dominant faith of Gujarat as early as the twelfth century. The worship of *Viṣṇu* also remained popular, and the proximity of Dwaraka provided a potent impetus to the devotees of *Kṛṣṇa*; but a majority of Banias in Gandhi's day still adhered to Jainism. Jaina influence on Gandhi can be clearly seen in his acceptance and practice of *anekāntavāda*, 'many-sidedness of reality'; in his penitential suffering for self-purification and also for the benefit and moral upliftment of fellow human beings. But he was not attracted to the idea of Jaina retirement from the world and self-sequestration as a monk, withdrawing from the quotidian concerns of society to stay undefiled by deleterious *karma*. His life, instead, unfolded as a story of the deepest involvement with the world and its problems, social, economic, physical and political. *Nirvāṇa* for him lay in identifying himself with all humankind; in striving to allay their fears and calming their tempers; in solving their conflicts; in preaching as well as practising non-violence. *Ahiṁsā* (non-violence) is not abstention from or cessation of *karma*, and must, as it does, express itself in positive, practical action to relieve the distress of all animate creation. Educative and ameliorative, concerned and curative *karma* would certainly not blemish the pristine purity of the soul; nor, indeed, tarnish its transparency!

The concepts of *satyāgraha,* truthfulness and non-violence, together with fasts, dietary taboos, minimization of clothes and possessions, naturopathic cures and the pursuit of *brahmacarya* (continence, celibacy) owed as much, if not more, to Jainism as to Hinduism. The concept of non-violence as an absolute value expressing and emphasizing the illimitability of ethics in Gandhi's thought doubtless owed a great deal to Jainism, the first philosophy in the world to prescribe it.

Notwithstanding his debt to Jainism, and later on in life to Buddhism as well, Gandhi always called himself a *Sanātanī* Hindu, and regarded both Jainism and Buddhism as philosophical movements arising out of Hinduism, and remaining part of the Hindu world.[11] His faith, his code of conduct and his ethics were principally derived from the Hindu tradition. His values were forged by the stories of the Epics and the *Purāṇas.* His mother, as we know, was a devout worshipper of *Kṛṣṇa*; and the depth of her faith impressed her young son as much as the discipline and piety that informed the observance of her rituals. Her ardour of faith sank into his soul, though the rituals taxed his credulity. Her formative influence was indeed enduring; and the close rapport between mother and son helped shape Gandhi's sense of duty along with an understanding of what he should and should not do. And her influence became even more pronounced after his father's death. The story of Gandhi's life as told by him has only reverence for his mother!

The story of *Śravaṇa* left an indelible stamp on his consciousness, as it does on the hearts and minds of countless Indians. The son's total dedication to his blind parents, and his death in an act of their service is an example that stirs many a heart! *Mātṛ devo bhava:* Mother is God. *Pitṛ devo bhava:* Father is God. So say the *Upaniṣads.* If one desires ever to see God and know God, one can do so only in the loving care and protection provided by one's parents. To serve them, therefore, is to serve God, and express one's gratitude to one's Maker. Gandhi never forgot this lesson; and never forgave himself for his remissness in the last fleeting minutes of his father's life.[12]

---

11 'I do not regard Jainism and Buddhism as separate from Hinduism'. Cf. Stephen Hay in S. Ray (ed.), *Gandhi, India and the World,* Bombay, 1970, p. 22.

12 Rev. Joseph Doke: 'When Mr. Gandhi speaks of his parents, those who listen realize that they are on holy ground.' Cf., *M.K. Gandhi: An Indian Patriot in*

This filial devotion was signally reinforced by the epic legend of Rāma narrated in Tulasī's *Rāmāyaṇa*, which was read to his father by Ladha Maharaj, a great devotee of Rāma. He left his audience including young Gandhi spell-bound by the dulcet cadences of his recitation, and the fervour of his elucidation. Monia had already learned from his nurse Rambha the efficacy of *Rāma-nāma*, repetition of Rāma's name as a safeguard against fear. That faith in Rāma and the protective, magical potency of his name never forsook Gandhi, and was on his lips with the last breath of his life. Indians have believed in the historical existence of Rāma since the early centuries BC. That ancient, unwavering, constant belief is indeed far more important than any other palpable archaeological or literary evidence. They celebrate Rāma's birthday with fasts and prayers on the 9th of the month of *Caitra* every year; and the Indian astrologers are familiar with Rāma's horoscope and the constellation of stars under which he was born. The story of Rāma is recited in countless voices throughout the length and breadth of India. Poets and writers of every Indian language have told and retold his story; and allusions to his example suffuse Indian consciousness. His entire life-story is enacted every year in popular theatre in cities and villages in India, and outside India wherever Indians or people of Indian origin are to be found in residence, culminating in the festival of *Dashehrā* marking the victory of Rāma over Rāvaṇa; of good over evil.

The story of Rāma travelled beyond India to lands and islands near and far, finding expression in their art and literature illustrating the ethical values that he embodied and upheld, providing yardsticks for proper behaviour and exemplary conduct in the context of our common humanity. What are those values? Rāma as a son, Rāma as a brother, Rāma as a monogamous faithful husband, Rāma as a warrior, Rāma as a protector of the oppressed and down-trodden, Rama as a defender of personal and national honour and Rāma as an ideal ruler, provided a paragon of perfect propriety worthy of universal emulation. Hence kings in India and abroad sought to link themselves to his genealogy; to adopt his name, as they also did in Thailand.

It is these values that make him relevant beyond any specific time and place. He is an incarnation of divinity in action to alleviate the distress of common humanity; to confront evil and defeat and destroy it. Rāma as God

---

South Africa, Akhil Bharat Sarva Seva Sangh Prakashan, Varanasi, 1956, p. 22; cf., Pyarelal, *op.cit.*, p.202.

Incarnate is not aloof but at once concerned, caring and compassionate, and active for the world's redemption. Like him, we, too, can rise to the true level of divinity that is innate in us all, through our dedication to the values that he upheld. Tulasī's *Rāma-carita-mānasa,* sung alike in royal courts and common cottages, became the popular Bible of those values, and came to be regarded by Gandhi 'as the greatest book in all devotional literature'.[13] In later life, Rāma became his *iṣṭa-devatā,* his personally preferred name of God, to whom he lovingly surrendered himself[14]: 'Rāma has now come into my home. To me....Rāma is all...My life is His. In Him I live....In the *Bhaṅgi* and the *Brahmin* I see the same *Rāma* and to them both I bow'. *Rāma, Khudā* and God meant and addressed the same essence of Ultimate Reality.

If Śravaṇa and Rāma infused him with filial devotion, Hariścandra, the unbending, resolute practitioner of truth, totally regardless of the most harrowing consequences in the play *Satya-Hariścandra,* taught young Gandhi the primacy of truth and truthfulness as values above compromise. In his own words, 'truth became' his 'sole objective.'[15] Śravaṇa and Hariścandra informed his sense of right and wrong, duty and morality. Hymns of the *Praṇāmīs* and *Kabīrpanthīs* deepened his spiritual awareness; and he was led to the 'conviction that morality is the basis of things, and that truth is the substance of morality'.[16] The medieval poet *Narasimha Mehtā's* worshipful songs addressed to *Kṛṣṇa* brought home the message that only those who identified with and felt the world's pain as if it were their own, were able to commune with the Divine; and were indeed able to see God. His composition '*Vaiṣṇava Jana*' became Gandhi's song at every epochal moment in his life.

Young Gandhi also chanced upon a copy of *Manusmṛti* in his father's collection, which failed to impress or convince him with its account of creation; and made him toy with the notion of atheism. Mystical speculation was not compatible with his dutiful sense of involvement with the world. And unconvincing rituals provoked a reaction of revolt, as did

---

13 *Autobiography,* p.24; cf., also *Collected Works,* 21, p.249: 'Nothing elates me so much as the music of the *Gita* or the *Ramayana* of Tulsidas, the only two books in Hinduism I may be said to know.'

14 Cf., 24:197.

15 *Autobiography,* p. 25.

16 *Ibid.*

the current caste prejudices and the pernicious practice of untouchability. His mother's command that if he ever came in contact with *Uka* the scavenger, who serviced their house, he should immediately wash away the defilement with a bath, left him protesting; like her incomprehensible instruction that if he touched any untouchable at school, he should then go and touch a Muslim. One pollution would neutralize the other! The boy questioned the purpose and propriety of the exercise. If *Viṣṇu* or God was immanent in all beings, he would surely be present in the person of Uka as well. Lord *Rāma* crossed the river *Gaṅgā* in a boat plied by a so-called untouchable who also washed his feet; and could never regard a human being as untouchable. Mohan argued, but still at the time obeyed his mother. The doubting, protesting boy was only twelve years old! He reminisced later about his boyhood dream of 'amity between Hindus, Muslims and Parsis', when he undertook his last fast in his unending quest for Hindu-Muslim *rapprochement*.[17]

Then, in his formative years, words of a Gujarati poem went straight to his heart, and were etched for ever on his mind:

> 'For a bowl of water give a goodly meal;
>
> For a kindly greeting bow thou down with zeal;
>
> For a simple penny pay thou back with gold;
>
> If thy life be rescued, life do not withhold.
>
> Thus the words and actions of the wise regard;
>
> Every little service twofold they reward.
>
> But the truly noble know all men as one
>
> And return with gladness good for evil done.'

The last two lines of this stanza quoted by Gandhi[18] convey the core of his life's message; the predominant purpose of his mission, the essence of his tireless endeavour!

---

17 Cf., *Collected Works*, Vol. 96, p. 330; Vol. 98, p. 235. In one of his speeches in Delhi in 1947, Gandhi hoped that the Muslims would fulfil his dream as a lad of twelve that the Hindus, Muslims and the other Indians would live together as brothers and friends. See *Gandhi's Delhi Diary, Prayer Speeches from 10.9.1947-30.1.1948*, Navajivan Publishing House, Ahmedabad, 1948, p.22.

18 *Autobiography*, p.25.

Gandhi recalled going to school at Porbandar; his difficulty in memorizing the multiplication tables; and also calling his teacher, together with the other boys, 'all kinds of names'.[19] But the family moved to Rajkot in 1876. His father was appointed Advisor to the Thakore or ruler of Rajkot in 1874, and became Diwan of the state in 1876. Kaba's younger brother Tulsidas replaced him as Diwan of Porbandar; and the family's connection with the Rana and the state remained close and strong.

In 1879 Gandhi was admitted to a school in Rajkot, not far from home. In his own words he was a 'mediocre' student. His attendance was patchy; and his result was nondescript, placing him in the lower half of his class.[20] He was, however, an honest and industrious student always trying hard to keep abreast of his class, with no interest in sport or other extra-curricular activities. He did well in the test for admission to High School, and was enrolled in the oldest High School of the region in 1880. This was the beginning of the study of English side by side with other subjects. English teaching received the highest attention with a solid ten hours every week to prepare the boys for a career in government service.

A retired head-master chanced upon young Mohan's records at school, and wrote a couple of books based on them, which do not contradict Gandhi's honest self-assessment. We are told that his performance was 'discouraging' to begin with; his attendance suffered owing to his father's illness in 1882; and he did not appear in the annual examination. From 1883 onward, his attendance became regular; and his performance improved.[21]

In Rajkot, Gandhi's parents enjoyed frequent visits to their home by practitioners and protagonists of various faiths including Muslims, Zoroastrians and Jains. His father's discussions with them found an inquisitive, avid listener in young Mohan, and laid the foundation of his tolerant, deferential attitude towards Hinduism with all its challenging variations, as well as other religions.[22]

---

19 *Ibid.,* p. 4.

20 Guha, *op.cit.,* p.25.

21 Cf., J.M. Upadhyaya, ed., *Mahatma Gandhi as a Student*, New Delhi, Publications Division 1965; and *Mahatma Gandhi: A Teacher's Discovery*, Vallabh Vidyanagar: Sardar Patel University, 1969; Guha, *op.cit.,* pp. 25-26.

22 *Autobiography*, p.24.

Life at school brought young Gandhi into close contact with boys from different castes and religions including Parsis and Muslims. His horizons expanded with this exposure to the reality of India; to its unity in diversity; to the cheek-by-jowl co-existence of different castes and religious communities. The Parsis, though not numerous, were the most educated and modernized. Three of his teachers, including the Head-Master, an Oxford graduate, were Parsis. Muslims constituted about 13 per cent of the population of Kathiawar. There were Christians too, but none in Gandhi's school. He had cultivated a definite dislike for them owing to the aggressive, abrasive and abusive criticism levelled by Christian missionaries at Hinduism and other religions. Some of them stood at a spot near the school gate, railing against the Hindus and their deities. Gandhi heard them just once, and turned away in shock and anger.[23] He had also heard that the new converts to Christianity were made to eat beef, drink spirits and liquor, and discard their traditional clothes for western outfits. All of this indeed was not entirely true; and a missionary named H R Scott identified himself in a letter to Gandhi in 1926 as one who had preached near his school, denying that he had ever abused Hindus and Hinduism, or that he ever made converts 'eat beef and drink liquor'. Gandhi accepted his word, but stood by what he wrote about Christian missionaries in his *Autobiography*.[24] In his new world at school and around, Gandhi imbibed new ideas independent of the family and its confines, from which he remained comparatively free during this period. He made new acquaintances; and cultivated new friendships. A special friendship developed between him and a Muslim boy, Sheikh Mehtab, who lived close to his home. Though his senior, Mehtab repeatedly failed in the annual examinations together with Mohan's elder brother Karsandas, so that all three of them became class-fellows. He came to Mohan via his elder brother, whose friend he had been, as both expressed and exhibited a total disregard for study. Mehtab was a tall and athletic dare-devil afraid of nothing and no-one, and afforded protection to diminutive Mohan from the bullies at school. Bound by, and chafing at the chains of a conservative, ritual-ridden household, young Gandhi was impressed by Mehtab's freedom of spirit; and the temperamental difference was the curious attraction that made them fast friends. Later, when his mother, eldest brother and wife sought to dissuade Gandhi from pursuing this friendship

---

23 *Ibid.*, pp. 24-25.
24 Cf., Pyarelal, *op.cit.*, p. 216.

further, he remained unmoved, determined, as he said, to reform and reclaim Mehtab to a life of discipline and rectitude. Mehtab was a keen sportsman excelling in athletics; Mohan was the opposite who had himself excused and exempted from gymnastics and sport in order to nurse his father. He admired the athletic triumphs of Mehtab, who was in his eyes a model of courage and physical prowess.

Gandhi was not yet 13, when he married Kasturba, who was a few months older. He describes his wedding at Porbandar, which was organized together with the marriages of his brother Karsandas and a cousin at the same time to curtail and contain the expenses involved. His father had to travel posthaste from Rajkot, where he had been preoccupied with pressing matters of state, to arrive on time at Porbandar for the wedding ceremonies. His coach overturned along the way; but he nevertheless made it, swathed in bandages, and wholeheartedly participated in the rituals and festivity. Kaba never fully recovered from his injuries; but young Mohan was at the time too immersed in the celebrations to take too much notice. He laments his early marriage in his *Autobiography*, and repeatedly expresses his strong opposition to child marriages in his speeches and writings, condemning the conspicuous consumption and meretricious display of Indian weddings.[25]

The young husband enjoyed sex without ever admitting it in his later writings. Kasturba became pregnant at sixteen. There is no mention of any tender moments, or merger of spirits; of emotional bonds transcending their duality. Some of these experiences would have been inevitable; but Gandhi was loath to say so! He admits that he was 'passionately fond of her'; and the thought of being with her at night was for ever 'haunting' him. 'Separation was unbearable'.[26] To quote him again: 'My passion was entirely centred on one woman, and I wanted it to be reciprocated. But even if there were no reciprocity, it could not be all unrelieved misery because there was 'active love on one side at least'.[27] For once, he places sex above mere catharsis; equates passion with love; and candidly admits that it was not misery. But, still, what a purblind statement! Only he loved her! Did she, or did she not respond in kind? Did she or did she not reciprocate?

---

25 *Autobiography*, pp.6-7.

26 *Ibid.*, p.10.

27 *Ibid.*, p.11.

FAMILIAL HERITAGE: CULTURAL CONDITIONING

He was always actively demanding as a sexual partner. And he was possessive too; jealous to the point of exasperation, even though Kasturba really gave no cause for jealousy. He tried to impose his authority over her; to teach her how to read and write; to make her submit to his will. She defied him, and did not always succumb or surrender to his wishes and commands. Matters were not helped by the fact that they were both the same age; indeed, Kasturba was a little older. A typical story of pubescent teen-agers trying to establish a pecking order; of the male trying to dictate; to assert his superiority over his female partner! But young Mohan was also timid and timorous, fearful in the dark, scared stiff of ghosts, snakes and burglars. Brave Kasturba had no such fears; and could often put him in his place with a curt riposte.

A sense of dissatisfaction with the state of things around him characterized the entire life of Gandhi; and it was no different when Mohan was at school. His nascent unease was nurtured by writers like Narmad and Govardhanram Tripathi, who sought to rouse the Gujaratis to a disquieting realization of their degrading subjection to the British. Both of them wrote against caste and the corruption of the princes, with their challenge to change India; to discard pernicious social practices that had outlived their utility; to reform and to rise, to reclaim India!

His dear friend Mehtab impressed upon young Mohan the need to eat meat in order to gain the strength and stature required to drive the British out of the country. Gandhi had repeatedly heard the popular verse of the poet Narmad:

> Behold the mighty Englishman
>
> He rules the Indian small,
>
> Because being a meat-eater
>
> He is five cubits tall.[28]

Mehtab assiduously taught Mohan how to eat and enjoy meat, which would enable Indians like him, with their added strength, to expel the British from India. And this friend also took him to a prostitute to help him indulge his manhood and enjoy sex outside wedlock as an expression of, and exercise in true masculinity. If we are to believe Gandhi, and there is no reason not to, he was so paralyzed by anxiety, that he could

---

28 *Ibid.*, p.15.

do nothing at all, and was driven out by the woman with some choice epithets of imprecation and abuse.[29] A strong, subconscious dread of deceitful immorality saved him from the imminent slide into depravity. Though at the time, as Gandhi would have us believe, he froze with shame at the failure of his manhood, the values imparted by parents, family and society came to his rescue. Gandhi writes of at least four more episodes of his life, recounting his retreat from a moral precipice almost at the last minute before it was too late! Mohan gave up meat-eating, not because he then thought it was morally impermissible; but deceiving his parents and family was. He would resume meat-eating only when his parents were no more; when he could openly do so![30]

Gandhi wasted an academic year owing to his marriage. So did his brother, who never really went back to school. His father never regained good health after the carriage accident on his way to the wedding; and was seriously ill in the later half of 1885. He was suffering from a fistula, for which the best treatment was a neat operation; but that was disapproved by the family doctor in view of Kaba's age and physical debility. His strength was slowly and surely ebbing away; and the prospects of survival became increasingly dim. His mind, though, remained unclouded, his thoughts lucid, and his words prescient, as when he said that young Manu (Mohan) would add a new lustre to his father's name, and be the pride of the family.[31]

Mohan nursed his father's wound; compounded and administered his medicaments; and massaged his legs every evening before going to bed. He would do so only when his father went to sleep, or else, told him to retire. This unflagging nursing instinct remained an integral characteristic of Gandhi's response to physical suffering throughout his life. Erik Erikson believes that Gandhi gained a special hold, a kind of maternal mastery over the person he nursed.

Gandhi writes that his mind hovered around his bedroom and pregnant wife Kasturba, even as he massaged his father's legs, waiting for the signal to be beside her. On the fateful night, his uncle took over to give him a break. Young Gandhi, exhausted in spirit, looking for the solace of love, woke up his wife to lose himself and his anxieties in her arms. But within the next

---

29   *Ibid.*, p. 30.

30   *Ibid.*, p. 17.

31   Cf., Pyarelal, *op.cit.*, p.202.

few minutes, a servant knocked on his door; his father was no more! His sense of shame never forsook him; sex became suffused with an odour of sinful dereliction; he was deprived of the last moments of his father's life; of the satisfaction of serving and nursing him to his last breath. He blamed his 'lust' for his departure from duty. He forgot that he had done nothing unnatural; that he had only sought release from his unbearable tension and consuming anxiety in his wife's embrace. But this is how the burden of past conditioning produces an effect and an impression, a sense of sin and sinfulness where none was intended, and none was incurred. Gandhi never owned up to the curative, healing and sharing effects of sexual love. This lack of realization and acceptance, this incapacity or studied unwillingness to comprehend the depth of love uniting two persons in a state of mind where each is both, only attests the tempering of his mind with 'values' he could not analyze, dissect or appraise for what they truly meant in the scheme of life. That is what dictated his lifelong striving to deny this essential truth of being and becoming. A sense of sin scarred his view of sex, even though he yet continued to have sex with his wife; and produced four sons out of their union.

The 'poor mite', his first child, did not survive the first week of its existence. Gandhi deplored the double shame of making love with his pregnant wife; and his absence from his father's bed-side during the last moments of his life. He accused himself of somehow causing the baby's death; and of his 'lustful' indulgence at a time when he was a student, and when all his energies should have been devoted to studies. But, then, he did not desist, even after his father's death from doing so, while he still remained a student. When he set sail for England, he left his wife behind with a young son to nurture and look after.

Kaba's death drew Gandhi even closer to his mother. His eldest brother Lakshmidas was now the head of the family. Gandhi immersed himself in studies; and in 1887, passed the Matriculation Examination. It was a creditable, if not an outstanding result, as only 823 out of a total of about 3000 students passed; and Gandhi's rank in the province was 404.[32]

He was then sent to Samaldas College at Bhavnagar to study for his Bachelor's Degree, but found it exceedingly hard to cope, and failed his

---

32 Cf., Gandhi, Rajmohan, *Gandhi the Man, His People and The Empire*, p.17; Guha, *op.cit.*, p.30.

first end-of-term examination. A dispirited Gandhi returned home for the summer vacation, when a friend and trusted well-wisher of the family, Mavji Dave infused him with a new aspiration with the suggestion that he should be sent to England to study Law and become a barrister. That would indeed enable him to claim the position of *Diwan* at Porbandar, as his ancestors had done before him. Times had changed, and the British would certainly not allow his appointment to the position without a degree, which in India would take longer to acquire, and would not really distinguish him from the others around. With an Indian degree, he could hope to be a teacher, but not a *Diwan*. Mohan, who found the going hard in India, embraced the idea with all his heart. He wanted to study medicine instead of law, to which his brother did not agree, as that was contrary to their father's wish. Dissection was not really compatible with their orthodox religious practices. Even though the advice came from a Brahmin, Mohan's mother was hesitant; the in-laws were against; the uncle was disapproving; the caste was up in arms at the idea, as travel to London would amount to self-inflicted pollution tainting the entire family. The family was also short of money.

Mohan pressed his mother and eldest brother to let him go; and offered his wife's ornaments to help finance the trip. Putli Ba consulted Becharji Swami, a Jaina monk who was originally a Modh Bania, and whom she wholly trusted for the right advice. Becharji Swami eased her concerns by administering three oaths to Mohan in her presence not to touch meat, wine or women overseas; and Putli Ba gave her consent. His mother's assent and blessing gave Mohan the strength to dismiss all dissent; his brother's support reinforced his resolution; and Lakshmidas managed to raise the requisite amount of money.

Mohan was summoned to face the leaders of his caste in Bombay, who argued with him and tried to dissuade him from his proposed voyage, but to no avail. He was determined, and calmly disregarded their fulminations and decision to deprive him of his caste. The tenacity of intent questioning the hide-bound command of communal elders presaged a strength of will and purpose that defied all species of opposition in later life.

His wife's anxiety and expostulations had likewise failed to deflect him from his resolution. In his *Autobiography*, he does not even mention her in this context, though a later line refers to his wife left behind with a baby. The excitement of travel to distant England to see 'the land of philosophers and poets, the very centre of civilization,'[33] and to become a barrister-at-law, rode roughshod over every other emotion. It was only later, in London, that he talked of parting from his 'sobbing' wife: 'I went to her and stood like a dumb statue for a moment. I kissed her and she said, 'Don't go'. What followed, I need not describe'.[34]

On September 4, 1888, on board the SS Clyde, Mohandas Karamchand Gandhi set sail for Great Britain.

---

33 Cf., Pyarelal, *op.cit.,* p.223.

34 Cf., Interview in *The Vegetarian* of London, 13 June 1891; Pyarelal, *op.cit.,* p.222; *Collected Works*, Vol.1, p. 45.

Chapter 2

In England: New Horizons

Quickened by curiosity, spurred by ambition, young Gandhi left for London in September, 1888, determined to become a barrister. On board ship, he shared a cabin with a lawyer from Junagarh, Mr. Tryambakrai Mazmudar, who was also going to London to qualify for the bar, and promised to look after him.

Ignorance of the West and its ways, its customs and its etiquette, its food and its drinks, aggravated by his limited knowledge of spoken English and the difficulty of understanding the accent, filled him with a measure of unease and anxiety. And to his dismay, all the passengers in his dining room, with the only other exception of Mazmudar, were English. He had his vows to observe, which added to his trepidation. He was a stranger to the drill of formal dining; innocent of the use of knives and forks. He did not know what to ask for. He did not know which items of food were strictly vegetarian. He could not drink any spirits or wine. It was hard to understand the conversation; harder to participate. His shyness made matters worse. He therefore confined himself mostly to his cabin; ate what items of food and fruits he had brought along with him; or else ordered some bread and vegetables to his cabin. He even shrank from moving around on deck, despite Mazmudar trying his best to draw him out of his shell, to make him mix and talk with people. His Indian friend and a kindly English passenger encouraged him to come to the dining table; and also tried to convince him that meat was necessary for providing proper and requisite nourishment in a cold climate, though without any success. He was a true son of his parents, the keeper and custodian of his father's high hopes, subject to his mother's spiritual discipline. His father's prophecy had indeed provided the impetus for the 'ambition' that took him to London.

In England: New Horizons

He reached Southampton on Saturday, the 29th of September, 1888, and suddenly noticed that he was the only man to disembark from the ship in white flannels, which made him overly self-conscious and uncomfortable. Gandhi and Mazmudar stayed in the Victoria Hotel near Trafalgar Square, one of the finest in London. He was impressed by its opulence, and later wrote of his room: '...I thought I could pass a lifetime in that room.'[1] He had letters of introduction to Dr. Pranjivan Mehta, Mr. Dalpatram Shukla, Prince Ranjitsinhji and Dadabhai Naoroji, of whom Mehta was the first he contacted. The doctor, pursuing higher medical studies together with law, came to see him the same evening, and became a lifelong friend and supporter of Gandhi's causes. Mehta provided his first initiation into British etiquette, and advised him to stay with a private family, so that he could gain an intimate knowledge of the people and their way of life.

The hotel was expensive; and so was the food. The tasteless vegetarian dishes left him hungry. All alone, far from his dear and near ones, he was teary and homesick, especially missing his mother. He does not specifically state any yearning for his wife and child. He must have doubtless missed them, but would not say so in so many words all those years later, when he wrote his *Autobiography*! His friend Mehtab in India served as a link between him and his family, including his wife. However, his mother and wife, who could not read or write, did not like or trust Mehtab. Gandhi knew it, and yet persisted with the arrangement.

Only the first twenty pages of his diary survive. His *Autobiography* is therefore the principal source of our information, apart from bits and pieces gleaned from recollections in his writings and records of conversation; and the unpublished manuscript of a 'Guide to London' written by him in 1893-94. There are three short letters from 1888; some documents detailing his studies; some stories told by his contemporaries; a few articles that he himself wrote on vegetarianism in 1891; and a farewell interview on the eve of his return to India.[2]

Gandhi moved from the hotel to an apartment, of which Mehta did not approve, and took Gandhi to a friend's house to stay there as a paying guest. The landlady meant well, but did not know what to cook for him. Oatmeal, spinach, bread and jam formed part of his vegetarian meals;

---

1 'Guide', *Collected Works*, Vol. 1, p.83.

2 Cf. Hunt, James D., *Gandhi in London*, 1993, p.2.

but there was no milk for lunch or dinner. Gandhi stayed hungry, as he was always too shy to ask for more. His friend Shukla, fearing that he would end up as a crank hell-bent on destroying his health, took him to a big restaurant in Holborn for a decent meal, before going together to the theatre. When Gandhi inquired whether the soup served was vegetarian, Shukla snapped, and asked him to leave. Gandhi had no dinner that evening, but accompanied his friend to the theatre; and the matter was no longer broached. In order to impress his friend, he now tried hard to become an English gentleman, at ease in polite society. He bought new clothes from the Army and Navy Stores; had an evening suit made in Bond Street; and purchased a silk top hat. He wrote to his brother for a double watch and chain of gold. Lakshmidas was kind enough to send one. He spent at least ten minutes each day knotting his tie and combing his hair. A friend who saw him in Piccadilly so smartly dressed, remarked on the fine cut of his clothes. He took private lessons in music, dancing, French and elocution, and bought a violin.

It took Gandhi three months to realize that he could never be a perfect Englishman. He woke up to the fact that he was not really there to become one, but to study. He saw that he had little or no idea of timing in music to make him a good musician; and his movements were too clumsy to make him an acceptable dancer. The attention to his attire, though, remained punctilious, whatever he chose to wear or not wear in later life. He always understood the propriety of apparel in relation to profession, as well as occasion. His chosen clothes became statements of his identity alike with people and purpose.

Gandhi passed himself off as a bachelor even though he had a wife and a son back home. There were no child marriages in England; and they would have looked down upon anyone who had been married as a child. He met a lady in Brighton, who helped him decipher a French menu in a restaurant. They struck up a friendship, and the lady invited him to dine at her house every Sunday. When introduced to young girls, Gandhi felt obliged to tell her that he was a married man, and thus 'purged' himself 'of the canker of untruth'.[3]

Of the addresses where Gandhi stayed in London, we know at least three, all of which belonged to middle class, well-to-do areas of London. Gandhi

---

3   *Autobiography*, p. 48.

was constantly asking his 'struggling' but kind elder brother for more money; but then felt a strong need to economize. He decided on renting only one room instead of two; and to cook some of his meals himself. So, he gave up his suite of rooms; moved to a single room apartment; and cooked his breakfast at home which consisted of oatmeal, porridge and cocoa. He had his lunch out; and had bread and cocoa for dinner at home. He reduced his expenses by half; and kept moving to places that were close to work, to which he could walk within half an hour. He walked eight to ten miles a day; saved fares and also stayed healthy. He kept a complete account of all his expenses, a habit that stood him in good stead throughout his life. As he tells us in his *Autobiography*, he kept accounts of very large amounts of public funds in later life; exercised the greatest economy; and always managed to have a surplus balance in the movements that he managed.

In his first year in England, he spent about twelve pounds a day. In the second year, he cut his expenses down to four pounds. He walked; he used postcards instead of envelopes; shaved himself; and read newspapers in the library. He had become an avid newspaper reader, and developed an interest in public affairs. He read the Liberal *Daily News,* the Conservative *Daily Telegraph,* and the *Pall Mall Gazette.* He bought a book by Dr. Nichol, *How to Live on Sixpence a Day.* He stopped drinking tea and coffee, and ate fruits and vegetables in season. The simplicity of life in no way detracted from his sense of fulfilment. Life was more in accord with the means of his family. He was more at peace with himself, as he was living the truth of his available means, and studying hard to savour the success that came his way.

He had enrolled in the most prestigious and expensive of the Inns of Court, called the Inner Temple, thus suddenly thrust into an upper-class world! He had to wear formal costumes to attend formal dinners in an institution steeped in tradition. Hence the silk shirts, starched collars, striped trousers, evening suits, silk hats and shining shoes! At the official dinners, he was quite appalled by people paying more for drinks than for food; and initially starved for want of a proper vegetarian meal. He discovered later that he could order one; and at the request of Gandhi and a Parsi student, they were then served fruit and vegetables. He was in great demand at the dinners, as his share of wine could be enjoyed by his mates at the table. He had to go through twelve terms spread over three years, and pass two examinations: one in Roman Law; and the other in Common Law.

He did not find his legal studies too onerous; and spent time familiarizing himself with his new surroundings as well as the English way of life. He felt he also needed a 'literary degree', and decided to broaden his education by taking the London Matriculation Examination, for which he had to study Latin, French, English, History, Geography, Mathematics, Mechanics, Chemistry, 'Heat and Light'. Though frightened by the syllabus, he realized, among other things, the importance of Latin for legal studies, as also for a deeper understanding of the English language. The 'aspirant after being an English gentleman' worked really hard, but failed the examination in January, 1890. Undeterred, he persevered; and passed quite comfortably at the second attempt in June of the same year. He recalled his visit to the British Resident at Porbandar prior to his departure for England to ask for financial assistance from the state for his studies in London, and Mr. (afterwards Sir) Frederic Lely's cold, curt, dismissive response: 'Graduate first and then come to me'.[4]

In his studies for the bar, Gandhi took no short cuts, but read all the text-books, and, as he tells us, the Roman Law in Latin. This would have been made possible by Thomas Collett Sandars' *The Institutes of Justinian; with English Introduction, Translation and Notes* 1859, which facilitated his comprehension of the original Latin.[5] He passed his Roman Law examination in March 1890, and stood sixth in order of merit in a group of forty successful examinees.[6] When in South Africa, he found his knowledge of Roman law very helpful, as reading Justinian made it easier to understand South African law.

The study of Common Law included the Law of Property, Common Law including Criminal Law, and Equity. Gandhi read *Principles of the Law of Real Property, Intended as a first Book for the use of Students in Conveyancing,* by Joshua Williams; *A Compendium of the Law of Property in Land,* by William Douglas Edwards; *The Modern Law of Real Property, With an Introduction for the Student*, and *The Modern Law of Personal Property* by Louis A. Goodeve. He studied *Principles of the Common Law* by John Indermaur; and *Commentaries on the Common Law, Designed as introductory to its Study,* by Herbert Broom, for the examination in Common Law. He had to read *The Principles of Equity, Intended for the*

---

4   Ibid., p. 39.

5   Cf. Hunt, *op. cit.,* p. 16.

6   Ibid., p. 17.

Use of Students and the Profession, by Edmund Snell; and *Leading Cases in Equity* by Frederick White and Owen Tudor to pass the examination in Equity. He found some of these texts, especially Snell's, quite taxing, but acquitted himself with credit in the Bar Finals, and stood 34th in a batch of 109, out of whom only 77 were successful.[7]

By the time he was called to the Bar in June 1891, Gandhi had acquired an easy mastery of the English language, and also useful knowledge of other languages and subjects. His perseverance brought to the fore his dormant intellectual capacity, fleeting glimpses of which were provided earlier by some school honours he won in India. Even though he later discounted the skills acquired through the years of formal education, Gandhi could not become the man he was, and could not achieve what he did in life without his mental training and academic equipment. Fischer's conclusion that Gandhi did not learn much as a student, and that he was a 'doer' unhappy in London, is certainly at variance with reality. He learned his lessons from life and its activities; but books, discussions, associations and reflection provided the ingredients of his personal development.[8] Fischer quotes Gandhi from *Young India* of September 4, 1924, where he said that his college days were before the time when his life actually began. According to Geoffrey Ashe[9], the time spent studying was a kind of 'preface' in which 'the ingredients were assembled, but they were still inactive. The world had yet to draw him out.' He enjoyed his friendships; he took active part in the activities of the Vegetarian Society; attended seminars and conferences; spoke to different audiences; derived inspiration and spiritual impetus from Theosophy and theosophists, and even associated with unorthodox, broad-minded, ethical Christianity.

His principal preoccupation in London was the study of law; but his social and spiritual disposition drew him to the vegetarians and the theosophists. He found time enough during the course of his studies to involve himself with both of those movements. He was steadfast in his devotion to vegetarian food; and did not succumb to any argument or persuasion to change course. He was very disappointed with English food and cuisine. A fellow Gujarati, B. M. Malabari puts it across in picturesque prose: 'in

---

7   *Ibid.*, pp.19-20.

8   Cf. Fischer, *The Essential Gandhi*, p. 29.

9   Ashe, Geoffrey, *Gandhi A Study in Revolution*, Heinemann, London, 1968, p. 46.

no respect, perhaps, does the average Englishman show himself so slow of imagination and wanting in taste as with respect to his daily food…as a rule the Englishman's dinner is plain and monotonous to a degree. The cook knows nothing of proportion in seasoning his food; knows little of variety, and has a rough, slovenly touch. The cookery is often worse than the materials, which may be seen any day hung up at the shops; carcasses of large animals and small, beef, veal, pork, mutton, ducks, geese, rabbits, chickens, all dressed and ready for use. The sight is invariably unpleasant, and the smell is at times overpowering if one happens to be near the shops. It is an exhibition of barbarism, not unlikely to develop the brute instincts in man.'[10]

Looking for a vegetarian restaurant called the *Porridge Bowl* of 278 High Holborn, Gandhi discovered *The Central* at 16 Bride Street, which filled his heart with 'child-like delight'.[11]

He enjoyed a hearty meal, and bought *A Plea for Vegetarianism* by Henry Salt, prominently displayed in the window. The book converted him to vegetarianism by choice, not under any obligation or oath. He had been a vegetarian, till then, in deference to a promise and a vow, hoping to become a meat-eater out in the open at a later day, and to enlist others to do so. He had indeed wished that all Indians should become meat-eaters to realize their full physical potential.[12] But he was now a committed vegetarian by choice and not by any sense of compulsion. His mother's code was now equally his, leading to the rejection of any other conceptions of manhood.

He read books written by Howard Williams, Anna Kingsford, Thomas Allinson and others. He enjoyed reading *The Ethics of Diet* by Howard Williams, who said that Pythagoras, Jesus and all the other great prophets and philosophers were vegetarians. Dr. Anna Kingsford's *The Perfect Way in Diet,* and Dr. Allinson's writings on health and hygiene advocated cures based on diet. [13] All these books moved Gandhi to begin his own experiments with his diet in order to improve his health; but he tells us,

---

10 Malabari, Behrami M., *The Indian Eye on English Life*, London, 1893, p. 45; Cf. Hunt, *op. cit.,* pp. 22-23.

11 Autobiography, p. 35.

12 *Ibid.*

13 *Ibid.*

'later on religion became the supreme motive'.[14] The injection of religion into diet was interesting. Many in the world do so. But is that religion; or prescribed morality; or a dictation of considered hygiene? He made a note of all the vegetarian restaurants in London and elsewhere, and could now eat in any of them. He also lived for some time in a vegetarian boarding house; and stayed at vegetarian places in Brighton, the Isle of Wight and Paris. He met Henry Salt at a vegetarian tea at *The Central* restaurant; and the author later remembered the fastidiously dressed Gandhi.

The vegetarians of London and their Society attracted Gandhi; and his association with them led to friendships with Englishmen, and helped bring him out of the Indian group and the Indian mind-set. It enabled him to understand the English better, and opened up his mind to new religions and trends of thought. He mixed with them; ate with them; and shared homes with them. It enabled him to socialize with some local people equipped with education, culture and curiosity; widened his horizons and enlarged his sympathies.

Gandhi met a young barrister, a theology graduate from Oxford named Josiah Oldfield, who rose to be the editor of *The Vegetarian*, and impressed him with his zeal and oratory. They became good friends, and at his invitation Gandhi attended the International Vegetarian Congress from 11 to 13 September 1890; and became a member of the Executive Committee of the London Vegetarian Society. The friendship deepened, and in the spring of 1891, Gandhi moved into Oldfield's residence in Bayswater. Both had a common interest in food as well as economy.[15] Gandhi regularly attended meetings of the Executive Committee till his departure in June of 1891. Despite his physical indisposition during part of this period, he discarded the doctor's advice to eat meat and drink beef tea. His last six months in London were otherwise free from any pressures of study or anxiety; and he made good use of them to pursue his favourite causes.

The vegetarian movement was not a 'coterie of cranks'[16], as some might be led to believe! Thoughtful people were attracted to it. Salt was nurturing a

---

14 *Ibid.*

15 Cf . Josiah Oldfield, 'My Friend Gandhi' in Chandra Shankar Shukla, ed., *Reminiscences of Gandhiji*, Bombay, 1951, quoted in Pyarelal, Vol. 1, p. 252.

16 Ashe, *op. cit.,* p. 33.

tradition derived from Shelley, drawing inspiration from Thoreau, Ruskin, Whitman, Edward Carpenter and others. Carpenter rejected civilization in its current form and sought a new beginning with the examination of food, sex and religion. Vegetarianism came to the fore. Some advocated free love, as Shelley did. Some stood for celibacy and restraint; and some for birth control. In matters of religion some professed agnosticism, while others perceived the cosmic truth in Christianity. The vegetarian call also attracted Tolstoy, who held up the standard of revolt against the ugly excesses of urban overcrowding and the hectic pace of industrial society destructive of unstressed life.

The vegetarians derived their original inspiration from India. Salt's father, an army officer, served in India. Salt was born in India, but educated at Eton and Cambridge. He published more than forty books, including the lives of Thoreau and Shelley. The principal consideration in the choice of food, he said, was 'not chemical, but moral, social, hygienic...'[17] He insisted that it was not human life alone that was sacred and lovable, 'but all innocent and beautiful life: the Great Republic of the future will not confine its beneficence to man'.[18] Salt was a Fabian, a friend of Sydney Olivier, one of the founders of the Fabian Society. He was also involved with an affiliated organization called the *Humanitarian League,* formed to press for ethical more than economic reform.

Vegetarians argued that human superiority made it ethically incumbent on them to protect animals rather than kill them. They also stressed that humans ate in order to live, not for enjoyment.[19] But were they right? Man eats to survive, but certainly enjoys his food. Hence the development of cookery and culinary craft in all human societies! Some in the vegetarian movement went as far as giving up eggs and milk as well. Some of them argued that man 'was not meant to do cooking but a frugivorous animal'.[20] This may, however, be called into serious question. In the beginning, humans were carnivores, if not also cannibals, before they learned how to cook on fire. The development of agriculture was a slow, long drawn-out, experimental process; and the clearance of forests to prepare the land for cultivation required tools and technology.

---

17 Cited in Guha, Ramachandra, *Gandhi Before India,* 2013, p. 43: 'Flesh-eating is a cruel, disgusting, unwholesome, and wasteful practice'.

18 *Ibid.*, p. 44.

19 *Autobiography,* p. 40.

20 *Ibid.*

Some of the vegetarian writers also advocated the rejection of 'all spices and condiments'[21] for reasons of health, even though we know from age-old usage and experience that many of these spices such as cloves and pepper, and turmeric, preserve food and guard against ailments. The Āyurvedic system of medicine makes widespread use of condiments to treat all kinds of diseases, aches and pains. And there is a strong belief buttressed by recent evidence that the use of turmeric prevents or delays the onset of Alzheimer's and dementia.

Gandhi was also impressed by the argument that vegetarian food was the least expensive. He gave up the goodies that he had brought from home; and developed a taste for boiled spinach. He ate only inexpensive vegetarian food. The mind, not the tongue, was the 'real seat of taste.'[22] He gave up tea and coffee as harmful, and took to cocoa. Both are nowadays credited with beneficial effects on human health. Gandhi did not know. In his dietary experiments, he once switched to cheese, milk and eggs. Eggs were a good substitute for starched food; and their consumption did not cause injury to any living creatures. They could not be equated with meat, he told himself, and did not therefore violate his vow. This according to Gandhi lasted for only about a fortnight, as he knew his mother would not exclude eggs from non-vegetarian fare. He stopped taking eggs, and that was the end of the experiment.[23]

Gandhi refers to 'three definitions of meat in England'[24]: the flesh of birds and beasts: so people ate only fish and eggs; 'the flesh of all living creatures': so people could still eat eggs. The third definition covered the meat of all living things and also all their products, which meant that eggs and milk also could not be taken. Avoidance of eggs made Gandhi 'give up several dishes' that he 'had come to relish'.[25] He did not give up milk, and followed his mother's interpretation of his vow, even though he noted that one could interpret a pledge to suit his purpose or his 'better knowledge'.[26]

---

21 *Ibid.*
22 *Ibid.*, p. 41.
23 *Ibid.*
24 *Ibid.*
25 *Ibid.*
26 *Ibid.*

Gandhi started a vegetarian club of his own in Bayswater, and persuaded Sir Edwin Arnold to become its Vice President, and Dr. Oldfield its President. Gandhi himself became its Secretary, but the club folded as he moved to another locality. This was his first attempt at organizing and running a public institution.

As a member of the Executive Committee of the London Vegetarian Society, Gandhi attended all its meetings, though always feeling hesitant to open his mouth and say anything at all. The movement had some zealous participants; and its principal financial benefactor, Mr. Hills became President of the London Vegetarian Society, and later of the Federal Union of twelve other societies.[27] Vegetarianism was yet in its infancy in the UK, a new idea, a new awakening, a new movement of dietary ethics, a new intimation and avowal of moral responsibility! Hills wrote and spoke for the cause with evangelistic zeal, quoted Christian scripture, and saw vegetarianism as a practical expression of the Gospel, inasmuch as simple food procured without violence was conducive to righteousness. Perfect physical life would bring salvation to the world and make man 'one with God by obedience to His will'.[28] This accords with the Vedantic concept of *tat tvam asi*, 'that art thou', with which Gandhi would have been vaguely familiar.

In an article titled 'Salvation', Hills wrote about self-control and moral discipline in a vein that anticipated Gandhi's speeches and writings of a later day: 'When he who is impure has learnt to loathe the sensual sins which war against the soul, when he has learnt to love the heavenly chastity, which is the sign and seal of God's abiding presence, then for him the process of salvation is begun - for in the body he has begun to know God'.[29] These sentences succinctly anticipate so much that Gandhi said and wrote in the years that followed on matters relating to *brahmacarya* or sexual abstinence. But I strongly feel that heavenly chastity cannot be incompatible with the will of God expressed in natural human relationships sanctioned by society, regulated by rules of conduct put in place for a peaceful life, free from strife. Sensual sins are only those that disturb the tenor of togetherness by impinging on the rights and happiness of others!

---

27 Cf. Hunt, *op. cit.,* p. 20.

28 *Ibid.*, p. 21; *The Vegetarian* 1, January 7 1888, 1.

29 *The Vegetarian*, 39, September 29, 1888, 401; cf. Hunt, *op. cit.*, p. 21.

One of the most influential and eloquent members of the Vegetarian Society, Dr. Allinson was also an ardent advocate of artificial methods of birth control. Hills, the President and principal provider of resources for the Society was, however, a stern puritan, and considered contraception unethical. He therefore moved a motion to expel Allinson from the Society. Gandhi opposed contraception, but did not want to impugn the liberty of others to preach and practise whatever they thought best. He prepared a speech to support Allinson, which was read for him by somebody else, as he could not muster the courage to make it. But Hills won the day, and the motion was carried. Gandhi voices a faint recollection that he thereafter resigned from the committee.[30] We learn elsewhere, though, that he remained active in the affairs of the Vegetarian Society; and attended all the meetings of the committee. Even when in South Africa, he in fact renewed his association with the Society; wrote articles for *The Vegetarian*; and was appointed an Agent for the London Vegetarian Society, which he proudly published on his letterhead. One of Gandhi's biographers, Ashe only tells us that Gandhi 'contemplated resigning himself', when Allinson was expelled from the committee.[31] Hunt, who wrote on Gandhi's activities in London, does not mention his resignation. If Gandhi resigned from the committee, what was it that made his recollection 'faint'? He often refers to his recollections, faint or otherwise, which may not always be accurate or total, and may be consciously and unconsciously selective. He cannot, it seems, always trust his recollection, which might be subject to deliberate or inadvertent edition, cut down in places, added to in others!

The vegetarian movement was indeed his first foray into social activism. He learned to participate in organization and action. He went to a Vegetarian Federal Union Conference at Portsmouth, where Henry Salt gave the main address on 'The Return to Nature'; and Gandhi presented a paper on 'The Foods of India'. He recounts how he narrowly escaped the allure of Eros at a boarding house where he stayed, when at a game of cards salacious jokes escalated into a situation with a female player, which would have certainly led to a sexual summation. He was 'moved…to lust' by a woman other than his wife.[32] A friend of his warned him just in the nick of time! 'God saved me', wrote Gandhi. God always did, according to him, in so

---

30   *Autobiography*, p. 44.
31   Ashe, *op. cit.,* p. 38.
32   *Autobiography*, p. 51.

many situations in his personal and public life. 'Supplication, worship, prayer are no superstition; they are acts more real than the acts of eating, drinking, sitting or walking. It is no exaggeration to say that they alone are real, all else is unreal'.[33] Did Gandhi pray when assailed by temptation, or immediately after it? Did prayer, 'an unfailing means of cleansing the heart of passions'[34], save Gandhi? Whatever does he mean by passions? Is it necessary to forget the body and its functions before one prays, when one prays, after one prays? Love and humility also arise from a sense of belonging, from physical and mental proximity, from an extension of those threads of connection, which in their highest reaches embrace the whole world. Love of the world, and submerging oneself in the service of the world, is also an expression of passion, an exercise of passion. *Kāma, krodha, lobha* and *moha* are often cited as undesirable passions, to be overcome, to be cast aside, to be eradicated! Of these, *krodha* alone is harmful and destructive of commonsense. *Kāma* is life-sustaining and life- regenerating, the fount of love and altruism. *Lobha*, synonymous with acquisitive desire, is a pre-requisite of provisions for life, though one can carry it too far to the detriment of others. It certainly needs limitation, as *kāma* requires restraint, but not rejection, to keep society on an even keel. *Moha* gives meaning and purpose to relationships, and a sense of belonging to all our associations and connections, to our entire familial and social context. Life devoid of attachment would be a desert of soulless toil. Of course, excess of anything is bad, which is true of *moha* as well, an inseparable, defining element of love!

Gandhi also spoke at other places; and addressed a conference at Ventnor on the Isle of Wight. His participation in the vegetarian movement placed him in a group of educated friends who had seceded, even if only partially, from the ways of the world around them. They had their doubts and their double standards evident in their lives; but Gandhi became an unqualified lover of simple life. He did not encounter any racial or colour discrimination; and the vegetarians also led him to meet people active in the theosophical movement. An uncle and nephew, Bertram and Archibald Keightley, provided his first contact with theosophy, and requested him to help them understand the *Gītā*. Gandhi had not yet read the *Gītā* in Sanskrit or even in a Gujarati version; but he now did so with his new

---

33   *Ibid.*

34   *Ibid.*, p.52.

friends, with the help of the English translation by Sir Edwin Arnold, titled *The Song Celestial*. He was deeply moved by its philosophy, and as he repeatedly tells us, the *Gītā* became his book of daily reference: 'I regard it to date as the book *par excellence* for the knowledge of Truth'.[35]

Bertram and Archibald Keightley also encouraged Gandhi to read Sir Edwin Arnold's *The Light of Asia*, which introduced Gandhi to the life and philosophy of Gautama the Buddha. They had placed their home in Notting Hill at the disposal of Madame Blavatsky, the founder of the Theosophical Movement; and took Gandhi to meet her, and also Mrs. Annie Besant, who had only recently joined the Society. Blavatsky aimed at reconciling religion with science, and Christianity with Hinduism, from which theosophy derived its principal inspiration. Her book, *The Key to Philosophy*, whetted Gandhi's appetite to read more about Hinduism, and 'disabused' his mind of the Christian propaganda that 'Hinduism was rife with superstition.'[36] Theosophy's pantheistic conception of God, emphasis on the oneness of all people, and faith in human capacity for perfection, left their unmistakable stamp on Gandhi's vision of God and man.

Mrs Besant's *How I became a Theosophist* anchored his theism, and buoyed up his faith.[37] The atheism of Bradlaugh failed to attract him. Theosophy brought Gandhi to study the *Gītā*. He went to hear Mrs Annie Besant: '...the words she uttered...have never faded from my memory. She said...that she would be quite satisfied to have the epitaph written on her tomb that she had lived for truth and she died for truth'.[38]

Vegetarianism and theosophy enabled Gandhi to be himself as well as a proud Indian, while at the same time drawing close to a privileged, educated group of people, who were attracted to these movements.[39]

The theosophical movement with its Indian philosophical focus attracted many. Sir Edwin Arnold translated the *Gītā* and wrote *The Light of Asia*,

---

35   *Ibid.*, p.48.

36   *Ibid.*, p. 49.

37   *Ibid.*, p. 50.

38   *Collected Works*, Vol 16, pp. 201ff. '...I ask no other epitaph on my tomb but 'SHE TRIED TO FOLLOW TRUTH' – Besant.

39   Cf. DiSalvo, Charles, *The Man Before the Mahatma, M.K. Gandhi, Attorney at Law*, Random House, India, 2012, p. 15.

a free adaptation of the *Lalitavistara,* presenting an account of the life, character and philosophy of Siddhārtha Gautama the Buddha. Carpenter read the *Gītā*; and Anna Kingsford cited *The Light of Asia* in her writings. The movement definitely helped produce Gandhi, as it shaped his ideas and action in most vital ways. According to his *Autobiography*, he did not join the Society. But we know that he actually did, and became an associate member for six months on the 26th of March, 1891, about three months before he left for home.[40] He appears to have deliberately understated his interest in theosophy and his debt to it. It certainly helped Gandhi sort himself out and determine what kind of a Hindu he really was, and wanted to be. It confirmed his confidence and pride in the Hindu faith; and assisted his eclectic acceptance of Truth abiding in all religions. His early years in South Africa were marked by a deep spiritual quest. Theosophy helped this process. A portrait of Mrs Annie Besant hung in his office.

The movement certainly shaped Gandhi's thought, as it also inspired men like Bernard Shaw and Chesterton. He came face to face with much new radical thinking; and acquainted himself with other religions. A Christian in a vegetarian boarding house told him that meat-eating and drinking were not scriptural obligations, and encouraged him to read the Bible. Gandhi found the *Old Testament* hard-going, yet persevered, without the text evoking either interest or understanding. The *New Testament* immediately attracted him; and the *Sermon on the Mount* gripped him. 'But I say unto you, that ye resist not evil: but whosoever shall smite thee on thy right cheek, turn to him the other also and if any man takes away thy coat, let him have thy cloak too.' Gandhi was immediately reminded of Shamal Bhatt's 'for a bowl of water give a goodly meal'. He saw in renunciation the highest form of religion, and tried in his mind to link the *Gītā*, the teachings of the Buddha that he learned from *The Light of Asia,* and the *Sermon on the Mount,* with one another.[41]

The dignity of every religion, and the basic unity of them all as repositories of ancient, fundamental truths, formed the core of Gandhi's approach to religion. Theosophy contributed to that receptivity and catholicity of spirit; but theosophy itself owed its tolerance and respect for different religious philosophies to what it learned from India, and from the examples of great Indian emperors such as Aśoka and Akbar. Gandhi's curiosity made him

---

40 Cf. Hunt, *op. cit.*, p. 32.

41 *Autobiography*, p. 49.

turn to other religious teachers to discover what they said and prescribed. Carlyle's *Heroes and Hero Worship* was among the many books he read, and was impressed by the chapter on the Hero as a prophet.[42] But in Chapter 21 of his *Autobiography*, titled *'Nirbala ke bala Rāma'*, he laid emphasis on the experience of religion as distinct from mere knowledge. He could not yet give a free rein to his spiritual quest, as his legal studies reclaimed his attention.

Gandhi found time to visit Paris as well as the great Exhibition of 1890. He had heard so much of the Eiffel Tower. He climbed it more than once; and had a meal in a restaurant on the first floor. He refers to the disparagement of the Tower by Tolstoy, who attributed its creation to minds befuddled by liquor and especially tobacco. Gandhi himself saw it as a toy, then and later when he wrote his *Autobiography*. Its huge height and scale was its sole attraction; and people climbed it like children. He failed to grasp or admire the imagination and great engineering skill evinced in its conception and construction.[43] He was indeed not alone in his attitudinal inability to embrace innovative, unfamiliar, ground-breaking forms of architecture. A group of French writers and artists had already protested when, in 1887, the foundations of Gustave Eiffel's 312-metre iron tower weighing 10,000 tonnes were excavated: 'We writers, painters, sculptors, architects, passionate fans of the beauty, until now intact, of Paris, hereby protest with all our force and our indignation, in the name of French taste… against the construction in the very heart of our capital of the useless and monstrous Eiffel Tower.'[44] But the French are still celebrating the 'monstrous' landmark symbolic of their capital city; and $38 million have been spent on great additions and improvements to it, to mark 125 years of its glorious existence.

The celebration of life, the merriment, the fashions, fun and frolic of Paris left him cold. Frivolities that provided escape from, or functioned as safety valves protecting lives from imploding and becoming insufferable remained unappreciated and incomprehensible. Gandhi does not talk of the grandeur of Paris, of its architecture and sweeping boulevards, or of its polished etiquette and cultural felicity. He admires only churches and their soaring spires; their generous, commanding interiors; their

---

42 *Ibid.*

43 *Ibid.*, p. 56.

44 Cf. *The Guardian Weekly*, 17.10.14, p. 44.

grave solemnity; and the display of faith in the prayers of the devoted. Life around in all its colours, in its expression of a medley of emotions, especially the warm glow of its creative capacity in physical love was nothing but unmitigated folly in a frame of mind conditioned by the culture of prohibitions! One cannot always be serious, high-strung and anxious in life; and to make it enjoyable, liveable and sufferable, there must always be room for entertainment, for song and dance and drama, sport and banter and unrestrained laughter. Gandhi only refers to the prayers of the faithful 'increasing the glory of God'[45], which is not easy to understand. Does the glory of God depend on, and arise only from human prayer?

Gandhi repeatedly refers to his shyness, which he often found insurmountable in his attempts to make a speech. He lost his nerve and even clarity of vision in fits of nervous anxiety on public occasions. He found it exceedingly hard to make a speech at Ventnor, even though he had already written one for the occasion. He describes how his 'vision became blurred,' and he 'trembled, though the speech hardly covered a sheet of foolscap'.[46]

If we are to believe him, he failed even in his last attempt to make a speech at a dinner that he gave just before he left London to return home. He had invited his friends to the Holborn restaurant, which had been persuaded to serve a strictly vegetarian meal. Gandhi refers to the West making an art of eating, especially on important occasions. Speeches are made; and Gandhi had carefully prepared one for himself. He began on a humorous note, but suddenly went blank with nervousness and could not say anything beyond 'I thank you gentlemen for having kindly responded to my invitation'.[47]

The Vegetarian, though, varied in its summation of the occasion: 'at the close Mr Gandhi, in a very graceful, though somewhat nervous speech, welcomed all present, spoke of the pleasure it gave him to see the habit of abstention from flesh progressing in England, related the manner in which his connection with the LVS arose, and in so doing took occasion to speak in a touching way of what he owed to Dr. Oldfield.'[48]

---

45 *Autobiography,* p.55.

46 *Ibid.,* p. 44.

47 *Ibid.*

48 *The Vegetarian,* June 13, 1891.

Was this shyness so incapacitating as to fail him or expose him to ridicule on almost all occasions? Or did he exaggerate? One wonders if there is a deliberate overstatement of his tongue-tying bashfulness in the *Autobiography*, in order to highlight or dramatize his later liberation from it. He knew his mind. He stuck to his convictions. He had the ideas. He had the words. He still could not muster the courage to mouth them, to express them. Arjuna in the *Mahābhārata* needed the inspiring, electrifying exhortation of Kṛṣṇa to overcome his trepidation-cum-hesitation to take up arms in defence of good over evil. Gandhi too needed the powerful rod of conscience quickened by the *Gītā* to snap asunder the shackles of shyness. The harrowing experiences and trials of South Africa finally unlocked his tongue and capacity for cogent speech. Gandhi tells us that even this shy hesitancy served him well, inasmuch as it helped the cultivation of clarity and brevity, and guarded against thoughtless expressions or statements that might needlessly hurt or provoke. It taught him to be economical with his words; and to restrain himself with greater ease. It made his words more circumspect and deliberate, so that he did not have to regret anything written or said in haste. If one spoke less, one would indeed be more careful with one's words!

London was the greatest city of the world, the central seat of a far-flung empire. It was also a great international city, attracting people from all over the world. It boasted a population of around six million, amongst whom there were about one thousand Indians.[49] It was also a great centre of education as well as industrial activity. Gandhi mingled largely with the middle class people of London, and met Christians, Hindus, Muslims, Theosophists, and occasional atheists. He heard Charles Bradlaugh, the great champion of the poor, and a friend of the Indians, in the House of Commons, and elsewhere.[50] He also attended Bradlaugh's funeral, and was quite perplexed by the presence of priests at an atheist's last rites. He also met Cardinal Manning, whose contribution to the resolution of a dock strike inspired Gandhi's later attempts at the settlement of labour disputes. He took many of these ideas with him in order to apply them, adjust them, develop them, and make them relevant and acceptable in the Indian context.

---

49 Cf. Guha, *op. cit.,* p. 38.
50 *Ibid.,* p. 51.

He was not much interested in British politics. He does not mention the Liberals or the Tories, the Communists or the Socialists. Marx had died only in 1883; but Gandhi remained untouched and unaffected by his thought, and did not make any attempt to see any Labour leaders. He does not mention the Fabian Society.

He had arrived in London with a letter of introduction to Dadabhai Naoroji, who had been thrice President of the Indian National Congress, and was a member of the British Parliament. His shyness prevented him from an early visit, but he attended meetings of the London Indian Society founded in 1865 by Naoroji and W C Bannerji; and heard Naoroji speak on many occasions. Though quite moderate in its plea for reforms in India, the Society was still viewed as radical at the time.[51]

Gandhi also attended meetings of Anjuman-e-Islam, later called the Pan-Islamic Society, which was founded by barrister Abdullah Al-Mamoon Sohraworthy, in 1886. This indicates his early awareness of Muslim aspirations; and a sympathetic concern for their welfare.

Gandhi also often visited the home of Miss Elizabeth Manning in Pembridge Crescent, Notting Hill, where Indian students were invited to tea under the auspices of the National Indian Association in Aid of Education in India, founded by Mary Carpenter in 1867. It was a British attempt to help the Indian students in the country; and Miss Elizabeth Manning was the current director. We have already spoken of Gandhi's interaction with the theosophists; with their leaders Madame Blavatsky and Mrs Annie Besant. Indeed, it was Blavatsky who provided the impetus for Gandhi's later rejection of formal education. Gandhi never found himself close to the Anglican establishment. The Queen's Golden Jubilee, Gladstone, Cecil Rhodes, the birth of Labour politics, current English literature, left him largely unconcerned. He was not at all interested in sport, with only a limited awareness of the theatre.

There is no doubt whatever that some of his most important ideas imbibed in London helped the evolution of his philosophy in later life. He spent the last days of his stay in London writing articles for *The Vegetarian* on the 'Foods of India'. In these articles he touched on the evil of infant marriage; on alcohol 'the curse of civilization', 'one of the most greatly-felt evils of the British rule' in India. The first series was condensed into a long

---

51 Hunt, *op. cit.,* p. 12.

article on 'The foods of India' in another journal. Gandhi looked forward to a time 'when the great difference now existing between the food habits of meat-eating in England and grain-eating in India will disappear, and with it some other differences which, in some quarters, mar the unity of sympathy that ought to exist between the two countries.' He also wishfully hoped: 'in the future, we shall tend towards unity of custom, and also unity of hearts'.[52]

In these articles he also referred with disapproval to the salt tax that was imposed by the British on India. In a letter published in *The Vegetarian* on April 28, 1894,[53] Gandhi spoke of the 'bond of sympathy that should exist between a vegetarian and a vegetarian in a land where there are so few of them'. He thought that 'the vegetarian movement will indirectly aid India politically also, inasmuch as the English vegetarians will more readily sympathize with the Indian aspirations...'. He hoped that vegetarianism and its practice in Britain would be conducive to firm adherence to principles, and would convince parents that it was possible to study in England without eating meat.

He became a formal member of three English organizations: the London Vegetarian Society; the Theosophical Society; and later, of the Esoteric Christian Union.

Though he passed his examinations and was called to the bar, he knew precious little about the nitty-gritty of an actual law practice; and had no knowledge of Hindu or Muslim law, or Indian law. He did not confide his fears or anxiety to Dadabhai Naoroji, when he met him. An Englishman, Frederick Pincutt reassured him that honesty and industry would be enough to steer him through the initial induction into a law practice. He had to read some more, learn a little more about Indian history, and also learn the art of sizing up people by looking at their faces. He read Lavator's book on the subject, without much profit.[54]

It is a little baffling to note that, so far in his story, he does not mention one person from whom he learned anything in particular; not any great teacher

---

52 M K Gandhi, 'The Foods of India', originally published in *The Vegetarian Messenger*, 1 May 1891; *Collected Works*, Vol. 1, pp. 36-41; cf Guha, *op. cit.*, p. 49.

53 *Ibid.*; *Collected Works*, Vol. 1, pp. 125ff.

54 *Autobiography*, p. 59.

at school in India; not any inspiring teacher of law or any other subject in London. He talks of his sundry experiences in England; his initial hesitation to proclaim his married status; his vegetarianism; his narrow escapes from trying temptations; God's hand in his protection from numerous pitfalls; and his waxing faith in the efficacy of prayer. He relates his anxieties, his sense of uncertainties, his doubts in his capacity and ability to face the realities of the legal world. He, however, devotes only limited space to the studies that occupied him, and for which he had gone to London. So many other things were always on his mind, claiming his time and attention; and it seems that he was always confident of himself with an undented self-belief, even if it was hidden behind and beneath his external diffidence described in so many vivid accounts of his dumbing shyness. He does not acknowledge any academic debts; he does not uphold any teacher; he does not applaud any lecturer. A great man's uniqueness owes precious little to the others around; his greatness is self-nurtured, self-sustained and self-expressed. But is it possible? Can it be true?[55] All great autobiographies, Erikson says, 'demonstrate that the writer in his youth had proved to himself that he had mastered every danger and yes, every ridicule, in such a way that as an adult he would be able to call all his virtues and all his values his own.'[56]

His stay in England familiarized him with the British and their language, which he now wrote as well as spoke with an easy authority. This knowledge of the people, their ways and their prejudices, their likes and dislikes, and their language, as also their laws, stood him in good stead throughout his life in his varied roles as a lawyer and leader, as a propagandist, as an organizer, as a speaker, as a writer, as a fighter for the causes dear to his heart, for human dignity and Indian independence. His sexual abstinence increased his incapacity to appreciate the beauty and value of sexual intimacy. He does not express any anguish of separation from his wife during this period; any word of longing. Nor does he mention anything of the British landscape, the land and the scenic beauty of nature. Rivers, lakes, hills and the undulating expanse of greenery, trees and shrubs, flowers and gardens do not hold his attention; nor does he mention any

---

55 Cf. Erikson, Erik H., *Gandhi's Truth*, New York, 1969, p. 144: 'Such a man never admits that he has learned anything essential from anybody, except where he chooses to ascribe to somebody else what he has already figured out for himself.'

56 *Ibid.*

visits to any museums, though he casually mentions the many museums of London. Two years and eight months gave him a good understanding of the people. He developed a definite affection for them and for their way of life, as also for the city of London. The first chapter of *The Guide to London*, which he wrote after his return, began with a question and an answer: 'who should go to England? It may be laid down broadly that all who can afford it should go to England.'[57] He changed his opinion in 1909.[58] But before that, he was unashamed of his attachment to London: '...so much attached was I to London and its environments; for who would not be? London with its teaching institutions, public galleries, museums, theatres, vast commerce, public parks and vegetarian restaurants, is a fit place for a student and a traveller, a trader and a 'faddist'-as a vegetarian would be called by his opponents. Thus, it was not without deep regret that I left dear London'.[59]

He had not taken any meat or wine; he had not succumbed to physical feminine attractions; and his vows stood the test of time and temptations. Two years and eight months taught him a great deal, and transformed him in more ways than one. He accomplished his principal goal by being successfully called to the Bar. And to raise the level of his education, he passed the Matriculation examination of the London University as well, which he was not required to do, but which demonstrated his curiosity and will to learn. He acquired a sartorial taste and cultivated a lifelong attention to dress as a statement of propriety and purpose. Residence in English homes facilitated the appreciation and cultivation of English manners and etiquette; and made it easier for him to mix and interact with people in social as well as professional spheres. Living away from home made him independent and self-reliant; able to make judicious use of his money and resources, and also to take care of his food and health.

He was interested in religion, and attracted to Christianity, but not enough to convert. Theosophy provided the window and impetus, which reassured his faith in Hinduism. It shaped and strengthened his eclectic inclinations. He remained an admirer of England and English heritage; believed that the British connection would benefit India, and looked forward to Indians playing an increasingly greater role in the process of governing India.

---

57 *Guide to London, Collected Works*, Vol. 1, p. 68.
58 Cf. Hunt, *Gandhi in London*, p. 6.
59 *Collected Works*, Vol. 1, pp. 50-51; Hunt, *op. cit.,* p. 36.

While he was completing his legal studies, certain apprehensions came to the fore. How would he function in the rough and tumble of the real world, as an attorney in an actual court? How would he curb and conquer his incapacitating shyness in public speaking? He had spoken well on more than one occasion; but the experience of drying up in speech through nervousness had an unsettling effect; and produced a feeling of anxiety about his future. The study and practice of Law enabled young Gandhi to find the strength, courage and words to address millions of people around him, and became pivotal to the birth of his non-violent non-cooperation.

There is no doubt that the essence of his education in England shaped a part of Gandhi for ever. It enabled him to understand the British, to agree with them as well as disagree; cooperate with them and also do the opposite; help them and oppose them; argue with them and fight with them if necessary, but always non-violently. He could and would always talk to them and try to understand them, and reason with them. Even when disagreement prevailed, he kept channels of communication open. He respected them, as they respected him. Even in the hatred of many, there was a grudging cognizance of his tenacity, of his determination, of his sincerity, and of his unique greatness. He understood them; they sometimes failed to do so, baffled by his logic or constrained by the commands of their policy. That Gandhi, at once their friend and foe, was 'born' in England!

Chapter 3

Back Home in India

Gandhi arrived in Bombay, and was received by his elder brother Lakshmidas, who took him to Dr. Mehta's house. The friendship that began in England blossomed into a close relationship between the two families. His brother then broke the sad news of his mother's death while he was yet in England. They had decided not to tell him till he came back, so that he could share his grief with the family, not alone and so far away from home. Gandhi was shattered, but tried as best as he could to contain his grief and go about life 'as though nothing had happened'.[1]

Dr. Mehta introduced Gandhi to a number of people. The man who made the deepest impression and became a life-long spiritual mentor was the poet Raychand or Rajchandra, a partner in the jewellery business of Dr. Mehta's brother. Raychand was a young man of about twenty-five, famous for his prodigious memory and power of recall. At Dr. Mehta's instance, Gandhi spoke a number of words from all the European languages that he knew, and to his great astonishment, Raychand repeated them in the same exact order in which they had been spoken. Gandhi was impressed, but not quite blown off his feet. What, however, commanded his respect was Raychand's deep understanding of the scriptures, his blameless character, and his ceaseless pursuit of self-realization. Gandhi cites a stanza from Muktānanda, which was ever so often repeated by Raychand:

'I shall think myself blessed only when I see Him

In every one of my daily acts....'[2]

---

1   *Autobiography*, p. 63.
2   *Ibid.*, p. 64.

Though a jeweller, and a connoisseur of pearls and diamonds, Raychand devoted every spare minute of his life to the study of scriptures, and spiritual reflection. Gandhi's discussions with him left an abiding imprint; and in 'moments of spiritual crisis', he turned to Raychand, who always provided a ready 'refuge'.[3]

Gandhi deems it necessary to let us know that he did not place the poet on a Guru's throne, which always remained vacant.[4] A reader of his *Autobiography* should not fail to note that Gandhi follows nobody; he makes his own discoveries; he takes his own decisions. He walks alone. He owns no leaders except one, Gopal Krishna Gokhale, with whom also he had some distinct differences of opinion. He mentions many; assuredly learns from them all; but passes them by. Raychand gave him a sense of certitude in the direction of his spiritual quest.

A section of his caste re-admitted him after he purged himself by a dip in a holy stream at Nasik; paid a priestly fee of Rs. fifty for a purificatory rite; and gave a caste dinner to propitiate the elders. The reluctant conformist hid behind the elder brother, 'taking his will to be law'. On his own admission, however, he did nothing to provoke the headman of the other hide-bound section that refused to accept him back into their fold, by desisting from visiting his in-laws and other relations who were forbidden to entertain him.[5] They were not unwilling to accord secret hospitality, of which he thought it best not to take advantage. He 'fully respected the caste regulations about excommunication'[6], and as a result, won the affection and co-operation of even those disgruntled, in the tasks that he undertook later. His docile submission to their rules disarmed all opposition.

Gandhi modernized his house; and made changes to the menu of food served. Oat-meal porridge and cocoa were introduced; tea and coffee were discouraged. Boots and shoes and European dress were adopted. He took it upon himself to teach his brothers' children and his son, and encouraged them to undertake physical exercise. He always loved and liked the company of children.

---

3   *Ibid.*

4   *Ibid.*

5   *Ibid.*, p. 65.

6   *Ibid.*

The reunion with Kasturba after his return from England was rocked by young Gandhi's baseless jealousy. His desire to educate her, to enable her to read and write, was defeated as much by his 'lust', as by his self-willed wife's resistance to his dictates warped by his false pride and unfounded suspicions. Stung by inexplicable jealousy, he did not trust anything she did. The two quarrelled, and he sent her to her parental home, permitting her to return only after he had 'made her thoroughly miserable'.[7] Was it some sense of inadequacy, or an ego always gnawing at him? When he wrote his life's story all those years later, he knew he was wrong. It was all his fault. Her misery massaged his self-image. The husband was more than an equal partner; a master who could order her about! But Kasturba had her own mind and power of will, and refused to be crushed by his callous conduct. The later messiah of non-violence was no less than a bully where his wife was concerned!

Though his brother Lakshmidas was a legal pleader at Rajkot, the idea of Mohan starting his practice there was discarded as beneath the dignity of a new barrister. Gandhi, therefore, went to Bombay to gain first-hand knowledge of Indian law and procedures of the High Court, and also to find some work for himself. Four or five months passed without any income to speak of, though his brother was trying hard to find briefs for him. Gandhi spent his time studying Indian law; the Evidence Act and Mayne's *Hindu Law;* but still lacked the confidence to conduct a case in a court of law. In his *Autobiography* he likens his plight to that of a 'bride come fresh to her father-in-law's house'![8]

He went to the High Court daily to listen and learn from legal stoushes between the leading lawyers, but felt that he was not yet conversant enough with Indian law to grasp the intricacies of the arguments; and often dozed off. He doubted if he learned anything at all, which may not be right. One learns, even unwittingly, from the cut and thrust of debates, from the vocabulary of colourful phrases used by the masters of their craft. Sombre details of cases are suddenly lit up by flashes of humour, even if, generally, the insipidity of routine arguments casts a soporific spell on the listeners. As Gandhi dozed off, others did too; and Gandhi was quite comfortable with the thought that he was not alone to do so!

---

7   *Ibid.*, p. 66.

8   *Ibid.*, p. 68.

Virchand, a friend who was preparing for a Solicitor's Examination, and sharing Mohan's dietetic experiments, told him that success at the Bar took years to come by. Aimlessly waiting for a client, Gandhi pounced upon a chance to represent a woman called Mami bai, who was a defendant in a civil case in a Small Causes Court. He refused to pay the tout's commission on grounds of principle; charged Rs. thirty as his fee; but lost his nerve when he rose in the court to cross-examine the plaintiff's witnesses. He froze and could not utter a word. His head reeled, as he resumed his seat. He returned the fee and told the agent to engage another lawyer.[9] This was his first and last appearance before a judicial officer in India. As a boy, he had kept himself aloof from sports and playmates; and found it difficult to speak in public. In 1888, before journeying to London, he shivered as he stammered from his written notes in response to a farewell given by his class-mates at his High School. As a member of the Executive Committee of the London Vegetarian Society, he came to the meetings with prepared remarks, which, for want of courage, he asked one of his fellow members to read for him. And in his own farewell speech before leaving London, his delivery was marred by visible nervousness. For such a shy man, the combative, competitive tenor of lawyers' speeches posed a painful hurdle. He had to put on an act; he had to tell a story that carried conviction. He had to ask challenging questions; he had to tackle, deflate and discredit hostile witnesses through ruthless cross-examination. He had to rebut and refute the arguments of the opposing lawyer; respond to the judge's queries; and conclude with a convincing summation. He had to think on his feet; he had to respect the rules of evidence and procedure; he had to act and speak with palpable confidence. It proved hard, indeed impossible for Gandhi in this first instance. Consciousness of the mocking mirth, that his failure in court would have provoked, lingered long after the event! He did not face any court again till he went to South Africa.

His lack of ties to the business classes virtually closed that avenue of work. He had no close friends or relatives who could help him with clients in the Bombay legal world. And to compound his hardships, Gandhi refused to engage or pay any touts who brought clients and briefs to barristers. 'Faced with the choice of failing with honour or succeeding with dishonour'[10], he resolutely chose a path that was as uncertain as it was uneasy!

---

9   *Ibid.*

10 DiSalvo, *The Man Before the Mahatma: M.K. Gandhi, Attorney at Law*, Random House India Private Limited, Noida, 2012, p. 29.

He applied for a job as an English teacher in Bombay, but the Principal of the High School did not appoint him as he was not a university graduate. London matriculation was not enough. While he was in Bombay, though, he attended the High Court every day in order to learn whatever possible, and always walked to the court and back. He had always been fond of walking, which kept him in fine physical fettle; and commended it to everyone as a habit conducive to good health.

Bombay was a burgeoning city beckoning to Indians from every part of the country; a crucible of many communities carving out a future for themselves. Marathas, Gujaratis and Parsis were rising in prominence and prosperity. Gandhi does not tell us of any 'extra-curricular' interests or activities; does not evince any interest in music and the arts and the budding Bombay theatre. Lack of lucrative work and financial worry was certainly an inhibiting factor; but there was another persistent irritant that ruffled his peace of mind. He complains in a letter about the intransigence of a hard-headed elder of those Modh *Banias*, who still trained their guns of caste ostracism on him.[11]

He visited Raychand often in his shop, and held discussions with him, prompted by religious curiosity and ethical purpose. He was struck by the poet's simplicity; by his earnestness; by his transparent honesty; by his spiritual perspicacity. They talked of *ahiṁsā* or non-violence towards all living beings. Raychand pointed out that Banias in general abstained from harming life and eating non-vegetarian or *tāmasika* food, which tended to stir the lower appetites. But they exercised only selective compassion; and were strangers to courage; conspicuous for their cowardice. They must, said the poet, learn and cultivate the capacity for hard work from the *śūdra;* conquest of fear from the *kṣatriya*; and devotion to learning from the *brāhmaṇa*.[12] Such a precept, however, went against the grain of Gandhi's later statements based on the *Gītā* as he understood it, that one's duty performed badly is preferable to the efficient discharge of others' duties by an individual. Indeed, it took Gandhi painfully long to liberate himself entirely from the thraldom of caste and its compulsions in the

---

11 Cf. *Collected Works*, Vol. 1, pp. 56-57, Gandhi's Letter to Ranchhodlal Patwari.

12 Gandhi's 'Preface' to 'Srimad Rajchandra', p. 6; 'Speech on Birth Anniversary of Rajchandra', Ahmedabad, 16 November, 1921; *Collected Works*, 21, pp. 432-4; cf. Guha, *op. cit.*, p. 62.

choice of one's calling. The burden of preconceptions, reinforced by one's understanding or interpretation of scripture, is a powerful factor influencing thought and action. But we should not surrender our capacity for moral judgement to any scripture, whatsoever! In the ultimate analysis, I must decide what is right and morally unimpeachable; what I am good at; what I must do; what profession I embrace without regard for any prohibitive restrictions imposed by invidious texts. Reason, justice, fair-play, equality of opportunity, freedom of choice is what true morality should be about!! The accident of birth in a caste or class should never be allowed to restrict my choice.

Gandhi was already a published author before he left England. His articles had appeared in the *Journal of the London Vegetarian Society,* and elsewhere. He knew how to write. He drafted a memorial for a poor Muslim, whose land had been confiscated at Porbandar. It was commended by his friends, and helped renew his confidence in his own ability. But it did not bring him any money. Unable to stay in Bombay without an income, he returned home; set up an office in Rajkot; and earned about three hundred rupees a month drafting applications and memorials for his clients. The work found its way to him through Lakshmidas and his partner, who had a joint, settled practice. Gandhi was persuaded to give a commission to the *vakils* (lawyers) who briefed him. Lakshmidas argued that his fellow lawyer was now passing on the overflow of his work to Mohan, who should therefore rightfully pay the partner for the favour. His mental reservations notwithstanding, Gandhi could do no more than acquiesce in the arrangement.

Gandhi recounts a painful experience fraught with disastrous consequences for his professional prospects. He went to speak to the British Political Agent at Rajkot on behalf of his elder brother Lakshmidas, who was implicated in a case of disputed ownership of state jewellery between Rana Vikmat Ji and his grandson Bhav Singh Ji; and was forbidden to visit Porbandar without the Agent's permission. Gandhi had known this person in England, but found to his dismay and humiliation that the Englishman's attitude in India was very different, and far from friendly. He refused to listen to Mohan's plea on his brother's behalf; called Lakshmidas an 'intriguer'; and had Gandhi led out of his office by an orderly. Gandhi had been a very reluctant emissary for his brother; and learned his lesson not to go on any such errand ever after. He wrote a note to the officer asking him to apologize for his high-handedness, failing which he would sue him. The Englishman replied that Gandhi was free to do as he chose. Sir Ferozeshah Mehta, the leading legal eagle of Bombay, advised the young barrister to pocket the insult and move on. 'Tell him he has yet to know life', said the old veteran.[13] The bitter experience taught Gandhi not ever again to exploit his friendship with anyone in this fashion.

The brush with the Agent closed the avenue of fruitful legal practice in his court, where most of Gandhi's cases would have gone; and his position as a barrister in Rajkot became untenable. Any chances of his appointment to a judgeship or to his grandfather's office receded into the backwoods. The corrupt goings-on of Kathiawar courts weighed him down with deep disillusion; and even though he was able to earn enough for himself and his family, professional progress was devoid of cheer. He did some work to secure more powers for the Prince of Porbandar with only limited success, which was not enough to dissipate his disappointment. Just then, Lakshmidas received an unexpected offer for Gandhi from a Muslim firm in Porbandar. They had a big firm in South Africa, which was fighting a case there over their claim of forty thousand pounds. The case had been dragging on for quite some time. They had used the services of many *vakils* and barristers, but would like to use Gandhi to help them instruct their counsel better than they could themselves. This would provide an opportunity to the young barrister to see a new country, make new friends, and also make some money.[14]

Gandhi was tempted. His brother introduced him to Sheth Abdul Karim Jhaveri, a partner in the firm Dada Abdulla & Co. The Sheth told him that the job would not be too demanding. Gandhi had to assist the firm with its English language correspondence and act as an interpreter between the firm and its English lawyers. He was told that his employment would not go beyond the year and that he would be paid a sum of hundred and five pounds together with a first class return fare.[15] Gandhi realized that he was not really going there as a barrister, but as 'a servant of the firm'.[16] But his frustration with his current predicament helped him make up his mind. A

---

13 *Autobiography*, p. 72.

14 *Ibid.*, p. 73

15 *Ibid.*

16 *Ibid.*

new country and its people would indeed provide a new experience; and he could send money home to help his brother run the household.

Leaving India for South Africa was not emotionally as difficult as it had been to leave home for studies in England. His mother was no more. He was fed up with the political and legal intrigues of Kathiawar; defeated by the drudgery of drafting applications and petty petitions; disgusted with the need to pay commissions for the work that came to him. The South African opportunity promised an escape from a set-up far from satisfying. But parting from his wife was admittedly painful.[17] They also had another son, born on October 28, 1892, named Manilal. Gandhi's love for his wife, still laced with 'lust', was becoming 'purer'. They had still lived very little together; but he had 'helped her to make certain reforms'; and both felt they had to stay together to continue the process under Gandhi's role as a teacher.[18] He consoled her with the words that they would be together again in a year. And in less than five years, he left his wife and family for the second time, to sail to South Africa.

Coming events doubtless cast their shadows before! Right from the beginning of his career, his way was different from that of the world around him. He did not flout even in secret the caste restrictions to which he was subjected. He would just not do surreptitiously what he could not do in public. And his measure of success differed from the yardstick of other lawyers. He refused to pay any commission to a tout even for his first case. His adherence to truth limited the extent of his legal advocacy and practice, but not his vision of a lawyer's goal always in accord with truth and honesty. As he tells us later, he lost neither his conscience, nor really any income on that account! He kept his honesty; he observed his principles; he retained the respect of his peers and the public; he found true success, untainted by any dubious intent in unseemly pursuit of a dishonest goal!

---

17 *Ibid.*, p. 74.

18 *Ibid.*

Chapter 4

In South Africa: A Mahatma in the Making

It was in South Africa that Gandhi discovered and uncovered his true self. The personal humiliations, the racial tyranny and abuse of power, the brazen oppression, the studied mockery of royal proclamations, and the withering contempt for those ideals expressed in their blatant breach, rudely roused the young barrister from his comfort zone of usually expected social proprieties. He was jarred and jolted by the ugliness of colour prejudice; uncouth verbal abuse and brutal assaults; and the misguided immoral delight of the perpetrators. The reluctant rebel formulated a new vocabulary of revolt; and forged a new weapon to defeat the injustice and violence of the ruling class. Steadfast and unyielding, non-violent non-cooperation confronted the repressive commands of those in power. Baffled Government and bureaucracy piled oppression upon oppression, to no avail! A new philosophy, a new ideology came to the fore. A new moral challenge and an invitation to the perpetrators of tyranny to realize the folly and injustice of their ways made some of them uneasy in the execution of their iniquitous policies. Constructive dialogue explored the capacity of both parties to compromise in the interests of truth, justice and fair play.

Racial discrimination assails the sense of self in relation to others. The impediments and the inequities lacerate the soul, and inflict wounds that are hard to heal! Gandhi cannot help identifying himself with the misery of the Indians around him, and to his own surprise, stands up in strenuous protest to do what he can to dispel their despair; and channels their hopelessness into a chain of remedial thought and action. Gone is the old diffidence and the self-defeating reticence, replaced now by the indomitable will of a son and grandson of Diwans (prime ministers), whose resolution and purpose expresses itself from the very beginning in letters and notes of protest sent to officials and newspapers. South Africa takes note of his arrival, as he spells out his strident unwillingness to put up with what is ugly, unjust and morally indefensible; incompatible, indeed, with any notion of self-worth and dignity. *Satyāgraha* or soul-force is pitted against the tyranny of the state. Non-violent non-compliance with unjust laws defies the might of the law-makers. Voluntary self-suffering is offered as a penance for the excesses and enormities of those in power in the hope that they would see reason and find the capacity to correct their ways. And there is a ready willingness for honourable compromise!

Time and circumstance combine to create a person and shape his personality. Unavoidable involvement in a painful social situation generates a special awareness and a compelling sense of responsibility. It becomes impossible to melt into abject acquiescence. Any idea of retreat into the realm of apathy and unconcern is unbearable. Withdrawal is not an option. The emasculation of fear (*bhaya*), the enunciation of non-violence (*ahiṁsā*), the deliberate defiance of unjust laws, the self-effacing humility, the unflinching acceptance of punishment, the unfading smile, the unfailing forgiveness, sum up the transformation of an otherwise ordinary mortal into a true *Mahatma*!

Chapter 5

The Voyage

On April 24, 1893, full of high hopes and dreams, Gandhi set sail from Bombay, on his way to South Africa. Events that followed explain the 'birth' of the Great Soul.

They went via Lomu to Mombasa, and then to Zanzibar, where there was a change of boat. The Captain took him ashore, and into a brothel. Gandhi was ushered into a room where an African woman waited for him. Stung by a sudden sense of guilt and self-loathing, he did not know what to do. Anxiety and fear of the unknown, and the prostitute's unattractiveness became the operative factors in Gandhi's escape, where he sought to redeem himself with thanks to God: 'I came out just as I had gone in.'[1] He admits that he should have declined the invitation to go into the woman's room. He thinks aloud of many innocent young men who are drawn into these deeds by a false sense of shame and manliness; and gives the credit for his unscathed exit to God alone, as he had himself not refused to go into the prostitute's room. He tells us that the incident added to his faith in God, and to his capacity to 'cast off false shame'.[2] But all this had happened before! Gandhi describes this ordeal as 'the third of its kind'.[3] His willingness freezes into fear, strengthened by a sudden surge of moral repugnance at the very edge of the precipice. He retreats; and thanks God; but that faith in God did not thwart the initial impulse!

---

1   Gandhi, M.K., *An Autobiography or the Story of My Experiments with Truth*, Navajivan Publishing House, Ahmedabad, 2nd ed, re-printed 1959, p. 75

2   *Ibid.*, p. 76

3   *Ibid.*

Durban and Dada Abdulla

The next port of call was Mozambique; and then they arrived in Durban, also known as Port Natal, where he was received by Sheth Abdulla. He noticed that the Indians around were not accorded much respect, and even Sheth Abdulla was treated with studied condescension. Gandhi was disturbed by what he saw; but he also saw that the Sheth was used to it. People were looking at Gandhi with some curiosity, as he wore a frock-coat and a turban, and not the customary dress of the other Indians.

The Sheth took him to the firm's quarters. They could not immediately size each other up. The puzzled Sheth studied the papers that Gandhi had brought for him, and wondered whether 'his brother had sent him a white elephant'.[4] Gandhi's dress and living style were European and expensive; and the Sheth could not immediately think of any particular task with which he could entrust him. The case in question was proceeding in the Transvaal; and it would not serve any purpose if Gandhi was sent there at once. The Sheth was not even sure of Gandhi's ability or integrity; and he could not be asked to do anything else, for the company's clerks knew their chores better than the newcomer.

Head of one of the biggest firms in South Africa, Dada Abdulla was an intelligent man of the world with great common sense burnished by practical experience alike of business and life matters. With little or no formal education, he could yet talk in English, and was a proud votary of Islam. With no knowledge of Arabic, he still had a good knowledge of the *Koran* and Islamic literature, and enjoyed discoursing on his religion. It was from him that Gandhi acquired useful knowledge of Islam. As they came closer and understood each other better, they had serious discussions on a wide variety of religious matters.

Two or three days after Gandhi's arrival, the Sheth took him to a court in Durban. Both wore turbans. Gandhi was the first Indian to appear as an English barrister in a Durban court. The magistrate, eyeing him seated next to the Sheth's attorney, asked him to take off his turban. Gandhi refused, and left the court. A portent, indeed, of the experiences that followed!

The Sheth explained. Those wearing Muslim turbans might keep them on; but the other Indians had to take them off. One of the three distinct Indian

---

4   *Ibid.*

groups, the Muslim merchants called themselves 'Arabs'. The Hindus and the Parsis made up the other two. The Hindu clerks joined ranks with the 'Arabs' to command what little respect they could; the Parsi clerks called themselves 'Persians'; and these three groups mixed socially. But there was a fourth group, the largest, which comprised the Tamils, Telugus and North Indians, who worked in South Africa as indentured or freed labourers. They came to Natal bound by an agreement to serve for five years. The agreement was mispronounced as '*girmit*'; and the people under '*girmit*' were called '*girmitiyas*'. They were the first Indians to arrive in Natal in 1860, to be followed by others, only thirty-three years before Gandhi. 'Coolie immigration' was the 'vitalizing principle' providing the man-power for the sugar plantations, which ensured the economic viability and prosperity of the colony. Indeed, Indian indentured labour was the human subsidy paid for the pecuniary profitability of Britain's colonies.[5] They came mostly from the lower working class and castes; and some of them found work in the coal mines and the Natal Government Railways. Many went back home on the termination of their indenture; but the others stayed on, working as farmers, gardeners, fishermen and household servants. These people had no social relations to speak of, apart from business, with the other three Indian groups. Called *coolies* by the British, they constituted the majority of Indians resident in Natal, and for that reason, all Indians were called *coolies*. Another name for them was *sāmīs* derived from the Sanskrit *swāmī*, meaning 'master', which was a common suffix to South Indian names. The original meaning of the word was totally forgotten in the derogation of every Indian as a *sāmī*, not much different from a *coolie*.

Businessmen and traders came of their own accord, from the 1870s onwards. Largely from the west coast, mostly from Gujarat, they came at their own expense. Many of them were Muslims, Bohras, Khojas and Memons. There were a few Hindus and Parsis too; and they were all called 'passenger Indians'. The Muslim traders were erroneously called 'Arabs', which set them apart from the working-class Indians. They spread out across Natal and beyond; garnered an increasing share of the retail trade; bought land and buildings and became landlords. South Africa in the 1890s had four regions, consisting of the self-governing

---

5   Cf. *Natal Mercury*, 1865; Guha, *op. cit.*, p. 65. Cf. Also my 'Introduction' to *Indians Abroad*, edited by Singh, Sarva Daman, and Mahavir Singh, Hope India Publications/Greenwich Millennium, Gurgaon, 2003, pp.11-19.

Cape Colony under the Crown; Natal, a Crown colony; the Transvaal and the Orange Free State, which were Boer republics. In 1891, there were 35,763 Indians in Natal; 46,788 Europeans; and 455,983 Africans.[6] Some Indian merchants and labourers found their way to the Cape Colony in the south, numbering about 10,000 in a population of about 400,000 whites and 900,000 Africans.[7] The Transvaal had about 5,000 Indians, 120,000 whites, and 650,000 Africans.[8] Indian traders like Abdulla had come over to supply the needs of the Indian indentured labourers and other workers. They also set up brisk business with the Africans. Hard work combined with thrift and commercial sagacity accounted for their increasingly visible prosperity, which roused spiteful white ire together with a measure of nervousness as evidenced in the *Natal Mercury* around this time:

> We had no squalid coolies then,
>
> With truthless tongues and artful ways;
>
> No Arab storeman's unclean den
>
> Disfigured West Street in those days.
>
> The white man ran the Kafir trade,
>
> And was the boss in days gone by;
>
> But now the Hindoo takes our cash,
>
> 'Busts up' and straightway 'does a guy'.
>
> With a ha ha ha and a ho ho ho,
>
> Ramsammy soon will have to go.[9]

Gandhi was also known as a *coolie barrister,* just as Indian merchants were known as *coolie merchants.* Every Indian was a *coolie.* If a Muslim merchant protested that he was an 'Arab' and not a *coolie,* an Englishman would occasionally apologize. The turban was a statement of personal dignity; and being forced to take it off would be submission to an insult.

---

6   Cf. Guha, *op. cit.,* p.66.

7   Ashe, *op. cit.,* p.56.

8   *Ibid.*

9   *Ibid.*

Gandhi's thought of wearing a hat was dismissed by the Sheth's derisive disdain; only Indian Christians working as waiters in hotels wore hats and English clothes. The turban expressed their patriotic pride.

Gandhi took the Sheth's advice; wrote to the press to apprise them of the incident; and insisted on his right to wear his turban in court. The papers discussed the issue, and referred to him as an 'unwelcome visitor'.[10] South Africa suddenly became aware of Gandhi's arrival. He received a measure of support side by side with some severe indictment of his 'temerity'.[11] The turban remained a part of Gandhi's attire till he left South Africa. At a certain juncture, though, he agreed to take it off, to abide by the direction of the superior court.

Gandhi made good use of his first few days in Durban to make the acquaintance of many, including Christians, Parsis and Muslims, some of whom later played an active part in his campaigns. Abdulla Sheth received a message from his lawyer that he should either go himself or send a representative to Pretoria to help prepare his case. At the Sheth's instance, Gandhi studied the accounts with the clerks of the company; bought himself a book on book-keeping, and painstakingly apprised himself of the case. Abdulla said that his lawyer in Pretoria would find suitable lodgings for Gandhi; and instructed him to avoid familiarity with the other party, who were very influential and might bring unwelcome pressure to bear upon him. But Gandhi frankly told him that he would like to cultivate the friendship of the other party and try to bring about a settlement out-of-court, if possible. The talk of an out-of-court settlement with Sheth Tyeb Haji Khan Muhammad 'somewhat startled the Sheth',[12] who warned him to be on his guard against their wily adversary.

To Pretoria: A Fateful Journey

Gandhi left Durban, travelling first class by train. He refused to pay for a bedding despite the Sheth's advice. Saving five shillings seemed more important, even though the Sheth said that they had enough and to spare. When the train arrived in Pietermaritzburg at about 9 pm, a railway employee looked in and asked him if he needed a bedding. Again, Gandhi

---

10 *Autobiography*, p. 78.

11 *Ibid.*

12 *Ibid.*, p. 80.

declined. Then came a passenger, who looked at Gandhi, a 'coloured' man; went out and returned with a couple of officials. One of them told Gandhi to come out and go to a van compartment. When Gandhi protested that he had a first-class ticket, the official said that did not matter, and asked him again to go where he was told. Gandhi insisted on going in the first-class compartment, as he had been allowed to do so at Durban. The official still said that Gandhi must leave the compartment, or else he would call a policeman to push him out. 'Yes, you may. I refuse to go out voluntarily', said Gandhi.[13] A constable came along, took Gandhi by the hand and pushed him out of the compartment. Gandhi refused to travel in any other; and the train left without him. He sat alone in the waiting room, only with his hand bag. He had left his remaining luggage where it was; and the railway authorities took care of it.

Located at a high altitude, Pietermaritzburg was bitterly cold in winter. Gandhi 'sat and shivered', as his overcoat was in his luggage; and he could not muster the courage to ask for it, lest he should be subjected to further humiliation. His mind was a cauldron of contrary thoughts.[14] He had not come to South Africa to put up with such an ugly assault on his dignity and on his legitimate personal right to travel in a railway class he had paid for. Until then, he was a stranger to such a species of racial thuggery. Should he go back to India without living up to his obligation? He had a job to do; a task to complete. He had failed in Bombay; and he had not been able to carve a niche for himself in the legal set-up of Rajkot, commensurate with his qualifications or expectations. He could not run away from South Africa without doing his duty by the Sheth. Should he then struggle and strive to bring an end to the 'disease of colour prejudice', which was the cause of so many wrongs?[15] He could certainly brave his own hardships and suffering in pursuit of that imperative goal. As he said later: 'my active non-violence began from that date'.[16] He steeled himself to face the painful reality; and decided to take the next train to his destination. He sent a long telegram of protest to the General Manager of the Railway; and another to Abdulla, who at once met the Manager. The latter did not offer any apologies, but assured the Sheth that he had instructed the Station

---

13   *Ibid.,* p. 81.

14   *Ibid.*

15   *Ibid.*

16   Cf. Pyarelal, *Early Phase,* p. 298.

Master to make sure that Gandhi reached his destination in safety. The Indian merchants of Pietermaritzburg, alerted by Abdulla Sheth, came to commiserate with Gandhi, and told him that they had all suffered likewise; and, indeed, it was nothing unusual. Gandhi spent the day listening to these painful stories of discrimination till the evening train arrived. There was a berth reserved for him; and, wiser with experience, he bought himself a bedding. He arrived in Charlestown the following morning, from where he had to go to Johannesburg in a stage-coach, as there was no railway line. The coach also had to stay at Standerton for the night en-route to Johannesburg.

Gandhi had a ticket for the coach journey, but the white man in charge of the coach called 'leader' did not want to seat a 'coolie' inside the coach. He himself sat inside, and gave Gandhi a seat on one side of the coach-box. Gandhi swallowed his pride and pocketed the slight, for otherwise the coach would have left without him. He was sitting next to the coachman. In the afternoon, the 'leader' wanted to smoke; and in order to do so, wanted to sit on Gandhi's seat. He spread a dirty sack-cloth on the foot-board and told Gandhi: '*Sami,* you sit on this, I want to sit near the driver'.[17] Gandhi found it too much to bear; protested that he should have been accommodated inside the coach; and refused to vacate his seat. He would sit inside, but not on the floor. The man suddenly pounced on him, boxed his ears and tried to drag him down; but he held fast to the rails of the coach-box. The man was hurling obscenities at him, trying to beat and pull him down. Gandhi used all his strength to stay put where he was. Moved by the painful spectacle, some of the passengers told the conductor that Gandhi should be allowed inside the coach if he could not sit where he was. The 'leader' then stopped beating Gandhi, and let go of his arm, still swearing at him. As the coach rattled on its way, he kept glaring at Gandhi, telling him: 'take care…I shall show you what I do'.[18]

The coach arrived in Standerton, where Gandhi was relieved and happy to be received by some Indians, who had been asked to do so by Dada Abdulla. Gandhi told them of what he had to put up with; and they too tried to comfort him with stories of their own hardships. Not one to give up, Gandhi wrote a letter to the coach company's agent with a graphic account of his painful experience; and of the threat that had been made.

---

17 *Autobiography,* p. 82.
18 *Ibid.,* p. 83.

He was assured that he would be accommodated inside the coach on the journey from Standerton to Johannesburg.

The eviction from a first-class railway compartment was immediately followed by this atrocious assault. It decidedly shook Gandhi up; and it must have indeed been doggedly brave on his part not to turn his back on South-Africa there and then. It must have dawned on him that the perpetrator was only demeaning himself by his base act. The victim was inconvenienced, insulted and physically abused; but certainly not degraded by the vile conduct of the violent offender. One is reminded of the Buddha, who sat smiling through three days of abuse, till on the fourth day the abuser, tired of his tirade, failed to reappear. Asked by his disciple Ananda, how was it that he remained entirely unflappable, the Buddha said the abuse never reached or touched him. The abuser was defiling his own person like someone spitting at heaven to find the spittle descending on his own self. It is unlikely, though, that the conductor of the coach even realized the baseness of his conduct, or felt any sense of shame or remorse. Notions of racial superiority and mastery completely warp the mind, and blind people to the ugliness of their actions. The seeds of *Satyāgraha* were surely being sown in the fertile ferment of these experiences. Non-violent resistance was taking its uneasy birth. The resolution to challenge racial tyranny was crystallizing!

Gandhi writes that he had no wish to proceed legally against the 'leader' of the coach, who had assaulted him. The journey from Standerton to Johannesburg went without incident; but on arrival there, a man sent to receive him missed him. Gandhi took a cab to the Grand National Hotel, and asked for a room. The manager looked at him and politely told him that they were fully booked. Gandhi then took a cab to the shop of Abdul Gani Sheth, who was happy to see him. The Sheth had a hearty laugh when Gandhi told him what the hotel manager had said to him. The Sheth told him that he should not expect to find room in a hotel, whereupon Gandhi asked, why? The Sheth replied that he would know why, after staying there for some time. They did not mind 'pocketing insults' for making money, which was the only reason that they were there. The Sheth apprised Gandhi of the great hardships that the Indians suffered in South Africa. He said that the country was really not for men like Gandhi, who had to go to Pretoria and would have to travel third class to do so. First and second class tickets were never issued to Indians in the Transvaal. Gandhi blamed it on the lack of 'persistent efforts' on the part of Indians; but the Sheth told him that many representations sent to the authorities had proved futile, and Indians, as a result, got used to travelling third class.

Gandhi got hold of the Railway Regulations, and found that the language was imprecise. He told the Sheth that he would go first class, or else take a cab to Pretoria. The Sheth said the journey by cab would be more expensive and time-consuming, and so Gandhi wrote to the Station Master for a first class ticket, telling him that he was a barrister and always travelled first class. He needed to reach Pretoria at his earliest, and would therefore expect to get the ticket on arrival at the station. There was no time to wait for a written reply. Gandhi proceeded to the station immaculately dressed in a frock-coat and neck-tie, and asked for a first class ticket. The station master asked if he was the one who sent him the letter. Gandhi said yes, and also that he had to reach Pretoria that very day. He would be grateful for a ticket. The station master appreciated his feelings, and said that he would give him a ticket on condition that Gandhi would move to third class if asked by the guard to do so. He did not want Gandhi to sue the railway company, for that would involve him. Gandhi gave the assurance and got his ticket. Sheth Abdul Gani had come to the station to see him off, and was agreeably surprised. He warned Gandhi that the guard might still not leave him in peace. If not the guard, the passengers would make it hard for him to travel first class.

The train was on its way; and Gandhi was in first class. The guard came in at Germiston, and was not pleased to see Gandhi. He told him to go to the third class. Gandhi showed his ticket. 'That doesn't matter', said the scornful guard, and asked Gandhi again to get out and go to the third class. An Englishman, the only other passenger in the compartment, rebuked the guard and told him that Gandhi had a first class ticket; and he did not mind travelling with him at all. The guard growled that he did not care if the Englishman wanted to travel with a 'coolie', and left the compartment. Gandhi reached Pretoria without any further incident.

The shocking incidents fortified his self-assurance and brought it out into the open. The turban that he wore in court, the eviction from first class in a train, followed by his dogged travel in first class on the same line the next day revealed his tenacity of purpose. And then the gross and violent misbehaviour of the coach conductor, including the physical assault, failed to shake Gandhi's determination to sit inside the coach, which he finally did, on the last stage of his journey. He did not submit to these indignities. He protested. He sent letters and telegrams. His resistance was spontaneous and instantaneous. He retained his poise. He would not, he did not stay silent.

In Pretoria

There was no one at the station to receive him, as it would have been inconvenient for the lawyer to send a person on a Sunday. A black American took him to a small hotel owned by an American. The owner took Gandhi in on condition that he would dine in his own room. He assured Gandhi that he did not have any colour prejudice; but all his customers were European. They might take offence and even go away. Gandhi agreed; thanked the proprietor for accommodating him; and hoped to move elsewhere the next day. He sat in his room awaiting his dinner, when the proprietor came in to invite him to the dining room, as the other guests did not mind. Gandhi enjoyed his dinner.

Next morning, he called on the attorney A. W. Baker, who received him warmly, but told him that they did not expect him to work for them as a barrister, as they had already engaged 'the best counsel' for the case. He would use Gandhi's services to garner all the required information in the protracted and complicated case. Gandhi would make it easier for Baker to communicate with his client; and he would now receive all the information that he required through Gandhi. Baker referred to a 'fearful amount of colour prejudice'[19] around; but assured Gandhi that he would be able to persuade the poor wife of a baker to take him in as a paying guest. He took Gandhi to her house, spoke to her 'privately'; and she accepted Gandhi as a boarder.[20]

---

19 *Autobiography,* p. 86.
20 *Ibid.*

Chapter 6

Proselytizing Push of Christianity

Baker was a committed Christian and lay preacher.[1] Gandhi told him that he was a Hindu by birth, but did not know a great deal about his own religion, and even less of others. He was unsure of himself as to what his beliefs should be; and he wanted to make a conscientious study of his own religion, as also of others. Baker was pleased with what he heard. He told Gandhi that he was one of the directors of the South Africa General Mission. He had built a church with his own money, where he delivered regular sermons. He did not have any colour prejudice. He and his fellow-workers met every day to 'pray for peace and light'.[2] He invited Gandhi to join them; commended the Holy Bible; and promised to give him some religious books to study. Gandhi agreed to attend the one o'clock prayers.

He moved to his new lodgings. There was no immediate work for him to do. Baker's interest in him intrigued him. He wondered how far he should go in his study of Christianity; and how he could understand and evaluate Christianity without a proper knowledge of Hinduism. He made up his mind to study what he could; to make God his guide; and not to embrace any other religion without first properly studying his own.

He started attending the one o'clock prayer meetings, where he was introduced to a number of people including Michael Coates, a young man of strong Christian beliefs. Coates went out for long walks with Gandhi;

---

1 He was still writing to Gandhi, when the latter wrote his Autobiography, and untiringly talking of Jesus as 'the only son of God and the saviour of mankind'. *Autobiography,* p. 87.

2 *Ibid.,* p. 87.

and gave him a large number of books to read, which all talked of the infallibility of Christ and Christianity. Gandhi was moved by some, but not converted. He could not accept that Jesus was the only incarnation of God, and the only mediator between God and man.

Coates was an affectionate and persistent man still trying to convert Gandhi. He saw Gandhi wearing a *Vaishnava* necklace of *tulasī* beads; and saying that it was unbecoming to give in to superstition, offered to break it. Gandhi told him to desist. It was a sacred gift from his mother. He did not know and could not spell out its 'mysterious significance'; but his mother had put it around his neck in the belief that it would protect him. He would let the necklace remain where it was, until it wore out and broke away; and he would not care to get a new one. Coates could neither understand nor appreciate Gandhi's statement. He wanted to impress upon Gandhi his belief that salvation was impossible without the acceptance of Christianity. All good works availed of little or nothing without the intercession of Jesus. He introduced Gandhi to a number of Christians. One of them, a staunch follower of the Plymouth Brethren, told Gandhi that he could not understand the beauty of their faith. It seemed, from what Gandhi said, that he was continually thinking of his transgressions, trying to correct himself and atoning for them. This incessant struggle would bring him no peace, as it was impossible to bear the burden of sin. The man then emphasized the beauty and perfection of the Christian belief. Individual attempts at improvement and expiation did not go very far, even though redemption was a crying necessity. The Christians could transfer it all to Jesus, who was the only 'sinless Son of God'. 'It is His word that those who believe in Him shall have everlasting life. Therein lies God's infinite mercy. And as we believe in the atonement of Jesus, our own sins do not bind us. Sin we must. It is impossible to live in this world sinless. And therefore Jesus suffered and atoned for all the sins of mankind. Only he who accepts His great redemption can have eternal peace. Think what a life of restlessness is yours, and what a promise of peace we have'.[3]

Unconvinced, Gandhi countered: 'If this be the Christianity acknowledged by all Christians, I cannot accept it. I do not seek redemption from the consequences of my sin. I seek to be redeemed from sin itself, or rather from the very thought of sin. Until I have attained that end, I shall be

---

3   *Ibid.,* pp. 89-90.

content to be restless.'[4] Brimming with pity, the Plymouth Brother said that Gandhi's attempt was an exercise in futility; and invited him to give greater thought to what he had been told. And true to his word, the Brother consciously did things that were morally questionable, and told Gandhi that he remained undisturbed because of his faith. But Gandhi knew that so many other Christians did not subscribe to such a theory, and 'walked in the fear of God'.[5] His friend Coates believed in purity of thought and action, in self-purification, and was very upset by Gandhi's encounter with the Plymouth Brother. Gandhi reassured him that he was in no way prejudiced against Christianity, though he still had basic problems with the Bible and its current interpretation.[6]

---

4   *Ibid.,* p. 90.

5   *Ibid.*

6   *Ibid.*

Chapter 7

Indians in Pretoria

In the very first week of his arrival in Pretoria, Gandhi met Sheth Tyeb Haji Khan Muhammad, who was the most prominent Indian in town. Gandhi told him that he wanted to meet every Indian around, and to study their living conditions. He sought and received the Sheth's promise of help, and called a meeting of the Indians, in which he spoke of their plight in the Transvaal. This meeting took place at the residence of Sheth Haji Muhammad Haji Joosab; and most of those who attended were Meman merchants. Of the small number of Hindus in Pretoria, some were present at this meeting; but Gandhi's public life began with the noteworthy support of Muslims.

Gandhi tells us that this was the first public speech of his life. He felt none of the nervousness that characterized his efforts in India. The distance from home infused a sense of liberation, and helped him find his true self. He had prepared himself for the exercise, and spoke on 'truthfulness in business'.[1] He had often been told by merchants that truth was incompatible with business, which was a practical profession quite separate from religion. They could be truthful only to the extent that it suited them, and could not uphold 'pure truth'.[2] Gandhi emphasized their duty to be truthful, as all Indians would be judged by their conduct. Gandhi also stressed the need for greater hygiene, so that in matters of sanitation the Indians were not behind the English. He exhorted them to rise above all divisive distinctions. They were Indians first, and 'Hindus, Muslims, Parsis, Christians, Gujaratis, Madrasis, Punjabis, Sindhis, Kachchis, Surtis' only

---

1 *Ibid.,* p. 91.
2 *Ibid.*

later.³ He recommended the organization of a representative association, which could convey accounts of their hardships to the authorities, and work for the welfare of the Indian settlers. He offered his time and service to the extent possible. He made an impression. A discussion followed. Some of the people present offered to help with facts and information. Very few of those present knew English, and Gandhi encouraged them to try and learn the language. Age was no barrier to learning a language; and Gandhi offered to teach those who were willing to learn. Three young men expressed a desire to learn English if Gandhi was willing to go to their places to teach them. He obliged; but they were not as eager or enthusiastic as their teacher. Gandhi was patient. Two of his pupils acquired enough English to be able to make a fair living. His spirit of selfless public service came to the fore. He was prepared to go to great lengths to motivate, to help and to inspire! It was as though insistent intimations of his mission were leading him on!

The first meeting was followed by regular gatherings for discussion; and Gandhi came to know almost every Indian in Pretoria. He also met the British Agent in the city, who was sympathetic and agreed to help, though he did not command much influence. Gandhi also wrote to the Railway authorities pointing out the insufferable disabilities to which Indians were subjected. They wrote back that first and second class tickets would be available to Indians if they were properly dressed. This did not help much, as it was for the station master to determine who was 'properly dressed'.⁴

Papers dealing with the Indian situation alerted Gandhi to the cruel eviction of Indians from the Orange Free State. He made a serious study of the 'social, economic and political conditions of the Indians in the Transvaal and the Orange Free State',⁵ which proved 'invaluable' when he decided to stay on in South Africa after the conclusion of his case. His *History of Satyagraha in South Africa* details the painful conditions to which Indians in the Transvaal and the Orange Free State were subjected. A special law enacted in 1888 or earlier deprived Indians in the Orange Free State of all their rights. They could stay there only to 'serve as waiters in hotels

---

3   *Ibid.*

4   *Ibid.*, p. 92.

5   *Ibid.*

or to pursue some other such menial calling'.[6] All their petitions and representations fell on deaf ears. An Act passed in 1885, and somewhat amended in 1886, made it compulsory for all Indians to pay a poll tax of three pounds as fee for entry into the Transvaal. They could not own any land except in areas demarcated for them. Even that did not amount to real ownership. They did not have any franchise. There was a special law for 'Asiatics', who were also subject to laws formulated for coloured people. Under these laws 'Indians might not walk on public footpaths and might not move out of doors after 9 pm without a permit.'[7] There was some elasticity in the enforcement of this regulation in respect of Indians. Those passing as 'Arabs' were favoured with exemption, which was dependent on the whim of the policeman.

Gandhi had to bear the brunt of both these restrictions. He used to go out for a walk with Coates in late evening, and came back home around ten o'clock. As the police could arrest him, Coates took Gandhi to Dr. Krause, the State Attorney. They discovered that Krause and Gandhi were barristers of the same Inn. Krause was upset by the regulation and expressed his sympathy. He did not give Gandhi a pass, and instead gave him a letter authorizing him to be 'out of doors at all hours without police interference'.[8] This was a special favour; and Gandhi always kept this letter with him when going out, though, fortunately, he never had to make use of it. But the footpath restriction still landed him in trouble. He used to go for a walk past President Kruger's house to an open plain. He always went past the police patrol in front of the Presidential residence 'without the slightest hitch or hindrance'.[9] The man on duty changed from time to time. One day, a policeman suddenly pushed and kicked him into the street without either warning him or asking him to leave the footpath. Before Gandhi could utter a word, Coates, who happened to be riding by, said that he had seen everything and would gladly be Gandhi's witness in court if the latter proceeded against the policeman. Gandhi replied that the policeman treated all coloured people alike, and did not know who he was. He had made it a rule not to seek any redress in a court of law for any personal grievance. 'That is just like you', said Coates; but he asked

---

6   *Ibid.*, p. 93.

7   *Ibid.*

8   *Ibid.*

9   *Ibid.*, p. 94.

Gandhi to re-think about it, as such men needed to be taught a lesson.[10] Coates then asked the policeman to apologize to Gandhi, who had already forgiven him. Gandhi never went to that street again. He did not want a repeat occurrence.

Gandhi now knew of the disabilities and indignities suffered by Indian settlers not only from what he heard, read or studied, but from personal experience. He began to think hard about how they could bring about some improvement in the state of things. It was exceedingly hard for any self-respecting Indian to stay in South Africa. While he increasingly busied himself with public work, he was intensely stirred by an inner religious and spiritual quest. And in Pretoria he also came to grips with the realities of legal practice. He learned from senior barristers; gained confidence; and also discovered 'the secret of success as a lawyer.'[11] He never refers to himself or shows himself as a follower, though he did follow the advice of many mentors in the legal profession; and of Gokhale and others in the political sphere.

---

10   *Ibid.*

11   *Ibid.*, p. 95.

Chapter 8

The Lawyer

From the age of 18 till he was 45, the study and practice of law moulded the man as well as his character. It enabled him to defeat his diffidence; to develop his capacity to reflect and analyse; to grasp and marshal his facts; to present his arguments with cogent clarity; to think on his feet in the cut and thrust of legal and political debate. It made a public person of an extremely shy and taciturn man, initially hesitant in speech to the point of freezing in public delivery. It gave him courage to present his case and advocate his cause in different legal venues to often cold and unfeeling, unfriendly judges. The meek man, as a lawyer, learned to speak with conviction and authority; and to understand the art of the possible in his search for truth and justice. Compromise constituted principled, even if halting progress towards his cherished goal. To understand Gandhi, therefore, as a social and political reformer, we have to look at him and his work as a lawyer gradually merging with his over-riding mission of public service; of liberating the Indians in South Africa, if he could, from the thraldom of degrading laws and disabling or de-stabilizing rules and regulations. He sought to invest their lives with a measure of dignity through his legal practice; with the possibility of making an honest living without let or hindrance, against the naked intent of the white rulers to drive them out of the country.

The case that brought Gandhi to South Africa involved a huge amount of about 40,000 pounds claimed by Dada Abdulla from Tyeb Sheth of Pretoria. Gandhi studied all the intricacies of the case and his Sheth's claim with great diligence. He learned from what the attorney accepted from his preparation, side by side with what the latter found unnecessary or irrelevant. He learned more from what the counsel made use of, from the brief prepared by the attorney. He was now able to assess his own powers of comprehension and his own ability to garner and present the evidence that mattered. He had the capacity and the will to improve; and could not afford to fail. The case enabled Gandhi to understand book-keeping; and improved his capacity to translate from Gujarati into English. He had to live up to the 'absolute confidence' of the Sheth in his ability to deliver. His sincerity and diligence, and his dogged determination could lead only to success!

Gandhi now knew more of the case than both the parties. He commends the advice of a famous South African barrister, J. W. Leonard, to make the deepest possible study of the facts of a case before going to a court; and the law would 'take care of itself.'[1] Facts were synonymous with truth; and adherence to truth would inevitably, in the last analysis, prevail in a court of law. Gandhi realized that though his client's cause was just and true, the two warring parties could prolong the legal proceedings for a long time, at the expense of both, to the chagrin of both. He therefore approached Tyeb Sheth and advised him to go to arbitration. With the appointment of an arbitrator acceptable to both the parties, the case could be expeditiously resolved. Any prolongation of the case would multiply the mounting legal expenses of both to a degree that would be ruinous to both. Gandhi also realized that the winning party could never recover all the costs incurred. He felt a moral obligation to bring both the parties together, and did everything he could to persuade the Sheths to accept arbitration. And an arbitrator was duly appointed.

On April 25, 1894, John Livingstone, the arbitrator, summoned both the parties with their lawyers and witnesses to a hearing; but the proceedings were rudely disturbed by three Pretoria detectives who wanted to arrest Abdulla Hajee Adam, Dada's partner, for breach of customs regulations. They said that they also had a warrant to seize certain papers belonging to Abdulla to prove their charges. Baker read the warrant which only authorized seizure of the relevant books and nothing else. He identified the papers and even Abdulla. But when one of the detectives tried to seize Baker's papers relating to his current case, he resisted and proceeded to put them inside his briefcase. The detectives, however, wrested the papers from him, and also restrained him. They seized everything including Abdulla Mahomed's books and papers, Baker's private papers, and the

---

1 *Ibid.,* p. 96.

notes of the arbitrator. They then took handcuffed Baker through the town to the police office, where he was charged with resisting them. Abdulla was also arrested and charged. Both were bailed out. When the matter went to court, Justice Jorissen upbraided the authorities for disturbing the serious process of arbitration; ordered the return of all the papers, and asked Baker and Livingstone to keep them in their custody. The state should have sought a proper court order for Abdulla to surrender all the required documents to the authorities. A unanimous decision of the High Court totally exonerated Baker, dismissing all charges against 'a well-known and respectable citizen'; and condemned the behaviour of the detectives as 'vulgar, cruel and mean'.[2]

Gandhi learned an important lesson. He saw Baker being hustled and handcuffed by the three detectives. He saw him stand up for his rights against their high-handedness. He saw him march proudly and unashamed in handcuffs in defiance of the misuse of state authority. That would indeed be an instructive example influencing the future course of Gandhi's action!

The arbitration ran its course, and Dada Abdulla won the case. Full and immediate payment of a colossal amount of about 37,000 pounds and costs would have bankrupted Tyeb Sheth; who would have preferred death to insolvency. Gandhi persuaded Sheth Abdulla to accept his payment in easy instalments spread over a fairly long period of time. His tenacity and Sheth Abdulla's magnanimity in victory brought about this happy consummation. Both the Sheths felt relieved and happy; and both gained in public esteem. Gandhi was overjoyed. He had learned 'the true practice of law'.[3] He had successfully cultivated the capacity to commune and correspond with 'the better side of human nature and to enter men's hearts.'[4] He learned that a lawyer's true function was to unite parties rather than to aggravate the existing divisions. To quote his own words: 'The lesson was so indelibly burnt into me that a large part of my time during the twenty years of my practice as a lawyer was occupied in bringing about private compromises of hundreds of cases. I lost nothing thereby – not even money, certainly not my soul.'[5]

---

2   Cf. DiSalvo, *op. cit.,* pp.50-51.

3   *Autobiography*, p. 97. Gandhi's persuasion of the sheths to accept arbitration would have also been helped by the advice of senior lawyers involved in the case.

4   *Ibid.*

5   *Ibid.*

Gandhi's involvement in the case brought home to him a proper realization of the vast extent of the Sheth's trading activities, and the large amounts of money that Indian businesses were making. Their needs for legal representation would certainly increase with their prosperity; and an Indian lawyer would indeed serve their interests better, with significant monetary rewards for his labours.

Chapter 9

Spiritual Quickening

Genuinely concerned for Gandhi's spiritual welfare, Baker took him to a Christian convention in Wellington, and hoped that his presence in an atmosphere of religious fervour would encourage him to embrace Christianity. Gandhi assured him that he would have no hesitation in doing so, should he receive the call from his inner self.[1] He was moved by people praying for him, as he was also moved by the quality and content of many of the hymns. Three days of exposure to Christian faith and fervour, however, failed to move Gandhi to convert. He found it impossible to believe that he could gain salvation only if he became a Christian. He could not accept that 'Jesus was the only incarnate son of God, and that only he who believed in him would have everlasting life. If God would have sons, all of us were His sons. If Jesus was like God, or God Himself, then all men were like God and could be God Himself. My reason was not ready to believe literally that Jesus by his death and by his blood redeemed the sins of the world'.[2]

Gandhi had no difficulty in lauding Jesus as a great martyr; as a great exemplar of sacrifice; and as a divine teacher. He could not however accept him as the greatest or most perfect man ever born. He could not comprehend the miraculous virtue in Christ's crucifixion; he could not accept the redemptive effect of Christ's sacrifice for all the sins of his followers. He found nothing extraordinary in Christianity, that was not discernible elsewhere. He could not see Christianity as the greatest of all

---

[1] Gandhi refers to the hardships to which Baker submitted himself in the company of a coloured man. His efforts to conceal all this failed, as Gandhi could clearly see what was happening.

[2] *Autobiography*, p. 98.

religions, or as the most perfect of them all. Other religions, including Hinduism, also offered great examples of sacrifice for the world's welfare.

Gandhi was fully conscious of the fact that Hinduism as a religion was far from perfect. 'If untouchability could be a part of Hinduism, it could but be a rotten part of an excrescence. I could not understand the *raison d'etre* of a multitude of sects and castes. What was the meaning of saying that the Vedas were the inspired Word of God? If they were inspired, why not also the Bible and the Koran?'[3]

While the Christians tried to lure him into their fold, his Muslim friends sought to do likewise. Dada Abdulla encouraged him to study Islam, and never failed to dwell on the beauty of his faith. Gandhi bought a translation of the *Koran*, as well as a few other books on Islam, and began a proper study of the faith. He was in a kind of spiritual quandary. He sought guidance from spiritual authorities in India; and in 1894 wrote to his friend Raychandbhai, requesting him to throw what light he could, among other things, on the existence and incarnations of God; the nature of the soul; the age and authorship of the *Vedas* and the *Gītā*; the divinity of Christ and the content of Christian faith; the belief in *karma* and reincarnation; the concept of *mokṣa*; on limits, if any, on the practice of *ahiṁsā* (non-violence); and the way to end the world's inequities.[4] Raychandbhai was patient and persuasive. His answers are strongly reflective of his Jaina roots; of his faith in the many-sidedness of Reality. God has 'no abode outside the self', and is not the universe's creator. *Jīva* and *Ajīva* are eternal. Consciousness is an eternal, inalienable constituent of a *jīva*. It would not be right to believe that all religions arose out of the *Vedas* despite their great antiquity. Neither the *Vedas* nor the Bible contain the whole truth, which is multi-faceted. Allegorically only could Christ be the Son of God. The millennium of one's dreams may be unattainable; but one should still strive to embrace equity, and forsake injustice and immorality. Raychandbhai advised Gandhi to make an objective study of his own faith; and was himself 'convinced that no other religion has the subtle and profound thought of Hinduism, its vision of the soul, or its clarity.'[5]

---

3   *Ibid.,* p. 99.
4   Cf. Shrimad Rajchandra, a Gujarati book edited by Mehta, Mansukhlal R., 1914, pp. 292ff.; *Collected Works,* 1, pp. 90-91, 1958 edn.
5   *Autobiography,* p. 99.

Gandhi's friend Oldfield introduced him to the writings of Edward Maitland, who, like Indians, referred to God as both male and female, and held that Christ had to be discovered within himself by a person. This was a mystical union with Christ, quite in accord with the Hindu idea of Self and God, and the union of Self with Divinity.[6] Maitland sent Gandhi a copy of his book, *The Perfect Way*, written in collaboration with Anna Kingsford, and also his own *New Gospel of Interpretation*. Gandhi was deeply impressed by both the books. Many of the ideas in *The Perfect Way* came from Anna Kingsford, who believed that Christianity was a reiteration of ideas existing in older religions, explaining the inner life of the soul. Scripture was not historical but allegorical; and the 'doctrine of the exclusive divinity of one man' was false. It was necessary to realize 'the potential divinity of all men'.[7] This was a kindred stream of thought with which Gandhi could relate and identify himself, so much so, indeed, that he became an agent in Durban for the Esoteric Christian Union; and in November, 1894, published a letter in the *Natal Mercury*, upholding *The Perfect Way* as a new kind of Bible.[8] He commended the Union as an advocate of universality,'based on eternal verities and not on phenomena or historical facts merely'.[9] To the questions, 'whence and what art thou', and where do we go from here, Gandhi found 'complete, satisfactory, and consolatory' answers in *The Perfect Way*.[10]

Maitland also sent Gandhi Tolstoy's *The Kingdom of God is Within You*. He had heard of Tolstoy's thought from Salt and Madame Blavatsky, and had himself read one of his essays, but this book swept Gandhi off his feet with its compelling diction and brilliant advocacy of non-violence; with its repudiation of Christian orthodoxy; with its rejection of state oppression at home and aggression abroad supported by a pliant church with deceptive ritual. Power corrupts. Christ commands obedience as a teacher of truth; and 'inward perfection, truth and love' alone enable humankind to find through self-denial the source of life in God.[11] Tolstoy's Christ was not expiating for the sins of Christians, but was instead preaching the *Sermon*

---

6 Cf. Gandhi, Rajmohan, *op. cit.*, p.67.

7 Cf. Ashe, *op. cit.*, p. 64.

8 *Ibid.*

9 *Collected Works*, p. 139, 3 DEC, 1894. Cf. Adams, Jad, *op. cit.*, p. 67.

10 *Collected Works*, 1, p. 140.

11 Cf. Ashe, *op. cit.*, p. 65.

on the Mount. Tolstoy emphasized five commandments from the Sermon: do not hate; do not lust; do not hoard; do not kill; love your enemies. Gandhi immediately embraced the commands, which went straight to his heart. He said later that Tolstoy converted him to non-violence.

Tolstoy's freedom of thought and untrammelled pursuit of truth, together with his deep morality, impressed Gandhi far more than the books lent by Michael Coates. A Tolstoyan disciple of Jesus must rise against the evils of the state and class hierarchy; conscientiously object to what is unjust and unjustifiable; and secede as far as possible from the dispensations of an unjust society. He must always be non-violent; and he must strive to convert the ruling class to the cause of justice. He must be calm and resolute. 'There is one and only one thing in life in which it is granted man to be free, and over which he has full control....That one thing is to perceive the truth and profess it.'[12]

Gandhi also read other works by Tolstoy, including a tract written in praise of the peasantry and manual labour. These studies, however, did not lead to his conversion to Christianity, which his Christian friends had been hoping for. He kept up the correspondence with Edward Maitland for quite some time; and his exchange of thought with Raychandbhai continued until the latter's death.[13] Gandhi's Christian friends were disappointed by his unwillingness to convert, though he remained grateful to them for quickening his spiritual quest.

---

12 Cited in Ashe, *op. cit.,* p. 65. Tolstoy, Leo, *The Kingdom of God is withinYou,* World's Classics Edition, with other Peace Essays, 1936.

13 He read books that Raychandbhai sent him; and these included *Pancīkaraṇa, Maṇiratnamālā, Mumukṣu Prakaraṇa of Yogavāsiṣṭha, Haribhadrasūrī's ṣaḍdarśana Samuccaya,* and some more.

Chapter 10

Persuaded to Prolong His Stay in South Africa

With the settlement of the case that brought Gandhi to South Africa, he left Pretoria for Durban to return home to India. Abdulla Sheth hosted a day-long party to farewell Gandhi. While people met and mingled, Gandhi's eye caught 'a paragraph in a corner' of one of the papers captioned 'Indian Franchise'.[1] It talked of a bill being considered by the Legislature to take away the right of Indians to elect members of the Natal Legislative Assembly. He states that he was quite unaware of the bill, 'and so were the rest of the guests who had assembled there'.[2] Gandhi dramatizes his discovery.[3] The bill was being debated and reported upon in the local press for quite some time. It is hard to believe that Gandhi, who was an avid reader of newspapers, would have been unaware of it. It is possible that, though some of the literate Indians also knew about it, they had not been able to grasp its import and the consequences that would follow. But Gandhi could distinctly understand the train of disabling measures that would come after, to which he drew the attention of the people present. When asked, Sheth Abdulla told him that they knew little of these matters, and were always preoccupied with issues of trade which they could understand. Their trade in the Orange Free State had been dealt a death blow; and all their protests had been entirely unavailing. They read newspapers only to find out daily market rates, and little more. They did not comprehend the niceties of legislation; and their guides in these matters were their European attorneys. The educated

---

1 *Autobiography*, p. 100.

2 *Ibid.*

3 Maureen Swan characterizes Gandhi's version as 'highly romanticized'. Cf. Swan, Gandhi: *The South African Experience*, Ravan Press, Johannesburg, 1985, pp. 45-48.

Indians were generally Christians, who were controlled and manoeuvred by the white clergy, and therefore desisted from alerting the community to the intentions of the Government.

This dismayed Gandhi, who felt that Christians were still Indians and should therefore be reclaimed for the Indian cause. He warned the Sheth: 'this bill, if it passes into law, will make our lot extremely difficult. It is the first nail into our coffin. It strikes at the root of our self-respect.'[4] One of the guests asked Gandhi to cancel his passage back to India and stay for a month longer, to help them oppose the bill. Abdulla agreed that Gandhi should be persuaded to stay on. But who would pay his fees? Gandhi protested that he did not want any fees for public work, which would nevertheless incur expense; and funds would be needed to mount a movement against the bill. He had to study the local laws, and other attorneys would have to be consulted. Telegrams, travel and printed material would be needed to mount the campaign. Money was important; and even more important was the participation of many in the process. He could extend his stay by a month if those assembled wanted him to do so.

They all requested him to stay, and promised to help with both men and money. Gandhi agreed, and later wrote:'Thus God laid the foundations of my life in South Africa and sowed the seed of the fight for national self-respect'.[5] This was doubtless an epochal decision; a moment of transformation that made a barrister not only the leader of the Indians in South Africa, but also the keeper and guardian of their conscience. Critics of Gandhi like Lelyveld believe that Gandhi's main motive was to set up a legal practice in Durban.[6] But it would be wrong to conclude that his actions and decision to stay arose solely or even principally out of his personal predicament. He would have, of course, gone back to India to an uncertain future, to fight anew to secure a niche for himself in the Indian legal world. The memory of past stumbles and failure haunted him. But he had found his feet in South Africa. He had tasted success in the satisfactory resolution of the case that brought him to the country. He had gained greater self-confidence. He was much more certain of his abilities. He was conscious of his capacity to commune with people, and to guide them constructively towards the achievement of their desired goals. There

---

4   *Autobiography*, p. 100.

5   *Ibid.*, p. 101.

6   Lelyveld, *op. cit.*, p. 38.

was a painful situation confronting the Indian community, fraught with far-reaching consequences, which they did not clearly comprehend. The occasion called for a leader and path-finder. An opportunity arose. Gandhi clasped it, which was perhaps a dictate of destiny!

When Gandhi saw that news item in the paper, it reminded him of something that he must have been reading about in earlier newspaper reports. The implications of what was contemplated, what was proposed, and what was sought to be translated into legislation, suddenly roused him to a new sense of urgency. The others around certainly knew what was in the offing; but perhaps felt despondent and helpless, resigned to the inevitable. The memory of all his racial humiliations in South Africa, of his eviction from a first class compartment, of a policeman kicking him out of a pedestrian walkway, and many more such incidents to which he himself and others were daily subjected, made him feel that something needed to be done; a protest had to be mounted; and it was absolutely vital to fight for the defence of Indian franchise. They had a right to live in South Africa with a measure of dignity; and the spirit of resignation to the disabilities imposed on them had to be replaced by determination to stand up and be counted. When he pointed all this out to his assembled friends, he did not know that they would ask him to stay. Any interpretation of his action as an exercise only in self-promotion and aggrandizement would therefore be wrong and questionable. This was the beginning of his social engagement; of his solicitude and concern for social justice; and of his devotion to public duty. Little did he know then, that his sojourn in South Africa would come to an end only in 1914!

A meeting organized at the house of Dada Abdulla was largely attended, including the participation of many Christians. The volunteers enrolled included many Christian youths. The merchants included both Hindus and Muslims, heads of big firms. The gravity of the situation brought all classes of Indians together, regardless of religion, class, caste and region. 'All were alike the children and servants of the motherland'.[7]

---

7   *Autobiography*, p. 102.

Chapter 11

The Indian Response

Already in the process of enactment, the bill had passed its second reading; and the abject silence and absence of any opposition to its disabling clauses by Indians was cited in the legislative discussions as proof that they did not deserve the franchise. Gandhi literally jolted his countrymen out of their stupor to the need for urgent action. The unanimous support of the legislature for the bill failed to dismay Gandhi. A telegram was dispatched to the Speaker of the Assembly requesting postponement of any further discussion of the bill, which he agreed to do, for two days. Telegrams were sent to the Premier and many more.

A petition, dated June 28, 1894, was presented to the Legislative Assembly;[1] and a copy was sent to the press. A large number of signatures were obtained to add weight to the petition; and all this was done in the course of a single night. The petition, ably drafted, and cogently argued, refuted the argument that Indians did not know any institutions of representative government in their own country. Gandhi drew attention to local self-government in India's municipalities; to democratically elected councils of castes and the trading communities. He referred to the functioning of a representative parliament in the Indian state of Mysore. And he quoted statements by eminent Europeans in praise of Indians and their character. This petition was the first document from the pen of Gandhi. It shows a sharply focussed legal mind, which was bound to gain greater maturity and capacity for combative, compelling argument with practical experience and exposure to the rough and tumble of legal jousts in a variety of cases.[2]

---

1 *Collected Works*, 1, pp. 92ff.
2 Understandably, though, there was no dearth of critics in the colonial press. Cf. DiSalvo, *op. cit.,* p. 347, n. 5.

On July 1, 1894, he sent a set of five questions to the legislators of Natal, asking them if they conscientiously regarded the Franchise Law Amendment as a just measure without any amendment or change; and was it just to debar all Indians from voting despite their qualifications and interests in the colony? Would an Indian British subject never be qualified enough to become a full citizen with the right to vote? Did they consider it just that 'a man should not become a voter simply because he is of Asiatic extraction?' And did they want to keep the indentured settlers in a state of semi-slavery for ever?

On July 3, 1894, he led a delegation of Indians to the Governor of Natal. On July 4, he sent a petition to the Legislative Council of Natal; and followed it up with another on July 6, in which he quoted Lord Macaulay: 'Free and civilized as we are, it is to little purpose, if we grudge to any portion of the human race an equal portion of freedom and civilization.'[3]

Gandhi also wrote to the Indian statesman Dadabhai Naoroji, a member of the British Parliament, to apprise him of the situation in Natal; of what he was doing to counter the attack on Indian franchise without any personal gain to himself; of his heavy responsibility and inexperience; but also of the fact that he was the 'only available person' who could 'handle the question.' He requested Naoroji to help with his influence and advice in a letter that is marked by singular humility, but also clearly voices his self-belief and strength of purpose.[4]

He wrote to the Premier, and sent a letter to all members of the Legislative Council and the Legislative Assembly.[5] He cited the authority of W.W. Hunter to emphasize that Indians came from the Indo-Germanic stock; of Max Müller to highlight the loftiness of their thought and culture; of Sir H. S. Maine to praise their laws; and of many more to laud their achievements in art, music, mathematics, architecture, literature and administration. Gandhi did not mince his words when he said: 'To bring a man here on starvation wages, to hold him under bondage, and when he shows the least signs of liberty, or, is in a position to live less miserably, to wish to send him back to his home where he would become comparatively a stranger

---

3   *Collected Works*, 1, p. 110.

4   *Collected Works*, 1, pp. 105-106. He followed this letter up with many more to seek advice and assistance.

5   *Ibid.*, pp. 142ff.

and perhaps unable to earn a living, is hardly a mark of fair play or justice characteristic of the British nation.'

He drew attention to the election of Dadabhai Naoroji, an Indian, in 1893, to the House of Commons, lauded in the British Parliament and press alike as a uniquely desirable event; and boldly asked: 'Will you, then, follow them, or will you strike out a new path? Will you promote unity, 'which is the condition of progress', or, will you promote discord, 'which is the condition of degradation'?'[6] Gandhi anticipated an attack on Indian franchise in Natal in a letter that he wrote to *The Natal Advertiser* from Pretoria in September, 1893, pointing out that the miniscule number of Indians qualified to vote would not in any way affect the lives of the white settlers.[7]

The petition drew favourable comments from the press, and was duly discussed in the Assembly. This, however, failed to deter the passage of the bill on July 7, 1894. Despite their failure, the Indian community felt a new surge of unity and also the imperative necessity 'to fight for its political rights as for its trading rights'.[8]

It was decided to submit a new petition to Lord Ripon, the Secretary of State for the Colonies. Gandhi worked hard to draw up the petition, strengthened by ten thousand signatures. It was no easy task collecting the signatures from far-flung places across Natal; and Gandhi insisted that the signatories should fully understand the nature and contents of the petition. He found the volunteers. He enthused and encouraged them to do it in record time at their expense, regardless of all physical hardships in traversing a wide terrain and obtaining all those signatures. The petition was duly sent; and a thousand copies were printed for circulation. Indians were for the first time made fully aware of the conditions to which they had been subjected in Natal. *The Times of India* came out in support, as did the London *Times*. A new surge of hope heartened the Indian community, who thought that the bill would perhaps be vetoed. That hope, however, failed to find full fruition, when Joseph Chamberlain, who replaced Ripon as the new Secretary of State, told the Natal law-makers that the British Government would not accept the specific exclusion of 'Asiatics', meaning

---

6   *Ibid.,* p. 163.

7   Cf. 'The Indian Vote', September 29, 1893, *Collected Works,* 1, pp. 78-81.

8   *Autobiography,* p. 103.

Indians, from the electoral rolls; but would not mind a general exclusion if the existing Indian voters were not disenfranchised. The Natal Legislature accepted the directive, and a revised Act achieved the same purpose with a general exclusion of people from voting if they came from 'countries that have not hitherto possessed elective representative institutions founded on the parliamentary franchise...' Gandhi's campaign succeeded in saving only the existing Indian voters when the Act was duly approved by the Colonial Office in 1896.[9] He sought to content himself and his people with his statement that Indians did not crave any political power; but certainly took exception to their humiliating abasement in the first Franchise Bill. And that complaint had been upheld by the British government.[10]

---

9   Cf. Swan, Maureen, *Gandhi: The South African Experience*, p. 67; DiSalvo, *op. cit.,* pp. 96-97, and 347-8.

10 Cf. 'The Second Report of the Natal Indian Congress', post-October 11, 1899, *Collected Works*, 3, p. 101, 1960 Edn. Cf. DiSalvo, *op. cit.,* p. 360, n.4.

Chapter 12

Gandhi Stays On

Gandhi states that it became impossible for him to leave Natal at this juncture.[1] He clearly understood that the disfranchisement was only the beginning of the European colonists' campaign to nip Indian enterprise in the bud, and wipe out the growing Indian competition in business and trade. They wanted Indian labour to work on their plantations; but also to block all their economic and political progress. A battle loomed; a challenge beckoned! His Indian friends requested him to stay permanently in South Africa. He told them that it was impossible for him 'to stay at public expense.'[2] And to bring due credit to the community, he had to live in a style commensurate with the status of a barrister, which it would not be possible to do 'with anything less than £ 300 a year.'[3] The community had to find legal work for him to ensure that income, to make his stay in South Africa possible. His friends told him that they could easily collect that amount for his public work, and that he could also charge people for private legal work. But Gandhi resolutely declined to charge them anything for public work, as that would detract from his freedom and ability to express his opinions without fear or favour. About twenty merchants then gave him retainers for one year of their legal work; and Dada Abdulla bought furniture for Gandhi's household in lieu of the purse that they intended to give him on his departure. Abdulla paid the fees for his admission to the bar; and also for the law books that Gandhi had to buy to set up his practice.

---

1   *Autobiography*, p. 104.

2   *Ibid.*

3   *Ibid.*

Gandhi's application for admission to the Bar in Natal was stoutly opposed by the Law Society. One of the objections was that the admission of a coloured man was not even contemplated at the time when the rules for admission of advocates were framed. The growth of Natal was due to European enterprise, and Europeans should therefore predominate at the Bar. The admission of any coloured barristers would reduce them in time to a minority, which would seriously jeopardise their sense of security. And an Indian barrister would take away all Indian business from his European counterparts. Issues of race and likely loss of income fuelled the opposition; but on September 3, 1894, despite every obstruction, Gandhi was admitted to the Bar.

As soon as he was sworn in, the Chief Justice said: 'You must now take off your turban, Mr. Gandhi. You must submit to the rules of the Court with regard to the dress to be worn by practising barristers.'[4] He had refused to take off his turban in the District Magistrate's Court; but now took it off in obedience to the command of the Supreme Court. The discomfiture of turban removal was tempered by the triumph of admission.'I wanted to reserve my strength', he says, 'for fighting bigger battles'.[5]

Abdulla and other Indian friends remonstrated; but Gandhi replied that he could not 'disregard a custom of the Court in the province of Natal'.[6] Different circumstances call for different standpoints; and compromise is but an expression of the many-sidedness of truth. It is indeed an inseparable part of *Satyāgraha*. It often endangered Gandhi's life, and displeased or annoyed some of his friends. He calls it the pursuit of truth, which is 'hard as adamant and tender as a blossom.'[7]

The Law Society's opposition served as an advertisement for Gandhi in the whole of South Africa, and was, to his great delight, decried by most of the newspapers. The *Natal Witness* was scathing in its editorial:

'We cannot congratulate the Natal Law Society on its attempt to exclude an English Barrister, who happens to be an Indian by birth, from practice in this colony...And we make so bold as to say that the legal ability and

---

4   *Ibid.*, p. 106.

5   *Ibid.*

6   *Ibid.*

7   *Ibid.*, p. 107.

legal knowledge, as well as the educational standing, of a majority of members of this society are not such as to invite comparison…' It accused the Law Society of fanning 'the bright flame of bigotry and prejudice.'[8]

Gandhi rented a lovely villa at Beach Grove, a prestigious European suburb of Durban, with distinguished neighbours including Harry Escombe the Attorney General, who had moved his admission to the bar. The choice of residence was calculated to attract a measure of respect in conformity with the dignity of a barrister, as it also demonstrated an Indian's readiness to spend in order to lead a respectable life.[9]

---

8   *Natal Witness*, September 5, 1894; Cf. DiSalvo, *op. cit.,* p. 69.
9   *Autobiography,* p. 116.

Chapter 13

The Natal Indian Congress

Gandhi tells us that the only justification for his stay in Natal was the call of public duty. His legal practice would be no more than secondary to his preoccupation with public work. It was critically necessary to mount an unwavering agitation against the move to disfranchise the Indians. To do so, it was considered imperative to create a permanent organization, which would continually sustain the spirit of the movement. Gandhi suggested the name 'Congress' for this body, inspired by the Indian National Congress; and on August 22, 1894, with the support of Sheth Abdulla and others, the Natal Indian Congress came into existence.[1] Its seven objects included the need 'to promote concord and harmony among the Indians and Europeans residing in the colony'; to keep the people of India informed; to encourage Indians to study Indian history and literature; 'to inquire into the conditions of the indentured Indians and to take up proper steps to alleviate their sufferings'; and 'to help the poor and helpless in every reasonable way'.[2] As Gandhi would have it, 'the constitution was simple, the subscription was heavy'.[3] Those able to afford were exhorted to pay as much as they could; and donations were received with due gratitude. A new spirit of optimism swept across the community.

As secretary of the new organization, it fell to Gandhi to collect subscriptions. He persuaded the members to pay their dues annually in advance. He notes that people were often not as quick to pay as to promise. He adopted the principle that any work undertaken should only

---

1 *Ibid.,* p. 107.

2 *Collected Works,* 1, pp. 130-135.

3 *Autobiography,* p. 108.

follow the receipt and availability of the requisite amount of money. The Natal Indian Congress never incurred any debts. Gandhi's involvement in the foundation of this organization and its day-to-day operation provided priceless experience that stood him in good stead in the trying tasks that lay ahead. And his patient persistence showcased his matchless capacity for enlisting members, and collecting funds for public causes.

Gandhi also insists on the principle that the organization should not have more money than required. He laid down the rules of procedure at meetings which were held once a month or even once a week if so required. He kept proper accounts and insisted on giving receipts to people for whatever they paid. Meticulous account books served as the basis of 'truth in its pristine purity'.[4] We see the lawyer's training in full play, inculcating a sense of order and organization; and of economic integrity.

The Colonial-Born Indian Educational Association, established under the auspices of the Natal Indian Congress, brought the educated youths in touch with the Indian mercantile community, who could help them find suitable employment. They could also develop their debating skills and participate in public service through this body and the Congress.

The Congress had to do more in terms of propaganda. The English in South Africa and in England had to be apprised of the real state of things in Natal. The people of India had also to be told how painful the situation was in Natal. Gandhi addressed himself personally to the task, and wrote two pamphlets: *An Appeal to Every Briton in South Africa;* and *The Indian Franchise – An Appeal.*[5] The first highlighted the general condition of Indians in Natal; and the second was a brief account of the Indian Franchise in Natal. Written with painstaking care, they were extensively circulated; and won for Indians many new friends in South Africa. They also attracted meaningful sympathy in India, while also providing timely guidance to the Indian community in South Africa. Gandhi's organizing capacity and keen observation of ground realities, researching ability and mastery of evidence, and fast developing writing skills bear witness to his evolution as an advocate of social justice, as also to his indefatigable industry and clear sight of his goal.

---

4   *Ibid.,* p. 109.

5   *Ibid.,* p. 110.

Chapter 14

Inhumanity of Indenture

Indians in South Africa gained a sense of direction from all this activity, with increasing understanding of what they needed to do to improve their lot. The Natal Indian Congress consisted of the merchant and clerical sections of the Indians resident in the colony, but did not yet include the indentured labourers and the unskilled wage earners. They could not afford the subscription; and the Congress could only attract them by doing something to improve their lot. The Congress was hardly three or four months old, as was Gandhi's practice as a lawyer, when one day 'a Tamil man in tattered clothes, head-gear in hand, two front teeth broken and his mouth bleeding, stood before' him 'trembling and weeping.'[1] He had been brutally beaten by his master, a well-known European resident of Durban. His swollen face made it exceedingly hard for him to speak. He was crying at the memory of the vicious assault. His name was Balasundaram. He wrote an account of his harrowing experience on a piece of paper and gave it to Gandhi's clerk, who spoke Tamil. The clerk relayed to Gandhi the story of this indentured servant set upon by his cruel master. Balasundaram had first gone to the Protector of Immigrants, only to be turned away. He then sought redress with the local magistrate, who was shocked to see the plight he was in. His front teeth showed through his torn lip. His turban, in his hands, was soaked with the blood flowing from his head. The magistrate sent him to hospital, but kept the turban as vivid evidence of the atrocity.

Discharged from the hospital after several days of treatment, Balasundaram went straight to Gandhi's office.[2] Balasundaram requested the Indian

---

1   *Ibid.*

2   In the account given in *The Grievances of British Indians in South Africa: An*

barrister to sue his master, and liberate him from his indenture. Gandhi knew it would be hard if not impossible to win against a European master in a European court, and suggested his transfer to another master. He sent him to see a doctor, and secured a certificate listing the injuries he had sustained. Gandhi then approached the master, who hesitated, before agreeing to the transfer. But his wife was totally unwilling, as Balasundaram's services were indispensable. The master went to the Protector to withdraw his consent to any transfer; and the Protector wrung a withdrawal of his complaint from Balasundaram, together with his agreement to continue his indenture with his unrepentant master.

The so-called compromise shocked Gandhi, who knew what would happen to the hapless man consigned once more to the tender mercies of a master he had dared to defy. He hurried to the office of the Protector, who told him that Balasundaram had withdrawn his complaint, and showed him the piece of paper which he had himself quickly attested. The clear purpose was to dissuade Gandhi from proceeding any further. Not to be silenced, Gandhi insisted that he would still seek redress with the magistrate. He made a move in the magistrate's court; but also wrote to the master seeking his consent to the transfer of Balasundaram to a new master. The indentured worker was a virtual slave of his master, and could be criminally charged for leaving his service without due process. Gandhi took the poor man to the magistrate and filed an affidavit. Balasundaram's testimony and the visible proof of the master's savagery moved the magistrate. Gandhi could have pursued his case to a clear win; but, instead, repeated his suggestion of the man's transfer to a new master. The angry magistrate warned the master that the case would not end well for him; and accepting a transfer would be far more preferable. The master agreed, but the Protector would accept transfer only to a European, as Indians were not allowed to employ indentured labour. Gandhi's friend, Oswald Askew, himself an attorney, accepted the man's services, thus bringing the matter to a satisfactory conclusion.

Gandhi had quietly, calmly, but resolutely pursued his objective without making any unnecessary noises or loud speeches. He knew that truth and

---

Appeal to the Indian Public, commonly called the 'Green Pamphlet' owing to the colour of its cover, Gandhi tells us that Balasundaram had gone first to the Protector of Immigrants. But according to the *Autobiography* written 31 years later, he came to Gandhi first. The charge by some recent biographers that Gandhi embellished the story does not negate what he saw when the injured labourer came to him, and what he did for him.

justice were on his side. He did not want to subject the master to any retaliatory punishment. He knew what was possible under the system; what solution could be sought and successfully achieved. Compassion, active and steadfast, but not vociferous, a sense of justice tempered by an awareness of harsh realities, and a resolute course of action produced a result that would not exacerbate relations or inflame tempers.[3]

Service of the poor was his 'heart's desire'. In his own words: 'Balasundaram's case reached the ears of every indentured labourer, and I came to be regarded as their friend. I hailed this connection with delight. A regular stream of indentured labourers began to pour into my office, and I got the best opportunity of learning their joys and sorrows.'[4] Gandhi listened; and gave helpful advice. He could relate to them, feel for them, and identify himself with them. The realization that there was a man in Natal willing and eager to plead their cause and work for their betterment, surprised them; and filled them with joy and hope. Increasing contact with the indentured, and their service, sharpened his sense of social solicitude, and decisively delineated the contours of a *Mahatma* in the making.

Gandhi recalls that Balasundaram had entered his office with his headgear in hand. Gandhi had himself been asked to take off his turban in a court. The practice was symbolic of the humiliation of Indians by the white masters. Almost every Indian was forced to take off his headgear when visiting a European. Any other mode of salutation was not good enough. Balasundaram followed this practice even with Gandhi, who asked him to re-tie his turban; which he did, but not without hesitation. Gandhi muses: 'It has always been a mystery to me how men can feel themselves honoured by the humiliation of their fellow-beings.'[5]

In an 'Open Letter' to members of the Legislative Council and the Legislative Assembly, circulated among the European residents of Natal on December 19, 1894, Gandhi made a plea for sympathetic understanding

---

3 Ashe, *Gandhi, A Study in Revolution*, p. 61, tells his readers that 'Gandhi... practically blackmailed' Balasundaram's employer 'into letting his victim go.' An inaccurate, unfortunate choice of words, that betrays an unshakeable sense of British annoyance and exasperation with Gandhi despite the grudging admiration!

4 *Autobiography*, p. 101.

5 *Ibid.*, p. 112.

between the Europeans and Indians. He was forthright: 'If I am to depend upon one-tenth of the reports that I have received with regard to the treatment of the indentured Indians on the various estates, it would form a terrible indictment against the humanity of the masters on the estates and the care taken by the Protector of Indian immigrants. This, however, is a subject which my extremely limited experience of it precludes me from making further remarks upon.'[6]

DiSalvo says that Gandhi jumped to the rescue of Balasundaram, but did not care as much for the German businessman Max Sheurmann, who was evicted from premises owned by Dada Abdulla & Co.for non-payment of rent. Gandhi was the lawyer who secured the eviction. DiSalvo calls this 'uncompassionate', as Sheurmann later went to the Durban Circuit Court with an application for bankruptcy.[7] But likening of the two cases is inapposite and inaccurate, as Sheurmann was nobody's slave to be subjected to assault and battery with impunity. How would Gandhi know that he was in dire financial straits? His bankruptcy did not result from Gandhi's win on behalf of Abdulla. Businesses have to be financially viable to be able to pay others' dues. One cannot allow any business to operate from premises, the rent for which remains unpaid. It is not fair to blame Gandhi for Sheurmann's economic failure.

Gandhi fought cases involving issues of honour and justice for Indians; and won a symbolic victory in an out-of-court settlement for his client Ismail Hajee Adam, who was assaulted by a policeman. He also conclusively won an argument in the columns of *Natal Witness* against Justice Sir Walter Wragg, who questioned his ability to understand Muslim law and recommend a decision on that basis. It was a telling demonstration of his fearless challenge to authority on matters of law and principle.

---

6   *Collected Works*, 1, p. 160. Cf. also DiSalvo, *op. cit.*, p. 353, n. 114.

7   DiSalvo, *op.cit.*, p. 76.

Chapter 15

A Lesson Learned

An instructive event of 1895 had a portentous significance. The Natal Government Railway used to provide fuel to their Indian employees for cooking their meals in the barracks. The Railway suddenly decided to give them coal instead of firewood, which they found almost impossible to ignite for want of kindling. The desperate workers decided to get hold of firewood from the railway yard, but were arrested by police for doing so. There was a scuffle, in which some police officers were allegedly injured. The workers' leaders were taken to court the next day; but a hundred of their co-workers assembled and threatened to encamp there if their colleagues were not released. The Protector of Immigrants supported them and told the magistrate that they had not been able to cook any meals for seventeen days. The magistrate, quite sympathetic, observed that they had been 'labouring under an enormous grievance'. He found them guilty of taking what was not theirs, and chided them for their conduct against the police; but released them without prescribing or imposing any punishment.

The Railway was sill unmoved and unyielding. The workers, 250 of them, left their jobs the next day, and marched to the office of the Protector of Immigrants to demand firewood, so that they could cook and eat. They could not work on empty tummies. They would desist from work until their demand was conceded. The Railway agreed to make firewood immediately available; and the victorious workers resumed their duties.[1] We do not know if Gandhi acted as an advocate for the workers. He, however, wrote to the *Natal Advertiser* to complain about the coverage it gave to the case.

---

1 Cf. DiSalvo, *op.cit.,* p. 85; 'Coolies on Strike', *Natal Advertiser*, May 21, 1895

He referred in detail to the dialogue in court, which clearly indicates his presence there. Thus on May 20 and 21, 1895, he witnessed with educative effect the demonstrative power of determined disobedience. This was no doubt an object lesson, a primary precept in principled, courageous and calculated refusal to obey, which provided the impetus for social change.

The lesson was reinforced a month later. Two hundred fifty-five Natal Government railway workers walked off their jobs on June 25, 1895, in a dispute over their entitlement to a certain quantity of rations. They proceeded, as before, to the office of the Protector of Immigrants to lodge their complaint; but instead of any redress or assistance, they were arrested and charged. They had violated Section 101 of Law 25 of 1891, which prohibited leaving work together. The prescribed punishment for the offence was a fine of £ 2, or a maximum of two months' jail. Representing the workers, Gandhi suggested that the hearing be postponed and the case resolved privately between the workers and the Railway authorities. He had done this before, with success, in other cases. But the magistrate refused the request. The workers had violated the law; and the Railway official also insisted that he did not want to withdraw the charges. When asked by the magistrate whether his men would plead guilty or deny the charges, Gandhi instructed them to plead guilty. The magistrate sentenced them to a one- shilling fine or three days' jail in a lenient judgement; but they refused to pay the fine and proceeded to jail. Their resolution was clearly on display; and the authorities dreaded the prospect of providing food and beds for so many in jail for a whole three days. The workers then paid their fines and returned to work, but only after the magistrate assured them that the Railway would provide adequate rations. Gandhi learned anew the power of principled disobedience.[2]

He was not afraid of authority. When a magistrate named Lucas made remarks derogatory to the Natal Indian Congress in a judgement,[3] Gandhi wrote to the Colonial Secretary calling into question his *bona fides*, emphasizing his obvious bias against the Congress, and challenging the Government to investigate the Congress. The thought of appearing

---

2 Cf. *Natal Mercury*, June 26, 1895; DiSalvo, *op.cit.*, p. 86.

3 Lucas likened the Congress to 'an association of conspiracy – pernicious and fraught with danger to the whole community in the Colony of whatever race'. Cf. DiSalvo, *op.cit.*, pp. 89-90. The judgement was overturned by the Supreme Court.

before the magistrate in a case in future caused no unease, whatsoever. He showed purposeful persistence in his practice; and imperviousness to insult and derision by judges prejudiced against him and his clients. He never lost sight of the key issues, which accounted for his success. And the most important feature of his practice, well known to the judges, was his unswerving adherence to truth.

The Europeans in Natal needed Indian labour for the cultivation of sugarcane and manufacture of sugar. The Zulus were unsuitable for this kind of work. The Government of India was approached, and with their permission, Indian labour was recruited to develop sugarcane farms in Natal. These recruits were made to sign an agreement of indenture to work in Natal for five years, at the end of which they would have the liberty to settle there and to have full rights to own land. The Indians exceeded their expectations. They grew vegetables; introduced many Indian varieties and fruits such as the mango; and could grow them at much less expense. And they went beyond agriculture into trade; bought land and built on it. Labourers became owners of land and houses. They were followed by merchants from India, some of whom built up large businesses and alarmed the white traders, who could not easily stomach the idea of competition from Indians. Their happiness even with small profits, their way of life and inattention to sanitation, combined with their adherence to different religions, added to the aversion towards Indians. Hence the bills to deprive Indians of their franchise, and to impose a crippling tax on the indentured Indians!

The proposals to emasculate Indian enterprise and to get rid of Indians to the extent possible included the suggestion that the indentured labourers should go back to India on the expiry of their indenture; or else sign a new indenture every two years. If they refused to return to India or renew their indenture, they should be made to pay an annual tax of £ 25. The Natal Indian Congress mounted an intense campaign against the cruel proposal; and Gandhi believes that the Viceroy of India, Lord Elgin was thereby moved to reject the £25 tax, though he gave his consent to an annual poll tax of £3. Gandhi construed it as a dereliction of viceregal duty to the interests of Indians, as levying a tax of £12 from a family of four, including husband, wife and two children, regardless of their average income, never more than 14 shillings a month, was a cruel and indefensible imposition.[4]

---

4   *Autobiography*, p. 113.

A Lesson Learned

The 'Memorial to Lord Elgin', dated August 11, 1895, beseeching him to intervene or to stop any further emigration of Indian labour, presents a pathetic picture of the hopeless lot of the indentured:

'....Five years' indenture, your Memorialists submit, is long enough to undergo. To raise it to an indefinite period would mean that an Indian who cannot pay a poll-tax of £ 3 or return to India, must for ever remain without freedom, without any prospect of ever bettering his condition, without ever even thinking of changing his hut, his meagre allowance and ragged clothes, for a better house, enjoyable food and respectable clothing. He must not even think of educating his children according to his own taste or comforting his wife with any pleasure or recreation....'[5]

Submission to the injustice of this tax in a spirit of fatalistic resignation would have brought shame to both India and the Indians of South Africa. And It took a protracted, painful struggle of twenty years to finally secure its remission.

---

5   *Collected Works*, 1, p. 230. One wonders, though, whether Gandhi ever thought of providing any recreation for Kasturba!

Chapter 16

Immersion in Comparative Religion

While in England, Gandhi had read in Anna Kingsford's *Perfect Way in Diet* of a colony of monks and nuns of the Cistercian order, known as Trappists, in South Africa, noted for their silence, austerity and vegetarianism. In April, 1895, he visited their monastery situated on Mariann Hill, about sixteen miles away from Durban. He was impressed by their discipline and adherence to a tough time-table. The monks were vegetarian, though the 'more delicate' sisters were allowed meat for four days in a week. 'Grieved' Gandhi could not understand. None of them took any alcohol. They did not carry any money; and observed a strict vow of silence and chastity, while busy making shoes, furniture and kitchen pots. There was no racial feeling, nor any discrimination based on colour. The whites and the natives wore the same dress; and ate the same food. Gandhi wrote about this visit to *The Vegetarian,* heaping praise on the Trappists who proved 'that a religion appears divine or devilish, according as its professors choose to make it appear'.[1] The visit left a lasting impression, which is reflected in the management and discipline of the *ashrams* that he established; and in his own observance of silence on specific days in later life.

Gandhi tells us that his involvement in public service was motivated by his 'desire for self-realization'.[2] He felt that he could realize God only through service, which, for him, became the service of India. He came to South Africa to seek salvation from the intrigues of Kathiawar, and to earn a living. He, however, found himself searching for God, for self-realization and self-fulfilment through service of the poor and the deprived. His

---

1 *Collected Works,* 1, pp. 180-186.

2 *Autobiography,* p. 114.

Christian friends roused his 'insatiable' spiritual curiosity.³ He continued his religious correspondence with Raychandbhai; and read Narmadashankar's book called D*harmavicāra*; Max Mueller's *India-What Can It Teach Us*; and translations of the *Upaniṣads* brought out by the Theosophical Society. His understanding and appreciation of Hinduism deepened; but it did not in any way decrease his respect for other religions. He read Washington Irving's *Life of Mahomet and His Successors*, and also Carlyle's account of the Prophet in his *Heroes and Hero Worship*; and the Prophet rose high in his estimation. He studied *The Sayings of Zarathustra*. He pored over the works of Tolstoy, and was deeply impressed by *The Gospels in Brief, What to Do?*. His expanding mental horizon was lit up with an increasing awareness of the 'infinite possibilities of universal love'.⁴

All these books added to his knowledge of different religions, and assisted introspection, inculcating in Gandhi the habit of practising whatever appealed to him in his spiritual quest. He also began the practice of *yoga*, in which he did not proceed very far.

Gandhi continued to eat only vegetarian food. He tried 'vital food' consisting of 'fruit, grain, nuts and pulse, all raw', recommended by A.F. Hills as the 'diet of paradise', both in Bombay and Pretoria, only to find that it left him feeling weak, hungry and tired.⁵ It hurt his teeth. He went back to fruits and cooked vegetarian meals, extolling their goodness. But his Sunday visits to a family came to an abrupt end, when he impressed upon the couple's young son the desirability of eating fruits and vegetables instead of meat. The lady, worried about her son's health, did not like it; and Gandhi excused himself from visiting their house any more.

---

3   *Ibid.*

4   *Ibid.*, p. 115.

5   Cf. *Collected Works*, 1, pp. 81-86.

Chapter 17

Gandhi's Household

Gandhi's residence in Beach Grove consisted of a drawing room, a lounge, a dining room, and five bed-rooms. It was suitably furnished in consonance with his status as a barrister and representative of his community. He was a gracious host, and regularly invited his English friends and Indians to dinner. His office clerks, and a friend of his boyhood days, Sheikh Mehtab, resided and boarded with him. They had a cook, who was treated as a member of the family; and Mehtab managed the household. He, sadly, betrayed Gandhi's trust in more ways than one.

Gandhi caught Mehtab with a prostitute in the house one day, and asked him to leave forthwith. Mehtab was defiant, but apologized and left when Gandhi threatened to call the police. Gandhi admits that his 'infatuation' with this 'evil genius' had hitherto blinded him to his unfaithful conduct.[1] He had cultivated the friendship of Mehtab at school knowing full well that he was a shady character, but hoping to reform and reclaim him to a life of blameless conduct. His family, including his mother, eldest brother and wife had remonstrated with him and warned him; but he had persisted with his mission to reform his misguided friend. From Gandhi's story as told by him, one gains the impression that this was the final parting of ways between the two long-time friends. But it was not really so. We find Mehtab writing to the *Natal Advertiser*, telling South Africans that Gandhi's *Green Pamphlet* distributed in India only restated what he had already said or written about the shameful treatment of Indians in South Africa.[2] We see him publishing poems in Gandhi's journals; singing songs

---

1   *Autobiography*, p. 118.
2   Cf. Guha, *op. cit.*, p. 109.

in praise of Andrews and Pearson; and participating in the *Satyāgraha* launched by Gandhi. Mehtab had followed Gandhi to South Africa; and married and settled there. His wife also figures in the story of Gandhi's movement. She courted jail, together with her mother, in the struggle for recognition of Indian marriages by South African law.[3] Though Gandhi refrains from naming Mehtab even once in his *Autobiography*, their friendship had been certainly extraordinary. The gulf between the two was not really bridged by the unacknowledged *rapprochement*. Gandhi's unforgiving characterization of his unnamed 'companion' so many years later makes that quite obvious. The idea that Gandhi did not name his friend in his *Autobiography* to spare any embarrassment to the latter's family and friends is a little difficult to accept, as he would have known that his readers and reviewers would immediately name Mehtab, as indeed they all did. Forgiveness is the foundation of a tranquil disposition. Even traces of reactive resentment for a friend's failings in the past disturb and detract from one's practice of *ahiṁsā* or non-violence in thought, word and deed. Gandhi fails to rise above his grouse against his friend despite the passage of years; despite Mehtab's positive participation in his campaigns in South Africa, which he entirely omits to mention. He seems to have forgotten the precept of *abhyudaye kṣamā*, forgiveness in one's rise to greatness! He forgets that the flesh is often weak; and to err is human! 'Only between like natures can friendship be altogether worthy and enduring', writes Gandhi: 'I am of opinion that all exclusive intimacies are to be avoided; for man takes in vice far more readily than virtue. And he who would be friends with God must remain alone, or make the whole world his friend.'[4] He certainly tries to befriend the world; but finds another intimate friend in Hermann Kallenbach a few years later.

---

3   Cf. Guha, *op.cit.*, pp. 501, 507.

4   *Autobiography*, p. 14.

Chapter 18

Public Service and the Practice of Law

More than two years passed by. Gandhi forged a happy relationship with the people; and knew that they needed him. He had a lucrative practice. At a mass meeting convened by the Natal Indian Congress in September,1895, he told an audience of more than a thousand that he would go to India to promote their cause in their motherland; and would return with his wife and children to properly settle down in South Africa. And he would also persuade Indian barristers to come to South Africa to help the community.

Before he could go, though, he had to fight some important cases to defend Indians in the South African courts of law. In a controversial case on race relations, he scored a clear victory against the highhandedness of the police, and the brazen prosecution of the charges against two Indians in court by the Police Superintendent Richard Alexander himself. John Lutchman Roberts and Samuel Richards, Indians who had adopted European names after their conversion to Christianity, were stopped by a policeman on their way back home at 9.30 pm after a stroll. A Durban law allowed police to arrest a coloured person wandering between the hours of 9 pm and 5 am without a pass from his employer, if he could not give a good account of himself. The two young men were properly dressed. They told the constable that they were walking back to their house just minutes away from Durban's gardens. They told him that they were both employed. One of them was a clerk of Gandhi; and the other was a school teacher. The police officer still arrested them and took them to the police station. Bail was refused; and they had to spend the night in jail.

On February 20, 1896, the Police Superintendent represented the Crown, and Gandhi appeared to defend his clerk and his companion. The cross-examination of a defendant by the Superintendent clearly displayed the contempt held against Indians. Gandhi argued that both men had given a good account of themselves, and their arrests, therefore, were entirely unwarranted. The magistrate agreed, and immediately discharged the defendants. Gandhi urged the police to be a little more 'charitable and considerate towards the Indian community...'[1]

The Police Superintendent gave a scornful, racist interview to the *Natal Mercury*, which was resolutely rebutted by Gandhi in a long lucid letter to the journal. That the Indians were sons of indentured workers was no offence; and no argument against them. 'A man's worth, not his birth, is taken into account in judging him.' The presumption of innocence should be equally applicable to everyone. The police could certainly use better judgement; and the cold, harsh treatment of the two Indians was totally unnecessary, and uncalled for.[2]

Gandhi fought an important case on behalf of Dada Abdulla and Co., against James Matthew Adams, captain of one of their ships, the S.S. *Courland*. Adams sued the Company for wrongful discharge from service, and for the reimbursement of money he had spent on management of the ship. Gandhi defended the Company with a counterclaim against the captain, accusing him of cheating the Company. He stood undaunted by the scornful sneers of the opposing counsel, the hostility of the judge, and the unfriendly gallery. The case tried his mettle; his toughness and his tenacity; his tireless perseverance and attention to detail; his unfaltering focus on the central issue in the case; and above all, his adherence to truth. When the exasperated judge at one point asked him if he had read the shipping law, Gandhi frankly said 'No'. Yet, with his dogged marshalling of facts and evidence, he won part of his counterclaim, and minimized the damages awarded to Adams.

'Have you read your shipping law?', was a short, sharp question. Gandhi's honest, short answer showed his devotion to truth, in the practice of which he did not waver.[3]

---

1 'Out After Hours', *Natal Mercury*, February 21, 1896; DiSalvo, *op.cit.*, 94, 359, n.69.

2 *Cf.* 'Letter to *The Natal Mercury*', March 2, 1896, *Collected Works*, 1, pp. 297-300; also DiSalvo, *op.cit.*, pp. 359-360.

3 Cf. DiSalvo, *op.cit.*, pp. 97-105, for a detailed discussion of the case.

Chapter 19

India

On Tuesday the second of June, 1896, more than a thousand people applauded him as he gave a two-hour long speech, rich in intellectual content and relevant substance, at the new Congress Hall. The timorous lawyer of an earlier day, with his throat choked by nervousness, was nowhere to be seen. The transformation was total. The spirit upheld the physique. And on Friday the fifth of June, 1896, about five hundred Indians, including some of the most prominent merchants of the community, took him from his home to his ship, and loudly cheered, as he set sail for India. In the words of Parsi Rustomji, a Congress colleague, 'words could not express the kindness shown by Mr. Gandhi to poor Indians'.[1]

He would educate public opinion in India, and activate greater interest in the fate of Indians residing in South Africa. He would tell them about the crippling tax of £3 exacted from every Indian, the abolition of which was imperative to secure their future in South Africa.

He taught himself Tamil during the course of the voyage to Calcutta; and studied Urdu with the help of a *munshi* (clerk) travelling with him. He would thus be able to cultivate a more meaningful relationship with the Tamils and Muslims. The going was hard, but he persevered; and made fair progress in both. He points out that most of his reading since 1893 took place while he was in jail. His Tamil improved in South African jails, and his Urdu in the Yeravda jail. He rues the fact that he would never really be able to speak Tamil or Telugu.

---

1 Cf. 'More Recognition', *Natal Mercury*, June 5, 1896; cf. DiSalvo, *op.cit.*, p. 76.

Gandhi recalls with gratitude the great affection that he received from the Tamils and Telugus in South Africa. These people were all largely illiterate, but they nevertheless became soldiers in their great struggle for justice and a better life. Gandhi's inability to talk to them in their languages was made up for by their broken English or Hindustani, which made communication possible for the prosecution of their campaign. Gandhi's observation that only those unable to speak proper English learn to speak Hindustani is true even today. The knowledge of English, lamentably, becomes an impediment to the learning of other Indian languages.[2]

Gandhi's vegetarian food led to interesting conversations with the ship's Captain, a Plymouth Brother. He had already had discussions with Plymouth Brothers in South Africa. The Captain held that if people had faith in Jesus and his sacrifice, their sins would be assuredly redeemed. Faith was therefore more relevant and more essential than mere morality. Any religion that subjected a person to irksome moral constraints was no good to the good Captain! God has created the animal world and vegetables alike for the enjoyment of humankind. Gandhi insisted on equating religion with morality; but the Captain was happy in the security of his faith. The amicable exchange failed to budge either.[3] Twenty-four days passed. The voyage came to an end. Gandhi landed at Calcutta.

He immediately took a train to Bombay; but, on the way, stayed for a night at Allahabad and met Chesney, Editor of *The Pioneer*, an influential newspaper published from the city. The Editor gave a patient hearing to Gandhi's account of the sad plight of Indians in South Africa, and promised to take note in his paper of anything Gandhi wrote. Chesney also said that he could not support all Indian demands, as he had to understand and assess the viewpoint of the colonials as well. Gandhi told him that the only thing he asked for was a balanced study of the situation, and the 'barest justice' for Indians in South Africa.[4] This unplanned interview with Chesney began the process which led to the vicious attack on Gandhi on his return to South Africa.

---

2   *Autobiography*, p. 120.

3   *Ibid.*

4   *Ibid.*, p. 121.

The Green Pamphlet

Gandhi proceeded to Rajkot via Bombay, where he brought to completion a pamphlet that he wrote on his way to India, entitled *The Grievances of The British Indians In South Africa.*[5] It came to be known as the *Green Pamphlet* because of its covers.[6] He used a very temperate tone and deliberately understated the harshness of the Indian predicament in South Africa. The pamphlet provided a succinct summary of the abuses suffered by Indians in South Africa, with repeated references to court cases in which Gandhi, together with others, sought justice for the Indian victims of European mistreatment. He deliberately, distinctly disowned any inclination to draw attention to the woeful plight of the Indians under indenture, and instead focussed attention only on the legal disabilities to which all Indians were subjected. It was a clear, convincing statement of the problems confronting them in South Africa.[7]

Ten thousand copies were sent out to papers and leaders of all the parties in India. *The Pioneer* took editorial notice of the pamphlet; and summaries of the article were cabled by *Reuters* to England and Natal. The cable consisted of just three lines in print, though it exaggerated Gandhi's account, not in his own words. The pamphlet had been written in a strong but restrained, respectful strain. Everything he wrote had already been repeatedly and openly said by him in Durban. But people still did not savour the thought of their attitudes and action being exposed to the glare of publicity in India.

All the newspapers in India devoted space to discussion of the question. Gandhi used school children as volunteers to help post these pamphlets to various places and people around; and this was his first attempt to enlist the support of volunteers.

The Plague and Gandhi's Obsession with Hygiene

There was a sudden outbreak of plague in Bombay; and Rajkot was also

---

5   According to DiSalvo, *op.cit.*, p. 365, n. 10, he wrote the pamphlet during the course of his journey, not in India over a period of more than a month, as stated in his *Autobiography*.

6   Cf. *Collected Works*, 2, pp. 2ff.

7   Gandhi is not yet free from bias against the indigenous Africans, and resents the equation of Indians with the 'natives'.

gripped by panic. Gandhi offered his services to the State to help with sanitation and hygiene. The State appointed him to a committee; and he stressed the need for keeping latrines clean. The committee inspected latrines in every street; and the poor people accepted all the suggestions to improve theirs. To Gandhi's dismay, some of the well-off people even refused the inspection of their toilets, and to listen to any talk of improvements. They found the toilets of the rich much more unclean than those of the poor. Gandhi's preoccupation with cleanliness and hygiene was called his 'essential foreignness' by Sri Aurobindo, who saw in him a European, indeed a 'Russian Christian in an Indian body', in his obsession with latrines and the disposal of their contents.[8]

When Gandhi went to inspect the untouchables' quarters, only one member of the committee agreed to go with him. Others regarded the very idea as 'preposterous'.[9] Gandhi tells us that this was the first visit of his life to a locality of untouchables. When requested by Gandhi to let him inspect their latrines, the surprised residents told him that they had none, as they went out into the open. Latrines were only for the rich. Gandhi then asked for permission to inspect their houses, which was readily given. He was delighted to look at the interior of these nondescript hutments, which were spotlessly clean. No outbreak of plague could occur in these quarters. The committee also went to inspect the *Vaishṇava Havelī* (temple), whose priest was a family friend of the Gandhis. He welcomed their suggestions; but Gandhi did not know if they were acted upon. He was pained by the lamentable state of cleanliness in a place of worship despite the *śāstric* prescription for inner and outer cleanliness.

Gandhi's Love of the British

Gandhi talks of his heart-felt loyalty to the British constitution, and equates it with his love of Truth. He is conscious of the shortcomings of British rule, but nevertheless believes that it is beneficial to the British subjects. His equation of the British constitution with Truth makes one feel uneasy, in as much as its tenets and values were not equally applied to the governance of the Empire. Gandhi disregarded the defects and thought only of the benefits, which made him join in the singing of the National

---

8   Cf. Lelyveld, *op.cit.*, p. 37.
9   *Autobiography*, p. 122.

Anthem.¹⁰ Though the colour prejudice in South Africa was a travesty of any British idea of fair play, Gandhi lulled himself into the belief that it was only a 'temporary and local' problem.¹¹ To quote him: 'I therefore vied with Englishmen in loyalty to the throne. With careful perseverance I learned the tune of the 'national anthem' and joined in the singing wherever it was sung.'¹²

He taught the national anthem to his family and to others; but parts of the text made him feel uncomfortable with his devotion to *ahiṁsā* becoming more pronounced. Lines such as 'scatter her enemies, and make them fall; confound their politics, frustrate their knavish tricks', caused unease. The enemies, so-called, were not necessarily 'knavish', nor necessarily wrong, just because they were enemies.

Queen Victoria's diamond jubilee was drawing near; and Gandhi accepted his appointment to the committee in Rajkot to help organize the celebrations. A few years later, in 1903, he referred to the 1858 Proclamation of the Queen as 'the Magna Carta of the British Indians', and described the Indian Revolt of 1857 in words that would surprise and hurt most Indians today: '....At one time the cloud looked so black that even the final result had become a matter of uncertainty. An appeal was made to the worst superstitions of the people of India, religion was greatly brought into play, and all that could possibly be done by the evil-minded was done to unsettle people's minds, and to make them hostile to British rule....'¹³ Indeed, 'it was the Indians' proudest boast that they were British subjects.'¹⁴

---

10 *Ibid.,* p. 124.

11 *Ibid.*

12 *Ibid.*

13 *Indian Opinion,* 9-7-1903; *Collected Works,* Vol. 3, 1960, p. 357.

14 *Collected Works,* Vol. 3, 'Congratulations To British Generals', Gandhi's Brief Speech at Durban on March 14, 1900, p. 136; Reported in *The Natal Mercury,* 15-3-1900, and *The Natal Advertiser,* 15-3-1900.

Chapter 20

The Roving Publicist

Gandhi sought to increase public awareness of the Indians' plight in South Africa by organizing meetings in Bombay and elsewhere. He met Justices Ranade and Tyabji; and Sir Pherozeshah Mehta, who agreed to organize a meeting, and introduced him to some important people.

The enormous crowd at the meeting brought about a relapse of Gandhi's nervousness. The old timidity resurfaced once more. He found himself trembling, and, despite Mehta's urging, spoke very feebly. Dinshaw Wacha came to his help, and read his speech with great force and clarity. The audience listened with great attention and applause. 'Sir Pherozeshah liked the speech.' Gandhi was 'supremely happy'.[1] In this speech, too, Gandhi decries the 'desire to degrade us to the level of the raw Kaffir...'

Writing a neatly-argued cogent speech in his office was not the same thing as delivering it to a large audience. He had to hone his skills a lot more; boost his confidence a great deal; and fortify his morale with total self-belief to be able to stand up and lord it over enormous, astronomical numbers of Indian audiences. The South African platform would continually add to his self-confidence; the justice of his cause would steel his determination; the spirit of insistence upon truth, *satyāgraha*, would impart the strength of conviction to his words. Self-mastery and identification with his audience would invest his later speeches with an indomitable purpose, with an assertive urgency! The audiences would hang on every word, each whisper, every intonation in respectful silence. But not yet!

Gandhi's attempts to lure Indian barristers to South Africa did not prove successful. He, however, remained determined, despite dissuasion by

---

1 *Autobiography*, p. 127.

some, to go back and do whatever he could to improve the lot of his countrymen there. He cites the *Gītā* to justify his resolution, which he could also do, if he so desired, to accept the advice of his friend Pestonji Padshah to stay and work in India. Pestonji told him that he was needed more in India, where he could help alleviate the grinding poverty of his countrymen, and win self-government for the country. India's liberation would 'automatically' improve the lot of Indians in South Africa.[2] The *Gītā* tells us:

> 'Finally, this is better, that one do
> His own task as he may, even though he fail,
> Than take tasks not his own, though they seem good.
> To die performing duty is no ill;
> But who seeks other roles shall wander still.'[3]

The question is, who decides what is one's task, and what is others'? Who allocates tasks? A person decides for himself or herself. There is no divine dispensation. Gandhi went as a lawyer to South Africa, but found himself leading the South African Indians' struggle for dignity and survival. He had to assume unpremeditated roles; carry out self-selected tasks; shoulder painfully trying responsibilities; and suffer self-inflicted, clearly foreseen consequences of his actions. He was himself the director and actor.

The passage of the *Gītā* is not in accord with what he does himself; with his personal freedom of thought and action. No one should arbitrarily choose for us; no one should compel us. If society and its set-up dictate and allocate duty, choose one's occupation for him or her, and make it contingent on birth in a class or caste, that would indeed be a travesty of justice and fair play. Passages of the *Gītā* that purportedly prescribe such a dispensation are indeed unacceptable, and open to categorical rejection. Any idea of pre-ordained congenital duty to society is indeed utter anathema. Gandhi, though, is not yet free from the textual tyranny of social divisions!

He went to Poona, and met B.G.Tilak, R.G. Bhandarkar and G.K. Gokhale to solicit their support for his cause. He was charmed by Gokhale, and felt as if they were 'renewing an old friendship':[4]

---

2 *Ibid.,* p. 128.

3 *Ibid.* It is not a literal translation of the verse III. 35.

4 *Autobiograpy,* p. 128.

'Sir Pherozeshah had seemed to me like the Himalaya, the Lokmanya like the ocean. But Gokhale was the Ganges. One could have a refreshing bath in the holy river. The Himalaya was unscaleable, and one could not easily launch forth on the sea, but the Ganges invited one to its bosom. It was a joy to be on it with a boat and an oar.'[5]

Bhandarkar agreed to preside over a meeting, in which all these great men would participate; and Gandhi was happy. His cause was gaining due publicity.

He then proceeded to Madras, where he was met and welcomed with great enthusiasm. At a public meeting supported by some of the most prominent citizens of Madras, the audience listened to Gandhi's speech with rapt attention, and was deeply moved by the story of Balasundaram. Gandhi recalls the rush of people to buy the *Green Pamphlet*. Ten thousand copies of a second revised edition were quickly printed. Popular enthusiasm for the cause of Indians in South Africa made Gandhi the recipient of great affection, even though the conversations with the local leaders and people were only in English and not Tamil. The local press praised him for his accurate and unexaggerated description of the trying conditions of life faced by Indians in South Africa; and called upon Britain to prevent the enactment of any discriminatory laws against British subjects in the colonies.

The next stop was Calcutta, the capital of the Raj, the seat of the Viceroy, and the throbbing centre of Indian nationalism. To his dismay, though, the bigwigs of Bengal gave him a cold shoulder. Surendranath Banerji, the 'idol of Bengal', talked of local difficulties that totally preoccupied the people, who would take little interest in Gandhi's work. The editors of papers, the *Amrit Bazar Patrika* and the *Bangabasi*, treated him with dismissive disdain, which failed to dent his resolution to try and see the editors of other papers. He met Ellerthorpe of *The Daily Telegraph*, who invited him to the Bengal Club, where he was staying. An Indian could not be taken into the club's drawing room, whereupon his host took him to his own room, and apologized for the local English prejudice. He met the Anglo-Indian editors of *The Statesman* and *The Englishman*, who at once grasped the importance of Gandhi's problem. He gave them long interviews, which they published in full. Saunders, the Editor of *The*

---

5   *Ibid.,* p. 129.

Englishman, 'placed his office and paper' at Gandhi's disposal. 'He even allowed me', Gandhi tells us, 'the liberty of making whatever changes I liked in the leading article he had written on the situation…'[6] Saunders had been won over by Gandhi shunning exaggeration, and sticking to the truth. His painstaking interrogation of Gandhi, and his realization that the latter was presenting an impartial picture of the reality in South Africa, moved him to support Gandhi. 'We win justice quickest by rendering justice to the other party.'[7]

Just when Gandhi was beginning to feel optimistic about holding a public meeting in Calcutta, he received a cable from Durban asking him to return as soon as possible, as the parliamentary session was going to begin in January. He left Calcutta for Bombay to prepare his family for the voyage.

Gandhi recalls the arrangements he made for his wife and children, who were accompanying him for the first time to South Africa. The 'highest religion' of a Hindu wife is 'implicit obedience to her husband'.[8] Gandhi justifies it by pointing out that usually the husband is literate, the wife is not. He therefore acted as a teacher in more ways than one. He wanted his family to look civilized by adopting dress and manners that were as close to the European standard as possible. They would have to be role models for the community. He made the family adopt the *Parsi* style, which was considered the most advanced in India. Kasturba wore the *Parsi* saree, and the boys *Parsi* coats and trousers. They all wore shoes and socks. He also made them use knives and forks at the dinner table. They gave them up later, only when he did so. Thus, once the family got used to new ways of dressing up and eating, he made them change again and revert to the old, which would have been as difficult for them as the first change. He consoles himself with the thought that the family felt freer and happier after discarding these modes and measures of 'civilization'.[9]

---

6   *Ibid.,* p. 131.

7   *Ibid.*

8   *Ibid.,* p. 135.

9   *Ibid.*

Chapter 21

To South Africa

Gandhi set sail for Durban on the steamship *Courland* on November 30, 1896, with his wife and two sons, as well as the son of his sister, who had just lost her husband. This boat had been recently bought by Dada Abdulla, who offered Gandhi and his family a free passage to South Africa. Another steamship called the *Naderi* owned by Dada Abdulla, set sail for Durban at the same time, both arriving at their destination on the 18th of December.[1]

No passengers were allowed to disembark without a thorough medical examination; but the authorities imposed an unjustifiably long quarantine on both the ships on the ground that India had an outbreak of plague.

There were other factors at work behind this delay in disembarkation. A movement was already afoot to prohibit the entry of Indian labour into Natal, when a single sentence summary of Gandhi's *Green Pamphlet*, distributed in India, was relayed to South Africa by Reuters: 'A pamphlet published in India declares that the Indians in Natal are robbed and assaulted, and treated like beasts, and are unable to obtain redress'. This warped summary was construed as a wicked calumny; and the *Natal Mercury* accused Gandhi of uttering 'infamous falsehoods'.[2] The press deliberately distorted the accounts of Gandhi's writing; and his estranged friend Sheikh Mehtab rose to his defence in a letter to the *Natal Advertiser*, in which he told them that Gandhi had said no more than what he had done in his 'Open Letter' and 'Appeal' addressed to the European population of Natal. He asked Gandhi's detractors to read those two pamphlets again to

---

1 Cf. *Collected Works*, 2, p. 372.
2 Cf. Guha, *op.cit.*, p. 108.

accept that the Indians were indeed 'shamefully treated'.[3]

When a Sugar Company sought the Government's assistance to import a few brick-layers, carpenters, fitters and blacksmiths from India in August, 1896, ferocity of the opposition made them withdraw their application. The working class of Durban went up in arms against the importation of Indian labour into the state, shouting that they would be thrown out of jobs by cheap Indian artisans. Incipient protest at the ground level swelled into mass meetings, at which the Government was asked to protect the interests of the Europeans. Several ships arriving in Durban in August and September with indentured labourers, returning residents, as well as new migrants, added to their fear of being swamped by them. In various meetings held, they spouted their unmitigated contempt for Indians.

The *Courland* and the *Naderi* sailed into this surcharged situation, with the frayed tempers of the European population wickedly put on edge by the press as well as others, including Gandhi's neighbour Harry Escombe. Gandhi was quite unaware of the storm he had stirred by his speeches and writings in India. The unease of the white workers, their sense of insecurity, and lastly the fear of plague being transmitted to Natal through the Indian immigrants created an explosive atmosphere. Gandhi was portrayed as the arch villain; and the *Natal Advertiser* urged decisive action against him and his 'advanced guard of the Indian army of invasion...'.[4] A meeting attended by some 2000 men asked the Government to send the ships back, allowing only the indentured workers to disembark. Gandhi was accused of conspiring to change the demography of Natal; of masterminding the 'Asiatic invasion'. They threatened to give him 'something more' than what they had already given him!

The two ships carried 617 Indians, including Gandhi and his family. About half of them were bound for the Transvaal; the rest were residents returning to Natal; and only a small minority were new migrants. But the white residents of Durban demanded the repatriation of them all. Large meetings were organized every day. All kinds of threats were aired; and they also sought to persuade Dada Abdulla and Co. to send them back. They offered to indemnify the company, which, however, did not budge in its determination to disembark the passengers, regardless of any

---

3   *Natal Advertiser,* 17 September, 1896, cited in Guha, *op.cit.*, p. 578, n. 27.

4   Cf. Guha, *op.cit.*, pp. 111 and 578, n.33.

costs involved. Sheth Abdul Karim Haji Adam, managing partner of the company, kept Gandhi fully informed.

Gandhi had earned the grudging respect of many South African whites, some of whom opposed these tactics. But they were outnumbered by those amongst whom there were some rich and powerful people; and the Government was also on their side. Escombe, a prominent member of the cabinet, made no secret of his support for the rabble-rousers. But the quarantine was failing to coerce the Indians into returning home. Threats were addressed to Gandhi and the others. They would get their passage money back if they went back home; or would otherwise be pushed back into the sea. Gandhi was constantly on the move amongst the passengers keeping up their morale; and sent messages of support to the other ship as well. He did not know any passengers on the two ships except a couple of relatives. Agonizing days went past each other at anchor; and Christmas arrived. At a celebratory party, Gandhi described the Western civilization being principally based on force, which was not true of the Eastern. The Captain of the ship asked: 'Supposing the whites carry out their threats, how will you stand by your principle of non-violence?' Gandhi said: 'I hope God will give me the courage and the sense to forgive them and to refrain from bringing them to law. I have no anger against them. I am only sorry for their ignorance and their narrowness. I know that they sincerely believe that what they are doing today is right and proper. I have no reason therefore to be angry with them.'[5]

Ahimsā in thought and deed is for the first time firmly affirmed! Gandhi states his belief in the efficacy of non-violence for the resolution of disputes that might otherwise explode into violence. The passage also suggests that the ship's Captain was already aware of Gandhi's advocacy of non-violence in the prosecution of policies that he and his followers devised. The smile on the Captain's lips hinted only at his incredulity!

On the 11th of January, a reporter of the *Natal Advertiser* went on board to interview the Captain, who told him that nobody knew Gandhi before he boarded the ship. The next day the reporter came again to talk to Gandhi, who refuted every charge that was levelled against him. He gave the journalist copies of all the speeches that he had made, which clearly showed that he had said nothing new; and that his statements in India

---

5   *Autobiography*, p. 139.

were milder than the ones that he had already made in South Africa. He had 'nothing whatever to do' with bringing any passengers to Natal. Many of them were old residents returning; most of them were bound for the Transvaal; and there were no blacksmiths or carpenters on board. He referred to the glory of the British Empire arising out of their rule over India; and to the folly of Natal not to recognize that their prosperity depended on the introduction of Indians and their labour into the colony. Any protest against the introduction of free Indians into the Colony was unpatriotic, as well as disruptive of imperial harmony. He had not advised anyone to institute legal proceedings against the Government for illegal detention, nor did he wish to do so. He had returned to Natal not to make money, but to act as an interpreter between the two communities.

At last, on January 12, 1897, the ships were permitted to disembark their passengers, but to begin landings on the 13th. The Viceroy of India had weighed in with an appeal; and the Secretary of State for the Colonies cautioned against disrupting imperial harmony during the celebrations of Queen Victoria's Diamond Jubilee. News of the Government's submission to pressure provoked about 5,000 Europeans representing various vocations to march to the harbour to block the disembarkation. Escombe, who was Attorney- General, rushed to the harbour when he heard of it, and spoke to them. He told them that he sympathized with their cause. They were right to show their force, but not to ill-use it. They could not legally stop the landings. The passengers on the ships were innocent men, women and children, who knew nothing of the strong feelings against them. Natal would remain a white colony. He would support a special session of Parliament to deal with the issue of Indian immigration. He asked them to go home, and not to do anything that would make their Queen sad in the sixtieth year of her reign. They agreed to demonstrate without violence, but reserved their ire for Gandhi.

Escombe informed the Captain that Gandhi's life was in danger; and that, therefore, he and his family should be advised to land at dusk. The Superintendent of the Port would escort them home. Gandhi agreed; but soon afterwards, Laughton came to the Captain and told him that he would like to take Gandhi with him if there was no objection. He was a legal advisor of the Agent Company, and in that capacity, he was not in any way bound to follow the advice of Escombe. Kasturba and the children would drive to Rustomji's house, and Gandhi could follow them on foot in

Laughton's company. Things were quiet. The whites had all dispersed. He did not want Gandhi to enter the city like a thief. Gandhi agreed. Kasturba and the children drove safely to Rustomji's house; and Gandhi went ashore with Laughton to walk for about two miles to the house. Some youngsters recognized Gandhi and shouted 'Gandhi, Gandhi'! They were joined by half a dozen more. Laughton hailed a rickshaw, but the youngsters would not let Gandhi get in. The frightened rickshaw boy ran away. Gandhi and Laughton kept on walking, but the crowd swelled, and they could not go any further. They separated Gandhi from Laughton, and pelted him with 'stones, brickbats and rotten eggs'.[6] They snatched away his turban, and began beating and kicking him. Gandhi almost fainted, but kept on standing, clutching the railings of a house. The battering and boxing went on. The Police Superintendent's wife, passing by, saw what was happening. She knew Gandhi. She came up, opened her umbrella and stood between him and the crowd. This stopped them, as they could no longer hit him without injuring Mrs Alexander. An Indian eyewitness informed the police station, and the Superintendent sent policemen to form a protective ring around him and escort him safely to his destination. They came just in time. He was taken to the police station, where the Superintendent advised him to take shelter. Gandhi, though grateful, declined the invitation, and said that his attackers would surely realize that they were being unfair, and would quieten down. He had not lost his trust 'in their sense of fairness'.[7] And that faith in the basic goodness of humankind, and their capacity for remorse and self-correction never forsook him, despite repeated shocks of dismay and disappointment.

The Police escorted him to Rustomji's house, where the ship's doctor ministered to his injuries. Gandhi's optimism was sadly belied by the whites surrounding Rustomji's house. The crowd was in an ugly mood, with people shouting, 'we must have Gandhi'.[8] The Superintendent of Police did all he could to humour the crowd; but advised him to escape in disguise if he wanted to save the house and his family from imminent violence. Gandhi had bravely sallied out of the ship with Laughton despite the danger that lurked. But now he left in disguise, as not only did the safety of his family matter, but also that of his friend's house.

---

6   *Ibid.*, p. 140.

7   *Ibid.*

8   *Ibid.*

They made him put on an Indian constable's uniform with a Madrasi scarf on his head. One of the two detectives who accompanied him was disguised as an Indian merchant with paint on his face to make him look like one. They stole out of the house to a carriage that was waiting for them at the end of the street, and drove back to the same police station where Gandhi had earlier turned down the Superintendent's invitation to shelter. Gandhi tells us that Alexander, the Superintendent, kept the crowd at Rustomji's house in good humour by singing 'Hang Old Gandhi on the sour apple tree', while he was affecting his escape. Alexander then informed the crowd that there was no use staying there any longer, as Gandhi had made his escape. Some of them laughed, while others were still incredulous. The Superintendent asked them to appoint one or two representatives, whom he would escort into the house to see for themselves. If they found Gandhi, he was theirs. If not, they should disperse. The representatives went in, but came back with the news that Gandhi was no longer there. The disappointed crowd dispersed, many appreciative of the police officer's tact, some fuming!

The Secretary of State for the Colonies, Chamberlain cabled the Government of Natal asking them to bring Gandhi's assailants to book. Escombe personally expressed his regret to Gandhi for the assault and the injuries he had sustained. He said he would arrest and prosecute any assailants identified by Gandhi, who characteristically replied that he had no desire to prosecute anyone. He could identify one or two, but did not consider it prudent to punish them. They had been misled. They had been misinformed that he had exaggerated his accounts of the condition of Indians resident in Natal and South Africa. They felt that they had been subjected to great defamation; and their indignation was due to this deliberate misreporting. Part of the blame lay with Escombe himself and his colleagues, as they did not care to check the accuracy of the reports by Reuters. Gandhi had no wish to have anyone punished; and hoped the realization that he had neither misrepresented nor exaggerated the situation in South Africa, would make people feel contrite about their violence.

Escombe asked Gandhi to say so in writing, as he had to inform Chamberlain. Gandhi could consult his friends and take time to arrive at a considered decision. But he also said that if Gandhi waived his right to sue his assailants, that would certainly help the restoration of peace, and add to the latter's reputation. Without any hesitation or ado, Gandhi immediately expressed in writing his intent to sue no one!

This is the decisive, defining moment in Gandhi's story. He stands battered but unbowed before ugly violence. Invincible courage defies deathly blows. Hard knocks burnish the Great Soul. His astounding capacity to forgive, to bear and forbear, comes to the fore, and shames even his enemies. This is *ahiṁsā* in thought and practice. But the fierce attack reveals the gaping racial divide that Gandhi seeks to overcome; and his opponents vow only to widen!

Even though the press decried the violence and the attack on Gandhi, the *Natal Mercury* still accused him of inciting the people, and then marching through the centre of the city. Laughton immediately sent them a long letter, in which he lauded Gandhi's ability, integrity and honour, together with his courage 'to vindicate himself before the public.' He asked Durban to apologize, to 'express regret handsomely and generously'. [9]

A week later, Mrs. Alexander, acknowledging a gift that Gandhi sent her, deplored 'the gross injustice' done to him by her 'countrymen'. And her husband Alexander, the Superintendent of Police, regretted his inability to do more to protect Gandhi, and hoped that the latter would, like Christ, forgive his accusers, 'for they know not what they did.'[10] Alexander's unfeigned apology is all the more remarkable in view of the fact that he and Gandhi had clashed with each other in the law courts before Gandhi's visit to India.

---

9   *Natal Mercury*, 16 January 1897; Guha, *op.cit.*, p.119.
10 *Ibid.*, pp.120 and 579, n.52.

Chapter 22

Gandhi Settles Down

It was an unnerving introduction to their new home for Kasturba and her two sons. Gandhi settled down once more, and rose in public estimation, which also helped his professional practice. His victory and vindication, though, came at a price. He now came to be viewed as a danger.

Gandhi received two letters from M.A. Jinnah, dated January 21 and July 24, 1897, the contents of which are unknown, but we now know that they knew each other from that year.[1] Jinnah's first letter might have expressed commiseration and support for Gandhi after the deadly attack on him in Durban; and the second might have explored the possibility of legal practice there independently, or in partnership with Gandhi. This is not unlikely, as Gandhi was trying to lure Indian barristers to South Africa; and Jinnah was then, like Gandhi before him, struggling to establish himself in Bombay.

Harry Escombe, elected Prime Minister of Natal in March, 1897, proposed four new pieces of legislation in fulfilment of the promises he had given to the demonstrators against Gandhi and Indians. The Quarantine Act, the Uncovenanted Indians Act, the Immigration Restriction Act, and the Dealers' Licences Act, were all devised to put a stop to Indian immigration; make life insufferable for the resident Indians, and deal a death-blow to all Indian competition against the Europeans. The Indian struggle against their disfranchisement brought about a tactical decision that no act would be passed against them on openly affirmed grounds of race or colour. These bills were therefore so worded that, without invoking

---

1 Cf. Guha, *op. cit.,* pp. 129-30.

race or colour, they would subject the Indian residents of Natal to cruelly crippling restrictions.

The Quarantine Act, prohibiting the disembarkation of any person coming from any place infected with the plague or other disease, was in its application really meant to securely bar the entry of Indians into the Colony. The Uncovenanted Indians Act provided for Indians to purchase and carry passes showing their free status, so that the police would not harass or arrest them. Indentured workers leaving their place of work without permission were subject to arrest. The pass system proved most irksome; and the police officers were given immunity against any liability for unfair arrests. Indians rightly protested against 'almost a license to arrest with impunity any Indian they choose.'[2]

The Immigration Restriction Act and the Dealers' Licences Act were doubtless the most invidious and hurtful in subjecting Indians to studied travail. The first permitted the much needed import of Indian indentured labour, but prohibited the immigration of those who could not write 'the characters of any language of Europe'. The second made it mandatory for every wholesale and retail business in Natal to have a licence. Officers appointed by the Town Councils would refuse permits to people who could not keep their books in English; whose premises were not provided with proper sanitary arrangements; and those who could not afford suitable accommodation for their employees, apart from their stores and warehouses. The officers were given unqualified discretion to decide; to issue or refuse a licence for wholesale or retail trade. An aggrieved trader could appeal only to the Town Council without any hope of redress, as the officers in question were actually putting into effect 'voiced public opinion'.[3] There was no provision for recourse to a court of law against the verdicts of these officers and their Town Councils. The sole purpose of the Act was to make Indian businesses unviable. Naked and unashamed, racial prejudice dictated state policy!

The Dealers' Licences Act was brutal in both its intent and application. Gandhi appealed to the Supreme Court. It forced the Councils to go through due process and give reasons; but did no more. There was no relief.

---

2   *Collected Works*, Vol. 2, 1959, 'Petition to Mr. Chamberlain', p.337.
3   Cf. 'Restriction on Immigration', *Natal Witness*, April 1, 1897; DiSalvo, *op.cit.*, p.122.

Gandhi was afraid of asking whether the law permitted the Town Councils to refuse licences to applicants simply because they were Indians.[4] And, then, the Privy Council disallowed appeals from the Town Councils to the Supreme Court. New applicants would as a result be unable to gain licences. Business owners would not be able to sell their businesses, or bequeath them to their successors. They would not be able to set up businesses in new locations. They would not be able to split businesses among partners. They would find it exceedingly hard if not impossible to start new businesses on the completion of their indentures. Meetings, petitions and litigation proved altogether unavailing!

The Indian community became inevitably more conscious of the dangers that lurked; of the trials that loomed; and Gandhi became increasingly more involved in public service. The bills were translated into Indian languages and properly explained to the community. Petitions were sent to the Colonial and Home governments. Joseph Chamberlain was far less sympathetic than his predecessor Lord Ripon towards the Indians. Yet Gandhi insisted that the number of Indian immigrants was negligible; they were not in any kind of competition with the Europeans; and they made a positive contribution to the community. The Europeans did not want Indians to take up free residence in Natal after serving their indentures; but they still wanted indentured servants. The status of the Indian British subjects had to be clarified. Gandhi pleaded for a reiteration of the British Government's wish that Indians should be accorded equal treatment.[5]

Chamberlain did not respond; and told a gathering of colonial prime ministers in London that he 'quite sympathize(d) with the determination of the white inhabitants of these colonies.... that there shall not be an influx of people alien in civilization, alien in religion, alien in customs.'[6] When Gandhi read this in the newspapers, he wrote in despair to Dadabhai Naoroji, urging him to do what he could to stem the tide of racial discrimination. Despite Gandhi's desperate petitions to the Natal Parliament, the Assembly and the Council, and to the Secretary of State for the Colonies, the new Acts became reality. All his pleas to uphold the

---

4 Cf. DiSalvo, *op.cit.*, pp.139-40.

5 *Ibid.*, p.124. He makes the point that Gandhi failed to argue that if the Government allowed this anti-Indian Act to pass, the Indian community would do what they could to cut off the supply of indentured servants.

6 Cited in Guha, *op.cit.*, p.126.

'British name and the Constitution' fell on deaf ears. Escombe, who had no qualms about making money from Indian clients as a lawyer, steered these laws through Parliament. But when he lost his prime-ministership owing to a rift in his party in September 1897, he asked Gandhi 'to convey to the Indians the value' he 'set on their good opinion'. Guha suggests that he was fishing for Indian clients in the courts of law.[7]

The Natal Indian Congress grew in strength; and attracted new members and funds, which now amounted to £5000. Gandhi persuaded the members of the Committee to buy a property, which was leased out, with a body of trustees duly appointed to look after it. The rent was used to defray the expenses of the Congress. This was Gandhi's first experience in the management of a public institution. But once he departed from South Africa, people started quarrelling, with the result that the property's rent had to be deposited and kept in a court of law.

Gandhi changed his opinion regarding these matters after greater experience with the management of many public institutions. He no longer wanted public institutions to have permanent funds, which could be the cause of moral downfall. When an institution ceased to enjoy public support, it lost its right to exist. If institutions had permanent funds at their disposal, they could flout public opinion and act arbitrarily against it. Gandhi cites the example of many religious trusts that do not submit any accounts; and the trustees become virtual owners accountable to none. He excepts institutions, which cannot function without permanent buildings at their disposal. He tells us that the great campaign of *Satyāgraha* in South Africa was conducted over a period of six years without recourse to any permanent funds, even though large amounts of money were collected and spent.

---

7   *Ibid.*, p.127.

Chapter 23

The Gṛhastha (Householder)

For the first time in her married life, Kasturba found herself managing her home independently, together with her husband in Durban. His office clerks, Hindus and Christians, Gujaratis and Tamils, stayed with him as members of the household. Gandhi always treated them as his family members, like his own kith and kin. This, though, became a cause of strife between him and his wife, who found it hard to carry out the chores involved. The rooms in Gandhi's house had chamber pots, which Gandhi and Kasturba cleaned. The clerks who felt quite at home, cleaned their pots themselves. The Christian clerk, a son of untouchables, had newly arrived; and Gandhi considered it his duty to clean his pot to make him feel at home. Kasturba cleaned the pots of others, but was reluctant to clean the newcomer's. She hated the thought of Gandhi cleaning the pots, and did not like doing so herself. Gandhi recalls her unwillingness, and her sense of coercion, when he describes Kasturba coming down the ladder, pot in hand, her eyes red with crying, tears rolling down her cheeks. He delights in telling his readers that he was 'a cruelly kind husband', determined to teach his wife; and subject her to his will in an expression of his 'blind love for her'.[1] However noble the sentiment of self-effacing service may be, Gandhi's tyrannical imposition of his will on his wife, and the way he did it, does not endear him to us. He goes on: 'I was far from being satisfied by her merely carrying the pot. I would have her do it cheerfully. So I said raising my voice- I will not stand this nonsense in my house.'[2]

Unable to contain her pain, she shouted:'keep your house to yourself and let me go'. Gandhi is brutally candid in his description of what he did. The qualities of kindness, forgiveness, forbearance and compassion

---

1 *Autobiography*, p.204.
2 *Ibid.*

totally forsook him, as he dragged her to the gate opposite the ladder. Just when he was going to open the gate to throw her out, she cried, choked with tears, 'have you no sense of shame? Must you so far forget yourself? Where am I to go? I have no parents or relatives here to harbour me. Being your wife, you think I must put up with your cuffs and kicks? For Heaven's sake behave yourself, and shut the gate. Let us not be found making scenes like this!'[3]

This happened in 1898. As far as he was concerned, his wife was his plaything, born to carry out his command, not 'a partner in the husband's joys and sorrows'. He tells us that he changed; and his ideas changed in the year 1900, till in 1906 he took a specific vow. His 'carnal appetite' progressively abated to the point of almost total suppression; and his domestic life came to savour greater peace and happiness.

Gandhi does not express any sense of compunction at the ugly roughness of his treatment of Kasturba. He felt ashamed, but not sorry, when told by her that he was breaching the limits of decency; violating the vow of reciprocal respect for his spouse. He shut the gate that he had opened in a fit of rage. They could not really leave each other. Gandhi remembers so many of their fights, which nevertheless ended in peace. Kasturba always won with her 'matchless powers of endurance'.

Gandhi calls this narrative a sacred recollection; an exceptional lesson, indeed, in the precept and practice of *ahiṁsā*. He admits that they do not make a perfect couple, and that they do not always think alike. Gandhi, the self-effacer in the eyes of the world, is not really one in his relationship with his wife. He is imperious, dictatorial and demanding. He seeks to reduce his wife to a mere cipher, when he asserts that she has perhaps no ideals other than his own,[4] and that with no formal education, she is intellectually far beneath him. He forgets that ideals do not have much to do with formal education. They are imbibed from interaction at the level of the family, and in the context of one's social experiences, observations, struggles, disappointments and successes. Like Gandhi, Kasturba was also a sensitive, perceptive, active human being, with her own set of values; with her own ideas of right and wrong; with her own vision of happiness with commitment to the welfare of those around her!

---

3   *Ibid.,* p.205.

4   *Ibid.*

He concedes that she may not approve of everything he does. But he says he never cares to discuss things with her. He does not think that any discussion would be fruitful. She was not educated by her parents. And he did not educate her when he should have done so! But he credits her with a common quality of most Hindu wives who regard their husbands as demi-gods, and unwittingly follow their lead. The pliant Kasturba does not take exception to Gandhi's 'endeavour to lead a life of restraint.'[5] What else could he expect? Would his wife protest? Would she vociferously verbalize her disappointment at his unwillingness to respond to her sexual urges, her natural need for physical closeness, for losing herself and finding comfort and reassurance in her husband's caressing arms? He did not care. He did not want to know. He took things for granted. He took her for granted. He convinced himself that theirs was 'a life of contentment, happiness and progress.'[6] It seems as if he never really tried to peep into the recesses of his wife's heart, to read her thoughts, to feel her needs, to fulfil them. The self-righteous man in pursuit of his own brand of purity, of his own concept of Truth, of his own goal of *mokṣa*, of his own communion with the Ultimate Reality, was oblivious of the reality on the ground; of his wife's individuality, which he deliberately drowned in his own. Gandhi, trying to be so unique, striving to practise *ahiṁsā*, to rise above the intellectual and moral level of his contemporaries, to blaze a new trail of truthful action, to campaign for the equality of the sexes, never accorded any equality of status to his wife. He never respected her capacity to think for herself and decide for herself; and seemed to think that she was incapable of doing so, and would therefore be entirely happy to walk behind his shadow. His behaviour amounted to bullying coercion to exact her obedience, her compliance, which he then self-satisfiedly interpreted as her willing espousal of all his ideals; her total identification with all his goals. Was that not what a Hindu wife was expected to do? We must, however, respect Gandhi for his uncompromising candour; for his making an open breast of all these incidents reflective of his ideas as well as attitude. We know it all, simply because he chooses to tell us!

The influence of his spiritual mentor Raychandbhai was steadily pushing Gandhi towards abstinence from sex. Though he and his wife slept in separate beds, nature yet had its way, with repeated episodes of coition.

---

5   *Ibid.*

6   *Ibid.*

They had two more sons. Ramdas was born in May 1898; Devadas in May 1900. The birth of Devadas became a trial of skill and fortitude for Gandhi. Neither the doctor nor the mid-wife could come in time; and he himself helped the safe delivery of the baby. His careful study of the subject certainly helped; and he tells us, he was not nervous. He insists on parents learning to take proper care of babies; and attributes his children's good health in later life to the time and effort he devoted to their well-being.

Education of Children

When Gandhi arrived in Durban in January 1897 with his ten-year old nephew, and two sons, nine and five respectively, they could have been admitted to schools for European children as a special favour, as Indian children were not otherwise admissible. They could certainly go to one of the schools established by the Christian missions; but their medium of instruction was only English; and Gandhi did not like their curriculum. He tried himself to teach them, but could not do so regularly; and could not find a suitable Gujarati teacher either. He engaged an English governess, even though he was not quite satisfied with the arrangement. The boys learned Gujarati from Gandhi, who talked to them only in Gujarati. He did not want to send them back to India, as he thought the young children should stay with their parents. A house in good order provided the right atmosphere for children to learn things they could not imbibe in hostels. He sent his nephew and elder son to residential schools in India, only to call them back a few months later. The eldest son later broke away from Gandhi, and went to India to join a High School in Ahmedabad. The other three sons never went to a public school, but received some regular instruction in an improvised school which Gandhi himself started for the children of *satyāgrahīs* in South Africa.

Gandhi knew that these arrangements were far from adequate. He failed to give enough time or attention to his sons, who were justly uneasy and unhappy about it. Whenever they met people with matriculation certificates or university degrees, they were stung by a strong sense of deprivation. But Gandhi tries to set his conscience at rest with the argument that, if the boys were sent to school, they would have missed out on essential education based on constant contact with the parents, and experience of life. Any artificial education in England or South Africa, staying away from him, would never have inculcated in them the spirit of simplicity and service that he taught them. And 'their artificial ways of living' would have seriously hindered and handicapped his own work for the public. Gandhi admits that the inadequate literary education he gave them left him as unsatisfied as they were. But he still maintains that he did what he could, to the best of his capacity. He has no regrets about not sending them to public schools. He sees in the 'undesirable traits' of his eldest son a reflection of his own unregulated early life.[7] While Gandhi regards his school years 'as a period of half-baked knowledge and indulgence', his eldest son had quite a different opinion in the matter. He thought that his father's earlier years were the brightest period of his life; and the later changes arose only out of 'delusion miscalled enlightenment.'[8] Many people asked Gandhi why he did not give his boys proper school and university education. Did he have the right to thus deprive them, and limit their potential? Why did he not allow them to gain proper degrees and credentials? Why did he not allow them to decide on their own careers?

Gandhi is unrepentant; indeed, calmly complacent! He confidently tells us that his boys did not suffer in comparison with other young men of their own age in terms of knowledge; and there was little that they could learn from them. He muses about the difference that 'disciplined home education' can make; and weighs the results due to changes introduced by parents in their children's lives. He talks of the lengths a votary of truth traverses in his experiments with truth; and stresses the sacrifices a votary of truth makes in pursuit of his goal. If he had provided for his sons the education that other children could not get, he would have done so only at the cost of his own sense of self-respect. He would have 'deprived them of the object-lesson in liberty and self-respect', which he 'gave them at the cost of their literary training'.[9] He goes on to emphasize that liberty is a thousand times preferable to learning.

It is difficult to understand Gandhi's logic; and to be convinced by his argument. There is no inherent clash between liberty and learning. Any consideration of truth is quite extraneous, and does not come into the situation. This kind of esoteric sophistry does not condone the deprivation of his sons in respect of their education. Gandhi knew that he had little or insufficient time to teach them. How many Indians in South Africa could

---

7   *Autobiography,* p.146.

8   *Ibid.*

9   *Ibid.,* p.147.

afford an English governess to teach their children? And what would she teach them? What kind of syllabus was acceptable to Gandhi? Was the emphasis on Gujarati so vital in a multi-lingual environment? His eldest son had a valid and potent point in his reminder that his father's status in society was entirely due to his education and qualifications. And his own education in England was the stuff of dreams in Gandhi's homeland. How many could afford what he managed to find the means for? And it did not compromise his sense of self-respect. Not everyone lived in a fancy villa in a white suburb of Durban. Not everyone dressed and ate like them. That was all due to Gandhi's education and training in the legal profession. His denigration of his student days and the knowledge that he then acquired was less than honest, and did not in any way accord with his devotion to truth. It also failed entirely to justify Gandhi's reluctance to send his sons to school. His own devotion to liberty was not in any way handicapped by his education, which only enabled him to stand up for himself and others around him in defence of freedom.

In 1920 Gandhi asked students in India to boycott their schools and colleges, which he called 'citadels of slavery'; and advised them that 'it was far better to remain unlettered and break stones for the sake of liberty than to go in for a literary education in the chains of slaves'.[10] He traces this advice to its source in relation to his own sons. The beginnings of the freedom movement in India do not correspond with the situation in Gandhi's household in South Africa, where he was himself living in European style; using knives and forks at the dining table; dressing in western style and doing all his work in the English language. The imposition of his will on his sons, and their subjection to his choices amounted to paternal despotism out of tune with *ahiṁsā*, which he identified with Truth. The aspirations of the sons were of no consequence; the father knew better. The equation of the situation in South Africa at the turn of the century with the Indian freedom struggle in 1920 was indeed a late afterthought to justify the fatherly tyranny!

---

10 *Ibid.*

Chapter 24

Spirit of Public Service

Gandhi was constantly gaining ground as a barrister and winning recognition for his legal skills and ability. But he was not at ease; that was no longer his aspiration. Instead of running a merely 'money-making' business, he wanted to render ameliorative service that made a difference. He wanted to lift the Indian community up from the pits of racial and official oppression; from their own social divisions; from their indifference and inattention to matters of their own health and hygiene. One day a leper knocked at his door. Gandhi dressed his wounds and offered him food and shelter. But he could not keep him indefinitely, and therefore sent him to the Government hospital for indentured labourers.

He wanted to engage in humanitarian work on a permanent basis. Parsi Rustomji's generosity helped the establishment of a small charitable hospital headed by the kind and compassionate Dr Booth, who treated his patients free of charge. Gandhi took time off from his office to work for one or two hours every day as a compounder in the hospital dispensary. This service took about two hours of his time every morning; and gave him a great sense of peace and satisfaction. He talked to the patients, understood and explained their complaints to the doctor; and then dispensed the medicines prescribed. This brought him into close contact with the poor and suffering Indians, who came as indentured workers from the south and north of India. In mid-1899, he enlisted the services of a second Indian London-trained lawyer, Rahim Karim Khan, to help cope with the volume of work in his practice. Khan's presence provided the time needed for work at the hospital; and the experience proved useful when Gandhi offered his services to nurse the sick and wounded soldiers in the Boer War.

With Khan to mind the practice in his absence, Gandhi proceeded to the Transvaal, where the Boers were subjecting Indian traders to an agonizing licensing procedure, seeking to segregate and push them to 'out-of-town rural locations'.[1] Gandhi pleaded their case to the State Secretary; but on his return to Durban found himself defending Indian businesses there from administrative oppression. While Indians were being targeted everywhere, the British, in charge of Natal and the Cape Colony, were turning increasingly hostile towards the Boers, who governed the Transvaal and the Orange Free State. More than a quarter of the world's gold in 1898 came from the Transvaal. The British decided to extend their control and supremacy over the Boers, whom they also accused of enacting anti-Indian legislation, one of the reasons cited for the action taken against them. Ten thousand soldiers were brought in from India and the Mediterranean; many more from the United Kingdom. Hostilities broke out in October, 1899.[2]

The Boer War

Indians in the South African Republic, viewed as unfriendly British subjects by the Boers, hurried across the border into Natal for shelter. Gandhi and the Natal Indian Congress swung into action to raise money and find accommodation for them. And though he and the Indians sympathized with the Boers suffering like them from calculated British oppression, he hastened to help Britain in the conflict. He had tirelessly argued for equal treatment of Indians with the other colonists, as they were all British subjects. If he demanded any rights as a British citizen, it became his duty to help defend the British Empire. He thought of India's 'complete emancipation only within and through the British Empire'.[3] The weight of his profession also bent him towards the British. So many members of the Natal bar actively joined the British war effort. Gandhi felt that it was expedient and necessary for the Indians to demonstrate their loyalty to the British at such a time of trial, and that it would certainly facilitate their struggle for rights. They would be able to earn the respect of their rulers and the British colonists. He proceeded, therefore, to organize an Indian Ambulance Corps with the help of other Indians; and despite the initial official refusal to use their services, Gandhi's persistence finally led to their acceptance. The average Englishman, Gandhi tells us, viewed

---

1 Cf. DiSalvo, *op.cit.*, p.147.

2 Cf. Guha, *op.cit.*, p.135.

3 *Autobiography,* p.156.

Indians as cowards, always unwilling to risk anything except for their own self-interest. But when the Boers came across as formidable adversaries, the services of Gandhi's Ambulance Corps were grudgingly accepted. The great majority of the Corps of eleven hundred people were indentured Indians; and they were used within the line of fire during the course of hostilities. They discharged their allotted tasks with unflinching bravery and commendable efficiency; and were mentioned in dispatches. War medals were awarded to the leaders, including Gandhi, who protested in a letter to the Colonial Secretary against singling him out for mention in General Buller's dispatches.[4]

The Indian community forgot their regional and religious differences and gained in prestige. Official appreciation and praise in the press for Gandhi and the Indians led people to believe that there would be expeditious redress of their grievances. Sir John Robinson, Prime Minister of the Colony, loudly complimented Gandhi upon 'his timely, unselfish, and most useful action in voluntarily organizing a corps of bearers for ambulance work at the front at a moment when their labours were sorely needed in discharging arduous duties which experience showed to be by no means devoid of peril.'[5] But as the immediate future revealed, Indian optimism remained as misplaced as it was unfulfilled. The colonial authorities quickly poured cold water on hopes of any acknowledgement of Indian rights. The British Home Government added to the depth of Indian despair by insisting that all the anti-Indian laws enacted by the Boers would be strictly upheld by the new administration. Boer laxity in enforcement would be replaced by cold, unfeeling, pitiless efficiency! The Indian grievances against the Republican Government were part of the British justification for the war against the Boers, as clearly specified in the declaration of Lord Lansdowne at Sheffield in 1899: 'Among the many misdeeds of the South African Republic I do not know that any fills me with more indignation than its treatment of these Indians.'[6] The Polaks suggest that Gandhi may have, all unconsciously, received his first suggestions regarding the method of civil disobedience when, the Boer

---

4 *Collected Works*, Vol. 3, p.181. A fine illustration of Gandhi's true humility!

5 Cited in DiSalvo, *op.cit.*, p. 381, n.44.

6 Cited in Polaks, H. S. L., and M.G.,'Mohandad Karamchand Gandhi: Greatest Figure in Modern India,' in Rushbrook Williams, ed., *Great Men of India*, The Home Library Club, The Times of India – The Statesman Associated Papers of Ceylon Ltd., 1939, p. 320.

Government having refused to issue any more trading licences to Indians, the British Agent at Pretoria recommended them to tender the licence-fees and, if the licences were still refused, to trade without them. Later, when the Government threatened to prosecute for trading without licences, the British Agent warmly approved of the advice given to the traders to pay no bail or fines, but to go to jail.'[7] The British Agent in Pretoria had assured Gandhi: 'if the Transvaal became a British Colony, all the grievances under which the Indians laboured would be instantly redressed.'[8] But that was before the war! DiSalvo dubs Gandhi's Boer strategy 'a spectacular failure'.[9] The victors forgot all their earlier reassuring rhetoric.

Gandhi had hitherto very largely represented only the business class in his legal work. A happy outcome of raising the Ambulance Corps was the establishment of close, abiding links between him and the poor indentured workers, whom he vigorously defended in court against charges made by their masters in the months that followed. He did not even charge fees, as the court referred to his 'philanthropic motives'.[10] His solicitude for the persecuted Indian indentured servants and their defence helped ease, even if it could not erase the pain of blighted hope!

His practice flourished. He learned a lot from Laughton, his senior by many years; won a lot of cases; assisted many profitable settlements out of court; and made a lot of money. He rose in popular esteem; and was invited to speak at public functions. He spoke well, and made an effect, as when he spoke on the famine in India. Gone was the old hesitancy, the old paralysing timidity! He spoke to large audiences with self-assurance and palpable authority. He had found his feet. European racism made him stand up and be counted! But try as he might, the Dealers' Licences Act was not repealed; and to add insult to injury, the Durban Town Council segregated rickshaws for 'Europeans only', who refused to use those that carried 'dirty' Indians.

---

7 *Ibid.*

8 Gandhi, *Satyagraha in South Africa, Collected Works,* Vol. 29, pp.69-70.

9 DiSalvo, *op.cit.,* p. 150.

10 Cf. DiSalvo, *op.cit.,* pp.382-383, n.53.

Beginnings of Austerity

Gandhi was a wealthy man making considerable amounts of money, which facilitated a life of 'ease and comfort'. But he now decided to reduce his expenses. He got rid of the washerman, and began to wash his own clothes. He taught his wife also to do so. He did not mind his fellow-barristers laughing at his first attempt at washing his shirts and collars. He had already become 'impervious to ridicule'[11]; and enjoyed the additional benefit of treating his friends to so much mirth. He became quite an expert at washing his clothes and collars; and a few years later persuaded Gokhale during his visit to South Africa that he could carefully iron his scarf, which was a treasured gift from Mahadev Govind Ranade. Gokhale hesitated; but the result was quite satisfactory.

Gandhi had secured his freedom from the washerman. He then proceeded to free himself from visits to the barber. An English hair-cutter in Pretoria had refused to serve him. Gandhi bought a pair of clippers and cut his own before a mirror. He did the front 'tolerably right', but the back not so well. The result excited a lot of laughter in the court. Friends asked if the rats had been at his hair. Gandhi told them that the white barber would not touch his black hair, which made him decide to do it himself. He did not blame the barber, for if he had served Gandhi, he might have lost his custom. Gandhi makes the telling point that Indians did not let their barbers cut the hair of the untouchables. He repeatedly realized in South Africa that his treatment at the hands of the Whites was a sample of the sin of Indians in their own country. That is why he was not angry. He understood!

Gandhi talks of his simplicity and passion for self-help. In his later life, in so many situations, he spoke against machines that deprived people of work and livelihood. There were no machines involved here. But if a man did everything himself without any division and distribution of labour, many would lose their livelihood and their means of living. Did Gandhi think of that while embarking on his course of self-help.[12] We must however do justice to Gandhi, as some of these changes to his lifestyle were also forced upon him by practices of racial segregation exemplified in the refusal of the white barber to cut his hair.

---

11 *Autobiography*, p.154.

12 *Ibid.,* p.155.

Sanitation and Service of India

Gandhi refers to the European perception of Indian slovenliness, uncleanliness and disregard for sanitation in and around their houses. There was a basis for it in reality! Gandhi urged his fellow Indians to improve their houses and clean up their surroundings to beat the charge and change the perception. When an outbreak of plague was feared, he undertook a house-to-house inspection with the approval of the authorities. The community voluntarily improved their sanitation, so that they would not be subjected to any official oppression. But Gandhi had difficulty, including 'some bitter experiences,' in rousing the community to do its duty. He was at times ignored, and even insulted. The reformer is not infrequently viewed as a menace; and met with contemptuous opposition. Gandhi nevertheless created a greater awareness of sanitation and hygiene amongst the Indians, which was appreciated by the authorities. They saw that he was not only agitating for the redressal of Indians' grievances, but was also at the same time trying to insist upon his countrymen lifting their game and leading lives that did not pollute the environment.

Gandhi also tried to kindle in the hearts of his compatriots a sense of their duty to India, the land of their origin. The settlers went out of their way to help their motherland in the famines of 1897 and 1899. Some Englishmen also responded to Gandhi's appeal. Indentured Indians made a significant contribution. And from then on, Indians always responded with help to India in times of need. Gandhi equates his service of Indians in South Africa with his increasing realization of Truth.[13] What is this Truth? To him, it seems, Truth is synonymous with the service of these despondent Indians.

---

13 *Ibid.,* p.159.

Chapter 25

Brahmacarya (Sexual abstinence)

Parents who realize their responsibilities would, according to Gandhi, have sex only when they desire children, never for the 'fulfilment of their lust'.[1] The idea that 'the sexual act is an independent function necessary like sleeping or eating', is decried by him as 'the height of ignorance'.[2] 'The act of generation should be controlled for the ordered growth of the world.'[3] He wants people to contain their lust 'at any cost' and gain the knowledge required to take care of the physical, mental and spiritual welfare of their children. He brings Divinity into this dispensation to safeguard God's glory with a controlled and 'ordered growth of the world'.[4] The advice inexplicably comprehends and communicates God's purpose to incorrigible humanity! How does arbitrary abstinence accord with God's glory? How did God communicate His command to Gandhi? How and why does the purpose of God clash with the compulsions of contrary human nature? Only Gandhi knows. Who would, in the world of mere mortals, heed this cold command to total sexual abstinence, except only when intercourse takes place for the sake of progeny?

Gandhi started thinking seriously of celibacy or total sexual abstinence. He says that he was devoted to the ideal of monogamy ever since his marriage; and his fidelity to his wife was 'part of the love of truth'.[5] It seems as though the love of truth, which kept him on the straight and

---

1 *Autobiography*, p.148.
2 *Ibid.*
3 *Ibid.*
4 *Ibid.*
5 *Ibid.*, p.149.

narrow, was more important and more compelling than his love for his wife. We may recall Gandhi's lack of reluctance in going to a prostitute during the course of his first voyage to South Africa, even though he came out of that room without performing the act. The thought of his wife was not the deterrent that it should have been; the unattractiveness of the woman, the sudden sense of loathing and the fear of God, which he calls the saving grace of God, brought him out untainted from the ordeal. We may also recall an earlier episode in Rajkot, where married Gandhi's nerve failed him in a prostitute's quarters; and another trying incident in England, where he was restrained from the brink by a friend's timely warning. He remembered God; he remembered his word to his mother; he did not mention or emphasize any sense or obligation of fidelity to his wife. It appears that his faithfulness to his wife owed more to his fear of God, and to the word that he had given to his mother!

Now in South Africa, he agonized about the importance of observing *brahmacarya* in his relations with his wife. He recalled how, in a discussion with Raychandbhai, he had praised the love and devotion of Mrs. Gladstone for her husband. The poet asked: 'which of the two do you prize more, the love of Mrs Gladstone for her husband as his wife, or her devoted service irrespective of her relation to Mr Gladstone? Supposing she had been his sister, or his devoted servant, and ministered to him with the same attention, what would you have said? Do we not have instances of such devoted sisters or servants? Supposing you had found the same loving devotion in a male servant, would you have been pleased in the same way as in Mrs Gladstone's case?'[6]

These words of Raychandbhai gradually worked on Gandhi, who unjustly rates the devotion of a servant a thousand times higher than a wife's to her husband. Gandhi takes the wife's devotion for granted, as something 'perfectly natural'. Equal devotion between master and servant is extraordinary. Gandhi wonders whether his faithfulness to his wife arises from the fact that she is the instrument of his 'lust'? 'So long as I was the slave of lust, my faithfulness was worth nothing. To be fair to my wife, I must say that she was never the temptress. It was therefore the easiest thing for me to take the vow of *brahmacharya*, if only I willed it. It was my weak will or lustful attachment that was the obstacle.'[7] One reads this

---

6 *Ibid.*

7 *Ibid.*

passage with rising resentment at Gandhi's obsession with himself at the expense of his wife, who comes across only as a plaything to be used or distanced at will. The comparison of wifely devotion with that of a sister or servant is irrelevant and in bad taste. Love has many manifestations, many incarnations, which merit equal appreciation, but which cannot be subjected to questionable comparisons. Gandhi demeans the depth and piety of sexual union with its equation only with lust and nothing more. The longing to lose one another in the embrace of love, to demolish the physical barriers in search of a true unity of being and becoming is put to shame by his repeated references to 'lust' in his descriptions of conjugal closeness. His spiritual preceptor Raychandbhai considered female genitals used for sexual gratification unfit 'even for a worthy receptacle for vomiting', which I, unlike Gandhi, find absolutely appalling![8]

Gandhi talks as if only he mattered. The wife's acquiescence was a matter of course. She had no say; supposedly no will of her own. Gandhi resolved twice to abstain, but failed. He did not want to have any more children. But he did not want to use any methods of birth control. He had been deeply influenced by the ideas of A. F. Hills of the London Vegetarian Society, who laid the greatest emphasis on self-control rather than birth control.

Gandhi decided on self-denial; and refers to 'endless difficulty' in the practice of his resolution.[9] They stopped sleeping together; and he deliberately went to bed only when he felt 'completely exhausted' after the day's work. He found all this unavailing; but with hindsight believes that the final vow was the outcome of these 'unsuccessful strivings'.

The news of Raychandbhai's untimely death at the age of thirty-three in May, 1901, greatly grieved Gandhi, who had ever so often turned to his spiritual mentor for advice in matters relating to life and religion.[10] He had helped enlarge Gandhi's spiritual horizons by exhorting him not to succumb to the tyranny of any text; and to appreciate essential ethical

---

8   Cf. James Laidlaw, *Riches and Renunciation: Religion, Economy and Society among the Jains*, Oxford, Clarendon Press, 1995, p.237; cited in Guha, *op.cit.*, p. 196.

9   *Autobiography*, p.150.

10 *Collected Works*, Vol.3, 1960, p.193. In his letter to Revashankar Zaveri, dated May 21, 1901, Gandhi says: '...whenever there is a little leisure, the mind reverts to it.'

precepts in all religions, which were at once perfect as well as imperfect when viewed from different points of view. The void left behind by him was partially filled by Gopal Krishna Gokhale, who gave Gandhi invaluable guidance in public life.

Chapter 26

Gandhis Return Home

Gandhi at this point felt that his work in South Africa was done; there were others to help after him; and India beckoned. Mere 'money-making' was certainly not his goal.[1] His friends reluctantly accepted his wish to return home, on his promise to come back to South Africa within a year if they needed him. The Indians of Natal, where he had lived most of the time, showered him with their love; organized farewell functions; and gave him costly gifts. These gifts included expensive items in gold, silver and diamonds. Gandhi was in a painful dilemma. If he accepted the presents, he could no longer feel that he had served the community without any personal benefit. But for a few from his clients, most of the gifts were given to him for his service to the community. His clients had also helped him in his discharge of public duty. An important gift was 'a gold necklace worth 50 guineas' meant for Gandhi's wife. Gandhi asserts that even this gold necklace had been given for his public work; and could not therefore be any different from the rest of the gifts.

He had 'a sleepless night'.[2] It was not easy to give up expensive gifts. But he felt even more uneasy with the thought of keeping them. How could he justify keeping the gifts to his wife and children, whom he had been training to a life of service which 'was its own reward'.[3] Gold watches, gold chains and diamond rings were out of place in his simple life. How could he keep all this jewellery, while he had been telling people to free themselves from the lust for jewellery? He therefore decided not to keep them, and drafted a trust document in favour of the community.

---

1   *Autobiography*, p.150.

2   *Ibid.*, p.160.

3   *Ibid.*

Next morning, he discussed the matter with his wife and children. He knew that it would not be easy to persuade his wife. He convinced his children first, so that they might help him convince their mother as well. But Kasturba protested. She was not satisfied with Gandhi's logic. He might not need them, she said; his children might not need them. Brainwashed by him, they would do as he desired. She could understand if he did not permit her to wear them. She was, however, thinking of her would- be daughters- in- law. They would certainly need them. And what of the future? Anything might happen. 'I would be the last person to part with gifts so lovingly given', said Kasturba.[4] They argued. There were tears. But the children tutored by Gandhi, and Gandhi himself remained 'unmoved'.[5] He told her that the children were yet to marry; and when they did so, they would know how to look after themselves. He would not have for his sons any brides in love with ornaments. And if ornaments were at all needed, he would get them. He was there to be asked.

Dismissively, Kasturba reminded him that he had taken away all her ornaments. She could not ever imagine Gandhi buying any for his daughters-in-law. He was trying to make *sādhus* (hermits) of her sons. She would not return the ornaments. And Gandhi had no right to her necklace.

Gandhi asked her if the necklace was given to her for her services or his? To which she replied that any service rendered by him was as good as rendered by her. She had toiled for him without cease. What was that, if not service? He had forced her to slave for all kinds of people despite her bitter tears and tireless remonstrance.

Gandhi's persistence defeated poor Kasturba; and with her 'extorted' consent, all the gifts received in 1896 and 1901 were included in a Trust Deed and deposited with a bank, to be used for the needs of the community in accordance with the wishes of Gandhi or the Trustees. Gandhi later drew funds from the Trust to help the community, without touching the Trust money. And at the time Gandhi wrote, the fund was still there. It was drawn upon in times of need; and it had been continually accumulating its proceeds. Gandhi says that he never regretted this step, and that his wife also came to realize that it was a correct decision. Gandhi insists that 'a public worker should accept no costly gifts'.[6]

---

4   *Ibid.,* p.161.

5   *Ibid.*

6   *Ibid.*

A reading of this account reinforces the perception of Gandhi's prepossession with himself; with his own self-certitude without any regard for, and without any or little appreciation of the sacrifices and services of his pliant, submissive wife. She had stood shoulder to shoulder with him, enabling him to render all his services to the common cause of the community. He was brimming with self-belief. He did everything himself. He was loath to share the credit with his wife, or duly or adequately recognize her services so silently rendered. The wife became an unacknowledged means to the realization of his lofty goals. The goals may be lofty. The ideals may be most laudable. But their pursuit and their realization requires the active association and assistance of one's partner. That indeed calls for full appreciation, proper acknowledgment, and grudging if not spontaneous gratitude to one's partner. And that is missing in Gandhi's account of his achievements. His great altruism, his great sacrifices, his great understanding of unimpeachable propriety notwithstanding, he is too full of himself; regardless of the contribution of Kasturba, which made it all possible. He knew it in his heart of hearts; he spells it out in Kasturba's words, reluctant to say it himself! Why?

In October, 1901, the Gandhis sailed back to India via Mauritius, where the resident Indian community gave a garden party in his honour. Gandhi encouraged them to educate their children; and to participate in politics. [7]

They reached Bombay towards the end of November, 1901; and proceeded to Rajkot. He settled his family there, and himself took a train to Calcutta to attend the 1901 session of the Indian National Congress. Sir Pherozeshah Mehta was also travelling in a special coach reserved for him in the same train to attend the Congress session. Gandhi had a brief meeting with him on the way, and requested him to take up the South African Indians' issue at the Congress. But he was told:'it seems nothing can be done for you. Of course we will pass the resolution you want. But what rights have we in our own country? I believe that, so long as we have no power in our own land, you cannot fare better in the Colonies.'[8] He could do no more than move his resolution.

---

7   Cf. *Collected Works*, Volume 3, 1960, pp.210-211.

8   *Autobiography*, p.162.

Chapter 27

Calcutta and the Congress

They arrived in Calcutta. Gandhi was put up in the Ripon College[1], where Tilak also came to stay. Gandhi recalls the Durbar which Tilak held seated in his bed, being visited by a constant stream of people, and the peals of laughter that punctuated the accounts of misdeeds of the ruling race. Gandhi is at his vivid best in his detailed description of the disposition of the camp. He is as amused as dismayed by people delegating responsibility from one to another, the volunteers continually quarrelling with each other. If Gandhi asked one to do something, he asked another to do it; who then asked someone else to do it. Gandhi made friends with some of the volunteers, and gave them an account of what they did in South Africa; and 'they felt somewhat ashamed.'[2] Gandhi tried to instil in them 'the secret of service'. The annual sessions of the Congress lasted only three days. The volunteers were always changing, and could learn hardly anything in such a short period of time.

Gandhi had a clear view of the stark spectacle of untouchability even there. The Tamil kitchen was set far apart from the others. While eating, the Tamil delegates found the sight of others polluting. A special kitchen was therefore made for them in the college compound, which was duly surrounded by a wall of wickerwork. The thick swirling smoke inside was suffocating; and in Gandhi's words,'it was a kitchen, dining room, washroom, all in one – a close safe with no outlet. To me this looked like a travesty of *varnadharma.*'[3] Gandhi was aghast at the sight of such

---

1 *Autobiography*, p.162. According to Guha, *op.cit.*, p.145, he stayed at the India Club.

2 *Autobiogrphy*, p.163.

3 *Ibid.*

untouchability amongst the Congress delegates; and wondered how painful its extent would be in the society they represented.

Let us hear Gandhi himself: 'There was no limit to insanitation. Pools of water were everywhere. There were only a few latrines, and the recollection of their stink still oppresses me. I pointed it out to the volunteers. They said pointblank – 'that is not our work, it is the scavenger's work'. I asked for a broom. The man stared at me in wonder. I procured one and cleaned the latrine. But that was for myself. The rush was so great, and the latrines were so few, that they needed frequent cleaning- but that was more than I could do. So I had to content myself with simply ministering to myself. And the others did not seem to mind the stench and the dirt.'[4]

Gandhi goes on: 'But that was not all. Some of the delegates did not scruple to use the verandahs outside their rooms for calls of nature at night. In the morning I pointed out the spots to the volunteers. No one was ready to undertake the cleaning, and I found no one to share the honour with me doing it. Conditions have since considerably improved, but even today thoughtless delegates are not wanting, who disfigure the Congress camp by committing nuisance wherever they choose, and all the volunteers are not always ready to clean up after them. I saw that, if the Congress session were to be prolonged, conditions would be quite favourable for the outbreak of an epidemic.'[5]

Gandhi went to the Secretary of the Congress, Janakinath Ghoshal, to ask him if he could help in some way; and was told to help with the latter's correspondence. Ghoshal was pleased with Gandhi's efforts, who even buttoned his shirt for him as an act of attention to his old age. The Congress session enabled Gandhi to see some of the great Indian stalwarts like Gokhale and Surendra Nath Bannerji,; and also to critically observe a lack of proper organization. Prominence of the English language in the deliberations of the Congress pained him.

Gandhi was overawed by the grand array of elders and leaders in the vast pavilion of the Congress. Only excerpts of a lengthy presidential address were read out; and a long list of resolutions were rushed through. With Gokhale's support, Gandhi was allowed to read out his resolution on South

---

4   *Ibid.*

5   *Ibid.,* pp.163-164.

Africa, which he did with his characteristic nervousness in the presence of great Indian leaders. He was given five minutes to address the Congress, but he mistook a warning bell from the President to stop only after three; and the resolution was unanimously carried. He was not quite satisfied with the pace of deliberations, which did not give the delegates any time to understand and properly consider the resolutions. The summary treatment disappointed him, though the stamp of the Congress delighted him.[6]

Gandhi intended to stay for about a month at the India Club in Calcutta after the Congress session; but was persuaded by Gopal Krishna Gokhale to go and stay with him. The great Indian leader had taken a liking to him; and took him personally to his quarters. He wanted him to work for the Congress. And Gandhi wanted to meet people to apprise them of his work in South Africa.

Before, however, he went to Gokhale's residence, he met some Indian grandees staying at the India Club, who discarded their normal Indian attire and changed into trousers and shining shoes, with turbans on, to attend a Darbar held by Lord Curzon. Gandhi was hurt to see that they had shed their fine Indian dresses for this occasion. He describes another Darbar years later at Banaras, when Lord Hardinge laid the foundation stone of the Hindu University. Gandhi attended the function at the invitation of Pandit Madan Mohan Malaviya. The assembly was aglitter with the glistening finery of the rajas and maharajas in attendance. In Gandhi's own words: 'I was distressed to see the maharajas bedecked like women – silk pyjamas and silk achkans, pearl necklaces round their necks, bracelets on their wrists, pearl and diamond tassels on their turbans and, besides all this, swords with golden hilts hanging from their waistbands. I discovered that these were insignia not of their royalty, but of their slavery'.[7] Gandhi was told that they were only following orders to wear all these meretricious adornments to add to the pomp and circumstance of the viceregal presence. His equation of these personal sartorial decorations with 'sins and wrongs that wealth, power and prestige exact from man' is somewhat incomprehensible. What have clothes to do with any sins and wrongs? A person's clothes may present a painful contrast to the rags of the people steeped in poverty, and may therefore be in bad taste in the eyes of some. But they may not necessarily be the badges of 'sins and wrongs'.

---

6   *Ibid.*, p.161.
7   *Ibid.*, p.168.

If no one wears any finery, and if people discard jewellery altogether, arts and crafts and their practitioners would cease to exist. Gandhi forgets that the Hindu gods in the temples he himself visited are bedecked with heavy jewellery and ornaments. That has been the time-honoured tradition illustrated in old Indian paintings and sculpture!

Gokhale was very impressed with Gandhi's sparse needs, self-help, cleanliness and hard work. He praised Gandhi, and introduced him to many people, including the great Sir P. C. Ray. Gandhi learned a great deal from Gokhale, whose consuming concern was the state of the country and the struggle to secure its freedom.'To see Gokhale at work was as much a joy as an education. He never wasted a minute. His private relations and friendships were all for the public good.'[8] Gokhale was a great devotee of Ranade, whose authority in so many matters was the last word for him. Gandhi even tried to reform the life and habits of Gokhale, whom he asked why he kept a horse and carriage, and did not use the public tram cars. Gokhale replied that, given his public profile and work, it would be most difficult for him to go about in tram cars. Gandhi also pressed upon him the necessity for some exercise and walks, but was told that Gokhale's preoccupations did not leave him with much time to do so. The two formed an affectionate, abiding relationship.

Gandhi walked around Calcutta and met a number of people. He mentions a Bengali Christian leader, Kalicharan Banerji, who was also active in the Congress. This man told him that he could have no hope of absolution from the original sin, in which Gandhi also believed, until and unless he surrendered to the saving grace of Jesus Christ. Gandhi's affirmation of his belief in the 'original sin' is interesting, even if it does not find an echo in any Indian tradition.[9] New ideas were developing. A new philosophy was taking root. A new conviction was sprouting. Service with humility, good-will without qualification towards friends and adversaries alike, would become the bedrock of Gandhi's *Satyāgraha* or insistence upon Truth.

Gandhi also describes his visit to the Kāli temple, and his sense of revulsion at the sight of dumb, driven sheep taken to their slaughter at the shrine, and the blood and gore that added to his horror. He prays for the birth of a great man or woman who will be able to persuade people to do away

---

8   *Ibid.*, p.169.

9   *Ibid.*, p.171.

with this practice. He finds it hard to reconcile the intelligence, knowledge and sensitivity of Bengal with this ugly sacrificial slaughter at the Kāli temple.[10]

Gandhi tried to acquaint himself with the tenor of Bengali life; their beliefs and their rituals. He met a number of Bengali leaders, and read a biography of Keshav Chandra Sen. He attended a celebration of Brahmo Samaj at the house of Maharshi Devendranath Tagore, and heard some captivating Bengali music, which secured a place in his heart for ever.

He went to Belur math to see Swami Vivekananda, but was sad to learn that the Swami was very ill at his Calcutta residence; and could not be seen.[11] He met Sister Nivedita in a 'Chowringhee mansion', the splendour of which shocked him.[12] He met her again; but though he admired her love for Hinduism, he failed to see how their points of view could coincide.

Gandhi met the leading citizens of Calcutta, and on January 19 and 27, 1902, gave a couple of public lectures, in which he drew attention to the woeful plight of Indians in South Africa. He proposed to conquer the intense hatred of the white colonials against Indians with love; and detailed the work of the Indian Ambulance Corps in the Anglo-Boer war.[13] In his introductory remarks, Gokhale described him as ' a man made of the stuff of which heroes are made.'[14]

Gandhi's stay with Gokhale facilitated his work in Calcutta, and laid the foundation of his close contact with Bengal in the years that followed. He paid a flying visit to Rangoon to meet his friend Pranjivan Mehta, who was, despite his medical credentials, running the family jewellery business there. Gandhi noted the listless indolence of the monks and the laziness of the Burmese men; but was impressed by the freedom and industry of the Burmese women. He did not like the 'innumerable little candles' burning inside the Golden Pagoda, though he had admired the candles in Notre Dame, when he visited Paris as a student in London. Burma presented a replication of India's subjection to the British and their interests.

---

10 *Ibid.*, p.172.
11 *Ibid.*, p.173.
12 *Ibid.*, p.173.
13 *Collected Works*, Vol.3, pp.216-217, 219-224.
14 Cf. Guha, op.cit., p.147.

He took leave of Gokhale on the completion of his work in Calcutta. He talked to him about his intention to travel across India in third class railway carriages to see the country and acquaint himself with the difficulties of third class passengers. Gandhi preferred the ordinary to the mail trains, as they were less crowded and the fares were cheaper. He proceeded to Banaras in third class; found the compartments dirty; and points out that there was hardly any improvement in the years that followed. The difference between first and third class was painful. The dirty habits of the passengers, and their lack of consideration for each other, added to the indifference of the Railway authorities to their comforts. Gandhi's description of third class travel is truly telling: 'These unpleasant habits commonly include throwing of rubbish on the floor of the compartment, smoking at all hours and in all places, betel and tobacco chewing, converting the whole carriage into a spittoon, shouting and yelling, and using foul language, regardless of the convenience or comfort of fellow-passengers. I have noticed little difference between my experience of the third class travelling in 1902 and that of my unbroken third class tours from 1915 to 1919.'[15] The unfortunate truth is that this state of affairs continued right down to the 1950s and beyond. His serious illness in 1918-19 forced him to 'practically' give up third class travel, which remained for him 'a matter of constant pain and shame.'[16]

---

15 *Autobiography*, p.175.

16 *Ibid.*, p.176.

Chapter 28

Banaras

Gandhi gives us a vivid account of his stay in Banaras. He put up with a *paṇḍā* (priest), whom he chose for his comparative cleanliness out of a throng that surrounded him at the station. He was lodged in the upper storey of a house, in the courtyard of which there was a cow. Even though Gandhi told the *paṇḍā* that he would not give him more than a rupee and four *annas*, the *paṇḍā* accorded him every facility. Gandhi went to the river, had his holy dip, did his *pūjā*, and went to the Kāśī Viśvanātha Temple for a glimpse of the deity. He was upset and pained by the experience. He had to approach the temple through a very narrow, dirty lane. There was maddening noise. There were swarming flies; aggressive shop keepers; and the jostling pilgrims. 'Meditation and communion' were out of the question in such an insalubrious and noisy quarter. The entrance to the temple filled one's nostrils with the stink of rotting flowers. Gandhi gives a hilarious account of his encounter with the temple *paṇḍā*. The dirty maintenance of the temple interior made Gandhi loath to give any substantial *dakṣiṇā* or donation. He therefore gave a *pie*, which was contemptuously thrown away by the *paṇḍā*, who said that Gandhi would go straight to hell for this insult to God. Gandhi replied that he was quite prepared to accept his fate; but it did not behove the *paṇḍā* to curse him. Gandhi told him again to accept the *pie*, or else he would take it away. 'Go away' said the *paṇḍā*, and abused him some more. Gandhi was happy with the thought that he had saved a *pie*. As he started walking away, the Brahmin *paṇḍā* called him back and asked him to leave the *pie* there. He would not be as mean as Gandhi was, because refusal of the *pie* would hurt Gandhi. And Gandhi and his *pie* were irretrievably parted!

Gandhi tells us that he has been to Kāśī Viśvanātha twice since; but 'afflicted' as he is 'with the title of *Mahatma*', the experience has not been unlike the one described above.[1] 'People eager to have my *darshan* would not permit me to have a *darshan* of the temple. The woes of *Mahatmas* are known to *Mahatmas* alone. Otherwise, the dirt and the noise were the same as before.'[2] He is appalled by the 'hypocrisy and irreligion' rampant at these holy places; and cites a passage from the *Gītā: ye yathā māṁ prapadyante tāṁstathaiva bhajāmyahaṁ.* He translates it freely as 'whatever a man sows, that shall he reap'.[3] Gandhi's faith in the inexorable law of *karma* is total. Evasion of *karmic* consequence is not possible. 'There is thus hardly any need for God to interfere. He laid down the law and, as it were, retired.'[4]

Gandhi also called on Mrs. Annie Besant who lived in Banaras, and was convalescing from a bout of illness. He then visited Agra, Jaipur and Palanpur on his way back to Rajkot.

---

1   *Autobography*, p.177.

2   *Ibid.*

3   *Ibid.* This is the first line of Gītā, IV.11, which means: 'However men approach me, so do I welcome them'. Gandhi's translation elsewhere is: 'In whatever way men resort to Me, even so do I render to them.' Cf. Mahatma Gandhi, *The Bhagvad Gita According to Gandhi*, Translated by Mahadev Desai, Important Books, USA, 2013, p.25.

4   *Autobiography*, p.177.

Chapter 29

In Bombay Again

Gokhale wanted Gandhi to settle down in Bombay, practise at the Bar, and share some of his burden of public work, which meant working for the Congress. Gokhale's advice fell on receptive ears; but Gandhi remembered his past experience as a barrister in Bombay, which did not make him feel over-confident. He therefore decided to start his practice first at Rajkot. Kevalram Dave, himself a lawyer, whose father had advised and helped send Gandhi to England, brought him three briefs. With his friend's ready assistance and his own hard work, Gandhi won an important case at Jamnagar. He won all these cases, which boosted his self-confidence.

Dave insisted on Gandhi moving from Rajkot and setting up his practice at Bombay. So he did, with the money he received from Natal, and took chambers in Payne, Gilbert and Sayani's offices.

Gandhi tells us that though he settled in Bombay, God put him to a test. Soon after he moved into his new house, his second son Manilal was laid up with typhoid. The boy also developed pneumonia, and became delirious at night. The doctor said that medicines would not do much, but eggs and chicken broth would be good for the patient. Gandhi was in a quandary. He had to decide for his ten-year old son. He told the Parsi doctor, a very good man, that they could give none of those two things to the boy as they were vegetarians. The doctor insisted that the boy's life was in danger. Milk diluted with water would not be nourishing enough. 'I think you will be well advised not to be so hard on your son,' said the doctor. He served many Hindu families; and they never objected to whatever he thought was necessary.

Gandhi agreed that the doctor was right in prescribing whatever he considered good and necessary for the patient. But his responsibility as a father was 'very great'.[1] If the boy was an adult, they would have respected his wishes; but as he was a minor, his father had to decide for him. According to Gandhi, such an occasion was a true test of a man's faith. 'Rightly or wrongly it is part of my religious conviction that man may not eat meat, eggs, and the like. There should be a limit even to the means of keeping ourselves alive…Religion, as I understand it, does not permit me to use meat or eggs for me or mine even on occasions like this, and I must therefore take the risk that you say is likely.'[2] Gandhi told the doctor that he would resort to some hydropathic remedies; and requested him to help check the boy's pulse, chest and lungs, and keep the father abreast of his condition. The doctor agreed. Gandhi told his son about the conversation he had with the doctor; and Manilal asked his father to go ahead with the hydropathic treatment.

Gandhi gave his son Kuhne's treatment, including hip baths, and gave him orange juice mixed with water for three days. The boy's temperature went up to 104 degrees. He would become delirious at night. Gandhi was racked by doubt and anxiety. If something happened, what would the world say? What would his elder brother say? Could they find another doctor? Could they consult an Āyurvedic physician? Did he have any right as a parent 'to inflict' his 'fads' on his progeny?

Gandhi's mind was a cauldron of contrary thoughts. He also had a feeling that God would be very pleased to see that he was giving his son the same treatment that he would give himself. He had faith in hydropathy, hardly any in allopathy. The doctors only experimented with medicines and could not guarantee cures. One's life depended on God, and it was right to continue the treatment with faith in God.

Gandhi gave his son wet packs to bring the temperature down. So it went on, and the fever gradually went down. He kept his son on diluted milk and fruit juice for full forty days. Finally, he succeeded in defeating the obstinate fever. Gandhi tells us that Manilal is the healthiest of his boys. He does not know whether the boy's recovery should be attributed to God's mercy, or to hydropathy, or to careful nursing and Gandhi's dietary

---

1   *Autobiography*, p.180.
2   *Ibid.*

dispensation. Gandhi personally believes that it was God's grace that saved his honour. It seems as though in Gandhi's eyes his 'honour' is of greater consequence than the life of his son. He plays God or the agent of God's will. He knows what God wills, and what God commands. His blind belief in the vegetarian commandment of God is a travesty of a universal rule of nature, in which life has always depended on life. Gandhi was himself not above eating eggs in England at a certain juncture in his experimentation with different types of food. He forgot that, when he decided to discard the doctor's advice for his son! No parent should have such an unethical authority to refuse a doctor's advice and prescription in face of such a daunting danger. A child's life hangs in the balance. The doctor says one thing, but the father does another. Quackery luckily helps the child's recovery, which is construed as the will of God, and the vindication of the father's faith. To an ordinary mind like mine, such an attitude, and such obstinacy, does not merit any approval whatsoever. It is irrational; it is callous; it is incomprehensible; it is unpardonable! It is little more than an abject acceptance of fatalism and of predestination, with feeble hydropathy only serving as a salve for the father's conscience. There is no doubt that Gandhi loved his son. The passages describing the son's illness and the father's treatment move one to tears. But the lasting feeling is one of exasperation; of disbelief at the superstitious insensibility of a great man.

Gandhi hired a fine bungalow in Santa Cruz and moved his family there. It was a better house and a healthier environment. He travelled first class from Santa Cruz to Churchgate, and took pride in the fact that he was the only first class passenger in the compartment. He did better in his profession than expected. His South African clients often gave him work to do; and he earned enough to support his family. He was not yet able to secure any work in the High Court, where he attended the hearings of many cases; but often found himself dozing in the 'soporific breeze'.[3] Sir Pherozeshah was not very encouraging, when he told him that he 'would be foolishly wasting away in Bombay' his 'small savings from Natal'.[4] Gokhale, though, visited him often in his chambers; and introduced him to many more people. Gandhi was settling down.

---

3   *Ibid.*
4   *Collected Works*, Vol. 3, 1960, 'Letter to Devchand Parekh', August 6, 1902, p.261.

A persuasive American insurance agent convinced him to take out a small life policy. He thought of his wife and children. He thought of his wife's ornaments, most of which he had sold. If something happened to him, his brother, who had 'so nobly filled the place of father', would have to bear the burden of supporting his family. Gandhi could not bear the thought, and took out a policy for Rs. 10,000. But then he received a cable from South Africa asking him to return immediately, as Chamberlain was expected there; and they needed his help and guidance to safeguard their status in the new scheme of administration. Gandhi remembered his promise; and told them that he would undertake the journey as soon as they sent him money. The fact that he was yet unable to find his feet in the High Court would certainly have been a factor influencing his decision. Despite strong dissuasion by Sir Pherozeshah Mehta[5], who told him that he would not be able to achieve much there, he left for South Africa, where he had awaiting an assured and appreciative clientele. As he did not think he would be staying there for more than a year, he kept the bungalow in Bombay, where his wife and children could stay on. One of the five youths who accompanied him to South Africa was his nephew Maganlal Gandhi, who became one of his chief lieutenants in the country. Leaving his wife and family behind was painful; but he was getting used to the vagaries of life. 'All else but God that is Truth is an uncertainty.'[6] Gandhi calls the quest for that Truth 'the *summum bonum* of life'. And that Truth would doubtless express itself in the service of South Africa's oppressed Indian community!

---

5   Gandhi, Rajmohan, op. cit., p.94.

6   *Autobiography*, p.184.

Chapter 30

In South Africa Again

Gandhi arrived in Durban in the third week of December, 1902; and immediately busied himself drafting a petition on behalf of the Indians residing in Natal, and accompanying the deputation that submitted it to Chamberlain on the 27th.

The Secretary was specially requested to relax the licensing laws; and to provide schools for the education of Indian children. He recognized that the grievances had substance; but the best course for the Indians was to win over the Europeans, in whose midst they had to live. The Imperial Government could not meddle too much in the affairs of self-governing colonies; he would do what he could, but not very much. Chamberlain was in South Africa not to improve the lot of the Indians; but to woo the English and the Boers, and to receive from them a gift of 35 million pounds! Indians were deeply disappointed. He had gently told them that might was indeed right!

Chamberlain went from Natal to the Transvaal. Gandhi had to prepare and submit a petition to him on behalf of the Indians there as well. Indians intent on returning to the Transvaal now needed the recommendation of a new Asiatic Department to secure the necessary permits. Sadly, no permit could be procured without payment of bribes. With the help of Alexander, the Police Superintendent of Durban, Gandhi secured one; and was immediately on his way to Pretoria. He drafted the memorial to be submitted; but discovered that the officers wanted to exclude him from the deputation to wait upon Chamberlain. Some of them, newly arrived from India and Ceylon, had brought with them the autocratic effrontery that they cultivated in those countries. The South African officers practised a certain amount of courtesy in their dealings with people even if they were coloured, which was not the case in autocratic India and Ceylon.

The Chief of the Department, W. H. Moor, formerly of the Ceylon Civil Service, told Gandhi that a permit had been issued to him by mistake; and that he had no business to be there. The Asiatic Department was there to protect the Indians. He did not offer Gandhi and the others any seats; did not give Gandhi any opportunity to speak; and asked him to go away. As Gandhi left the room, the officer vented his spleen on his companions.

Gandhi was rattled, but inured to such slights. The discourteous treatment was followed by a letter to inform them that Gandhi's name had been omitted from the deputation, as he had already met Mr Chamberlain in Durban. Gandhi's friends were so incensed that they proposed not to wait on Chamberlain at all with any deputation. He, however, persuaded them to carry their deputation with an Indian barrister named George Godfrey in his place. Chamberlain sought to explain Gandhi's exclusion by saying that it was better to hear someone new instead of the same person over and over again. Undeterred and untiring, Gandhi wrote another petition for the Indians in Cape Town, to be presented to Chamberlain when he visited their city.

Gandhi was taunted by some in the community telling him that they had helped in the war only at his instance, which proved utterly futile. But he was still firm in his view that they had done the right thing; and, later if not sooner, that would bear good fruit. He told his friends that though his immediate task was now practically done, he would not like to return to India even if they permitted him to do so. The community was in great danger of being 'thoroughly robbed' and 'hounded out of the country'.[1] The insult with which he had been hit was only a foretaste of what was in store for the entire community. 'It will become impossible to put up with the veritable dog's life that we shall be expected to lead'.[2] He wanted to get enrolled in the Transvaal Supreme Court, and start working there. He was confident that he could deal effectively with this new oppressive department. He viewed it as an opportunity. He had been unable to halt the anti-Indian legislation in Natal. If he could persuade Britain to put aside the anti-Indian laws of the Boers in the Transvaal, that would logically

---

1 *Autobiography*, p.192.
2 *Ibid.*

make the anti-Indian laws of Natal untenable. He would be much more than a barrister making money, exerting himself in every way possible to secure a better deal and a tolerably respectable existence for his fellow Indians.[3] He discussed the matter with his delighted Indian friends, and made up his mind to set up his practice in Johannesburg. On March 31, 1903, Gandhi applied for admission as an attorney to the Supreme Court of the Transvaal. The bar did not oppose, as they could discover no defensible grounds for objection; and on April 14, 1903, he was duly admitted.

---

3   Cf. Maureen Swan, *Gandhi: The South African Experience*, pp.92-93.

Chapter 31

Life in Johannesburg

With the help of his English friend Louis Walter Ritch, manager in a commercial firm, Gandhi managed to rent suitable rooms for his office in the city's legal quarters; and thus began another chapter in his South African story. The practice prospered. Most of his clients were Indian, who kept him occupied with their applications for re-entry into the Transvaal after the war; for relaxation of the trading laws; and for permits needed for inter-provincial travel. Four Indian clerks and a secretary called Miss Dick, fresh from Scotland, helped cope with the volume of business. Miss Dick managed the funds and the accounts with great diligence and integrity to win Gandhi's complete confidence; and later asked him to give her away in marriage. Ritch also joined the practice by getting himself articled under Gandhi, thus providing much needed relief from the burden of work.

The Asiatic Department in Johannesburg were gleefully harassing the Indians, Chinese and other Asians, doing nothing whatsoever to protect them. They were smuggling people into the province on payment of bribes, and refusing admission to the rightful applicants. People came to Gandhi for help; and he approached the Police Commissioner with a fair amount of evidence. The Commissioner gave him a patient hearing; examined the witnesses; and was convinced that the complaints were correct. He knew that it was not easy to convict a white offender against coloured people with a white jury; but nevertheless assured Gandhi that he would pursue the matter and have the guilty arrested. Warrants of arrest were issued against two, about whose guilt Gandhi had the clearest proof. One of them absconded; but the Police Commissioner managed to have him arrested and brought to the Transvaal. They were both put on trial, and despite clear proof of their guilt and the additional charge that one of them had absconded, the white jury declared them not guilty. Both Gandhi and the Police Commissioner were disappointed; but the two officers were still dismissed by the Government, as their guilt had been so clearly established. The Asiatic Department was forced to clean up its act, which gave some respite to the Indian community. Gandhi's prestige went up. His business picked up. The community was able to save large amounts of money that would have otherwise greased the palms of dishonest officials. Always intent on inventing 'new engines of torture', the Department had been a source of 'terror to the people'.[1]

Gandhi did not obstruct the appointment of these two officers later to the Johannesburg Municipality, demonstrating an essential attribute of *Satyāgraha* and *ahimsā*, which he developed and practised in his struggle against official tyranny. Gandhi emphasizes that *ahimsā* alone leads one to the Truth. It is quite in order to stand up against an unjust system, but not against the authors of the system, which would be 'attacking oneself'.[2] It is the sin and not the sinner that you are fighting against. But the reference to 'attacking oneself' restates the Indian philosophical position that one has to see oneself in others, and the others in one's own self. Gandhi believes that we are children of the same Maker; and that we carry within ourselves aspects of the Divinity that brings us into being. The immanence of Divinity in us all invests us with an infinite potentiality; and we should desist from harming others, inasmuch as doing so would amount to hurting ourselves, and slighting the Divinity within us. Gandhi does not say so here, but he is restating the well-known Indian belief – *ātmavat sarvabhūteṣu yaḥ paśyati sa(ḥ) paṇḍitaḥ*. He who looks at all living beings as he looks at himself, is truly wise.[3]

---

1 Cf. DiSalvo, *op. cit.*, pp.189-190, 398, 39.

2 *Autobiography*, p.203.

3 *Ibid.*

Chapter 32

Statement of Faith in Human Equality

Gandhi tells his readers that he deals with people of many creeds and communities; and very seriously states: 'I have known no distinction between relatives and strangers, countrymen and foreigners, white and coloured, Hindus and Indians of other faiths, whether Musalmans, Parsis, Christians or Jews. I may say that my heart has been incapable of making any such distinction. I cannot claim this as a special virtue, as it is in my very nature, rather than a result of any effort on my part...'[1] We admire and applaud such a straightforward affirmation of our collective humanity without any invidious distinctions in Gandhi's thoughts. He is instinctively inclined to embrace such an inclusive image of humankind. But like any other human being, he too rose to this wonderful realization only through his experiences and inner growth in the rough and tumble of real life. When he went to South Africa, and faced the degrading racial assaults on his dignity, he protested, and refused to submit to his humiliation by the whites. He told them that he came from a race that was related to their own, and that spoke languages that formed part of their own linguistic family. He did not at that time seek to identify himself with the blacks of South Africa, for whom he used the common pejorative term *kaffir*. He referred to their inferior culture and lack of education, and pleaded for distinction between Indians and *kaffirs*. It was later that he realized that this distinction was basically false and misplaced. He stopped using the word *kaffir* for the blacks, and in some of his writings and statements praised their humanity and racial majesty. We can therefore understand that a man takes time to take stock of his surroundings; to come to grips with the intricacies and difficulties of inter-racial human relationships; and to come to the final realization that all distinctions are

---

1   *Autobiography*, p.204.

man-made; are activated by selfish motives; and are justified only in terms of narrow racial self-aggrandizement at the expense of others. Moral justification for this kind of exploitation and subjection of different races is out of the question. Reality, though, dictates pursuit of policies that are limited on grounds of feasibility, on the premise of possibility. It is from the establishment of a principle, from the gain of a limited objective that one can proceed to the chase of the final goal seeking equality of one and all in the policies of state. Gandhi took his time to clearly and categorically state his firm and final conviction of the equality of all despite their racial and religious differences. The conviction would have been there even earlier, but Gandhi knew the limits of what was immediately possible; and what was achievable in the fullness of time. We may thus understand how Gandhi came to his great vision of human unity in diversity. There is no dearth of denigrators who are suddenly rising and writing to denounce Gandhi as a racist, which he certainly was not. He took time to grow up, to study, to struggle, to understand and state his final position in the quote given above. And, as he said elsewhere: 'By a long process of prayerful discipline I have ceased over forty years to hate anybody.'

Like anyone else, he evolved, his thinking evolved, his vision evolved; and it was only painfully, gradually, that an ordinary lawyer, a man of the world with common ambitions and common dreams grew far above them to become the *Mahatma*, who identified himself with the meanest of humankind. *Mahatmas* are not born. Men and women through their thoughts, deeds, service and sacrifice attain sainthood.

Chapter 33

Spiritual Striving

Christian influence had kindled his spiritual quest during his first stay in South Africa. Now in Johannesburg, he was drawn to theosophy by his friend Ritch, who came originally from England immersed in theosophy, and helped the establishment of the Theosophical Lodge in the city. Gandhi fraternized with the practitioners of this all inclusive, syncretic ideology without formally joining the Society. He heard readings from theosophical books; and addressed the members on occasions, drawing their attention to the gap between their precept and practice of brotherhood.

The theosophists wanted to get what they could out of Gandhi as a Hindu. He told them that he had not studied Hindu scriptures in the original; and most of what he knew came from translations. But his theosophist friends had faith in '*samskara* (tendencies caused by previous births) and *punarjanma* (rebirth)...'[1] They felt that Gandhi could still be useful to them owing to his birth legacy. He read Swami Vivekananda's *Rājayoga* as well as M.N Dvivedi's work of the same name with some of these friends. He also read the *Yogasūtras* of Patañjali and the *Bhagavad-Gītā* with some of them. Gandhi already had great faith in the *Gītā*, but now made a deeper study of it. He memorized thirteen chapters, while trying to understand it; and 'the *Gītā* became an infallible guide of conduct.' It became his 'dictionary of daily reference.'[2] Whenever in doubt he turned to it to find 'ready solution of all' his 'troubles and trials'.[3] He was deeply affected by the ideas of *aparigraha* (non-possession) and *samabhāva*

---

1 *Autobiography*, p.194.

2 *Ibid.*, p.195.

3 *Ibid.*

(equability). It was easier said than done. 'How was one to treat alike, insulting, insolent and corrupt officials, co-workers of yesterday raising meaningless opposition, and men who had always been good to one? How was one to divest oneself of all possessions? Was not the body itself possession enough? Were not wife and children possessions? Was I to destroy all the cupboards of books that I had? Was I to give up all I had and follow Him?' Gandhi tells us that he got his answers straightaway. He could not follow God, to whom he referred as 'Him', unless he gave up all he had.[4] He discovered religion in Snell's book on jurisprudence, which enabled him to understand the true meaning of the word 'Trustee'. Gandhi's interpretation of *Gītā's* non-possession meant that a person seeking salvation had to behave and act as a Trustee in relation to his own possessions. Even though he had complete control over his possessions, he should not regard them as his own. These two concepts of *aparigraha* and *samabhāva* required a new understanding of one's relationship with things and people. He was drawing on both the East and West to experience 'a change of heart, a change of attitude'. He increasingly felt that all his work in South Africa was 'in the name of God and for His service'.[5] He could not tell how long he would have to stay; he might never return to India. He now thought that it was a mistake to take out an insurance policy in India. He felt 'ashamed' of being converted to the acceptance of insurance by the agent. He told himself that his father-like brother would not mind supporting his widow and children in case of his death. But why should he assume that he would die earlier than the others? The real protector was God Almighty, not Gandhi, nor his brother. By taking out the insurance, he argued, he had deprived his wife and children of 'self-reliance'. They should be able to take care of themselves. The world was full of the poor beyond any count. Who looked after them? He should count himself as one of them.[6]

This is incredible drivel; an abject acceptance of fatalism, of predestination, of cruel or felicitous chance. This is a deliberate imposition in Gandhi's thoughts on the limitless kindness of his father-like elder brother despite the latter's rather straitened circumstances. This is throwing his wife and children to the wolves. This is a false identification with the poor of the

---

4   *Ibid.*

5   *Ibid.*, p.193.

6   *Ibid.*

world. He was not poor. He was not living like the poor. He had at his command, with his careful planning, whatever he needed to lead a life of comparative comfort and dignity. The only possible way to look at it is to treat it as selfish, self-serving obedience to God's will only as he understood it, in so far as life at the time of this introspection did not leave much wanting. Blind faith in God's mercy is at odds with Gandhi's struggle at the social level for the redress of wrongs and social and political injustices. Gandhi had left a Trust behind made up of the proceeds of gifts he had received from his friends in South Africa, when he left for India in October, 1901. This Trust had been set up to stand the community in good stead in case of future needs. He forgot the principle when he castigated himself for taking out this personal insurance; and when he misconstrued it as an affront to Divine Providence.

Gandhi wrote to a friend in India to let his insurance policy lapse, and recover anything that was possible. The loss of premiums paid would be bearable. He was newly convinced that God would take care of him and of his wife and children, as He was their Creator. And a few months later, in 1905, he wrote to his elder brother Lakshmidas that from that point onwards, he should not expect anything from him. He had paid him all that he could save so far, but no more! Any future savings would be pressed into the service of the community. Gandhi's family was no longer his immediate or extended family in the common sense of the term. The world was his family now. The brother who had helped him become what he was, could fend for himself. He was no longer Gandhi's concern. The sudden sundering of the sibling cord was exceedingly painful to the elder brother who was shaken, and found it hard to understand. He wrote to Gandhi in the strongest terms to remind him of his debt and duty. He told Gandhi that he should not act wiser than his own father, who had always looked after his extended family. Gandhi replied that he 'was doing exactly what our father had done. The meaning of 'family' had but to be slightly widened and the wisdom of my step would become clear.'[7]

Gandhi's brother had gone totally out of his way to provide for Gandhi; to support his ambition to go to London to study Law and become a barrister; to provide the money needed; to shell out more to pay for his gentlemanly

---

7 *Autobiography,* p.196. Cf. *Matthew* 12: 46-50 for the answer of Jesus, when told that he was abandoning his mother and brothers; Adams, Jad, *Gandhi: Naked Ambition*, Quercus, London, 2011, p.81.

pursuits and fashionable living. He helped Gandhi on his feet as a lawyer in India. And he found the opening that made it possible for Gandhi to go to South Africa. He looked after and provided for Gandhi's family while the latter was away. In joint Indian families, where the elder brother assumed the responsibilities of the father to look after his younger siblings, it was morally incumbent on the younger brothers to help the joint family with part of their income when they began to earn. Morality apart, it was also a duty in terms of traditional Hindu law. Any money sent by Gandhi to his elder brother up to that point, whatever the total, could never really repay the debt owed. Lakshmidas had every reason to feel cheated and deeply disappointed. Gandhi could have given away whatever he wanted in the practice of *aparigraha*; but he should have always saved something for his elder brother throughout the latter's life. As it is, the elder brother did not live very long after this painful parting of ways. An amount of 100 rupees, or even a little less a month was certainly not too much for Gandhi to afford for his brother. He could have spent the rest on whatever he held dear in the discharge of his responsibilities to the wider world. Mere acknowledgement of gratitude by Gandhi, and expression of distress, was not enough to absolve him from a valid charge of hurtful unconcern. The assertion, nevertheless, of Gandhi's devotion to his elder brother does not convince a sceptical reader. His attitude and his action alike betray a self-righteous callousness unmindful of the sense of deep desolation and discomfiture felt by his brother. I personally find it inexcusable, despite Gandhi's enlightenment through the *Gītā* that his family now included the entire Indian community in South Africa. If one is to really go by the *Gītā*, Gandhi had to include all the whites and blacks of South Africa in his family. *Udāra caritānāṁ tu vasudhaiva kuṭumbakaṁ*: to people of generous disposition, the whole world, the whole earth constitutes one family. Gandhi could not rightfully exclude his elder brother and his family from this vision of oneness. The wider view of human unity should not, and does not exclude or destroy the bonds of the immediate family.

Gandhi tells us that his elder brother stopped all communications with him. He acknowledges that the acuteness of his brother's misery arose out of the latter's love for him. The elder brother in Gandhi's own words 'did not so much want my money as that I should be well behaved towards the family.' Gandhi tries to convince himself and his readers with the statement that his brother realized the rightness of Gandhi's step when he was near death's door. Lakshmidas wrote him 'a most pathetic letter', in which he apologized to Gandhi, and entrusted his sons to his care, asking him to bring them up as he wished. The brother sent him a telegram that he would like to come to South Africa to see him. Gandhi said he could; but Lakshmidas died before his wish could be fulfilled. Gandhi did nothing for his sons. He seeks to salve his conscience by telling us that he could not draw them to himself.[8] The devotee of Rāma failed to recall the totally self-effacing devotion of Bharata and Lakṣmaṇa to their elder brother!

Gandhi's increasing devotion to simplicity and sacrifice made him a vegetarian with a vengeance. He patronised a vegetarian restaurant in Johannesburg run by a German, who was also a believer in Kuhne's hydropathic treatment. He even helped the restaurant with money; but it closed down owing to financial difficulties. He found time and money for these fads, while he washed his hands of any financial responsibility for his brother and the joint family back home.

Gandhi cites another example of his misplaced generosity, when he lent 1000 pounds of Trust money, with the consent of his client Badri, to a lady to help her run a vegetarian restaurant. The money could never be recovered; and Gandhi had to make good his client's loss out of his own pocket. He learned the lesson that he could not help others' causes with borrowed money.[9]

---

8 *Autobiography*, p.196.

9 *Ibid.*, p.197.

Chapter 34

'Indian Opinion'

The Indian community in South Africa was in sore need of a printing press, and in 1989, Gandhi lent money to a friend named Madanjit Vyavaharik to establish one in Durban, called the International Printing Press. In 1903, Madanjit came to him with the idea of using the press for publishing an Indian journal called *'Indian Opinion'*. Gandhi embraced the proposal with ready alacrity; and agreed to support the journal with at least one article each week, and if necessary, with money as well. Mansukhlal Nazar, an old associate, became the first editor, though Gandhi did most of the work, and also wrote the editorials. The first issue, out on June 4, 1903, consisted of Gujarati, Hindi, Tamil and English versions. The journal would, as Gandhi said in the first issue, draw public attention to the unjust social and political treatment to which the Indians were subjected, and would also point out the faults of Indians with unhesitating candour.

Indian opinion certainly filled a lacuna; and provided a mirror of Indian opinion to everyone interested. It enabled Indians to express themselves through letters and comments published in the journal.[1] As Madanjit wanted to go back to India, Gandhi took over the press and the journal in March-April, 1904; and the annual cost of publication amounted to Rs. 30,000, if not more. Gandhi had to discontinue the Indian language versions, and soon discovered that it could not support itself without his financial input. Stopping the journal would have amounted to a loss of face. Gandhi tells us that he had to spend all his savings to run it. In retrospect, though, he feels that the exercise had been worthwhile. The community benefited from it; and it was never a 'commercial concern'.

---

1   Cf. Gandhi, Rajmohan, *op.cit.*, p.99

During the years 1905-06, Gandhi raised *Indian Opinion* to a significant level of authority and influence. He kept himself abreast and fully informed of the course of events in India and supported Gokhale for Presidentship of the Indian National Congress. He wrote about the iniquity of the Salt Tax and the need to abolish it; and fully supported the boycott of British goods and the use of *Swadeshi* to defeat the proposed partition of Bengal, while at the same time emphasizing the imperative need for communal and inter-religious harmony. And in South Africa, he continued to raise the Indians' level of awareness in relation to hygiene, sanitation and self-discipline. The new idea of *Satyāgraha* also came to the fore not to submit to unjust laws and ordinances, regardless of any consequences, with readiness to suffer and go to jail if necessary in the struggle for justice and fair play.

Indian Opinion reflected the course of his life from one week to another, as he wrote for it and laid down the 'principles and practice of *Satyāgraha*'. He wrote for it continually for ten years until 1914. The only gaps occurred when he was in prison. Gandhi feels content with the thought that his writing for the journal provided a wonderful training in self-restraint. He always desisted from exaggeration. He never wrote to please. The paper became pivotal to the *Satyāgraha.* It provided authentic accounts of the campaign and of the plight of Indians in South Africa. It enabled Gandhi to commune with the world around him; to comprehend human nature; and to create a personal relationship between the editor and the readers. He received letters, which both commended or criticized him. He established a close rapport with the community. He could hear what they thought and felt. He also learned what it meant to be a responsible journalist. Through the journal he nurtured a special relationship with the community, which made a vital contribution to the viability and success of *Satyāgraha.*

Gandhi realized the power of the press for good as well as evil, which invested the editor's task with a great responsibility. He knew that this power could be easily misused, and therefore insisted that it must be exercised with control and caution, and a sense of service to the community.[2]

Lectures at the Theosophical Lodge

Gandhi gave lectures on Hinduism at the Theosophical Lodge in Johannesburg. He talks of the ultimate reality or *Brahman*; of the soul

---

2 *Autobiography,* p.211.

or *ātman* being dragged into *saṁsāra* through *karma*, and striving to find salvation through self-realization. He describes Buddha as a social reformer, and treats his philosophy as integral to Hinduism leading to a reformation and final absorption of Buddha and Buddhism into Hinduism through acceptance, not rejection. Gandhi's statement, though, that the Buddha believed in God, has been labelled as a deliberate distortion of Gautama's message.³ He lauds the logic of Jainism, and its injunction of unqualified non-violence or *ahiṁsā*, synonymous with ethics without limits! There is no doubt that so many of Gandhian principles and practices can be traced back to the inspiration of Jainism. To suffer for self-purification as much as the betterment of fellow human beings and for their moral upliftment is the emulation of Jaina ideals of non-violence, non-possession and expiation. *Ahiṁsā* necessarily evinces itself in positive and practical action to relieve the distress of animate creation.

His emphasis on the identical ethical precepts of all religions, and acceptance of them all as the repositories of Truth, leads him to advocate tolerance and respect for one another in our common realization that we arise out of the same source of being and becoming, despite the differences of our religious diction; our modes of prayer; our doctrinal formulations; and our divergent rituals. He talks of Kabīr and Nānak and their attempts to synthesize Hinduism and Islam by laying stress on the core of both; on God the father; on humans as God's progeny; on their inalienable common identity; on the inefficacy and distraction of rituals;⁴ on the need to find our Maker within ourselves and to realize, proclaim and practise our fraternal equality to find justice and happiness now and in the hereafter. Gandhi is frustrated by the fact that the precepts aimed at demolishing distinctions ended only in the establishment of new religious orders; the erection of new divisive walls separating us from one another. New barriers arose, where the great teachers laboured to raze the old into oblivion.

Though Gandhi accommodated all sects and superstitions in his commodious tent of *Sanātana* Hinduism, he called the *Ārya Samāj* a cult despite their acceptance of the *Vedas* and rejection of meaningless rituals;

3　Cf. Bharati, Agehananda, 'Gandhi's Interpretation of the Gita', in S.Ray (ed.), *Gandhi, India and the World*, p.42.

4　Cf. Emperor Aśoka's characterization of numberless rituals as exercises in futility. See his Rock Edict IX; Bhandarkar, D.R., *Aśoka*, Calcutta University, Calcutta, 1955, p.93.

and their advocacy of female emancipation and education for both sexes without any caste distinctions; abolition of child marriages and support for the remarriage of widows; their campaign against untouchability, and for inter-caste marriages; and their cries for *swadeshī* and *swarāj*.[5] The defensive militancy of the Ārya Samāj frightened him. Their criticism of other faiths threatened the inter-religious solidarity of the South African Indians, which Gandhi was trying so hard to foster.

---

5   Cf. *Collected Works*, Vol. 5, p.48.

Chapter 35

Earth and Water Cures

Gandhi talks of his increasing simplicity and of his steady aversion to medicine. While in Durban, he had felt a certain weakness and rheumatic discomfort; but felt well after Dr. P. J. Mehta's treatment. He stayed healthy in India. In Johannesburg, though, he suffered from constipation and headaches, which he overcame with a specific diet and regular use of laxatives. He decided to forego breakfast, which got rid of the headaches, and confirmed his belief that he had been eating too much. But the constipation was still there. Kuhne's hip baths helped only partially. Somebody gave Gandhi a book called *Return to Nature* by Adolf Just, who prescribed earth treatment and fresh fruit and nuts as the natural food for humankind. Gandhi undertook earth treatment with very good results. He applied a bandage of clean earth moistened with cold water to his abdomen before going to bed. He removed it either in the middle of the night or in the morning. And 'it proved a radical cure'.[1] Gandhi continually gave that treatment to himself in later life, as well as to his friends. He was never disappointed. He affirms his faith in these earth and water treatments and recommends them to all his friends. Gandhi refers to two serious personal illnesses, but says that a person can always be cured by a regulated diet, and water and earth treatments. He scoffs at people running to doctors, and swallowing all kinds of medicines. This results only in curtailing the life of a man, who 'by becoming the slave of his body instead of remaining its master, loses self-control and ceases to be a man.'[2]

Gandhi continued his earth treatment and dietary experiments. He also wrote a series of articles in Gujarati for publication in *Indian Opinion*,

---

1   *Autobiography*, p.198.
2   *Ibid.*, p.199.

which were later published in an English translation as a *Guide to Health*. He tells us that this little book made a profound influence on the lives of many in the East and the West.

Gandhi stresses the spiritual quest which motivated all his writing, including this book. He expresses a sense of deep distress that he has not been able to practise some of the precepts of his book. He is convinced that 'man need take no milk at all, beyond the mother's milk that he takes as a baby. His diet should consist of nothing but sun-baked fruits and nuts. He can secure enough nourishment both for the tissues and the nerves from fruits like grapes and nuts like almonds.'[3] He forgot that humankind progressed from the state of nature to civilization through the knowledge of fire and the art of cooking. The evolution of culinary skills raised humans from savagery to cultured existence. He also forgot that fruits like grapes, and nuts like almonds, were not always and everywhere easily available, and even where they were, they were beyond the financial means of the vast majority of humanity. Gandhi theorizes that a man living on fruits and nuts would find it easier to restrain his libido and other passions. Even though solid substantiation of his statement may not be easy, he still asserts that he and his co-workers believe in the Indian proverb that 'as a man eats, so shall he become'. He says that he has explained it all in the book, notwithstanding the reader's sense of bafflement!

Back in India years later, he found it necessary to give up some of his theories in practice. A dietary error made him sick in Kheda, and he found himself 'at death's door'. He tried hard to regain his health and strength without milk, without success. He asked doctors, *vaidyas* and scientists to recommend a substitute for milk. *Mūng* water, *mowhrā* oil, and almond oil were suggested. Gandhi tried them all, wearing himself out.[4] The Indian *vaidyas* (Āyurvedic doctors) tried to convince him with verses from *Caraka* that religious dietary restrictions had no place in therapeutics. They could not help him without milk. The doctors who recommended things like beef tea and brandy could not even think of a diet without milk. Gandhi tells us that he could not take the milk of a cow or a buffalo, as he had taken a vow not to do so. When he took the vow, he had only cows and buffaloes in mind. He therefore resorted to an escape strategy when he took goat's milk instead, as mother goat was not in his mind when he took

---

3   *Ibid.,* p.200.

4   *Ibid.,* pp.200-201.

his vow. He admits that he violated the spirit of his vow by taking goat milk, because he wanted to live in order to lead a campaign against the Rowlatt Act. He needed strength and good health to fight the Government; and that put paid to any idea of giving up all kinds of milk. And thus was abandoned one of the 'greatest experiments' in his life.[5]

Gandhi does not doubt the beneficial properties of milk, and therefore advises his readers not to give it up unless advised by those competent to do so. He realizes that milk is the best light nourishment for people suffering from debility; but continues to look around; and requests his readers to let him know if and when they discover a vegetable substitute for milk.

Gandhi heard people say that the soul does not eat or drink. That is the function of the body. What you eat is not important. What you do is. He is, however, convinced that a person hankering to see God 'face to face' has to live in His fear, and has to restrain both his thought and speech, which is not possible without dietary restraints in terms of both quality and quantity. As the use of the pronoun 'Him' indicates, he views God in a masculine image. His 'firm conviction' may not impress his readers; but he seems happy and self-sure in his pursuit of the Divine Vision. The correlation between food and drink and the spiritual quest is a statement of faith.

---

5   *Ibid.*, p.201.

Chapter 36

European Friends

Gandhi tells us that he writes from week to week as the Spirit dictates, with no plan, no diary or documents to fall back upon. All the great and small steps of any moment in his life 'were directed by the Spirit'. How much does he believe in the autonomy of his Spirit to take decisions and act upon them, and then taking personal responsibility for their consequences? Is he responsible, or is the impersonal Spirit responsible? He refers to the Spirit with a capital 'S'. Is it God synonymous with Truth, as he ever so often tells us? An ordinary human being would, as he should, assume and accept responsibility for his thoughts and actions, as only then would the sequence of *karma* and *saṁsāra* affect him and condition his existence. We know that Gandhi believed in both as axiomatic, beyond any doubt or disbelief!

Gandhi has not seen Him, or known Him. But he subscribes to the world's faith in God in full measure. His faith in God is 'ineffaceable'; and he equates it with experience. He concedes that this equation may be called into question as at variance with Truth; and contents himself with the statement that he does not know how to spell out his 'belief in God'.[1]

He repeats that he writes his story as the Spirit prompts. Now that he proceeds to write about his English friends, he sees 'a serious problem'. If he omits something that is relevant, Truth will suffer. But it is not easy to decide what is relevant and what is not. He is sceptical even of the 'relevancy' of the entire autobiographical essay. It is best here to quote him:

---

1   *Autobiography*, p.206.

'I understand more clearly today what I read long ago about the inadequacy of all autobiography as history. I know that I do not set down in this story all that I remember. Who can say how much I must give and how much omit in the interests of Truth? And what would be the value in the court of law of the inadequate *ex parte* evidence being tendered by me of certain events in my life? If some busybody were to cross-examine me on the chapters already written, he could probably shed more light on them, and if it were a hostile critic's cross-examination, he might even flatter himself for having shown up 'the hollowness of many of my pretensions.'[2]

Gandhi did not voice any such doubts or reservations when writing about Indians. Suddenly, when he proceeded to write about Englishmen, he became cautious and apprehensive, and a little uncertain as to what he should include or exclude. It seems as though he is exercising a double standard here; and two scales of assessment to the material furnished by his memory as to its importance and relevance in one case or the other. An ordinary reader would find Gandhi's difficulty inexplicable, and Gandhi's caution in the context of European connections selective of his Truth, and therefore detracting from its authenticity, certainly from its totality. Gandhi agonizes about the usefulness and propriety of his autobiographical exercise, but nevertheless carries on in the belief that there is no objection from the 'voice within'.

Gandhi had many European friends. Some of them became dear friends, close associates, soulmates and partners in his campaigns for social and economic justice for Indians in South Africa. As a student in England, he could count Josiah Oldfield, Henry Salt and members of the London Vegetarian Society among his friends. In his first year in Pretoria, he enjoyed the love and solicitude of A.W. Baker and Michael Coates. In Durban, he won the respect and friendship of F.A. Laughton and R.C. Alexander. In Johannesburg, amongst others, he met four Europeans who became firm friends to stand beside him and assist him through thick and thin in his great undertakings. L.W. Ritch, Albert West, Henry Polak and Hermann Kallenbach not only cultivated his abiding friendship, but also zealously participated in the pursuit of his causes.

L.W. Ritch, an English Jew, drew Gandhi close to the Theosophical Lodge in Johannesburg. He got himself articled to Gandhi, and joined his legal

---

2   *Ibid.*

practice. The lone Indian barrister struggling to secure for his compatriots a place under the Transvaal sun needed all the help he could get; and Ritch served him and his movement with abiding loyalty.

In the Alexandra Tea Room, the only vegetarian restaurant in town, to which he went for his meals, Gandhi met Albert West, also from England, who was a regular visitor. They discussed vegetarian food, Kuhne's baths, earth poultices and fasting, while the others talked of gold and diamonds. They became close friends; and West, a printer, helped Gandhi with the publication of *Indian Opinion*.[3]

Gandhi met Henry Polak, too, at the same restaurant. Polak came from a European Jewish family that had moved to England, where his father worked for a newspaper, and the young man studied at the University of London. His love for a Christian girl was viewed with some misgiving by his family, who sent him to South Africa; but before he did so, he got formally engaged to her. Sub-editor of the *Transvaal Critic* in Johannesburg, Polak saw Gandhi seated at a table in the restaurant; and the sight of a 'quiet, slender, pleasant looking man' did not correspond with his mental image of 'a big, aggressive fellow, who had been a sergeant-major of an East Indian Ambulance Corps during the Boer War'.[4] They found that they had common interests. Both of them admired Tolstoy, and talked about Adolf Just, the author of *Return to Nature*. The friendship blossomed; and Polak became an important participant in Gandhi's campaigns in South Africa.

About this time or a little later, Gandhi met Hermann Kallenbach, also Jewish, who was originally from Lithuania, but grew up in Prussia, where he studied to become a qualified architect. A tall and athletic man of muscular physique, Kallenbach was an enthusiastic skater and swimmer, fond of fishing and many other sports. Proficient and prosperous in his profession, he loved luxuries, the theatre, and the company of women.[5] But 'a vein of other-worldliness in him' made him turn to theosophy and Tolstoy, a little restless with spiritual curiosity! Introduced to each other by a common client, P. R. Khan, they found mutual attraction in qualities that they did

---

3 Cf. Guha, *op. cit.*, pp.164, 585, n.33; Albert West, 'In the Early Days with Gandhi – I', *Illustrated Weekly of India*, 3, October, 1965.

4 Cited in Guha, *op. cit.*, pp.164-165.

5 CF. Lev, Shimon, *Soulmates: The Story of Mahatma Gandhi and Hermann Kallenbach*, Orient Blackswan, New Delhi, 2012, p.3.

not share. Gandhi was an exemplar of *dama* (self-control), *tyāga* (sacrifice) and *apramāda* (diligence)[6]; of spiritual striving and equanimity. History was repeating itself. The attraction of Gandhi and Mehtab to each other in his student days also derived from their different dispositions. One had what the other did not; and their togetherness, therefore, filled each other's need for a part of the other. At their very first meeting, Kallenbach wanted Gandhi to tell him something about the Buddha's renunciation.[7] The two became soulmates. Kallenbach's personal and financial contribution to Gandhi's movement definitely helped its success; and the transformation of Gandhi the man into a *Mahatma* became one of the epochal events of world history.

Gandhi was the only educated Indian professional in Johannesburg. His European friends filled a gap, as they discussed issues of religion, ethics, politics and social justice, apart from their common interest in vegetarian food and natural remedies for human maladies. The shared awareness, first- hand or otherwise, of invidious distinctions, painful prejudices and persecution, drew the Jews closer to Gandhi. As the drama of the *Satyāgraha* unfolded, they became his unflinching comrades and lieutenants, helping him and the Indian community with their wholehearted participation.

Sonja Schlesin, a young Jewish girl of seventeen from Lithuania, was introduced to Gandhi by Kallenbach, and became his secretary after the departure of Miss Dick. Brash but sincere, at times too frank and outspoken for comfort, she worked for Gandhi with unflagging zest on a low salary, refusing to accept any rise. Gandhi totally trusted her ability and integrity; signed letters drafted by her unchanged; and saddled her with great responsibility. Thousands of people came to her for help and advice; and when most of the leaders were in jail during the *Satyāgraha*, she led the movement; handled the voluminous correspondence; and even managed the *Indian Opinion*. Gokhale was impressed by 'the sacrifice, the purity and the fearlessness' of Sonja. In Gandhi's words: 'Her courage was equal to her sacrifice. She is one of the few women I have been privileged to come across, with a character as clear as crystal and courage that would

---

6 *damastyāgo'pramādaśca eteṣvamṛtamāhitaṁ, Mahābhārata.*
7 *Autobiography*, p.242.

shame a warrior'.⁸ Gandhi tried to have her articled to him, so that she could become a lawyer; but the application was rejected by the Law Society because she was a woman.⁹

Of the other Jews who were attracted to Gandhi, we know of two businessmen, William M. Vogl, a draper, and Gabriel Isaacs, a jeweller. Gandhi went more than once to a synagogue with them. Isaacs was a member of the Phoenix Settlement; and collected subscriptions and advertisements for the *Indian Opinion*. In 1908, he offered to become a nominal owner of some of the *satyāgrahīs'* shops when the Government adopted the policy of auctioning their goods. In 1909, Gandhi sent him to Delagoa Bay to help *satyāgrahīs* who were being deported to India. He also helped Gandhi with the *Indian Opinion* in the *Satyāgraha* campaign from 1906 onward; and went to jail together with the others in the Great March of 1913.¹⁰

Gandhi and his friends were ill at ease with the current civilization with its concomitant colonialism and violence; willing and able to criticize their traditions in quest of an all-inclusive utopia. Gandhi, with a genius for acts of innovative symbolism, demonstrated the peaceful and productive proximity of different races in residence at the Phoenix Settlement and the Tolstoy Farm; and his friends subscribed with him to the ideal of human brotherhood. Ritch brought about the exchange of letters between Gandhi and Tolstoy, who reinforced Gandhi's faith in non-violence.¹¹

Gandhi had English friends living with him in Durban. The house was full of both Indians and Englishmen. Indians and Europeans alike tried his patience at times; and poor Kasturba shed some 'bitter tears'; but he had no regrets. He did not change his conduct to suit them, and often bent them to his will. This was Gandhi's way of seeing the same God in himself and others. He had stayed in English houses in his student days, when he conformed to their mode of living in England. Now two

---

8   *Ibid.,* p.209.

9   Cf. Gandhi Rajmohan, *op.cit.*, p.155.

10 See Chatterjee, Margaret, *Gandhi and His Jewish Friends*, Macmillan Acedemic and Professional Ltd., London, 1992, p.50.

11 Gandhi also raised his voice against 'the silent and insidious opposition' to the Jews in South Africa. Cf. *Indian Opinion*, 14. 10. 11; *Collected Works*, Vol. 11, p.167-8; Chatterjee, Margaret, op.cit., pp.32-33.

Englishmen, both theosophists, lived as family members, and adopted the Indian style in many ways. Gandhi repeated the practice, when he moved to Johannesburg.

This was also Gandhi's liberation in practice from the constraints of caste contacts, though he was yet far from fighting fully free from the shackles of *varṇa* and *jāti*. He seemed to equate them with divine order; and it was only much later that he categorically rejected heredity as a determinant of profession; and the boundaries of caste for purposes of marriage.

Chapter 37

Coolie Locations and the Plague

Gandhi deplored the ill-treatment of the so-called 'untouchables' in India, and of the Jews in Europe. Indians in South Africa were receiving the same treatment as the so-called *Āryas* in India meted out to the *Anāryas*. This segregation and mistreatment affected all Indians, including Hindus, Muslims and the Parsis. Contemptuously called 'coolies', Indians in South Africa were forced to live in quarters that were known as 'coolie locations'. There was a location in Johannesburg, where the Indians had acquired their plots on a lease of ninety-nine years. The population increased, but the area of the location did not. The municipality had in place an unsatisfactory arrangement to clean the latrines, but beyond that did not care to provide any other kind of sanitation, or roads or lights. Most of the Indians were poor farmers; only a few traders, with little or no education. They could not help themselves without the direction and close supervision of the municipality. Municipal neglect and Indian ignorance compounded the insanitary conditions. Instead of improving things, the municipality secured from the legislature an authority to destroy the location and disperse the settlers. But the residents had proprietary rights; and were entitled to compensation. A special tribunal was set up to try the cases of land acquisition. A tenant dissatisfied with the offer of the municipality could appeal to the tribunal; and the municipality had to pay if the award was greater than its own offer. Gandhi, engaged as their legal advisor by most of the tenants, told them that he would be satisfied with the costs awarded by the tribunal if they won. He would charge a fee of ten pounds on every lease, half of which he would set aside for building a hospital or a similar institution for the poor. Gandhi fought seventy cases, of which he lost only one.[1] The fees became substantial in total, out of

---

1 *Autobiography*, p.213.

which sixteen hundred pounds were 'devoured' by the *Indian Opinion*. Most of his clients were ex-indentured labourers from Bihar; and there were some from South India. One of their leaders, Badri became a close associate of Gandhi and played a prominent role in the *Satyāgraha*. Gandhi became 'more their brother than a mere legal advisor, and shared in all their private and public sorrows and hardships.'[2]

Abdulla Sheth called Gandhi *bhai* (brother);and was followed by others, who all addressed him as *bhai*. Everyone's 'brother' loved it specially when the ex-indentured Indians called him *bhai*!

The municipality now owned the location, but it could not remove the Indians immediately before finding another location for them. Sanitary conditions went from bad to worse, as neither the tenants nor the municipality cared. There was a sudden outbreak of black plague in one of the gold mines in the vicinity of Johannesburg. Some Indian mine workers caught the infection, and brought it to their location. Gandhi went to the location, and helped confine the infected patients to a single house. He and his friends nursed the patients totally regardless of the danger of infection. Gandhi treated three of the patients with earth bandages to their heads and chests. Two of them survived. The other twenty who were treated otherwise, died in that go-down. The experience fortified his faith in the earth treatment. Gandhi sent a critical letter to the press accusing the municipality of neglecting the location after gaining possession of it, which helped the outbreak of plague. This letter impressed many, and gained for Gandhi the friendship of Rev. Joseph Doke and Henry Polak.

Polak, like Gandhi, loved a simple life, and always tried to practise anything that inspired him. He had the capacity to radically change the course of his life in accordance with his changing ideas.

Gandhi requested Albert West to take charge of the *Indian Opinion* in Durban, while Madanjit was preoccupied with the care of patients with Gandhi. West left for Durban on a salary of ten pounds per month and a share of the profits. 'He remained a partner of' Gandhi's 'joys and sorrows,' till the latter left South Africa.

Gandhi helped the municipality with its work to stamp out the disease from Johannesburg and around. He persuaded the Indian residents of the

---

2   *Ibid.*

location to vacate their houses and move to a camp, where they had to live for a few days under canvas. He persuaded them either to deposit their monies in banks as fixed deposits, or to entrust him with their savings, which he himself deposited in banks. The monies entrusted to Gandhi and deposited by him in a bank amounted to nearly sixty thousand pounds. The Indians who knew nothing about banks till that point of time, learned to invest their money in banks. The location was burnt down by the municipality to destroy the source of infection.

Gandhi's fearless help to the poor Indians during the outbreak of the plague raised him in their estimation. His business increased; but so did his responsibility.

Gandhi's Birthplace, Porbandar

Gandhi's Mother, Putlibai

Gandhi's Father, Karamchand Gandhi

Gandhi, aged 7

Alfred High School, Rajkot

Gandhi and friend, Sheikh Mehtab, c.1883

Mohandas Gandhi, right, with his brother, Lakshmidas Gandhi, 1886

Members of the Vegetarian Society, London, 1890. Gandhi sits in the front row right.

Young Gandhi, barrister-at-law

Dr. Pranjivan Mehta, Gandhi's friend and benefactor

Raychandbhai (Rajchandra), Gandhi's spiritual mentor

Founding members of the Natal Indian Congress, 1895

Gandhi with the stretcher bearers of the Indian Ambulance Corps during the Anglo-Boer War, South-Africa, 1899-1900

Kasturba with three sons, from right to left, Harilal, Ramdas, Manilal, and nephew on the left, Gokuldas, 1901

Gandhi with Henry Polak, Sonja Schlesin, and colleagues at his office, Johannesburg, 1905

Gandhi as a practising barrister, Johannesburg, 1906

Gandhi with colleagues at Phoenix Settlement

Gandhi at Tolstoy Farm with early settlers

Gandhi with Kallenbach and Sonja Schlesin, 1913

Thambi Naidoo

Parsi Rustom ji

Maganlal Gandhi, Nephew

A. M. Cachalia

Henry Polak

Millie Polak

Albert West

Leung Quinn, Chinese Satyagrahi leader

Rev. J. J. Doke

Harilal, eldest son of Gandhi

J. C. Smuts, Gandhi's redoubtable adversary

At the reception for Gokhale in Durban, 1912

G. K. Gokhale with Ratan Tata, England, c.1914

Gandhi and Kasturba, 1914

Gandhi in the garb of an Indian indentured worker, 1914. The white clothes mourn the death of Satyagrahis in police firing.

Gandhi with C. F. Andrews and W. W. Pearson, 1914

Chapter 38

'Indian Opinion': Phoenix Settlement

West found *Indian Opinion* in a bad way. He told Gandhi that there was no question of a profit. As a great deal of reorganization was necessary, he would stay on and try to put things right regardless of profit or loss. Gandhi had thought of a profit only because Madanjit had given him an optimistic report. A public worker, Gandhi realized, should say things only if he had proof of their accuracy. To do otherwise was to depart from the truth. Gandhi confesses that he has not been able to entirely curb his credulity, due to his desire to do more than what is practicable or possible. This optimism and ambition often weighed upon his co-workers as a worry.

Gandhi left for Natal after hearing from West. Polak came to the station to see him off, and gave him a book to read on the way, Ruskin's *Unto this Last*. Gandhi was so gripped by the book that he finished it during the twenty-four hour journey. Not only that, he made up his mind to fashion his life after the ideals he imbibed from the reading. He translated it into Gujarati, and called it *Sarvodaya*, welfare of all.

He saw the reflection of his 'deepest convictions' in the book; and learned three special lessons. In his own words:

1. 'That the good of the individual is contained in the good of all.
2. That a lawyer's worth has the same value as the barber's inasmuch as all have the same right of earning their livelihood from their work.
3. That a life of labour, i.e., the life of the tiller of the soil and the handicraftsman is the life worth living.'[1]

---

1   *Autobiography*, p.221.

He was familiar with the first precept. He realized the second fully only after reading Ruskin. He had never thought of the third. As Gandhi saw it, the second and the third statements were actually anticipated in the first. Gandhi resolved to translate these ideas into real practice.

Gandhi discussed the book with West, and told him that he wanted to act on the principles laid down in it. He proposed to establish a farm, and to move the *Indian Opinion* to it. Everyone living on the farm would perform manual labour; draw the same wage; and in their spare time work for the press. With the approval of West, a monthly wage of three pounds per head was laid down, regardless of nationality or colour. Those reluctant to go and live on a farm on bare maintenance could continue to draw their current salaries, but should try to live up to the new ideal to become members of the settlement.

Madanjit considered it a foolish idea. It would destroy the venture; the workers would run away; the press would have to shut down. Chhagan lal, Gandhi's cousin, working in the press, agreed to move, even though he was a family man with a wife and children to look after. Govindaswami, the machinist, also accepted the proposal. The remaining workers refused to join the scheme, though they agreed to work in the press wherever it was located. Gandhi bought a farm called 'Phoenix' consisting of twenty acres with a little spring and nice fruit trees; and added another eighty acres of land to it.[2] Indian carpenters and masons helped build a shed for the press. Gandhi and his friends took about a week to move to this new settlement, which was two and a half miles from Phoenix station, and fourteen miles from Durban. John L. Dube, the prominent Zulu leader who later helped found the African National Congress, had an establishment not far from Gandhi's Settlement.

Gandhi tried to persuade some friends and relations to join him. But they had come to South Africa to make money; and Maganlal was the only one to give up his business for ever to stand beside Gandhi, and help him all the way. Maganlal's 'ability, sacrifice and devotion' earn Gandhi's praise.[3]

The Phoenix Settlement was thus established in 1904; and the *Indian Opinion* was published from there despite every possible hardship. The

---

2   *Autobiography*, p.222.

3   *Ibid.*

first issue went through some vexatious teething problems during its publication, as the oil engine to power the press refused to start, making Gandhi and his friends use a hand-wheel to do the initial printing for some time. They worked throughout the night; but the engine suddenly came to life in the morning, and the remaining work was easily done. The first issue of *Indian Opinion* from Phoenix was thus despatched on time on December 24, 1904. At a later stage Gandhi and his co-workers used hand-power only to publish their paper, which he described as 'the highest moral uplift for Phoenix'.[4] This equation of morality with manual work sounds prescient, when one looks at the atmospheric pollution threatening the climate, and the new machines replacing manpower for purposes of production. Gandhi could only vaguely imagine human inventions that are now pushing large numbers of men and women into unemployment with the loss of all kinds of jobs in so many sectors of human activity.

Gandhi intended to progressively retire from practice and live a simple life at Phoenix, based on the fruits of manual labour. But the vital work at Johannesburg could not be left unattended. On his return he told Polak of what he had done after reading Ruskin's book. Polak, himself a lover of simple life, was delighted and asked if he could also participate in the new scheme. Gandhi could not be happier. Polak left his post at *The Critic*, and proceeded to Phoenix. He won everyone's heart with his warm affability; but then Gandhi called him back to Johannesburg to join his office and qualify as a lawyer, as Ritch was going to England for his legal studies. Always trustful, Polak returned, and signed his articles with Gandhi. A Scottish theosophist named McIntyre also joined Gandhi's busy firm as an articled clerk. Gandhi's dream of him and Polak finally retiring at Phoenix never materialized!

---

4   *Ibid.,* p.224.

Chapter 39

Return of Kasturba

Though Gandhi had promised Kasturba that he would come back home within a year, he did not see that happening for quite some time; and decided to call her and the children to South Africa. Harilal, his eldest son at school in Bombay, now 16, stayed on, as Kasturba and the other boys took a boat to South Africa in the last quarter of 1904. Their third son Ramdas broke his arm during the voyage, which was treated and put in a sling by the ship's doctor. On disembarkation, the doctor instructed them to have the wound dressed by a qualified medical practitioner. Gandhi the quack, full of faith in his earth treatment, asked his son if he would like his father to dress his wounds. What could the eight-year old say? Gandhi washed the wound and applied earth poultices for a month, till it was totally healed. The healing process was not any longer than it would have been under a doctor's treatment. Gandhi became even more confident of his doctoring experiments. He tried his ideas on his comrades and companions with earth and water and fasting treatments 'in cases of wounds, fevers, dyspepsia, jaundice and other complaints, with success on most occasions'.[1] At the time of writing though, Gandhi admits that he does not feel as confident as he did in South Africa. He is now more aware of 'obvious risks'.

He defends his experiments with the statement that doctors also do the same with their theories and ideas. As a further justification for 'novel experiments', he says that one must begin with oneself, which hastens the discovery of Truth. And God is always there to protect one who is honest in his experiments. It is rationally impossible to agree with this line of argument. Honesty is not synonymous with credulity. Blind faith may not

---

1 *Autobiography*, p. 226.

always meet with the approval of God, who, one would suppose, expects a certain amount of caution and discrimination on the part of his believers. It is one thing to try a novel experiment with oneself, and quite another to try it on one's son who is only eight years old, and not really able to rationally and independently decide for himself. If something had gone wrong, and if his son's wound got infected, who would be responsible? Fads fed by credulity cannot be justified by satisfactory outcomes, which are no more than fortunate flukes. I find it hard to praise Gandhi for what he did; and happily relates![2]

A nice two-storey house with a garden in prestigious Troyeville became the home of the Gandhis in Johannesburg. They had a servant, who was treated as a member of the family, and helped by the children in his work. Ruskin's teaching led to carefully cultivated simplicity. Gandhi encouraged everyone to do physical work. They ground their own flour; and followed Kuhne's recipe to make their own unleavened wholemeal bread. Gandhi trained his children to help with cleaning the toilets; and gave them a good education in sanitation and hygiene.

Soon afterwards, Kasturba had new company. Polak moved in, when Gandhi invited him to stay with them. Gandhi never shrank from cultivating close contacts; and living together with Europeans. Polak, already engaged, wanted to save some money before proceeding to marry. Gandhi convinced him to go ahead and marry, as he was now living with them; and household expenses should not worry him at all. Polak called Millie, his bride-to-be, to South Africa; and they went through a simple marriage without any religious rites. Millie was a Christian, and Polak was a Jew. The Registrar postponed the registration of their marriage, as their best man Gandhi was a coloured man. Gandhi went to the Chief Magistrate, who laughed and wrote a note for the Registrar; and the marriage was duly registered.[3]

Millie Polak was a new arrival from England. Occasional minor differences between her and Kasturba did not hurt the harmony of the household. Gandhi stresses his belief that every family consists of people of different temperaments. Any distinction between heterogeneous and homogeneous families is only a matter of imagination. The whole world is one family.[4]

---

2   *Ibid.*, p. 227.

3   *Ibid.*, p. 227.

4   *Ibid.*, p. 228.

As his ideas about *brahmacarya* were still evolving, he wanted all his bachelor friends to get married. When West went to visit his parents in England, Gandhi asked him to get married if possible. Phoenix would be their common home, as they had all decided to become farmers. West returned married, with his wife who was a lovely young woman from Leicester with some practical experience of shoe-making. Gandhi admired 'her moral purity of heart'.[5] He encouraged his Indian friends likewise to marry and settle down at Phoenix, which became a little village with a dozen families living there.

Education of Sons

Gandhi was, on his own admission, willing to sacrifice his sons' literary education to enable them to fulfil other obligations. He was aware of his sons' grievance on that score, which was voiced on more than one occasion. Gandhi pleads partially guilty. He wanted to give them a literary education; and tried to do it himself. There were so many inevitable hiccups. He did not engage any private tutor for them; but made them walk five miles with him to his office and back home. The exercise was good for them; and Gandhi sought to instruct them with his talks during these walks. This happened when his attention was not distracted or claimed by someone else on the way. The eldest son Harilal was in India; but the others were brought up in Johannesburg and thus taught by him. Gandhi says that an hour of regular literary education imparted by the father to his sons would have been adequate and ideal. But, regrettably, that did not come to pass. Gandhi's eldest son openly expressed his distress in public and private; but the other sons forgave their father in view of the unavoidable circumstances. Gandhi is 'not heart-broken over it'; and his qualified regret only concedes that he did not come across as an 'ideal father'.[6]

He gave precedence to service to the community over literary training. He might have been wrong, but he was genuine. He did all he could to build up their character. That is the parents' principal duty. Gandhi makes a curious self-serving statement that if his sons have been 'found wanting', that has been due not to any 'want of care' on his part, but to 'the defects

---

5   *Ibid.*

6   *Ibid.*, p. 229.

of both their parents'.⁷ This is no less than an invidious insinuation that any moral lapses on the part of his sons can be blamed more on the mother than the father. This is at once disingenuous and indefensible; and does great injustice to Kasturba. If the sons do anything right, the credit goes to Gandhi. If they do anything wrong or untoward, the blame is in a lawyerly turn of phrase fastened on Kasturba.

Gandhi refers to 'heated discussions' between him and Polak on the question of giving an English education to his children. Gandhi regards it as an act of betrayal on the part of Indian parents to 'train their children to think and talk in English from their infancy'.⁸ The children are deprived of their spiritual and social heritage; and become unable to serve their country. For that reason, he always talked to his children in Gujarati, which Polak did not like. He told Gandhi that he was compromising their future. If they learnt a universal language like English from their early childhood, they would have a great advantage over others throughout their lives. Gandhi and Polak failed to convince each other. Gandhi maintains that his conviction has only deepened with time. It may be interesting and relevant to mention in this context the fact that English is a lot more common in its usage in India today than it was in Gandhi's time. So much so, that some people in Eastern UP belonging to the depressed classes have established a temple dedicated to Goddess English, who alone would enable them to demolish the distance between them and the higher classes through her cultivation and mastery! English, its knowledge and its use would enable them to contend against their competition on a comparatively more level playing field. What would Gandhi think of this? And what would he say of the wide currency of English in Indian life, and of the infusion of a medley of English words into every spoken Hindi sentence? And that would also be true of other Indian languages. You cannot constrain culture and linguistic contact. You cannot contain language and inhibit its growth and interaction with the living world around. The scouts of linguistic purity in countries like France are only fighting a losing battle against the realities of modern life with its lightning capacity for contact and linguistic interaction. Language grows as it flows. Increasing international and inter-linguistic contact only points to the inevitability of give and take between different languages, and to the

---

7   *Ibid.*, p. 230.
8   *Ibid.*

compelling necessity to find a medium that is universally intelligible. To be unilingual is to confine and contract one's vision of the human reality around oneself, limit one's understanding of the world and its problems, and deny oneself any opportunity of communicating directly with speakers of other languages. The deletion of distances and our consequent residence in a global village makes it imperative for those who can do so to learn more than one language. Bilingualism and multilingualism will certainly help weld humankind into the one family that Gandhi dreamt of.

Gandhi did not know if he convinced Polak as to the correctness of his view. Polak could not convince Gandhi. It is quite possible that he tired of arguing with Gandhi, whose obstinacy he found insuperable. It is interesting to hear Gandhi saying so, for elsewhere he tells us that Polak never argued with him; and accepted whatever he said. In this case, however, in the matter of the children's education, Polak seems to have gone out of his way to totally disagree with Gandhi, because he was sure that he was right and Gandhi was wrong. Gandhi himself would not be where he found himself; would not be able to find new ideas from the likes of Ruskin; and would not be able to translate them into action without a knowledge of English. He would not be able to practise law in South Africa without a sound knowledge of English. He would not be able to propound his principles and philosophy of *ahiṁsā* and mount his movement of *Satyāgraha* without his own capacity to communicate with the world around him in the English language.

Twenty years later Gandhi felt even more convinced of the rightness of his decision for his children. He admits that his sons 'have suffered for want of full literary education.'[9] But he puts himself at ease with the thought that their knowledge of the mother tongue had helped them and their country. How, only Gandhi knows, and does not tell us. If he had done otherwise, his sons would have appeared like foreigners in their own country. The boys became bilingual because Gandhi was surrounded by English friends. They could speak and write English without any difficulty, as they were living in a country where English was the principal spoken language. Gandhi deliberately denied himself credit for the acquisition of English by his sons, which only happened as a matter of course in the social situation not of their choosing, but of their father's. This haphazard learning process could only be enhanced by a proper attempt at their literary education. Chance

---

9   *Ibid.*

and situation defeated Gandhi's determination to confine his children's education largely to Gujarati. There are better ways of inculcating the pride of patriotism than rigid theoretical formulations affecting the scope of general, broad-based education.[10]

---

10 *Ibid.*

Chapter 40

Inroads upon Indian Livelihood

Every law that in any way discriminated against the British was expeditiously annulled after the defeat of the Boers. But all anti-Indian laws were carefully compiled into a manual; and any loopholes were studiously plugged. The Transvaal Government headed by the Governor Lord Milner decided on serious action to force Indians to live and do business in remote locations called *bazaars*, away from centres of trade and commerce; away from customers. Their 'insanitary habits' were cited as the reason for increasing white hostility; but the clear motivation was the removal of all Indian commercial competition. Milner wanted Indian workers for the mines and the railways; but hated the sight of Indian traders and hawkers. The notorious 'Bazaar Notice' emphasizing compliance by the end of 1903 rang alarm bells for all Indian businesses, though it exempted 'those Asiatics who were trading outside Bazaars at the commencement of the late hostilities…' It also exempted higher-class Indians from the residential requirement. The White Leaguers were up in arms at the exemptions. Their boisterous protest voiced through public meetings and chambers of commerce was resisted by the British Colonial Secretary, who expressed 'reservations about dispossessing Indian merchants who had traded before the war with either tacit or explicit government approval'.[1]

Gandhi met Milner on May 22, 1903, to convey his people's anxiety and unease at 'the constant changes of passes and permits'.[2] The Governor pointed to the strident white opposition to Indians settling wherever they chose; and reiterated the need for bazaars for Asians only. In December,

---

1 DiSalvo, *op. cit.*, p. 192.

2 Cf. Guha, *op. cit.*, p. 156.

1903, the Legislative Council of the Transvaal decided 'to appoint a Commission to investigate the cases of those Asiatics who traded in towns before the war without licences, and to report what vested rights or interests they may reasonably claim in respect to such trade...'[3] The Commission's judgements in the first few cases put before it did not give much hope to Gandhi, who withdrew the claims of twenty clients submitted to it.

One choice for Indians was to stand fast, stay put, and refuse to apply for permits. Gandhi talked of doing so in *Indian Opinion* in January 1904. He asked Indians to make 'respectful representations to the Government'. They should 'firmly decline to give proof to the Receivers of Revenue, offering to do so before the Commission...If summons are issued and penalties imposed for carrying on trade without a licence, the persons prosecuted should rise to the occasion, decline to pay any fines, and go to gaol. There is no disgrace in going to jail for such a cause; the disgrace is generally attached to the offence which renders one liable to imprisonment, and not to the imprisonment itself. In this instance, the so-called offence would be no offence at all, and it would be a most dignified course to adopt.'[4] The idea occurred, the thought flickered, as in his desperation Gandhi toyed with the notion of principled and deliberate civil defiance of legal injustice. He was cautiously exploring the idea of breaking an unjust law on principle. *Satyāgraha* was showing the first symptoms of life in mental incubation. But when the Government indicated that it would refrain from prosecuting Indians until the Commission's work was done, Gandhi asked his readers to be patient; and expressed his faith in the system finally delivering justice.

The Indians could either take their case to the Government and plead for accommodation; or go to courts of law to establish their claims. As their experience with the courts had often been painfully disheartening, they pursued the first alternative.

Gandhi was also in constant contact with two prominent Indian leaders in London. Dadabhai Naoroji, a former member of the British Parliament, sent nineteen letters to the India Office on Gandhi's behalf testifying to

---

3   'Asiatic Traders', *Transvaal Leader*, December 22, 1903; DiSalvo, *op. cit.*, p. 400, n. 65.

4   'A New Year's Gift', *Indian Opinion*, January 14, 1904; DiSalvo, *op. cit.*, p.196.

the 'younger man's persistence and the older man's patriotism'.[5] Sir M. Bhownaggree, a current member, asked a series of questions in Parliament, calling the anti-Indian legislation in South Africa a scandalous exercise. With all the information received from Gandhi, he sent a long letter in September 1903 to the Secretary of State for the Colonies, with a vivid account of the 'disabilities and indignities' heaped on the British Indians in the Transvaal. He warned that 'the continuance of the state of affairs in South Africa' would undermine 'the affection of the Indian people for King and Empire'.[6] The letter found its way to Milner, who asked his deputy Lawley to draft a suitable reply. Lawley was blunt in his response that the 'redemption of pledges' mentioned by Bhownaggree was 'among promises which it is a greater crime to keep than to break.'[7] Indians were acceptable as labourers, but certainly not welcome as educated professionals. If their children got educated, they would pose an undesirable challenge and danger to the white supremacy. Milner's reply to the Imperial Government spoke of stopping the 'indiscriminate influx of the Asiatics'; and called 'the attempt to place coloured people on an equality with whites in South Africa...wholly impracticable, and...in principle wrong.'[8]

Lord Curzon, Viceroy of India, was scathing in his criticism of Milner and his policies pandering to 'the prejudices of a small colony of white men in South Africa', totally regardless of the sentiments of 300,000,000 British subjects in Asia.[9] Gandhi also repeatedly cited Curzon's speech at the Guildhall, London, in which he said:

'....Unless we can persuade the millions of India that we give to them absolute justice as between man and man, equality before the law, freedom from tyranny and injustice and oppression, then your empire will not touch the hearts and fade away.'[10]

Bhownaggree referred to the despicable treatment of Indians in South Africa in a number of questions in the British Parliament; and also told

---

5 Guha, *op. cit.*, p. 166.
6 Cited in Guha, *op. cit.*, p. 167.
7 *Ibid.*
8 Cf. *Ibid.*, pp. 168, 586, n. 40.
9 Cited in *Ibid.*, pp. 176, 177, 586, n. 65.
10 *Selected Works*, Volume 4, Navajivan Trust, Ahmedabad, 1960, pp. 251-52.

the press that 'the Indian subjects of the King were being actually worse treated than they were under the Boer rule'. Gandhi on his part encouraged the Indians to continue their 'constitutional effort' in the hope that the British would heed their united persistence.

When all else failed, the only recourse left to the Indians was to knock once again at the doors of the judiciary. In January, 1904, Gandhi talked of the necessity of asking the Supreme Court to settle the question whether residence included trade. That was where they could test the Government's right to refuse licences to Indians to trade outside locations. As Gandhi said elsewhere, 'the Law 3 of 1885 requires Indians to reside in locations; it says nothing as to trade...'[11]

Conciliation had proved utterly infructuous; the last recourse was the highest judiciary. An Indian trader, Habib Motan went in appeal to the Supreme Court when the Government denied him a general licence. He had traded without any restrictions before the Anglo-Boer conflict. He should not be arbitrarily confined to a location. The Supreme Court concurred; and held that Law 3 did not give the Government any power to force Indian businesses to operate only in locations. Chief Justice James Rose-Innes was emphatic and unambiguous in his judgement that 'some definite provisions...would surely have been inserted' into the law if the legislature intended to confine Indian businesses to locations. His opinion was supported by the two other members of the court, Justices Solomon and Curlewix.[12]

Victory in court negated the need to think of civil disobedience. Gandhi advised Indians to exercise restraint in applying for licences everywhere, which would assuredly rouse the fears and hostility of the whites. Indians, however, took out licences in numbers regarded as large by the whites, who immediately began to talk of the 'Asiatic peril'.[13]

---

11   *Indian Opinion*, January 14, 1904.

12   Cf. DiSalvo, *op.cit.*, p. 402, n. 97.

13   *Rand Daily Mail*, 'Asiatic Trading', June 8, 1904; DiSalvo, *op. cit.*, p. 402, n. 102.

Chapter 41

Evolution of Ideas

Gandhi's spiritual evolution proceeded apace with his legal and political understanding. He advised Indians to exercise self-restraint in pursuit of their legitimate aspirations; and placate with persistent persuasion the whites' opposition. The recourse to judiciary was an act only of last resort. He was exploring how suffering and sacrifice could catalyse attitudinal change and social justice. He talked of sacrifice as the law of life. Nothing comes free. We pay a price for everything we enjoy. There is no gain without pain, no success without sacrifice. The salvation of the community called for sacrifice, for submerging the self in the whole, for unity, for giving to the community what one could do without, which should in no case be too much. He cited the sacrifice of Christ for the salvation of his followers. 'The Americans bled for their independence'.[1]

The very livelihood of Indians was threatened. They faced destructive sequestration in ghettoes. They had to gird up their loins to counter this onslaught. They had to unite against this common danger. They had to be ready to sacrifice personal gain and comfort in their struggle for justice; they had to put their money where their mouth was! Patience, persistence and self-control were all imperative pre-requisites in the looming fight for justice and fair play, for vital living room under the South African sun!

All this is easier said than done. Gandhi gave it a meaning and purpose by his own emerging attitude to the wealth generated by his legal practice. He understood the value of money, without which nothing could be done.[2]

---

[1] *Indian Opinion*, January 21, 1904.

[2] Cf. DiSalvo, *op.cit.*, p. 202.

But he refused to fight cases based on untruths. When, in the middle of a case, he discovered the deception of his client, he immediately closed his argument and requested the magistrate to dismiss the case. The money so assiduously earned was not spent by him on conspicuous consumption. He readily sacrificed a significant amount of his own interests for those of Indians and their causes. He spent thousands of pounds on the publication of *Indian Opinion*, the all-important voice of the Indian cause. A big chunk of his income supported the Phoenix Settlement, from where the *Indian Opinion* came to be published. And he spent significant amounts of money on the continuous Indian campaign for social and economic justice.

Gandhi also emphasized the need for forgiveness and charity, and love even for one's oppressor. Willing endurance of undeserved suffering would shame the tyrant into remorse and reform. Self-suffering without malice and anger would ultimately reform the oppressor. He had already provided personal proof of his practice of these qualities. Civil disobedience, if all else failed, would indeed be strictly bound by these principles!

Gandhi's struggle in South Africa had totally transformed the man. His refusal to submit to tyranny or accept inequality and to acquiesce in unjust laws and the injustice that followed, marked the awakening of his dormant inner spirit, of which he himself was perhaps only dimly aware. The physical assaults and the painful blows, instead of weakening his resolve, incrementally increased his determination to protest and to disobey laws that were morally indefensible without any violence towards the perpetrators; and to suffer without bitterness the punishments that followed. He sought through self-suffering to kindle in the hearts of the law-makers and enforcers stirrings of compunction and soul-searching, hopefully leading to corrective action. *Satyāgraha*, the insistence upon Truth synonymous with justice, non-violent non-cooperation with an unjust government with its unjust laws, opposed soul-force to the heavy-handed iniquity of the authorities. Acquiescence in injustice and iniquity was tantamount to cowardly, collusive acceptance, and an indication of an abject willingness to take more of the same. That was not on! But while fighting his opponents with weapons of non-violent non-cooperation, he would always leave the doors open to negotiation. There was no point of no return. He was always willing to negotiate and to compromise, to concede where necessary, without prejudice to basic morality, humanity and justice. In his busy legal practice, too, he always aimed at mediated settlements rather than protracted litigation. The human predicament always provided room for give and take, for a finally profitable compromise!

As far as the plight of the Indians in South Africa was concerned, they could, through their disciplined, determined suffering, ultimately bring about a change of heart amongst their rulers. The willing acceptance of punitive suffering for espousing Truth and demanding justice would ultimately chasten the hearts and minds of the rulers. They would progressively, if only slowly, realize the folly of their ways, and amend their laws. But would they, really? Would they be able to rise, and how much, above their own profit and interests, to redress the grievances of the Indians and the other disadvantaged and exploited sections of the community? Would they forsake their fancied racial superiority, and dilute their absolute authority to accommodate the Indians? Would they easily agree to amend the order of relationships between the whites and the Indians? Would they accept the principle of racial equality? Gandhi's optimism verged on the unreal in South Africa of the first decade of the twentieth century. It would take a whole century to enthrone worldwide the principle of racial and human equality, with the reality often at variance with the ideal!

Gandhi devoted many columns of *Indian Opinion* to the praise of British heroes, who made their country great. In his piece on Nelson he went on to say: '...Those who have faith in God recognize that the British do not rule over India without His will. This too is a divine law that those who rule do so because of the good deeds they have done before.'[3] Will the attribution of British rule over India to Divine Will absolve all their atrocities as acts of Divine retribution for the Indians' acts of omission and commission? He admired Tolstoy, and martial heroes, all at once, at one and the same time! His applause for the heroes would naturally accept their violence!

On the second of September, 1905, he wrote about his neighbour near Phoenix, the African reformer John Dube, who had acquired 300 acres of land to impart education to his people, to teach them 'various trades and crafts' and prepare them 'for the battle of life'. Gandhi referred to an 'eloquent speech' by Dube to a group of visiting Englishmen, in which he said that 'it was unfair to burden' them 'with taxes; also it was like cutting down the very branch one was sitting on....They worked hard and without

---

3 *Collected Works*, Vol. 5, p. 117, 1961 Edn.; *Indian Opinion*, 28 October, 1905, Gujarati version.

them the whites could not carry on for a moment. They made loyal subjects and Natal was the land of their birth. For them, there was no country other than South Africa; and to deprive them of their rights over lands, etc., was like banishing them from their home.'[4] Gandhi's horizons were slowly but surely widening, as he was becoming increasingly conscious of the legitimate rights and aspirations of the African people.

---

4   *Collected Works*, Vol. 5, p. 55, 2.9. 1905, from Gujarati.

Chapter 42

The Zulu Rebellion

Gandhi was settling down at Johannesburg. But the Zulu 'rebellion' in Natal upset the tenor of his life. A Zulu revolt erupted in April, 1906 against the imposition of a poll tax of £1 per head on every male African. The Government wanted to force the Zulus into paid employment, apart, of course, from raising revenue. The chiefs told the Natal Government that the villagers would find it hard if not impossible to pay the tax. The Government turned a deaf ear to their protests. The arrival of the police to collect the tax by force sparked the Zulu 'rebellion' led by its main leader Bambatha; and it quickly spread across Natal. Gandhi admits that the Indians had never had any quarrel with the Zulus. But they were in Natal only by virtue of the British power; and their very existence depended upon it. It was therefore the Indians' duty to render whatever help they could; and if possible, to organize an ambulance corps. He believed that 'the British Empire existed for the welfare of the world'. His sense of loyalty precluded any justification of the Zulu uprising; and did not admit of any qualms of moral discomfort, when he decided to help the British Government as best as he could. He wrote to the Governor, offering to organize an Indian Ambulance Corps. The offer was immediately accepted. Kathryn Tidrick[1] writes that he offered Indians' services to fight for the Government, which is not exactly right. Gandhi only said that the Indians were also capable of being trained, if necessary, to fight in defence of the colony. 'For fifteen years now the whites have accused the Indians that, if it came to giving one's life in defence of Natal, they would desert their posts of duty and flee home', Gandhi wrote on June 23, 1906.[2] And to quote him again:'work in the field...is just as useful and

---

1 *Gandhi: A Political and Spiritual life,* I.B Taurus London, 2006, p. 73.
2 *Collected Works,* Vol. 5, p. 362.

The Zulu Rebellion

quite as honourable as the shouldering of a rifle.' It is also true that the whites had no intention, whatsoever, to impart military training to Indians and arm them with rifles.[3] It is interesting, though, to hear Gandhi, the advocate of non-violence, referring to rifle-wielding soldiers in affirmative terms. The news published in the *Indian Opinion*[4] that twelve of the rebels were 'condemned to death and blown up at the mouth of a cannon' as punishment for killing two white policemen, would have made Gandhi wince, but not waver in his resolution to lead the Ambulance Corps!

He broke up his home at Johannesburg, and sent his wife and children to Phoenix. He himself went to Durban and got together a party of twenty Indian men, including a few from North India, and several ex-indentured men from South India. There was also one Pathan. The merchants, as before, provided money and the goods. Gandhi was given the temporary rank of Sergeant Major. They remained on active service for about six weeks, often close to the line of fire. Gandhi admits that on arrival at the scene of operations, he saw little that could be characterized as a 'rebellion'.[5] There was no resistance. He was unutterably shocked by the brutality of the whites; and felt relieved on hearing that his main task was going to be to nurse the wounded Zulus. Many of them had been ruthlessly whipped into writhing agony. Their wounds festered; but the whites would not treat them. The medical officer welcomed the arrival of the Indian Ambulance Corps, and provided the bandages and medicines needed to treat them. But as the Indians busied themselves with the treatment of their wounds, many whites tried to dissuade them from doing so. Gandhi and his men still attended to the wounded, while the whites heaped the vilest abuse on the Zulus. The soldiers stopped interfering after a while; but surprised by Gandhi's composure, some of the higher officers in the force thanked him. He also acted as a compounder, dispensing medicines for the white soldiers. Training under Dr. Booth came in handy!

The crying shame was that the wounds of the Zulus were not incurred in battle. They had been arrested as suspects and mercilessly flogged. Among them were also "Zulu friendlies", who had been mistakenly shot at despite the badges that they carried. Polak tried to visualize Gandhi's grief and unease at 'allying himself' even in a healing role 'with those capable

---

3   *Ibid.,* pp. 233-234.

4   *Ibid.,* p. 266.

5   *Autobiography,* p. 231.

of such acts of revolting and inexcusable brutality'.⁶ But those sworn to *ahiṁsā* could nevertheless help mitigate the misery inflicted by war and violence.

Gandhi talks of long marches up to forty miles a day across difficult terrain. This so-called rebellion brought home to him the unspeakable horrors of war, which in this case was a merciless man-hunt and not really a war. Many Englishmen said so to him. The soldiers' rifles exploded 'like crackers in innocent hamlets'.⁷ Gandhi saw it all, 'swallowed the bitter draught', and went on nursing the injured Zulus. No one would have cared for them or attended to them, if he and his men had not been there. This provided a kind of salve to his conscience. In his long marches across this thinly populated part of Natal, he 'often fell into deep thought'.⁸ Joseph Doke, Gandhi's first biographer, notes the 'great reserve' with which he spoke of this horrid experience. 'What he saw he will never divulge…It was intolerable for him to be so closely in touch with this expedition. At times, he doubted whether his position was right.'⁹

He had seen so much blood-curdling cruelty; so much violation of black bodies. The memory of gore, filth and suffering haunted him. Despite the passage of many long years crowded with all his campaigns, he remembered with horror 'the atrocities committed on the Zulus'. 'What has Hitler done worse than that?', he asked his physician Sushila Nayar in 1943.[10] Aversion to sadism, sexual sadism, led to Gandhi's vow of celibacy.[11]

---

6   Polak, Henry S.L., 'Mr. Gandhi A Sketch', in *Speeches and Writings of Mahatma Gandhi*, Madras, 1919, xii.

7   *Aurobiography*, p. 233.

8   *Ibid.*

9   Cited in Lelyveld, *op. cit.,* p. 69.

10   Cf. Lelyveld, *op.cit.*, p. 70.

11   Cf. Erikson, *Gandhi's Truth*, p. 194.

Chapter 43

Brahmacarya (Celibacy)

The sight of soldierly savagery in the suppression of the rebellion dried up in Gandhi's heart and mind any desire to bring new life into being. He brooded over *brahmacarya* and what it meant. Self-realization was not possible without *brahmacarya*. One could not give his entire heart and soul to the service of humanity without it. He would therefore find himself wanting, if he did not take a solemn vow to embrace *brahmacarya* in order to serve humanity.

Unwillingness to take a vow is a clear symptom of weakness, of the desire to escape the consequence of a resolution. That is why people shirk the juncture of a final, binding decision. But they might say that views are always subject to change. Is it therefore wise to bind oneself with a vow? Gandhi, however, insists that it is 'a lack of clear perception that a particular thing must be renounced.'[1] He cites the poet Nishkulananda: 'renunciation without aversion is not lasting'. I find this 'aversion' to an act of love that binds people together and remains the backbone of social order, utterly repugnant. There is no need to hate, decry or denounce what you don't want to do any more. No lapse of morality is involved. No injury to anyone is involved. There is no deleterious social consequence. Where is the need for aversion? You decide not to do a thing any more. That is enough. There is no need to quote a poet and to talk of aversion. Gandhi says that with the departure of desire a vow of renunciation is a natural corollary. To an ordinary person, the extinction of desire or the death of libido would not lend any credit to a vow of renunciation. To one though, who resolves to abstain despite the drive of desire, the journey ahead is only a story of painful self-denial. It does not deserve any laudation. It is also

---

1   *Autobiography*, p. 151.

an act of unfeeling injustice to one's partner, as two persons are involved. The acquiescence of the partner is not synonymous with consent. It is only an acceptance of dictation, a submission to the partner's command!

He felt that he would have many more occasions in life demanding of his service to the people around him. The pleasures of family life and procreation would be incompatible with the idea of total commitment to communal welfare. He was completely drained and exhausted, so much so, that he lost his appetite for sex; and thought that his involvement in any tasks of such a demanding nature would leave him no respite to attend to the needs of his wife and children.

He tries to draw a line between the flesh and the spirit, as if the two are unrelated and incompatible, and can exist independently of each other. He says that he would not have been able to fling himself into the fray of social service, if his wife had been pregnant. Society, though, subsists on the life of the *gṛhastha* or the householder, whose modes of activity include the obligatory and unavoidable duty of giving physical love to his spouse, and bringing new life into this world. *Brahmacarya* would be suicide. The society, to which the *brahmacārin* seeks to dedicate his services, would itself cease to exist if everyone followed the concept of continence by denying himself or herself the natural expression of mutual love and the physical bond of belonging. The so-called incompatibility of physical sexual love and social service fails to wash and carry any conviction!

Gandhi, however, became quite impatient to take the vow of *brahmacarya;* and the idea of limitless service sustained it. The so-called 'rebellion' was over. The Ambulance Corps was discharged. Gandhi received a letter of thanks from the Government. Back at Phoenix, he discussed the subject with his mates; and decided to take the vow of *brahmacarya* for life. The *brahmacarya* that he had been fitfully practising since 1900, was sealed and sanctified by a public vow in the middle of 1906. He and his wife were both thirty-seven years old. And that was the end of their union as lovers!

Gandhi writes that he took the vow only 'after full discussion and mature deliberation'.[2] But he also tells us that he had not discussed anything with his wife; or shared his thoughts with her. Who was he discussing the matter with? He only 'consulted her at the time of taking the vow.

---

2   *Ibid.*

She had no objection.'³ It has been said in Gandhi's defence that Indian husbands did not often care to discuss serious issues with their wives in his day and age. But we also know that Gandhi was a very widely travelled man, who had lived amongst different people in three continents; who had shared homes with Europeans, and seen how they treated their wives and women. Was the 'Indian' in him impervious to all that influence? Kasturba is taken for granted. Gandhi is full of himself. He only refers to the 'great difficulty' that he had in making up his mind. He doubted his strength to control his passions. Putting an end to 'carnal relationship with one's wife' was unheard of. But Gandhi 'launched forth with faith in the sustaining power of God'.⁴ One wonders what God had to do with it. Why add to the work of God? This imposition on God is inexplicable!

Gandhi celebrates his observance of the vow for the preceding twenty years at the time of writing; expresses a sense of 'freedom and joy'⁵; and tells us that the vow became 'a sure shield against temptation'.⁶

He makes the claim that the observance of *brahmacarya* leads to, and makes a reality of *Brahma* realization. And he tells us that he did not owe this knowledge to any study of the Śā*stras*. This awareness came to him with his own experience. He read the scriptures only later. We are not, and cannot be privy to a man's inner thought processes, but what he says leads us to believe that this realization on his part was independent of any preconception or belief based on the legacy of scriptural lore. It is a little hard to believe that this correlation between *brahmacarya* and *Brahman* was an original, independent realization by Gandhi unaffected and untouched by any statements in the scriptures, which he says he read only later. Where did he then gain an idea of *Brahman* and of the efficacy of *brahmacarya* in leading to that blissful realization? These ideas form the basis of floating preconceptions influencing common Hindu thought and conversation. The profession of originality without any debt to common beliefs widely entertained in Indian society without any knowledge or study of the scriptures, does not carry conviction.⁷

---

3   *Ibid.*
4   *Ibid.*
5   *Ibid.*, p. 197.
6   *Ibid.*
7   *Ibid.*, p. 198.

Gandhi exults in his growing 'knowledge' that *brahmacarya* protects his body, mind and soul. It is no longer a penance. It is pure 'consolation and joy'.[8] He sees 'fresh beauty' in it every day. But why does he talk of 'consolation', and what does he mean thereby? It seems as though 'consolation' consists in the comfort that his self-denial is leading him to *Brahman*. This only demonstrates the power of faith, which may not stand the scrutiny of scientific reason. He goes on to tell us that it was not easy even at the age of 56. He likens it to 'walking on the sword's edge', and stresses the 'necessity for eternal vigilance'.[9]

He found it essential to control the palate in his pursuit of *brahmacarya*. Total control of the palate made *brahmacarya* easy. With his dietetic experiments Gandhi concluded that a vegetarian *brahmacārī's* food should be 'limited, simple, spice-less, and, if possible, uncooked.'[10] But as we know, the knowledge of fire and the ability to cook food on fire formed a most significant basis of human development and superiority over the other animals around them. Going back to uncooked food amounted to an unravelling of all the progress achieved in the preparation of food over thousands of years.

The consumption of fresh fruit and nuts for six years convinced him that they constituted the ideal food for a *brahmacārī*. It gave him 'immunity from passion'. His difficulty increased when he started drinking milk. He had no doubt that milk makes it very difficult to observe *brahmacarya*. He says that it may not be necessary for all *brahmacārīs* to give up milk, as different kinds of food produce different effects on different people. A lot of experimentation is called for. Gandhi was still seeking a fruit-substitute for milk, which would be equally efficacious in building up muscles, and equally digestible. He consulted doctors, *vaidyas* and *hakīms* (*Āyurvedic* and *Yūnānī* Indian physicians),who were unable to suggest an equivalent substitute. He knew that milk was a stimulant, but desisted from advising people to give it up.

According to Gandhi, careful selection and restriction of diet is not enough by itself in the observance of *brahmacarya*. Fasting is equally necessary. The senses have to be held in check; and fasting certainly helps. Fasting

---

8   *Ibid.*

9   *Ibid.*

10 *Ibid.*

without control of the mind, and hankering for delicacies on the termination of the fast, will not control the palate or the lust. Fasting helps only when one's mind develops a distaste for things denied to the body. The mind is the seat of all sensuality, for which reason it has to be controlled. A fasting man may not be free from passion, but the suppression of, and freedom from sexual passion is not possible without fasting. Gandhi therefore prescribes fasting for practitioners of *brahmacarya*.

Control of the senses makes one a *brahmacārī*. The *Brahmacārī* uses his eyes 'to see the glories of God', while the others around him see only 'frivolity'. The *brahmacārī* listens only to the 'praises of God', while the others listen only to 'ribaldry'. They may all keep late hours; but the *brahmacārī* is preoccupied with prayer, while the others are steeped in 'wild and wasteful mirth'. The *brahmacārī's* inner self is a 'temple of God'; but the others' revelry makes their inner selves a 'stinking gutter'. They stand far apart from each other, and as time passes, the distance grows.[11]

It is an utterly incomprehensible differentiation. The negation of life and its natural urges, the rejection of nature and its flow would be at loggerheads with the purpose of God and the scheme of creation. The acceptance of life would not divorce one's mind from the thought of God, and of gratitude to God. How can the 'temple of God' be established in the mind of a person who denies and discards his or her true nature in contradistinction to one who accepts life with its natural joys and legitimate enjoyment with proper ethical discipline without causing any hurt or grief to anyone around? Gandhi's attempt at distinguishing a *brahmacārī* from common humanity, and the language used to do so, is an exercise in verbal violence. How can an ordinary law-abiding, nature-loving, life-accepting mind of a person be likened to a 'stinking gutter'? A life-denier becomes divine. But a grateful recipient of life and its natural flow is likened to a low-life. So much of Gandhi's thinking in this regard is warped by superstitious cultural preconceptions, even which he refuses to acknowledge when he tells us that many of his ideas correlating God-realization with *brahmacarya* came to him without any thought of, or study of the *Śāstras*, which happened only later.

---

11 *Ibid.*, p. 153.

He is quite conscious of the difficulties involved, 'staring' him 'in the face'. He likens a life without *brahmacarya* to animal existence. The capacity for self-restraint is a principal human attribute; and Gandhi applauds the 'extravagant praise of *brahmacarya* in our religious books'.[12] He talks of the 'wonderful potency' of *brahmacarya*, which is not confined to mere physical restraint; and does not admit of 'even an impure thought'.[13] Any normal human being would stridently reject the ascription of 'impurity' to legitimate sexual expression, which is little less than wilful smothering of the very life principle. What does Gandhi mean by purity as opposed to 'impurity'? In ordinary human understanding, purity is synonymous with hygiene in the physical sense, and with nobility and generosity of disposition with reference to others in life. Purity of conduct would normally be understood in terms of action calculated to help rather than hinder others; of kindness and compassion and the capacity for personal sacrifice to alleviate the suffering of others. What has sex to do with it? It has been suggested that Gandhi's increasing indifference to sex and the struggle to contain and, if possible, extinguish his libido arose out of a pathological prepossession with sanitation and hygiene. The fear of insanitation and maniacal loathing for physical uncleanliness, which he associated with sexual activity, tended to emasculate his sexual desire. Gandhi's view of a *brahmacārin* was that of a person who had entirely excised his libido, so much so that he would not and could not even dream of sex.[14]

At the time of writing his *Autobiography*, Gandhi is candid enough to tell us that his pursuit of *brahmacarya* has been fraught with difficulties. He feels 'fairly safe', even though 'complete mastery over thought' is yet distant.[15] He is still groping around to find the key that will shut out all 'undesirable thoughts'. He admires the teaching and examples of old saints and sages, which nevertheless lack infallible prescriptions for the attainment of *brahmacarya* amounting to a total sublimation of libido in its extrication from one's physical self. The freedom he seeks comes only from God's grace. The old seers with their legacy of '*mantras*, such as *Rāmanāma*'help; but total mastery over thought comes only from God's

---

12 *Ibid.,* p. 234.

13 *Ibid.*

14 *Ibid.*

15 *Ibid.*

grace. Fearful of his fallibility, he for ever seeks Divine succour in his struggle for the achievement of 'perfect *brahmacarya*'. He forgets that even Lord Rāma remained deeply devoted and attached to his wife Sītā, and became utterly disconsolate when she was abducted by *Rāvaṇa*. The agony of her abduction and the pain of parting is conveyed in verses that poignantly describe her physical beauty and charm sorely missed by *Rāma*. The loss of physical proximity and her warm embrace becomes too much to bear.[16] How can *Rāmanāma* then help extinguish the spark of sexual desire? Only Gandhi knows!

Gandhi talks of 'control of the senses in thought, word and deed'. He waxes eloquent on the limitless scope of renunciation and *brahmacarya*. One can clearly see the influence of both Jainism and Hinduism on such a frame of mind. Gandhi tells us that the control of mind and thought is an unceasing exercise in order to thwart the constant onslaught of passions. The existence of God within helps one to control his or her mind. It is not easy, but it remains the highest goal. Gandhi repeats that *brahmacarya* is impossible of attainment by 'mere human effort'. This is what he realized when he came back to India. He had till then believed that a fruit diet would be enough to defeat all passions. He does not elaborate; and leaves the matter for later discussion. He seems to make *brahmacarya* a precondition for the realization of God; and equates faith in God with one's confidence in the pursuit of his goal. He cites the *Gītā*, 2.59-

Viṣayā vinivartante nirāhārasya dehinaḥ

Rasavarjaṁ raso 'pyasya paraṁ dṛṣṭvā nivartate.

'The sense-objects turn away from an abstemious soul, leaving the relish behind. The relish also disappears with the realization of the Highest.'

Gandhi's ideas and understanding of *brahmacarya* will always be challenged and called into question. Whimsical, weird, eccentric, intolerant, misconceived, unnatural, impossible, unrealizable?

Āhāra nidrā bhaya maithunaṁ ca

Sāmānyametad paśubhirnarāṇām... (Bhartṛhari)

---

16 Cf. ŚrīmadVālmīkīya Rāmāyaṇaṁ, Paṇḍita Pustakālaya, Kāśī, 1951, *Araṇya*, 62.4, 13, 18.24; also Singh, Sarva Daman, 'Terracottas from Manwā Ḍīh (Sitapur) in *Journal of U.P. Historical Society*, Vol. XVIII, (N.S.), Parts I – II, 1970, pp. 1-5.

'Eating, sleeping, fear, and sex are all common to animals and humans.'

There are certain basic needs and appetites that are inseparable from our natural physical existence. Denying them does violence to our nature; eschewing them runs contrary to the laws of creation; and seeking to extinguish them goes against the grain of reality. Restraint cannot be magnified to engulf and negate life and its physical free flow, out of which arise all our activities, our creativity, and meaningful, fruitful exertion sustaining us and all others around us with loving concern and compassion. *Brahmacarya* understood and prescribed as sexual abstinence between loving couples is an unnatural and merciless misconstruction of cultured self-control and discipline in conformity with the ethical restraints of human civilization. Love and physical fulfilment of love within the bounds of accepted social norms has never impeded or thwarted social service, or the capacity for constructive engagement with the problems of people around us. The so-called *Brahmacārīs* are as a rule entirely dependent on the charity of copulating couples running normal households in society.[17] *Gṛhastha* or the household is the mainstay of society, the guarantee of its continuity; the source of its contentment; the basis of its stability; the bedrock of its order. That is why *gṛhasthāśrama* is spoken of as the most excellent order of existence.[18]

In so many ways, in so much of his thinking, in so many of his practices and prescriptions, Gandhi the non-violent revolutionary was as hidebound, as conservative, as much a prisoner of superstitions, supposed verities derived from the old *śāstras* and literature, as the vast majority of his countrymen and women were. The thought that the conservation of semen purifies the blood and gives immunity from disease and infection, and bestows almost superhuman powers on the self-denying and self-defying *brahmacārīn*, has no basis in science and medicine. It is a belief that he endorsed without any scepticism. Unnatural negation of nature and rejection of basic instincts, the founts of love and belonging, charity, compassion and tenderness, can never be conducive to inner calm and outward tranquillity. In one's eagerness to transcend one's nature, one will have little time, energy or will left to devote to the tasks of the world around, to the service of others. The battle within will at all times be self-

---

17 Cf. *Manusmṛti*, VI. 87, 89; also my *Polyandry in Ancient India,* Motilal Banarsidass, Delhi, 1988, 'Introduction', pp. 1-2.

18 *Manusmṛti, op.cit., gṛhastha ucyate śreṣṭhaḥ.*

consuming, debilitating and distracting from life's battles to be fought on so many other fronts, leaving one often disgruntled, disheartened, despondent and desolate! Unnatural emasculation of instincts and self can never lead to happiness or deliverance. Satiation of legitimate love and libido is certainly preferable to the constant smothering of smouldering passions, which one may seek to suppress, because one cannot totally extinguish them. Even Gandhi said that following *brahmacarya* was like walking on the sharp edge of a sword. Where is the need to do so? And where is the hard evidence to prove that such self-abnegation enables one to conquer or transcend physical suffering and mortality? All the scientific data to date point to sexually starved people dying early; single people suffering and dying early; widows and widowers afflicted by disease and loneliness dying early. There is no joy, no fulfilment, no elongation of longevity, no immunity from disease and physical suffering, no transcendence, physical or spiritual, in the arbitrary, unnatural continence of *brahmacarya*. Science and medicine, and life as we know and live it, do not support Gandhi's assertions about *brahmacarya*. Belief is not synonymous with reality! In a pamphlet entitled *General Knowledge about Health*, however, Gandhi wrote about the conservation of the male's reserved 'generative fluid' investing him with exceptional physical and mental vitality, citing his own example with a sense of unblushing certainty.[19]

We cannot deny humanity its true nature. Men and women will love one another and have sex with one another. Sex can never be only for purposes of procreation, as it is the fulfilment of love and the undeniable need to belong! Gandhi wasted so much of his time, intelligence and effort to defeat the invincible logic of *kāma*. We cannot bottle or throttle the flow of life. Its natural course brooks no obstruction, cultural, 'spiritual', or whimsical. Life must indeed go on, within the varying values and constraints of society in the contexts of time and place.

And what do we make of homosexual attraction, love and sexual union in both human and animal worlds? Procreation forms no part of those impulses and relationships. As the world increasingly accepts the naturalness of same-sex relationships, one would have to go beyond the link of sex only with procreation; and recognize it as the consummation of attraction between two individuals in bonds of love without any reference to, or need for progeny, as an essential consequence of sex.

---

19   Cf. *Collected Works*, 12, pp. 45-52, 26.

Gandhi himself could never forget, and was for ever obsessed with sex. He thought of it till the very last days of his tortured existence amid the bloodshed and butchery of communalism gone berserk all around him. He thought of it; he wrote about it; he talked about it, only to deny himself and others its physical consummation; to tirelessly advocate *brahmacarya* as he interpreted it; to try and transform any vestigial urges into self-rejection and sublime self-forgetfulness, if the state of the body and mind thus realized can be so described. Even those close to him were perplexed and puzzled by his trials and tests of self in the closest possible proximity to temptation. Was such an exercise at all essential, if not desirable or easily comprehensible in the eyes of his immediate associates and companions? What was it? Whimsical eccentricity? Or restrained surrender to the need for physical contact and warmth without any sex, when he felt disconsolate and lonesome, defeated and desolate, emotionally deflated by the savagery around him, in need of a female's soothing touch and warmth, and motherly ministering without any carnal content or activity? The young, caring, loving, and suffering female companions, buffeted by the inhumanity all around them, overflowed with an irrepressible, natural affection for the ever so frail Mahatma, whose attenuated, bruised, tired frame was kept alive and going only by the indomitable strength of his will!

India produced teachers of sex, who recognized its centrality in the scheme of life; who emphasized its sanctity and beauty in human relationships; and therefore proceeded to write manuals to enable humankind to attain the highest possible levels of sexual joy and fulfilment. The joy of sex is a happy concomitant of the process of creation; a source of love that overwhelms and overflows; and brings people close to the source of life, to God. Hence the gods of Hindu mythology are soaked in sex; and the entire gamut of sexual relationships is in evidence in their activities. The human saints (*ṛṣis*) are not far behind! We have all heard of Parāśara, Bṛhaspati and Dīrghatamas.[20] Gandhi's irrational attitude towards sex, overlaid with a sense of guilt and sinful impurity, amounted to the denial of an ineradicable primal instinct, of the basis of human relationships and the spirit of sharing, giving, receiving and sacrificing in the intimacy and togetherness of our existence. Any reference to sex as sinful, impure and unclean is a travesty of the truth of life's ceaseless, joyous renewal. Gandhi was tireless in repeated reiteration of his search for Truth. One may ask, what and which Truth? Denial of one does not lead to the discovery of another!

---

20   Cf. my *Polyandry in Ancient India, op. cit.*, for the activities of these sages.

Tolstoy's essay 'The First Step' might have provided an added impetus with its emphasis on abstinence for leading a good life. Lusts of gluttony, sloth and carnal love had to be defeated. The basal passions had to be extinguished.[21]

Gandhi sees his *brahmacarya* as an exercise in 'self-purification', which a person wedded to nature will find incomprehensible. He, however, views it as a preparation for action in the struggle that loomed. He has only forsaken pleasure, not his responsibility in society. The service of the household would give way to the service of the community. He is embracing *vānaprastha* without repairing to the forest. He would not bury himself in solitude detached from the world around him. He would indeed be ever more active in his *Satyāgraha*, like Bhīṣma of the *Mahābhārata*, who willingly embraced celibacy and renounced his ancestral throne, but stood steadfast to serve his society.[22] He would steadily retreat from the obligations of the *gṛhastha* (householder) not for freedom from action, but for freedom for action. *Satyāgraha* would be much more than 'passive resistance', which may be sometimes regarded as a weapon of the weak. It would be a fearless pursuit of truth and justice without recourse to any violence. The term *Satyāgraha* arose out of suggestions in the *Indian Opinion*. Maganlal Gandhi came up with *sadāgraha (sat*=truth+ *āgraha*=force, insistence), which Gandhi changed into *Satyāgraha*; and that became the standard name of his movement.

---

21 Cf. 'The First Step', in *The Complete Works of Count Tolstoy,* Vol. XIX, Translated and Edited by Leo Wiener, Boston, Doma Estes and Company, 1905, pp. 391-2 ff.; Guha, *op. cit.,* pp. 198, 589, n.48.

22 Cf. Guha, *op. cit.,* p. 197.

Chapter 44

Mokṣa

Gandhi thinks *of mokṣa*, and tells his readers that the name and the grace of God are the ultimate resource leading to that realization. He tells us that he understood this Truth only after his return home to India.[1]

He told his son Manilal that *mokṣa* was 'nothing but release from the cycle of births and deaths'. He had asked Raychandbhai some years ago to explain what *mokṣa* was. It is generally understood as liberation from the cycle of births and rebirths. Raychandbhai explained that it meant deliverance from the bondage of the body, and from attachment. A person, still living, could be certain of attaining *mokṣa*. The *ātman* still living in a body could become conscious of its pure essence, and of its absolute otherness and freedom from all relations. It is therefore possible to experience *mokṣa* while still living. The soul yet in the body may thus feel or experience full liberation. Raychandbhai does not equate it with, or understand it as absorption into godhead, or merger with Divinity. He also denied that the entire world could be materially destroyed or merged with God.

Gandhi tells us: 'I am impatient to realize myself, to attain *moksha* in this very existence…freeing my soul from the bondage of the flesh…I want to identify myself with everything that lives.' There is a painful contradiction in the statement. If the soul becomes conscious of its 'absolute otherness' and freedom from all relations, why would it bother with the world and its ills, and attempt any amelioration? How would it identify with everything that lives? Such *mokṣa* is supreme selfishness, total absorption into self without any concern for the world around. Is this liberation, or self-aggrandizement enthroned? Raychandbhai was a Jaina; and did not

---

1 *Autobiography*, pp. 153-154.

believe in the soul losing itself and merging in God or godhead. For him the soul was eternal, and in its disembodied, pure and pristine state resided for ever at *Siddhaśilā*, the heaven of the Jainas.

Call it *mokṣa* or *nirvāṇa*, if you will, but if it means only individual salvation without any association with, or without any benefit to the rest of creation including humanity, its pursuit is no different from any desire for self-advancement in our worldly context. God, if we believe in one, is the source and cause of creation, the base of its being and becoming, pervading every pore of all its manifest forms, for ever inseparable! *Mokṣa*, if it means that the soul departs from this world to become one with God, or to reside in close proximity to God, without anything more to do with this world, would run counter to the will and purpose of God, who remains inherent in, and incessantly concerned with the welfare of the world and its progression towards everlasting peace and happiness. *Mokṣa* that rends asunder any relationship with the world, and forsakes any concern for its well-being, is a narrow, narcissistic consummation for the soul! I do not agree with such a concept; I do not seek such a destination. For me, the liberated soul, like God, its parent and master, must for ever remain part of the Divine purpose to sustain creation with compassionate concern and requisite association. If God can incarnate Himself or Herself to redress the world's distress, how can the liberated soul stay apart, aloof and unmoved? If God can repeatedly reincarnate to redeem our world, why can't the liberated soul as well? The great men and women of the world born from time to time to lift its people from the darkness of despair, to relieve their pain, to allay their anxieties, and to solve their problems, are the reincarnations of the liberated souls, parts of God and God's purpose. The other, selfish kind of *mokṣa* would be a contradiction in terms, as it would run counter to the purpose of the world and its Maker!

If God inheres His or Her creation, if God always resides in His or Her creation, if God keeps it going through a ceaseless cycle of births and deaths, should I seek to escape from the world? Why should I seek Him or Her elsewhere and not here? Why should I not strive to be one with Him or Her by identifying myself with His/Her creation; by doing what I can and must, to improve the lot of the world around me; by doing a little of what God supposedly does, in order to please Him or her; in order to realize and advance the purpose of God's will as I understand it! That conscious existence in God, that oneness with God my Father and Mother, will be my *mokṣa* here and now, not somewhere else with all links broken with His/Her world, where I woke up to find my being! I do not seek a state beyond comprehension, beyond any palpable experience, beyond any bounds, beyond any expression or communication! That would indeed be extinction, or in other words, what we generally mean by death. I do not see any attraction or allurement in such a prospect of unimaginable, indefinable, incorporeal union with the Divine! Such a species of *mokṣa* is nothing short of wilful, irretrievable self-annihilation. Who does it help? What good does it do?

In 1913, Gandhi wrote to Jamnadas Gandhi, brother of Magan and Chhagan about *avatāras*, God assuming a human form like Rāma, Kṛṣṇa and others: '[They] were divine incarnations, and we, too, can be like them when immense *punya* (merit) has accrued to us. The *atmans* about to attain *moksha* are so many divine incarnations...*Avatar* is, and always will remain a necessity...'[2]

If *mokṣa* means liberation from ignorance, passions and anger, it is understandable. But it makes no sense if all that self-denial leads to irretrievable, irreversible exit from the theatre of life into a state of unrelieved nullity, void, or oneness with the Divine, never to return. If the Divine returns as an incarnation, or as a multiplicity of *ātmans* or souls, the one-way ticket to nowhere is not a very tempting quest or destination. It may sound sacrilegious, but perfection of the soul should certainly not lead to a nebulous, amorphous, incomprehensible state of being, from which there is no escape or return!

---

2 *Collected Works*, 12, p. 126, 2 July, 1913.

Chapter 45

Tram Cars

The city of Johannesburg introduced a new electric tram system in February, 1906. But they soon introduced policies to prohibit Indians from travelling with the Europeans. The Indian claim that they were entitled to 'the same facilities as any other community', was totally rejected by the whites. The city authorities, however, suspended the new restrictions until the system became fully functional. In the interim, they would run separate cars for the Europeans and the 'coloureds'. Gandhi sent a wealthy Indian merchant E.S. Coovadia to board a European tram car together with one of Gandhi's law clerks, William J. Macintyre. This was his first experiment in civil disobedience. There was no opposition in the first instance; so they boarded a second European car. This time, though, the conductor said that he would permit Coovadia to enter the car only if he was a servant of the white European with him. As this was not the case, and Coovadia said that he was not, the conductor prohibited him to board the car.

Coovadia duly filed a criminal complaint against the conductor, as the city's existing traffic by-laws required the conductors to take all passengers without any discrimination. The need for segregation had not yet formed any part of considerations. The Magistrate found the conductor guilty; the city authorities announced that they would appeal to the Supreme Court; but did not do so. Gandhi made Coovadia try to board another European car; and he was again refused permission to board. Another case was filed; and once again, the conductor was found guilty. Gandhi had succeeded in embarrassing the city. The city, not to be defeated by his manoeuvres, repealed the by-laws, and thus brought into play an earlier Boar regulation imposing a ban on coloured people travelling with Europeans. In May, 1906, Gandhi sent another prominent Indian, Abdul Gani, chairman of the

British Indian Association, to board a European tram-car in the company of H.S.L. Polak, working as a lawyer in Gandhi's office. The conductor told Gani that he could not sit in the car; but Gani refused to get out. The police arrived, together with a tram inspector. Gani agreed to get off the tram-car, to be arrested for interfering with its operation. With the repeal of the by-laws, the culprit was not the conductor, but Gani. The city, however, did not prosecute Gani, which denied Gandhi the opportunity to fight them in court. Gandhi could have sent successive waves of Indians to the tram-cars and thus forced the authorities to pack their jails to the point of overflowing. The city would be compelled to respond; but Gandhi obviously did not think of doing so in the first half of 1906. He resorted to the tactic later. He was still reflecting on civil disobedience on a large scale as an instrument designed and directed to engineer social change; to affect changes in law; to soften if not totally demolish racial injustice and segregation. It was a beginning; a limited exercise to take test cases to the courts for adjudication. He was progressively pondering the nexus between 'self-suffering, public sympathy, and curative institutional reaction'.[1] He was not yet quite ready to use large-scale civil disobedience; he did not yet quite understand how to use it with purpose and discipline, to steer society, politics, and law towards constructive, curative outcomes. It did not take him long to realize the power of mass civil disobedience, as he contemplated the failure and futility of his test cases to bring about any reform to speak of. New tram regulations published in May 1907 denied Indians the use of regular tram-cars. The dogs of European masters were welcome.[2]

---

1   DiSalvo, *op. cit.*, p. 214.

2   *Ibid.*; 'Those Tramway Bye-Laws', *Indian Opinion*, May 25, 1907.

Chapter 46

Return to Johannesburg

Gandhi settled Kasturba at Phoenix, where she had at least some members of the extended Gandhi family, with whom she could converse in her native language, and from whom she could derive a measure of emotional support. He then returned to Johannesburg to a small house, which he shared with Henry and Millie Polak. Millie's attempts to make the place a little more pleasant were defeated by Gandhi's austerity. Gandhi the glutton for simplicity would not have rugs on the floors, or any pictures or paintings on the walls to hide their bare ugliness. He asked Millie to open the windows and view the sunset. The Polaks finally made him agree that a pleasant interior in no way challenged the beauty of nature. Other things apart, Gandhi was too obsessed with what he ate and what he could do without. He insisted that sugar, onions and milk should not form a part of their diet. Millie, however, insisted on the use of milk as it was absolutely essential for nutrition. Millie was highly impressed by his unremitting diligence.

Harilal

Gandhi's eldest son Harilal was at best an indifferent student. He went to many schools without any progress to speak of. He did not come to South Africa with his mother and brothers. Gandhi was dissatisfied with his attitude and conduct towards his parents. The son did not write regularly to them; and what they heard from others was disquieting. Young Harilal was in love with a girl named Chanchal, daughter of Haridas Vora, a friend of Gandhi. Even though the father did not approve of marriage at such an early age, Gandhi's brother Lakshmidas gave his blessing; and the marriage took place on May 2, 1906. Unhappy Gandhi wrote to his brother: 'It is well if Harilal is married; it is also well if he is not. For the present at any rate I have ceased to think of him as a son.'[1]

Gandhi also refused to reimburse the expenses incurred by Lakshmidas in the celebration of Harilal's marriage. While he was annoyed that Harilal did not heed his advice not to hurry into marriage, Kasturba saw the faults of both father and son in their fraught relationship. She persuaded Harilal to come to South Africa with his wife; and when he did, the meeting between the father and son was thankfully devoid of any bitterness.[2]

---

1   27th May, 1906, *Collected Works*, Vol. 5, pp. 334-5.
2   Guha, *op, cit.,* pp. 203-4.

Chapter 47

The Civil Rights Campaigner

Gandhi was no longer interested in a prosperous practice. The lawyer safeguarding the commercial concerns of Indian clients was slowly but surely assuming the role of a civil rights lawyer. His law practice and political activism became closely intertwined. In August 1906, the Transvaal Government proposed several measures to make serious inroads upon Indian interests and freedom of movement in their territory. Of these, the Asiatic Law Amendment Ordinance dubbed the 'Black Act' aroused great alarm and loud opposition. Published in a *gazette extraordinary*, the ordinance had been purposely drafted to 'shut the gate against the influx of the Asiatic population. The author, Lionel Curtis, Assistant Colonial Secretary of the Transvaal, smugly congratulated himself for proposing something great for the future of the whites not only in the Transvaal to begin with, but to be followed by similar legislation in the rest of South Africa, and hopefully, in all other white colonies of the British empire.

Gandhi took a copy to study and translate it into Gujarati in Johannesburg, where he was now staying with his friend Kallenbach. Every Indian, male or female, eight years or older, needed to acquire a new certificate of registration from the Registrar of Asiatics, and provide finger and thumb prints as well as other marks of identification to the authorities. Failure to do so would incur a fine, imprisonment and/or deportation. They had to carry these certificates at all times, and produce them on demand to the police and other government officers. They were otherwise liable to arrest, and even expulsion from the Transvaal. Police officers could, if they so wished, enter private houses for inspection. When Gandhi explained it to a small gathering of Indian leaders, they viewed it with great dismay and indignant anxiety. They had already undergone registration in accordance with Law 3 of 1885 and the Peace Preservation Ordinance of 1903. There was no need for any more. There was no respect for them as British subjects. They were instead being treated as common criminals, as 'finger prints are required by law only from criminals.'[1] The naked hatred for Indians shocked Gandhi as much as the other Indians, to whom he explained the ramifications of the offensive law. It was the first step to hound them out of the country. If the Indians did not put up a fight, the law would be copied and enacted in every province of South Africa. They had to unite; they had to be calm; they had to think; and they had to resist without violence.

Gandhi led a delegation to Pretoria to meet Patrick Duncan, the Colonial Secretary. He was told that 'the Asiatic Act would be unacceptable to the Indian community under any circumstances and the registration would simply not take place.' Gandhi told Duncan that the Indians would go to jail rather than comply; and he would himself be the first to do so. But Duncan gave no hope; and the *Indian Opinion* accused the British of killing the Indians 'by inches'.[2] The Legislative Council spared the women, but passed the ordinance almost as it was first drafted.

Gandhi's friend R. Gregorowski, a prominent Pretoria lawyer, told him that the penalties for refusing to register were very severe; and advised him to lead a delegation to London to plead their case before the new Liberal Government. Gandhi agreed to do so, but not before gauging the mood of the community, for which a public meeting was announced. Gandhi laid the groundwork for this meeting in the columns of *Indian Opinion*:

'...if, disregarding our attempts at gentle persuasion, the Government enforces the Ordinance, Indians will not abide by it; they will not register themselves, nor will they pay fines; they will rather go to gaol. We believe that, if the Indians in the Transvaal firmly stick to this resolution, they will at once be free of their shackles. The gaol will then be a palace to them. Instead of being a disgrace, going to gaol will enhance their prestige. And the Government, for its part, will realize that it cannot with impunity go on humiliating Indians....It is our duty to make some sacrifice for the sake of others. We do not realize there is real beauty in this: that it is thus that we

---

1   Gandhi, M.K., *Satyagraha in South Africa, Collected Works,* Vol. 29, p. 85; DiSalvo, *op. cit.,* p. 408, n.50.

2   Cf. *Collected Works*. Vol. 5, p. 412; Guha, *op. cit.*, p. 205.

please God and do our true duty.'³

A day later, Gandhi's impassioned address to the Hamidiya Islamic Society exhorted them to break the law and brave the consequences:

'Let the accusation of breaking the law fall on us. Let us cheerfully suffer imprisonment....If...we...unite and offer resistance with courage and firmness, I am sure there is nothing that the Government can do....I would only advise you not to register yourselves again. If the Government sends us to gaol, I shall be the first to court imprisonment. And if any Indian is put to trouble because of his refusal to register afresh in accordance with the Draft Ordinance, I will appear in his case free of charge'.⁴ And he invited them to close their businesses and attend a mass meeting on Tuesday, September 11, 1906.

This momentous meeting was held at the Empire Theatre, packed to capacity, and overflowing, with more than three thousand Indians, who came from all parts of the Transvaal. There was not a seat left; no standing space unoccupied; hundreds of disappointed Indians found no room to participate. Patrick Duncan, the Colonial Secretary, invited by Gandhi to attend, did not come himself, but sent Montford Chamney, Protector of the Asiatics, in his place. Abdul Gani, President of the British Indian Association, presided, and spoke in stirring Hindustani. He exhorted his audience to defy the law, refuse to re-register, and unflinchingly go to jail. 'There are moments in the life of a community', he said, 'when resistance... becomes a vital necessity and a sacred duty, and...such a moment is now at hand for us if we would be called men.'⁵ There was loud acclamation with a full-throated shout: 'we shall go to gaol, but will not register ourselves again.'⁶

Five resolutions were passed, categorically expressing the Indian revulsion against the ordinance; calling upon the Government to withdraw

---

3   'Russia and India', September 8, 1906, *Collected Works*, Vol. 5, p. 414, 1961 Edn.

4   'Speech at Hamidiya Islamic Society', September 9, 1906, *Collected Works*, Vol. 5, p. 418.

5   'British Indian Protest', *Rand Daily Mail*, September 12, 1906; DiSalvo, *op. cit.*, pp. 218, 408, n.59.

6   Cf. Guha, *op.cit.*, p. 207.

it; approving a delegation to be sent to London; and authorizing the Chairman to forward the proceedings to the governments in the Transvaal and London. The fourth resolution was indeed the most far-reaching in its intent and implications: ' In the event of the Legislative Council, the local Government, and the Imperial authorities rejecting the humble prayer of the British Indian community of the Transvaal in connection with …the Ordinance, this mass meeting…solemnly and regretfully resolves that, rather than submit to the galling, tyrannous, and un-British requirements laid down in the above Draft Ordinance , every British Indian in the Transvaal shall submit himself to imprisonment and shall continue to do so until it shall please His Gracious Majesty the King-Emperor to grant relief.'

Haji Habib, a respected merchant, moved the resolution, and said it would be an honour to court imprisonment for the cause. He then declared with God as his witness that he would never abide by the detestable law.[7] The audience wholeheartedly concurred; and each of the three thousand men present solemnly pledged by raising their hand to go to jail rather than obey the ordinance. When Gandhi saw the audience taking an oath and making a pledge, he felt a sense of misgiving. He looked upon a pledge and an oath as a very serious commitment both in the eyes of God and the world. One who broke his pledge would make himself a sinner in the eyes of the world. He felt that the crowd did not quite appreciate the seriousness of its pledge. He was the one who had called for disobedience, and he therefore thought that the assembly needed his counsel. With the permission of the chair, he rose and reminded his audience with carefully chosen words of the consequences that would follow their action. It is best here to go to parts of his speech:

'You must understand what is this responsibility, and as an advisor and servant of the community, it is my duty to fully explain it to you…we may have to go to jail, where we may be insulted. We may have to go hungry and suffer extreme heat or cold. Hard labour may be imposed upon us. We may be flogged by rude warders. We may be fined heavily and our property may be attached and held up to auction…Opulent today we may be reduced to abject poverty tomorrow. We may be deported. Suffering from starvation and similar hardships in jail, some of us may fall ill and even die. In short, therefore, it is not at all impossible that we may have to

---

7 Cf. Yogesh Chadha, *Rediscovering Gandhi*, Century, London, 1997, p. 115.

endure every hardship that we can imagine, and wisdom lies in pledging ourselves on the understanding that we shall have to suffer all that and worse. If someone asks me when and how the struggle may end, I may say that if the entire community manfully stands the test, the end will be near. If many of us fall back under storm and stress, the struggle will be prolonged. But I can boldly declare and with certainty, that so long as there is even a handful of men true to their pledge, there can only be one end to the struggle, and that is victory.

A word about my responsibility: if I am warning you of the risks attendant upon the pledge, I am at the same time inviting you to pledge yourselves, and I am fully conscious of my responsibility in the matter. It is possible that a majority of those present here may take the pledge in a fit of enthusiasm or indignation but may weaken under the ordeal, and only a handful may be left to face the final test. Even then there is only one course open to someone like me, to die but not to submit to the law.'[8]

The crowd listened to him in pin-drop silence. He was spelling out the consequences they might face as result of civil disobedience. Within minutes though the jail-going resolution was unanimously passed, and deafening cheers rocked the city centre. Only a few hours later, a fierce fire gutted the premises!

This was an entirely new course of action. Gandhi was establishing a new relationship between himself and the Indian residents of South Africa. Some scholars attribute Gandhi's switch from petitions to protests to the influence of Henry David Thoreau. But Gandhi had not yet read Thoreau. James Hunt suggests the influence of Nonconformists against the Education Act in England.[9] It seems, though, that the events in India in 1905-06 were more pertinent in their influence on Gandhi's thinking. As he himself wrote in *Indian Opinion*, the resolution adopted on September 11, 1906, was 'unique' in the sense that the Indians had not yet done so anywhere else. But with reference to India itself, it could not be considered unique because Indians had been resorting to *hartāls* since

---

8   Gandhi, *Collected Works*, Vol. 29, *Satyagrahain South Africa*, pp. 88-90; DiSalvo *op. cit.*, pp. 219-220.

9   James D. Hunt, *Gandhi and the Non-Conformists: Encounters in South Africa,* New Delhi, Promila and Co., 1986, Chapters 3 & 4.; Guha, *op. cit.*, pp. 208-209, 591, n. 21.

time immemorial. The word *hartāl* signifies the withdrawal 'of support and services' from people to the authorities or vice-versa; from employees to the employers or vice-versa. Gandhi likened the fateful resolution passed at their meeting to the age-old concept of Indian *hartāl*.[10]

The Chinese, who as fellow Asians would also be subject to the ordinance, were present at the Empire Theatre meeting; and the Chinese Consul-General in Johannesburg urged Lord Selborne to withhold his sanction to the offensive measure, a wanton violation of international law.

Gandhi's address to the Empire Theatre audience and speeches elsewhere posited the acceptance of jail for conscientious objection to unjust laws, while vaguely referring to it as a course of action that would lead to success. Going to jail illustrated and affirmed unswerving adherence to principle. How would it lead to success? That was a question yet to be clearly answered. Should an Indian quietly submit to his conviction and punishment as tools of propaganda against the excesses of the Government? It was an experiment in the making.

Gandhi and Haji Ojer Ally were selected as members of the deputation that would wait upon the Imperial Government in London. They arrived in Southampton on October 20, 1906. Not to lose any time, Gandhi gave two press interviews the same day, in which he stressed that the restrictions imposed upon Indians in the Transvaal should not humiliate; and should not detract from the liberty of those who were already settled in the country. He swung into breathless action in stitching together a powerful deputation to wait on the Secretary of State for the Colonies Lord Elgin, a former Viceroy of India.

A day before they met Elgin, Gandhi and Ally spoke to more than a hundred members of Parliament in the Grand Committee Room of the Westminster Palace. Many members spoke, including Sir Henry Cotton, who presided; and a unanimous resolution supporting the objectives of the deputation was forwarded to the Prime Minister.

Headed by Sir Lepel Griffin, the deputation had 14 members including Sir Henry Cotton, Sir Muncherjee Bhownaggree, Dadabhai Naoroji, Ameer Ali, John D. Rees, Harold Cox, Lord Edward Lyulph Stanley, Sir George

---

10 *Indian Opinion*, 6th October, 1906; *Collected Works*, Vol. 5, p. 461, 1961 Edition; Guha, *op. cit.*, pp., 209-210.

Birdwood, Thomas Thornton, Sir Charles Dilke, Sir Charles Schwann, H.O. Ally and Gandhi himself. They met Elgin on November 8, 1906.[11]

Elgin surprised Gandhi with a letter that he had received from two Tamil South Africans, C.M. Pillay and William Godfrey, which stated that Gandhi was a well-known agitator who had made money out of his work, and was responsible for causing a rift between the Indians and Europeans. Pillay was an opponent of Gandhi; and Godfrey, one of the seconders of the Fourth Resolution on September 11, was peeved at his exclusion from the delegation. Most of the signatories of Pillay's petition did not even know what they had signed or appended their finger-prints to; and disavowed their association with its contents in a communication to Elgin. On the day the delegation met the Secretary, though, it was an unfortunate distraction. In a forceful speech, Griffin told Elgin that the Indian position in the Transvaal had become worse than it was under the Boers; invidious legislation of this kind was incompatible with the protection promised by the British flag; and, 'indeed, with the exception of the Russian legislation against the Jews, there is no legislation comparable to this on the continent and England.' Indians were 'the most orderly, honourable, industrious, temperate race in the world, people of our own stock and blood.'

Gandhi presented his case with great sobriety and suasion, urging just and proper treatment of Indians as British subjects, asking the Secretary to withhold royal assent to the offensive ordinance and appoint a commission to consider the principle involved, together with the adequacy of the already existing laws. Other members of the delegation added weight to his submission. H. O. Ally appealed for justice: 'We are content that the white man should be predominant in the Transvaal, but we do feel that we are entitled to all the other ordinary rights that a British subject should enjoy'. Elgin, however, resorted to equivocation; drew attention to the difficulties of the white communities in the Empire; and promised to do what he could in accordance with his responsibility.

Gandhi met his old friends in London, including Josiah Oldfield, and Henry Polak's father and sisters. He also met Shyamji Krishnavarma, the learned Indian linguist and barrister who advocated the use of violence if necessary for gaining India's independence, and established India House

---

11   Cf. James D. Hunt, *Gandhi in London*, Revised Edition, Promilla & Co., New Delhi, 1993, pp. 68 ff.

in Highgate, London, to accommodate and train Indian students for the struggle. Gandhi spent two nights in India House, where he preached peaceful disobedience to convert Krishnavarma to non-violence. Vinayak Damodar Savarkar, a recent arrival from India, was one of the young men who listened to these serious discussions between the two.[12] In 1948, he would be one of the accused in Mahatma Gandhi's murder trial!

Gandhi worked exceedingly hard, getting in touch with newspaper editors, leaders of all persuasions, and other notables with influence in society. Five thousand penny-stamps were used to approach every possible supporter. His intelligence, astounding industry and organizing capacity came into full play in getting together a powerful coalition of influential leaders to oppose this law; and he did everything he could to publicise its transparent injustice. The power of his personality was on splendid display; and his persistence, rewarded by notices in newspapers, alarmed the Government in the Transvaal. Selborne wrote to the Secretary asking him to approve the ordinance; and insinuating that Gandhi had a vested interest in the traffic in permits.

Gandhi and Ally also met Winston Churchill, Undersecretary of State for the Colonies, on November 27; but received little more than a smile and a pat on Ally's back. Churchill warned Gandhi that self-governing Transvaal with a new government would enact an even harsher law. This was Gandhi's first and last meeting with the man who would be the most obdurate opponent of India's independence in the years ahead!

Gandhi also organized a powerful deputation to wait on John Morley, the Secretary of State for India; and a select group of British statesmen met the Prime Minister Sir Henry Bannerman on the Indians' behalf. The Prime Minister assured them that he would discuss the ordinance with Lord Elgin.

Gandhi also set up a South Africa British Indian Committee, supported by Sir Lepel Griffin, Dadabhai Naoroji and Sir M. Bhownaggree, to represent Indian concerns in the Imperial capital. L. W. Ritch, Gandhi's friend and associate, now a qualified lawyer in London, became its Secretary. And at a farewell function in Hotel Cecil, attended by many members of Parliament and a former Governor of Bombay, Gandhi pointed to some South African Indian students in the room, who viewed their return home

---

12 Cf. Gandhi, Rajmohan, *op. cit.,* p. 119.

with great trepidation, as they would also face cruel discrimination and dispossession like the other Indians: 'Here, in England, they will become barristers or doctors, but there, in South Africa, they may not even be able to cross the border of the Transvaal.'[13]

Elgin had told Gandhi and Ally that the Imperial Government would not countenance discrimination against Indians; but he also quietly assured the London representative of the Transvaal Government that, once they were granted self-rule, they could pass the same law again; and London would not stand in the way. Placation of the Boers was far more important than any justice to the Indians. Blissfully unaware of the duplicity, Gandhi the optimist believed that London would do the right thing by the Indians, as indeed they seemed to do, when Royal Assent to the ordinance was withheld.

Gandhi arrived back in South Africa in the third week of December, 1906. Responsible government was introduced in the Transvaal on January 1, 1907. Elections held in the third week of February, brought the Het Volk party to power. Louis Botha became the Prime Minister; and J. C. Smuts the Colonial Secretary. The same measure was introduced into the Transvaal Assembly on March 20, 1907; went through three readings in a day; and was then approved by the Legislative Council. On March 22, the gazette notified its passage; and in June, 1907 it received royal assent, laying bare the truth of Imperial trickery. Gandhi was deeply disappointed that Britain did nothing to safeguard the interests and well-being of Indians before granting independence to the Transvaal. The whites regarded the law as vital to the preservation of their supremacy. The British and the colonists could not be more callous in their treatment of the Indians; in their utter disregard for the service rendered by Indians to the Empire in the hour of its need! A meeting with Smuts on April 4, 1907, proved utterly infructuous.[14]

The intentions of the white masters were spelled out by Smuts in words of unmistakable purpose: Indians were 'detrimental to the everlasting prosperity of south Africa...the object is not persecution, but a stoppage of the influx of Indians.'[15]

---

13   *Collected Works*, Vol. 6, 1961, p. 246.

14   Cf. Guha, *op.cit.*, p. 233.

15   His speech cited in 'Johannesburg Letter': Smuts' Speech, *Collected Works*,

Registration began on July 1, 1907. Indians were shocked and saddened. Gandhi was emphatic in his refusal to accept any: '...if British Indians choose to submit to the serfdom which the legislation seeks to impose on them, I can only say that we deserve the Registration Act. We are undoubtedly put upon our mettle, and it remains to be seen whether, as a body, we shall rise to the occasion...It will be churlish and sinful for myself and my fellow-workers to turn aside from a course which has been dictated by a conscientious purpose.'[16]

The first permit office went to work in Pretoria. Indians organized public meetings, in which the implications of the law were explained; and oaths of resistance were renewed. Indian pickets moved from house to house; and posters of strident protest appeared all over Pretoria:

> 'Boycott the permit office – By going to jail we do not resist, but suffer for our common good and self-respect – Loyalty to the King demands loyalty to the King of Kings – Indians be free!'[17]

Registration officers moved from place to place; permit offices were opened in all the Indian locations; but there were few willing to register. Volunteers picketing the registration offices had strict instructions to be polite to everyone including those who wanted to register. They had to go quietly to the police station if arrested; and suffer in silence, if treated brutally.

On July 31, the last day of registration, two thousand Indians held a meeting in the grounds of the Pretoria mosque. William Hosken, a member of Parliament and a friend of Gandhi and the Indians, came to address them. Botha and Smuts had sent him to persuade the Indians to register. He told them to do so, and not to 'dash [their] heads against a wall'.[18] He told them that Botha respected them, but was helpless in view of the unanimous will of the whites. Gandhi translated his speech for the Indians, but warned: 'If we submit to the law, there is no guarantee that the legislation will be final. The natural consequences of such legislation would be segregation

---

7, p. 285, 1962 edn.

16 'Passive Resistance', May 13, *Johannesburg Star*; cf. DiSalvo, *op. cit.*, p. 230.

17 Cited in Chadha, *op. cit.*, p. 124.

18 *Collected Works,* Volume 29, *Satyagraha in South Africa*, p. 109.

The Civil Rights Campaigner

in locations and finally expulsion from the country.'[19] Prophetic indeed!

Indignant speakers said that they would rather die than register; and the Passive Resistance Association was formed to regulate the struggle. It was later renamed the Satyāgraha Association. Gandhi also enlisted the participation of the small Chinese community likewise affected by the law. *Indian Opinion* helped sustain the spirit of the resisters, who chivalrously gave the Government advance notice of their plans. Every Indian was a lion in a lamb's garb, wrote Gandhi. Those who violated their vow lost their manhood and Indian honour; and those who honoured their vow added to their manhood and India's honour.[20]

On July 20, 1907, Gandhi spoke to the Natal Indian Congress in Durban about the 'divide and rule' tactics of the Government of India: 'Today India gets the kind of justice that the cats got from the monkey in the well-known fable. The Government succeeds by setting the two cats – Hindus and Muslims – against each other. Here it is not so. Both the communities are united, hence our courage will bear fruit.'[21]

Gandhi posted a petition signed by 4,522 Indians to Smuts, asking him to repeal the Act. The signatories were men from all walks of life, from all categories and castes, from all religions, from towns and villages. Gandhi thought the numbers would convince the General of the determination of Indians to boycott registration; but Smuts hoped that their resolution would wilt and waver with the passage of time.

The British Indian Association elected a new chairman, Essop Mia, who, on November 4, 1907, sent a letter drafted by Gandhi to the President of the Indian National Congress, asking for prime importance to be given to their struggle in the parleys of the forthcoming session. They were rising in protest against 'an insult that is levied against our race and our national honour':'…our movement of passive resistance merits the approval of all religious men, of all true patriots, of all men of common sense and integrity. It is a movement so potent as to compel the respect of our adversaries by virtue of our very own non-resistance, of our willingness to suffer; … because we consider that our example, on a small scale in this Colony…may

---

19   Cf. Chadha, *op. cit.*, p. 125.
20   *Indian Opinion*, 6 July, 1907.
21   *Collected Works*, 7, pp. 113-15.

well be adopted by any oppressed people, by every oppressed individual, as being a more reliable and more honourable instrument for securing the redress of wrongs than any which has heretofore been adopted.'[22] The three delegates sent to attend the Surat session of the Indian National Congress were all Muslims. In his letter to Gokhale Gandhi stressed the fact that they were Indians first and foremost in their struggle for basic rights and dignity. He suggested to the senior leader that Hindu-Muslim solidarity should become a special feature of the Congress. As early as 1907, his mind was already at grips with the vital importance of Hindu-Muslim unity in India.[23] Owing to a disturbance at the session, however, the Surat Congress could not pass any resolution on South Africa. Sir Surendranath Banerjea sent Gandhi a cable from the Congress Camp: 'Our sympathies and support. Courage.'[24]

Gandhi denounced resisters who threatened violence against Indians seeking permits. Some of them obtained their permits under police protection, which demonstrated the folly and futility of violence. Some prominent Indians secured their permits in secret at night, and not at any public office. But by 30 November, 1907, the last date for registrations, only 511 out of 13,000 Indians living in the Transvaal sought registration.

Gandhi differentiated between the 'passive resistance' of the British Non-conformists against the Education Act of 1902, and his own, which was certainly not a weapon of the weak, and was totally devoid of violence. In December, 1907, he called it the firmness and force of Truth, synonymous with *ahiṁsā*, non-violence and love. He had recently discovered Henry David Thoreau, who was extensively quoted in the pages of *Indian Opinion* in vindication of disobedience to unjust laws. Gandhi would find in his steadily unfolding *satyāgraha* 'the moral equivalent of war'.[25] What he saw and heard at Shyamji Krishnavarma's 'India House' in London, and the nascent eruptions of terrorism in Bengal thoroughly alarmed him. His *satyāgraha* would render recourse to political violence redundant, and undesirable!

---

22 'Essop Mia to Rash Behari Ghosh', 4 November, 1907, *Collected Works*, Vol. 7, 332-4; Guha, *op.cit.*, p. 253.

23 *Collected Works*, Vol 7, p. 376, Letter of 22 November, 1907.

24 Tendulkar, D. G., *Mahatma,* in Eight Volumes, Volume 1, Times of India Press, Bombay, 1951, p. 107.

25 Cf. Gandhi, Rajmohan, *op.cit.*, p. 114.

The Civil Rights Campaigner

The arrest of a Hindu priest Ram Sundar Pandit on November 8, three weeks before the extended limit for registrations expired, gave Gandhi the opportunity to find answers to a few questions. Should an Indian quietly submit to his conviction and punishment in order to gain public sympathy? Should he on the other hand rebut the Government's charges and in his spirited defence publicise the Indians' argument and campaign against registration? Was it possible to make use of conviction and punishment as tools of propaganda against the excesses of the Government?[26] Ram Sundar had arrived in South Africa in 1898 to cater to the religious needs of the Hindu community. He lived in Natal for seven years, and then, in 1905, received an invitation from the Germiston Hindu community to serve their needs in the Transvaal. He got a temporary but renewable permit from the Transvaal Government, which enabled him to settle down at Germiston. He made some stirring speeches against the Ordinance and led the locals to picket the registration officials. The Government refused to renew his permit; and he refused to register. He disregarded their advice to leave the Transvaal, and was arrested and jailed. He refused offers of bail, preferring to stay in jail to await his trial.[27] On November 14, 1907, he appeared before the Germiston Police Court. Gandhi was his defender. Every available seat in the court-room was taken by both Indians and Europeans. Hundreds of Indians stood outside the court office. Gandhi entered a plea of 'not-guilty' on his client's behalf. Montford Chamney, the Registrar, told the court that the priest had received a series of temporary permits. The last expired on September 30, 1907. The Registrar refused to renew his permit and ordered him to leave the Transvaal. Gandhi replied to the Registrar together with a letter from Ram Sundar stating that he was needed by the community, and would therefore refuse to leave. There was no one else to replace him.

Gandhi argued that the registrar had not renewed Ram Sundar's permit simply because he was an opponent of the Ordinance. Chamney said that he had received complaints that Ram Sundar was preaching about matters that were non-religious, and that made him an undesirable person. Gandhi asked the Registrar if Ram Sundar had at all been warned. 'No', was the answer. Gandhi enquired when was it that the Registrar received the complaint in question. The Registrar said that he could not recall. Gandhi

---

26 Cf. DiSalvo, *op. cit.,* p. 221.
27 'Trial of Ram Sundar Pundit', *Indian Opinon,* November 16, 1907.

asked him to produce the complaints. He would not!

The magistrate, however, said that he had to 'administer the law as he found it'. Gandhi tried to make the Government justify the non-renewal of Ram Sundar's permit. The Government would not do so. The court did not help. The prosecutor asked if the accused had urged Indians not to register by picketing the sites of registration. Gandhi could not tell a lie and therefore told the court that his client was indeed the 'chief picket'. The accused denied any complaints against him. He had not assaulted anyone; and his activity, including picketing, was always non-violent. He would go to jail for his religion, but refused to leave the Colony. He was 'quite prepared to die for his religion'.[28]

The magistrate was impressed by the 'very able' argument of Gandhi; but stressed that he was 'unable to criticise the law; and had only to administer it as it was placed before the court'. Ram Sundar was pronounced guilty, but awarded only a month in prison without hard labour, a gentle verdict which suggested or implied the court's unstated disapproval of the prosecution.[29]

Ram Sundar was led to jail to a chorus of cheers from the Indians present. Gandhi and the leaders of the community decided at a mass meeting to observe a strike the next day, not to do any business to demonstrate their disapproval of the Government's policies and action. This was the beginning of *hartāl* or strike used as a weapon in Gandhi's campaigns in India. A resolution adopted at the meeting praised the Pandit for going to jail to uphold a principle; and announced the intent of thousands to follow his example.

Gandhi had sought the disapproval of the court for the prosecution, which came in a symbolic light sentence. Gandhi had also found a hero who was willing to suffer for the cause, to illustrate and emphasize the need for sacrifice in pursuit of justice. There was doubtless a dichotomy between Gandhi's legal obligation to defend his clients, and his public role to find a willing victim of official tyranny. Court conviction brought to the fore a seeker of salvation through self-suffering.

Gandhi lavished praise on Ram Sundar in the columns of *Indian Opinion*.

---

28 *Indian Opinion*, November 23, 1907.

29 Cf. DiSalvo, *op. cit.*, pp. 221-225.

A 'guiltless' man 'serving the spiritual needs of his countrymen' was flung into prison; but by going to prison the Pandit had 'opened the gate of our freedom'. Ram Sundar was assigned a separate cell in the European wing of the prison, where he could receive visitors and hold discussions with them. When Gandhi went to see him in jail, he said his only sorrow was that he was not given hard labour. Gandhi published his interview with him, in which the Pandit expressed his resolve to go to jail again for the community's sake, and wondered why other Indians had not been arrested. That, he said, would be the prelude to freedom.[30]

Smuts complained to Lord Selborne that 'the Indians headed by the lawyer Gandhi' construed any concessions made to them as signs of weakness. The Governor asked David Pollock and William Hosken, two liberal whites respected by the Indians, to help find a formula for *rapprochement* between the Government and the resisters. Gandhi reiterated his request for repeal of the Act, letting the Indians register themselves with 'full identification particulars', without any degrading coercion. The matter of finger-prints could be resolved later. Gandhi also demanded the replacement of Chamney, who was incompetent and lacked both legal ability and sympathetic understanding. But Smuts refused to budge.[31]

At a mass meeting attended by 2000 or more Indians at the Fordsburg Mosque on November 24, 1907, Gandhi was the principal speaker. He boldly declared that their petition had to go straight beyond earthly authorities to the Divine Dispenser. They could give their finger-prints in jail if asked to do so. The goal of their struggle was 'freedom from slavery', not mere opposition to finger-prints. He told his audience that their cause was also attracting white sympathy, as indeed it was!

The Friend published in Bloemfontein bemoaned the 'martyrdom that the Asiatics are now undergoing...their suffering is voluntary, and marks their refusal to comply with what they consider a degrading law'. It called for acceptance of the offer of voluntary registration made by the British Indians. The Ordinance would otherwise 'drive the self-respecting class of Indians out of the colony and retain only the moral rabble within it. A law which...expels the best and keeps the worst stands self-condemned.'[32]

---

30 *Indian Opinion,* December 7, 1907.

31 *Collected Works,* Vol. 7, pp. 409-11, 422, 446.

32 *The Friend,* quoted in *Indian Opinion,* 23 November, 1907; cf. Guha, *op. cit.,*

In a long, lucid letter to the *Transvaal Leader*, David Pollock pointed out that ninety-five per cent of Indians were still unregistered on December 1, 1907, and therefore liable to arrest and even deportation. It was not possible to jail or deport thousands of conscientious objectors, who would certainly boost the movement for Indian home-rule. He appealed to the Government to stop harassing the Indians; repeal the Asiatic Act; and issue certificates of domicile to all Asiatics who were lawful residents of the colony.

When Ram Sundar came out of jail, Gandhi was with him. They were received with great enthusiasm by leaders of the community; and a rally was held at the Fordsburg Mosque attended by hundreds of Indians. It is worthy of note that the Pandit and Gandhi went to a mosque for this rally. Ram Sundar spoke with great spirit and expressed his steadfast resolution to court arrest and rearrest in defiance of the Act. He would not leave the colony, nor submit to the requirements of the new Registration Law.[33] Ram Sundar exhorted his countrymen to keep up their fight, and go to jail like him if necessary. The fiery speech was greeted with loud cheers. He was a martyr in their cause. Gandhi had found a laudable disciple. The Government immediately issued an order asking him to leave the Transvaal within seven days, or face further imprisonment. Suddenly, the Pandit lost nerve, and sped to Natal with his family. The flight of the hero sent waves of shock across the entire community. Gandhi, sadly disillusioned, was scathing in his comment: 'as far as the community is concerned, Ram Sundar is dead as from today. He lives to no purpose... Physical death is to be preferred to such social death... Having meanly betrayed the people of Germiston, his community, himself, and his family, he has fled like a coward in fear of imprisonment.'

Gandhi understood the abiding significance of his movement. He wrote: 'Indians in the Transvaal will stagger humanity without shedding a drop of blood... It is because I consider myself to be a lover of the Empire for what I have learned to be its beauties that, seeing, rightly or wrongly, in the Asiatic Law Amendment Act seeds of danger to it, I have advised my countrymen at all costs to resist the Act in the most peaceful, and shall I add, Christian manner.' As he wrote later, the Act spelt 'absolute ruin for the Indians in South Africa... It was a question of life and death for

---

p. 258.

33 *Transvaal Leader*, December 14, 1907; DiSalvo, *op. cit.*, p. 410, n. 97.

them… The community must not sit with folded hands. Better to die than to submit to this law.'[34]

The intentions of the white masters were also unhesitatingly clear, as set forth in the words of Jan Smuts:'We have made up our minds to make this a white man's country, and, however difficult the task before us in this matter, we have put our foot down and shall keep it there.'[35] But Gandhi was equally emphatic and clear in his conviction: "True victory will be won when the entire Indian community courageously marches to the gaol – when the time comes – and stays there as if it were a palace."[36] He defended resisters in court; wrote to the press; wrote articles for *Indian Opinion;* wrote to Smuts; and pleaded the cases of railway workers who had been sacked owing to their failure to register. It was a phenomenal explosion of energy and will-power.

Gandhi was called on December 27 and told that he and some of his fellow Indians would be arrested. He promised to present himself and the other defendants in court the following day. In the evening he gave a fiery speech at the Hamidiya Islamic Society Hall; and called the Government's action un-Christian and uncivilized: 'If Jesus Christ came to Johannesburg and Pretoria and examined the hearts of General Botha, General Smuts and the others…he would notice something strange, something quite strange to the Christian spirit…Some sections of the Act [were] savage, and they were only worthy of an uncivilized Government…. He would give the same advice that he had ventured to give them for the last fifteen months.'[37]

On December 28, 1907, ten defendants including Gandhi, who did not have any registration, were arrested and put on trial. Gandhi pleaded guilty, as he conscientiously objected to the law. The Indians told the Magistrate that finger-printing was against their religion and an affront to their human dignity. Only criminals were subjected to this kind of finger-printing. At Gandhi's own prompting, the Magistrate asked him to leave the colony within forty-eight hours. Gandhi expressed at a public meeting his and his colleagues' readiness to be re-arrested, as they were not going anywhere;

---

34 Cited in DiSalvo, *op.cit.,* pp. 230-231.
35 Cited in *Johannesburg Letter*, Smuts' Speech, *Collected Works*, Vol. 7, 1962 edition, p. 285.
36 'Indians in the Transvaal' February 2, 1907, *Collected Works*, Vol. 7, p. 306.
37 *Collected Works*, Vol. 5, p. 418, 1961 edn.

and advised his people to fight to the bitter end. It was a struggle for self-respect, not against Europeans. God was on the Indians' side, as theirs' was a just cause. On January 1, 1908, the Rev. Joseph J. Doke, Head of the Central Baptist Church in Johannesburg, visited Gandhi in his chambers. He had travelled across India, and was a sympathetic observer of the Indian struggle led by Gandhi, who repeatedly invoked Jesus and the Christian spirit in his struggle for justice without malice, without violence in word and deed, and with love for his opponents. He saw 'a small, lithe, spare figure', 'a refined earnest face', 'a direct fearless glance', and 'the smile that lighted up the face...and simply took one's heart by storm'.[38] In reply to Doke's question how far he was prepared to make a martyr of himself for his cause, Gandhi resolutely stated that he was 'willing to die at any time, or to do anything for the cause'.[39]

Gandhi presented himself before the Magistrate on January 10, 1908, and was sentenced to two months imprisonment without hard labour, even though he asked for the heaviest penalty, which was six months imprisonment with hard labour including a fine of £500.

The same Johannesburg jail where his first sentence began, housed Mandela, also a lawyer, about 54 years later. How times change! South Africa, free from the scourge of apartheid, chose the site of the jail for its new Constitutional Court to honour their memory. Gandhi's arrest and imprisonment pained the Indians, but also some whites and even blacks, as some could even then clearly realize that Gandhi's struggle in its scope and essence, transcended race, colour and class alike. Among the many voices raised to support Gandhi and his cause, that of John L. Dube, the great African reformer and Gandhi's neighbour near Phoenix, in his newspaper *Ilanga lase Natal,* lauded the courage of Indians, and upheld their 'fair claim to justice'. It was a generous gesture.[40]

Both in Natal and the Transvaal, many Indian stores remained closed as a mark of respect for their leader. In his congregational sermon, the Rev. Joseph Doke praised the 'heroic struggle' dictated by Gandhi's conscience, and the display of inherent human nobility in consonance and accord with

---

38   Cf. Doke, Joseph J, *M.K. Gandhi*, pp. 6-8.

39   Joseph Doke, *M.K. Gandhi: An Indian Patriot in South Africa*, London, London Indian Chronicle, 1909, pp. 5-6, 9.

40   Cf. Guha, *op. cit.*, p. 267.

the teaching of Christ in stark contrast with the callousness of Christians to the suffering of Indians and the Chinese. Henry Polak spoke of the global importance of the 'race fight' which would help decide whether the 'Asiatic peoples' would be doomed to eternal subjection, or treated, as they should be, as 'fellow human beings', not as 'slaves'.[41] Kallenbach spoke of Gandhi's character and conduct; he had not seen 'a more conscientious, more honourable or better man'.[42]

'A lesson in True Manliness' in the *Basutoland Star* mocked the Transvaal Government 'known all over the world as being very harsh and inconsiderate in its treatment of all persons of colour', 'almost driven to climb down from its high pedestal by the exhibition of manly qualities by the Indians'. The paper supported both the ends and means of the movement.[43] In the words of Guha, 'this statement of solidarity is made more remarkable by the fact that it was unprompted, unsolicited and... unrequited'.[44] The *Natal Mercury* warned that Smuts' policies would make martyrs of Gandhi and his associates and lead to 'unforeseen results, both here and in India'.[45]

Gandhi organized himself in jail, 'enjoyed it', and read the *Gītā*, Bible, the Koran, Carlyle, Samuel Johnson, Walter Scott, Tolstoy, Huxley, Ruskin, Plato and Bacon. He discovered that Socrates was the first philosopher to say that it was preferable to suffer than to wrong others. He had worked to his uttermost capacity outside jail, stretching himself beyond limits. Imprisonment imposed relief from countless concerns, but also hurt the movement. People were losing courage, and reluctant to go to jail. The waning momentum worried Gandhi; but a new opportunity arrived with the visit in prison from Albert Cartwright, editor of the *Transvaal Leader*, who was sympathetic towards the Indian cause, and whom Gandhi regarded as a friend.

In their meeting on June 21, 1908, both agreed that the dispute could be

---

41 Cf. *Transvaal Leader*, 13 and 15 January, 1908.
42 Letter to the editor, dated 14 January, published in *Transvaal Leader*, 16 January, 1908.
43 'Passive Resistance and the Native Mind', a remarkable article published in *Transvaal Leader*, 16 January, 1908; Guha, *op. cit.*, p. 270.
44 *Ibid.*, p. 270.
45 *Natal Mercury*, 7 January, 1908; Cited in Guha, *op. cit.*, p. 266.

resolved if the Indians registered voluntarily after the repeal of the Act. Cartwright re-visited Gandhi on January 28, with a draft of the letter, which he wanted the Indian resisters to send to the Government. Gandhi amended the letter to ensure that Indians who registered voluntarily should be free from the Act's application; and also to clarify the position of the Transvaal Indians at the time outside the colony's boundaries. He then signed it, as did another Indian leader, Thambi Naidoo, and the Chinese leader, Leung Quinn. This letter was the basis of the agreement with Smuts. According to Gandhi, he and Cartwright had agreed upon the repeal of the Act and voluntary registration by the Indians.

Cartwright took Gandhi's letter to Smuts, and conveyed to Gandhi its acceptance by the General. This letter was unfortunately not as unambiguously drafted as one would wish; and that provided the ground for the clash of two opposing wills. Both Gandhi and Smuts had some similar and comparable experiences. They were both almost the same age. Both went to England to study law. Both were students of philosophy and religion. Both dabbled in journalism. Gandhi led his people in a non-violent struggle. Smuts led his men in the Anglo-Boer War. Both practised law in the Transvaal. Both relinquished their practices to lead their people. Smuts' study of Christ and Christianity at Cambridge failed to impress him with the fact that Christ was a coloured Asian and that he would be totally out of place and utterly unwelcome in white South Africa. Gandhi was a champion of the Indian cause for justice. Smuts was an unapologetic white supremacist, who wanted to strengthen and preserve the white monopoly in the society, economy and political set-up of the Transvaal.

On January 30, 1908, Gandhi was taken to Pretoria to meet Smuts. In a cordial conversation Smuts said that he accepted Gandhi's amendments, but also told him that the English-speaking whites were keener than the Boers to enforce the new Act. The General commended the commitment of the Indians, and added: 'I have consulted General Botha also, and I assure you that I will repeal the Asiatic Act as soon as most of you have undergone voluntary registration ...'[46]

Smuts told Gandhi he was no longer a prisoner; and all the others would also be released. With the train fare lent by Smuts' secretary, Gandhi arrived in Johannesburg at 9 p.m., and went straight to the mosque at Newton, where

---

46 *Satyagraha in South Africa, Collected Works,* Vol. 29, p. 128.

he addressed a crowd of about one thousand Indians around midnight. He explained the terms of the settlement to the leaders and the people present, and said: 'The responsibility of the community is largely enhanced by this settlement. We must register voluntarily to show that we do not intend to bring a single Indian into the Transvaal surreptitiously or by fraud.'[47] Mir Alam, one of the Pathans at the meeting, angrily asked Gandhi: 'It was you who told us that fingerprints were required only from criminals. It was you who said that the struggle centred round the fingerprints. How does all that fit in with your attitude today?'[48] Gandhi explained that the circumstances had changed. There was a difference between being forced to salute someone, and doing it of one's own free will. The rugged Pathan, an ex-army man and a client of Gandhi, could understand none of this, and rudely accused him of selling the community to Smuts for £15,000. He said he and his fellows would never give their fingerprints, nor allow anyone else to do so. 'I swear with Allah as my witness, that I will kill the man who takes the lead in applying for registration.'[49]

Gandhi assured the audience that those who had sworn not to give fingerprints would not be forced to do so. He promised to help anyone who wanted to register without providing fingerprints. But he did not like threats in the name of God; and would indeed take the lead in providing his fingerprints. If he were to die at the hands of a brother, he would embrace death without any hatred or anger towards his assailant. Even the assailant would later repent, and realize Gandhi's innocence.[50]

Smuts, however, breached the agreement by refusing to repeal the Act. DiSalvo points out that 'Gandhi's January 28 letter focuses on the suspension of the operation of the Act – not its repeal.'[51] Gandhi meant that the Act would stay suspended during the process of voluntary registration, and would then be repealed. The letter did not exactly say so, though it referred to an exchange of voluntary registration for repeal: '... We have repeatedly offered to undergo voluntary registration if the Act was repealed...' That was a painful oversight on the part of Gandhi, who

---

47   Cited in Tendulkar, *Mahatma*, Vol. 1, p. 110.

48   *Ibid.*

49   *Ibid.*

50   *Ibid.*, p. 111.

51   DiSalvo, *op. cit.*, p. 255.

thought it was 'not possible during the Parliamentary recess to repeal the Act...'[52]

Gandhi wrote that the General had accepted the demands made in his letter. A letter from the acting Assistant Secretary to Gandhi, however, did not mention repeal, but promised supplementary action by Parliament. Chamney, the Registrar of Asiatics, gave Gandhi a hint that repeal was not really agreed upon. Gandhi wanted to see Smuts again, but was not allowed to do so. He therefore wrote to Smuts on February 1 to express his misgivings. He met him on February 3, 1908, and claimed that at this meeting they both agreed that, if the Indians registered voluntarily, the Act would be repealed.[53]

Gandhi announced in the columns of *Indian Opinion* complete success of their campaign.[54] Many Indians were however incensed at Gandhi's capitulation on the demand for fingerprints. He sought to assuage their anger with the argument that compulsion in the requirement for fingerprints constituted the principal humiliation, which would form no part of volunteering one's fingerprints. And he would be the first to do so. He failed to fully foresee the anger welling up amongst some of them, so much so that he was set upon by some Pathans while on his way to Chamney's office to register and give his fingerprints. This was February 10, 1908. The main assailant was Mir Alam, who had already threatened him in no uncertain terms on January 30. He was struck on his head from behind with a rod of iron, and as he fell, he was dealt more severe blows with staffs and kicks. He lost consciousness, and might even have lost his life, but for the adroit use of his umbrella by his companion Thambi Naidoo to ward off some of the hefty blows, and the timely arrival of the police. Gandhi's life was saved. The assailants were arrested. Rev. Joseph Doke, who was fortunately passing by, took him to his house to take care of him. Gandhi's forehead bled, his lips bled, and two of his front teeth came loose. After being patched up, Gandhi, still undeterred, decided to go ahead and register. Chamney came to Doke's house to take his fingerprints. In great pain, he could scarcely move his hands, but persisted with the task that he had undertaken to complete. Chamney's moist eyes at that

---

52 *Ibid.*, p. 416, n. 13.

53 *Collected Works*, Vol. 8, p. 65, 1962 edn.

54 'A Dialogue on the Compromise', *Indian Opinion*, February 15, 1908; Cf. DiSalvo, *op. cit.*, p. 418, n. 7.

moment illustrated for Gandhi the power of self-suffering: 'I had often to write bitterly against him, but this showed me how a man's heart may be softened by events'.[55]

In a short message to the community, Gandhi requested that no steps be taken against the assailants. 'Seeing that the assault was committed by a Musalman, or Musalmans, the Hindus might probably feel hurt. Rather let the blood spilt today cement the two communities indissolubly.'[56]

He stayed with the Dokes for about ten days recovering from the ordeal under their kind care; and then moved to the house of Kallenbach for rest and recuperation. Despite his repeatedly stated wish not to prosecute the assailants, they were sentenced to jail, as other eye-witnesses gave evidence against them at their trial.

---

55 *Satyagraha in South Africa, Collected Works,* Vol. 29, p. 139; Tendulkar, *Mahatma,* Vol. 1, p. 112.

56 *Ibid.*

Chapter 48

Kallenbach

The attack on Gandhi provided an emotional impetus to a desire for settlement. Indians went ahead with registration. And on his return from Durban in March, 1908, Gandhi moved in with Kallenbach to live with him at his residence. Doke visited them often, as he was writing a biography of Gandhi; and mentions a rolled-up mattress on which the latter slept.[1] The house on Pine Road was called the Kraal, as it featured many traditional African elements. And later, they lived in an isolated 'tent' in Mountain View on Linksfield Road near Johannesburg for seven months. It became an intense personal relationship, the depth of which is conveyed by Gandhi's letters to Kallenbach. They were preserved in the private Kallenbach Archive in Haifa, Israel; but were put up for sale by Sotheby's in 1986, and purchased by the Government of India.[2] It appears that Gandhi and Kallenbach came to a mutual agreement to destroy each other's letters to save them from the prying eyes of posterity; but while Gandhi lived up to his part of the deal, Kallenbach carefully kept his treasure. And after his death, they were faithfully preserved by his niece Hanna Lazar. Kallenbach's letters are therefore scarce; and only a few survive. But Gandhi's outpourings of love and emotion now form the subject matter of scholarly discussion and debate.

Gandhi and Kallenbach were both ardent admirers of Tolstoy, who experienced a personal crisis in middle age, and gave up alcohol, tobacco

1 Cf. Lev, Shimon, *Soulmates: The Story of Mahatma Gandhi and Hermann Kallenbach,* Orient Blackswan, New Delhi, 2012, p. 25; Doke, J., *M.K. Gandhi: An Indian Patriot in South Africa,* Government of India, New Delhi, 1967, pp. 76-7.

2 Published in a Special Volume: CW XCVI (Supplementary Volume VI), New Delhi, Publications Division, Government of India, in 1994.

and meat; did hard manual work in the fields; split wood, made shoes and shared life with the serfs. Deeply attracted to Hinduism and Buddhism, he sought to give up sex; became a votary of religious tolerance and simplicity; and an advocate of non-violence and pacifism. Gandhi's progress towards non-possession, and together with him, Kallennbach's towards austerity and abstinence was boosted by the example of Tolstoy. The great author had stopped writing the kind of novels that made him famous. Gandhi also increasingly viewed his legal work as an obligation, not a vocation. Personal development and social reform became his principal preoccupations, even if he continued his fight against discrimination and injustice. Tolstoy had rebelled against and rejected institutional Christianity including that of the Russian Orthodox Church; and called upon his readers to harmonize their lives 'with the moral foundations one considers to be true, regardless of the demands of family, society, and government.'[3] Gandhi and Kallenbach opted for that goal; and their life together in a 'living laboratory' involved introspection, self-examination, strict ascetic self-discipline and austere living. The most stringent levels of self-abnegation brought about mental and spiritual changes. The two, living together, did all their housework without assistance from any servants.

Gandhi had shared homes with Europeans before. He had lived with Josiah Oldfield in England; and with Herbert Kitchin, Henry and Millie Polak in South Africa. He and Kallenbach lived sporadically together, between 1908 and 1914. They were apart from each other only when Gandhi was in jail; or visiting Phoenix; or when one of them was overseas. Their relationship, therefore, became so much more intimate, so much more philosophically close. They shared living quarters at Tolstoy Farm after its establishment in 1910; and spent time together in London on the eve of Gandhi's departure for India in 1914. The years 1906-9 were the most crucial in the development of Gandhi's spiritual and social ideas; and by 1909 he had hammered the heterogeneous elements of his philosophy derived from both the East and West into an ordered whole. He had a clear, unclouded vision of his goals; and of his priorities.[4] Kallenbach was the closest witness to this fraught process of self-denial and self-suffering delivering the 'Mahatma' to the world.

---

3   Cf. Guha, *op.cit.*, pp. 287, 600, n. 56.

4   Cf. Bhana S., and G. Vahed, *The Making of Political Reformer Gandhi in South Africa* 1893-1914, New Delhi, Manohar, 2005, pp. 11, 19.

Following the attack on Gandhi by the Pathans, Kallenbach acted as his body-guard with a loaded pistol in his pocket that Gandhi knew nothing about. The latter's reprimand, when he learned of it, included a reference to Ruskin and Tolstoy, who would not have approved.[5] Kallenbach accompanied Gandhi to meetings, where he listened for hours to speeches in Indian languages he did not know a word of, braving hunger and plain physical fatigue.

Gandhi made Kallenbach economize and save every penny, as if he was spending public money and not his own; and brought his personal expenditure down from Rs. 1200 per month to Rs. 200. Kallenbach felt hurt if Gandhi offered to pay his share of the household expenses; and told Gandhi that he had already saved him a lot more. It was a deliberately designed hard life they led! In June 1908, Kallenbach wrote to his brother Simon: 'we cook, bake, scrub and are cleaning the house and the yard; we are polishing our shoes, and are working in the flower and vegetable garden.' 'A vegetarian according to his religious convictions', and yet 'an extraordinarily good and capable person', his Hindu housemate was changing his ways.

Kallenbach gave up meat and alcohol; and told his brother: 'for the last eighteen months I have given up my sex life.'[6] Gandhi had taken a vow of celibacy. Kallenbach joined him. The Hindu-Jaina ascetic tradition was quite cognizant and prescriptive of continence; but celibacy or sexual abstinence were neither known to Jewish heritage, nor in any way applauded or upheld by the Jews. It was an agonizing, difficult departure from the norm for the highly sexed, fun-loving Kallenbach. But by subjecting himself to ruthless discipline he 'gained in character – strength – mental vitality and physical development...' Gandhi was trying hard to convert himself and Kallenbach, by embracing austerity and detachment from worldly pleasures, as did some of his other friends under his influence. Kallenbach wrote to his brother that, with his steady financial income, he planned to go to study in London; and that Gandhi also intended to do so, to study medicine there. And they hoped to live in London together, as they did in Johannesburg. Guha points out that this unrealized intent of Gandhi to study medicine in London, like his friend Pranjivan Mehta who was both a doctor and a barrister, has escaped the attention of the Gandhi

---

5   Cf. Lev, *op.cit.*, p. 15.

6   Cf. Guha, *op.cit.*, p. 287.

biographers.[7] But that was not to be! Smuts did not repeal the Act; and Gandhi did not leave!

Kallenbach loved Gandhi as an elder brother; held him in the highest esteem; and tried exceedingly hard to live up to his ideals. They discussed sex all the time, as it lay at the root of their struggle between the body and soul, between the flesh and spirit. Gandhi sought 'purity' through *brahmacarya*, in readiness for the struggle of *Satyāgraha*!

Gandhi and Kallenbach practised their fasting and dietary experiments in concert; discussed changes in their food; and the greater pleasure they derived from those changes. Gandhi deplores this delight in taste and its expression in their mutual conversation. 'It was wrong to have dwelt upon the relish of food.'[8] As Gandhi would have it, eating is meant only 'to keep the body going'. Pleasing the palate is out of order. The function of sense organs is to keep the body and soul together, in service of the soul, and when that happens, the relish of food disappears. That according to Gandhi is what nature intends. God alone knows where Gandhi got this intimation of the intentions of nature! Gandhi seems to equate the denial of nature with 'symphony with nature'.[9] There is a thing called over-indulgence, just as there is a thing called self-crucifixion. Gandhi forgets the principle of the golden mean, of moderation between extremes. He should have heeded the advice of the Buddha, who came to the great realization of *majjhimā paṭipadā* ('middle path') before his enlightenment. Self-punishment is not conducive to bliss either of the spiritual or material variety. But willing self-suffering to touch the heart of the oppressor is at the very core of *satyāgraha*.

---

7   *Ibid.*, p. 289.

8   *Autobiography*, p. 237.

9   *Ibid.*

Chapter 49

Back at Work: To *Satyāgraha*

Gandhi went back to his work, looking after his clients. He inducted Polak into his practice; and had him admitted to the bar to help meet the increasing workload of his commercial clients. Polak, though, began his legal career largely with representing cases of the Indian civil disobedience movement.

On March 5, 1908, Gandhi was attacked once more, while addressing a meeting in Durban. But the assailants rushing towards the podium were blocked by the protective crowd that surrounded and saved him.[1] Gandhi wrote to his son Harilal that the still angry Pathans might kill him: 'what if they kill me?... most of the teachers have such a fate'.[2] An eerie premonition!

The movement gained momentum in less than two months after Polak's swearing in. It was gradually dawning on everyone that the Government was not really going to repeal the Act notwithstanding the Indian compliance with the undertaking to register voluntarily. A sense of outrage was acute in the Indian ranks. Gandhi and his associates accused Smuts of going back on his pledge to repeal the noxious Act. They drew attention to a speech Smuts had made; to their own clear recollection of the negotiations; and to the correspondence between Gandhi and Smuts. But Gandhi had not been careful enough to state unambiguously in his letter that voluntary Indian registration was contingent upon the repeal of the act by the Government. He claimed that Smuts had assured him orally that repeal would follow voluntary registration by the Indians.

---

1 'A Disorderly Meeting', *Indian Opinion,* 7 March, 1908.
2 From undated letters, probably written in 1908, in Parikh, *Gandhiji's Lost Jewel,* p. 139; cf. Rajmohan Gandhi, *op. cit.*, p. 129.

BACK TO WORK: TO *SATYĀGRAHA*

On May 18, 1908, Gandhi was the only non-white participant in a debate at the Johannesburg YMCA on the topic: 'Are Asiatics and the Coloured Races a menace to the Empire?' The labour of Africans and Asians had made the Empire viable and what it was, said Gandhi, opposing the motion. What would the British Empire be without India? 'South Africa would probably be a howling wilderness without the Africans'. He looked forward to the East being energized and 'quickened with the Western Spirit', and the directionless West being imbued with a purpose by the East. He called upon the colonists to raise the status of Indians, immigrants just like them; to allow them to 'live freely without being restricted, move freely without being restricted, own land and trade honestly'. Though it was premature to speak of political rights for Indians and Africans, they would have them, in the fullness of time, as bringing that about was the mission of the English race. He looked forward to a commingling of races, and to the burgeoning of a civilization that the world had not yet seen. It took him fifteen years to develop this vision of Eastern and Western, Indian, African and European unity. The future foreshadowed here would be the realization of the old Indian ideal of *vasudhaiva kuṭumbakam*. He forgets the pejorative *kaffir*, as he looks at the proud though bowed African. The colour of the skin ceases to define any false divisions![3]

Smuts refused to repeal the Act. The fact that Gandhi could not secure a written pledge from him enabled the General to deny that he had ever consented to do so. The omission or oversight on the part of Gandhi might have been attributable to his faith in Smuts, and his hope that the General would keep his word. This lack of attention to detail became the basis of what followed. Gandhi's insistence that a pledge was broken, and Smuts' assertion that a repeal was never promised, simply meant that the Indians felt short-changed and painfully betrayed. Smuts had played them false. Gandhi would not take it lying down. He wrote to Chamney on May 26 requesting a return of his application for registration, and all the other associated papers. He referred to the breach of a clear agreement between him and Smuts. The Government had 'no legal right to the documents', which he had given to the Registrar 'only as a matter of grace and not in

---

3 'Speech at Y.M.C.A.', *Collected Works*, Vol. 8, pp. 242-246. Hunt, *op.cit.*, pp. 137-8, points out that Gandhi gave voice in this speech to 'the ideology of the Hindu Renaissance – the contrast and mutual dependency of the spiritual East and the material West.' He was well on the way to disillusionment with the modern civilization.

virtue of any law.' He asked Chamney to return his papers by May 29. The latter did nothing, but informed Smuts, who invited Gandhi to a meeting on June 6, 1908. Gandhi asked Smuts to honour his promise to repeal the Act, now that the Indians had registered voluntarily. Smuts, however, said that he had given no such assurance, and refused to commit himself to repeal the Act. Albert Cartwright also failed to move the General's mind towards 'Justice and Righteousness.'[4] Gandhi wrote to Smuts again to nudge and ask him if people could be told that the Act was going to be repealed. If the answer was 'no', he would ask Chamney to return his application form. And if the Government did not agree to return the papers, he would move the Supreme Court for an order to compel it to do so.

Smuts called him to another meeting in which they talked about amendments to the Act. Gandhi wanted the Act to permit pre-Boer War residents and possessors of Boer-issued certificates to register voluntarily; and the educated Indians to enter, like the Europeans, after passing a test, which Smuts refused to accept. Gandhi then wrote a letter to Smuts in which he carefully laid down his position. They met again on June 22, and at this meeting Smuts expressed his willingness to repeal the Act, but he wanted to amend it in ways that Gandhi found unacceptable. Dissatisfied and disappointed with the position of Smuts, Gandhi requested the return of his voluntary application papers. Smuts told him that he was free to go to the courts.

Gandhi wrote: '…General Smuts was willing to repeal the offending Asiatic Act…This shows that General Smuts was, and still is, under promise to repeal the Act…but he wanted to break the spirit of it… The position of the Asiatics is simple. They must revert to the condition that prevailed in January last in this matter. And they have been advised to withdraw their voluntary application forms. General Smuts has declined to return them. If he had the courage to face the passive resisters, he would return them without much ado.[5]

On June 23, 1908, a man called Ebrahim Ismail Aswat filed a petition with the Transvaal Supreme Court for the return of his application papers. That became a test case for the return of the voluntary registration papers of all

---

4   Cf. Guha, *op. cit.*, p. 280.
5   'Letter to the press', June 22, 1908, *Collected Works*, Volume 8, p. 306-307, December 1962 Edn.

Indians. By not repealing the Act as promised, the Government breached the terms of an agreed deal; and a breach entitled the Indians to reclaim their voluntary papers. It was argued on the Indians' behalf that the applications had been voluntarily tendered with a clear understanding that the act would be repealed. There was no repeal. Therefore, the entire process of registration was null and void. The judge said there was no clearly written pledge to repeal the act; and Gandhi's statement that the pledge was orally given by Smuts was denied by Smuts and Chamney. He therefore decided that Smuts had not made the promise or given the undertaking; and ruled that once Aswat gave the document to the government, it became their property.

The Indians would not get their papers back. They had no such entitlement. Gandhi did not have any assurance of Smuts in writing. However, if recourse to the courts of law for redress failed once more, it heralded a new movement, a novel change of direction, which involved deliberate civil disobedience in defiance of unjust laws and official tyranny. Gandhi's negligence in clearly spelling out his prerequisite position for voluntary registration, and his failure to get Smuts' promise of repeal in black and white provided the basis of *Satyāgraha* in opposition to, or non-compliance with a patently unjust legislation. The mistake became the mother of *Satyāgraha*, of civil disobedience for truth and justice. It armed resisters with the resolution to suffer for their cause with love and without bitterness; without resorting to invectives; without any violence in thought and deed. They needed to move the hearts of the perpetrators with rising public sympathy; to put moral and public pressure on them to do the right thing. Civil disobedience could be a powerful weapon against tyranny; withdrawal of consent to obey unjust public laws could force the Government to see reason with increasing public support for fair play.

Gandhi's doctrine of civil disobedience was steadily evolving under pressure of events. He could visualize the prospect of social change and reform through civil disobedience and self-suffering to mould and influence public opinion, to make the Government see reason. His incarceration with about 200 Indians for disobeying the act had taught him a thing or two. The press apprised him of Smuts' painful dilemma in dealing with resistance in the garb of civil disobedience. The General openly conceded that he could not exact obedience from the Indians. And if he arrested them all, the jails of the Transvaal were not big enough to hold them all. Gandhi could clearly comprehend from the concession that Smuts made, that a government can function only with the willing consent of the governed. A large body of persons intent on civil disobedience could exert immense, sometimes overpowering pressure for change in the right direction. These were lessons Gandhi used to great effect later in the much larger theatre of Indian politics.

Up till then, only tentative steps had been taken in the development of *Satyāgraha*, not with any great success. But, from the very beginning, Gandhi clearly understood and appreciated the importance of dignified, stoic self-suffering in rousing public sympathy; in influencing public perception; in affecting change; in prompting governments to act for the greater good of everyone concerned; in prodding, pressing and pushing ameliorative, corrective, curative action. 'Passive resisters depend upon creating public opinion... it will not be denied that their suffering has at last made some pubic men in this colony think'.[6]

In full view of society, self-suffering would assuredly rouse sympathy and activate the natural inner springs of compassion. That is why Gandhi said before his imprisonment that 'he had sufficient faith in human nature to believe that when the colonists saw husbands torn away from their wives, when colonists found that their wives were left to be starved to death, and husbands stranded... then the colonists of the Transvaal themselves would tell General Smuts that he had not received a mandate to treat human beings in that fashion'.[7]

He repeated this elsewhere: '... when they saw the British Indians would suffer... they would ask General Smuts to stay his hand and keep his promises, and to repeal the act on the conditions he agreed upon'.[8] He wrote to Doke that 'passive resistance' meant 'self-imposed suffering of an acute type, intended to prove the justice of the cause, and thus to bring conviction home to the minds of colonists'.[9] What followed was an

---

6   'Letter to editor', December 31, 1907, *Johannesburg Star*.

7   Meeting of Chinese: Mr. Gandhi's Exhortation, December 31, 1907, *Johannesburg Star*.

8   Speech at mass meeting, August 10, 1908, *Collected Works*, Volume 8, p. 436.

9   Letter to Doke, July 25, 1908, *Collected Works*, Volume 8, p. 399, December 1962 edn.

interesting tussle between the instincts of the lawyer, intent upon defence of the resisters, and the desire to make a moving spectacle of self-suffering powerful enough to engender sympathy and change in social attitudes.

A student of Gandhi's life trying to chalk out his inner growth, his incipient idea that self-suffering would move hearts and minds becoming a conviction, would be almost at his wit's end to understand these thoughts striking roots in Gandhi's mind despite his exposure to the unrelenting, remorseless cruelty of the colonists towards the Zulus. Had he discerned any inklings of compassion; any pangs of contrition in any quarters; any hint of corrective will and action? If they had already demonstrated their opacity to such sentiments, why would their hearts suddenly melt for the British Indians? Gandhi still thought they would. He had to jolt his community into a new awareness of their dire predicament. He had to persuade them to suffer for their cause, for their dignity, for their future. He had to convince them and fortify their will to go to jail in a brave, unbending assertion of their basic humanity. That would oblige even Smuts to bend!

Gandhis' great faith in the courts and his hope that the Supreme Court would order the Government to return their papers, were certainly misplaced. It was too much to expect the Supreme Court to undermine the writ of the very Government, of which it was itself an important part. The court would certainly not countenance any defiance of law and the Government of the day by thousands of Indians. It was nothing but wishful thinking on the part of Gandhi, as the court system had clearly demonstrated its subservience to the Government on so many occasions. Gandhi had his successes in a few places, but not enough really to rock the Government's boat or halt its operations.[10]

Indian Opinion warned of the resumption of *Satyāgraha*. If the court did not help with the return of their papers, the Indians could achieve the same purpose by burning their own permits and certificates of registration. Gandhi hoped that the threat of burning their certificates would persuade Smuts to honour the original accord. He therefore advised the Indians that there was only one remedy. They had to ignore the Government and its law; burn their certificates of voluntary registration when necessary to do so; and refuse to affix their fingerprints or signatures on any documents,

---

10   Cf. DiSalvo, *op.cit.*, p. 268.

or to give their names when asked by the police to do so. They could tender the licence fee; but if the licence was refused, 'they should carry on trade without one...we want to go to jail'.[11] Imprisonment would be willingly accepted. Gandhi would provide legal assistance, 'free of charge as usual', to all resisters. The *Satyāgraha* would be for Indians who had Boer certificates of residence; for residents of the Transvaal who were currently outside the colony; and, of course, for the educated Indians.

Smuts wanted to make the repeal of the Act contingent upon an agreement to completely ban the entry of Indians into the Transvaal. But Gandhi wanted the Government to except educated Indians, who should be allowed to enter, as they could under the existing law. Excluding or barring only educated Indians, not the other educated immigrants, would be a very invidious act of discrimination. The rights of educated Indians, like Gandhi himself, were vitally important; a racial barrier was anathema; white supremacy could certainly not last for ever! Smuts countered with his opinion that the current law did not allow even the educated Indians to enter the colony. In point of fact, though, Indians able to write and understand English were not barred by the law as it currently stood. This was the Immigrants' Restriction Act of 1907.

Gandhi found a client to mount a test case to prove that he was right and Smuts was wrong. Sorabji Shapurji of Natal, a Parsi proficient in English volunteered to enter the Transvaal, while Gandhi was announcing the Indians' readiness to burn their registration certificates. If the authorities refused him entry, Gandhi could mount a test case to prove that they were wrong, and had no right to do so. The law did not bar educated Indians from entering the colony.

Gandhi forewarned Chamney, and told him that Sorabji was proficient in English, apart from being a man of means. Sorabji was surprisingly allowed to enter without any let or hindrance on June 24, 1908. Smuts and Chamney knew that their legal position was anything but strong; and did not want to provide an instance for purposes of propaganda to their undaunted adversary.

Sorabji found his way to Johannesburg. The police kept an eye on him, but did nothing else. But then, they arrested him on July 4. They did not

---

11 'Johannesburg Letter', before July 2, 1908, *Collected Works*, Volume 8, p. 329.

accuse him of being a prohibited immigrant. He was arrested as he had failed to register. This, too, was done to deny Gandhi the legal forum to challenge Smuts and the Government. On July 8, Sorabji was presented before magistrate H.H. Jordan for his trial. He pleaded not guilty. Gandhi told Chamney that his officers did not ask Sorabji at the border whether he qualified under the IRA to enter the Transvaal. He pointed out that Sorabji had the requisite English qualifications, and also that he was a man of sufficient means. Gandhi clearly showed that Chamney had no ground to stand upon.

The magistrate discharged Sorabji. But he was re-arrested and recharged with the same offence. He had failed to register under the Act. Even though the magistrate was impressed by Gandhi's 'very subtle and very able arguments', the only consideration for him was that Sorabji was not registered. He ordered him out of the colony within seven days.

On July 20, 1908, Sorabji was once again before the magistrate. He had not left the colony; and said that he had deliberately disobeyed the court's order; and would do so again and again as a matter of principle. Gandhi pointed out to the court that a principle was at stake. It was an issue of conscience. Sorabji was sentenced to one month's imprisonment with hard labour. He could not be charged under the IRA, as he clearly qualified under its provisions. His example provided so many opportunities to publicize Gandhi's interpretation of the IRA, and its correctness.

Sorabjis' indomitable stand made him a hero, and an inspiration for the others to emulate. He told his Indian compatriots he would never comply with the unjust law; he would never leave the colony; he would always refuse to register; and he would gladly go to jail as many times as they sentenced him. Gandhi gave him the praise that was his due in columns of the *Indian Opinion*.

The ignominious escape of Ram Sundar Pandit had shamed the Indians' resolution to stand up, suffer and be counted without wilting under tyranny. Sorabji was a breath of fresh air; an icon of Inflexible will; a herald of revolt against oppressive injustice; a beacon of determination and hope!

With the hopes of Indians dashed by the intransigence of the Government, Gandhi laid down the next step they had to take. Indians in possession of licences would return them to the Government; would trade without them;

and would stay ready for arrest and imprisonment. *Satyāgraha* flickered into life once more. So many hawkers surrendered their licences to be returned to the Government. They were comparatively poor Indians eking out a living from the sale of fruits, vegetables and other items from the baskets that they carried around. Their disobedience was calculated to convince the Europeans that the struggle was based on a principle. The Indian suffering would help bring about a change of mind; a change of attitude. So Gandhi hoped!

The normal sentence for hawking without a licence was a week in prison. Thambi Naidoo, the Tamil stalwart of *Satyāgraha*, an unflinching supporter of Gandhi, had led his people since July 1907, when they stoutly opposed finger-printing and registration. When Gandhi struck a deal with Smuts, Thambi supported him. But when Smuts reneged on his word, Thambi Naidoo stood undaunted in the vanguard of the struggle once more, leading his people into jail. He was a true passive resister suffering in proud silence without complaint. The Gujaratis wavered, but under Thambi Naidoo's banner, the Tamils provided solid support to Gandhi and his movement. Thambi had saved Gandhi's life from the savage attack of the Pathans; and he was there yet again, to suffer for the cause with resolution and purpose, regardless of the serious personal consequences for him; for his family and business. Men like him helped make Gandhi what and who he was! Gandhi was not lacking in fulsome acknowledgement of the sacrifices and suffering of a *satyāgrahī* 'with few equals', a happy and prosperous family man, who was now 'a proud pauper, a true patriot, and one of the most desirable of citizens of the Transvaal, indeed of South Africa...'[12] He was sentenced to jail for the third time within a month in the last week of July, 1908.

Unlicensed hawkers were arrested from July 20 onwards. Gandhi and Polak defended them; and told the court that they were not professional hawkers; but were protesting against the policies of the Government. Till early October 8, Gandhi represented 58 resisters in court. In some cases he instructed his clients to plead not guilty. In others he asked them to plead guilty. The leader of civil disobedience, himself representing the persons charged in court, presented a paradoxical display of defiance as well as compliance!

---

12   Cf. Guha, *op.cit.*, p. 294.

The judges decreed that the defendants could pay a fine, or else go to jail for two to seven days, generally with hard labour. The defendants invariably opted for jail. Gandhi intended to advance the public debate through these trials; and succeeded in doing so by repeatedly apprising the media of the painful predicament of Indians many times over.

The Government made an exception of 14 Indians who were exempted from giving thumb impressions. Gandhi insisted that this unfair partiality was indefensible; but the magistrate, in compliance with the dictates of the Government, did not allow him to see the list. This magisterial submission to the will of the Government, right or wrong, moved Gandhi away from the courts to embrace civil disobedience.

Only a few decisions, and they were exceptions, questioned and quashed the high-handedness of the authorities; and even those rare victories and vindications in courts of law could easily be nullified and wiped out by fresh Government decrees or action.

In several cases Gandhi fought against convictions on grounds of procedure without success. Defence on technicalities unrelated to the issues of civil disobedience detracted from the moral merits of non-cooperation and consequent self-suffering and self-sacrifice. Such tactics, if successful, could only lengthen the duration of civil disobedience by other means, and defeat any discrimination only for a limited amount of time. Gandhi perhaps intended to soften the impact on Indian volunteers, while at the same time hoping against hope that the authorities might have a change of heart and do the right thing.

In some cases, Gandhi offered no defence whatsoever. A group of 6 Indians in one case were charged on July 28, 1908, with hawking without any licence. They pleaded guilty. Gandhi said that he would not call any witnesses; and told the magistrate that he had been instructed by the prisoners to ask for the severest possible punishment for them. P.C. Dalmahoy, the magistrate imposed a fine of £1 on five of them or seven days in prison. The sixth person, Thambi Naidoo, was, however, sentenced to a fine of £2, or fourteen days in prison, owing to his previous convictions.

One of the 6 accused was Gandhi's own son Harilal. His eldest son was on trial for unlicensed hawking. Gandhi made no attempt to defend his son or the others. Harilal was 20, when he decided to participate in the

Satyāgraha. He came across from Natal, determined not to register, and started hawking fruits without any licence. To quote Gandhi: 'I have advised every Indian to take up hawking. I am afraid I cannot join myself since I am enrolled as an attorney. I therefore thought it right to advise my son to make his rounds as a hawker. I hesitate to ask others to do things which I cannot do myself. I think whatever my son does at my instance can be taken to have been done by me. It will be part of Harilal's education to go to jail for the sake of the country'.[13]

Harilal, as he said, represented him and his ideal of self-suffering arising out of civil disobedience unmitigated by any legal argument in extenuation, or any legal tactic, or procedural misstep in prosecution, to soften or ward off any blow of punishment. He must appear in court as a paragon of willing self-suffering to uplift and sanctify the struggle for justice; to activate the dormant founts of compassion; to ignite soul-searching in the European community. He wanted to assist and enable them through his and his country-men's self-suffering to rise above narrow self-interest to grant Indians the basic freedoms without which their lives would be devoid of any dignity; their future would be bereft of any hope and sense of security; and their economic survival would become impossible!

Harilal did not contest any charges. His attorney was a silent spectator, as he was arraigned and sentenced. That set an example for emulation. Gandhi made himself quite clear in the columns of *Indian Opinion*: '... Satyagraha is easy for those who understand it well... I do not, strictly speaking, defend them but only send them to gaol. If we have acquired real courage, there should be no need for me to present myself in court. I thought it only proper that I should make this experiment in the first instance with my son... Since there were others with him in Johannesburg, I attended the court, but asked for the maximum penalty for him and for his associates. It was their misfortune that they did not get it.'

Gandhi acted as a defence lawyer for ordinary *satyāgrahīs*. He explained why they acted as they did; he made it as difficult as possible for the prosecution to procure a sentence against them. The true *satyāgrahīs*, like his son and his associates, needed no such defence. They accepted their punishment in silence. Their lawyer stood silent, as they stood silent. Silent

---

13 'Letter to Indian Opinion', August 8, 1908, *Collected Works*, Vol. 8, p. 432, 1962 edn.

submission to punishment would present a picture of their suffering for a cause, for an unexceptionable principle, for justice, for fairplay. And they hoped to move hearts and minds. They hoped to bring about change, not through violence, not through conflict, not through angry confrontation and demonstration, but through self-suffering.

Gandhi explained in the *Indian Opinion* that those willing to undergo imprisonment should do so without the need for a lawyer or Gandhi to defend them. He was still prepared to defend Indian *satyāgrahīs* arrested against the law. He would go anywhere needed. The best way, though, was to undergo any sentence imposed without recourse to any lawyer.

He was willing and ready to defend those who wanted to avoid or resist jail if possible. He would find and highlight any and every extenuating circumstance, and use every procedural tactic to achieve his goal. But there were those who wanted to illustrate and publicize the justice of their cause through silent self-suffering as a moral expression of their civil resistance. Their silence was their defence and their exculpation! Their suffering was an attempt at cleansing the self as well as the minds of their adversaries. They did not need a lawyer. They needed only themselves, their sense of right, their sense of moral conviction, and their fortitude to bend the will of the tyrant. That is how civil disobedience was shaping itself!

In an interview to the *Star* Gandhi said: 'When I talk of equality of treatment in the eye of the law, the idea is jeered at... To my mind it is the only thing that binds the Empire together.'[14]

It was decided to publicly burn the certificates on Sunday July 12, 1908. The threat had to be more than mere vociferous shouting in thin air. They did not do so on the day at the request of Albert Cartwright and William Hosken, who tried to build a bridge between Gandhi and Smuts once more, without success. Smuts even sought to malign Gandhi when he said that the latter was fleecing permit-seekers, and charging Muslims even more! Gandhi decried the 'damnable lie'.[15] The tactic of 'divide and rule' was at work!

Gandhi then announced that the voluntary registration certificates were in

---

14 *Collected Works*, Vo. 9, p. 30, 1963 edn; cf. also, 'Petition to Secretary of State for Colonies', *Collected Works*, Vol. 8, pp. 28-29.

15 Cf. Guha, *op. cit.*, p. 291.

possession of the British Indian Association, and a decision to burn them would await knowledge of the Government's intended legislation. Weeks passed. Nothing happened. Smuts had uncompromisingly demanded a complete ban on the entry of Indians into the Transvaal as a necessary condition for repeal of the Act. Indians demanded an exception for educated Indians to continue to enter the colony. That was indeed no more than the current law allowed. Smuts spurned the Indian demand to retain the status quo. And to regularize the voluntary registration of Indians with new legislation, he proceeded with the Validation Bill in Parliament to achieve his goal.

The Indians lost no time to petition the Transvaal Parliament against the Bill. Their plea was ignored. Tired and desperate, they set a date for burning their certificates. Gandhi wrote once more to Smuts to inform him of the date, still beseeching a fair solution. The minister was unmoved.

On August 16, 1908, some 3000 Indians gathered in the grounds of the Fordsburg Mosque. People had come from all over the Transvaal, and all available space was taken. When they could not find any room on the ground, they sat on the rooftops around. The Chinese were represented by their leader Leung Quinn. 1500 certificates and 500 trading licences had been surrendered, to be consigned to flames.

The first to speak was the chairman of the British Indian Association, Essop Mian, followed by Gandhi, who told his audience that he was giving them his well-considered advice as their lawyer. He outlined the careful course he had pursued to finally find it imperative to tell them what to do. He had thought about everything; and he had prayed for guidance. The Indians, he said, could either disobey the law and accept the resulting suffering, or else meekly submit to the humiliation and ignominy of the Validation Act. He chose and advised disobedience and suffering. He wanted them to burn their certificates. There was thunderous applause!

Gandhi's evocative words were charged with his memorable eloquence. He explained the significance of their struggle: 'To my mind its significance did not commence with a demand for the repeal of the Asiatic Act…It is open to the Government of the Colony to give a repeal of this legislation today, to throw dust into our eyes and then embark upon other legislation, far harsher, far more humiliating, but the lesson that I wanted to learn myself, the lesson I would have my countrymen to learn from this struggle is this: that un-enfranchised, unrepresented though we are in the Transvaal, it is open to us to clothe ourselves with an undying franchise, and this consists in recognizing our humanity, in recognizing that we are part and parcel of the great Universal Whole, that there is the Maker of us all ruling over the destinies of mankind and that our trust should be in Him rather than in earthly kings, and if my countrymen recognize this position, I say that no matter what legislation is passed over our heads, if that legislation is in conflict with our ideas of right and wrong, if it is in conflict with our conscience, if it is in conflict with our religion, then we can say we shall not submit to that legislation.'

Gandhi said that they would not use any physical force. They would accept the penalties. He refused to call this defiance. It was a 'perfectly respectful attitude for a man or a human being who calls himself man.' He asked British Indians to wage their struggle with this method; and to exhort their countrymen to adopt this method.[16]

Gandhi questioned the integrity of Chamney, Registrar of Asiatics. He called him utterly ignorant and totally incompetent. Chamney was present when, according to Gandhi, Smuts gave a pledge to repeal the Act. Chamney himself thereafter confirmed it to Gandhi; but then denied the existence of this promise in an affidavit to the Supreme Court. He was a liar, and his presence in office was an insuperable obstacle to peace in the colony. There was repeated applause.

Then the deed was done. A huge black cauldron full of these certificates and licences was set alight by Yusuf Mian with a roar of wild applause. The Chinese also flung their certificates into the fire. Lo and behold! Among those present to participate in the protest was Mir Alam, who had attacked Gandhi with murderous intent on February 10, 1908. The Pathan apologized, and Gandhi hugged him; there were no hard feelings.[17] This was the first of many bonfires that figured in Gandhi's long-drawn-out struggle against the exploitative and iniquitous policies of the British raj. And half a century later, black nationalists enacted an identical form of protest against Apartheid by burning the passes that they were required to carry. The similarity of action does not require any documentary proof of

---

16 'Speech at mass meeting', August 16, 1908, *Collected Works*, Vol. 8, p.456, 1962 edn.

17 Cf. Tendulkar, *op.cit.*, p. 116.

inspiration.[18] A sculpted iron cauldron on a tripod outside the Fordsburg Mosque commemorates Gandhi's protest in post-Apartheid South Africa.

A day later, Smuts asked Gandhi to see him. This meeting was attended by the Prime minister Botha, Sir Percy Fitzpatrick, Leader of the Opposition, William Hosken, Albert Cartwright and Leung Quinn. Following three hours of talk, the Government finally agreed to permit the pre-war residents to return and register; and not to register children under sixteen. They would also permit people to give their signatures instead of thumb impressions, when applying for trading licences. But they would not allow the admittance and immigration of educated Indians. They would not repeal the Act of 1907; but they would let it remain a 'dead letter'.[19]

Three days later, Smuts brought a new bill to the Parliament with concessions relating to the Boer certificates and minors; but educated Indians were deliberately barred. He admitted the awkward position of the Government dealing with passive resistance. The jails were full of Indians from one end of the country to the other. This was indeed undesirable; and he had therefore decided to release Gandhi and the others. The bill was passed within twenty-four hours of its first reading.

Indians were no doubt unsatisfied. The Black Act still stood in place, to be evoked at any time at the sweet will of the Government. Educated Indians found the gates of entry into the Transvaal bolted and barred. On August 23, 1908, there was another mass meeting, and bonfire of more certificates, outside the Fordsburg Mosque! Gandhi wrote to Smuts, asking him to show statesmanship to resolve the dispute simmering for almost two years. But his plea was ignored.

Gandhi was always and ever learning, with his eyes and ears open; with his mind receptive; with an unceasing, inexhaustible capacity for compromise and self-correction; always seeking to improve his understanding of the world and its people; of his own friends and so-called foes, whom he never regarded as enemies. Sometimes he tried to win with words; sometimes with silence. He evolved; his ideas evolved; and his tactics evolved in the

---

18 Cf. Lelyveld, *Great Soul: Mahatma Gandhi and His Struggle with India,* p. 14, where he talks of the need for corroboration despite the popular perception of a connection.

19 Cf. Guha, *op. cit.,* pp. 300, 602, n.7; Tendulkar, *op. cit.,* p. 117.

rough and tumble of life, in accordance with necessity. He might have been growing rigid in matters of personal, physical concern; but he was always approachable and ever malleable in dialogue and discussion on issues of social, economic and political relevance.

He was acutely aware of the attributes of self-suffering, but not yet fully appreciative of its place and function in *Satyāgraha*. His ideas and his strategies were still in a state of gradual, progressive evolution. He knew that self-suffering could evoke sympathy and spontaneous assistance. Lawyers and legal procedure could, however, seriously diminish its impact, which Gandhi did not immediately grasp. DiSalvo thinks that Gandhi and his fellow lawyers detracted from the perception of Indian misery, self-suffering and martyrdom, with their approach to Indian cases between July and early October 1908.

Gandhi stridently called upon his countrymen to 'fill the jails'. An unending stream of Indian jail-goers would 'tire out the government', which would be forced to give in. Civil disobedience would mean disowning the power of Smuts and his government to govern. Gandhi also wanted to make use of Indian disobedience and suffering to dent the apathy of the British, and translate their sympathy into some corrective action to assuage Indian concerns. Indian *Satyāgraha* could stir people's minds, provoke debate and bring change for the better. The threefold strategy consisted of 'withdrawing consent, advancing the debate, and creating political change'.

Prominent Indians came into the Transvaal from Natal to challenge the Government's interpretations of the IRA. Harilal came to the border again, and was allowed to go through. But they finally arrested him on August 10, as he had not registered under the Act, and his defiance was too public to be ignored. Gandhi repeated what he had done at his son's previous trial for hawking without a licence. Harilal pleaded guilty. Gandhi requested the magistrate to order him to leave the colony within 24 Hours. The magistrate, though, gave Harilal seven days to leave the Transvaal. He did not leave; and was again in the dock on August 19. An Indian lawyer, Godfrey, also offered no defence, and no statement. Harilal pleaded guilty, and was sentenced to one month's jail with hard labour.

In other cases, Gandhi asked his clients to plead not guilty, and strenuously argued in their defence, without success. His friend and associate Henry

Polak also defended Indians, who tried to exercise their 'right of entry as educated immigrants, pre-war residents, or because they held permits under the Peace Preservation Ordinance'.[20] Legal and procedural defences were mounted to wear out the prosecution; to publicize the truth of gross injustice amongst those who read newspapers; and to goad and encourage the authorities in England to do something.

Fighting every case in court provided good publicity for the Indian cause; contributed to the ongoing debate; and sought to strain the Government and its resources to a point where they would perhaps comprehend the futility and gross injustice of their Act and its intent. But a *satyāgrahī* resister steadfastly refusing to mount any defence, and silently embracing any punishment presented a different spectacle of studied self-effacement and self-suffering,[21] which would make people morally uneasy and inquisitive about the factors that made men resort to desperate self-harm and self-imposed misery.

Gandhi, however, also wanted to demonstrate the gross injustice of multiple registrations to which Indians were subjected. That would become patently perceptible only when cases were tried, arguments were advanced, statements were made to spell out in full public view the morally indefensible nature of the law or laws in question. Two methods were therefore used to achieve two purposes: to demonstrate the iniquity of the Law; and to rouse the sympathy of those whose intervention could mend matters. The first method exercised the intellect; the second touched the heart-strings of some, if not all. So there were those who did everything legally possible to avoid suffering, and accept punishment only when it was inevitable. But there were those cheerfully embracing suffering without mounting any defence whatsoever, to tug at the emotions of human sympathy and compassion. Gandhi had not yet quite understood the distinction between the two methods in relation to public reaction.[22] The crossing of borders, the refusal to register, the burning of certificates, the repeated acts of defiant disobedience failed to placate Smuts, or move the British Government to take any remedial measures.

Many Indians in Natal held old rights of domicile in the Transvaal. They

---

20   Cf. DiSalvo. *op.cit.*, p. 286.

21   *Ibid.*

22   DiSalvo, *op. cit.*, p. 288.

were also proficient in English. Big businessmen like Sheth Daud Mohamed and Parsi Rustomji came to the Transvaal on August 18 to demonstrate their support. They went round the Transvaal towns collecting certificates to burn; but were arrested after a week, warned and deported to Natal. Not to be denied, they re-entered the Transvaal on August 31, and resumed their campaign, visiting Indian homes in Johannesburg and raising 200 pounds for the movement. They then proceeded to Heidelberg and Standerton to continue their collection; but were arrested again, and on September 8, sentenced to a fine of 50 pounds or three months' jail with hard labour. They cheerfully opted for jail.[23] Indians in the Transvaal hawking without licences were arrested, tried and jailed, for periods ranging from four days to three months.

Notwithstanding their limited resources, working class Tamils of the Transvaal were much more enthusiastic than the Gujarati merchants in their passive resistance. One-fourth of them had been to prison at least once by the end of August, 1908, risking all they had for upholding the dignity of the larger community.[24]

Gandhi approached the Transvaal Government with a new suggestion. A certain number of educated Indians, not more than six, should be allowed entry into the Transvaal every year. He had come in as a lawyer; and did not want other educated Indians to be refused entry into the Transvaal altogether. With proper education, Indians could doubtless prove themselves equal to any competition, whatsoever! It was a matter of principle; of national pride!

One Johannesburg paper called his demand very reasonable. The Transvaal Government had 'for the first time in the history of the Empire' enacted a law that 'in no circumstances, under no conditions, shall the people from another of the imperial states set foot here.'[25] The Government dreaded the prospect of more Gandhis than one, as they also dreaded any demand for greater rights. They could not view with equanimity even a distant semblance of racial equality! The Government resorted to resolute

---

23 *Collected Works*, 8, pp. 481; 9, pp. 3,8, 13, 29; Tendulkar, *op. cit.*, p. 117; Guha, *op.cit.*, p. 302.

24 *Collected Works*, 9, p. 4; Dayal, Bhawani, *Dakṣiṇa Afrīcā ke Satyāgraha kā Itihāsa*, Saraswati Sadan, Indore, 1916, p. 24; Guha, *op.cit.*, p. 302.

25 Cf. *Transvaal Weekly Illustrated,* 12 September, 1908.

repression. The shops of merchants who had participated in the *Satyāgraha* were shut down. And their goods and wares were seized and auctioned.

At a meeting of the British Indian Association on September 7, 1908, Gandhi asked for financial provision, as he had suspended his legal practice. It was decided that the work done by Henry Polak and Sonja Schlesin would be financed by the Association. Gandhi's, and his family's needs, would be paid for by Kallenbach, who now became his personal financier.[26] At about this time, Gandhi and Kallenbach started calling each other Upper House and Lower House. The Lower House was in charge of finance in accordance with the Westminster system. They continued to use these nicknames for each other in all their correspondence till 1917, and then again in mid-1930s. Kallenbach was allowed to incur any expense only after the approval of Gandhi, who was always advising restraint and economy, telling him to treat his own money like public funds. Gandhi, with complete faith in his friend, appointed Kallenbach chief executor of his will.[27]

Visit to Phoenix

Gandhi went to Phoenix towards the end of September, 1908, to devote some time and attention to the small school operating there. The principal was a Gujarati gentleman named Purushottamdas Desai. Albert West and John Cordes also taught at the school. The curriculum was in Gujarati as well as English. Boys were instructed in the religion of their choice. Desai taught Hindus the Hindu religion. West looked after the Christian boys, instructing them in their faith; and a visiting *Maulvi* taught the Muslims. Cordes, a theosophist, taught those who sought unorthodox spirituality.

Gandhi typically took special care of what the boys ate. Green vegetables, fresh fruit, pulses, rice, bread, milk, ghee, sugar and groundnuts were provided. Tea, cocoa and coffee were prohibited, as they were produced by men 'who work more or less in conditions of slavery.'[28] Gandhi wanted the school to take boarders from different parts of Natal.

In an interview to *Natal Mercury*, Gandhi said that the Transvaal Indians

---

26 Cf. Lev, Shimon, *op.cit.*, p. 16; *Collected Works*, Vol. 9, p. 602; *Indian Opinion,* 15 September 1908.

27 Lev, *op.cit.*, p. 17.

28 Cf. *Collected Works*, 8, p. 85; 9, pp. 135-9.

were fighting for 'the honour of India, and for a principle'. Any restrictions should not be based on race or colour. They could make the education test as difficult as they wished. Exclusion on racial grounds was not acceptable. The brightest jewel in the British Crown could not be used for target practice from every possible quarter.[29]

Gandhi crossed into the Transvaal with fifteen others, and was arrested at Volksrust on October 7, 1908. He could not show any registration papers as he had burnt his certificate; and declined to give his thumb impression, which would have amounted to compliance with the Act. He was remanded to Volksrust prison for a week, as he refused to avail of any bail. Produced before a magistrate on October 14, he said he had advised his companions to enter the colony; and asked for the maximum punishment, which was three months' hard labour. The prosecutor also demanded the maximum sentence, as Gandhi's sin was admittedly greater. But the magistrate felt sorry to see him in this situation brought on by his belief that he was suffering for his country. He was sentenced to pay a fine of 25 pounds, or imprisonment with hard labour for two months. He cheerfully chose imprisonment, declaring himself 'the happiest man in the Transvaal'; and in a message to his people, exhorted them to 'keep absolutely firm to the end. Suffering is our only remedy. Victory is certain'.[30]

He was housed in the Volksrust jail; made to dig pits, break stones and work with road gangs as part of the hard labour; and also assigned a sweeper's job for some time. Two weeks later, they took him to Johannesburg, and marched him through the streets in convict garb to the prison, where he was lodged with hard-core convicts serving time for murder and other serious offences. He was appalled by scenes of obscenity around him; and the fear of possible sexual assault kept him awake for a night, drawing strength from passages of the *Gītā*. A few days later, he was moved to another cell full of Indians, where, however, he was one day bodily lifted and tossed out of a doorless lavatory that he had just occupied by 'a strong, heavily-built, fearful-looking native'.[31]

A meeting held in Caxton Hall in London on October 16, 1908, protested against the imprisonment of Gandhi. Sir M. Bhownaggree presided; and

---

29   Interview to *Natal Mercury, Collected Works,* 9, pp. 77-9.

30   *Collected Works*, Vol. 9, p. 104.

31   Cf. Gandhi, Rajmohan, *op.cit.*, p. 128.

Lala Lajpat Rai, Savarkar, Kharpade, Bipin Chandra Pal and Dr. Ananda Coomaraswamy spoke. Two resolutions were adopted; and the inhuman treatment of Indians in South Africa was severely condemned. A protest meeting in the Transvaal on October 18 was attended by about 1500 people, who came from all parts of the Colony to express their anguish and indignation at their leader's incarceration. The principal speaker A.M. Cachalia warned the Government that Gandhi's sentence would make each one of them a leader in their own right, adding greater strength and purpose to the movement.

Chapter 50

Fortitude of Kasturba

On November 4, Gandhi was moved back to Volksrust, where he heard of Kasturba's serious illness and haemorrhage from Albert West at Phoenix. The doctor was apprehensive of the worst; and West therefore asked Gandhi to pay the fine and get out, to be with his wife. That, Gandhi said, was 'impossible'. 'If Mrs. Gandhi must leave me without even the consolation a devoted husband could afford, so be it'.[1] Painfully competing loyalties were at play. He owed alike to his family; society and community! He certainly loved his wife, as she wholeheartedly loved him. They had been faithful partners for more than 25 years. But the interests of the community had precedence. Gandhi wrote to Manilal, so that he could read his letter to Kasturba. He had offered whatever he had to the 'Satyagraha struggle'. He could just not pay the fine. He asked for a daily bulletin on her health. There were tender words of consolation and encouragement: '...you will recover. If, however, my ill-luck so has it that you pass away...there would be nothing wrong in doing so in your separation from me while I am still alive. I love you so dearly that even if you are dead, you will be alive for me. Your soul is deathless. I repeat what I have frequently told you that if you succumb to your illness, I will not marry again...If you die, even that death of yours will be a sacrifice to the cause of Satyagraha...'[2]

Guha[3] writes: 'According to custom and tradition, part of the duties of a Hindu wife was to make sure that she did not predecease her husband.' But that is no doubt incorrect. There is nothing more dreadful and undesirable

---

1 *Collected Works*, Vol. 9, p. 105.

2 *Ibid.*, 'Letter to Mrs. Kasturba Gandhi', November 9, 1908, p. 106.

3 Guha, *op.cit.*, p. 308.

than widowhood; and every Hindu wife therefore wishes to die before her husband as a *sadhavā, saubhāgyavatī* or *suhāgin,* bedecked with all the marks and adornments of the married state in her funeral ceremony.

Gandhi was released from jail in early December.

He tells us that his wife Kasturba had three serious illnesses, in which she came back from death's door. He attributes her cures and recovery to 'household remedies'. In the last week of December, 1908, Gandhi went to Phoenix to be with Kasturba, who was very ill, suffering from frequent haemorrhage. He moved her to Durban to stay there under the care of Dr. Nanji, a Parsi, the best Indian doctor in town, and a supporter of the *satyāgraha*. A surgical operation without chloroform helped, even though it gave her indescribable pain. She was brave, but extremely weak and utterly emaciated. The doctor and his wife nursed her with the greatest care, and told Gandhi that he could go to Johannesburg. There was no cause for anxiety; and they would look after her. A few days later, he heard that her condition had got worse; she was suffering from pernicious anaemia; and had become too weak even to sit up in bed. The doctor sought Gandhi's permission to give her beef tea. Gandhi immediately replied in the negative, but also said that she should herself be consulted if she was fit enough to decide. The doctor refused to consult the patient's wishes and asked Gandhi to come. If the doctor was not free to prescribe the diet he considered necessary for his patient, he would not take any responsibility for Kasturba's life.

Gandhi arrived by the next train available, and met Dr. Nanji, who told him that he had already given beef tea to Kasturba. Gandhi protested that this was an act of fraud, to which the doctor curtly retorted that the prescription of any medicine or food for a patient was a doctor's prerogative. Doctors loved deceiving patients or relatives, whenever they could save lives by doing so. Even though Gandhi was grateful to the doctor, he told him that he would never allow him to feed meat or beef to Kasturba, 'even if the denial meant her death.'[4] If Kasturba herself agreed or desired to take beef or meat, he would have no objection. The doctor was adamant and told Gandhi that he would not treat Kasturba if he was not free to give her anything to eat, which was meant to bring her back to health. If Gandhi did not agree, he would ask him to remove his wife from under his roof. He did not want to see her die owing to Gandhi's obduracy. When Gandhi asked if he had to remove her immediately, the doctor protested that he had

---

4   *Autobiography,* p. 328.

never told him to do so. He only wanted to be free to treat her to the best of his ability, so that he and his wife could nurse her back to good health. If Gandhi found it impossible to understand the doctor's sense of obligation to his patient, the latter would have no alternative left but to ask him to take his wife away.

One of Gandhi's sons, who was with him, agreed with his father that they should not give beef tea to his mother. Gandhi then spoke to his wife; but tells us that she was 'too weak to be consulted in this matter'. When asked, his submissive wife, with her will wilted by disease and debility, additionally weighed down by the burden of lifelong dietary prohibitions, replied that she would certainly not take any beef tea. She would prefer death to pollution of her body with what the doctor prescribed. Gandhi tells us that he reminded his wife of the fact that many Hindu friends gladly ate meat and drank wine as medicine. If she so wished, she did not have to follow him. Kasturba, battered by haemorrhage and illness, asked her husband to take her away. Gandhi was 'delighted.' When told that he was going to take her away, the doctor lost his temper and accused Gandhi of unfeeling callousness. Without mincing words, the doctor told him that he was behaving shamefully in discussing the matter with her in her precarious condition. Kasturba was too weak to be removed. She could very easily die on the way. If, however, Gandhi still so wished, he could take her away. The doctor would not keep her under his roof if he was not free to give her anything to eat, including beef tea.

Gandhi conveniently or blindly forgot that he had himself enjoyed meat in the company of his boyhood friend Mehtab, while at school, and the heavens had not fallen. His wife's very life was at stake. But that was less important than his religious convictions and slavish abidance. He took his wife away at once. The weather was wet. It was raining. They had to cover some distance to get to the station. They took the train from Durban to Phoenix, from where the settlement was two and a half miles away. Six men took Kasturba in a hammock from the station to the farm. Gandhi felt secure in his faith in God, while the ailing wife tried to comfort him with words such as 'nothing will happen to me. Don't worry.'[5] At Phoenix, a Swami came to convince Gandhi that religious texts including Manu allowed the consumption of meat, but Gandhi was unmoved. His vegetarianism did not require any scriptural sanction. Kasturba could not herself read any texts; but held fast to the convictions of her forefathers.

---

5   *Ibid.*, p. 239.

It seems that Kasturba recovered somewhat under Gandhi's care; but her recuperation had a setback when she began to haemorrhage again. Hydropathic treatment proved of no avail. Despite her misgivings about Gandhi's treatment, she gave in, but did not improve. Gandhi's remedies were failing. He then asked her to give up salt and pulses. She did not agree, and challenged Gandhi to give them up, if he could do so. Gandhi told her that he would give up anything without hesitation if advised by doctors to do so. He totally forgot the great contradiction between this statement and his disagreement with Kasturba's doctor in Durban. He told his wife that he would henceforth give up salt and pulses for one year. Poor Kasturba was shocked, and promised to stop taking salt and pulses, and pressed Gandhi to take back his vow. He, however, told her that he could not go back on his vow; and restraint would always do him good. The poor woman melted into tears. Gandhi regards this incident as an exercise in *satyāgraha*; and calls it 'one of the sweetest recollections' of his life.[6]

Even though Kasturba's condition was delicate, and she was not yet out of danger, Gandhi had to go back to Johannesburg. Painfully pressing problems weighed on his mind. He wrote to Kallenbach: 'I fear that my departure next week will send her to her grave.'

Kasturba began to improve. Was it the food without salt and pulses, and the changes in her diet? Was it Gandhi's exaction of obedience to the other rules of life that he laid down? Or was it the 'mental exhilaration' arising out of this incident? Gandhi does not know, but tells us that the haemorrhage stopped, and his reputation as a quack soared. He himself felt better after giving up salt and pulses. It helped him control his senses. He abstained from both salt and pulses for a long time, and only once ate both in London in 1914. Gandhi tried a diet without pulses and salt on a number of his co-workers in South Africa; and tells us that the results were good. Medical opinions may vary, but 'all self-denial is good for the soul'. A man practising self-restraint has to eat differently from a 'man of pleasure'. *Brahmacarya* demands dietary restraints not observed by common humanity.

---

6   *Ibid.*, p. 241.

Chapter 51

Towards a Union of South Africa

The idea of South Africa as a united state had been brewing ever since the Boer War. In May, 1908, an intercolonial conference of the four territories was organized to discuss the modalities of a federation. A 'National Convention' followed, with meetings in Durban and elsewhere. The examples of Canada and Australia, and economic considerations provided an impetus; but they also had a very large native population to consider, besides the Indians who added another element to the issues that they had to tackle. The Boers predominated at these parleys; and it was decided to seek a 'union of white races in South Africa'. Though the coloured voters in the Cape were an undesirable nuisance, they would not be deprived of franchise for the time being. In the rest of South Africa only whites would vote; and the Union Parliament would be free from the taint of colour. Lord Selborne's proposal to give a small measure of qualified vote to the natives and the coloureds was ruled out of order.

Two dissenting voices of a brother and sister sounded an alarm over the idea of building a grand structure 'upon unsound and sinking foundations'.[1] W. P. Schreiner, a former prime minister of Cape Colony, protested against creating a vertical barrier separating people on grounds of colour, and consigning the coloured races to the ranks of an unprivileged class deprived of any voice or representation. His sister, the writer Olive Schreiner, was even more outspoken and forthright in her view that 'all persons born in the country or permanently resident here should be one in the eye of the State.' She could vividly visualize the twenty-first century, in which 'it will not always be the European who forms the upper layer.' She spoke of the Europeans who 'loved freedom and justice'; of the natives, 'one of

---

1 Guha, *op. cit.*, pp. 312, 604, n.41.

the finest breeds of the African stock'; of the Asiatics, 'sober, industrious and intelligent'; and stressed that this 'heterogeneous mass' of humanity would form the nation of South Africa on a true basis of peace![2] That, indeed, was a delineation of Gandhi's dream projected in his speech to the YMCA a few months ago, but with a much sharper focus!

The Times of London published a letter signed by twenty-six European residents of the Transvaal in the first week of 1909. They included William Hosken, seven clergymen, a number of accountants, the jeweller Gabriel Isaacs, the draper W.M. Vogl, and the lawyer A.W. Baker. The signing priests included Joseph Doke and Charles Phillips. The letter was to let the British public know that 'an important body of sympathizers in the European section of the community' was 'grieved and hurt at the treatment being meted out to the Asiatics for no apparent purpose at all'. The letter lauded the 'courage and self-sacrifice' of the passive resisters who came from 'all faiths and castes'. Morality and the imperial interest alike dictated the concession of their just demands. If the passive resisters were deported, they would certainly spell trouble by garnering the sympathy of receptive audiences in India.[3]

---

2   'Olive Schreiner on Colour', *Indian Opinion,* 2 January, 1909.

3   *The Times,* 6 January 1909.

Chapter 52

Flagging Satyāgraha

Though Gandhi had given up his practice, he was back in court defending the *satyāgrahīs*. Some Indians, tired of the struggle, began to queue up for registration when the new amended Act became operative. And that revived picketing by the passive resisters led by Thambi Naidoo. People were losing hope; the traders and Gujaratis were reluctant to go to jail; but the Tamils were steadfast in their passive resistance. Gandhi praised the Tamils, and the Parsis, too, for their courageous persistence; and excoriated the timorous businessmen for their lack of will to bear any hardship. He cited 'the great Thoreau' who 'said that one sincere man is more than a hundred thousand insincere men'.[1]

Harilal

Harilal, Gandhi's eldest son, had already been twice in and out of jail. When not in jail, he worked for the movement in Johannesburg. His wife Chanchal at Phoenix felt forlorn without him; and he missed her terribly. They had a baby daughter, with whom they could spend little or no time together. The separation was most painful, and the days ahead looked bleak as Harilal prepared for a third term in jail. Back but briefly at Phoenix, the son confided his concerns to his father, who wrote back: '...I see that you will have to undergo imprisonment for a long period...The struggle is likely to be a prolonged one...Let me know what arrangement should be made in regard to Chanchal during your absence...'[2]

---

1 *Collected Works*, Vol. 9, pp. 130-32, 159-60, 184, 187, 193-4.
2 Cf. *Collected Works*, Vol. 9, p. 173, 'Letter to Harilal Gandhi', January 27, 1909.

Gandhi had already written to Chanchal on January 16 to help her understand that it would be good for both of them if she gave up 'the idea of staying with Harilal for the present.' 'Harilal will grow by staying apart and will perform his other duties. Love for you does not consist only in staying with you.'

Gandhi did not know how long the struggle would last. He hoped that Lord Curzon, who had condemned the 'odious' treatment of Indians in South Africa as India's Viceroy, would use his good offices during a private visit to persuade Botha and Smuts to do the right thing by them. Curzon could not find the time to meet Gandhi; but asked the Indians to give him a full statement of their case to enable him to talk it over with the generals. In his reply to Gandhi on February 2, 1909, Curzon wrote that Botha and Smuts had assured him 'of their anxiety to treat the British Indians with liberality and justice.' He felt that the matter 'would be taken up as a broader issue later between the Union and Home Governments.'[3]

Gujarati merchants were deserting the *Satyāgraha*. The Pathans had already attacked him twice. On January 29, Gandhi wrote to his nephew Maganlal:

'...My enthusiasm is such that I may have to meet death in South Africa at the hands of my own countrymen. If that happens you should rejoice. It will unite the Hindus and the Mussalmans. In this struggle a twofold inner struggle is going on. One of them is to bring the Hindus and the Muslims together. The enemies of the community are constantly making efforts against such a unity. In such a great endeavour, someone will have to sacrifice his life. If I make that sacrifice, I shall regard myself, as well as you, my colleagues, fortunate.'[4] An early presentiment of yet distant martyrdom!

Gandhi had been arrested at Volksrust on January 16, 1909, once again for his inability to produce a registration certificate; but was released on his own recognizance. He had come to Natal to look after the seriously ill Kasturba. We have already narrated that story!

He sent Harilal across the border to the Transvaal to court his third arrest and term of imprisonment in the second week of February; and on February

---

3   *Collected Works*, Vol. 9, p. 173, f.n.2.
4   *Ibid.*, p. 175.

25, was himself brought to trial before a magistrate at Volksrust. He told the court that he would continue to incur the penalties as long as justice was denied to a section of the citizens; and was sentenced to pay a fine of fifty pounds, or three months' imprisonment with hard labour. He chose prison.

Gandhi was happily surprised to find himself in the company of Parsi Rustomji and Harilal amongst the fifty or so *satyāgrahīs* in the Volksrust jail. The food served was 'nice and clean'; and the hard work included repairing roads and weeding crops. A week later, though, he was transferred to Pretoria, and allotted a cell marked 'isolated'. The other prisoners were all Africans. He slept on a hard bed without a pillow; and the food served included the hated mealie pap. He was made to polish floors; and forbidden to write letters in Gujarati despite his plea that his letters would serve as medicine to his seriously ill wife. He consoled her with a message via Albert West that he was 'all right'; and that she should carefully continue with her treatment; and adhere to her diet. He did not want to disturb her in her delicate state with any account of the trying conditions in which he still kept his spirits up. The news of his shabby treatment was, however, conveyed to the Governor Lord Selborne, and to London, by David Pollock and Henry Polak. Conditions improved. Smuts sent him a couple of books on religion; and Gandhi asked the boys at Phoenix to make a pair of sandals for the General. The leniency certainly owed something to the splendid tribute that Gandhi received from Lord Ampthill in the House of Lords. The Indians were opposing 'humiliating and offensive and unnecessary' laws. Their leader devoted 'all his means and most of his time and energy to public service and the purest philanthropy...This is the man who is leading this movement, and with him there are several hundreds of others who...will protest to the bitter end, whatever be the extremity of ruin or misery it brings upon them. In these circumstances it is simply fatuous to say that they have no good reason for undergoing suffering of this kind.'[5]

Smuts also received a strong letter from an old Cambridge friend H.J. Wolstenholme, asking him 'to concede in time with good grace what is sure eventually to be won by struggle.'[6]

---

5   Speech of 24 March 1909 cited in Guha, *op.cit.*, pp. 322, 605, n. 68.
6   Cf. *Ibid.*, p. 323.

In jail, as before, Gandhi read some thirty books in English, Hindi, Gujarati, Sanskrit and Tamil. He read Tolstoy, Emerson, Thoreau and Carlyle; the *Manusmṛti, Patañjali Yoga Darśana,* the *Upaniṣads, Gītā* and the Bible. Every stint in jail added to his inner growth. Kathryn Tidrick[7] says that though Ralph Waldo Trine is not mentioned in the list of authors read by Gandhi, he certainly came across Trine's work around this time. He asked Hermann Kallenbach to read 'Trine's book' in a letter that he wrote on the eve of his departure for England. Trine had outlined a practical creed for successful living inspired by Emerson's Transcendentalism; and held that the acquisition of virtue led to power over people and events. Spiritual power, synonymous with 'soul power', arose out of a person's oneness with God through acts of love and service to fellow human beings. The true seeker, free from fear and self-interest, would be so empowered by the will of God as to be able to transmit potent influences to the far corners of the world. 'Soul-force', in Gandhi's view, in its purest form, possessed the same power.[8] He studied Tamil books to express his 'sincere' gratitude to the Tamils,'who had done so much in the struggle…'[9]

The procession of Indian *satyāgrahī*s into jails continued unabated in the last months of 1908 and early 1909. Gandhi's friend of boyhood days Sheikh Mehtab published his Gujarati poems in the *Indian Opinion,* praising the bravery and sacrifices of men like Parsi Rustomji, M.C.Anglia, Sorabji Shapurji and Thambi Naidoo. While the Muslim poet used Hindu imagery to foster goodwill and solidarity between the Hindus and Muslims, a Hindu poet Jayshanker Govindji celebrated the courage of Ahmed Cachalia, undaunted by the rack and ruin of his business when he went to jail.[10] Gandhi said that'men like Mr. Cachalia and Mr. Aswat are rare in this world. If the Hindu businessmen display even half as much strength, they

---

7 *Op.cit.*, pp. 88-89.

8 Gandhi returned to Trine, and read his *My Philosophy and My Religion* (1921), in Yeravda jail in 1923, and also in 1933, as he recovered from a 21 day fast. The fast for 'self-purification' arose out of 'a yearning of the soul to merge in the divine essence…How far I have succeeded, how far I am in tune with the Infinite, I do not know.' *Collected Works* 23, p. 178, 3 January 1923; *Collected Works* 25, p. 84, 4 September 1924; *Collected Works* 55, p. 257, 8 July 1933. Trine's best known book is entitled *In Tune with the Infinite.*

9 Cf. Tendulkar, *op.cit.*, p. 121.

10 Cf. Guha, *op.cit.*, pp. 324, 605, n. 71.

can serve the movement...'¹¹ Cachalia, Chairman of the British Indian Association, called upon the Indian merchants to face voluntary poverty with unflinching fortitude.¹²

One of the few letters that Gandhi wrote from jail was addressed to his son Manilal, who was 17. It was a truly tender epistle brimming with fatherly love, but also with the resolute espousal of poverty: 'This much is clear that you are not to work as a barrister or a doctor. We are poor and wish to remain poor...Have faith that since you are serving others, you will not suffer privation.'¹³

In April 1909, in Pretoria jail, Gandhi heard of the death of Kallenbach's mother. He conveyed his condolences in words that came straight from his heart: 'Need I say that among those of whom I think daily you are one? I am not with you in body but I am always with you in spirit...'¹⁴

The *Satyāgraha* ebbed and flowed, with varying levels of intensity. The Government could not subdue it; but a sense of fatigue and frustration afflicted both the parties. On May 24, 1909, Gandhi was released from Pretoria Prison. He was greeted with bouquets and garlands by a large crowd of Indians at the prison gates; and addressed another crowd at the Pretoria Mosque asking for donations to revive the bankrupt British Indian Association. He told the businessmen to lighten their pockets for the cause of the community; and then proceeded to Johannesburg, where he was received by a large crowd including some Chinese and European friends, such as Joseph Doke. He was taken in a procession from the railway station to the Hamidiya Mosque, where he made a moving speech asking people to join the movement in larger numbers.

Two weeks later, he spoke to the Germiston Literary and Debating Society on 'The Ethics of Passive Resistance'. Soul-force never caused suffering to others, he told his liberal white audience. The colonists should not therefore object to the use of this force in attempts to redress any grievances. The natives could also use soul-force to seek remedies for

---

11 *Collected Works*, Vol. 9, pp. 184, 185.

12 Cf. Tendulkar, *op.cit.*, p. 122.

13 Gandhi, Prabhudas, *Jeevan Prabhat,* p. 148; Gandhi, Rajmohan, *op.cit.*, p. 130.

14 *Collected Works* 96, p. 6; Gandhi, Rajmohan, p. 131.

their problems without causing any harm, whatsoever. If they 'could rise so high as to understand and utilize this force, there would probably be no native question left to be solved.' Gandhi was evolving; his horizons were expanding. The future would indeed be drastically different from his current world![15]

Disunity and disaffection in the Indian ranks led to the decision to send a deputation to London to highlight their grievances in deliberations for the Union of South Africa. Swan says that the economic losses suffered by the merchants and petty traders made many of them desert the *Satyāgraha*.[16] Haji Habib, H.O. Ally and others formed a British Indian Conciliation Committee to negotiate with the Government. Habib held Gandhi responsible for the debacle of his agreement with Smuts at a meeting on June 6, 1909; and protested at the description of those who had registered as 'blacklegs' in *Indian Opinion*. They wanted to petition Smuts for relief and bring the struggle to a conclusion; and also demanded a deputation to London. Gandhi had no objection to either. The approach to Smuts proved utterly nugatory. 'The British', Gandhi hoped, 'would view the imperial question from an imperial rather than a parochial point of view.'[17] On June 13, the British Indian Association nominated five men for the delegation: Ahmed Cachalia, V.A. Chettiar, Gandhi, Nadeshir Cama and Haji Habib. The meeting also decided to send a deputation to India to enlist greater support in the mother country; and raise funds for the struggle. Henry Polak, N. Gopal Naidoo a Tamil Hindu, N.A. Cama a Bombay Parsi, and M. Coovadia a Bombay Muslim, were nominated; and both the deputations were confirmed at a mass meeting on June 16, 1909. Arrests and imprisonment curtailed their numbers; only Gandhi and Habib proceeded to London; and Polak went alone to India.

---

15   *Collected Works*, 9, pp. 243-4.
16   Swan, *op. cit.,* p. 175.
17   Cf. Tendulkar, *op. cit.,* p. 123.

Chapter 53

London

Gandhi and Haji Habib left Johannesburg for Cape Town *en route* to London on June 21, 1909. Gandhi wrote to Henry Polak, with detailed instructions on briefing the press; and meeting people and parties for soliciting support in India. He advised Polak to have his articles translated into the major Indian languages; and to circulate them throughout the country. He asked Polak to bring for him a copy of *Ṣaḍ-darśana Samuccaya*, a manual of the six schools of philosophy, from India.[1]

In an interview to a newspaper in Cape Town, Gandhi made no secret of his 'great fear that under the Constitution, it will be a union of white races against British Indians and the Coloured races'; but still hoped that the Imperial Government would act with justice before it sanctioned the union of the four colonies.[2]

A friendly Indian crowd was present at Cape Town to see Gandhi and Habib off, as they boarded the *SS Kenilworth Castle*. Gandhi caught the eye of the writer Olive Schreiner, who had also come there to see some friends off. As she specially came on board ship to give him a warm handshake, her friendly gesture was noticed by many whites around. Gratified Gandhi construed it as 'a tribute to passive resistance.'[3] He was quite familiar with her thoughts on race, which had been reprinted in the *Indian Opinion*.

---

1 Cf. Guha, *op. cit.*, p. 328.
2 *Collected Works*, Vol. 9, pp. 267-8.
3 *Ibid.*, pp. 270, 287: 'Fancy the author of 'Dreams' paying a tribute to passive resistance'.

Mir Alam, the Pathan who had attacked Gandhi with murderous purpose, but later made peace with his victim and participated in the *satyāgraha*, was arrested and deported with many others to India by the Government. He wrote to Gandhi from India to inform him that he was propagating the news of *Satyāgraha* all over the country; and would carry it as far northwest as Afghanistan. The letter arrived just after Gandhi left for London. Polak published it in the *Indian Opinion*, and sent Gandhi a copy to cheer him up. It was a touching proof and vindication of the power of forgiveness added to self-suffering![4]

Gandhi thought the community would derive greater strength and benefit from the prisoners in comparison with the deputation. He warned the community against building any high hopes. 'It should... be remembered that this deputation is not going on behalf of the *satyāgrahīs*...For them following truth is itself a victory...the *satyāgrahī* must continue to seek opportunities for imprisonment.'[5]

Gandhi was no longer a little-known man. He was the progenitor of a new philosophy of thought and action; a paragon of the power of self-suffering, who had been thrice to prison; twice with hard labour, for a total of about six months. The world had taken notice of him and his movement; and of the pitiable plight of Indians in South Africa. Millions in India had already heard of him, and of his epic struggle against white tyranny. And Polak was on his way to India to drum up more support for the cause. Gandhi was sceptical of the likelihood of achieving anything worthwhile in London at a time when Johannesburg, not London, was the real centre of action.

Gandhi singled out two issues concerning the Indians in the Transvaal for action. He sought repeal of Act 2 of 1907; and recognition of the status of highly educated Indians, so that no more than six per year should be admitted as residents by right, and not merely as temporary residents on permit.[6] A successful resolution of these issues would do little to alleviate the misery of Indians groaning under ruthless segregation and discrimination; and immigration into the Transvaal would still remain

---

4   Cf. 'A Suggestive Letter', *Indian Opinion,* 10 July 1909; Guha, *op.cit.*, pp. 328-29.

5   'Letter to Transvaal Indians', From Gujarati, *Collected Works* 9, p. 259-60.

6   Cf. Hunt, *op.cit.*, p. 104.

almost totally impossible. What really mattered, and was most important to Gandhi, was the issue of legal equality. He was 'fighting for the right of cultured Indians to enter the Transvaal in common with Europeans'.[7] As Hunt puts it, 'it was for the honour of India. The end was pure because it was unselfish, and in Satyagraha the means were pure because they were nonviolent. In this conjunction of pure end and pure means Gandhi recognized a mighty new power at work.'[8]

In stark contrast with the punitive rigour of life in jail, Gandhi found himself and his colleague wallowing in First Class luxury on his way to England. 'Too much pampered' throughout the voyage, they disembarked at Southampton on the tenth of July, 1909, and stayed at the Westminster Palace Hotel in London. Gandhi's friend Dr. Pranjivan Mehta had also come to London to admit his son to school; and was staying at the same hotel. Gandhi surprised Ritch in his office; called on Sir M. Bhowanaggree; and wrote to Lord Ampthill, Chairman of the South African British Indian Committee. Henry Polak's unmarried sister Maud acted as his secretary.

London was in great ferment. On July 1, 1909, a young Indian student named Madanlal Dhingra, under the spell of Savarkar, shot an India Office aide Sir Curzon Wyllie to death. He claimed that he had every right as an Indian patriot to kill the man; and disputed the right of the Lord Chief Justice at the Old Bailey to pass any sentence on him. In his statement from the dock, he said that his act was 'an humble revenge for the inhuman hangings and deportations of patriotic Indian youths.' 'As a Hindu', he went on, 'I felt that wrong to my country is an insult to God…Poor in wealth and intellect, a son like myself has nothing else to offer to the Mother but his own blood, and so I have sacrificed the same on her altar. The lesson required in India at present is to learn how to die, and the only way to teach it is by dying ourselves. Therefore, I die, and glory in my martyrdom.' 'My only prayer to God', he continued, 'is may I be reborn of the same Mother, and may I re-die in the same sacred cause till the cause is successful and she stands free for the good of humanity and to the glory of God'.[9] Winston Churchill called the speech 'the finest ever made

---

7 *Collected Works* 9, p. 506. Message to the Indian National Congress.

8 Hunt, *op.cit.*, p. 105.

9 Cf. Tendulkar, *op.cit.*, p. 125.

in the name of patriotism'.[10]

Gandhi was categorical in his condemnation of violence: 'India can gain nothing from the rule of murderers – no matter whether they are black or white.'[11]

Lord Ampthill was Gandhi's main advocate and adviser in London. The former Governor of Madras (1900-1906), and Acting Viceroy of India (1904), was the same age as Gandhi. He was sympathetic to the plight of the British Indians in South Africa, many of whom had found their way to that land from the Madras Presidency. Even though he was generally apathetic to any reforms in India, he was sincere and wholehearted in his support for Gandhi and his cause. Sixty letters were exchanged between the two in about four months. Ampthill preferred the quiet, personal, diplomatic approach to a public one; and advised Gandhi not to make any public statements or issue any press releases without first conferring with him. He said he had also been able to enlist the support of Lord Curzon for their cause. Gandhi abided by his advice, contrary to a public approach advocated by Sir M. Bhownaggree. Gandhi was charmed by the honesty, courtesy and humility of Ampthill.

The two ex-Viceroys had taken the initiative out of Gandhi's hands. Even though they were sympathetic towards the British Indian victims of racial tyranny in South Africa, their principal concern was the power and stability of the British Empire. Even though Gandhi had confined his minimal demands to matters of honour rather than substance, they proved unequal to the task of meeting them. When asked by Ampthill if he had any links with the revolutionaries, Gandhi said his movement was an eloquent protest against their violent methods. They had neither received, nor would they ever accept a single farthing from 'the party of sedition'.[12]

Ampthill obtained Gandhi's agreement for the proposal that there should be a numerical limit of six on the entry of educated Indians, but that it be set by the Governor, keeping it out of the law-books. Even though apprehensive, Gandhi conceded. Ampthill met Smuts; and Gandhi met

---

10 *Ibid*. Cf. also Datta, V.N., *Madan Lal Dhingra and the* Revolutionary *Movement*, Vikas Publishing House, New Delhi, 1978, pp. 38-41.

11 *Indian Opinion,* 14 August 1909; *Collected Works*, 9, pp. 302-3.

12 *Collected Works* 9, p. 320. Gandhi to Ampthill, July 29.

Lord Crew. Smuts did not agree, and advised Crew of his willingness to repeal Act 2 of 1907, but not the equally restrictive Act 36 of 1908. He would also admit up to six 'approved Asiatics' per year, but only on temporary permits. He would not remove the racial bar from the law: 'We cannot recognize in our legislation the equal rights of all alike to emigrate to South Africa. Under our special circumstances we leave the door as wide as possible to white immigrants, but we could never do the same to Asiatic immigrans.'[13]

Even though the mediation of Lord Ampthill failed to deliver, he was unwavering in his support. He told the delegates that in the work-a-day world they had to give and take: 'We cannot have everything that we desire. I would therefore strongly advise you to close with this offer. If you wish to fight for the principle's sake, you may do so later on…'

Habib spoke in Gujarati, and Gandhi translated, to convey his acceptance 'on behalf of the Conciliation Party', which constituted the majority of the community. Gandhi thanked Ampthill for all his efforts; but also expressed his inability to accept what was on offer: 'The Indians for whom I speak are comparatively poor and inferior in numbers, but they are resolute unto death. They are fighting not only for practical relief but for principle as well. If they must give up either of the two, they will jettison the former and fight for the latter.'

Lord Ampthill was gracious in his response: 'You must not suppose that I will give you up. I too must play the gentleman's part. Englishmen are not willing at once to relinquish any task they have undertaken. Yours is a righteous struggle, and you are fighting with clean weapons. How can I possibly give you up? But you must recognize my delicate position. The suffering, if any, must be borne by you alone, and therefore it is my duty to advise you to accept any settlement possible in the circumstances. But if you, who have to suffer, are prepared to undergo any amount of suffering for principle's sake, I must not only not come in your way but even congratulate you. I will therefore continue as President of your Committee and help you to the best of my ability.'[14]

Gandhi met Lord Crew once more on September 16, 1909; but the latter

---

13   Smuts to Crew, August 26, 1909. Cd. 5365, pp. 32-34; Cf. Hunt, *op. cit.*, p. 112.

14   Gandhi, *Satyagraha in South Africa, Collected Works,* Vol. 29, p.185.

disregarded the Ampthill-Gandhi proposals in favour of those by Smuts. Gandhi's mission to London met with failure.

Letters to Polak and Kallenbach

Gandhi kept in constant touch with Polak, Kallenbach and others with his regular correspondence. His letters to Kallenbach from London are honest, sincere, frank and unabashed in his profession of love and regard for his friend. They were trying to live a life of extreme self-denial in their common pursuit of a genuine transcendental experience; of spiritual awakening that went beyond the bounds of physical barriers. Gandhi was touched when, in one of his letters, Kallenbach referred to Kasturba as mother: '...That you should describe Mrs. Gandhi as your mother shows your ultra-regard for me. You have reached a stage in which you refuse to recognize my limitations. How shall I retain such an exalted standard?'[15]

In another, Gandhi refers to Kallenbach's portrait on the mantelpiece opposite his bed; and to items of toiletry. He had perhaps taken to London Kallenbach's shaving kit and other accessories, which reminded him of his friend amid the frustrations of a fruitless mission. Gandhi took a vow of celibacy in 1906. He sought throughout his life to live up to it. He always lauded it; recommended it; imposed it on his workers in the movement; and urged his sons to practise it. In all his correspondence with Kallenbach, an insistent theme of untiring tenacity is continence and the need for total abstinence. He always keeps warning Kallenbach, asking him not to let his defences down; to keep himself pure and unsullied by the taint of any sexual indulgence. Spiritual growth was incompatible with sex and the satisfaction of 'lust'. Those addicted to indulgence were of no use to society; and were incapable of any purposeful social service. Even married men had to abstain, to render any worthwhile service to society. Kallenbach was a heterosexual male with a strong libido held in check only by Gandhi's restraining presence!

The Suffragettes

Gandhi made use of the time in London watching the progress of the women's movement for suffrage. The Women's Social and Political Union was verging on violence in response to the refusal of the Liberal Government to introduce a women's suffrage bill in Parliament. On June

---

15 Cf. Lev, *op.cit.*, p. 19.

29, the WSPU held their ninth Women's Conference, and marched to the Parliament in their thirteenth attempt to present a petition to the House of Commons. The march was halted by mounted police, as Prime Minister Asquith refused again to receive them. Small bands of women then raced from nearby buildings with copies of their petition towards Parliament. Some of them threw stones and smashed the windows of some Government offices in Whitehall. They were put on trial on July 12, and were sentenced to a month in prison. But they went on a hunger-strike; and the baffled Government released them. At a mass meeting on July 29, 1909, at St. James' Hall, the hunger strikers were presented to the audience. Gandhi was there. He wrote a long article praising their determination, organization, bravery and hunger-strike; but made no mention of the stone-throwing.[16]

Gandhi met Mrs. Emmaline Pankhurst, the leader of the WSPU, at this gathering. She repeatedly went to jail with her daughters for the cause; and often pursued her own much more belligerent campaign. The suffragettes often resorted to acts of violence like stone-throwing and window-smashing, which alarmed Gandhi. He praised their courage; but decried their deeds of violence.

Many people were disturbed and disappointed by the violence. A more moderate group, the Women's Freedom League was formed under the leadership of Mrs. Charlotte French Despard, ready to participate in civil disobedience without violence and damage to property. Their most noteworthy campaign was the vigil they maintained outside Parliament ready to present their petition whenever the House was in session. The completion of 10,000 hours of picketing by the end of September impressed Gandhi.[17]

Mrs. Despard had worked in the slums of south London, and established clubs for workmen and boys; and one of the first child welfare centres in the country. Deeply religious in disposition, she wore simple black clothes, and lived amongst the poor. A vegetarian and a theosophist, she was also politically active. One of the WFL moves involved refusal to pay taxes, on account of which the Government seized and sold her property. But her admirers bought back her furniture at auctions to defeat the designs of the Government. She was arrested in August for trying to present a petition

---

16 Cf. Hunt, *op. cit.*, p. 128.

17 *Ibid.*, p. 130.

to the Prime Minister.[18] Surely, her ideas would provide an inspiration to Gandhi in the development of his own. Though some of her followers sometimes swerved from the path of non-violence, she certainly showed the way!

There is no doubt that Gandhi did learn a thing or two from the women's suffrage movement. 'If they had based their fight on pure *satyāgraha,* they could have changed conditions all over England and the change would have had repercussions throughout the world.'[19]

Letters to Manilal

Gandhi wrote to his son Manilal on August 10, 1909, that 'very few Indians need marry at the present time...A person who marries in order to satisfy his carnal desire is lower than even a beast. For the married, it is considered proper to have sexual intercourse only for having progeny...I want you to...conquer your senses...I want to bind you not to marry even after the age of 25...If you do not think of marriage even at the age of 25, I think it will be to your good.'[20]

He wrote to Manilal again on September 17 and 27 to calm his restlessness and address his anxiety about his education. The son had asked what he was going to do. Gandhi told him that his present duty was to serve his parents, to study as much as he could, and to work in the fields: '...You must be definite on this point at least – that you are not going to practise law or medicine... we are poor and want to remain so...The true occupation of man is to build his character...I feel like meeting and embracing you; and tears come to my eyes as I am unable to do that. Be sure that Bapu [father] will not be cruel to you. Whatever I do, I do it because I think it will be in your interest. You will never come to grief, for you are doing service to others.'[21]

Gandhi did care, but in his own way, in which there was little room for any compromise!

Failure of Diplomacy

---

18 *Ibid.,* p. 131.
19 *Collected Works,* Vol. 9, p. 489.
20 *Collected Works* 9, pp. 352-353.
21 *Collected Works* 9, 'Letter to Manilal Gandhi', pp. 435-436.

In his absence, the English pages of *Indian* Opinion were edited by Rev. Doke, as Henry Polak was also away in India. Harilal sought, and got his fourth term of imprisonment. Gandhi was happy when he heard of it, and wrote that he too was 'itching to join him'.[22]

Towards the end of September Gandhi knew that diplomacy had failed to deliver; and felt free to speak about his mission, as also about matters of interest to him. In October and November, therefore, he spoke from a number of platforms. In his address to the Gujarati Literary Conference on October 5, he pleaded for the pride of place for one's mother tongue; and lauded the languages of India and the conferences held to celebrate them. It was important to preserve and enrich India's literary legacy.[23]

'The Ethics of Passive resistance' was the topic of his talk to the Union of Ethical Societies on October 8. The brutalizing effect of war was contrasted with the kind of character nurtured by *Satyāgraha*: 'Self-restraint, unselfishness, patience, gentleness, these are the flowers which spring beneath the feet of those who accept, but refuse to impose, suffering...'[24] Soul force, said Gandhi, 'is far superior to brute force, and..is invincible.' Bipin Chandra Pal, the fiery Bengali orator in the audience, remarked in question time that soul force needed to be backed by physical force. Gandhi replied that it would then cease to be soul-force.[25]

On October 13, Gandhi spoke on 'East and West' at a meeting of the Hampstead Peace and Arbitration Society. John Sankey, who as Lord Chancellor presided over the Round Table Conference in 1931, was in the audience. To say that the East and West could never meet was to propagate a doctrine of despair. It was his firm belief that the people of the East and West could live together peacefully in perfect equality. But he was alarmed by the mad rush and pace of the modern civilization typified by its railways, telegraphs and telephones, which did not really help the 'moral elevation of man'. He was upset by the glorification of the body at the expense of the soul. People were travelling around too much; the holy city of Banaras had become 'unholy' owing to the mad rush of both desirable and undesirable people, who flocked to the city. Modern

---

22   Letter to Polak, *Collected Works* 9, p. 513, also 522.
23   *Ibid.,* pp. 457-60.
24   *Collected Works,* Vol. 9, p. 471.
25   *Collected Works,* Vol. 9, p. 474.

civilization, the cause of India's ills, made India and Britain each other's enemies.²⁶ We can clearly discern the influence of Carpenter! The revolt brewing within him against the ills of civilization, spilling over into these lectures, would soon find a sustained vent in his *Hind Swaraj*.

He also spoke to Indian students at a *Vijaya-daśamī* (Dashehra) Festival dinner on October 24. Gandhi extolled Rāma's willing acceptance of exile to prepare himself for governing his kingdom; the austerities of Lakṣmaṇa; the purity and suffering of Sītā; and their devotion to duty. These qualities were needed to liberate India; to be the basis of a new victory of Truth over Falsehood.²⁷ But while Gandhi spoke of Sītā and her suffering, Savarkar spoke of the redoubtable Durgā and her rage. While Gandhi worshipped the steadfast discipline of Rāma, Savarkar spoke of the slaying of Rāvaṇa, obliquely signifying that violence alone would ultimately deliver.

The recourse to bloodshed and murder, and the talk of violence haunted Gandhi, and disturbed his equanimity. He repeatedly returned to the issue in his speeches and writings. In a letter to Lord Ampthill dated October 30, 1909, he referred to the rising Indian 'impatience of British rule'; and pointed out that the people did not disapprove of violence: 'I have practically met no one who believes that India can ever become free without resort to violence.'²⁸

Gandhi spoke to the Indian Social Union on October 30; and on November 7, to the Indian students at Cambridge, where he met Teja Singh, President of the militant Sikh organization in Canada.²⁹

Gandhi had brought along with him the manuscript of his first biography by the Rev. Joseph J. Doke, entitled *M.K. Gandhi: An Indian Patriot in South Africa*. Lord Ampthill wrote a fine introduction, in which he commended the passive resistance movement, and urged the Empire to be true to its principles. Doke likened Gandhi's simplicity, truthfulness, fearlessness and readiness to court death in pursuit of justice to the qualities of 'the Jew of Nazareth'. The New Testament and the Sermon on the Mount had roused Gandhi 'to the rightness and value of passive resistance'. Doke appealed

---

26 *Collected Works*, Vol. 9, pp. 475-6.

27 *Ibid.*, p. 498.

28 *Ibid.*, p. 509; cf. Hunt, *op.cit.*, pp. 126-7.

29 Cf. *Ibid.*, pp. 133-35.

for proper Christian action; for repeal of the racial laws; for building 'a new Jerusalem, whose beautiful gates are ever open to all nations; where no colour-bar is permitted to challenge the Indian, and no racial prejudice to daunt the Chinese; into whose walls even an Asiatic may build those precious stones which, one day, will startle us with their glory.'[30]

Dr. Pranjivan Mehta paid for the publication. Gandhi bought the lot of 600 copies; sent some for purposes of review; and shipped half of the remainder to the publisher G.A. Natesan in Madras. The rest were sent to South Africa.

Shortly before leaving London, Gandhi organized a gathering of his Indian and English friends; and exhorted them to help the passive resisters. A meeting was held on October 23 with the help of the Muslim League; and it was decided to circulate a petition to support the Indian cause and raise money for hard-pressed passive resisters.

A farewell dinner hosted by the Reverend F. B. Meyer on November 12, 1909, was attended, amongst others, by Sir M. Bhownaggree, Sir Frederick Lely, many members of Parliament, and Motilal Nehru, father of Jawaharlal, the first Prime Minister of independent India. Lely, the former administrator of Kathiawar states, who had refused young Gandhi a scholarship from Porbandar, was living in retirement in London. In his speech at the function he remembered his friendship with Kaba Gandhi, and said that the father, 'had he been alive now, would have been proud of his son.'[31]

In his speech, Gandhi described the struggle in South Africa as 'one of the greatest of modern times.' It was so 'because of the great principle at stake, because of the pure ideal for which they were fighting and, lastly, because of the pure methods they had adopted in endeavouring to attain that ideal'.[32] It was doubtless 'a combination of great principle, pure ideal and pure methods.'[33]

---

30 Doke, Joseph J., *M.K. Gandhi: An Indian Patriot in South Africa*, The London Indian Chronicle, London, 1909, pp. 7-8, 23, 84, 92-3.

31 Cf. Guha, *op. cit.*, p. 357.

32 *Collected Works*, Vol. 9, p. 542.

33)Hunt, *op.cit.*, p. 132.

In a letter to Curzon, Ampthill gave candid expression to his sense of dismay at a Liberal Government putting 'an actual "colour" bar' in place for the first time in the history of the Empire; and sought the former's support for a motion that he intended to move in the House of Lords.[34]

---

34 Cf. Guha, *op. cit.*, p. 610, n. 79.

Chapter 54

Henry Polak in India

While Gandhi was doing all he could in London to win friends and influence the people in power to do justice to the Indians in South Africa, his emissary Henry Polak was very active in India. Immediately on arrival in Bombay, he met newspaper editors, industrialists, lawyers including Jinnah, nationalists, and the patriarch Dadabhai Naoroji. Gokhale helped him with the resources of the Servants of India Society. He wrote a pamphlet on the situation in South Africa; and Sir Jehangir Petit offered to bear the cost of its publication. Polak's experience in India raised Gandhi even higher in his esteem.

A large public meeting in the Bombay Town Hall on September 14, 1909, was attended by many knights and notables, including Mohammad Ali Jinnah. Gokhale, the main speaker, saluted the courage of 'the indomitable Gandhi, a man of tremendous spiritual power, one who is made of the stuff of which great heroes and martyrs are made.' Gokhale spoke of 'the splendid manner in which the whole movement has been managed. Hindus, Muslims, Parsis, all hold together as one man. Surely a man who can achieve this must represent a great moral force, and must not be lightly judged...I am sure, if any of us had been in the Transvaal during these days we should have been proud to range ourselves under Mr. Gandhi's banner and work with him and suffer with him in the great cause.'[1]

In his speech, Polak laid emphasis on Indian solidarity in the Transvaal, where all religions, castes and classes were united in their struggle. He called Gandhi a 'saint and a patriot, who would gladly allow his body to be torn asunder by wild horses rather than compromise his honour and that of his country.'[2]

---

1 Cf. Tendulkar, *op.cit.*, p. 135.
2 Cf. Guha, *op. cit.*, pp. 344, 608, n. 36.

Polak travelled from Bombay to Gujarat, and then to Madras and other South Indian towns, addressing meetings to apprise people of the Transvaal struggle and the great principle at stake. G.A. Natesan published his pamphlet in two parts, *The Indians of South Africa: Helots within the Empire and How They are Treated*. The pamphlet sought to rouse Indians to a sense of their duty: '...The Transvaal Indians have understood that upon their efforts depended whether or not this race-virus should infect the rest of South Africa and the rest of the Empire, whether India would not have to suffer and drink deep of the cup of humiliation. What of this has India realized? Have the bitter cries from the Transvaal Indians penetrated the ears of their brethren in the Motherland?'[3]

Polak also wrote a brief biography of Gandhi at the request of Natesan, which was published anonymously. In *M.K. Gandhi: A Sketch of His Life and Work*, Polak wrote of Gandhi's extraordinary love of truth, generosity, and sense of public duty: 'One feels oneself in the presence of a moral giant, whose pellucid soul is a clear, still lake, in which one sees Truth clearly mirrored.' Gandhi, according to Polak, lived 'for God and for India.' And his supreme desire was 'to see unity among his fellow-countrymen.' He had united the Hindus and Muslims in South Africa to showcase 'the possibility of Indian national unity and the lines upon which the national edifice shall be constructed.'[4]

Polak's travels, talks, speeches and writings added immensely to India's awareness of Gandhi and his *Satyāgraha* in South Africa. In a letter the disciple wrote to the master: 'I don't believe any other country could have given you birth.' The Government kept a close watch on Polak. He was shadowed; his mail was tampered with; and the people he stayed with were interrogated.

Polak found his way to Rangoon, where he enjoyed the hospitality of Dr. Pranjivan Mehta. Talks between the two prompted Mehta to write a letter to Gokhale, in which he described Gandhi's life as 'that of a great Mahatma', whose mind was totally preoccupied with the idea of his motherland. This

---

3 Polak, H.S.L., *The Indians of South Africa: Helots Within the Empire and How They are Treated*, G. A. Natesan&Co., Madras, 1909, Part 1, pp. 4,21,70 ff; Part 2, pp. 16-17, 22-23, 41, 43-44.

4 Anon., *M.K. Gandhi: A Sketch of His Life and Work*, G.A. Natesan & Co., Madras, 1910.

was a few years before Tagore, in 1919, called Gandhi a Mahatma; and the title became synonymous with the great man. Gandhi never saw or knew of this letter expressive of Mehta's incredible prescience![5]

Polak went from Rangoon to Calcutta, where a large meeting, attended by the leading lights of Bengal, protested against the treatment of Indians in the Transvaal. He then crisscrossed U.P. and the Punjab, addressing numerous meetings. In Banaras, Annie Besant presided over one, and spoke with her characteristic eloquence. She also contributed Rs. 30 to a collection of Rs. 1,000 at the meeting, to help the Transvaal passive resisters.

Polak attracted the attention of Aurobindo Ghose, who had already written on the 'possibilities of passive resistance in India.'[6]

Aurobindo belonged to a school of thought diametrically opposed to the gradualist moderation of Gokhale. Securing his approval and approbation for Gandhi's *Satyāgraha* in South Africa side by side with the wholehearted support of Gokhale was no mean achievement for the persuasive power of Polak's speeches and writings in India.

---

5 Cf. Guha, *op.cit.*, p. 349.

6 Cf. *Bande Matram*, 11 to 23 April, 1907. Aurobindo wrote of 'The Great Glory of the Transvaal Indians': '...they, ignored by humanity, are fighting humanity's battle in the pure strength of the spirit, with no weapon but the moral force of their voluntary sufferings and utter self-sacrifice... The passive resistance which we had not the courage and unselfishness to carry out in India, they have carried to the utmost in the Transvaal under far more arduous circumstances, with far less right to hope for success...they have contributed far more than their share to the future greatness of their country.' ('The Transvaal Indians', first published in *Karmayogin*, 11 December, 1909. See Guha, *op. cit.*, p. 609, n. 53).

Chapter 55

HIND SWARAJ: Collision of Cultures

London stood stone-deaf to Gandhi's pleas for justice to the Indians in South Africa. Dispirited and disillusioned, he told his hosts at his farewell party that the struggle he was involved in was a matter of national honour. As they could not in principle meet violence with violence, they had to resort to passive resistance. One had to raise objections to laws that were unjust; to dispensations that were morally flawed and therefore unacceptable. He cited the Biblical example of Daniel, who found it impossible to accept the laws of the Medes and the Persians.

In the third week of September 1909, he read G.K. Chesterton's article on 'Indian Nationalism' in the *Illustrated London News.* The author had been reading the *Indian Sociologist* published by Shyamji Krishnavarma; and found the ideas in it 'not very Indian, and not very original'. He railed at 'a conquered people demanding the institutions of the conqueror.' If an Indian wanted to resuscitate and revive his pre-British past, if he wanted to go back to his Indian system of self-rule, to institutions that were the products of Indian genius in response to India's needs and India's psyche, Chesterton could understand. If an Indian preferred an unapproachable Maharaja to a legion of British masters, he could understand. If an Indian sought his own brand of religion and 'spiritual comforts' instead of the so-called 'peace' imposed on India by the British, he could understand. If on that basis an Indian asked the British to go, and leave the Indians to themselves, he could understand. But the Indian radicals were aping the West, embracing its violence.[1] Gandhi sent long excerpts from this article for publication in *Indian Opinion*;and expressed his own concern for the

---

1 G.K. Chesterton, 'Our Notebook', *Illustrated London News,* 18 September 1909.

preservation of India's own age-old legacy. Madanlal Dhingra's violence appalled him; Savarkar's bloody-minded precepts and prescription of violence shook him to the core.

The idea that civilization is a kind of disease came from Edward Carpenter, who believed that pre-civilized man was comparatively free from disease, with a more 'harmonious and compact' social life. Modern civilization is violent, steeped in materialism and limitless consumption. It is selfish, ego-inflating, obsessed with the body, and also machine-mad. It is afflicted by a spirit of pervasive discontent, so that we always want to get more; and we always want to go from one place to another. This restlessness is a mental disease. Carpenter pleaded for 'a return to nature and community of human life.' He recommended open-air living, and a clean and pure diet of fruits and grains. A vegetarian diet helped control one's passions by avoiding internal disunity and disease. This was music to Gandhi's ears!

The type-written draft of *A letter to a Hindoo*, written by Leo Tolstoy to Taraknath Das, editor of the revolutionary journal *Free Hindustan* published from Canada, was brought to Gandhi by his friend Pranjivan Mehta;[2] and a serious discussion followed. Das had asked Tolstoy whether Indians could resort to force and terrorism to evict the British from India. The British held India because, according to Das, the Indians failed to defend themselves with requisite force. Tolstoy told Das that he was wrong: 'you say that the English have enslaved your people and hold them in subjugation because the latter have not resisted resolutely enough and have not met force by force. But the case is just the opposite. If the English have enslaved the people of India it is because the latter recognized, and still recognize, force as the fundamental principle of the social order.'[3] 'It is not the English', Tolstoy said, 'who have enslaved the Indians, but the Indians who have enslaved themselves.'[4] 'Do not resist evil,' he continued, 'but also yourselves participate not in evil, in the violent deeds of the administration of the law courts, the collection of taxes and, what is more important, of the soldiers, and no one in the world will enslave you.'[5] Tolstoy's argument for rejection of the English civilization by Indians, and

---

2 Cf. Hunt, *op.cit.*, p. 133, n. 95.
3 Tolstoy, Leo, *Recollections and Essays*, London, 1937, pp. 426 ff.
4 *Ibid.*, p. 427.
5 Cf. *Collected Works*, Vol. 10, p. 4, English version of Gandhi's Preface.

for non-violent non-cooperation with the British convinced Gandhi. And he convinced Mehta that violence was not the way to get rid of the British and their rule over India.

Gandhi's direct correspondence with Tolstoy began around this time; and continued till the latter's death a year later. He wrote to Tolstoy from London on October 1, 1909, with an account of his campaign in South Africa, seeking his blessing. He also requested permission to publish and distribute 20,000 copies of the *Letter to a Hindoo,* and also to omit the dismissive reference to 'reincarnation' in the text, as the Hindus came to terms with many things in their lives in accordance with their belief in it. Tolstoy was prompt in his response; and gracious enough to allow the excision, even though personally, he gave no credence to reincarnation. The struggle of 'our dear brothers and co-workers in the Transvaal' pleased him. He referred to 'the same struggle of the tender against the harsh, of meekness and love against pride and violence…' in Russia as well.

Gandhi translated Tolstoy's *Letter to a Hindoo* on his voyage back to South Africa, and wrote Gujarati and English prefaces for it. He drew attention to Tolstoy's non-violence and opposition to industrialism and militarism like that of the Japanese. Personal commitment and action was the need of the moment. 'If we do not want the English in India we must pay the price.'[6] Gandhi introduced his Gujarati readers to Tolstoy and his philosophy:

'An oppressor's efforts will be in vain if we refuse to submit to his tyranny…Slavery consists in submitting to an unjust order, not in suffering ourselves to be kicked. Real courage and humanity consist in not returning a kick for a kick. This is the core of Tolstoy's teaching.'[7]

On November 10, 1909, a few days before he left Britain, Gandhi wrote a second letter to Tolstoy, in which he described the struggle of the Indians in the Transvaal as 'the greatest of modern times'. If successful, 'it will be not only a triumph of religion, love and truth over irreligion, hatred and falsehood, but should hopefully serve as an example to the millions in India and to the down-trodden in other parts of the world.' He also sent with this letter a copy of *M.K. Gandhi: An Indian Patriot in South Africa,*

---

6   *Ibid.,* p. 4.

7   *Ibid.,* p. 1.

by the Rev. Joseph Doke. Tolstoy did not read it immediately as he was very ill; but when he did later, he was delighted.

The thoughts of Chesterton, Carpenter, Tolstoy, and of the Indian extremists, whose supposedly radical ideas only stemmed from the colonial values and ways of the West, provided the subject matter for a prolonged exchange of views with Dr. Pranjivan Mehta. These discussions would crystallize in the text of *Hind Swaraj*!

Gandhi wrote to Henry Polak that the mere change from British to Indian rule would not benefit India at all. India had to forget what it had learned in the last fifty years. India should discard machine-made clothing, irrespective of where it was made, in Europe or India. He felt that he was doing violence to his 'sense of what is right,' whenever he sat inside a train or motorbus. He was also now fully convinced that any idea on his part of studying medicine was entirely wrong. Modern hospitals 'perpetuate vice, misery and degradation'. If there were 'no hospitals for the cure of venereal diseases', we would see 'less sexual vice amongst us.' The treatment of venereal diseases in hospitals was an 'abomination'.[8]

That is indeed a strange, insensitive statement. Would there be less vice if there was no treatment? Gandhi was kidding himself. Human nature cannot always be denied, whatever the rigour of cultural or spiritual conditioning! If we become apathetic spectators of suffering due to human frailty and lack of discipline, we are closing our eyes to an ineradicable component of human existence and human behaviour. We are turning our eyes and ears away from others' distress, pain and suffering; we are non-violent only in relation to our actions to escape personal defilement. Our *ahiṁsā* is then concerned only with us; with our purity; with the progress of our soul and its cleansing in accordance with strict Jaina teaching. We are selfish, unconcerned, uncaring and callous, if our non-violence does not translate into compassionate remedies for those who suffer, and whom we can help, regardless of their fall from the path of rectitude. The promontory of principle is sometimes too steep and slippery to negotiate; and falls are inevitable. At times such as these, Gandhi's *ahiṁsā* shrinks into the confines of self, bereft of mercy, bereft of compassion, bereft of the need for kindness, forgiveness and meaningful assistance! *Ahiṁsā* is no longer true to itself, if it fails to translate into effective, helpful action!

---

8   *Collected Works*, Vol. 9, pp. 477-82.

This inner tumult and swirl of ideas shaped the text of *Hind Swaraj* written by Gandhi like a man possessed. 30,000 words flowed from his pen at a pace of febrile intensity in a matter of nine days between November 13 and 22, 1909, on board the *SS Kildonan Castle*, on his way back to South Africa. When the right hand tired, he wrote with the left, which he also did later, throughout his life.[9] This laconic testament of Gandhi's philosophy is presented, like the *Upaniṣads* and the *Gītā*, in the form of questions and answers between the Reader and the Editor. Ideas are broached; and questions are asked. The answers address socio-political concerns, and present simple expositions of philosophy; observations on the meaning of existence with total rejection of violence and weapons of mass destruction, and of the civilization that produces and uses them. The reader is advised to go back to the old Indian civilization in its pristine purity to achieve personal self-rule and national self-government, with soul-force or *satyāgraha* as the instrument of achievement.

Twenty chapters discuss 'the condition of India'; 'the condition of England'; what freedom signifies; what is meant by passive resistance; and what is 'true civilization'. Indian nationalism and the Indian National Congress receive their due critical assessment. Dadabhai Naoroji is praised as the 'Grand Old Man of India', who prepared the ground for people who could speak of Home Rule. Gandhi pays homage to Hume, the founder of the Congress, and to Sir William Wedderburn, who were good Englishmen and true friends of India. He salutes Gokhale for his devotion to India; for his service to India; and calls him a pillar of Home Rule. The moderation of men like Naoroji and Gokhale provided the stepping stones to the country's progress towards the distant goal of freedom. The sight of the Congress torn apart by differences between the Moderates and the Extremists makes him sad. If people hold views other than our own, that does not make them enemies of the country.

Gandhi points to the awakening of India brought about by Bengal's partition. The unrest is productive of discontent, which is good for India. The Congress has created an awareness of India as one nation; and the atrocity of Bengal's partition has helped to rouse India's people from a state of stupor and hopelessness. This, indeed, is the most glaring of the many injustices to which his countrymen have been subjected; and 'the

---

9 Cf. Gandhi, Rajmohan, *op. cit.,* p. 141.

salt tax is not a small injustice.'[10] In his discussion on *Swaraj*, Gandhi goes on to lament that 'we want English rule without the Englishmen. You want the tiger's nature, but not the tiger; that is to say, you would make India English... This is not the Swaraj that I want.'[11]

A chapter is devoted to the 'pitiable' plight of England. Gandhi compares the British Parliament, the 'Mother of Parliaments', to 'a sterile woman and a prostitute'. Harsh, but true, says Gandhi! 'That Parliament has not yet, of its own accord, done a single good thing. Hence, I have compared it to a sterile woman.... It is like a prostitute because it is under the control of ministers who change from time to time.'[12] He cannot 'recall a single instance in which finality can be predicted for its work.' This is Gandhi perhaps at his eloquent best in vituperative, verbal violence! He attributes the ills of England to modern civilization, though he recognizes the industry and enterprise of the people, and the basic morality of their thought.

In his answer to the question what civilization means, Gandhi refers to an English writer who calls this civilization a disease. Carpenter attributed man's decline into civilization and ill-health to his prepossession with the body and its demands. Gluttony was the main cause of disease requiring doctors, who helped people continue with their indulgences. With death kept at bay, nature was denied its due; and life became longer, leading to profligacy and license, detracting from human health and values. Gandhi repeats the hypothesis. People make the welfare of the body the sole object of their lives. They live in better-built houses; wear better clothes; and rush from one place to another at great speed by rail. People are trying to travel to any part of the world within a few hours by air. If this is called civilization, machines would take over from men. Modern warfare and weapons make it possible for one man to kill thousands. People in the past worked in open air; but they now work in mines and factories. Enslaved by monetary temptations and the lure of luxury goods, they suffer from new diseases that they had never known before. The number of hospitals goes up; and doctors keep busy researching to find new cures. Gandhi castigates the West's preoccupation with material goods at the expense

---

10 *Autobiography.*, p. 23.

11 *Hind Swaraj Or Indian Home Rule*, Navajivan Trust, Ahmedabad, Revised New Edition, 1990, p. 27.

12 *Ibid.*, p. 28.

of religion and morality;[13] and criticizes the constituents of Western civilization, such as parliaments, newspapers, machinery, manufacturing, railways, systems of education, and weapons of wholesale destruction. The Prophet Mohammed would regard it as a 'Satanic Civilization'. The Hindus, of course, call it the age of *Kali*, the Black Age. 'Civilization is not an incurable disease', but the English people, 'at present afflicted by it',[14] deserve our sympathy. True civilization is the moral mode of life which teaches man how to master himself.

Gandhi discusses how and why India was lost. The English did not take India. We gave it to them. 'They are not in India because of their strength, but because we keep them.' The English merchants found a footing in India only because the Indians helped them. Indian rulers sought their help in their fights with each other. Hostility between the Hindus and Muslims enabled the Company to exploit our differences, and gain control over the country. We gave it to them. The causes that helped the occupation of India, also aided the British retention of India. The English statement that they took India by the sword, and hold India by the sword, is entirely wrong. They are there only because we keep them. Unfortunately, we quarrel amongst ourselves; and strengthen their position.

Gandhi believes that India is being destroyed by modern civilization. His first complaint is that 'India is becoming irreligious.' 'We are turning away from God'. Our 'worldly ambition' is detracting from our 'religious ambition.' For Gandhi, life and religion go together, inseparable from each other. The so-called peace given to India by the English is only nominal. They have emasculated and made cowards of the Indians. We have to conquer fear in order to become strong. How can we be strong if we fear our own brethren?

Gandhi blames the railways, lawyers and doctors for making India poorer; and says it is time we woke up. It was only with the help of railways that the British tightened their hold on India. The railways have spread diseases with the movement of people in large numbers from one place to another. They are also to blame for the increasing frequency of famines in India, because people do not sell their produce where it is needed, but in the dearest markets. The ability of unwanted elements to travel from one

---

13   *Ibid.,* p. 33.

14   *Ibid.,* p. 34.

place to another has made the holy places unholy. The railways propagate evil.

Gandhi insists that Indians constituted one nation before the British arrived in the country. 'One thought inspired us. Our mode of life was the same.' The British succeeded in dividing us. The ancestors of Indians established holy places in the far corners of India, like Setubandha in Rameshwaram in the South, Jagannath in the East, and Haridwar in the North. India is 'one undivided land so made by nature'.[15]

To the question how Indians can be one nation when they are divided as Muslims, Parsis, Christians and Hindus, Gandhi's answer is: 'India cannot cease to be one nation because people belonging to different religions live in it.' Foreigners coming into a country do not destroy a nation. They become part of it by merging in it. India has an infinite capacity for assimilation. Almost every man has his own religion; but that does not mean that they are not members of one nation. If the Hindus believe that India is only for them, they are delusional. The Hindus, Muslims, Parsis and the Christians are all fellow countrymen. It is in their own interest to live in unity. Nationality and religion are not 'synonymous terms'.[16] The Hindus and the Muslims have learned to live together in peace with one another. They come from common ancestors. The change of religion does not make enemies of people. The Muslim's God is no different from the Hindu's God. There are different roads leading to the same goal. There is no need to quarrel; but we do, simply because we are enslaved; and then we take our quarrels to a third party, asking it to decide for us. As we advance in true knowledge and greater understanding, we will realize that we have no quarrel whatsoever with those who may follow a different religion. India has always been a spectacle of unity in diversity.

Asked for his views on cow protection, Gandhi says that the cow is a most useful animal. But he respects a Muslim or a Hindu as much as a cow. He would not kill a Muslim to save a cow. He would urge the Muslim to join him in protecting the cow. But if the Muslim would still insist on killing a cow for food, Gandhi would let him do so, because he could do no more. A person could, if he so wished, give his own life to save that of a cow,

---

15 *Ibid.*, p. 43.
16 *Ibid.*, p. 45.

but could not take his brother's. This was the true dictate of religion.[17] Gandhi goes on to say that 'Cow Protection societies may be considered Cow- killing societies.'[18] There is no one around to protect the cow from cruel ill-treatment by the Hindu, who does not really care for her or her progeny. As it is not allowed to kill a fellow man, a devotee of *ahimsā* can only plead, and do no more![19]

Gandhi points out that the *Quran* and the *Gītā* have so many passages that would be acceptable to both the Muslims and the Hindus. There can be no quarrel between them if one of the two decides that he would not quarrel. 'An arm striking the air will become disjointed'.[20] To the question whether the English would allow the Hindus and Muslims to live in a spirit of amity and goodwill, Gandhi answers that a third party cannot separate two brothers who want to live in peace. 'We should be ashamed to take our quarrels to the English.'[21] Even if we quarrel, we should never seek the assistance of a third party. We should never hire lawyers and go to the English courts of law.[22]

Gandhi devotes a chapter to the lawyers of India. It is a wholesale denunciation of the legal system. He calls into question the character and conduct of lawyers. They chase riches, not the interests of their clients. They do not care to settle any quarrels. Others' disputes give them joy; and they multiply them, as that brings more money. People going to courts for settlement of their disputes become 'unmanly and cowardly'.[23] It is as savage to use a third party to resolve a dispute as it is to do so by fighting. The judges are not infallible, and often hand out wrong decisions. The parties know what the truth is, and what is right; and can therefore settle their disputes themselves without recourse to any third party. To characterize going to a court as 'a sign of savagery', though, seems somewhat intemperate!

---

17 *Ibid.*, p. 46.
18 *Ibid.*, p. 47.
19 *Ibid.*
20 *Ibid.*, p. 48.
21 *Ibid.*, p. 49.
22 *Ibid.*
23 *Ibid.*, p. 51.

Lawyers have added to the quarrels between Hindus and Muslims, and helped establish English authority. Their greatest disservice is tightening of the English grip on India. British rule is strengthened by the law courts acting as arbiters of the Indians' fate. The English could not rule over India, if they only had English judges, English pleaders and English police. They could rule over India because they had Indian Judges, Indian pleaders and Indian police. Gandhi calls the legal profession 'as degrading as prostitution'.[24] It teaches immorality. If some lawyers are mindful of the public interest, they do so 'as men rather than as lawyers'. Lawyers can certainly do some good in the personal realm, in their personal capacity. A measure of autonomy is an inalienable part of the human condition and human action. The constraints arising out of the law and its institutions do not entirely extinguish a lawyer's personal ability to act for the good of the community. Personal morality is the imperative desideratum on which the fabric of *Hind Swaraj* is woven, and the case of *Hind Swaraj* is argued. Gandhi provided a personal example of moral integrity in his own legal practice; and helped settle his very first case in South Africa through mediation by bringing the two opposing parties together, and persuading them to settle on terms satisfactory to both. Society, says Gandhi, will be better off without lawyers. He wants to rid India of the apparatus and accessories of the Western civilization. He wants to go back to an authentic Indian way of life in small happily-knit communities characterized by common observance of traditional morality. Such a society would consist of people practising self-control to live together without any need for lawyers, and lower and higher courts, or the regulatory, binding paraphernalia of modern life. Lawyers' tricks and convoluted arguments would become irrelevant; and their hair-splitting dexterity would then be out of place, and unnecessary!

The utopia of his imaginary construction, though, never existed in India. Life was doubtless simpler; but there were always good and bad people; people who had discipline and self-control; people who lived by principles; and people who did not. Adjudication of disputes was an ineluctable necessity, even if the judicial process was not as rigidly structured as it became at a later day; and there was a great deal of consensual democratic element in the dispensation of justice. Anthony J. Parel draws attention to the influence of Maine on Gandhi's attack on the legal system. Traditional Indian villages had their own councils, which wielded both 'quasi-judicial

---

24 *Ibid.,* p. 52.

and quasi-legislative powers'. The new 'adversarial court-system' of the modern utilitarian state dealt a death-blow to the village as 'the ultimate unit of national life'. As economic power ebbed from the villages to the cities, the judicial and legislative functions of the village councils were usurped by the lower and higher courts established by the British. And a new breed of lawyers enabled the acquisitive urban middle class to feed itself fat on the mounting misery of the hapless peasantry.[25] For Gandhi, the penury of the peasant was one of the worst aspects of the modern civilization in India.

His own personal experience in South Africa transformed Gandhi the lawyer into Gandhi the law-breaker. His repeated return to the courts in search of justice, compassion and fair play ended in despair heaped on disappointments. The chapter on lawyers in *Hind Swaraj* arose out of the judiciary's unwillingness, pusillanimity and opacity to pleas for justice from Gandhi and his associates. We see Gandhi here clearly contemplating his resignation from the legal profession. Recourse to law had frustrated him. *Hind Swaraj* is a scorching statement of that frustration!

The next chapter discusses doctors. Gandhi wanted to become a doctor to serve his country. But not now. He was finally dissuaded, when a South African medical student told him in London that he had to dissect about fifty frogs during the course of his medical studies. Gandhi calls quacks 'better than highly qualified doctors'. Doctors prescribe medicines only to cure diseases, but not habits. The medicines therefore 'result in loss of control over the mind.' As Gandhi puts it: 'I have indulged in vice. I contract a disease, a doctor cures me, the odds are that I shall repeat the vice. Had the doctor not intervened, nature would have done its work...'[26] Gandhi is wrong. Instead of acquiring mastery over myself, I would have succumbed to a pitiable end, full of suffering, shame and social rejection. The diffusion of infections, like aids in our own times, would have decimated entire populations. This cold morality devoid of any compassion shocks the reader. Gandhi accuses doctors of taking up the profession to make money and gain honours; and forgetting the basic purpose of service to humanity.

---

25 Cf. Anthony J. Parel (ed.), *Hind Swaraj and Other Writings,* p.xlii; DiSalvo, *op.cit.,* p. 302.

26 *Hind Swaraj,* p. 53.

What is 'true civilization'? Gandhi mentions many old civilizations that are dead and gone. India is an exception, as its old civilization, sound at the core, still survives. Westerners charge the people of India with indolence; with an incapacity to change themselves. Gandhi is quite happy with the fact. Why should we change what is tried and tested and true? Civilization shows the path of duty. Duty and morality mean 'good conduct'.[27] Gandhi thinks that India has nothing to learn from others in this respect. India's seers told us to discard pleasures and luxuries. Indians have been happy with the same plough and their simple cottages since time immemorial. Indian education has remained the same as before. India has been free from 'life-corroding competition'. People followed their old trade or occupation, and charged a regulation wage. Indians could invent machinery, but deliberately desisted from doing so, because they did not want to become slaves. It was important to keep life simple; to secure the self-worth and autonomy of humankind; to sanctify the work they did with their hands and feet; to guard against the degradation of humanity by the supremacy of the machine. That kept people healthy and happy.

Large cities were undesirable, as they would enable all kinds of vices to flourish; and the poor would be exploited by the rich. Small villages provided the true venues of happiness. The kings with all their weaponry and mastery of the earth were still considered inferior to the 'Rishis' and the 'Fakirs', wandering seers wedded to asceticism and learning. India was therefore able to teach rather than learn from others. Indians had their own courts, lawyers and doctors. They were not considered superior to others; and did not behave like robbers. There was justice; and people avoided the courts. Agriculture was the main occupation; and that, indeed, was true Home Rule. Paradoxically, therefore, the way forward for Indians led back to India's past. Gandhi asks people to go to these villages of India to see what life is like without the railways and the hallmarks of modern civilization. He recognizes the fact that there are many blemishes and many evil practices in Indian society; but tells us that reformers have always sought to eradicate them. The Indian civilization elevates the moral being of man. The western civilization increases immorality. The Indian civilization believes in God. Western civilization is Godless. Gandhi therefore tells 'every lover of India to cling to the old Indian civilization

---

27 *Ibid.,* p. 55.

even as a child clings to the mother's breast.'²⁸ As he sees it, the superiority of ancient Indian civilization arises from the primacy of humans instead of machines and money; from its non-violence; from its morality; from its spirituality.

Gandhi, though, had no first-hand knowledge of Indian villages. The village idyll is at variance with the harsh realities. The hierarchical structure of society condemned the lower classes to abject misery and ruthless exploitation. There was no competition because there was no permissible scope; no possibility for ambitions to soar beyond allocated ambits of compulsory, hereditary duty; no education; no medical facility; and no means of reasonably easy transport, as there were no roads to speak of. And Gandhi was content with the thought of rural illiteracy! Gandhi was dreaming. Recession into a glorious, untarnished utopian past of his imagination was as impracticable as it was impossible to resurrect or achieve in any approximation to his ideal. But he was preparing himself; trying to convince and persuade himself to take the plunge into a life of public service; to give up his legal practice; to give up earning money as ordinary mortals do; to propose and let God dispose! *Hind Swaraj* is an ardent expression of a dream. It is an earnest essay in convincing himself!

'Unquestionably the best', Indian civilization has survived a succession of shocks.²⁹ The enslaved are only those affected by the Western civilization. He excludes himself, despite his Western education, association with Western people, his study of Western writings cited at the end of the book, and his use of a Western language. 'It is swaraj when we learn to rule ourselves.'³⁰ Each of us has to personally cultivate and experience this swaraj. 'If the English become Indianized, we can accommodate them. If they wish to remain in India with their civilization, there is no room for them...'³¹ 'We brought the English, and we keep them...our adoption of their civilization makes their presence in India at all possible.'³²

Merely having the reins of government in Indian hands would not make India happy. So many Indians groan under the misrule of Indian princes.

---

28 *Ibid.*, p. 57.
29 *Ibid.*, p. 58.
30 *Ibid.*, p. 59.
31 *Ibid.*
32 *Ibid.*, p. 60.

We do not want to free India by recourse to assassinations. Madanlal Dhingra's was a blind and misguided love of India. It is a great mistake not to realize the connection between means and ends; 'there is just the same inviolable connection between the means and the end as there is between the seed and the tree.'[33] Violence will, but non-violence will never distort the outcome. If Indians tell the British that they will petition them no more, as their just demands are always rebuffed, and that they will cease dealing with them altogether, the rulers will have no option but to climb down. 'Love-force' and 'soul-force' expressed in and through 'passive resistance' is indestructible. It defeats the power of arms.[34] Intense discussions with the extremists in London added an element of acute urgency to the contents of this text.

'The force of love is the same as the force of the soul or truth.'[35] History is unfortunately only a chronicle of wars. Peace causes no upheavals to attract the attention of the historian. We owe our lives to the force of love and truth, not war. People and nations largely live in peace; but history is regrettably preoccupied with the cruel interruptions to peace.[36] 'Soul-force, being natural, is not noted in history.' Passive resistance secures rights by personal suffering. It rejects 'resistance by arms.' Do not accept anything against your conscience. If we do not like a law applying to us, we do not obey it, and 'accept the penalty for its breach.' We are using soul-force. 'It involves sacrifice of self.'[37] If we find certain laws unjust, we 'do not submit to the laws', without hurting anyone. 'That we should obey laws good and bad is a new-fangled notion.' Do not obey laws repugnant to your conscience. To obey them is 'unmanly'. Obedience to unjust laws will promote slavery.[38] Passive resistance is the only way to challenge unjust laws and defeat brute force.

'Passive resistance, that is, soul-force, is matchless. It is superior to the force of arms.'[39] A passive resister will refuse to obey an unjust law repugnant to

---

33 *Ibid.,* p. 64.
34 *Ibid.,* p. 68.
35 *Ibid.,* p. 69.
36 *Ibid.,* p. 70.
37 *Ibid.,* p. 71.
38 *Ibid.,* p. 72.
39 *Ibid.,* p. 73.

his conscience, regardless of consequence, clearly demonstrating that he is neither weak nor a coward. He who is prepared to welcome even death as a 'bosom friend', is a true passive resister. It is a weapon of the brave. In India, passive resistance has always been commonly used. People ceased to cooperate with rulers when they became oppressors. Gandhi's nationalism is far more indigenous than that of the radical extremists, as it embraces both culture and politics. As Hunt points out, he, too, is ready to lay down his life for his cause, which is no less radical.[40]

Passive resistance for the deliverance of the country requires chastity, poverty, truthfulness and fearlessness.[41] Chastity for Gandhi means abstinence from sex, which depletes a man's 'stamina', and makes him an 'emasculated' coward. A husband and wife making love are likened to animals. Gandhi would prohibit sex except only for progeny. A passive resister would not even have that limited recourse to sex, as he would have no desire for children. A married man can remain perfectly 'chaste'. Fearlessness would come through non-attachment. Voluntary poverty would add to the firmness of resolution and action.

Gandhi scoffs at the introduction of compulsory education by the Maharaja Gaekwar in his state. He pares down the meaning of education to mere 'knowledge of letters', which is an instrument as often used as abused.[42] A peasant works honestly and hard to earn his bread. He has basic knowledge of the world around him, and behaves properly with his parents, children, neighbours and others. He knows and obeys the traditional 'rules of morality'. He cannot write even his own name, as he does not read or write. The knowledge of letters will not 'add an inch to his happiness'![43] This denigration of compulsory education, and portrayal of an illiterate peasant as an ideal human being imbued with natural social morality and responsibility is nothing but the glorification of animal existence, with the world of learning closed; with the scriptures of any religion inaccessible; with the flights of fancy in prose and poetry unapproachable; with the sciences seeking to understand the universe a prohibited domain. Basic animal functions with a slightly higher understanding and application

---

40   Cf. Hunt, *Gandhi in London*, Promilla & Co., New Delhi, 1993, p. 148.
41   *Hind Swaraj*, p. 75.
42   *Ibid.*, p. 77.
43   *Ibid.*, p. 78.

of morality would be the pinnacle of felicity! Gandhi knew little about India's villages; their closed societies and ruthless social divisions; their tyranny and exploitation of the lower classes without compunction as a matter of God-given right and Divine dispensation; their imprisonment in superstitions; their gross religious practices; their inability to secure proper medical treatment; their paucity of clothes and proper nutrition; and their utter ignorance of the world around them. That, for Gandhi, was a millennium of unalloyed bliss! Alberuni, who came to India with the invader Mahmud of Ghazni, was astonished and shocked by the self-conceit of Indians who thought that they knew everything; that there was nothing they could learn from others. What was the result? They were beaten out of their wits by foreign invaders, and before they could do anything, they were treated as ignorant heathen by their new masters. But Gandhi would leave the peasant undisturbed in his world of unlettered bliss!

Gandhi practised what he preached, when he deprived his sons of any formal, structured, academic, institutional education. He stayed smug and unmoved when the boys grumbled; and the eldest, Harilal, never forgave him for his serious, in the son's eyes, dereliction of fatherly duty!

That India had a very old civilization was demonstrated and emphasized by the study of Sanskrit, the *Vedas*, the great Epics and the Indian philosophical texts in the West. Scholars, both Westerners and Indians, and men like Vivekananda and Rabindranath Tagore were giving a new content to Indian minds, filling them with an increasing awareness of their past greatness. That is why Gandhi repeatedly called India's civilization the best. But even the ancient best had its blemishes! The lofty heights of religion, philosophy, literature and the arts notwithstanding, life for the lower classes was often nasty, brutish and short. The idealized paradise of the myth-makers does not really correspond with the harsh realities of the past, which consisted of both good and bad; happiness and suffering; peace as well as violence!

Gandhi quotes Huxley to explain liberal education in terms of the body trained to obey one's will, a clear intellect capable of logical thinking, a mind conversant with the 'fundamental truths of nature'. But how would Gandhi understand a quote from Huxley without any ability to read? He says that the sciences he studied did not help him control his senses. Education, elementary or higher, does not help control of one's senses, 'does not make men of us'. And he blames it for man's inability to do his duty. A strange, incredible charge! Education is a primary necessity, a mental process of progress, a means of satisfying natural curiosity. Gandhi forgot the ancient Indian indictment of parents who do not educate their children: *mātā śatru pitā vairī yena bālo na pāṭhitaḥ*. A mother and father are enemies of their children, if they fail to educate them.[44] Control of the senses is dictated by social necessity to make it possible to live together in peace and harmony; and as we have already seen elsewhere, morality is not the prerogative and practice of human-kind alone. Education enforces it by enabling us to understand its value, its efficacy and its necessity! Gandhi wants to relegate us to a less than human level of mental growth and conduct!

Gandhi says that lower and higher education has been of no use to him; and his life would have been as useful without it. Who would believe it? He is trying to prove 'the rottenness of this education'.[45] He does not want to make this education compulsory. 'Character-building... is primary education.' 'Our ancient school system is enough.' Gandhi forgets that the ancient school system was based on class and caste, and closed to vast sections of society. It was a state of institutionalized discrimination, painful to those who were excluded and consigned to the unrelieved darkness of ordained ignorance. Have we not heard the painful story of Ekalavya and Droṇācārya in the *Mahābhārata?* Education, past and present, does help the inculcation of moral values!

Gandhi accuses the British of imposing dated systems of education on India; and says that English speaking and its use has enslaved India. It is both true and false! It was truer in Gandhi's days than ours. The imposition of a foreign language is a blighting burden on a child. It stifles our languages; and makes us feel inferior. But it also opens windows, enlarges horizons, more so today than before. Gandhi is right when he says that Hindi should be the national language of India; and also when he exhorts North Indians to learn Tamil, and the South Indians to learn Hindi.[46] But his plea for the replacement of the study of sciences with religious education is a recipe for dwarfing our ability to understand ourselves, the world and the universe

---

44 *Vidyā dhanaṁ sarva dhanaṁ pradhānaṁ*: learning is the greatest wealth - Bhartṛhari.

45 *Hind Swaraj*, p. 79.

46 *Ibid.*, p. 81.

around us. 'To restore India to its pristine condition',[47] we would have to close our eyes to current realities; bury our heads in the sand! In the present age of instant communication and fast travel, distinctions between the Eastern and Western civilizations fall to the ground as increasingly false, irrelevant, contumelious remnants of the past. The present state of the world admits only of a global culture with a global consciousness and responsibility for the preservation of our earth and its environment.

Gandhi wept when he read R.C. Dutt's *Economic History of India*. It brought home to him the stark exploitation and the ruin of India by the machinery of the West. 'Machinery is the chief symbol of modern civilization; it represents a great sin.'[48] It is desolating Europe, making men and women work in abysmal conditions, or else, throwing them out of work. He does not want Indians to use cloth produced by the mills of Manchester, or for that matter, cloth produced by the mills in India. He implores Indian mill-owners not to open more mills, but on the other hand to 'gradually contract their business'.[49] Indians should use handloom cloth; and should discard all machinery they can do without. When asked whether it would be good or bad to use a printing press to spread his message, Gandhi resorts to the old adage: 'sometimes poison is used to kill poison'.[50]

Gandhi's identification of machinery with evil can be understood only with reference to the relentless exploitation of the working class in hopeless working conditions, detrimental alike to their health and mental sanity. Tools and machines, simple and complex, otherwise symbolize the progress of humankind from savagery to civilization. It is indeed most desirable to engage in productive physical exertion; but there is only so much that human hands can do in a place-time context. Machines have definitely made life easier and more human, if they have also created new problems to contend with. The telegraph, criticized yet used by Gandhi, has gone, superseded by new super-fast technology, which continually breaks new barriers. The development of artificial intelligence with all its promise also contains a serious threat to human autonomy. Automation poses an alarming challenge to the contracting scope of human employment. The

---

47 *Ibid.*, p. 82.
48 *Ibid.*, p. 83.
49 *Ibid.*, p. 84.
50 *Ibid.*, p. 85.

lawyers and doctors are still here; and the world can do with many more hospitals. The peasant's life, though, continues to be a soulless grind dependent on the vagaries and caprice of nature, always held hostage by market forces that the farmers cannot control!

Petitioning the British is an exercise in self-derogation. Those who maintain peace under British pressure will fight when they go. Let it happen if it must! If we must fight before we find peace, so be it! We do not need a third party to mediate and 'protect the weak'.[51] This 'protection' is our undoing. Home rule is possible only with this realization. How prescient, when we recall the blood-bath in the wake of India's partition, and the displacement of millions! A partition that solved nothing!! A partition that created problems defying all attempts at solution!!!

Gandhi tells the British that they can remain only as servants of the people, not as masters. If they act against our will, we will not help. But let us not blame them. 'They came because of us, and remain also for the same reason.'[52] We can be free only through suffering. Self-rule is real Home Rule. It begins with an individual's rule over himself, translated into self-government at the political level. Indians of all religious persuasions constitute one nation fully entitled to *swaraj* or Home Rule.

Petitioning had failed to achieve its purpose; but violence and bloodshed was indeed immoral. The British would not just quit or walk away without pressure. Violence would invoke counter-violence. It would also deteriorate into a habit in the Indians' dealings with each other; and that would be sad and disastrous! The formulation and prescription of *Satyāgraha* was a revolutionary strategy that was neither moderate nor extremist in its joust with the rulers. It was an altogether original attack on arbitrary privilege and inequality, unjust, immoral laws and official oppression. The Transvaal *Satyāgraha* had vindicated its moral superiority as well as its efficacy as a political tool of constructive non-cooperation.

Gandhi concludes his text with a dramatic declaration of attitude and intent:

> 'I bear no enmity towards the English...but I do towards their civilization...I have endeavoured to explain [Swaraj] as I

---

51 *Ibid.,* p. 87.
52 *Ibid.,* p. 91.

understand it, and my conscience testifies that my life henceforth is dedicated to its attainment.'

The man of destiny has his gaze fixed firmly on India. His *Satyāgraha* would be the instrument of her deliverance! Unmistakable intimations of his mission 'to spread truth and non-violence among mankind' had stirred him as early as 1906 in the dark and pathless tracts of the Zulu country racked by the cruel British suppression of the so-called *Bambatha rebellion*.[53] In 1937, he wrote of his first awareness of 'the mission for which I was born', when he took the vow of *brahmacarya*.[54]

An appendix lists twenty books recommended for reading; and we can clearly see that his criticism of the West and its civilization is based on the anxiety gnawing at the hearts of many Western writers. Six books by Tolstoy, two by Thoreau, two by Ruskin, and the others by Sherard, Carpenter, Taylor, Blount, Mazzini, Plato, Max Nordau and Maine inform and influence the pages of *Hind Swaraj*. The works of two Indian writers, *Economic History of India* by R.C. Dutt, and *Poverty and Un-British Rule in India* by Dadabhai Naoroji, add substance to his condemnation of the British rule in India.

The spirited dialogue between the Reader and the Editor allows the juxtaposition of contrary ideas in recognition of the multi-dimensional nature of reality. *Hind Swaraj* is a total repudiation of the West and its values because of their main ingredient, brute force, used for the exploitation of the world. India has her philosophies of love and non-violence, peace and tolerance, which alone suit India. Violence is totally forsaken. 'Killing is evil in all circumstances'.[55] When G.D.H. Cole said it might be necessary to resort to arms and violence to stem the tide of brutal aggression and slaughter of innocents, Gandhi insisted that pacifism was 'a more effective weapon in the long run'.[56] And in 1921, he reiterated the condemnation of modern civilization in *Hind Swaraj*, which taught the gospel of love in place of hate; and replaced violence with self-sacrifice.[57]

---

53 He said so to the Viceroy Lord Linlithgow in 1942. Cf. *Collected Works* 77, p. 50, 31 December, 1942.

54 *Collected Works* 65, p. 111, 18 April, 1937; Cf. Tidrick, *op.cit.*, p. 72.

55 *Hind Swaraj*, p. 11.

56 *Ibid.*, p. 10.

57 *Ibid.*, p. 14.

He preaches a religion which includes and transcends all religions, based on duty synonymous with quintessential morality, to which we all alike subscribe, side by side with our allegiance to different religions. Religions do not divide, should not divide, and should not be used to divide humankind. India has been, and remains a composite nation made up of Hindus, Muslims, Christians, Parsis and others alike, inextricably bound by culture and common ethnicity.

Gandhi rejects machinery as evil. It damages the environment, reduces human fitness and throws people out of work. It makes a few rich at the expense of many. But the use of machines to exploit labour should be blamed on their owners, not on the machines. The ultimate offender is man, who must determine what is beneficial and what is harmful; what is profitable in the short term, but deleterious in the long term. Delisle Burns points to Gandhi's 'fundamental philosophical error' in investing machinery with an evil property, calling it evil.[58] Machines are neither good nor bad; they can be used and misused. There are machines and medical techniques that save human and animal lives. But, then, Gandhi would perhaps not like to save lives with surgical operations and transplants! He would let nature take its course. He would not appreciate that nature gave humans the intelligence and the capacity to devise new tools and methods of treatment to save lives; to promote longevity; to make the lives of those alive more meaningful to them and to the others around! Condemning the practitioners of medicine for vivisection would rule out operations which cure ailments and cease pain; and make life sufferable. From a doctor's point of view, the march of civilization is nothing but the progressive conquest of disease and reduction of physical suffering through medication and surgery down the ages. India was the first country in the world where plastic surgery and cataract operations were performed. Gandhi would not countenance medical research and the development of new treatments for known and hitherto unknown diseases. His blind opposition to vaccination against small-pox is an exercise in false, incomprehensible morality! He would not allow the use of alcohol in any shape or form in any medication. He forgets that the ancient Indians drank *soma* and *surā*; and the *Āyurvedic* pharmacopeia includes and prescribes the use of alcoholic potions in so many *āsavas*. Religion does not come into it. Spirituality does not clash with it. Morality is not hurt or damaged by it. Hallucinogenic drugs are used as much for the treatment of diseases and management of pain, as for

---

58 *Ibid.*, p. 7.

generating a heightened spiritual awareness or state of ecstasy. Alcohol has been 'a prime mover of human culture from the beginning, fuelling the development of arts, language and religion.'[59] Our ape-ancestors ate fermented fruit on the floors of forests; and that certainly 'preadapted' us 'for consuming alcohol'.[60] Great leaps forward in human history, from the beginnings of farming to the origin of writing, have 'a possible link to alcohol.'[61]

Gandhi is right when he says that all human beings are entitled to equality and self-rule. Inequality imposed by the state is totally unacceptable. Exploitative institutions like empires and their blatant discrimination against their subjects are alike unjust and unethical. Unjust laws must be disobeyed; but the disobedience must be non-violent; the resistance must be passive. Love your opponent even when you oppose his oppression. Love-force or soul-force always wins, as it does not in any way hurt those it opposes. Self-suffering will kindle the conscience of the tyrant; and prompt correction and progress towards justice and fair play. Right means alone guarantee right results. Self-concern takes care of the body. Concern for others takes care of the soul. He throws a life-line to the English rulers of India by telling them that they can stay as servants, not masters, of the people.

The streak of fanaticism and intolerance in many passages of *Hind Swaraj* does some violence to the precept of *ahiṁsā* in writing, as it would in speech and action. When questioned about the extreme nature of his total rejection of the paraphernalia of modern life, Gandhi conceded that he was visualizing only the ultimate goal, yet distant and unrealizable. The present could not be immediately disowned and discarded. He would not shy away, for the present, from using the current instruments of government and human movement. Reversion to the state of nature would take time. But he would ideally reject all machinery, as he would his own body, 'not helpful to salvation'. He would accept machinery only if, like the body, 'it subserves the growth of the soul.'[62]

---

59 Cf. *National Geographic*, February 2017, 'A 9,000-Year Love Affair', pp. 30-53.

60 *Ibid.*, p. 44.

61 *Ibid.*, p. 38.

62 *Hind Swaraj*, p. 9.

Gandhi identifies culture as the core of conflict between India and England. Rejection of the English culture was a pre-requisite to the liberation of India. But was it? Look at India today. So many elements of India's contemporary culture attest her untiring, undiminished assimilative capacity! When told, however, that civilization must be mended, not ended, he agreed that it was not irreparable! But 'the renunciation of London in 1909 marked the intellectual divide between Mr. Gandhi, Barrister-at-Law, and Mahatma Gandhi. The popular title did not appear for many years nor was the transformation completed in an instant, but after *Hind Swaraj* the direction was set.'[63]

The Gujarati original and the English translation of *Hind Swaraj* were both banned in India. Gandhi addressed a letter of complaint to the Home Secretary, Government of India; but the prophet of *ahiṁsā* who wrote the book in a hurry to debunk and discredit the violence of the Indian extremists, cut no ice with the humourless bureaucrats of the Raj.[64]

A decade later, 'except for withdrawing the word "prostitute" used in connection with the British Parliament which annoyed an English lady,' Gandhi would not wish to make any change at all in the text of *Hind Swaraj*.[65] Again, in 1938: '...after the stormy thirty years through which I have since passed, I have seen nothing to make me alter the views expounded in it...The reader may balance against this the opinion of a dear friend, who alas! is no more, that it was the production of a fool.'[66]

Gandhi sent a copy of *Indian Home Rule* to Tolstoy, who acknowledged in his letter dated May 8, 1910, that passive resistance was 'a question of the greatest importance not only for India but for the whole of humanity.' Tolstoy also spoke of Gandhi's biography by Rev. Doke: '...your biography...interested me much deeply and gave me the possibility to know and understand you better.'[67]

Tolstoy had noted in his diary the closeness of Gandhi's work to his own.

---

63 Hunt, *op.cit.*, p. 157.
64 *Cf.* Guha, *op. cit.*, pp. 375-76.
65 *Cf.* Chadha, *op.cit.*, p. 165.
66 Segaon, July 14th, 1938, *Aryan Path – Special Hind Swaraj number,* published in September, 1938.
67 *Collected Works* 10, p. 505, 1963 edn.

He wrote again to Gandhi on September 7, 1910, a long letter on receipt of the journal *Indian Opinion*: '...The more I live – and specially now that I am approaching death – the more I feel inclined to express to others the feelings which so strongly move my being, and which...are of great importance. That is, what one calls non-resistance, is in reality nothing else but the discipline of love underperformed by false interpretation. Love is the aspiration for communion and solidarity with other souls, and that aspiration always liberates the source of noble activities. That love is the supreme and unique law of human life, which everyone feels in the depth of one's soul....

'That law of love has been promulgated by all the philosophies – Indian, Chinese, Hebrew, Greek and Roman. I think that it has been most clearly expressed by Christ, who said that in that law is contained both the law and the Prophets...Christ knew also, just as all reasonable human beings must know, that the employment of violence is incompatible with love, which is the fundamental law of life...

'...the life of the Christian people is an absolute contradiction between their profession and the basis of their life; contradiction between love recognized as the law of life, and violence recognized as inevitable in different departments of life...

'....Is killing always a crime?... 'yes, always'.

'....your work in Transvaal, which seems to be far away from the centre of the world, is yet the most fundamental and the most important to us supplying the most weighty practical proof in which the world can now share and with which must participate not only the Christian but all the peoples of the world.'[68]

The advocate of violence to liberate India, Shyamji Krishnavarma poured scorn on *Hind Swaraj,* and denounced Gandhi as 'an admirer of Jesus Christ' trying to preach and practise 'the extreme Christian theory of suffering.' Gandhi had identified his *ahiṁsā* and *Satyāgraha* with India's spiritual legacy; and violence with the West and its ways. 'Krishnavarma counterattacked by linking Gandhi with a supposedly 'western' religion'.[69]

---

68 *Collected Works* 10, pp. 512-514.
69 Gandhi, Rajmohan, *op. cit.,* p. 143.

As his grandson rightly asserts, 'Gandhi's strategy did succeed, in South Africa and India.'[70] The British were often outmanoeuvred and at their wits' end; and the Indians sincerely felt that they stood on higher moral ground than their adversary. And his leadership definitely discredited and discouraged the practitioners of terror!

On board ship, Gandhi also found time to write a number of letters side by side with his preoccupation with *Hind Swaraj*. In a letter to Manilal, the father reiterated the importance of morality and *brahmacarya*. Experience was the real school. Bapu had to be trusted! The son's eagerness to study was a cause of anxiety for both![71] And in another letter to his third son Ramdas, Gandhi apologized for not being able to bring anything from Europe for him, as he liked only things Indian.

In a letter to Maganlal, dated November 27, 1909, Gandhi confided to him that he was prepared to induct Manilal into the struggle if the son so wished, and if his mother agreed! That would indeed do good to his restless spirit![72]

---

70 *Ibid.*

71 *Collected Works*, 10, pp. 70-1.

72 *Collected Works*, 10, pp. 81-2.

Chapter 56

Gandhi Returns

The voyage which began on November 13, ended when Gandhi disembarked at Cape Town on November 30, 1909, to be greeted by the welcome news that Ratanji Jamshedji Tata had donated Rs. 25,000 to the Satyāgraha Fund. The timely gift rescued the Phoenix Settlement, the *Indian Opinion,* and the *Satyāgraha* from dire financial straits. The son of Sir Jamshedji Tata, founder of the first steel mill in India, was a friend of Gokhale, and an informed benefactor of the Servants of India Society. He was watching developments in the Transvaal with keen interest; and was pained by the failure of Gandhi's mission in London. He kept abreast of the public meetings held in India in support of the cause; but felt that sympathy and support must translate into meaningful monetary assistance to relieve 'destitution', and help the movement. He sent Gokhale a cheque for Rs. 25,000, with a letter in which he expressed admiration for 'a spectacle of great nobility of aim, resoluteness of purpose and strength of moral fibre with which we Indians are not usually credited.'[1]

Gokhale informed Gandhi by telegram; and encouraged others to emulate Tata's munificent gesture to lend financial support to Gandhi and his colleagues in their determination to do or die for the honour of their country. The appeal bore fruit, as other donors, big and small, came forward. J.B. Petit forwarded £750 from Bombay. Pranjivan Mehta sent as much from Rangoon. Donations came in from India, London, Mozambique and Zanzibar.[2] Surely, the help received could not be more timely! Over

---

1 Ratan Tata to Gokhale, 29 November, 1909, File No. 242, Part I, Gokhale Papers, NAI; Guha, *op.cit.*, p. 612, n. 4; *Collected Works*, 10, pp. 98-99.

2 Cf. Tendulkar, *op.cit.*, p. 138.

3,000 Indians had been imprisoned; and more than 200 had been deported. Hundreds of families had been reduced to ruin and unspeakable suffering. Even the otherwise somnolent Indian princes evinced interest in passive resistance.

The Bengal Provincial Congress Committee suggested Gandhi's name for presiding over the forthcoming session of the Indian National Congress. Asked for a message, Gandhi wrote:'...I am unable to think of anything but the task immediately before me, namely, the struggle that is going on in the Transvaal. I hope our countrymen throughout India realize that it is national in its aim, in that it has been undertaken to save India's honour. I may be wrong, but I have not hesitated publicly to remark that it is the greatest struggle of modern times, because it is the purest as well as in its goal as in its methods. Violence in any shape or form is entirely eschewed...Self-suffering is the only true and effective means to procure lasting reforms....'

And he told the Congress, with utter conviction: '...for the many ills we suffer from in India passive resistance is an infallible panacea...it is the only weapon that is suited to the genius of our people and our land....'[3]

There is no modesty or hesitation in the prescription. The tone of certitude brooks no contradiction! He has formulated a new philosophy of action defying the might of the oppressor with loving non-violence; challenging unjust laws with resolute non-compliance; and defeating any chastisement with willing self-suffering. 'The greatest struggle of modern times', as he repeatedly calls it in his communications to Tolstoy and the Indian National Congress, proclaims the primacy of *ahiṁsā* and *satyāgraha* as universally applicable tools of social and political correction.

At the Congress session presided over by Madan Mohan Malaviya, Gokhale moved a resolution on South Africa, memorable for its praise of Gandhi:

'...it is one of the privileges of my life that I know Mr. Gandhi intimately and I can tell you that a purer, a nobler, a braver and a more exalted spirit has never moved on this earth...He is a man who may be well described as a man among men, a hero among heroes, a patriot among patriots, and

---

3 Cf. Tendulkar, *op.cit.*, pp. 135-6.

we may well say that in him Indian humanity at the present time has really reached its high watermark.'⁴

Rs. 18,000 were collected for the relief of Indian *satyāgrahīs* in South Africa. Malaviya, the President, sent Gandhi a cable expressing the appreciative support of the Congress; and another to Botha asking for much needed relief to the Indians. The Nizam of Hyderabad sent Rs. 2,500; and the Muslim league under Aga Khan's leadership also collected Rs. 3,000 for the Passive Resistance Relief Fund.⁵

Gandhi and Habib journeyed to Johannesburg from Cape Town, and were welcomed by a large crowd at the railway station. He spoke the next day at a meeting of Tamil ladies to thank them for their brave support to their men in and out of jail. On December 5, 1909, Gandhi addressed a large gathering of about 1,500 people at the Hamidiya Mosque. He emphasized the significance and global repercussions of their struggle; and thanked Ratan Tata for his generous gift to the campaign. And he thanked Henry Polak for his 'magnificent efforts' in India, which moved the people to help their cause.⁶

The *Satyāgraha* was due for renewal. In a letter to *Indian Opinion,* Gandhi announced that he would soon be in jail once more. His second son Manilal, now seventeen, would also court arrest in step with his father's belief that going to jail or suffering 'similar hardships with a pure motive for the motherland is the truest kind of education.'⁷

Gandhi found his way to Natal and Phoenix in the third week of December, and Kasturba was happy to see him. He spoke to a cheering crowd in Durban on December 20, and announced that some young men including his son Manilal and Joseph Royeppen, the Cambridge-educated barrister, would be accompanying him to the Transvaal in the hope of being arrested and jailed.

Gandhi crossed into the Transvaal with six companions on December 22, 1909; but to their surprise, they were allowed to pass through without

---

4   *Speeches and Writings of Gopal Krishna Gokhale,* G.A. Natesan & Co., Madras, Third Edition, p. 726.
5   Cf. Tendulkar, *op. cit.*, p.137.
6   Cf. Guha, *op. cit.,* p.387.
7   *Ibid.*

being arrested. The *Transvaal Leader* remarked that the authorities did not want to give the Congress session at Lahore any opportunity to criticize the Transvaal Government for their treatment of Indians.[8] It was at this session that the Rev. C.F. Andrews gave all the money in his wallet to the Passive Resisters Relief Fund.

Not to be outmanoeuvred by the Government, Gandhi sent Royeppen and Manilal back to Natal, to return to Johannesburg and hawk without a licence. The purpose was twofold: to break the law; and also to show that selling fruits and vegetables was no less honourable than the work of a clerk or lawyer. They were then arrested, and sentenced to ten days' jail with hard labour.[9]

The Tamils were foremost, as before, in offering *Satyāgraha*, and bravely, stoically, facing every hardship. In a letter to Gokhale, Gandhi gave the highest praise to Thambi Naidoo, 'perhaps the bravest and staunchest' of them all.[10] The Tamil women refused to be outdone by their men; and two of them came into Gandhi's office to take off all their ornaments and jewellery, and say that they would not wear them until the end of the struggle.

Guha speaks in superlative terms of the loyalty, industry and sympathy of Sonja Schlesin for Gandhi and the Indian cause. Rushing around on her bicycle, she visited the passive resisters in jail, carrying food and messages for them from relatives who could not go. With the leaders in and out of jail, she managed the Passive Resistance Fund; kept meticulous records; and helped families and individuals in need of urgent financial assistance.[11] Years later, Gandhi was fulsome in his tribute to the 'young girl', who 'soon constituted herself the watchman and warder of the morality not only of my office but of the whole movement.'[12]

The *Satyāgraha* had brought men of the mettle of Thambi Naidoo and Parsi Rustomji to the fore. In February, 1910, Rustomji came out of jail after enduring a year-long captivity; and spoke of the heartless treatment

---

8   Cf. Tendulkar, *op.cit.,* p.136.

9   *Indian Opinion*, January 1910; Guha, *op. cit.*, p. 388.

10   *Ibid.*

11   Guha, *op.cit.*, p. 388-9.

12   *Satyagraha in South Africa, Collected Works*, Vol. 29, p. 146.

to which he had been subjected. He went to Natal to restore his shattered health, and to put his business, in a state of ruin, back into shape. In a defiant statement to the press, he warned the Government that he remained unsubdued and unbroken in spirit, and would stand ready to go to jail again.

Two English friends of Gandhi, J.C. Gibson, a lawyer, and Charles Phillips, a non-conformist minister and colleague of Joseph Doke, offered to approach the Government to explore the possibility of a compromise. Always open to the idea, Gandhi told them that the Government had to repeal the existing legislation to enable the *bona fide* residents of the Transvaal to enter and devote themselves to their occupations and trade. The Government also had to modify the laws to 'enable any Asiatic immigrants of culture to enter the Colony on precisely the same terms as Europeans'. If the Government granted these two concessions, that would 'finally close the struggle, and remove the question from the arena of Indian politics.'[13]

---

13 *Collected Works*, Vol. 10, p. 119.

Chapter 57

Indentured Labour for Natal

On February 25, 1910, Gopal Krishna Gokhale moved a Resolution in the Imperial Legislative Council of India to empower the Governor-General in Council 'to prohibit the recruitment of indentured labour in British India for the Colony of Natal.'[1] In a moving speech, Gokhale drew attention to the 'intense feeling among all classes of His Majesty's subjects in India' on this issue; and pointed out that 'the whole of the Indian problem in South Africa' had 'arisen out of the supply of indentured labour to Natal'. They now had the indentured; the ex-indentured and their descendants struggling painfully hard to eke out a living as free Indians; and traders and other Indians who had gone to South Africa on their own to cater for the needs of the indentured. If not slavery, indenture was not really far removed from it, with those bound by it subjected to insufferable inhumanity. The contempt heaped on them was also inflicted on traders and other Indians of independent means.

The total population of Indians in the four colonies, recently federated into the South African Union, was about 1,50,000; of whom 1,20,000 lived in Natal; about 15,000 in the Cape Colony; and about 13,000 were entitled to reside in the Transvaal, though they were not more than 6,000 at present owing to the on-going struggle for the past three years. The export of Indian indentured labour to Natal began in 1860, and except for a brief period of eight years between 1866 and 1874, continued till the present. There were about 40,000 Indians under indenture in Natal; about 65,000 ex-indentured and their descendants; and about 15,000 members of the Indian trading community. A person could remain in Natal after the end of his five-year indenture as a free individual on payment of an annual

---

1 *Speeches and Writings of Gopal Krishna Gokhale, op. cit.*, pp. 509-518.

licence fee of £ 3 for every male above 16 years of age and every female above 13. Gross and cruel ill-treatment by the employers was the main grievance of those indentured; and the Protector of Immigrants, a local government employee, in effect provided no protection to speak of. The suicide rate among the indentured was double of what it was among the ex-indentured. It was a tale of unrelieved misery.

Natal had been rescued from doom and gloom by Indian labour. 'Durban was absolutely built up by the Indian population.' But during the last fifteen or twenty years, the colonists of Natal had been trying to 'get rid of the Indian element there.' The imposition of the annual levy on the ex-indentured by the Act of 1896 was the most painful exaction from men and women of exceedingly limited means. A bill to exempt women was being whittled down in committee to grant discretionary powers to magistrates to decide who would or would not be so exempted. This 'cruel impost' was paid by ex-indentured Indians over and above the £ 1 poll tax, which everybody had to pay in Natal. It had 'broken up families'; it had 'driven men to crime'.

Who were the people, asked Gokhale, 'called upon by the Colony to pay this annual licence of £ 3 for the right to remain in the Colony?' They were those broken by the sordid cruelties of indenture, with no stomach to indenture again; and also unable to go back to India, as they had been unable to save anything, and could look forward only to poverty compounded by ostracism, as they had lost caste by going to South Africa.

The Indian trading community was also under attack. Their political franchise was withdrawn in 1896; and there were continuing attempts to deprive them also of the municipal franchise. Licences to trade had been arbitrarily revoked or refused; and the aggrieved were not even allowed to appeal to the Supreme Court.

Gokhale turned his attention to the dismal scene in the Transvaal. Indians could not enjoy any political or municipal franchise in the Transvaal. They could not hold any immovable property. There was a policy to confine them to locations. Since 1907, they had shut their doors 'in the face of all Indians, who were not here before the war, no matter what their status or qualifications may be.'

'Alone among British colonies, the Transvaal has placed statutory disabilities on His Majesty's Asiatic subjects in the matter of entering that colony. Alone among British colonies, the Transvaal has sough to inflict galling and degrading indignities and humiliations on His Majesty's Indian subjects. The protest which the Indian community of Transvaal has made against these disabilities and indignities during the last three years has now attained historic importance…..India has no reason to be ashamed for the part which her children have played in this struggle. The Indians in the Transvaal have suffered much for the sake of conscience, and of country, but they have done nothing unworthy. And they have throughout been most reasonable. They have not asked for unrestricted Asiatic immigration into the Transvaal. They have only insisted that there shall be no statutory disabilities imposed upon their race, and that legislation subjecting them to degrading indignities shall be repealed.'

Gokhale's Resolution recommended that 'the Governor-General in Council should acquire statutory powers to prohibit altogether if necessary the supply of indentured labour to the colony of Natal.' Gokhale's appeal was 'to those immutable principles of justice and humanity which alone can form the enduring foundations of a great empire.' And he asked: 'First, what is the status of us, Indians, in this Empire? Secondly, what is the extent of the responsibility which lies on the Imperial Government to ensure to us just and humane and gradually even equal treatment in this Empire? And, thirdly, how far are the self-governing members of this Empire bound by its cardinal principles?'

More than a dozen speakers, including Jinnah, affirmed their wholehearted support for the Resolution, which was unanimously passed. With effect from July 1, 1911, Indians would no longer be sent to give their lives away in the coal mines and sugar-plantations of Natal. The coverage of the Indian debate and Resolution in the papers, contrary to Gandhi's expectations, did nothing to alleviate the lot of Indians in the Transvaal.

Chapter 58

The Transvaal Satyāgraha

Harsh and heartless measures of the Transvaal Government dashed all hopes of relief. A number of prisoners, including Manilal were placed in solitary confinement. Some of the *satyāgrahīs* were sent to the Portuguese port of Delagoa Bay, and deported to India. Almost destitute when they arrived in India, their heart-rending stories made painful reading in the Indian press. These stories were conveyed by L.W. Ritch to the Colonial Office in London. The Transvaal officials had sadistically deported some of the poorest, helpless, vulnerable people to India.

On the first of June, 1910, the Union of South Africa came into being, in which the whites alone enjoyed political power. Only they would be members of Parliament. They would have a Westminster type of government with a Prime Minister nominally under a British Governor-General. But, in contradistinction to Canada and Australia, the white settlers of South Africa were but a tiny minority of the total population despite their appropriation of the African land and ruling rights over it.

Gandhi's letter of June 2, 1910, informed the press that Indians suffered fresh arrests on the day of the Union. 'A cultured Indian and representative Parsee, Mr. Sorabji, who has already suffered six terms of imprisonment, was rearrested...; and is now under order of deportation.' The others arrested included 'the barrister and Cambridge graduate', 'Mr. Joseph Royeppen.' He asked, with a searing sadness, what such a union would mean to the Asiatics. They could only view it as 'a combination of hostile forces arrayed against them.' Was it meant 'to crush by its weight and importance Asiatic subjects of the Crown?' Gandhi applauded the discharge of the Zulu chief Dinizulu on the occasion as a gesture that would 'naturally fire the imagination of the South African natives.' Could not the rulers of the land exhibit 'a new benignant spirit' by conceding the demands of the Asiatics 'held...to be intrinsically just by nine out of every ten intelligent people in this continent?'[1]

Tolstoy Farm

The *Satyāgraha* was losing steam. Only the poor Indians lent wholehearted support, as the rich merchant class closed their hearts and minds to pleas for financial and physical support. Gandhi wanted to establish a cooperative centre where the dependants of poor *satyāgrahīs* could be housed and provided for, and where they could learn to live simply, in peace and harmony with nature and one another. The Transvaal was where the struggle was; where the Indians could buy land only in locations.

The white antipathy towards Asians was challenged by the sympathetic actions of some white men and women such as Kallenbach, Ritch, Polak, Sonja and others. On May 30, 1910, Kallenbach bought and donated a farm outside Johannesburg to the Indians. Gandhi was under great financial strain. Families of the jailed or deported *satyāgrahīs* had to be taken care of. Passive resisters who had lost their jobs had to be provided for. Ratan Tata's generous assistance went part of the way to ease his burdens; money received from other quarters in India and elsewhere kept them afloat; but the gift of 1,100 acres of land in Lawley, 21 miles from Johannesburg, was a true saving act. 'Passive resisters and their indigent families' could live on the farm 'free of any rent or charge.' Kallenbach and Gandhi named it 'Tolstoy farm'.

Nearly two miles long and a three-quarter mile wide, the farm had about a thousand fruit-bearing trees and a small house. Oranges, apricots and plums grew aplenty in season; and two wells and a spring supplied the water needed. Lawley, the nearest railway station was about a mile away. Gandhi, Manilal and Kallenbach were the first residents of Tolstoy Farm. They were joined by Thambi Naidoo and his family. Gandhi and Kallenbach proceeded to build houses on the farm to accommodate the *satyāgrahīs*, some of whom arrived on the fourth of June. The settlers came from Gujarat, Tamilnadu, Andhra and North India; and included Hindus, Muslims, Parsis and Christians. There were about 40 young men, two or three old men, five women, and thirty children of whom five were girls.

---

1   *Collected Works,* 10, p.263; *Indian Opinion,* 11-6-1910.

Shooting was prohibited on the farm. Gandhi was prepared to provide meat for those who wanted it. But out of respect for him and Kallenbach, who had become a vegetarian, everyone including Christians and Muslims agreed on a vegetarian diet. In the common kitchen, Christian women were entrusted with cooking, helped by Gandhi and others. The food was simple; and the time and number of meals were fixed. Everyone did his and her own cleaning. People took turns to clean the common pots. Drinking and smoking were prohibited.

The use of machinery was to be avoided, unless inescapably necessary. Hired labour was also to be used as little as possible. The East and West had to be incrementally brought together.[2]

The friendship between Gandhi and Kallenbach, who decided to live and teach on the farm, became closer and more intense. Many of Gandhi's close companions and *satyāgrahīs* were not sold on life-long service, and would not want to do hard work with their hands. They were asked to help with money and materials. The Gandhi family, Kallenbach, and members of other castes and communities used to hard labour, would work on the farm.

The arrival of Kasturba in late July to join Gandhi brought the family together after a period of five years, during which Gandhi was mostly engrossed in work at Johannesburg, and could manage only brief visits to Phoenix. The boys were travelling all the time from one place to the other.

Kallenbach supervised the construction of separate residences for men and women, as even married men had to lead celibate lives on the farm. Kallenbach built a house for himself; a building to serve as a school; and a carpentry and shoe-making workshop. Until the buildings were constructed, everyone lived in tents for a couple of months. Physical labour helped even the weak become strong on Tolstoy Farm. The ideas that Gandhi and Kallenbach imbibed from their joint study of Tolstoy and Ruskin in the Kraal and at Mountain View, were now translated into practical action on Tolstoy Farm. Simple living, manual labour, self-sufficiency and non-violence became the watchwords of their life together, and on the farm. As Gandhi put it: 'We are trying to seek the root of every activity in religion.'[3]

---

2   Cf. *Indian Opinion*, 18 June 1910. Also Tendulkar, *op.cit.*, pp.142-146.

3   Cf. Hunt, D.J., *An American looks at Gandhi*, Promilla, Delhi, 2005, p.26; Lev, *op. cit.*, p. 13.

The settlers worked hard on the farm. Everyone, young or old, not occupied in the kitchen, had to spend some time gardening and looking after the fruit trees. If people had to go to Johannesburg on some errand or other, they did so on foot. Only on community business could one go by rail, and that in third class. A person wanting to go on a pleasure trip had to walk to Johannesburg and back, and had to carry home-baked bread made from coarse wheat flour ground at home, home-made marmalade and groundnut butter. Sometimes people including Kallenbach and Gandhi walked the 21 miles to and back from Johannesburg the same day. The journey began at 2.30 a.m.; it took six to seven hours to reach Johannesburg. Gandhi tells us that one day he walked 55 miles.[4] He made too great demands on himself, as well as others!

Hygiene was strictly enforced. One could not find refuse anywhere on the farm. All rubbish was consigned to neatly dug trenches and covered. Waste water was used for watering trees. Food and vegetable refuse was converted into manure. A square pit received the night soil, fully covered with excavated earth.

They had to make some use of African labour on the farm. Working with the Africans gave Gandhi a better idea of their painful position in their own land. 'The negroes alone are the original inhabitants of the land. We have not seized the land from them by force; we live here with their goodwill. The whites, on the other hand, have occupied the country forcibly and appropriated it to themselves.' This was a new realization, a new understanding of the truth, a new awakening! The worshipper of British values and institutions was becoming conscious of the moral illegitimacy of their power![5]

'I regard the Kaffirs, with whom I constantly work these days, as superior to us,' he wrote in a later letter to Maganlal.[6]

Small industries were started on the farm in pursuit of self-sufficiency for the resident families. Kallenbach learned how to make sandals at the Trappist monastery at Marian Hill, and taught Gandhi, who then taught the art to the other settlers. They started making and selling sandals.

---

4   Cf. Gandhi Rajmohan, *op. cit.,* p.150.

5   *Indian opinion*, 22 October 1910; *Collected Works*, Vol. 10, p.340.

6   *Collected Works*, Vol. 10, p. 308.

Kallenbach, a fine carpenter side by side with being a highly qualified architect, introduced carpentry into the farm curriculum; and they made all kinds of things, big and small, for daily use.

As a School-master

Though Gandhi had railed against the introduction of compulsory education by the ruler of Baroda in his state in *Hind Swaraj*, ridiculing the knowledge of reading and writing as of no use, he found it necessary to make arrangements for the education of the resident boys and girls at the farm. A school, therefore, became functional in June for the education of the young. They included Hindu, Muslim, Parsi and Christian boys, as well as some Hindu girls. Gandhi found it impossible and unnecessary to engage special teachers for them. Qualified Indian teachers were exceedingly hard to find; and would not even agree to go to a farm twenty-one miles away from Johannesburg. The small salary would not attract anyone. They had little money to spend. Gandhi had his own ideas about education, and did not give any credit to the current system. He wanted to experiment with his own. He was convinced that only parents could impart true education. External help should be minimal. Tolstoy Farm was a family. He was its father. It was therefore his responsibility to teach and train the young. He knew that his conception and idea of education was not entirely perfect. The young people at the farm had been reared in different environments. They did not subscribe to the same religion. They had not been with him since their childhood. It was not easy for him to live up to the responsibility that he sought to assume for himself. He nevertheless felt that he could help mould their character 'through the culture of the heart'; and started living amongst them as their 'father'. Building of one's character was the true foundation, on which later education would be based. The other things could be learned at a later day by the children on their own, or from their friends around the world.

Gandhi was however conscious of the need for literary education, and began some classes with the help of his mates Kallenbach and Pragji Desai. He also sought to make them physically fit through the work that they did together with the others at the farm. This work included every chore from cooking to scavenging. He made everyone, young and old, to work in the kitchen as well as the garden. The heavy work outside gave them good exercise. He was a strict disciplinarian. The regularity of life at the farm together with nourishing food and clean air and water added to the health of the residents.

Gandhi also emphasized vocational training. So, he, Kallenbach and the others taught shoe-making, carpentry, as well as cooking to the students. All this was new, for the Indian children in South Africa in general learned only reading, writing and arithmetic. The teachers always worked with the students, and made them do things only together with them, which made the process of learning more cheerful.

Physical and vocational training of the boys and girls came through the practical work that they were made to do. Literary instruction was a more demanding and difficult proposition. Gandhi could not find enough time to devote himself to the task. He taught the children only after his physical work for the day, when he needed to rest. He found it hard to stay awake. The mornings were taken up by farm work and the domestic chores. The school began only after the mid-day meal. Three periods were allotted to literary training, and the languages taught included Hindi, Gujarati, Tamil, Telugu and Urdu. The pupils were taught in their own languages; but English was also taught. The Gujarati Hindu children were taught a little Sanskrit, while elementary history, geography and arithmetic were taught to them all.

Gandhi undertook himself to teach Tamil and Urdu. He had learned a little Tamil during his voyages and in jail. His knowledge of Urdu was also not great. He knew only a little Sanskrit, which he had learned at High School. Even his Gujarati was only of a school standard. He knew his shortcomings, but loved the languages of his country; and had great confidence in his teaching capacity. He also banked on the ignorance and generosity of his students.

He never hid his shortcomings from his students, and that was why they loved and respected him. His main task was to encourage them to learn themselves. He enabled them to overcome their lethargy. He enthused them to learn. And he supervised. By doing so, he was able to manage boys of different ages learn different subjects in one and the same class. He did not put much value on text-books; and did not make much use even of the ones that they had. The teacher was the best text-book. Gandhi remembered what he learned from his teachers more than what he learned from his school books. The eyes and the ears teach more than books. It was hard for the students to learn from books; and remember what they read in their books. He gave them the gist of what he read in many books. It was comparatively easier for them to digest and retain what their teacher told them or taught them. They found reading hard; but they enjoyed listening to their teacher. Gandhi tried to make his subjects interesting to grab his students' attention and help their memory. Their curiosity as well as their receptivity was reflected in the questions that they asked. That was a measure of Gandhi's success as a teacher.

Spiritual 'Training'

Gandhi was equally concerned with the spiritual 'training' of his students, by which he seems to mean development, not necessarily depending on any religious texts. He wanted his students to have some knowledge of their own scriptures; and did what he could to make that possible. Gandhi talks about the 'training of the spirit', which had to do with the development of character leading to 'knowledge of God and self-realization'. That was indeed an intangible, indefinable goal, and can perhaps be understood only in terms of one's relationship with the world, one's identification with the sentient world, and with humanity in particular. Any education which he called 'training', would hinder rather than help a person without cultivation of 'culture of the spirit'. This culture of the spirit would be incomprehensible if it did not mean one's identification with the joys and sorrows of the world around. Gandhi does not say it here in so many words, but certainly seems to believe so.[7]

Gandhi is critical of people's belief that 'self-realization is possible only in the fourth stage of life, i.e., *sannyāsa* (renunciation).'[8] He mocks this spiritual exercise in old age, when the depletion of one's physical energies and mental capacity makes any progress difficult, if not entirely impossible. He would like a person to strive for 'this invaluable experience' at a much earlier stage. He made his young pupils memorise hymns and recite them. He also read books on morality to them. But books were not enough. Physical exercise developed the body. Intellectual exercise developed the mind. 'Exercise of the spirit' was absolutely essential to develop the spirit. And this 'entirely depended on the life and character of the teacher'.[9]

---

7   *Autobiography*, p. 249.

8   *Ibid.*

9   *Ibid.*

A liar could not teach his students to be truthful. A coward could not inculcate the spirit of bravery. One could not teach self-restraint without self-discipline on his own part. Gandhi therefore sought to be a role model for his students. They thus became his teachers by motivating him to lead a life that they could emulate. Any discipline prescribed for his students first applied to the teacher.

Gandhi always reasoned with his students to keep them in line. Only once did he strike a rebellious student with a ruler, not without great personal anguish. He knew that the boy of seventeen was strong enough to strike him back, but, instead, he cried and asked for Gandhi's forgiveness. Never again did Gandhi use any form of corporal punishment to tame the wild spirit of his students. And he himself felt a pang of remorse at his lapse into violence. That had brought out the lurking 'brute' in him.

Gandhi tells us that he opposes any form of corporal punishment, and remembers that only once did he physically punish one of his sons. He says that the use of the ruler was probably wrong, as he had felt angry and wanted to punish. He would have considered it justifiable if the blow was only 'an expression' of his 'distress'. He thinks that his action arose out of anger as well as distress. However, distress is not always separable from anger, and cannot justify violence, if legitimate anger cannot do so! Gandhi desisted from correcting misconduct through corporal punishment in future. He used 'the power of the spirit' instead, to correct errant conduct.

Kallenbach told Gandhi that some of the boys at the farm were 'bad and unruly', and could be a bad influence on his own sons. But Gandhi insisted that he could not keep his sons apart from the others. He had to treat them all equally, teach and train them equally. He trusted his sons to discriminate between the good and the bad, and act and behave as desired. Gandhi is satisfied that his sons did not come to any harm as a result of this experiment. It had a wholesome effect on the boys in the sense that it got rid of any sense of self-superiority in them. Their education was at once a test and a code of discipline. The requisite element was the vigilance of guardians and teachers.

The education of children of different backgrounds brought together imposes an additional burden of responsibility on their teachers. It is not easy to discharge that duty, but it is not impossible!

Teaching the doctrines of four religions, Hinduism, Zoroastrianism, Islam and Christianity, was by no means an easy task. Gandhi studied books on these religions to do them justice; and wrote *Niti Dharma or Ethical Religion*, which was published in 1912. He taught his pupils to respect all religions; and exhorted them to live like blood brothers. Children learned to look at one another's religion with a measure of understanding and charity, and shared the joy generated by their festivals. Hindus fasted with the Muslims during Ramadan; and the Muslims did likewise at Hindu festivals. Feelings of warm fraternity bound them together.

Co-education at Tolstoy Farm bore Gandhi's daring imprint. He carefully explained the duty of self-restraint to his pupils; and sent boys and girls to bathe in the spring at the same time. He did not heed the misgivings of Kasturba. To quote him:

'This was my experiment. I sent the boys reputed to be mischievous and the innocent young girls to bathe in the same spot at the same time. I had fully explained the duty of self-restraint to the children, who were all familiar with my Satyagraha doctrine. I knew, and so did the children, that I loved them with a mother's love…Was it a folly to let the children meet there for a bath and yet to expect them to be innocent? My eye always followed the girls as a mother's eye would follow a daughter….There was an element of safety in the fact that they went in a body…Generally, I also would be at the spring at the same time….

…One day one of the young men then made fun of two girls…The news made me tremble…I remonstrated with the young men, but that was not enough. I wished the two girls to have some sign on their person as a warning to every young man that no evil eye might be cast upon them, and as a lesson to every girl that no one dare assail their purity…What mark should the girls bear so as to give them a sense of security and at the same time to sterilize the sinner's eye? This question kept me awake for the night. In the morning I gently suggested to the girls that they might let me cut off their fine long hair…At first the girls would not listen to me. I had already explained the situation to the elderly women who could not bear to think of my suggestion but yet quite understood my motive, and they had finally accorded their support to me.' Gandhi concludes: 'This act of mine was not without its effect on the entire life of the settlers on the farm.'

This irrational, impulsive, inexplicable act was certainly tainted by violence. And the memory haunted him twenty years later, and perhaps throughout his life. He himself usually followed the 'mischievous boys' and the 'young girls' to the spring with presumably 'sterilized' eyes; but was not there on this day. Thus, he knew that something similar or worse could happen at any time. Yet, he persisted with the perverse practice. When he heard of what happened, what did he feel? Was it rage, or anxiety, or remorse? Erik Erikson surmises that 'the question which kept him awake all night, then, was 'what mark should the girls bear to sterilize the sinner's eye?' '[10]

Cutting off a woman's hair was either a ritualistic act, as when a would-be Christian nun was shorn, or a Hindu widow was shaved; or else an act of punishment for a heinous crime. Gandhi cut off the locks of innocent girls; and let off the naughty boys with a mere reprimand. How did the girls' mothers feel? How did the other women on the farm feel? Gandhi does not tell us. He prevailed on them. Gandhi's guilty hand trembled at the thought even twenty years later. He himself said elsewhere that truth 'excludes the use of violence because man is not capable of knowing the absolute truth and therefore is not competent to punish.' In this instance, though, we do notice self-righteous excess usurping spiritual power!

It was a constant challenge to educate the boys and girls under his charge. He had to 'touch their hearts'. He had to share their joys and sorrows. He had to help solve their problems. He had to direct their youthful energy and aspirations into right channels.

Gandhi slept in an open veranda, and the boys and girls slept around him. Everyone slept on the floor, and had a couple of blankets for spreading on the floor and for covering, and a wooden pillow. This, too, was an experiment in living close to one another without any thought of sex. Gandhi's practice of sleeping in proximity to young women to earn spiritual merit arising out of self-restraint might have already begun at Tolstoy Farm.

Three meals were served every day. Bread and wheaten 'coffee' was served at six in the morning; rice, dal and vegetable at 11 a.m.; and wheat pap and milk, or bread and 'coffee' at 5.30 p.m. At about 7 p.m., the settlers

---

10 Erikson, Erik, *Gandhi's Truth: On the Origins of Militant Nonviolence*, W.W. Norton & Co., New York, 1969, p. 240.

said their prayers; sang *bhajans* (spiritual songs) in English, Hindi and Gujarati; and sometimes heard passages from the *Rāmāyaṇa* or books on Islam. Everyone retired to sleep at nine at night.

Chapter 59

Self-Restraint

Gandhi sought 'purity' through *brahmacarya* in readiness for the struggle of *Satyāgraha*. He subjected himself to strict dietary contol. He admits that the initial changes were 'largely hygienic', but then religion regulated his new experiments. He saw a clear relationship between passion and palate; and therefore resorted to fasting as well as restricting his diet. He discovered that one could become as fond of fruits as of other forms of food. Taste had to be curbed, and to do so, one had to fast, which became important for Gandhi, who had only one meal a day on holidays, or else fasted. And fasting also became his preferred tool of atonement.

Life is a process of ceaseless discovery. Gandhi realized that his fasting made him enjoy his food even more, and that disturbed him. As he was aiming at self-restraint and victory over his palate, he went from one kind of food to another, progressively limiting the amount of his intake. He was upset by the realization that he was still relishing in a greater measure the different kinds of food that he was eating. Taste and relish were proving obdurate opponents of self-abnegation.

Gandhi considered it unseemly to talk about the taste of food in his discussions with his friend Kallenbach; and any sense or expression of delight was indeed undesirable.[1] One should eat only to ensure proper physical function, with the sense organs duly serving the body and the soul. This rejection of a sensory function, which facilitates the process of eating instead of making it an unpleasant, forced exercise, is an arbitrary denial of nature miscalled by Gandhi 'symphony with nature'![2]

---

1 *Autobiography*, p. 237.
2 *Ibid.*

The dietary changes that began with Kasturba's illness, led to others inspired by men like Raychand Bhai, who had told him that 'milk stimulated animal passion.'³ Gandhi understood that milk was not necessary to support the body, but giving it up was not easy. While Gandhi was weighing up the need to give up milk for self-restraint, he read accounts of the tortures inflicted on cows and buffaloes by their keepers. He discussed the harmful effects of milk with Kallenbach; and both of them gave it up at Tolstoy Farm. Gandhi then decided to live on a diet of pure fruit, which had to be the cheapest available. They wanted to live like the poorest people. The fruit diet did not need any cooking. Did raw ground-nuts, bananas, dates, lemons and olive oil really constitute a cheap diet of the poorest of the poor?

Gandhi emphasizes a close connection between food and *brahmacarya*; but reminds his readers that it is much more a matter of the mind. An 'unclean' mind cannot be purged by fasting. It is only ceaseless 'self-examination, surrender to God and, lastly, grace' that helps get rid of 'the concupiscence of the mind'.⁴ Calling the sexual urge 'unclean', and considering a mind influenced by it tainted is indeed objectionable, and contrary to the very flow of life. It is this perception of filth in sex that progressively castrates him. Bent on curbing the primary elements of human nature itself, Gandhi talks of the 'intimate connection between the mind and the body'; and bemoans the 'carnal mind' lusting for 'delicacies and luxuries'. Fasting, together with so many dietary restrictions, is therefore required to extinguish this 'lust'. The carnal mind must be curbed; and to do so, one must eat 'clean' food that does not stimulate; and fast from time to time. Gandhi emphasizes a healthy correlation between dietary restrictions and the mental exercise of self-restraint in one's bid to defeat human nature; and feels very satisfied about it. To justify *brahmacarya* or celibacy on the ground that he was reducing all his needs for going to jail in his *Satyāgraha*, is neither right nor praiseworthy. To get over attachment to one's partner to go to jail is neither necessary nor desirable. To desist from loving someone to prepare oneself for the loneliness of jail is to punish one's beloved companion even before it is forced by circumstances. The logic is cruel, and sadly, fails to convince!

---

3   *Ibid.,* p. 242.
4   *Ibid.,* p.243.

Fasting

He had given up milk and cereals. He was living on a fruit diet. He added fasting to it in his pursuit of 'self-restraint'. Kallenbach joined him in the exercise. Gandhi had been used to occasional fasting and taking and keeping of vows, following the example of his mother. He learned from a friend that fasting helped the observance of *brahmacarya*. He began strict fasting, and took only water when he did so. He started practising his fasts on holy *Vaishnava* and *Śaivite* occasions, and his first fasting experiment coincided with *Ramadan* at Tolstoy Farm, where he encouraged the Muslim residents and the others to observe all their religious customs. He made sure that the Muslims said their daily *namāz*; and the Christians and *Parsis* continued with their religious rites. He encouraged everyone to observe fasts, as he did himself. It was a happy family, in which the importance of fasting was realized by one and all.

Gandhi thus popularized the practice of partial and complete fasting at the Farm, all in the pursuit of self-restraint. He says he benefited from fasting in his progress towards self-restraint; but did not know if the other inmates of the farm were likewise affected. He was told by some of his friends that fasting in fact stimulated their 'animal passion', as also their palates. Gandhi therefore falls back on the mind in insisting that self-restraint is principally a cultivated and assiduously cherished property of the mind. Fasting and any associated discipline helps self-abnegation. It is only a means to an end, and not the end itself. He therefore recommends both physical and 'mental fasting'. He is seeking to deny, disable and destroy the very impulse that governs and ensures the continuity of life and the basis of human relationships. He cites the *Gītā* to convince his readers:

> 'For a man who is fasting his senses
>
> outwardly, the sense-objects disappear,
>
> leaving the yearning behind - but when
>
> he has seen the Highest,
>
> even the yearning disappears.'[5]

When you quote the scripture, you expect acceptance, not dissent!

---

5   *Ibid.*, p. 245.

The three most powerful influences on Gandhi had been Raychandbhai, Tolstoy and Ruskin. Tolstoy was writ large over life at Tolstoy Farm. Gandhi explained the principles of Tolstoy in an article published in *Indian Opinion* as early as 1905:

1. Do not accumulate wealth.

2. Regardless of the evil done to you, always do good. That is God's commandment and His Law.

3. Do not fight, do not take part in fighting.

4. Political power leads to evil; it is sinful to wield any.

5. Man is born to discharge his duty to his Creator. He should therefore worry more about duties than rights.

6. Agriculture is the true occupation of man. It is against Divine Law to establish large cities, employ hundreds of thousands to mind machines in factories, so that a few can roll in riches by exploiting the poverty and helplessness of the many.[6]

They are in perfect accord with Gandhi's own; and Tolstoy Farm provided the testing ground, where he could try to translate them into reality. As he wrote later: 'My faith and courage were at their highest in Tolstoy Farm'.

---

6   *Indian Opinion*, 2-9-1905, [From Gujarati].

Chapter 60

The Travails of Satyāgraha

The deportees attracted the attention of India, and evoked feelings of great bitterness. The governments in Madras and Bombay found their presence most embarrassing. They were being treated as martyrs. But the deportations neither demoralized nor defeated the resisters. Indian sympathy quickened by their suffering led to donations that poured into the 'Passive Resistance Fund Account' of the Natal Bank in Johannesburg. Gandhi had given most of his earnings to the cause; and so had Kallenbach. Ratan Tata made another donation of Rs. 25,000. His note to Gokhale conveyed his anguish: '...It is pitiful to see a handful of Indians suffering and fighting for the rights of a whole nation, whilst that nation sits inertly and watches the struggle with absolute indifference.'[1] The letter accompanying the cheque expressed 'the admiration and good wishes of all true Indians' for Gandhi's 'noble work'.[2]

Polak, crisscrossing India over a period of nine months, raised with his oratory and enthusiasm over 50,000 rupees from people big and small, in amounts big and small. The donors included Hindu maharajas, Muslim Nawabs, Parsi millionaires, Christian clergymen, and members of India's middle class.[3] After almost a year in India, he returned to South Africa in the last week of August, 1910. The farewell meeting in Madras listened to a great tribute by the inimitable Annie Besant: 'Himself of a persecuted race, whose blood has been shed in every country in Europe,' 'he had not allowed himself to be soured and embittered by the suffering of his

---

1   Cf. Guha, *op. cit.*, p.399.

2   *Ibid.*, p. 400.

3   Reports in *Indian Opinion*, 3 September and 5 November 1910.

kinsfolk. He has shown himself to possess a heart softened and…he finds in the suffering of others a reason for taking the cause of the other.'⁴

From Madras, he took a train to Bombay, and boarded a ship to South Africa. There were about 400 Indians present to receive him at Durban, Gandhi among them! Some of them had been inspired to go and welcome him back to South Africa by Gandhi's old friend of boyhood days, Sheikh Mehtab, whose poems in *Indian Opinion* galvanized his Indian audience to support the *Satyāgraha*. He also asked his readers to shoot disunity between the Hindus and Muslims down with the arrow of unity.⁵

Gandhi and Polak spent a few days at Phoenix, and on October 4, 1910, went to the port to receive a shipload of Natal Indians deported from the Transvaal to Madras and Bombay, returning home. Polak told a reporter that the *Satyāgraha* would continue, 'one of suffering on the part of our people, who intend to go on enduring these hardships until they make the authorities ashamed of themselves.'⁶

Erosion of Faith in Legal Redress

The final blow to any hope of redress from the courts of law was delivered by the signal case of 21 resisters who had been deported to India from the Transvaal. They returned, but were not allowed to land at a series of ports. They finally proceeded to Durban, where Frederick Laughton, from whom Gandhi had learned a great deal, succeeded in receiving an order from the Natal Division of the Supreme Court restraining the officers at the Durban port from deporting the Indians, and ordering to let them disembark. The order was duly telegraphed to Durban; but the Immigration Restriction Officer defied it, and refused to let the Indians land on the ground that they could not meet his demand to first post security.

Laughton immediately went back to the Supreme Court and asked for the officer to be held in contempt of the Court's order. When asked if the officer had acted against the Court's order, and whether the Government was willing to arrange the Indians' return voyage from Delagoa Bay, the Government lawyer brazenly declared that 'the Government was not prepared to assent to the course requested by the Court.' The Court

---

4   Report in *Indian Quarterly*, August 1910.

5   Cf. Guha, *op.cit.*, p.615, n.47.

6   Cf. Guha, *op. cit.*, p. 401.

then sought to save face by talking of a 'misunderstanding on the part of the officer.' The Court frankly admitted its impotence in the statement that it 'would make no comment on the action of the Government in the matter', and felt that it could not order the Government to do anything.' The Indians could return at their own expense, but would have to pay a £100 bond on arrival demanded by the Immigration Restriction Officer, who had 'misunderstood' the Court's earlier order.[7]

The bond of £100 demanded by the officer was beyond the means of most; and that was the entire intent of the demand in order to defeat the attempts at disembarkation. The sensational surrender by the court to the intransigent defiance of the Government rudely rocked and reduced the authority of the judiciary to rein in the excesses of the Government to ensure a proper rule of law; to bring about change though a corrective, ameliorative judicial process. Gandhi could not but clearly comprehend the Government's intention to bar the entrance of Indians into the country at any cost. Legal procedure and propriety were indeed expendable!

It made Gandhi realize the futility of any attempt at the defence of Indian rights in the courts of South Africa. One of the men on board ship, named Narayansami, who like so many others spent weeks on open deck without sufficient clothes, of which they had been robbed, could not stand the cold and died on deck. Gandhi accused the Government of 'legalized murder.' Litigation was proving totally ineffective as an instrument aimed at social justice. The case of the deportees was a clear signal of failure! Gandhi gave up his practice, but not his use of the law, by breaking it! In DiSalvo's words, 'when Gandhi first stood before the court in South Africa to plead guilty and accept his punishment, defendant Gandhi abandoned lawyer Gandhi, declaring instead his faith in the world – and the law – as they should be.'[8] The study of law, the practice of law, the use of law to fight oppression and tyranny, and the defiance of unjust laws made Gandhi what and who he was, to leave his indelible impress on the pages of world history!

---

7   'The Passive Resisters: A temporary Victory', *Rand Daily Mail*, October 15, 1910; Cf. DiSalvo, *op.cit.*, p.438, n.78.

8   *Ibid.*, p. 312.

The Struggle Continues

Keen to get arrested, Gandhi kept crossing into the Transvaal and back to Natal without papers. In early November he crossed again into the Transvaal; and took with him some other Indians including a woman named Sodha and her children. The police said she was an illegal alien, but Gandhi managed to get the case adjourned, and took her and her children to Tolstoy Farm. The request to Smuts to let her stay until the release of her husband from jail was refused; and Gandhi appealed to Christian public opinion against the harassment of a harmless, destitute woman. One of her two children was eight months old, and the other three years. She was tried and sentenced to a £10 fine and a month's jail. Gandhi secured her release on bail pending an appeal.

On January 6, 1911, Leung Quinn returned from his deportation to Ceylon, and immediately proceeded to the Transvaal to join the struggle once more. He met Gandhi at Tolstoy Farm, before he was sentenced on January 19 to three months' rigorous imprisonment for non-possession of any registration certificate.

In London, Lord Ampthill and the South African Committee finally persuaded the Imperial Government to send a despatch in October 1910 to the Union Government of South Africa recommending the repeal of Act 2 of 1907. It asked for the removal of the racial bar, and for non-racial legislation regulated by administrative control to limit the future Indian immigration to a minimum number of highly educated men.

That is what Gandhi had been agitating for. The Coronation festivities would take place in June. A measure of placation would help make peace with India and the Indians. The Government published the proposed bill on February 25, 1911 in the Union of South Africa Gazette Extraordinary. The existing legislation would be repealed. There was no explicit protection for the wives and children of domiciled Asiatics. A language test was specified for new entrants into the Transvaal, but whether the Indians passing that test would be allowed in was not clearly or unambiguously stated. Gandhi wrote to the Minister of the Interior, who said that educated Asiatics admitted under the new bill would not be made to register. Gandhi wanted clarification of the position of women and children. When the Government did so, he would 'advise the community in the Transvaal to send a final acquiescence, and passive resistance will then naturally end.'[9]

---

9   *Collected Works*, Vol. 10, p.426; cf. pp.409-425.

On March 9, 1911, Gandhi wrote to Maganlal that the struggle might come to an end. Once the *Satyāgraha* ended, most people would probably leave Tolstoy Farm; but he and his family would stay on for some time to partly repay Kallenbach with their physical labour the amount of £600, which he had spent on the buildings alone. How could he leave Kallenbach alone after the struggle was over?

In this letter he also wrote about Kasturba's illness, who had a 'sudden attack of acute pain.' She was most probably menopausal; and Gandhi could not pay her immediate attention owing to his preoccupation with negotiations. She got angry, 'burst into tears and made it appear as if she would die.' After the initial shock, Gandhi recovered his sense of humour, and said with a smile: 'Nothing to worry about if you die. There is plenty of wood. We shall cremate you on this farm itself.' She laughed, and half the pain suddenly disappeared. As part of his treatment for her, Gandhi suggested that she should give up vegetables and salt altogether. 'She should live on wheat and fruits only. If she so desired, she could take saltless rice with ghee. When she said that even he could not do it, he immediately said: 'From today I give up salt, vegetables, etc.' For the last one month, therefore, they had been taking their food without salt, vegetables and pulses. The result was indeed miraculous. The bleeding stopped right away; and Gandhi 'got the incidental benefit of extra self-control.'[10] It was as if Providence was more than willing to let her recover!

The bill had anything but smooth sailing. It evoked stiff opposition from the Orange Free State members of Parliament, who objected to General Smuts' declaration that 'as a limited number of Asiatics would be allowed, under the bill, to enter the Union, every year, there could be no limitation on their right to travel about or settle in any part of the Union territory.'[11] They wanted to totally block the entry of Asiatics into their province. Gandhi opposed any racial bar, and categorically stated that 'there can be no playing with the snake of racial legislation. The virus of racial legislation in the Orange Free State will speedily attack the whole nation.'[12] Indians in the Orange Free State were indeed very few, which was an effective disincentive; but to say that no Indian could legally enter and reside in a province of the Union was wrong and unacceptable. Smuts called it an 'absolutely new contention', which would exasperate the Europeans and

---

10   *Ibid.,* pp. 446-447.

11   Cf. Tendulkar, *op. cit.,* p.153.

12   *Ibid.,* p.154.

complicate matters. Gandhi interpreted it in a letter to Doke as Smuts' bid to inflame the whites.[13] That is indeed what Smuts was doing. He said he did not want the retail trade to fall entirely into the hands of Indians, which was a far-fetched fear!

Gandhi knew what was possible, and what was not. He wanted to secure 'the rights of individuals and their families in the provinces in which they already lived, and an opening the door for a small, incremental immigration of a few educated Indians a year.'[14] The moderate case was hurt by the extreme demands of the radicals, such as P.S. Aiyar, the Tamil journalist of Durban, who wanted free immigration, and the removal of all provincial barriers. Gandhi was, on the other hand, asking only for six new entrants a year, which was met with pervasive unwillingness.

Gandhi met Smuts on March 27, 1911. When the General said that the Free Staters would never consent to the entry of Indians, Gandhi reminded him of his duty 'to persuade them.' Smuts also said that it had hurt him to imprison the passive resisters, 'who suffer for their conscience'.

There was another meeting between the two on April 19, 1911. Smuts told Gandhi that he could defeat the Free Staters in the Assembly, but not in the Senate. 'I want time', said the general; and asked Gandhi to postpone the agitation. The whites were only a handful beside the Kaffirs; he did not want Asia to come in. He asked Gandhi personal questions about his living, assets and income. When told that Gandhi was living as a poor farmer on Tolstoy Farm, the general said that he would try to visit him some time.[15]

In his reply to Smuts that evening, Gandhi wrote of the proposed truce for a year; but emphasized the difficulty of keeping passive resistance in check if the matter was 'not closed during this season.' He asked for three assurances:

1. That in the next session the existing legislation will be repealed.

2. Passive resisters with the right to do so could freely register in the Transvaal.

3. Pending legislation, up to six educated passive resisters in the Transvaal would be allowed to remain as 'educated immigrants'.

---

13 *Ibid.*, 10, pp.491-2.

14 Cf. Guha, *op.cit.*, p.406.

15 *Ibid.*, pp.407-8.

If these conditions were met, he would persuade his people to suspend passive resistance. The General's secretary replied that these conditions were acceptable. The General hoped that they would try and be able to achieve a more lasting solution.

The truce was in place. Gandhi also secured the release of the Chinese passive resisters together with the Indians. A meeting in the Hamidiya Hall of Johannesburg accepted the settlement, notwithstanding the lurking suspicions from past experience. The *Star* welcomed the closure of an unpleasant chapter, and asked Gandhi about his future. He replied that he was handing over to L.W. Ritch his legal practice in Johannesburg. His immediate task was 'to provide for the care and education of the children whose parents are now in necessitous circumstances.' He would retire to his farm in Natal to work on the land, and dabble in Indian thought and Tolstoyan philosophy.[16]

A banquet was held at the Masonic Lodge in honour of the whites who had helped the movement. William Hosken had become a firm advocate of passive resistance. As chairman of an active committee of Europeans, he had helped raise funds for the struggle since 1908. The loss of his seat in Parliament in 1910 failed to deflect his sympathy and support for the Indians. Among the sixty European guests present, the Dokes, Kallenbach, Ritch, Sonja Schlesin, Hosken, Gabriel Isaac, William Vogl and his wife, David Pollock and Edward Dallow, were all there. Henry Polak missed the banquet, as he was away in England visiting his family.

Hundreds of Europeans had supported the Indians in a variety of ways. Gandhi's friendship with them stood unscathed by his opposition to white laws, and his moral objections to aspects of their civilization. *Indian Opinion* published a touching tribute to them and to the committee chaired by Hosken in memorable words that almost certainly flowed from Gandhi's pen.[17]

---

16   *Star*, 28 April 1911.

17   'Successful Banquet in Johannesburg', *Indian Opinion*, 17 June 1911; cf. Guha, op.cit., pp. 411-2.

Chapter 61

The Parting of Ways: Harilal

Harilal, Gandhi's eldest son, was a star *satyāgrahī*. Between July 28, 1908, when he was twenty years old, and January 9, 1911, he had been to jail as many as six times. Gandhi mentioned his son's passive resistance to official injustice with pride in a letter to Tolstoy. Yet the relationship between the father and son was under great strain in the last months of 1910. Harilal was twenty-two, only eighteen years younger than his father. His wife and daughter wanted to visit India; and he wanted to go with her. Gandhi protested poverty. Money was scarce. She could accompany someone else to India. How could Harilal suddenly turn his back on the continuing struggle? She therefore went alone with her two-year old daughter without him; and Harilal courted arrest once more. But he was both unhappy and angry. Now that the provisional settlement was in place, he wanted to go to India and take the matriculation examination. His wife had just given birth to a baby boy. He wanted to be with her. Gandhi wrote to him on March 5 to say that he would not 'stand in the way' of his 'studies and other ambitions'.[1]

Harilal attended a function for *satyāgrahīs* in Johannesburg, collected his things, a photograph of his father, and went to Delagoa bay to board a ship to India. He wanted to live and study in the Punjab, and not in Ahmedabad, where his father would be able to monitor his activities.[2] Gandhi searched for him throughout Johannesburg. A Parsi friend told him that Harilal had borrowed twenty pounds from him, presumably to pay for his passage.

---

1   *Collected Works*, 10, pp. 428-429.
2   Cf. Dalal, Chandulal Bhagubhai, *Harilal Gandhi: A life*, edited and translated from the Gujarati by Tridip Suhrud, Orient Longman, Chennai, 2007, pp.28-29.

Joseph Royappen told him that Harilal had gone to Delagoa Bay *en route* to India. When the news spread, some Muslim friends of Gandhi expressed their disappointment at not being told that Harilal wanted to study law in England. They would have gladly paid his expenses.

Gandhi's friend Pranjivan Mehta had given two scholarships for Phoenix boys to study in London. Though they were actually meant for Gandhi's sons, he first chose Chhaganlal, and then a Parsi student, Sorabji Adajania. Mehta offered a third scholarship, which Harilal was too proud to accept. He wanted to do it on his own, with subsistence provided by his father. In father-son discussions, Gandhi had mentioned the names of great men like Shri Ramakrishna, Swami Dayananda Saraswati, Shivaji and Rana Pratap, who rendered priceless service to India without any English education. But the son cited the names of Ranade, Gokhale, Tilak and Lajpat Rai, who had also served India with nobility and distinction.[3]

Harilal had left a letter for his father, saying that he was following a call of duty. He still respected and loved his parents, and would follow their teachings. Apart from study, he wanted to earn. He would study in the first place. It would be nice if the father could send some money. If the struggle was renewed, he would come back from wherever he was to participate, and court imprisonment. The letter was an outpouring of 'affection, anger, anguish, ambition.'[4]

He was recognized by the officials, who informed Gandhi. Kallenbach rushed to Delagoa bay, and brought him back to Johannesburg on May 15, 1911. Father and son talked throughout the night. Gandhi recounted the conversation in a letter to Maganlal. Harilal felt 'much unsettled'. He was angry with the father. He felt that Gandhi had 'kept all the four boys very much suppressed'; that he 'treated them as of no account'; and that he had 'often been hard-hearted.' He had 'put them and Ba last'.[5]

Two harsh and barbarous jail terms of six months had done great damage. Harilal wanted to go to India to carve out his own future. While Gandhi

---

3   Cf. Desai, Pragji, 'Satyagraha in South Africa', in Chandrashekhar Shukla, ed., *Reminiscences of Gandhiji*, Vora and Co., Bombay, 1951, pp.82-83.

4   Guha, *op. cit.*, p.414

5   *Collected Works*, 11, pp. 77-78.

was totally preoccupied with the community and the India of his dreams, Harilal sought a meaningful career to realize his self-worth. The special relationship that he looked and pined for as the eldest son, was denied by the father absorbed in the trials of the community. He was just one of the many around; and he found the rules of discipline irksome.

Following the overnight discussion, Gandhi announced on May 17 that Harilal was leaving. Many went to the Johannesburg station to see him off. Pragji Desai, who was present, tells us that Gandhi kissed his son, gently stroked his cheek, and said in a voice tremulous with emotion, 'If you feel that your father has done any wrong to you, forgive him.'[6]

In the letter to Maganlal cited above, Gandhi says: 'He has now left with a calm mind...his education should be for the most part in Gujarat...I have left him free...'

Harilal wrote about it some years later: '...obeying your orders I returned. I remained steadfast in my views. Therefore, instead of giving me a patient hearing you mutilated my thoughts and clipped my wings. You made me give up the idea of going to Lahore, and instead made me stay in Ahmedabad. You promised to give me thirty rupees for monthly expenditure. You did not allow me to measure my capabilities; you measured them for me.'[7]

Gandhi as a father

Gandhi was more at home with the needs of young children than with those of adolescents and adults. He could not comprehend the tumult in youths' minds, their mixed emotions, and their yearning for freedom and untrammelled self-expression. He could not see that reason often took a back seat to youthful impetuosity. The son's ambitions collided with the convictions of the father. The son's need for self-satisfaction was at loggerheads with the father's drift towards asceticism and self-denial. Gandhi attributed his son's recalcitrance and revolt to ideas that Harilal imbibed from his reading of a Gujarati novel by Govardhanram Tripathi, in which the hero, disillusioned with his father, leaves home in a bold bid

---

6   Cf. Parikh, Nilam, *Gandhiji's Lost Jewel: Harilal Gandhi*, National Gandhi Museum, New Delhi, 2001, p.33

7   Dalal, *Harilal Gandhi*, Appendix 1, p.134, from a letter written in 1915 or 1916.

to understand himself.[8]

In the community, and among his European followers, Gandhi was looked up to and venerated; and his was almost always the last word. He was used to leadership and compliant deference. Harilal's waywardness was hard to take! Gandhi forgot that he had himself been free to choose his path and career as a young man. His father was not there to veto his wish to study in England. And his mother was not there to disagree with his decision to go to South Africa. He had been free to plough his furrow, to choose his career, cultivate his convictions, and act on them. But with his children, he was the authoritarian, intolerant father figure of the old Hindu tradition. He would decide for them. His disenchantment with modern civilization precluded the possibility of his sons seeking a modern education. Only he knew what was good and wholesome for them. Only he knew what would lend meaning and purpose to their lives. Only he knew where their happiness lay. Only he knew how they would feel fulfilled; how they would realize their potential and hidden capabilities; how they would help India redeem itself! He wanted Harilal and Manilal to practise celibacy, as he had done so. And he wanted them to be exemplary *satyāgrahīs*. He wanted to emasculate them with emotional and moral blackmail. The poor boys were only on the threshold of youth and manhood, when the self-opinionated, fanatical father foisted on them his ideology of life-negation and self-willed castration in order to serve society, as if otherwise, they would be able to do nothing useful; and would become incapble of rendering any worthwhile service to humanity in India or anywhere else!

He wanted them to be perfect *satyāgrahīs*. Only celibates could be! Only they could court arrest. Only they could go to jail. Only they could till the land. Only they mattered. The rest of humanity caught in the coils of their natural compulsions could not balance and harmonize their lives with simultaneous devotion to duty, social responsibility and necessary sacrifice. The father's fads and uncompromising, dictatorial commands were entirely antithetical to the spirit and meaning of *ahiṁsā*, tolerance of dissent, and the co-existence in love and peace of contrary ideals and ideologies. On the wide worldly plane, though, Gandhi was a messiah of inter-communal and inter-racial tolerance and goodwill. He did not see any contradiction between his intolerance at home and tolerance abroad!

---

8   Cf. Guha, p.616, n.13

The sons' disagreements galled him; made him more stubborn; more impatient. They could not be permitted to go beyond the possibility of redemption! Though Gandhi had travelled widely, and interacted with people of three continents, if not more, he failed to rise above the die-cast Indian paternal dictatorship of his day. In that respect, the great visionary remained blinkered in his view of fatherly duty beside fatherly authority. The sons could not be allowed to strike out on their own in search of their true calling, in any attempt at uninterrupted self-fulfilment! Gandhi was just like any other Indian father of the day! There was no originality, no novelty, no democracy, no understanding, no concession in his commands to obey and do as told!

In his own orbit of work, association and activity, among his own people, he was the leader; he was the mentor; he was the path-finder. Raychandbhai and Tolstoy were dead; Gokhale was not close by. The sons' dissent was incomprehensible.

He had a singular capacity for friendship across race, gender, religion, language and geography. He loved them all. And they loved him to a degree of adoration. Even his white friends, despite occasional arguments, accepted his lead. Gandhi could not understand Harilal's unexpected recalcitrance and rejection of his father's dream. Even though he let Harilal go, he believed that he was right. The son was going astray!

It was hard to let go. Ten days after Harilal left for India, Gandhi sent him a list of Gujarati books to read; and asked him to make it a habit to read Tulasī's *Rāmāyaṇa*. He was also asked to read the books listed in *Hind Swaraj,* and to write regularly and in detail to his father.[9] When Harilal intended to take French as a subject for matriculation, Gandhi tried to dissuade him and asked him to take Sanskrit instead. Gandhi also asked him to discard his 'infatuation' with matriculation; and chided him for his passion for his wife Chanchal.[10] Harilal failed thrice in three years to earn the coveted matriculation certificate. 'Cards and gambling elbowed out studies.'[11]

Gandhi had second thoughts, and offered twice to send his disgruntled

---

9   Cf. *Collected Works*, 11, pp.94-95.

10   *Collected Works*, 11, pp.165-7; 315-6; 333-4.

11   Gandhi Rajmohan, *op. cit.,* p. 154.

son to study in England on condition that the latter would return to South Africa to serve the *satyāgrahīs* after the completion of his studies. Harilal was peeved by the delay in the offer and the condition attached; and refused to accept it.

Chapter 62

Life at Tolstoy Farm

The middle months of 1911 were spent at Tolstoy Farm. Gandhi put in several hours of physical labour every day; and taught at the school from 10.30 to 4. The students, like their teacher, did not eat salt, vegetables and pulses between Monday and Saturday. Fruits like apples and bananas, bread with olive oil, rice and sago porridge formed part of their meals. Dinner for everyone was at 5.30 p.m. Gandhi spent the rest of the evening on his correspondence before retiring. Once a week, he visited Johannesburg, where L.W. Ritch was looking after his clients. He did not want to practise law again.

Pranjivan Mehta was pressing Gandhi to go to India, which needed him more than South Africa. Mehta published a series of articles in *Indian Review* of Madras, which were later brought out in a book form. 'No Indian in modern times', said Mehta, 'has succeeded so well in bringing the Hindus and Mahomedans together on a common platform as Mr. Gandhi.' What impressed Mehta most was that Gandhi practised what he preached. Nothing would deter him from his path once he decided upon a particular course of action. 'No earthly temptations' could ever sway him. It was impossible to find a man like him, 'who lives the ideal life he preaches.'[1] Gandhi, too, wanted to go to India, but thought that his work in South Africa was not yet done. He wrote to Mehta that he knew his work lay in India, and that he had no delusional dreams of reforming and saving the entire world.[2]

In the last week of July, 1911, *Indian Opinion* wrote about a move to unite

---

1   Mehta, P.J., *M.K. Gandhi and the South African Indian Problem*, G.A. Natesan & Co., Madras, 1912, pp.21-22, 26-32ff.

2   *Collected Works*, 11, pp. 165-7.

all the native associations of South Africa. Pixley Seme, a young Zulu attorney educated in the United States and London, emphasized that they would not in any way countenance the use of force. They had seen and learned from the non-violence of the Indian struggle. They did not say anything specific about passive resistance, but it was not unlikely that they might use it in certain eventualities.[3]

Pixley Seme visited Tolstoy Farm some time in 1911. 'Mr. Gandhi told Dr. Seme about his passive resistance movement and how he had settled the women and children on the farm. He remarked on how satisfactorily it had all worked out.'[4] This reveals personal links between Gandhi and the initiative for native African unity.

Seme published an article in the last week of October, urging the formation of a united South African native Congress. He pleaded with patient persuasion for sinking the tribal feuds and rising above the divisive rivalries to recognize that they were one people.[5] Seme must have seen the heterogeneous mix of the residents of Tolstoy Farm. Races, languages and religions commingled, as well as cultures. The spectacle would have inspired a vision of possible, viable South African native unity. Pixley Seme's efforts led to the formation of the South African Native National Congress in January 1912; and John Dube, Gandhi's neighbour at Phoenix, was elected its first president. The African leaders also, of course, knew of the Natal Indian Congress; and would certainly have heard of the Indian National Congress.

The South African Native National Congress arose out of the blacks' deliberate disempowerment by the white rulers of the Union of South Africa, who gave them no voice or representation at any level in matters of legislation and administration. The stated objective was the promotion and creation of national unity to defend the rights and privileges of the

---

3   'A Native Union: The Lessons of the Passive Resistance Movement', *Indian Opinion*, 29 July 1911

4   This information comes from a memorial written by Pauline Podlashuk, a Jewish lady of Russian extraction living in Johannesburg. She might also have helped translate Tolstoy's letter to Gandhi. Cf. Guha, *op. cit.*, p. 617, n.41.

5   Cf. Edward Roux, *Time Longer than Rope: The Black Man's Struggle for Freedom in South Africa*, University of Wisconsin Press, Second Edn., Madison, 1964, p.110.

native population. *Indian Opinion* congratulated Dube on his election as President; and published two paragraphs from his 'excellent' message to his countrymen. 'The first-born sons of this great and beautiful continent', said Dube, they 'were the last-born children' of the British Empire, 'just awakening into political life.' The whites, the Indians, the Cape Coloureds preceded them. 'They had therefore to tread softly...along the..path illuminated by righteousness and reason...that will surely and safely lead us to our goal, the attainment of our rightful inheritance as sons of Africa and citizens of the South African Commonwealth....by dint of our patience, our reasonableness, our law-abiding methods and the justice of our demands... by the nobility of our character, shall we break down the adamantine wall of colour prejudice and force even our enemies to be our admirers and friends.'[6] It sounds as though Gandhi is speaking. Both were patient, principled pursuers of justice, unperturbed by the lack or slowness of reform.

Though neighbours at Phoenix, the two met only rarely, as Gandhi was mostly away in the Transvaal. Yet, the similarity of their views is unmistakable. Both decried racial prejudice; but both counselled patience and politeness in their attempts to secure fairness and justice from their opponents.

Tolstoy farm had fashioned a smooth, disciplined mode of life for its residents. The provisional settlement had suspended the Indian *Satyāgraha*. It was an opportune time for Kallenbach to visit his family in Europe. But before he left, both he and Gandhi signed a document in legal format, which stated: 'Lower House is to proceed to Europe on a sacred pilgrimage to the members of his family...Lower House is not to spend any money beyond necessaries befitting the position of a simple-living poor farmer. Lower House is not to contract any marriage tie during his absence. Lower House shall not look lustfully upon any woman....The consideration for all the above tasks imposed by Lower House on himself is more love and yet more love between the two Houses – such love as, they hope, the world has not seen. In witness whereof the parties hereto solemnly affix their signatures in the presence of the Maker of all this 29th day of July at Tolstoy Farm.'[7]

---

6 'The awakening of the Natives: Mr.Dube's Address', *Indian opinion*, 10 February 1912.

7 An Agreement, 29 July 1911, *Collected Works*, Vol. 96, pp. 62-3.

As we have seen before, Kallenbach, in charge of finances, was the Lower House; and Gandhi was the Upper House. The extraordinary agreement indicates a very intimate and special relationship between Gandhi and Kallenbach, who found it exceedingly difficult to withstand temptation during his European sojourn. Gandhi kept reminding him in their correspondence of the condition of sexual abstinence in the agreement.

Kallenbach tried hard to control his attraction to Judith, his flirtatious niece; and wrote to Gandhi about it. In his reply, Gandhi told him: '…You are one of those spiritual rope-walkers…Beware then: think of the articles of our agreement, and God willing you will be safe….'[8]

On the final leg of his journey, in mid-December, Judith accompanied Kallenbach to England, to study at a boarding school. He boarded a ship to Africa on January 20, 1912. The entries for the period from December 28, 1911 to March 1, 1912, are mysteriously missing from his diary. Hunt suspects that Hanna Lazar, Kallenbach's second niece, deliberately destroyed these pages, because they contained details of his relationship with Judith.[9] The heterosexual Kallenbach could restrain himself only in the company of Gandhi, whose obsession with celibacy and sublimation of human sexual potency held him and the others around him in check. After Gandhi's departure from the scene, on his own return to South Africa after the war, Kallenbach had a long-term affair with Mrs. Alex Kennedy, the wife of his partner in his architectural business.[10] The absence of the strict exemplar of *brahmacarya* made all the difference! When Kallenbach returned to Johannesburg on February 11, 1912, he knew that he could not rise above temptation if he was far from Gandhi.

Obsession with celibacy

On the 16th of June, 1912, Gandhi wrote a letter to Kallenbach, in which he objected to those engaged in passive resistance getting married. Marriage was not for them! He wanted man and woman to view each other as brother and sister: 'As a passive resister I have come to the conclusion that marriage is not only not a necessity but positively a hindrance to public or humanitarian work…The possibilities for good if every woman looked

---

8   Gandhi to Kallenbach, *Collected Works*, 96, p.90.

9   Cf. Lev, Shimon, *op.cit.,* pp. 61,63, n.45.

10 Lev, *op. cit.*, p.21.

upon man as her brother and every man looked upon every woman as his sister are to my mind inconceivably grand. But such a consummation is not a probability. Those however who will follow a celibate life have certainly much greater and wider scope for their energy. My proposition holds good even for married people. They can change their outlook upon life and agree to live as brother and sister. Their love is then real and all the power for the animal in them having been driven out. I have been trying the thing in connection with Mrs. Gandhi...Self-restraint is no theory with me: it is a passion. No man or woman living the physical and animal life can possibly understand the spiritual or ethical...'[11]

Judith Brown cannot understand Gandhi's prepossession with celibacy solely in terms of the psychological effects of early childhood. She finds it hard to know 'what inner forces and ambiguities made celibacy so significant, indeed necessary, for this man in the prime of life.'[12]

I have also been intrigued and puzzled by this constant harping on celibacy. Despite his tireless emphasis on *brahmacarya*, and advice to married couples to keep their distance from their spouses even as far as sleeping in separate bedrooms, Gandhi himself drew sustenance from the physical propinquity of women around him, basking in their bodily warmth, and deriving comfort from their healing touch and soothing massage. The longing of the opposite sexes for each other is not simply expressed in sexual intercourse or activity; it is also naturally evidenced in their togetherness, in their company, in their acts and utterances of loving solicitude for each other. The mere fact of their presence together, their looking at one another, their talking together, is in essence nature in action with the sex instinct and attraction lending a unique warmth and meaning to human relationships. You may always be on your guard; you may always be holding yourself in check, in word and deed; but that does not negate nor demolish the basic source of myriad emotions investing relationships with inscrutable depths of meaning. Sex and the related pulsions of love, service and belonging do transcend the genitalia and coition, which represents only one important if imperative activity that binds, that overflows with self-effacing tenderness, that also brings new life into the world. Why did Gandhi view coition as ugly, as sinful, as

---

11 Cf. Lev, op.cit., p.27; also quoted in Hunt, D.J., and S. Bhana, *Spiritual Rope Walkers*, 2007.

12 *Gandhi Prisoner of Hope*, Yale University press, New Haven, 1989, p.86.

unclean, as polluting? Was it because a sense of sinful sex haunted him and never really left him ever since the day he was having sex with his wife just when his father was dying? Who knows? He did not immediately give up sex, though, after his father's death. He treated his wife and ministered to her physical needs when she was gravely ill. He also delivered his son Devadas at home, acting as a doctor and midwife when Kasturba gave birth to her fourth son. May be, the trauma of a baby's birth left a scar on his psyche, which he could never really shake off. A sense of guilt, a sense of sin, a sense of the physical distress of a woman in labour, inhibited his desire for sex, and its likeability! Witnessing the ugly abuse and torture of black bodies in the Zulu uprising also dealt a blow to any longing for sex.

Chapter 63

Satyāgrahīs

Sorabji Shapurji, one of the passive resisters who had been to jail as many as eight times, and ready to go back again if required, presented the case of the South African Indians to the Indian National Congress in Calcutta in December, 1911. The Congress offered its congratulations to Gandhi and the Transvaal Indians 'upon the repeal of the anti-Asiatic legislation of the province regarding registration and immigration.' It also asked the Government to abolish and to prohibit any further recruitment of Indian labour under indenture, 'whether for service at home or abroad.'[1]

Gandhi wanted to return to India with the final solution of the Transvaal grievances; but there was one more painful issue, a great cause of widespread affliction, which he needed to revisit and tackle before he left South Africa. This was the cruel annual tax of £ 3, that every ex-indentured Indian and his children had to pay in Natal. P.S. Aiyar, the Durban journalist, questioned why Gandhi was fighting simply for the entry of a few educated Indians into the Transvaal, instead of doing so for legal equality for Indians as British citizens, and for their free movement throughout the Union. The Natal Indian Congress had condemned the tax as 'oppressive, unjust and immoral.' Aiyar wrote that the tax amounted to 25% of the average annual income of an Indian in Natal. It taxed boys when 16, and girls when 13; wrecked many homes, and drove so many including young people into penury and untold privation. Despair and desperation bred immorality. Aiyar addressed his pamphlet to the whites, and to stir their conscience, called the impost patently unChristian.[2]

---

1 Cf. Tendulkar, *op.cit.*, p. 155.
2 Aiyar, P.S., *An Unjust Tax on Indian Immigrants: Appeal to the Empire, African Chronicle Printing Works*, Durban, 1911.

The pamphlet was sent to the Colonial Office in London. But when they asked the South African Government to give it sympathetic consideration, the Prime Minister Louis Botha brazenly replied that the prevailing white sentiment precluded any repeal.

With Gandhi largely preoccupied wih the struggle in the Transvaal, Aiyar was gunning for the leadership of Indians in Natal. Personal rivalries notwithstanding, the residents of Phoenix agreed that the tax was the single most oppressive, galling, destructive impost with a withering effect on people's lives. Albert West wrote to Gandhi in late 1911 that they should launch an immediate *satyāgraha* for its abolition. Gandhi was characteristically cautious, and specified the gradual steps leading to a *satyāgraha*. It needed a lot of groundwork and organization. They needed to collect people's signatures on petitions to the Prime Minister, to Parliament, to the Imperial Government, by the Natal Indian Congress aided by the other associations in South Africa. The final stage would be the refusal to pay any tax. The Congress would have to feed the wives and families of the jail-goers. Someone had to be in Durban, in charge of the movement. They needed to traverse the necessary steps leading to *satyāgraha*.[3]

Gandhi wote to Ratan Tata in April, 1912, with a report on the struggle, and of life on Tolstoy Farm, enclosing also a statement of accounts. Tata was pleased, and pledged a third gift of Rs. 25,000, which was announced at a public meeting in Bombay on July 31, 1912. A memorial dated 1 August 1912 to the Imperial Government urged them to put an end to the discriminatory practices against Indians in the Empire and the colonies. Indians would never acquiesce in the treatment of their compatriots abroad as inferior citizens.

Gandhi stayed in constant touch with the Ministry of the Interior during the first half of 1912, in connection with the new Immigration Bill. He raised the matter of the rights of domicile of women and minor children, the arbitrary powers of the immigration officers, the right of appeal to courts, and the right of inter-provincial migration for educated Indians.[4]

---

3   Gandhi to West, 27 November 1911, *Collected Works*, 96, pp. 93-4.

4   *Collected Works*, 11, pp.213-17, 227-8,231,241,254,264,275,556-8.

Smuts introduced a new 'Immigration Restriction Bill' in Parliament in May 1912. The General said that they wanted to do everything possible to attract white immigrants, and to keep the Asiatics out. They intended introducing an education test like Australia, which could be 'applied with rigour in the one case and treated with some laxity in the other.' That would enable the whites to come in; but would keep the Asiatics out. The bill still failed to pass through the Senate.

Some Indians in Natal sought to challenge Gandhi's leadership, and accused him of looking after the interests only of the *Banias* and Gujarati traders; but they were strongly challenged by Parsi Rustomji. Some others did not like Gandhi's caution, and felt that he had not taken up the issue of the £3 tax and its abolition in earnest. Gandhi's friends were concerned that some hotheads might try to harm him. Kallenbach asked Chhaganlal to watch out!

Gandhi gave away all he had in September 1912; and established a trust of the Phoenix Farm 'to follow and promote the ideals set forth by Tolstoy and Ruskin in their lives and works.'[5] Hajee Amod Johari, a Durban merchant, Parsi Rustomji, Kallenbach, Ritch and Pranjvan Mehta were the five trustees, among them a Muslim, a Parsi, two Jews and a Hindu. The inmates of the farm had to 'train themselves generally for the service of humanity'; and to publish *Indian Opinion* for the promotion of these ideals. He wanted them to cultivate better relations between Indians and Europeans; to promote purity of private life by leading pure lives; to start a school to educate children largely in their own languages; and to set up a sanitation and hygiene Institute.[6]

Gandhi would manage the trust while he lived; and would have two acres of land and a building for the use of his family. He would draw £5 a month like the other settlers. In case he died or left the farm, the trustees would select a manager from among themselves. The property was worth £5,130.4s.5d., a significant sum of money at the time.[7] L.W. Ritch had already taken charge of Gandhi's legal practice.

---

5   Cf. Tendulkar, *op.cit.*, p.156.
6   *Collected Works*, 11, pp.320-25; *Indian Opinion*, 14-9-1912.
7   *Ibid.*

Chapter 64

Gokhale's Visit

Gandhi had been pressing Gokhale to visit South Africa for quite some time. In England in 1911, Gokhale informed the Secretary of State for India that he wanted to go to South Africa to apprise himself of the situation there. The minister told the South African Government that he approved of Gokhale's mission, which assured official cooperation for the proposed visit.

Gandhi was 'simply overjoyed'.[1] Gokhale would be able to confer with the country's ministers on behalf of the Indian Government and the Empire; his words would carry weight; and they would find it hard to ignore his pleas for fair play. He could also raise pressing issues such as the oppressive £3 tax.

When the RMS *Saxon* docked at Cape Town harbour on October 22, 2012, a large Indian crowd was present to welcome Gokhale. Gandhi and a senior Muslim cleric went on board to greet him; and a great procession of fifty carriages with the guest seated in a coach and four drove him to the house of Gools, his local hosts. He was presented an address on behalf of the entire local Indian community. Senator W. P. Schreiner, head of the illustrious Schreiner family and a leading white liberal, gave praise to Gandhi's unselfishness of spirit at a large public meeting to welcome Gokhale. And Gandhi paid homage to the great Gokhale, his 'political teacher', whose name was sacred to all Indians. Gokhale told the Europeans that 'everything in India was open to all.' They could not 'shut the Indians out of their territory altogether without inflicting a very serious blow on the prestige of the Empire.' He had come in 'a spirit of compromise'; he only wanted to 'aid the cause of justice'. India was watching what

---

1 *Satyagraha in South Africa, Collected Works*, Vol. 29, p. 208.

was being done to her sons. There was 'a new awakening throughout the East...a new life throbbing, a new national consciousness everywhere.... there will be more and more self-respect in the future in[India's] dealings with such matters.'[2]

Gokhale also privately met J.X. Merriman, a prominent politician of Cape Town, who could not muster the courage to attend the public reception. Merriman was so highly impressed that he wrote to Smuts 'to do away with all the odious and illiberal machinery of repression' against the Indians: '... there are other and surely greater interests at stake than the conveniences of [white] traders and the prejudices of the [white] community.'[3]

The South African Government placed the state railway saloon at Gokhale's disposal. Mr. Runciman of the Immigration Department was assigned to escort Gokhale throughout the tour. Local mayors presided over every public meeting to welcome him.[4]

Gandhi had planned Gokhale's itinerary with great care, and was right beside him for four weeks of their travel across South Africa. Gandhi praised Gokhale at every meeting; and Gokhale emphasized justice and the Imperial interest in every speech. Indians of all persuasions, castes, communities and religions turned out to meet and greet them. Hindus, Muslims and Parsis conveyed messages to Gokhale. In Kimberley, the famous novelist Olive Schreiner was among the people who received him. Europeans and Indians ate together for the first time. The Mayor of Krugersdorp came to the station to receive Gokhale, which was resented by many whites who said the 'coolie gentleman' had come only to stir up 'strife'.[5]

Kallenbach designed an ornamental arch of welcome at the Johannesburg station. Rich carpets covered the railway platform. Gandhi, who called the love of gold a sickness, made sure that the welcome address presented to Gokhale at the station was 'engraved on a solid heart-shaped plate of

---

2 Anon., *Hon. Mr. G. K. Gokhale's Visit to South Africa*, 1912, Indian opinion, Durban, 1912, pp.4-7

3 Cf. Guha, *op. cit.,* p. 434.

4 Tendulkar, *op.cit.,* pp.156-7.

5 Cf. Report in *Indian Opinion*, 23 November 1912.

gold from the Rand mounted on Rhodesian teak.'⁶The plate had a map of India flanked by two gold tablets, 'one bearing an illustration of the Taj Mahal and the other a characteristic Indian scene.'⁷ Gandhi also made sure that Ellis, the mayor of Johannesburg, was present at the station to receive Gokhale. He deliberately sought pomp and ceremony, and white participation, as it was a matter of India's prestige. The scale and magnificence of the reception would add an additional thrust to Gokhale's talks with the ministers. The twin domes of the welcoming arch assumed the forms of the Muslim crescent and the Hindu trident.

Two Europeans, William Hosken and Joseph Doke, were among the speakers at the Johanesburg meeting. Hosken spoke of the recent imprisonment of 2,700 Indians out of a total of 9,000 in the Transvaal; and called it 'a horrible disgrace to our Christianity and our civilization.' Joseph Doke made a plea for 'justice for every man as a man' under the British flag. Gokhale praised Gandhi, who was 'the friend of everyone in the room', 'a great and illustrious son of India, of whom she [India] was proud beyond words, and he was sure that men of all races and creeds would recognize in him one of the most remarkable personalities of their time.'⁸

In an interview with the *Transvaal Leader* on October 30, 1912, Gandhi said that Gokhale wanted free and unhampered movement of Indians in the Union, and freedom of trade under conditions applicable to the whole community. They sought civic, not social or political equality. When asked about the Orange Free State, Gandhi said that the few allowed immigration should be able to go in, and move freely around the Union. The Free State barrier had to disappear in due course, or else, 'the Union will be a farce.'⁹

On November 1, 1912, Gokhale was a guest of the Chinese Association of Johannesburg for breakfast. Leung Quinn, the Chinese leader, spoke of the Asiatics standing 'shoulder to shoulder'; of 'a fraternity larger than that of common religion and race...' They looked forward to 'the reign of sweet reason instead of stupid prejudice' poisoning inter-racial relations.

---

6   Gandhi Rajmohan, *op.cit.,* p. 158.

7   Cf. *Satyagraha in South Africa*, p. 240.

8   Anon., *Mr. G. K.Gokhale's Visit to South Africa*, pp.13-16,17, 201.

9   *Collected Works*, 11, pp. 343-4.

GOKHALE'S VISIT

Gokhale spoke of so much in common between the two communities. Both were old peoples; and India had given China one of her oldest religions.[10]

Gokhale was not in good health, and stayed in Kallenbach's house in Mountain View for some rest. The views outside and the art inside provided a pleasant retreat. A three-room office was hired in the heart of the city, where he received visitors, and held a private meeting with leading Europeans, who could also apprise him of their problems and anxieties.

Gandhi could not resist the urge to show his revered guest how they lived and worked on Tolstoy Farm. They took Gokhale to the farm, where he stayed from the 2nd to the 4th of November.[11] Gandhi failed to realize that a mile and a half's walk from the Lawley railway station to the farm could be difficult for the frail guest; and it rained. Gokhale got wet and caught a cold. They put him up in Kallenbach's room, where a special cot was brought in for his comfort. But when he saw that they all slept on the floor at the farm, he too had his bedding spread on the floor. Gandhi and Kallenbach were in constant attendance. Gandhi cooked for Gokhale; and washed and ironed his special scarf with great care.

The next morning, Gandhi saw Gokhale pacing up and down the room weighing up the words he would use in a letter he was going to write. When asked by Gandhi why he was taking so long to write, Gokhale scolded him: 'You do not know my way of life. I will not do even the least little thing in a hurry. I will think about it and consider the central idea. I will next deliberate as to the language suited to the subject and then set to write. If everyone did as I did, what a huge saving of time there would be. And the nation would be saved from the avalanche of half-baked ideas which now threaten to overwhelm her.'[12]

No wonder, then, if 'the clearness, firmness and urbanity of Gokhale's utterances flowed from his indefatigable labour and devotion to truth.'[13]

They left for Natal on the 6th of November; stopped *en route* at the smaller mining and plantation towns like Newcastle and Dundee; and arrived in

---

10   *Indian Opinion*, 9 November 1912.
11   Cf. Tendulkar, *op.cit.*, p. 158.
12   Cf. Chadha, *op.cit.*, p. 176.
13   Cf. *Satyagraha in South Africa, Collected Works*, Vol. 29, p. 212.

Durban on the 8th. A meeting in the Town Hall attended by a large number of Indians was addressed, among others, by F.A.Laughton, KC, who had bravely tried to save Gandhi from a white murderous mob in 1897.

Gokhale presented prizes at a sports meet the next day; and heard from about sixty men who, one by one, told him of the iniquitous tax; their inability to pay it; and consequent imprisonment. Their harrowing tales were heard by the several thousand people who had come to attend the meeting from far and near on all kinds of transport, if not on foot. Their accounts given in Tamil and Gujarati were translated, so that Gokhale could understand; and the crowd was often moved to shout 'Shame! Shame!'[14]

Gokhale and Gandhi paid a visit to the Ohlange Industrial School on November 10, 1912; and discussed the native question with the Rev. John Dube. They were entertained by Zulu songs sung by the students.[15] This was a significant attempt by Gandhi to promote understanding between the native South African leader and India's foremost statesman.

Gokhale returned to the Transvaal, and on November 14, went to Pretoria. Botha was peeved by the fact that Gokhale had not gone to visit him first. He did not like the warm receptions accorded to Gokhale everywhere he went; and complained to the Governor-General that the visitor had raised 'false hopes' among the Indians. Gokhale's speeches, said Botha, had hardened the attitude of both the Dutch and English-speaking whites, who were 'more than ever opposed to any kind of concession'. But he would still 'meet him in the most reasonable spirit'.[16]

The Government did not concede Gokhale's request for Gandhi to accompany him to the talks. Gokhale asked Gandhi to prepare a historical summary of the Indians in the four colonies, to which he could refer. He and the others stayed awake the whole night preparing for the meeting. Gokhale carefully studied a long memo that Gandhi had drafted on the grievances of Indians including the £3 tax; and satisfied himself fully on every detail of every point. He then 'went over the whole ground again in order to make sure that he had rightly understood everything.'[17]

---

14 Anon., *Mr. G.K. Gokhale's Visit*, pp. 34-5; cf. Guha, op. cit., pp.436-7.

15 *Indian Opinion*, 23 November 1912.

16 Cf. Guha, *op.cit.*, pp. 437, 619, n. 70.

17 Cf. Gandhi, Rajmohan, *op.cit.*, pp. 158-9.

Gokhale's interview with Botha, Smuts and Fischer took a couple of hours. He urged the ministers to abolish the £3 tax, and allow the admission of a select number of educated Indians to the Transvaal. The next day, Prime Minister Botha and Gokhale met Lord Gladstone, the Governor-General, but separately. Gladstone sent a report to London: 'As regards the £3 tax, the Prime Minister told me that he thought it would be possible to meet Mr. Gokhale's views, though there might be strong opposition in Natal. From what Mr. Gokhale said I gathered that the Prime Minister had given him a satisfactory assurance.' Gladstone also hoped that the Immigration Bill would also be passed in a form that was acceptable. The Governor-General was 'convinced that the Prime Minister and General Smuts are sincerely anxious to put it through.'[18]

Gokhale was convinced that the demands of the Indians would be conceded. He told Gandhi after the interview: 'Gandhi, you must return to India in a year. Everything has been settled. The Black Act will be repealed. The racial bar will be removed from the immigration law. The £3 tax will be abolished.'[19] Gandhi was sceptical. He told Gokhale that he was not quite as hopeful, as he knew the ministers a little better. But he was happy that Gokhale had obtained this undertaking from the ministers. The promise made to Gokhale would be proof of the justice of their demands; and would redouble their fighting spirit if a renewal of the struggle became unavoidable. He doubted that he could return to India in a year, before many more Indians had courted imprisonment.[20]

In his farewell speech in the Pretoria Town Hall on November 15, Gokhale addressed 'the better mind of the two communities, European and Indian.' The Europeans were told that 'the Government must exist for promoting the prosperity not of the European community only, but of all its subjects.' The Indians were told that their future lay largely in their own hands: 'I pray to God that such a struggle...may not have to be waged again. But if it has to be resumed...remember that the issue will largely turn on the character you show, on your capacity for combined action, on your readiness to suffer and sacrifice in a just cause. India will no doubt be behind you.

---

18 Cf. Guha, pp.437, 619, n. 72.

19 As recalled in Polak, H.S.L., H.N. Brailsford and Lord Pethick-Lawrence, *Mahatma Gandhi*, Oldhams Press Ltd., London, 1949, pp.81-82; cf. Tendulkar, op. cit., p.158

20 Cf. *Ibid.*

Nay, all that is best in this empire, all that is best in the civilized world, will wish you success...Remember that you are entitled to have the Indian problem in the country solved on right lines. And in such right solution are involved not merely your present worldly interests, but your dignity and self-respect, the honour and good name of your motherland.'[21]

Gokhale was impressed by the loyalty and devotion of Gandhi's secretary Sonja Schlesin, and told Gandhi: 'I have rarely met with the sacrifice, the purity and the fearlessness I have seen in Miss Schlessin. Amongst your co-workers, she takes the first place in my estimation.'[22]

Gokhale spent the last weekend at Tolstoy farm, and on November 17, 1912, left Johannesburg for the Portuguese port of Lourenco Marques. Gandhi and Kallenbach went with him as far as Dar-es-Salaam, where Gokhale took leave of them to sail to Bombay. Gandhi wrote to him: 'I want to be a worthy pupil of yours...We have many differences of opinion, but you shall still be my pattern in political life.' And then Gandhi gave his senior comprehensive advice on food and exercise to 'get rid of his diabetes and add a few more years...to [his] life of service in [his] present body.'[23]

In his speech at a public meeting in Bombay on December 13, 1912, Gokhale lauded Gandhi to the skies: 'Only those who have come in personal contact with Mr. Gandhi...can realize the wonderful personality of the man. He is without doubt made of the stuff of which heroes and martyrs are made. Nay, more, he has in him the marvellous spiritual power to turn ordinary men around him into heroes and martyrs. During the recent passive resistance struggle in the Transvaal...2,700 sentences of imprisonment were borne by our countrymen... under the guidance of Mr. Gandhi to uphold the honour of their country. Some of the men... were very substantial persons, some were small traders, but the bulk of them were poor and humble individuals, hawkers, working men and so forth, men without education, men not accustomed in their life to think or talk of their country. And yet these men braved the horrors of jail life in the Transvaal and some of them braved them again and again rather than submit to degrading legislation directed against their country. Many

---

21 Anon., *Mr. Gokhale's Visit to South Africa*, p.4; Tendulkar, op.cit., p. 159.

22 Quoted in Gandhi's *Autobiography*.

23 Gandhi to Gokhale, 4 December 1912, *Collected Works*, 11, pp. 351-2.

homes were broken...many families dispersed, some men at one time wealthy lost their all and became paupers, women and children endured untold hardships. But they were touched by Mr. Gandhi's spirit that had wrought the transformation, thus illustrating the great power which the spirit of man can exercise over human minds and even over physical surroundings. In all my life I have known only two men who affected me spiritually in the manner that Mr. Gandhi does – our great patriarch, Mr. Dadabhai Naoroji and my late master, Mr. Ranade – men before whom not only are we ashamed of doing anything unworthy, but in whose presence our very minds are afraid of thinking anything that is unworthy....'

Gokhale went on to describe how Gandhi had fought for the country and its people for the last twenty years; how he had sacrificed himself and his splendid practice of five to six thousand pounds a year for the cause; and was living on three pounds a month like the poorest of the poor. Despite the agony of the long-drawn-out struggle, Gandhi's mind was entirely free from any bitterness towards his European adversaries. And even though the Europeans wanted to crush him, 'they honoured him as a man.'[24]

Gokhale debunked the radical critics of Gandhi, who said that he should have fought for free migration to South Africa. Such a demand and such a campaign would have provoked the implacable foes of Indians not only to shut and secure all their gates against them, but also to do everything possible to expel the resident Indian population from the country. The theoretical rights sought by Gandhi would in due course graduate into rights in practice; and the progress of Indians in their own country would doubtless improve their position abroad. Gandhi's self-effacing insistence on justice in tandem with his steady push for reform safeguarded the Indian community from any retributive wrath of the whites, while also at the same time striving for a fair deal.

Gokhale's visit was a fruition of Gandhi's endeavour to get India directly involved in the Indian struggle in South Africa. It also confirmed and strengthened Gandhi's status in South Africa in the eyes of the Government and the Indian community. And it made Gandhi famous in his motherland. P.S. Aiyar, the Tamil journalist, jealous of Gandhi, criticised him for relying too much on Kallenbach, Polak and Ritch, rather than Indians like him. 'The highest admiration and respect for Mr. Gandhi' was tempered by

---

24   Cf. Tendulkar, *op.cit.*, pp.159-60.

the emphasis on 'a considerable body of opinion outside the Trsansvaal', which was opposed to his 'views and conclusions.' In an interview, Gokhale told him how impractical and unachievable free immigration and free movement were in the context of current reality. Aiyar accused him of lecturing on the 'maintenance of the European civilization', and praising Gandhi as 'a wonderful personage', without achieving anything.[25] When Gokhale praised Gandhi again in a public meting in Bombay, Aiyar moaned that he had been hypnotised by Gandhi and Polak.[26] Aiyar was 'the only articulate opponent of Gandhi within the Indian community.'[27]

---

25 *African Chronicle*, 28 December 1912.

26 *Ibid.*, 28 December 1912 and 8 February 1913.

27 Guha, *op.cit.*, pp.442-3.

Chapter 65

Return to Phoenix

At the end of Gokhale's fruitful visit, Gandhi decided to move to Phoenix. There was no need for him to stay in the Transvaal after the formation of the Union. Immigration laws were now applicable to the entire Union; and any settlement with Smuts would also cover the whole country. At the beginning of 1913, therefore, he came to Phoenix to live there with his family, friends and disciples. Phoenix had always been home for the last eight years and more, even if he was largely away in Johannesburg, where his work and public responsibilities kept him. But every visit to Phoenix brought him joy, as it did to all the residents of the farm, and so much more to the children who loved him. Gandhi loved them, too, and laughed heartily in their company. He was not as good with the adolescents, specially his own boys, whose inner tumult eluded him.

With the release of the passive resisters from jail, most of the inmates left Tolstoy farm for their respective homes. Those that remained had mostly come from Phoenix. Gandhi moved them and the school to Phoenix. The settlement had grown in the past nine years. Some old settlers had gone; and new ones had come in. The plots of land were carefully cultivated; nice and neat hedges defined the lay-out; and the residents grew most of their own vegetables. Salads, fruits and pine-apples were cultivated. A couple of houses had been enlarged, with more furniture inside, and inviting curtains at the windows. A large one-room building was set up as a schoolroom.

The school had about thirty children. The teachers and their students did manual work on the farm from 6 to 8 a.m., and then had their breakfast. Gandhi took the boys to the classroom after breakfast; while the men went off to work in the press. Gandhi himself worked in the press in the afternoon, while someone else took charge of the students. They had their dinner at 5.30, which was followed by songs and prayer. From 7.30 till 9 p.m., Gandhi taught his son Manilal. He was waking up to a fatherly duty.

Gandhi's living-room served as the meeting place of the community. Every Sunday evening, all the inmates gathered there for an inter-faith religious service, which was a mix of the East and West. A book containing eighteen hymns taken from different sources, printed and bound at the Phoenix Press, was used for the musical service, in which one or two English members played the organ, while the others including Gandhi sang and enjoyed themselves. Gandhi usually began the service with a reading from the *Gītā*, followed by passages from the New Testament and other texts. 'Take my life, and let it be consecrated', and 'Lead, Kindly Light' were his favourite hymns.

Gandhi hoped to return to India by the middle of 1913. He was trying to persuade his friend Kallenbach to accompany him to Phoenix, and then to India. But Kallenbach was also in touch wih the Jews and Zionists, who were urging him to go to Palestine. While he was vacillating between Palestine and India, Gandhi came to Tolstoy Farm, packed his carpentry tools and some of his books on agriculture, and took them away to Phoenix, together with the other settlers. Gandhi handed a letter to Kallenbach before he left; and the latter felt hurt. Gandhi wanted him to decide for himself. He advised him to make very little use of his riches for his own comforts, and keep poverty and suffering as his goal: 'I was wrong in presenting India before you quite so soon and wrong in suggesting a study of Hindi.'[1]

Kallenbach moved after three weeks to Mountain View; and wrote to Gandhi to return his tools and books. Gandhi called his letter 'pathetic', and said he would send his things back. But Gandhi always stayed in Kallenbach's house when he went to Johannesburg; and the two discussed Kallenbach's questions about settling in Palestine. Gandhi counselled against; but it was on his advice later that Kallenbach bequeathed his entire fortune, in his will, to the Zionist movement.[2] Lev suggests that Gandhi learned of the idea of Zionism from Kallenbach in South Africa.[3]

---

1   Gandhi to Kallenbach, 8 January, 1913, *Collected Works*, 96, pp. 105-6.

2   Cf. Lev, Shimon, *op.cit.*, p.79.

3   *Ibid.*, p. 77.

The first issue of *Indian Opinion* in 1913 began a series, 'General Knowledge about Health' in Gujarati. It was based on Gandhi's wide reading, experience and experiments. He criticised modern drugs and dependence on them. Bad air, dirty toilets and open-air urination foul the atmosphere. Dumping of food peelings, garbage and spitting, for which Indians are notorious, add to the filth and spread of diseases. Contaminated water is a great source of sickness. Gandhi explained how to clean and purify the water at home before human consumption. Alcoholic drinks, tobacco, hemp and other similar substances are injurious to health, and waste hard-earned money. Chiles, spices and salt are all harmful, and need to be given up.

Gandhi spelled out ideal and preferred diets. The best is one that consists of fruits. Next come fruits and vegetables with no salt or spices; and after that a mix of vegetables and meat. The most harmful is a purely carnivorous diet. Those living 'exclusively on flesh' are not even worth thinking of. 'They are not healthy in any sense of the term.'[4]

---

4   *Collected Works*, 11, 428-30, 434-6, 441-3, 447-9, 453-5.

Chapter 66

Betrayal

The dream of an early return to India received a quick jolt when Gandhi saw the Government going back on its promises. Smuts told the House of Assembly that the Europeans of Natal were implacably opposed to the repeal of the £3 annual poll tax on ex-indentured Indians. On January 18, 1913, *Indian Opinion* sounded the alarm: 'We are in possession of information of the utmost importance to the Indian community...We may, next week, give the whole history of the matter, which bids fair to bring about a revival of passive resistance which we had hoped would not be necessary. We understand that the Government are not keeping their promise regarding those British Indians who, in terms of the settlement, should be given rights of residence in the Transvaal or the Union as the case may be....We warn the Government to be careful...if they do not...the seasoned soldiers in passive resistance will give a good account of themselves at the call of duty.'[1]

Gandhi wrote to Gokhale of the 'ever growing severity' of officials enforcing the Immigration Acts; and 'the great trouble and expense' to which the 'wives of lawfully resident Indians' were being subjected.[2] The provisional settlement was on the brink of break-down.

Indian Marriages

A judgement in the Supreme Court with far-reaching ramifications added fuel to the smouldering embers of dismay and discontent. Hassan Esop of Port Elizabeth married a woman called Bai Mariam when he visited

---

1 Cf. *Collected Works*, 11, p. 438.
2 *Collected Works*, 11, pp. 460-61.

India in 1908. He returned without her in 1909; but went back to India in 1912 to bring her with him to South Africa. On their arrival, the immigration officer did not allow her to land, and ordered her to return to India. In March, 1913,the husband's application for an order to restrain the Government from deporting his wife to India was rejected by justice Searle of the Cape provincial division of the Supreme Court. The judge observed: 'The courts of this country have always set their faces against recognition of these so-called Mahommedan marriages as legal unions'. A 'wife' could 'be repudiated the next day after the arrival by the husband.' When told that one wife should be allowed, the judge remarked: 'I do not know whether it is to be the first that comes, or the first that is married.' Both Muslim and Hindu laws permitted polygamy; but the judge paid no regard to the fact that Bai Mariam was Hassan Esop's only wife.[3] Only marriages celebrated according to Christian rites, and recorded by the Registrar of marriages, would thus be deemed legitimate. Hindu, Muslim and Zoroastrian marriages, which had never been registered, suddenly, instantly, became illegal in South Africa. What would the wives then be called? And what would be the legal status of their children?

Gandhi expressed his horror and frustration in no uncertain terms:

'…The meaning of the judgement is that every Hindu and Mahomedan wife is in South Africa illegally, and, therefore, at the mercy of the Government, whose grace alone can enable her to remain in this country. And no one will be blamed but ourselves if the future Indian wives – Hindu, Mahomedan or Parsee – are turned out. This is a state of things which our self-respect forbids us from tolerating. We hope that every Anjuman, every Association, and every Dharma Sabha will send respectful representations to the Government urging that the new Immigration Bill should be altered so as to admit the legality of marriages celebrated according to the recognized Indian religions. This request should be promptly granted…It is, indeed, a serious question for passive resisters to consider whether they ought not to include in their requirements a redress of this unthought of but intolerable grievance.'[4]

In the same issue of *Indian Opinion,* Gandhi emphasized that there was 'only one point at issue, whether or not a marriage solemnized according

---

3   *Cape Times,* 21 March 1913; cf. Tendulkar, op.cit., p.162.
4   *Indian Opinion,* 22-3-1913; CW,11, p.496

to the Muslim rites or under any religion other than Christianity was legal. The judge decided that such a marriage was not legal and that therefore the woman had no right to enter the Cape...This decision means that as from today all Hindu and Muslim wives living in South Africa lose their right to live there...a Hindu, Muslim or Parsi wife can live in this country only by the grace of the Government. It is quite on the cards that the Government will not permit any more wives to come in or that, if it does, it will be entirely as a matter of favour. We cannot conceive of a more degrading state of affairs. The remedy is entirely in our hands....We know that many battles have been fought to protect the honour of women....It will be nothing extraordinary if right now we sacrifice our wealth, our stocks, our businesses and start the fight...If we lose our honour, what remains of happiness?...'[5]

The Searle judgement threatened the validity of every Indian marriage and family. If rigorously implemented, it would rend families apart, men from wives, children from parents! A mass meeting of Indians held in the Hamidiya Hall of Johannesburg asked for remedial legislation to recognize the validity of marriages performed under the rites of 'the great religions of India.' If this did not happen, the community would be forced to resort to passive resistance for the protection of their women and their honour.[6]

Men were no doubt upset and angry; but the women, too, were incensed when told what the judgement meant to them, and to their status. Kasturba asked Gandhi: 'Then I am not your wife according to the laws of this country.' When Gandhi said yes, it was so, she suggested returning to India. That, replied Gandhi, would be an act of cowardice; and the difficulty would remain unsolved. She then asked if she, too, could join the struggle, and go to jail. Gandhi told her that she could; but 'her health was not good'; and she was a stranger to the 'hardships' of jail. Any weakening on her part after joining the struggle would be 'disgraceful'. If she succumbed to fear or terror, and apologized to the Government, he would not blame her. But 'how would it stand with me? How could I then harbour you or look the world in the face?'[7] The conceit of 'I' in relation to his wife, the thought of his self-image posed this ugly question to Kasturba. Self-effacement in relation to the wide world was not in order in his love for Kasturba. 'You

---

5   *Ibid.*, pp. 497-8.

6   *Indian Opinion*, 5 April 1913.

7   *Satyagraha in South Africa, Collected Works*, Vol. 29, p. 224.

may have nothing to do with me,' said Kasturba, 'if being unable to stand jail I secure release by an apology. If you can endure hardships and so can my boys, why can't I? I am bound to join the struggle.'[8]

The dutiful, devoted, undaunted Kasturba was ready to wage war for the Indian cause, for the Indian women's cause, for her husband's cause, her frail health notwithstanding! She had always stood resolutely right beside him, despite the tests and trials of their married life. She loved him, as, indeed, he too loved her!

Gandhi had up till now shielded women from the rough and tumble of *Satyāgraha*. This insult to Indian womanhood was a clear call for them to rise with their men to confront the perpetrators of legal tyranny! Gandhi would let Kasturba participate; and he would let the other women join her in defence of their honour. It would be a momentous departure from the seclusion and privacy of their homes! It had never happened before! It was totally out of bounds, and not even thought of as a possibility in India. Middle-class Hindu and Muslim women lived in *purda*; and moved outdoors only with members of their families. The *Swadeshi* movement in Bengal and Maharashtra had no female participants. The extremists and terrorists were all men. A small number of upper class women began to attend meetings of the Indian National Congress around 1910; but none of them went to jail. The struggle was viewed in male terms, requiring any sacrifices by men only. They could not even contemplate the prospect of their womenfolk being bullied and fed by male jailors who were neither related, nor of their caste.

In South Africa, though, Tamil wives of the *satyāgrahīs* in prison held a meeting in Germiston in 1909, and passed a resolution: 'As our religion teaches us that a wife may not be separated from her husband, we pray the Government to send us to gaol with our husbands, and to confiscate our property, if that be justice.'[9] But they were dissuaded from courting arrest.

Kasturba's bold move to seek imprisonment for the Indian women's cause might also have been encouraged by the feminist fervour of Millie Polak; while Gandhi's permission for her to do so would certainly have been inspired by the example of the suffragettes, and the readiness of the Tamil

8 *Ibid.*; cf. 'Conversations with Kasturba Gandhi', [Before April 19, 1913], *Indian Opinion*, 1-10. 1913; CW, 12, p.31.
9 Cf. Guha, *op. cit.*, p. 465.

women to go to jail. African women in the Orange Free State had also bravely returned their passes to the Government, and decided never to carry them.[10]

Gandhi wrote to Gokhale about the women's readiness to join the struggle; of Kasturba's 'offer on her own initiative' to do so. He did not want to 'debar her.'[11] In case the struggle took place, it would occasion much more suffering. He would gratefully accept help from people who knew him and wanted to extend their support; but would not appeal to the public in India for financial assistance. He asked Gokhale 'not to make any public appeal for funds.' Gokhale wrote back: 'We in India have some idea of our duty, even as you understand your obligations in South Africa. We will not permit you to tell us what is or is not proper for us to do. I only desired to know the position in South Africa, but did not seek your advice as to what we may do.'[12]

The Searle judgement ignited great indignation sweeping across the Indian community both in Natal and the Transvaal. The £3 annual impost on ex-indentured labourers and their families in Natal still stood unrepealed, a cause of widespread misery and disaffection. P.S. Aiyar organized a number of meetings to give voice to the people's suffering; and appealed to Prime Minister Botha to abolish the tax, without any success.

The draft of a new Immigration Bill, published in the Union Gazette Extraordinary on April 12, 1913, added insult to injury. The £3 tax stayed where it was. Qualifications for domicile were made even more strict. Inter-provincial migration was made even more difficult. Appeals to courts were not allowed; and the status of wives and children remained unclear and insecure. Armed with wide discretionary powers, officials could keep out 'any person or class of persons deemed...unsuited to the requirements of the Union or any particular Province thereof.'[13] Gandhi called the bill 'worse than its predecessor': '...the Government only want to give us what they must...they wish ill even to those who have established rights in the Union, and...by hook or by crook, they desire to compass our ruin....Unless the Government yield and amend the bill materially,

---

10 *Indian Opinion*, 2 August 1913, 'Native Women's Brave Stand'; cf. Guha, *op. cit.*, p. 465.

11 'Letter to G. K. Gokhale, April 19, 1913', *Collected Works*, 12, p. 41

12 Cf. Chadha, *op.cit.,* pp. 179-80.

13 Cf. Guha, *op.cit.,* p.448.

passive resistance must revive and, with it, all the old miseries, sorrows and sufferings. Homes, just re-established, must be broken up…we must learn the lesson again of finding pleasure in pain.'[14]

The Natal Indian Congress sent a telegram to the Governor-General warning that the Indian community would be constrained to oppose the bill with all its might, if the Government did not make the requested amendments. Gandhi went to Johannesburg to attend a large meeting of angry and excited people in the Hamidiya Hall. He told them that all the worst features of provincial laws were included in the new Bill; and the impending struggle might therefore be 'prolonged and fierce.' L. W. Ritch also spoke, and said that, as an Englishman, 'he would fight unto death', if he was treated like his Indian brothers.[15]

Abraham Fischer, the new Minister of the Interior, came from the Orange Free State. He was absolutely shameless in his opposition to Indians for the 'self-preservation of the white man'. And as a practitioner of monogamy like his fellow Europeans, he was not going to allow the privilege of polygamy to the Asiatics.[16] Voices of Liberal members of Parliament, such as Morris Alexander and W. P. Schreiner, who characterized the bill as a 'serious infringement', and a betrayal of the promises made to Gokhale, were drowned in the chorus of white hatred directed at the Indians.[17]

In an interview to *The Star* on or before April 28, 1913, Gandhi said the Indians would find the bill 'totally unacceptable', unless it honoured the fundamental principle of the compromise 'in respect of existing rights and the removal of the racial bar.'[18]

On April 30, 1913, A. M. Cachalia, Chairman of the British Indian Association of the Transvaal, sent the Governor-General a copy of the Resolution, unanimously passed at a meeting on the 27th, to start a *satyāgraha* against the bill if the objections and entreaties of the community went unheeded. Copies of the Resolution were sent to the Secretary of State for the Colonies, and to the Secretary of State for India.

---

14 *Collected Works*, 12, pp.13-14.

15 *Rand Daily Mail*, 23 April 1913; cf. Guha, *op.cit.*, p.449.

16 *Ibid.*, Speech of 30 April, 1913.

17 *Ibid.*

18 *Collected Works*, 12, p. 55-56; *The Star*, 28-4-1913.

Abraham Fischer even refused to recognize Gandhi as a leader and spokesman of the community. He would do nothing to overrule the Searle judgement, as only the union of one man to one woman certified by a marriage officer was a legitimate marriage according to the law of the land.

Sonja Schlesin, as Honorary Secretary of the Transvaal Indian Women's Association, sent Fischer a telegram on May 4, 1913, conveying their 'carefully considered position, in the light of the Searle judgement…the honour of Indian womanhood is affected by that judgement. Committee therefore respectfully trusts that the Government will be pleased to amend the law so as to recognize the validity of Indian marriages which have been duly consecrated according to the religious customs of the parties and are recognized as legal in India.'

The resolution also conveyed to the minister the determination of the women to offer passive resistance and court imprisonment side by side with men, if the Government turned a deaf ear to their entreaty.[19]

Henry Polak wrote a number of letters to the Government of India and the Colonial Office, highlighting the flaws of the bill, urging them to intervene. He also made constructive suggestions to make the necessary changes; and warned them of the imminence of passive resistance, and Gandhi's participation in the struggle, if nothing was done. Incensed Fischer was averse to any concession.

Gandhi's placid pursuit of good health and prescription of remedies for all kinds of ailments continued unaffected by his neck-deep involvement in the Indian struggle for existence in South Africa. He kept publishing in *Indian Opinion* articles on water treatments; enemas for relief from constipation, gas and flatulence; poor digestion and dyspepsia; earth cures and mud-packs for a variety of diseases; infectious diseases and their treatment; confinement and care of children; accidents such as drowning, snake-bites and burns, and the best ways to look after the victims.[20]

The Immigration Bill passed its second reading in May, 1913, despite the unanimous opposition of the Unionist party. Gandhi wrote that there

---

19 *Collected Works*, 12, p. 65.

20 *Collected Works*, 12, 67-9; 79-81; 102-4; 115-17; 118-19; 129-32; 135-137; 142-45; 149-51; 152-53; 156-60.

could be 'no question of compromise on points of existence or honour.'[21] He approached members of Parliament and Abraham Fischer, Minister of the Interior, asking for the abolition of the £3 tax; and for an acceptable resolution of the marriage imbroglio. The Minister replied that they would abolish the tax for women only; and that, if registered, marriages would be recognized. The inadequate concessions still broke the promise to Gokhale that the tax would be totally repealed for both men and women; and did nothing to address the fact that almost all Indian marriages were unregistered. Gandhi and the Indians had no other option but to reject them.[22]

The bill passed by the South African Parliament received Royal Assent on June 14, 1913. Lord Gladstone grumbled about the truculence of Gandhi and the Indians in his communication to London; and forecast a quick collapse of the Indian resistance. Polak wrote to Gokhale about the total betrayal; and said that he was 'thoroughly ashamed to have to call myself an Englishman today.'[23]

Gokhale was in London, from where he complained to the Government of India that the South African Government had again 'broken faith with the Indians.' If passive resistance became inevitable, he would return home and move a resolution to support it in the Imperial Council. Lord Ampthill, Gandhi's admirer, spoke in the House of Lords, criticizing the new Act, which took away existing rights of entry and re-entry; failed to recognize Hindu and Muslim marriages; and dishonoured the promise of South African Ministers to Gokhale that the £3 tax would be repealed. How would the Lords 'meet the untold scandal…if there shall be a renewal of passive resistance.'[24]

Gokhale was not well. Diabetes and related complications were wearing him down. The situation exercised him so much that he would return to India in hot and humid August to move a Resolution in the Imperial Council, if *Satyāgraha* broke out in South Africa. His friend William Wedderburn was so worried that he wrote to Gandhi. He requested Gandhi to beseech Gokhale to postpone his return to India; and if possible, to

---

21 *Indian Opinion*, 17-5-1913; CW, 12, p.72.
22 Cf. *Collected Works*, 12, pp.87-8, 90-91, 101, 574-5.
23 Cf. Guha, *op. cit.*, p.454.
24 *Ibid.*, p. 455.

postpone the passive resistance till the first of January, and meanwhile, try all possible means of compromise.[25]

Equally concerned with Gokhale's state of health, Gandhi explored the last remaining avenue of possible compromise. Fischer had made himself scarce and unapproachable. Gandhi knew Smuts. They had dealt with each other before. Even though Smuts was now Defence Minister, Gandhi decided to approach him. He went to the Transvaal in the last week of June, and requested an interview with the General. On July 2, 1913, he wrote a letter addressed to the Secretrary for the Interior, listing the changes that would obviate any necessity for passive resistance. Indians born in South Africa should be able to enter the Cape as before. Ex-indentured workers who had lived as free men in Natal for three years should be able to enter the province even if they had gone back to India. All monogamous marriages solemnized within the Union should be legalized. And one wife of an Indian should be allowed in, 'so long as she is the only one in South Africa, irrespective of the number of wives he might have in India.'[26]

A major strike by about 20,000 white workers in early July paralysed the mines around Johannesburg. They downed tools in protest against the managers demanding extra work for the same salary. The strike turned violent when the owners called in the police. The irate workers set fire to the offices of the newspaper *Star*, plundered shops, invaded railway stations and manhandled the railway staff. They then proceeded to the Rand Club, where they were confronted by armed police; and a dozen miners lost their lives. Gandhi and Kallenbach happened by chance to be nearby; and he wanted to nurse the wounded. Kallenbach dissuaded him; but on their way to Mountain View, Gandhi proposed that they should take only one meal a day in view of so much suffering. Kallenbach, however, persuaded him to stick to his sparse Phoenix diet.

Lelyveld speculates that the plan to call for strike action by Indian miners might have been worked out in the long discussions Gandhi had with Kallenbach at the time; and during the course of the meals they had at the home of Thambi Naidoo for three days in succession.[27] Was Thambi

---

25   *Ibid.*, p.456.

26   Cf. *Collected Works*, 12, pp.122-125.

27   Lelyveld, *op.cit.*, p. 109.

Naidoo inspired by the example of white workers to think of a strike by Indian miners, mostly Tamil?

Smuts, as Defence Minister, was deeply involved in the upheaval. When Gandhi repeated his request for a meeting, his secretary replied that the minister was so completely preoccupied with the current crisis, that he had no time to consider the terms of Gandhi's proposed compromise.[28]

---

28 Cf. Guha, *op.cit.*, p. 458

Chapter 67

Crisis at Phoenix

Still at Johannesburg, Gandhi received news that two residents of the Phoenix Ashram had a 'moral fall'. Any setbacks in the *satyāgraha* struggle would not have jolted him so much as this news did. The letter from Phoenix, no longer extant, was from his son Manilal. Kallenbach's diary alludes to its contents:

> 'Got letter from Manilal...for Mr. G[andhi] in which he makes a serious confession. Mr. G. came to my office and [I] broke the news to him and gave him the letter. He felt it most keenly. We both wired to Manilal. I decided to accompany Mr. Gandhi to Phoenix.'[1]

Manilal had confessed to sex with Jeki, daughter of Pranjivan Mehta, Gandhi's dear friend and benefactor. The boy was guilty of breaching his *brahmacarya* before wedlock. The fact that he did so with a married woman compounded his folly. Though herself young, Jeki was older than Manilal; and helped with teaching children at the Ashram. Deeply upset and angry, Gandhi immediately took a train to Phoenix. Kallenbach accompanied him.

Gandhi does not give any names in his *Autobiography*. He apportioned some blame to himself as a teacher, and decided to undertake a personal penance at the fall from morality of the two 'inmates', so that they could realize how much they had pained him. Neither are the two named, nor

---

1 Entry for 12 July 1913 in Hermann Kallenbach's Diary for 1912-13; cf. Guha, pp. 458, 622, n. 41.

is their fall spelled out. During the journey itself, he decided to subject himself to a fast of seven days and a vow 'to have only one meal a day for a period of four months and half'.[2] When attempts at dissuasion by Kallenbach failed, he too joined Gandhi in the observance of the penance. The anger gradually subsided. Pity took over. On arrival at Phoenix, he ascertained the details, and announced the form of his own penance. Everyone was pained to hear of it, as, according to Gandhi, they all felt that sinfulness was terrible. The bond between Gandhi and his male and female students became closer. Gandhi undertook an additional fast of fourteen days in connection with this matter a little later.

Manilal's biographer, Uma Dhupelia-Mesthrie describes the details of this incident.[3] Millie Polak also refers to it in her book as 'a case of deliberate seduction' on the part of Jeki, who was married and older.[4] She uses fictitious names to refer to the two offenders.

I agree with Guha when he says that blaming Jeki alone is not fair. Sexual attraction, despite Gandhi's lack of realization, always lurked as likely in the experiment in communal living. Manilal had been witness to the hot and passionate closeness of Harilal and Chanchal. He had seen the warmth of the physical bond between Millie and Polak. He was twenty, physically ripe for such a relationship. He and Jeki found themselves close to each other in the house, on the farm, at school, and when they went to the city. Jeki had stayed on at Phoenix to be guided and mentored by Gandhi, while her husband Manilal Doctor was back in Mauritius. She liked the attention Manilal paid her. The attraction was mutual, natural, unsurprising, and with hindsight, more than likely! Gandhi was partial to Jeki; and Kasturba's warnings had gone unheeded!

Gandhi made Manilal take a solemn vow, in expiation, to lead a strictly celibate life for a length of time to be determined by his father; and to marry only when his father permitted. Manilal had to wait till he was thirty-five, when in 1927, under pressure from Kasturba, Gandhi at last allowed him to marry. Jeki cut off her lovely locks; wore white traditional

---

2   *Autobiography,* p.252.

3   Dhupelia-Mesthrie, Uma, *Gandhi's Prisoner? The Life of Gandhi's Son Manilal,* Kwela Books, Cape Town, 2004, pp. 106-11.

4   Polak, Millie, *Mr. Gandhi: The Man,* pp.142-8.

widows' clothes; and gave up salt in her food as part of her atonement.[5]

I personally find the chastisement heartless and distasteful, with no trace of understanding, pity or pardon! Manilal had persevered at the press; and worked hard at the farm. He had gone and got arrested in *Satyāgraha*. But, then, he gave in to the temptation of sex with Jeki. Gandhi was trying hard to nurture his own clones in his sons. Harilal's intransigence irked him. Manilal's fall was even more painful. After a whole week's fast, Gandhi decided to take only one meal a day for a whole year! This would be his personal penance for the lapses of Manilal and Jeki; and for his own inadequate guardianship!

He does not lay it down as a teacher's duty to go on fasts to correct his students, even though in some cases it may be a 'drastic remedy'. It is possible only if and when there is a spirit of true love between the teacher and the taught. One may call into question the desirability of fasting to correct one's students, even if the teacher cannot absolve himself of responsibility for the improprieties of his students.

The first fast went smoothly, during the course of which Gandhi took only fruits. The second fast was not easy. Gandhi tells us that he suffered because he had not yet fully realized the 'wonderful efficacy of *Rāmanāma*'. He had also not yet become quite conversant with the technique required for fasting, the need for drinking lots of water even if one found it 'nauseating or distasteful'. He had taken daily Kuhne baths during his first fast, but failed to do so during the second; and did not also drink enough water. That gave him a parched throat and a sense of great weakness. Even his voice sank to a low note. He nevertheless dictated where writing was required; and derived his strength and comfort from readings of the scriptures and the *Rāmāyaṇa*. Even though the fast racked him, the experience stood him in good stead in the epic fasts that featured in his later political life.

Gandhi had already published the seventeenth chapter on *brahmacarya* in the on-going series on 'General Knowledge About health' in *Indian Opinion,* before he was buffeted by the news of the Jeki-Manilal affair. He went beyond the traditional Indian formulation of celibacy for the student and the old retiree (*saṁnyāsī*) to prescribe it for everyone. Conservation of the male's generative fluid invested a person with extraordinary powers.

---

5   Gandhi, Prabhudas, *My Childhood with Gandhiji*, pp.116-17; Polak, Millie, *op.cit.*, p.48; Dhupelia-Mesthrie, op.cit., p.110.

What would happen, though, if the world came to an end through the universal practice of *brahmacarya*? '...How is that any concern of ours? We are not God. He who has created the world will look after His affairs.'[6] Abstinence from sex for Gandhi meant freedom from any thought of sex, or any dream of sex, signifying the total deletion of one's libido. I find it utterly illogical to first reject a natural function of life designed by God; and then, through negation, force the hand of the Divine Artificer to invent other ways to keep creation going. Is this, too, a species of *satyāgraha?*

---

6   Cf. *Collected Works*, 12, pp. 45-52, 26 April 1913.

Chapter 68

Death of Rev. Joseph Doke: Declaration of Passive Resistance

Joseph Doke's death in the middle of August, 1913, saddened Gandhi. Touching tributes in *Indian Opinion* spoke of Doke's love for all humankind.'In a place where even men of religion are not free from the local prejudice against colour, Mr. Doke was among the few who know no distinction of race, colour or creed...Mr. Doke lives through his work of love and charity in the hearts of all who had the privilege of coming in contact with him.'[1] '...The Indian community of South Africa has lost one of its truest friends.'[2]

Gandhi went to Johannesburg to attend a memorial service on August 24, 1913; to pay his respects to 'a great and altruistic man', who always stayed untouched by colour prejudice. And on September 13, 1913, he announced in *Indian Opinion* that negotiations between him and the Government had failed; and *satyāgraha* would therefore be revived. 'The real object of our fight must be to kill the monster of racial prejudice in the heart of the Government and the local whites...There is only one way to kill the monster and that is to offer ourselves as a sacrifice. There is no life except through death. Death alone can raise us. It is the only effective means of persuasion...The only effective way of bringing about a change...is *satyāgraha*. It is a divine law that even the most hard-hearted man will melt if he sees his enemy suffering in innocence. The *satyāgrahi*

---

1 *Collected Works*, 12, pp. 167-173.

2 *Ibid.*, p. 171.

volunteers to suffer in this way…'³ Gandhi said he had 'no programme or plan of action'. The plan would 'unfold itself' as they proceeded.⁴

A letter from A.M. Cachalia, President of the Transvaal British Indian Association, dated September 12, 1913, drafted by Gandhi, to the Secretary for the Interior, informed the Minister that a decision to revive passive resistance had been reluctantly as well as regretfully taken, owing to the unwillingness of the Government to concede the demands submitted to them in repeated communications. The letter ended with a clear reiteration of five complaints:

'1. a racial bar disfigures the Immigration Act;

2. the rights existing prior to the passing of the Act are not restored and maintained;

3. the £3 tax upon ex-indentured men, women and children is not removed;

4. the status of women married in South Africa is not secured;

5. … a spirit of generosity and justice does not pervade the administration of the existing laws referred to herein.'⁵

Persistent appeals to Smuts and the other ministers for change of laws fell on deaf ears. Smuts made himself inaccessible. Members of Parliament did not listen. There was no other recourse left but *satyāgraha*!

---

3   *Collected Works*, 12, pp. 187-88.

4   *Ibid.*

5   *Collected Works*, 12, pp.183-86; cf. also pp. 192-95.

Chapter 69

The Scene

The Indian community in South Africa was much larger and more diverse in its make-up than what it was when Gandhi first came to the country twenty years ago. The number of Indians in Natal had tripled from over 40, 000 in early 1890s to about 135,000 in 1913. A large number of the indentured labourers worked in sugar plantations and the coal mines. Even before the import of indentured labour came to a halt in 1911, Indians had moved to the towns and villages of Natal on completion of their indentures, joined by their 'free' compatriots, to earn their living as farmers and traders. They were a visible part of Durban's population, dominating parts of the city with their numbers.[1]

The Transvaal had about 10,000 Indian residents. Some of them were successful, prosperous merchants; while the rest were petty traders and hawkers; clerks, hotel employees and other salaried workers. Indians in the Cape numbered around 6,500, some of whom were thriving traders and professionals. There were only 106 Indians in the Orange Free State according to the census of 1911.[2] Their microscopic numbers in the Free State made it the only province unaffected by the 'Indian problem.'[3]

There were so many Indians now who were born and brought up in South Africa. They had never been to India, with which they only had a distant emotional link. South Africa was the home they knew. It was the homeland

---

1 Guha, *op.cit.*, p.463.

2 *Ibid.*

3 Cf. Bhana, Surendra, and Joy Brain, *Setting Down Roots: Indian Migrants in South Africa, 1860-1911,* Witwatersrand University Press, Johannesburg, 1990.

where their future lay; where they would work and raise families, live and die. The new generation sought to educate itself to move into professional careers such as law, medicine and the public service. They even had a 'Colonial-Born Indian Association in Natal.'

Gandhi was conscious of the change in feelings and perception, though he thought he was, and remained an Indian. He knew he would return; but they would stay and suffer under the heel of oppressive governments. And that made him keen to arrive at a settlement with Smuts, which would safeguard the basic rights of Indians throughout the Union.

Gandhi proved himself a consummate master of tactics. The number of *satyāgrahīs* he could depend on was indeed small. The indentured labourers had not yet been told of the *satyāgraha*; nor had they been trained to take part in one. They could not read *Indian Opinion;* they did not know how to read! But Gandhi knew that his demand for the abolition of the crippling £3 tax touched a raw chord in thousands of hearts; and that they would certainly answer his call. They were well aware of his concern for their welfare. He had always helped them as a lawyer, often without any charge. He had worked in Dr. Booth's hospital dispensing free medicines to the poor. Everyone knew of the case of Balasundaram, the indentured worker rescued by Gandhi from the cruel clutches of his white master. They would undoubtedly follow his lead!

Gandhi was equally concerned with the plight of indentured Indian workers in the coal-mines of northern Natal, and on the sugar plantations. Any call for the repeal of the hated £3 levy would rouse them all, and draw them to the *satyāgraha*. He asked the Tamil women of the Transvaal to break the law by entering Natal. The Government would be reluctant to give any publicity to the *satyāgraha* by arresting women, because if they did, the news would spread rapidly in and outside South Africa. It would ruffle tempers and add a new thrust to the movement. If not arrested, the women would go to Newcastle, the coal-mining centre of Natal only thirty-six miles south of the border. Once there, they would advise and encourage the indentured Indian workers to go on strike. And 'if the labourers struck in response to the sisters' appeal, Government was bound to arrest them along with the labourers, who would thereby probably be fired with still greater enthusiasm.'[4]

---

4   *Satyagraha in South Africa, Collected Works,* Vol. 29, p. 223.

A group of sixteen people from Phoenix in Natal, including Kasturba, Chhaganlal's wife Kashi, Maganlal's wife Santok, Jeki (Jayakunvar, daughter of Pranjivan Mehta), would at the same time proceed to the Transvaal without any permits in order to court arrest and imprisonment. If asked by the border police to give their names and addresses, they would refuse to do so, to make sure of their arrest. For if they did, the police might link them to Gandhi, and deliberately ignore their *satyāgraha*. Four women and twelve men including Parsi Rustomjee and Ramdas, third son of Gandhi, left Durban for Volksrust on September 15, 1913, to cross the border into the Transvaal. Gandhi fortified the resolution of the departing mothers with comforting words expressive of their faith in God, who would take care of their children.

Gandhi, the theorist, ethicist and strategist, planned the whole movement with meticulous attention to detail. He wrote to Kallenbach to come from Johannesburg to the border to meet them at Volksrust, and 'simply watch as a spectator.' The resisters would not speak English; and would refuse to give their fingerprints. Only one of them would act as their interpreter. If arrested, they would ask for shelter at a police station. If they were not arrested, Kallenbach would take them to Johannesburg and accommodate them at Mountain View. But if they were, he would immediately inform Gandhi; meet the jail doctor and jailor and tell them of religious and health foods they might or might not take. The *satyāgrahīs* would not complain if their requests were ignored. Kasturba would be purely fruitarian.[5]

They were detained at Volksrust; and tried on September 23. All pleaded guilty to violating the Immigration Acts; refused to give any more testimony; and waived their rights to ask any questions. Sentenced to jail for three months, they were first housed in the Volksrust prison, and later shifted to Maritzburg.

A group of eleven women from Tolstoy Farm crossed the border from the Transvaal into Natal without the required immigration permits. One of them was pregnant; and six carried their babies in their arms as they had not been weaned.[6] Having cheerfully embraced the austere discipline of Tolstoy farm, they had no fear of any prison and its hardships. With one exception, they were all Tamils, including the wife of Thambi Naidoo.

---

5   *Collected Works*, 96, p.142.

6   Cf. Tendulkar, *op.cit.*, pp. 166-7.

They could therefore easily talk with the indentured workers in Tamil or Telugu. As Gandhi anticipated, they were not arrested, and ignored even when they hawked goods without permits at Vereeniging. They were detained for a few hours at Volksrust, but then allowed to go. They walked the 36 miles to Newcastle, and 'set about their work according to the plans previously settled.' The redoubtable *satyāgrahī* Thambi Naidoo, President of Johannesburg's Tamil Benefit Society, had himself accompanied them to the mining centre, where they were joined by Henry Polak and Hermann Kallenbach.[7] The women asked the magistrate in Newcastle to arrest them, as they had broken the law; but 'that canny officer refused'.[8] One of the women lost her baby on the way, but had pressed heroically on, saying: 'let the dead past bury its own dead, the living to work for the living.'[9] Their plea for action against the tax as well as the Searle judgement ignited a 'wildfire', as 'the pathetic story of the wrongs heaped up by the three-pound tax touched the labourers to the quick.'[10]

Fearful Indian traders of Newcastle were not yet quite forthcoming, but a Tamil Christian, D. M. Lazarus, who owned a small block of land and a house consisting of two or three rooms, threw it open to Gandhi and the women, who found food and shelter there. The house became a veritable *dharmaśālā*, a house of charity, where food was cooked for hundreds of *satyāgrahīs*. 'Men would come and go at all times and the kitchen fire knew no rest day and night.'[11]

Stirring articles by Gandhi in *Indian Opinion* called Indians in every town of every province to fight and court arrest. Removal of the £3 'blood tax' was 'the central point of the struggle.' Participation in the struggle for the removal of this tax was the primary duty of every Indian in South Africa 'to the poor men who are the victims of gold hunger on the part of the employers of indentured Indian labour.'[12] 'The obnoxious £3 tax must go

---

7   Desai, Ashwin, and Goolam Vahed, *Inside Indenture: A South African Story, 1860-1914,* Madiba Publishers, University of Kwazulu Natal, Durban, 2007, pp. 348, 361; Gandhi, Rajmohan, *op.cit.*, p. 162.

8   *Natal Witness*, 18 October 1913.

9   *Natal Mercury*, 16 November 1913.

10 Gandhi, *Satyagraha in South Africa, Collected Works,* Vol. 29, p.226.

11 Tendulkar, *op. cit.*, p. 168.

12 *Collected Works* 12, p.206.

at any cost. That is a debt we owe to the defenceless Indians, and to Mr. Gokhale.'[13] The strident demand for the abolition of this tax that hit the poorest the hardest, brought them to the fore; and made it a struggle of the masses against the ruling race for a measure of equity and justice! Gandhi was breaking new ground! He had put up a stiff but fruitless fight when the tax was first imposed. But this would doubtless be a fight to the finish!

Indians had to show their true mettle: '...we are capable of dying for our honour and an honourable existence in South Africa, not by fighting them bodily, but by a process of voluntary suffering which at once purifies and dignifies.'[14]

Gandhi was anxious and worried, as many in Natal resented his lead; and he did not know how many in the two provinces would come forward to answer his call. He had found it hard to persuade members of the merchant class to volunteer as passive resisters in the last *satyāgraha*. Under immense stress on September 25, he became angry with the children at breakfast before leaving Phoenix for the Transvaal, which he regretted soon afterwards in an apologetic letter to Maganlal: '...I felt ashamed within myself even as I was on the way – I reproached myself...Plunged as I have been in the affairs of South Africa, I think I can be entirely free only in India. But please warn me whenever I take upon myself too heavy a burden...But I would ride all the horses and that is why God ordained my fall. Surely this is not the first occasion when such a thing has happened to me. This time, however, the lesson has been brought home to me. I will now change myself a little.'[15]

He was trying to 'ride all the horses' at one and the same time. He wanted to be an ideal father, teacher, and fighter against racial tyranny; a physician and health consultant; a dietician and preacher of a new sex code. Everything concerned him, and claimed his attention, leading to an occasional loss of focus, and temper. He suddenly recognized the urgent need for self-correction!

The journey to the Transvaal was marked by some unpleasantness when the conductor at Ladysmith station asked Gandhi and his companions

---

13   *Ibid.*, p. 188.

14   *Ibid.*, p. 195.

15   *Ibid.*, pp. 209-10.

to vacate the compartment in which they had been seated by a railway official at Durban. It was one of the cleaner and more comfortable third class compartments, which, they were told, were meant for Europeans only. When Gandhi pointed out that the compartment was not so labelled, and the conductor at Durban had placed them there, the man said that he was now in charge; and they had to obey him. The Station Master told Gandhi that the conductors could shift passengers from one compartment to another as many times as they chose. Gandhi and his companions stayed put in the hope that they would be arrested; but a man named Windon recognized him and told the conductor, who then held his peace. He said he was only doing his duty. But when Gandhi replied that, if so, he should have him arrested for disobeying instructions, the conductor did not oblige.[16]

The officer on duty at Volksrust detained Gandhi's four companions, but did not arrest him. He went on to Johannesburg, where he addressed two meetings on the 28th of September; one of men, and the other of women, who expressed their eagerness to court arrest and go to jail.[17]

On September 29, passive resisters including Gandhi's son Manilal went out hawking without any licences, but were not arrested. They went out hawking again on the 30th; but were then arrested and sentenced to a fine of £1, or imprisonment for seven days with hard labour. All opted for jail.[18] Two of Gandhi's sons were in jail; and he wrote to the eldest, Harilal, on October 17, 1913, to come back to South Africa with his wife to take part in the movement: 'Both of you may come over here and get arrested…It is likely that I shall be in gaol when you arrive.'[19]

The *Transvaal Leader* wrote on September 30, 1913, that the Indian passive resistance movement was collapsing for want of money, martyrs and resisters. Merchants were unsupportive; and general support was very scanty. The exhortations of Gandhi and Cachalia were, according to the paper, met with growls of protest and defiance; and declarations of 'contentment with the present order of things.' The paper said that Gandhi would not be able to find more than 150 passive resisters ready to go to

---

16 *Ibid.*, pp. 211-3.
17 *Ibid.*, pp. 215-17.
18 Tendulkar, *op.cit.*, p. 166.
19 *Collected Works*, 12, p. 242.

jail. The Indian traders were 'making no secret of their antagonism to the passive resistance campaign.'[20]

Gandhi wrote to the newspaper that their story was bereft of truth: '... the proof of the pudding is in the eating, and time will show whether the movement collapses either for want of men or of money.'[21] The paper also printed three letters, from L.W. Ritch who said that 'right' was on the Indian side; from Kallenbach who refuted the charge that the resisters were mercenaries; and the third from about 40 merchants 'throughout the principal towns of the Transvaal', who said: 'We are in full sympathy with the movement, and...the merchants along with others are contributing both men and money to the movement.'[22]

General Smuts, Minister of the Interior once more, spoke of Gandhi 'suffering from one of his periodic attacks of mental derangement... attracted by the role of the prophet and martyr.' He expected the movement to collapse for want of support; and could not support polygamy. He wanted to repeal the £3 tax, but the 'narrow-minded' Natalians would not let him do so. They used the tax to force the workers to re-indenture, or to leave for India.[23] The choice before the ex-indentured was painfully stark, as the tax 'made the option of being a 'free' Indian in Natal incredibly difficult.'[24] Of the 10,800 Indian males required to pay the levy, less than a third had somehow managed to do so in 1913.[25]

Gandhi does not mention Sheikh Mehtab, his old class-mate and friend, by name in his *Autobiography;* and omits him altogether from his narrative after their quarrel at Gandhi's house years ago! Mehtab, however, supported his *satyāgrahas*; wrote and sang patriotic songs in Gujarati, Urdu and English to generate enthusiasm; and regularly visited Parsi Rustomji's house to express his support regardless of the opposition of many Natalian Muslim merchants to the current movement. His wife Bai Fatima was also inspired by the fighting spirit of the Transvaal women; and, on October

---

20 *Transvaal Leader*, 30 September, 1913.

21 *Ibid.*, 1 October, 1913; cf. *Collected Works*, 12, pp. 219-21.

22 Cf. Guha, *op.cit.*, p. 623, n.13.

23 Cf. Guha, *op.cit.*, pp. 470.623, n. 16.

24 Desai, Ashwin, and Goolam Vahed, *op.cit.*, p. 348.

25 *Ibid.*

12, sought to cross the border into Volksrust along with her seven-year old son and mother Hanifabai. When she refused to give her fingerprints, on October 13, she and her mother were sentenced to jail for three months. They were the first Muslim women to be jailed in the new *satyāgraha*.[26]

On October 12, Gandhi returned from the Transvaal to Durban, where he was criticized for making use of 'paid European workers' at a public meeting in the city's Union Theatre. He told the disgruntled questioner that Polak had been sent to London at the request of Gokhale. He then proceeded to Newcastle, where he was lustily cheered by the crowd as 'the brave son of India'. Thambi Naidoo's speech in Tamil made a deep impression; and the mine-workers voiced their zealous support for Gandhi and the *satyāgraha* in order to secure the abolition of the £3 tax.

Gandhi came back to Durban, where some sharp criticism of the founder's methods followed at a meeting of the Natal Indian Congress, on October 19, 1913. P. S. Aiyar had been fulminating in his *African Chronicle* against the ineffectiveness of passive resistance, which, he said, had outlived its utility. At the meeting, M. C. Anglia complained that Gandhi's methods had failed to raise Indians in the estimation of the whites; and that a professional and political agitator like him would only set the Government and the whites against them. But some people stood up to support Gandhi; passions ran high; the meeting was closed; and Gandhi was carried shoulder-high through the streets in a procession. As Gandhi explained, the critic was taken seriously by very few: 'It was really an attempt to bring about a schism in the Indian community and was not on the question of passive resistance by any means. I don't think there was any difference of opinion as to passive resistance.'[27]

Gandhi's followers held a meeting at Mr. Rustomji's premises, and a new body was formed and named the Natal Indian Association, with Mr. Dawad Mohamed as President, and Mr. Omar Haji Amod Jhaveri as Secretary. They were two of the most respected Muslims in the Indian community. A collection was taken; and a fund established to defray the expenses of the campaign.[28]

---

26 *Indian Opinion*, 15 October 1913; *Satyagraha in South Africa, Collected Works*, Vol. 29, p. 237; Gandhi, Rajmohan, op.cit., pp.162-3.

27 *Collected Works*, 12, pp.245-7.

28 *Ibid.*

In Newcastle, the women went from mine to mine to speak to the workers and meet their families. They spoke to their wives of the tyranny of the tax, and of the attack on the validity of their marriages. A number of mass meetings were held. The meeting at Farleigh Colliery was addressed by Mrs. Thambi Naidoo, Mrs. P.K. Naidoo and Mrs. T. Pillay, who explained the reasons and the need for the strike; and appealed to the workers to strike until the tax was abolished. Years later, Gandhi wrote that the 'mere presence of these women was like a lighted match-stick to dry fuel. Women who had never before slept except on soft beds and had seldom so much as opened their mouths, now delivered public speeches among the indentured labourers. The latter were roused and,...by the time I reached there, Indians in two coal mines had already stopped work.'[29]

Gandhi had warned the Minister of the Interior that the movement, once begun, would develop and follow its own inner logic, beyond control and prescription of any limits by the leaders. The 'marvellous awakening' pleased him, even as it 'perplexed' him. Lelyveld is delighted to interpret it as 'self-delusion, opportunism, or cunning, all of which were part of the leader's makeup in shifting proportions.'[30] But Gandhi had honestly forewarned the authorities. He had only reluctantly decided, as a last resort, on the miners' strike. He was now the leader of a mass movement. He arrived in Newcastle in Indian dress to identify himself with the oppressed Indian indentured workers.

Millie Polak describes how the Transvaal women also recruited the Indian railway employees. They 'travelled down the line, taking in the mines on their way, holding meetings and calling upon the men to refuse to work and to die as slaves, and at the call of these women, thousands... went on strike.'[31] The lot of the coal-miners was even otherwise hard and unenviable, as diseases of one kind and another, including chronic bronchitis and tuberculosis, played havoc with their health and happiness. As the poet Derek Walcott put it, 'hell was built on those hills.'[32]

On October 13, 1913, Gandhi addressed a mass meeting at St. Oswald's

---

29 *Indian Opinion, Golden Number*, December 1914; CW, 12, p.512; also see p. 246.

30 Lelyveld, *op. cit.*, p. 112.

31 *Indian Opinion*, 22 October 1913; *Golden Number*, p. 26.

32 Cf. Desai and Wahed, *op. cit.*, p.362.

School. Thambi Naidoo spoke in Tamil; Bhawani Dayal spoke in Hindi. Mrs. Thambi Naidoo and Mrs. P.K. Naidoo told the audience that 'they had left their homes and children for the sake of their fellow countrymen; and would not return till the struggle was finally over.' There was thunderous applause![33] Gandhi and the Passive Resistance Committee had rice, *daal* and other items of food sent to Northern Natal to feed the brave strikers.

On October 15, seventy-eight Indian workers at the Fairleigh Colliery went on strike in response to the exhortations of the female *satyāgrahīs*. They were followed by workers at Ballengeich, as the number of strikers steadily swelled to 2,000 within a week. And a week later, another 3,000 went on strike. The authorities could not leave the Transvaal women free any more. They were arrested on October 21; charged as 'vagabonds'; sentenced to imprisonment for three months with hard labour; and sent to jail at Pietermaritzburg. There, they joined the batch of female prisoners from Phoenix; and the picture of Kasturba and other respectable, innocent women in jail stirred Indian hearts both in South Africa and India with deep indignation. Sir Pherozeshah Mehta, who had been hitherto indifferent to the South African *satyāgraha*, spoke at a public meeting in the Bombay Town Hall in no uncertain terms, when he said that 'his blood boiled at the thought of these women lying in jails herded by ordinary criminals, and India would not sleep over the matter any longer.'[34]

Gandhi addressed large crowds of striking workers and their supporters in Durban, Newcastle, Hattingspruit and other towns in Natal. On October 20, the Justice Minister asked the Attorney-General of Natal if it was legally possible to put a stop to Gandhi's action. The Attorney-General in turn asked the magistrates to inform him whether Gandhi had 'contravened any law during the last few days.' The Attorney-General told the Minister on October 22 that he could not glean any information from the magistrates which would make it possible to take immediate action against Gandhi. He cited newspaper reports of the meeting of the Natal Indian Congress to point out that Gandhi was not fully supported; but dreaded the 'disastrous effect of any action taken against him.[35]

Gandhi addressed a meeting at Newcastle on October 22; and another

---

33 Ibid., p.363.

34 Cf. Gandhi, *Satyagraha in South Africa, Collected Works*, Vol. 29, p. 226

35 Cf. Desai and Vahed, *op.cit.*, p. 363.

at Dannhauser the same day. Around 4,000 miners were on strike by the end of October.[36] The Minister of Justice advised against hasty action; and asked for a proper investigation of the 'cause and the possible attitude the Indians wish to take.'[37] The Attorney-General was constantly fishing for information that would enable them to prosecute Gandhi. They could not yet lay their hands on him.

Gandhi told the mine-owners on October 25 that the workers were not striking against the mining conditions. They had no quarrel with the mine-owners; nor had he himself. 'The object of the strike was not to hurt' the mine owners, 'but rather to invite suffering on ourselves.'[38] The employers had two scores of worry. The Indian workers performed jobs that demanded greater skill, requiring 'more intelligence than is usually possessed by the average native.' The second nagging worry was whether Gandhi would also recruit the African workers to go on strike. Gandhi assured them that he had no intention to ask the Africans to stop work, as the strike was against the £3 tax.[39] He told them that the miners in Dannhauser, Newcastle and Dundee would 'court arrest and imprisonment in Natal, or, failing that, cross the border to the Transvaal and be arrested there.' The miners would go back to work as soon as the tax was abolished. But passive resistance against other grievances would continue. When the mine-owners said that they would write to the Government to repeal the tax if the strikers returned to work, Gandhi replied: 'This, the *satyāgrahīs* could not agree to.'[40]

John Dube, the respected leader of the Africans, referred to the Whites' apprehension of the blacks joining the strike in his paper *Ilanga*. There were a number of commentaries, the first of which said : 'We wish you the best Gandhi;' 'Go for it Gandhi.'[41]

In a statement to Reuters, Gandhi stressed that they were not fighting for

---

36 Bhana and Vahed, *Political Reformer*, p. 115.
37 Cf. Desai and Vahed, *op.cit.*, p. 364.
38 *Collected Works*, 12, pp.512-3.
39 'We do not believe in such methods', he told *The Natal Mercury*, in an interview dated October 25, 1913. Cf. *Collected Works*, 12 p.253.
40 *Indian Opinion, Golden Number*, December 1914; *Collected Works*, 12, p.512.
41 Cf. Lelyveld, *op.cit.,* p.114.

any political rights. They knew and accepted that implacable pre-existing prejudice made it unavoidable to put strict limits on immigration from India. He repeated in his speeches and statements that the demands of the striking workers were most modest, and unquestionably reasonable. They wanted the Government to do no more than honour the pledge to abolish the £3 tax; and amend the marriage laws to validate Indian marriages.

On Octobeer 26, Smuts denied in a speech that they had promised any tax repeal to Gokhale. They had only told him that they would reconsider the matter. But he had done this before. Going back on their word was not unknown to him and his colleagues in Government. He said the £3 tax was clearly specified in the contract signed by labourers in India before they came out to Natal. In a telegram to the mine-owners he told them that repealing the tax under Gandhi's pressure would be a 'public disaster'. The Minister of Justice also told the Ladysmith magistrate that the Government had consulted the Natal members of Parliament after the departure of Gokhale; and they did not agree to the repeal of the tax except for women and children. A repeal of the tax while the strike was on would have unwelcome, unforeseen consequences. The Justice Ministry also said that the abolition of the tax was not one of Gandhi's original demands; but was added 'to influence Natal Indians.'[42] The Government translated its message to the miners into Tamil, and distributed it at the coal-mines.

The Government and its ministers were certainly prevaricating; and disingenuous. Gokhale had been given a clear indication that the tax would be repealed. He said so to the Governor-General, whose communication to London corroborated it. Gokhale also told a highly placed official of the Indian Government that 'ministers have promised him, and quite publicly, that the Natal £3 licence tax will be revoked.'[43] Gandhi had the truth and the workers alike on his side! Abolition of the abominable tax was one of the principal purposes of the *satyāgraha*.

Striking workers told Sergeant W. Mann of the South African Mounted Rifles that promises made to Gokhale to repeal the tax were not honoured; and that the situation had also become very difficult for women. 'Free' Indians and their descendants should not have to pay any tax of the kind. Railway workers in Newcastle and Dannhauser also went on strike.

---

42   Cf. Desai and Vahed, *op. cit.*, pp. 364-5.
43   Cf. Guha, *op.cit.*, pp. 472, 624, n.30.

Gandhi's explosive energy was in overdrive. He was everywhere in the last few days, spending long hours on the trains to go to places, meet people, attend and address meetings. He and C.R. Naidoo addressed a meeting of three thousand men, women and children at Hattingspruit on October 28. The audience 'promised to carry out the strike to the bitter end,' until the tax was abolished. A little later, on the same day, they spoke to an audience of some eight thousand men and women, who had gathered at a Hindu Temple ground in Dundee to listen to them. They were joined there by Thambi Naidoo; and jail was described in their speeches as a better option than the tax and indenture. A considerable number of people contributed to a collection for the families of the *satyāgrahīs*. After Thambi Naidoo's speech at Ballengeich, about 300 people left for Newcastle. The Attorney-General had not yet been able to find any incriminating evidence to arrest Gandhi![44]

Gandhi's adversary P.S. Aiyar had been deprecatingly dismissive of passive resistance. Journalistic duty now forced him to devote columns in *African Chronicle* to the progress of the movement; to praise the courage of Kasturba and the other women; to report on the arrests and the strikes. Many of his own workers deserted their posts to join the strike, forcing him to drastically reduce the size of his journal.[45]

The striking *satyāgrahīs* left the collieries and plantations for Dundee and Newcastle, where they could not be forced back to work. Gandhi was there to lead them. He was in command, clear-headed and resolute. To keep them out of the reach of mine-owners and their agents, Gandhi and his associates decided to take them to Charlestown, which was thirty-five miles away. The rules of the march were spelled out to them. They would get a daily ration of only a pound and a half of bread and an ounce of sugar for each individual. They would take with them only their essential clothes; and would not touch anyone's property on the way. They would welcome arrest; and patiently put up with abuse, and even flogging. Gandhi also announced the names of those who would lead the march in the event of his arrest.[46]

They walked. Gandhi led the first batch, as shouts of *Vande Mātaram* ('Salutation to Mother [land]'), *Rāmchandra kī jai* ('Victory to

---

44 Desai and Vahed, *op.cit.*, p. 365.

45 Cf. Guha, *op.cit.*, p.473.

46 Cf. Tendulkar, *op.cit.*, pp.169-70.

Rāmachandra', God Viṣṇu Incarnate) and *Dwarkānāth kī jai* ('Victory to Kṛṣṇa, Lord of Dvarikā') rent the air. They cooked their own rice and *daal* on the way, spent the first night in the open, and made it to Charlestown the next day. Thambi Naidoo led a group of three hundred workers and their families; and Albert Christopher led another batch of around 250.

The Government could have arrested the striking workers; but were not quite enthusiastic to do so. Accommodating and feeding them in jail would be by no means easy. But Gandhi wanted to force their hand by illegally crossing into the Transvaal and courting arrest, with thousands in tow. A seasoned walker, he decided to march with them right across the border all the way to Tolstoy farm in Johannesburg, despite the daunting distance.

In Johannesburg, a public meeting held on October 29 was attended by a large number of Indians and European sympathizers such as W. Hosken, L.W. Ritch and Sonja Schlesin. It was the auspicious day of Dashehra, celebrating the victory of good over evil. But the rejoicing associated with the festival had been replaced by 'sadness and mourning', said S.K. Patel, presiding over the meeting. Ritch was, however, positive in his appreciation of the *satyāgrahīs* using lofty 'weapons of the soul, and not the weapons of the mob'. The audience stood up as a mark of respect for the women in the thick of battle. A large collection was taken in cash and kind; and personal items donated on the spot were auctioned for extraordinary prices. A quiet procession, led by two men with black flags, marched through the main streets of the city.[47]

The authorities infiltrated the resistance in search of evidence to arrest Gandhi. Even though they found a few ready to provide bits and pieces of information, they could not persuade the latter to make any 'sworn declarations'.[48]

On November 3, 1913, Charlestown presented a bustling spectacle, likened to an Indian bazaar by a press reporter.[49] Gandhi took upon himself the additional responsibility of serving food. He could tell them that food was not plentiful; and they had to be content with tiny portions to enable everyone to eat. By distributing food with his own hands, he was establishing a new standard; setting a new example; making no distinctions

---

47 *Indian Opinion*, 5 November 1913; cf. Guha, *op.cit.*, p. 475.

48 Cf. Desai and Vahed, *op.cit.*, p. 367.

49 *Natal Advertiser*, 10 November 1913.

between class, caste and religion; assuming a new responsibility; and expressing his solicitude for his followers in his caring action. As he described the scene:

'Many arrived on foot, while women mostly came by train. These were put up wherever there was space in the houses of Indian merchants of Charlestown....Our food was cooked in the mosque premises. The fire had to remain lit all the twenty-four hours. The cooks came from among the strikers. During the final days, four to five thousand persons were being fed....'[50]

Two grimly resolute women did not stop, and came to Charlestown even when one's baby died of exposure on the way; and the other's slipped from the mother's arms into a running stream, which she was crossing. They still refused to grieve; and one of them said: 'We must not pine for the dead who will not come back to us for all our pining. It is the living for whom we must work.'[51]

Gandhi also made sure of sanitation and hygiene; and the marchers joined him in the tasks of sweeping and scavenging. As he wrote later: 'Much can be done if the servant actually serves and does not dictate to the people... Where the leader himself becomes a servant, there are no rival claimants for leadership.'[52] This awareness stood him in good stead in India.

It was not easy to keep such a large crowd of hard-working people idle in Charlestown; and the danger of some epidemic breaking out dictated the urgency of movement. It was therefore decided to march to the Transvaal, and, if not arrested on the way, go on to Tolstoy Farm. The Government was duly informed that the strikers did not want to stay or claim any rights there, but if not arrested, would proceed to Tolstoy farm. They would go back, if the Government promised to abolish the £3 tax. But the Government, misled by their informants, disregarded the notice in the belief that the strikers would soon tire and turn back. In reply to Gandhi's last-minute plea to Smuts, the latter's secretary had told him: 'General

---

50 *Indian Opinion, Golden Number*, December 1914; *Collected Works*, 12, p.516.

51 Tendulkar, *op.cit.*, p. 170.

52 *Satyagraha in South Africa, Collected Works*, Vol. 29, p. 235; Cf. Gandhi, Rajmohan, *op,cit.*, p.164.

Smuts will have nothing to do with you. You may do just as you please.'[53]

Collections flowed in to help meet the daily expenses. The merchants loosened their purse-strings to donate; and Gokhale promised to send £2000 a month for six months, collected from the people of India. A large European bakery agreed to supply bread at each halting place; and even the railway officials helped with the delivery of bread on time.

On November 6, 1913, a party of about 3,000 left Charlestown at daybreak. A mile-long procession made it to the border, with Gandhi and Kallenbach in the rear. About 2,000 men, 127 women and fifty-seven children crossed the border around 11.45 a.m.

'The crossing of the Natal border into Transvaal was an epic moment in South African history. Mounted police massed to block the way. Without any apparent coordination, miners, women with children in their arms, and older men weakened by a meagre diet, were seized by a collective effort. They rushed past the startled police and cheered themselves on. The mounted police took a while to get ahead of the march and watched as the 'criminals' casually sat down on the Standerton Road, and shared their limited rations.'[54]

Gandhi talked to the police, who did not arrest them. Despite the decision to leave the women behind at Charlestown before embarking on this long march, it had proved difficult to contain their enthusiasm; and some of them had, therefore, joined this procession. Gandhi sent Kallenbach back to look after the remaining women and children at Charlestown.

Gandhi was arrested the next day near Palmford, and 'charged with having brought unauthorized persons into the Transvaal.' The procession carried on, as there was no other arrest. Produced before the magistrate at Volksrust, Gandhi asked for time, as he had to make necessary arrangements for the people who had gone ahead, and those who had been left behind. The objection of the Government pleader was overruled by the magistrate who said that bail could be declined only in a case of murder. Gandhi was asked to furnish a bail of £50; which was immediately paid by a Volksrust merchant.[55]

---

53   Cf. Tendulkar, *op.cit.*, p. 171.

54   Desai and Vahed, *op. cit.*, p. 368; cf. Henning, C.G., *The Indentured Indian in Natal, 1860-1917*, Promilla & Co., Delhi, 1993, p. 180.

55   *Collected Works*, 12, pp. 516-17.

Kallenbach, who had come to Volksrust to attend Gandhi's trial, immediately took him in a car to rejoin the marchers. A press reporter climbed in with them; and saw stragglers on the way lining up to salute Gandhi, 'calling him 'Bapoo', or father.'[56] Their arrival and reunion with the procession about thirty miles from Volksrust put a new heart into their followers, who enthusiastically pressed forward, with Gandhi in the lead.

The local Europeans in Volksrust, just outside the Transvaal border, met to discuss the march; and some of them threatened to shoot the Indians if they crossed. Kallenbach attended the meeting, heedless of the risk to himself, and put the Indian case to them. The procession, when it arrived, passed in peace through the town.

Smuts had reckoned that leaving Gandhi free would make the latter's task of managing and feeding his hordes impossible to handle; and the dispirited, hungry strikers would want to be sent back home to Natal. That would be the last gasp of their resistance. But that did not happen!

The march continued. They spent the night of 7th November by the riverbank at Krorndraai. On November 8, though, they were stopped at Standerton, and Gandhi was arrested with five 'ringleaders.' The whole crowd surged around the court grounds, saying that they could not proceed further without their leader. Released on bail of £50 once more, Gandhi returned to the march with his column.

His old adversary Montford Chamney arrived from Johannesburg with a posse of police to arrest him. Smuts had decided to push the illegal entrants back into Natal. Police halted the column at Teakworth near Greylingstaad on November 9; a Cape cart with Chamney and a police officer drove up; and the police officer told Gandhi that he was under arrest. He had already covered more than half the way to Tolstoy farm. More than two thousand Indians under Gandhi's command in the desolate veldt, sworn to non-violence, held their peace while the solitary police officer took him away. Gandhi was proud of the fact that the authorities were so trustful of his non-violence.[57]

Kallenbach met him on the train that would carry him away. The police officer permitted Kallenbach to enter Gandhi's coach and talk to him for

---

56 *Transvaal Leader*, 8 November 1913; cf. Guha, p.476.
57 Cf. Gandhi, Rajmohan, *op. cit.*, pp.66-7.

about fifteen minutes. Gandhi asked him to avoid arrest, as his freedom was essential to provide advice and help to the strikers. They did not foresee that their next meeting would be in jail.[58]

In Dundee, Gandhi was charged with prompting the strike and inciting the workers. Bail was rejected, and he was bundled off to prison. Guha reproduces a 'remarkable letter' that Gandhi wrote to the magistrate from prison, in which he drew the latter's attention to a significant number of men, women and children, who had to be left behind owing to their infirmity, fatigue or illness; and also those who had become separated from the main body of marchers. He gave details of people who needed immediate help and attention. He also wrote that about 150 resisters had probably entered the Transvaal without a leader. They had to be looked after, fed and provided for. If people were thrown back across the border, they would try to re-enter. They should be charged under law, or otherwise taken care of.[59] This letter expresses his keen concern for the participants in the struggle; and disproves Smuts' allegation that Gandhi was looking forward to free himself from their responsibility.

On November 11, Gandhi was tried at Dundee for inducing indentured labour to leave Natal for the Transvaal. His lawyer told the court that he would not plead in mitigation in accordance with his client's instructions. Gandhi pleaded guilty with the statement that he was honour-bound to organize the strike in view of the promise made by Smuts to Gokhale. He was sentenced to a fine of £60, or imprisonment for nine months, with hard labour. He elected to go to jail, with a parting message to the strikers: 'No cessation of the strike without repeal of the £3 tax. The Government, having imprisoned me, can gracefully make a declaration regarding the repeal.'[60]

He was tried again at Volksrust three days later, for bringing prohibited immigrants into the Transvaal. He pleaded guilty, but pointed out that none of the men under his command left the column; and produced a witness to prove that the whole exercise was a protest against the £3 tax; and that they would have all gone back to work if the tax was revoked. People had willingly subjected themselves to unspeakable suffering on his advice, in

---

58 Lev, Shimon, *op. cit.*, p.94.
59 Guha, *op. cit.*, pp. 477-8.
60 *Collected Works*, 12, pp. 263-4; Tendulkar, *op.cit.*, p.175.

order to melt the hearts of the authorities and the white inhabitants of the land. They were all, otherwise, like him, law-abiding members of society. Three more months in jail was the verdict.

Polak took charge of the march after Gandhi's arrest. They spent the night at Greylingstaad, where they were joined by Cachalia, and told that the Government had made arrangements to arrest the entire body of marchers. They found their way to Balfour on November 10, where three special trains were waiting to deport them to Natal. The marchers asked for Gandhi Bhai, on whose advice alone they would board the trains. They were, however, told by Polak and Cachalia that resistance to arrest was not in order in a peaceful *satyāgraha*; and were persuaded to surrender and entrain peacefully, without any untoward incident. 2,000 soldiers of *satyāgraha*, deprived of their homes, jobs and beloved leader, were flung into improvised prisons.

The trainloads of marchers taken back to Natal were summarily tried and jailed for leaving their work and crossing illegally into the Transvaal. They suddenly realized that they could not go back to work even if they wanted to. But the closure of the mines would cripple all industries. The Government did something utterly horrible. They decreed that the mines would be considered 'branches' of the Newcastle and Dundee prisons. The white foremen were appointed 'prison warders'; and strikers were forced underground into the mines at the point of whips and guns. They were beaten with sticks, fists, sjamboks or whips made of rhino or hippo hides. They would not receive any pay for six months for the hard labour to which they were sentenced. Indentured labour was deliberately degraded into slave labour. The authority of the Government degenerated into beastly brutality in defence of a law that was totally unjust; and even more injustice in defence of injustice; even more cruelty in defence of entrenched cruelty! Magistrates acted as prosecutors, judge and jury; and told the strikers that they had authorized the floggings. Desai and Goolam Vahed provide blood-curdling accounts of the ruthless repression to which they were subjected. Some were deported to India.[61] It was a heart-wrenching spectacle of self-suffering in full view of the world.

Polak and Kallenbach were arrested on November 10. Both of them were happy and unruffled. Polak had encouraged the Indians to confront the

---
61 Cf. *Inside Indenture*, pp. 370 ff.

Government and court arrest; and found it honourable as an Englishman to do so himself for their just cause.[62] Kallenbach philosophized that self-suffering was an essential part of passive resistance to secure redress from tyranny; and was in accord with the precepts of almost all religions including Judaism.[63] Kallenbach described his arrest 'in greatly romanticised detail' in a letter, in which he said that he 'felt very happy indeed...' to go to jail.[64]

Kallenbach and Polak, who had been arrested at different places, met each other the following morning, when they were produced before a judge. In his statement to the judge, Kallenbach said that he was an intimate friend of Gandhi. When the petitions of 'voiceless and voteless' Indians for the redress of their grievances fell on deaf, unreceptive ears, Gandhi showed them the only effective means of securing justice through passive resistance. He fully subscribed to the method as a long-time follower of Tolstoy.

Polak drew attention to his close and long association with the South African Indians. He had been the editor of *Indian Opinion*, their weekly newspaper. And he was an ardent supporter of their passive resistance movement as an Englishman, as a Jew, and as a lawyer. As an Englishman, he found it impossible to be a silent spectator of the repeated breach of faith by the South African Government towards fellow British subjects of Indian nationality. As a Jew, it was 'impossible' for him to associate himself, 'even passively, with the persecution of any race or nationality.' And, 'as a member of the legal profession,' he proved his loyalty to the Crown by giving to the Indians 'the only advice..possible.. as an honourable man who places justice before loyalty and moral law before human law.'

Polak accused the Government of dishonouring a promise they had made to Gokhale to repeal the £3 tax, doubtless 'a relic of barbarism'. Gokhale was his personal friend, revered by millions in India. The tax either forced Indians back into the dark abyss of servitude, or else drove them out of

---

62 Cf. Polak's letter to Lord Ampthill cited by Guha, *op.cit.*, pp.480, 624, n.51.

63 He wrote a long letter to his sister to explain and justify his going to jail. Cf. Sarid, Isa, and Christian Bartolf, *Hermann Kallenbach: Mahatma Gandhi's Friend in South Africa*, Gandhi Informations Zentrum, Berlin, 1997, pp.34-61.

64 Lev, Shimon, pp.94-96,104; Kallenbach to Janet, 10 November 1913. Kallenbach Archive.

South Africa, which had been transformed into a land of promise and plenty by their bone-grinding labour. He would not be a passive participant in this deliberate deed of heartless betrayal!

Gandhi, Polak and Kallenbach were put on trial on successive days. Gandhi facilitated the prosecution by providing the necessary evidence against Kallenbach, who said that 'as a European', he deemed it 'a privilege to have been associated with the movement.'[65] He was sentenced to three months' imprisonment without hard labour.

As in the case of Kallenbach, Gandhi also appeared as a witness against Polak, who was duly convicted, and sentenced to three months' jail without hard labour. They passed a few days together in the Volksrust jail, before the Government decided to separate them. On November 18, Gandhi was transferred to Bloemfontein, where no one was allowed to see him. He was the only Indian there.[66] Kallenbach was sent to Krugersdorf; and Polak to Boksburg.[67]

L. W. Ritch, another staunch Jewish supporter of Gandhi and the *satyāgraha*, ran Gandhi's law practice in his absence, and tirelessly defended the leader and the movement in his communications to the press. He castigated Smuts for citing the pronouncement of triple *talaq* by the Muslims in defence of new marriage laws imposed on Indians; and pointed out that it was viewed, when it happened, as a rare scandal. The common and easy incidence of divorce among the South African Europeans was far more alarming.[68] He accused the Government of pursuing repressive policies of neglect and segregation against Indians, comparable to the atrocities heaped on the Jews in Russia.[69]

Yet another Jew, steadfast in her devotion to Gandhi and the Indian cause was Sonja Schlesin, Gandhi's secretary, who had come down to Natal to help the strikers. She was visible everywhere, performing the tasks assigned to her; writing to Gokhale; assisting the strikers; visiting jails;

---

65 *Indian Opinion*, 26 November 1913.
66 Tendulkar, *op.cit.*, p.176.
67 Lev, Shimon, *op.cit.*, p. 99.
68 Letter from Ritch in *Rand Daily Mail*, 21 October 1913; Guha, op.cit., p.482.
69 Letter from Ritch in *Transvaal Leader*, 31 December 1913; Guha, *op. cit.* p. 482.

getting medical assistance for the sick and the victims of atrocities; and keeping the press and the Government informed of the vile acts of cruelty and violence.

There was another reason for the Draconian repression. Any thought of joining the strike by the Africans had to be put out of their minds by the pitiless punishment meted out to the Indians. The black miners at Ballengeich had demanded a wage rise from £3 to £4, taking advantage of the situation.[70] The use of excessive force was intentional, and calculated to instil fear.

The authorities hoped to break the back of the strike in northern Natal by imprisoning Gandhi and his lieutenants, and forcing the workers underground. But the strategy went horribly wrong. The strike generated its own inner momentum, resulting in a spontaneous surge. The policy of blood and iron, meant to crush the *satyāgraha*, failed dismally, and indeed had a diametrically opposite effect. Indignation swept from the coal-fields across to the sugar plantations on the Indian Ocean coast. The news of Gandhi's arrest and imprisonment ignited a firestorm of protest. 20,000 labourers struck work throughout Natal. It was the height of the harvest season. A spontaneous wave of walk-outs hit the plantations and sugar refineries, where three quarters of the work-force consisted of indentured Indians. The strikes were without precedent in scale and scope; and wholly self-organized in the sugar plantations of the South. The idea of calling out the plantation workers had occurred to Gandhi; but he had not done so. He had never campaigned in their midst. They heard of protests and strikes in the northern mines, and of Gandhi's arrest, which agitated and angered them. Entirely spontaneous, their participation in the strike was remarkable for its solidarity with their co-workers in the north. A rumour ran rampant that Gokhale was coming back to secure the repeal of the £3 tax. Many thought that Gandhi had asked them to down tools. Some strikers moved into nearby towns from the plantations. Some came to Phoenix.[71]

The first walk-out from a sugar estate on the north shore took place at Avoca, not far from Phoenix. Sugar refineries on the south shore were crippled by

---

70 Cf. Desai and Vahed, *op.cit.,* p.373.

71 Cf. Swan, Maureen, 'The 1913 Natal Indian Strike', *Journal of Southern African Studies*, 10:2, 1984.

strikes. By the middle of the month, the great majority of Natal's 60,000 Indian workers were on strike.[72] Indian street cleaners, water-carriers, household servants, hotel and restaurant workers and waiters, railway men and boatmen deserted their posts and paralysed Durban, where the strike was almost universal. Other cities were likewise affected. The unaffordable £3 tax had been clapped on them on purpose, to trap them underground, or chained to their jobs, for a long time. Large numbers had no option but to reindenture. It was exceedingly hard to see any light at the end of the tunnel. Their despair evoked their great response!

The plantation workers, subjected to official cruelty and violence, retaliated in kind at a number of estates, as they were not really abreast of Gandhi's prescription of self-restraint and non-violent self-suffering in the face of pitiless repression. There were some pitched though unequal encounters; sticks and knives were brandished against mounted police and firearms. Some sugarcane fields were set on fire. The panic-stricken farmers sent their families to the comparative safety of the cities. The army was mobilized. Gandhi was in jail at Bloemfontein, where, according to Rajmohan Gandhi, 'no Indian could see' him, 'or carry messages from him'. But the newly formed Natal Indian Association, fully awake to the developing situation, sent food to a north coast sugar estate when the employers cut off the rations of their workers.

At Mount Edgecomb, the son of the plantation owner tried to force the striking workers back to work with the support of mounted police. He fired four shots from his revolver, one of which killed an indentured worker named Patchappan, who was one of the eight killed or mortally wounded on November 17, 1913.[73]

An indentured labourer named Soorzai, badly beaten up at a nearby plantation, sought refuge at Phoenix, but died of his injuries.[74] Only one white named Armstrong in the whole of Natal was charged 'with having gone too far.' He just seized two Muslim Indians, not his employees; made his African workers tear off their clothes and hold them, while he repeatedly hit them with sjambok and fists. He pursued them, and twice again repeated the onslaught. The story found its way to Fleet Street. Downing Street

---

72 Cf. Gandhi, Rajmohan, *op. cit.*, p. 167.

73 Cf. Lelyveld, *op.cit.,* pp. 121-2.

74 *Ibid.*

asked for a report. Armstrong was fined a hundred pounds; but was quite unapologetic. He wanted 'to teach the whole tribe a lesson.'[75]

Ashwin Desai and Goolam Vahed provide a vivid account of the widespread extent of the strike, with searing descriptions of official cruelty and violence. They posit that 'the combative spirit of plantation workers in coastal areas was important in forcing Smuts to the negotiation table.'[76] But it was not so much the violence in the 'combative spirit' as the readiness to go on strike and paralyse the economy, that was the compelling factor no longer possible to ignore. The strike was a display of collective will in strong, irrepressible resistance. Decades of oppression, individual protests and devious forms of covert resistance led to a spontaneous eruption of anger and action. Gandhi's invitation to strike was the catalyst; his call was the trigger; his incarceration was the matchstick to a dry haystack; the arrest of the marching miners was the provocation that sparked the conflagration. The fact that 'it was outside the control of Gandhi and his coterie of leaders' in widespread parts of Natal does not negate the initiation of the strike by him; the organizing of the great march by him; the supervision of its orderly progress by him. It was only when Gandhi and his associates were flung into prison, the march was halted and the marchers were herded back to the mines converted into prisons, that the resulting resentment led to the unpremeditated eruption of the general strike. Pent-up frustrations and anger burst forth. The miners and the plantation strikers deserve their due credit for rocking the boat of the Government; but the main actor who brought it all about, directly and indirectly, was Gandhi. The authorities knew how to deal with violence. They were at a loss to tackle and put a lid on non-violent passive resistance. The opprobrium of international opinion, the condemnation by India's Viceroy, and the expression of guarded but real concern by the Imperial authorities forced Smuts and Botha to hide their faces with the fig-leaf of an Inquiry Commission, which made the recommendations leading to the subsequent agreement between Smuts and Gandhi.

The strike had spawned its own logic, its own momentum fed by memories of continual exploitation, repression and cruel conduct. Desai and Vahed are right to point out that 'there were experiments with armed struggle. Sticks and knife caches were hidden along roads, cane fields were torched,

---

75 *Ibid.*, p. 124.

76 Desai and Vahed, *op.cit.*, p.376.

policemen ambushed, White farmers besieged and taken hostage. So threatening did these acts become that reinforcements were sent from as far afield as the Eastern Cape.'[77]

'The specificity of rebel consciousness'[78] doubtless craves comprehension. It is the transparent misery arising out of the £3 tax, which made re-indenture peak in 1912, at the rate of over 95%. Gandhi said so, too, repeatedly telling the mine owners and the Government that the march would cease if the tax was repealed. Seventy-five-year-old Harbat Singh took part in the strike and died in jail. When asked by Gandhi why he was putting his life in danger, he replied: 'What does it matter? I know what I am fighting for. You have not to pay the £3 tax, but my fellow ex-indentured Indians have to pay that tax, and what more glorious death could I meet?'[79] The tax at once guarded against the paucity of labour, also serving white racism by limiting the number of free Indians. It sustained both re-indenture and repatriation!

Shared suffering with little prospect of relief or abatement induces a spirit of shared frustration and resentment, a sense of solidarity fortified by the common experience of iniquity. The strikers were not insurgents. It was not a communist or socialist kind of movement. They did not want to, and could not even dream of subverting the regime. They had a specific goal to achieve. The ebullition of emotion and anger at the betrayal of a pledge to revoke the tax led to their strike action; and the attempts at brutal suppression provoked retaliatory violence. The individual loses himself or herself in the crowd; his or her action in concert with the others makes it an upheaval of the crowd. Great movements are always made up of the participation of many, whose individual stories of trials and hardship shape their collective consciousness and response to their predicament. That is where leadership comes in to direct, define and articulate their response to enable them to converse with the authorities to arrive at some compromise and conclusion. Sadly, the fickleness and limits of human memory make it impossible to remember them all except a few, including their leaders. 'The iniquity of oblivion blindly scattereth her poppy.' And

---

77 Desai and Vahed, *op.cit.*, p. 393.

78 *Ibid.*, p.395.

79 *Indian Opinion, Golden Number*, p. 10.

history can never be exhaustive in its survey and analysis, as it is only an approximation to the reality in its detail and baffling complexity!

The strikers often spoke of a *Rajah* helping them, which was most probably a reference to Gokhale or Gandhi. The visit of Gokhale had been a most significant event. He was accorded 'state honours'. His tour, his meetings, his speeches, his receptions, stirred Indian pride and raised Indian expectations. They remembered it all, and the promise to repeal the tax. When that did not happen, they felt collectively betrayed. Their leader was betrayed, which was an assault on their dignity. Many believed that he would return, to set things right! The channels and networks active during his visit served later to add fuel to the fire of the strike.

The strike continued to spread. The army was called in. A big force of mounted riflemen was sent to the sugar country. The navy was put on alert. But the use of force failed again. A large meeting in Durban unanimously decided to continue the strike and refuse to work until the £3 tax was abolished, and Gandhi was released from jail.[80]

A meeting, on November 15, of about 1200 Indians in Pietermaritzburg expressed overwhelming support for Gandhi and the movement. A meeting, on November 16, at Johannesburg asked for the release of Gandhi followed by talks to resolve the situation. Durban was 'seething with the strike spirit.' A meeting of 3,000 Indians on November 16 gave cheers for Gandhi and the strikers. The strike was universal in the hospitals and the municipality, in the sugar plantations, coal-mines, railways, ships, shops and the hotels.

John Dube, the Zulu reformer, was an eye-witness to the conflict. Some Indian strikers congregated on a piece of open ground, and refused to move when asked by the police to do so. They were badly beaten, as mounted policemen ran through them, and yet declined to disperse. Their courage and endurance impressed Dube. He told a friend that he once considered plantation coolies crude and uncivilized; but had now 'acquired a sense of respect for all the Indians.'[81] Gandhi's precept of non-violence was at work!

---

80 Reports in *Natal Advertiser*, 14, 15, 16 November, 1913.
81 Cf. Hughes, Heather, *First President: A Life of John L. Dube, Founding Father of the ANC*, Jacana, Auckland Park, South Africa, 2011, pp.178-9; Guha, *op. cit.*, p.485.

In the last week of November, the leader of the Cape Coloureds, Dr. Abdurahman asked the annual conference of the African Political Organization: 'If a handful of Indians, in a matter of conscience, can so firmly resist what they consider injustice, what could the coloured races not do if they were to adopt this practice of passive resistance? We must all admire what these British Indians have shown, and are showing, in their determination to maintain what they deem to be their right.'[82]

The whites fumed against Gandhi and the Indians in angry letters to the press. But the distinguished lawyer F.A. Laughton said the £3 tax was illegal. Wages on the plantations were much below the market rates; and Indians were 'under no obligation either to leave Natal after the expiration of their indentures or to take out a licence if they remain.'[83] Strikes were not illegal! There was no law prohibiting them. The actions of the Government were entirely illegal.

Het Volk, the Boer Party in the Transvaal, called for the deportation of all Indians. The Government tried again to smash the strike in Natal by force, without success. Many victims of their tyranny sought refuge at Phoenix, where they were fed and looked after by Albert West and Maganlal Gandhi.

Apart from the indentured workers driven underground in the mines transformed into prisons, or otherwise jailed in Natal, around 2,500 Indians or nearly one-fifth of the Indian population of the Transvaal went to jail. Many of them did so several times. [84]

Reports of heartless excesses found their way to India and London. There was a surge of sympathy and support in India. A public subscription collected £5,000; and Gokhale asked who should he send it to. The Viceroy sent a series of telegrams to London, reporting widespread indignation and support for Gandhi and the *satyāgraha*.

South India felt the pain of the *satyāgrahīs* even more keenly, as so many of them were from the south. Natesan reprinted Polak's book on Gandhi to

---

82 Dr. Abdurahman and Passive resistance', *Indian Opinion*, 3 December, 1913; cf. Guha, *op.cit.*, p.485-6. Gandhi and his *ahiṁsā* were writ large over the movement!

83 *Transvaal Leader*, 22 November 1913.

84 Cf. Andrews, *Mahatma Gandhi's Ideas*, Allen & Unwin, London, 1931, p. 194.

raise money for the struggle. Rajagopalachari reprinted Gandhi's account of his experiences in jail to raise money to help. Gandhi 'must be ranked with the *Avatars*', said the rising lawyer in Salem. The booklet sold quite quickly, and Rajagopalachari sent a cheque for Rs. 1,500 to help the cause.[85]

Gandhi and his movement fired the imagination of many Indians. Many Englishmen in India sympathized with the Indian cause. In Porbandar, Major F. D. Hancock gave a state contribution of Rs. 1,000 to the fund for Indians in South Africa. Gokhale sent another £5,000 to Maganlal.[86] The great poet Tagore sent Rs. 100 to Gokhale as his 'humble contribution' to the cause.[87] The rich and the poor, the famous and the little-known, alike contributed to the fund. The Thakore and the Rani Saheb of Gondal, the Nizam, the Gaekwar and other Indian princes were also amongst them. Britons such as Ramsay MacDonald, Sir Murray Hammik, ex-acting Governor of Madras, and Sir Valentine Chirol sent donations. Gokhale was the moving spirit behind all these generous gestures. Chirol wrote to him: 'Few Englishmen who take a genuine interest in the welfare of India and have faith in the value of the British connection both for India and the Empire can fail to have been moved by the statement you made...'[88] Gandhi had touched the heart-strings of Indians and many Englishmen alike!

The Bishop of Madras, an Englishman, spoke with genuine feeling in his approbation of Gandhi: 'I frankly confess, though it pains me to say it, that I see in Mr. Gandhi, the patient sufferer for the cause of righteousness and mercy, a truer representative of the Crucified Saviour, than the men who have thrown him into prison and yet call themselves by the name of Christ.'[89]

---

85 Rajagopalachari, C., ed., *Mr. Gandhi's Jail Experiences: Told by Himself*, T. Adinarayana Cetti, Salem, 1913; cf. Guha, *op. cit.*, pp.488, 625, n.80.

86 *Ibid.*, p. 490.

87 *Ibid.*, p.491.

88 Cf. Tendulkar, *op.cit.*, p.179.

89 The Bishop of Madras, quoted in *Speeches and Writings of M. K. Gandhi: With an Introduction by Mr. C.F. Andrews, a Tribute by G.A. Natesan, a Biographical Sketch by Mr. H.S.L. Polak*, Second Edition, G.A. Natesan and Co., Madras, 1918, Appendix III, p. x.

Lord Hardinge, the Viceroy, was told by his advisers that 'there had been no movement like it since the Mutiny.' He was no less outspoken when he said: '...It is not easy to find means whereby India can make its indignation felt by those holding the reins of Government in South Africa.' He expressed 'the deep and burning sympathy of India and also of those who like myself, without being Indians, sympathize with the people of this country.' And he added: 'if the South African Government desires to justify itself in the eyes of India and the world, the only course open to it is to appoint a strong impartial committee, whereon Indian interests will be represented, to conduct the most searching inquiry, and...the Raj will not cease to urge these considerations on the Imperial Government.'[90] The Viceroy's intercession on behalf of the Indians in South Africa carried a great deal of weight, and, indeed, was most timely and called for.

There were many other notable supporters of the struggle. In a speech in the Bombay Town Hall, Sir Pherozeshah Mehta paid a moving tribute to Kasturba, 'one of the foremost heroines in the whole world.'[91]

A three-member Commission of Enquiry, all whites, chaired by Sir William Solomon, was appointed in less than a week after the Viceroy's speech; and within a week, they recommended the release of Gandhi, Kallenbach and Polak. The Commission had to perform two main tasks. The first, of course, was to whitewash the Government's misdeeds; the shootings and the sickening violence of beatings and floggings. The second was a settlement to signal the end of the *satyāgraha*, the scope and scale of which had indeed been without precedent. They had never seen or encountered such widespread, spontaneous protest. The Government had been painfully overstretched in the maintenance of law and order. The bravado of the newspapers did not correspond with the reality. The economy of Natal had received a body-blow. White workers did not want to work where the Indians did, in mines and plantations, and elsewhere. The suggestion of Gladstone that the Government should examine both the tax and marriage questions was now readily accepted by Smuts. He was in a most uncomfortable, unenviable position. He had broken promises; and encouraged the racial intolerance of the South African whites.

---

90 *Indian Opinion*, 3.12.1913 ; *Collected Works*, 12, 602-3; Hardinge of Penshurst, *My Indian Years*, London, 1948, p.91.

91 Cf. Guha, *op. cit.,* pp.492, 626, n. 90.

On December 18, Gandhi, Kallenbach and Polak were released from jail. Gandhi was not happy with the constitution of the Commission. He could trust the fairness of Sir William Solomon; but the other two members of the Commission, Lt. Col. Wylie and Edward Esselen were known for their anti-Indian views. In a public meeting in Johannesburg, he spoke against 'a weighted or packed Commission.' Instead of deferring to a Commission predisposed against Indians, he would prefer to go back to jail and 'allow the Indian case to stand upon its merits.' William Hosken begged him to control himself.

The next day Gandhi went to Durban to a victorious welcome. He was pulled by young men in an open carriage; he was smothered with flowers. He was wearing a new costume. Western clothes were shed to don the garb of the indentured labourer, the down-trodden son of the soil, wedded to the soil, sustaining life with the produce of his toil. He was barefoot, wearing a *kurtā* (tunic) and *lungī* (wrap-around). He had shaved his head except for a tuft on top, the *śikhā* of a Hindu, in mourning for the Indians who were killed in the *satyāgraha* confrontations with the police and the plantation owners. His sartorial sense had always made a statement of his intent and purpose. It always conveyed a message. His dress at Durban demonstrated his identification with the people and their causes. The bullets that felled the Indian workers, he said, had also pierced him through his heart. It would have been glorious for him to be struck down by one. It was a struggle 'even unto death.' Was it a repeated premonition of his assassination in 1948?

The presence of more than 6,000 Indians, snuffing out the earlier pockets of dissent, was a clear exhibition of their wholehearted support. The epic march was the epochal episode of Gandhi's stay in South Africa. The largest crowd he had ever drawn in Durban crowned his triumph! He urged them again to gird up their loins for more struggle, 'to suffer imprisonment, to march out…to strike, even though this may mean death.' Indians had no voice in the Commission. He wanted it to be enlarged to include members from the European community known to be free from bias. He wrote to Smuts suggesting the names of W.P. Schreiner and Sir James-Innes; but the request was summarily rejected.[92]

---

92 *Collected Works*, 12, pp.274-277; 599.

Gandhi said the Indians would boycott the Commission.[93] L.W. Ritch warned that the movement would be renewed if the Indians' demands were not conceded; and Gandhi's army would swell to 20,000.[94]

It was in the garb of an indentured labourer that Gandhi stood outside Pietermaritzburg Prison on December 22, 1913, to greet women prisoners including Kasturba, when they came out of the building. They had all been physically hurt and weakened by their prison ordeal; but the sight of Kasturba reduced to a mere skeleton shocked Gandhi. The strike would not have spread as it did without the women's participation, and their crucial contribution. Even on the day Gandhi was released, thirty-two *satyāgrahīs*, including five women, were sentenced to jail for entering the Transvaal without papers. And on December 22, 1913, a young girl named Valliamma Munusamy Mudaliar, only fifteen years old, was arrested along with her mother and other women on their return to the Transvaal almost two months after their departure from Tolstoy Farm to join the *satyāgraha*. Given the option of a fine of £5 or jail, they all opted for imprisonment for three months, with hard labour. Valliamma was already seriously ill when arrested; her condition deteriorated in prison; but she still refused to be set free on medical grounds. She was released only on February 11, 1914, after a provisional agreement between Smuts and Gandhi. Asked if she regretted going to jail, the emaciated but indomitable girl told Gandhi that she was prepared to court imprisonment for the cause yet again, even if she might die in captivity. She died soon afterwards.[95] Her martyrdom was a pure and perfect, fruitful sacrifice, which brought the aid of God to the seekers of liberty and justice! Gandhi wrote many years later: 'The name of Valliamma will live…as long as India lives.'[96]

Kathryn Tidrick believes that Kasturba 'was regarded as a prime candidate for martyrdom in the 1913-14 campaign.'[97] But despite her debility, serious

---

93 Lelyveld, *op. cit.*, p. 129, tells his readers that 'Gandhi made a show of boycotting the judicial commission but slipped comfortably into renewed negotiations with Smuts.' The language is in conformity with the entire tenor of the book.

94 *Natal Monitor*, 22 December 1913.

95 Cf. Desai and Vahed, *op. cit.*, pp. 369-70.

96 *Satyagraha in South Africa, Collected Works*, Vol. 29, p. 227; Gandhi, Rajmohan, *op. cit.*, p. 162.

97 Tidrick, Kathryn, *op. cit.*, p. 101.

illness and imprisonment, and Gandhi's quackery, she defied death, and hung on to dear life.

Writing about the death in jail of 'Immortal Hurbatsingh', the old ex-indentured labourer 'with no kith and kin', Gandhi observed: 'The whole Indian community mourns for him. His death, which ordinarily no Indian would have heard of, will...be known to the whole of India...he was a*satyāgrahī*; and as truth is eternal, even so a man who resolutely clings to truth is immortal.'[98] Hurbatsingh had spent 30 years in Natal as a labourer; 'had thought of India, India's honour and of India's *tapascharya* [sacrifice] in ancient times...it was no matter for grief if an old man like Hurbatsingh went to gaol for India's sake and died while in prison.'[99] It was the consummation of a quest; the ultimate offering to a cause!

Satyāgraha, Gandhi and the oppressed

Satyāgraha demanded and commanded *ahiṁsā* (non-violence) accompanied by self-suffering, and if necessary, martyrdom. It was a religious struggle in terms of the sacrifices the *satyāgrahīs* made, and were ready to make! Their motives were unimpeachable, inasmuch as they were campaigning for a future that would be more just and humane, even if they might not be there to benefit from it. *Satyāgraha* spelled self-sacrifice, not self-aggrandizement! Jail-going was part of the austerities or *tapascaryā* in pursuit of temporal justice and spiritual power!

Gandhi had fully identified himself with the indentured and the oppressed. He spoke of them, for them. So many of them had never heard or seen him. They were still having it tough on the farms, in the mines. He had made no promises to change their standard of living or terms of their employment except for advocating the end of indenture. They were all fighting a religious war for India, not narrowly confined to any particular religion, but uniting them all in the shared pursuit of basic human dignity. He would leave South Africa soon. Those left behind would realize and recall that they had received from him something most significant. They would be proud of standing up to power at his call; they would be proud of their courage of conviction; of their freedom from fear or a measure thereof,

---

98 *Indian Opinion* [From Gujarati], 7-1-1914 ; *Collected Works*, 12, p. 321.
99 *Indian Opinion*, [From Gujarati], 7-1-1914; *Collected Works*, 12, pp. 319-20.

that they cultivated under his command, under his guidance, inspired by his example!

Gokhale's Counsel

There was constant contact between Gandhi and Gokhale, who considered it a 'grave mistake' to boycott the Commission, depriving the Indians of the opportunity to present before it the evidence of untold cruelty towards them. Gandhi said that people were vociferous in their rejection of the Commission; and were pressing him hard for a march on Pretoria. When Gokhale told him that both the boycott and the march would humiliate the Viceroy, Gandhi asked for forgiveness, as he could not violate the pledge to boycott the Commission. Gokhale persuaded Lord Hardinge to depute a senior civil servant, Sir Benjamin Robertson, as the representative of the Government of India to the Commission. He briefed Sir Benjamin with painstaking care, so that the Viceroy's representative could convey the concerns of Gandhi and the Indian community to the Judicial Commission.[100]

Gokhale's counsel held Gandhi back. The march to Pretoria stood in abeyance. Meanwhile, Emily Hobhouse, the British social reformer, urged Smuts to be magnanimous; to 'readjust the marriage question and abolish that stupid £3 tax' before any march took place: '...never never will governmental physical force prevail against a great moral and spiritual upheaval.[101]

On December 31, 1913, the last issue of *Indian Opinion* for the year came out with the bold statement that 'the Satyagraha campaign, as carried on this time and still continuing, has hardly a parallel in history. The real credit for this goes to the Tamil and Hindi speaking brothers and sisters living in this country. Their sacrifice has been the highest of all. Some of them have even lost their lives, killed by the bullets of the white soldiers. As a tribute to their memory, we have decided to give Hindi and Tamil news in this paper.'[102]

This is Gandhi-speak. He is thanking the people for their love, devotion and sacrifices; for their loyal acceptance of his leadership. The gratitude

---

100 *Collected Works*, 12, pp. 276, 277-81, 283-4, 286- 289, 295-6, 301-5, 599; cf. Guha, *op.cit.*, p. 496.

101 *Ibid.*, pp. 497-8, 627, n. 106.

102 *Indian Opinion*, 31-12-1913 [From Gujarati]; *Collected Works*, 12, p. 311.

of the leader to his followers is in free flow, rather than any reference to what he did for them; how much he suffered for them; or the sacrifices he made for them.

Chapter 70

Negotiations and the 'Final Settlement'

Two other intermediaries, both English clergymen, were on their way to South Africa. When Gokhale heard that Albert West, Acting Editor of *Indian Opinion*, had been arrested on November 25, 1913, despite following Gandhi's instructions to do nothing to provoke or invite arrest, he requested his friends Andrews and Pearson to go immediately to help. C. F. Andrews and W.W. Pearson taught at St. Stephen's College in Delhi. Both were admirers of the great poet Rabindranath Tagore; and in close association with him at Santiniketan, the university he founded.[1]

Two years younger than Gandhi, Andrews had studied at Pembroke College, Cambridge, where he took firsts in Classics and Theology. He went to India with the Cambridge mission in 1904; and as an Anglican priest and lecturer at St. Stephen's, earned the respect and attention of both official and nationalist circles. He identified with the people of India; led a simple, celibate life; and made friends with a large number of people from all walks of life. He met Gokhale when he attended an Indian National Congress session in 1906; and the two became friends. He wrote to Gokhale to let him know if at any time he could be of some use to the national cause. Indians in South Africa in December, 1913, could certainly avail of his help. In his introductory note to Albert West, Gokhale described both Andrews and Pearson as 'great friends of India.'

---

[1] There are many biographies of C.F. Andrews, affectionately called *Dinabandhu*, 'brother or friend of the poor and down-trodden' by Indians. Notable among them are: Chaturvedi, Banarsidas, and Marjorie Sykes, *Charles Freer Andrews: A Narrative*, George Allen & Unwin, London, 1949; Tinker, Hugh, *The Ordeal of Love: C.F. Andrews and In*dia, Oxford University Press, Delhi, 1979; and O'Connor, Daniel, Gospel, *Raj and Swaraj: The Missionary Years of C.F. Andrews (1904-14)*, Peter Lang, Frankfurt, 1990.

A small dockside reception committee awaited their arrival in Durban on January 2, 1914. On disembarkation, Andrews looked around for Gandhi, who did not possess the commanding presence of Tagore. He saw Henry Polak, whom he had met before, and asked him if Gandhi was there. 'Polak turned to a slight ascetic figure, dressed in a white *dhoti* and *kurta* of such coarse material as an indentured labourer might wear.'[2] 'I stooped at once instinctively, and touched his feet [in the traditional Hindu gesture of reverence], and he said in a low tone: 'Pray do not do that, it is a humiliation to me.'[3] Andrews, however, told him that he would be similarly greeted in India!

The Indians in Durban organized a reception in honour of Andrews and Pearson. Andrews spoke with great feeling, and told them that India simmered with deep sympathy for their sufferings. Tagore had given him a Sanskrit *mantra* as his message to the South African Indians, which he recited in a lovely accent, profoundly moving his audience.[4] A friendly European speaker at the 'welcome' meeting, sister of the Speaker of the House of Assembly, Miss Molteno told the Indians: 'Only as you learn to call *Africa* your Motherland, can you become worthy children of her sacred soil.' They had no future if they lived apart, like strangers 'on an alien shore.'[5]

Indian Opinion published songs written by Sheikh Mehtab in honour of the visitors. Gandhi's old friend was now an enthusiastic passive resister and singer. His songs sung at this reception had 'been specially composed by Mr. Sheikh Mehtab as a tribute to the devotion of Messrs. Andrews and Pearson to the Indian cause.'[6] 'The two were now quite reconciled, notes Guha.[7] But Gandhi still omitted Mehtab's name from his autobiography; made no mention of his participation in the *satyāgraha*; of his poetical

---

2   Chaturvedi, Banarsidas, and Marjorie Sykes, *Charles Freer Andrews: A Narrative*, Publications Division, Ministry of Information and Broadcasting, Government of India, 1982.

3   Cited in Chadha, *op.cit.*, p. 186; cf. Gandhi, Rajmohan, *op.cit.*, p.169.

4   *Natal Mercury*, 5 January 1914.

5   Chaturvedi, Banarsidas, and Marjorie Sykes, *op.cit.*, pp.111-12.

6   *Indian Opinion*, 7 January 1914.

7   Guha, *op.cit.*, p.501.

exhortations to the resisters; and of his laudation of the leader. Gandhi was certainly less than forgiving!

That very afternoon Andrews gave an emotional sermon at the Indian Mission Church on St. Paul's Hymn of Love, in which he took his cue from Miss Molteno's message. She was in the audience, and came up to tell him: 'While you were speaking, the vision of a united Africa came so close I felt I could touch it with my hand. You must go forward with that message – they are all thirsting for that, Boer and English and Kaffir alike – and one day love will conquer.'[8]

Andrews and Pearson accompanied Gandhi to Phoenix the next day. Gandhi saw in Andrews an extraordinary capacity to reconcile, which would be helpful. But he was not very hopeful. He had heeded Gokhale's plea to postpone the march to Pretoria. The Commission, though, seemed stacked against the Indians. He could not compromise on the abolition of the £3 tax; or on the recognition of Indian marriages. He could not forget the bullets that felled Indians; and the brutal beating and flogging of the passive resisters. His boycott of the Commission was a matter of principle; a matter of honour. Andrews agreed that there must be no sacrifice of honour. He and Gandhi became friends soon enough; and within two or three days, they were calling each other Charlie and Mohan.[9]

In case of a resumption of *satyāgraha*, Gandhi would like his eldest son Harilal in India to come and participate; and so wrote to Gokhale. Manilal, the second son, was still in jail. The third, Ramdas had already been. The fourth, Devadas, still very young, helped run the Phoenix settlement. Their mother, broken in health, had just come out of prison. But Gokhale wrote back that he had asked Harilal to stay in India; and continue his studies. Harilal did not return.

Andrews persuaded Gandhi to meet Smuts. The formal boycott of the Commission did not exclude private talks between the two, who were seriously estranged from each other by the recent events. On January 6, 1914, Smuts received a letter from Gandhi requesting an appointment. The General said that he could meet him on the 9th or 10th.

---

8   Cf. Chaturvedi, Banarsidas, and Marjorie Sykes, *op. cit.*, pp. 111-2.
9   Chaturvedi, Banarsidas, and Marjorie Sykes, *op.cit.,* pp. 106-7.

NEGOTIATIONS AND THE 'FINAL SETTLEMENT'

Gandhi and Andrews proceeded to Pretoria to meet Smuts. Gandhi's 'extraordinary appearance, with a shaven head, his mourning suit of unbleached calico and his bare feet', startled a press reporter.[10] A general strike by white railway workers had just broken out, paralysing railway transport. Smuts became totally preoccupied with the strike that brought the country to a sudden halt. The white railway workers did not believe in non-violence; and the General had to declare martial law. He had to put Gandhi off again and again; and Andrews was impressed by Gandhi's great patience. They met briefly on the 13th; and Gandhi's 'kindly and courteous' attitude restored the old feelings of mutual respect between the two.

In view of the railway strike, Gandhi called off the march to Pretoria to protest against the unrepresentative and partisan composition of the Commission of Enquiry. He did not want to add to the Government's woes in the hour of their distress. Smuts was agreeably surprised by Gandhi's chivalry. Lord Ampthill congratulated Gandhi for being kind and considerate even to his opponent.[11] In a light, jocular vein, Smuts' secretary said to Gandhi: 'I do not like your people, and do not care to assist them at all. But what am I to do? I often wish you took to violence like the English strikers, and then we would know at once how to dispose of you. But you will not injure even an enemy. You desire victory by self-suffering alone and never transgress your self-imposed limits of courtesy and chivalry. And that is what reduces us to sheer helplessness.'[12]

Andrews hoped that the Commission would help find a solution; but if not, he was himself ready to join a march to Pretoria. 'There is nothing else to be done, and this may mean arrest,' he wrote to Munshi Ram (Swami Shraddhanand).[13] In a very brief meeting with Lord Gladstone on January 14, he told the Governor-General that the two non-negotiable demands of Gandhi were the repeal of the three-pound tax, and the recognition of Indian marriages. 'Nothing could shake Mr. Gandhi on matters of conscience.'[14]

F.S.K. Gregson, the Archdeacon of Natal, invited Andrews to deliver his message to the people of Natal. Gandhi accompanied Pearson to hear

---

10   Cf. Guha, *op.cit.,* p. 503.

11   Cf. Tendulkar, *op.cit.,* p. 179.

12   Cf. Chadha, *op.cit.,* p. 187.

13   *Ibid.*

14   Guha, *op.cit.,* p. 504.

Andrews' sermon, but was refused entry into the 'whites only' church. Recounting the incident to Tagore, Andrews lamented that 'Christianity in its present unholy alliance with the white race is utterly unable to cope with the evil [of racism].'[15] The 'meek and lowly' Christ could only be found among the Indian *satyāgrahīs*, 'the humblest and the lowliest and lost' in South Africa. 'If Christ had gone to that church, he also would have been turned away because he was an Asiatic', he recalled many years later.[16]

Gandhi met Smuts again on January 16; and they had a substantial conversation. Gandhi told the General what the Indians wanted: repeal of the three-pound tax; recognition of Indian marriages; entry of South African Indians into the Cape; and removal of the overt racial bar in the laws of the Free State. He reminded Smuts that the Cape was originally a British colony, with greater obligations to the British Imperial subjects. Sympathetic Smuts asked Gandhi to present these demands to the Enquiry Commission. But Gandhi said that he could not go back on the boycott of the Commission.[17]

In his report of the interview to the Colonial Office, Lord Gladstone referred to 'a sympathetic interest' that Smuts had in Mr. Gandhi 'as an unusual type of humanity, whose peculiarities, however inconvenient they may be to the Minister, are not devoid of interest...His ethical and intellectual attitude, based as it appears to be on a curious compound of mysticism and astuteness, baffles the ordinary processes of thought. Nevertheless, a tolerably practical understanding has been reached.'[18]

Letters and phone calls between Gandhi and Smuts kept the negotiations going. Smuts assured Gandhi that they had decided to grant the Indians' demands; but still needed a recommendation from the Commission. He understood that Gandhi was bound by his pledge to boycott the Commission; but he asked Gandhi not to prevent anyone willing to give evidence to the Commission; and to suspend the *satyāgraha* in the interval. By deciding not to present any evidence before the Commission, Gandhi and his associates were depriving themselves of the opportunity

---

15 Tinker, *The Ordeal of Love*, p.88.
16 Cf. Chadha, *op. cit.*, p. 188.
17 *Collected Works*, 12, pp. 324-326.
18 *Ibid.*

Negotiations and the 'Final Settlement'

to prove allegations of excesses and cruelty towards the passive resisters; but that was for them to think over. He asked Gandhi 'not to revive passive resistance until the Commission had reported and the Government had been given an opportunity of acting on the report.'[19]

Gandhi also had numerous discussions with Sir Benjamin Robertson, which dealt largely with the marriage question. The attitude of Robertson was that of a typical British civil servant; and he was often officious and bullying in his dialogue with the Indians.[20]

Andrews wrote a long letter to Gokhale to report on the progress of their negotiations. He admired Gandhi's goodness of heart and mind; but was concerned about the 'fragility of his nerves, on edge as a consequence of the crises he had faced these past few months.'[21]

Days of anxiety followed. An urgent telegram arrived from Durban; Kasturba was seriously ill. But Gandhi would not abandon his post of duty to be beside his wife. Then, finally, the letter from Smuts arrived, outlining the terms of the settlement. Gandhi construed the text as a studied insult to himself. He could not accept a phrase that the General wanted to insert in the proposed agreement. Though their interviews had been friendly, the letter was cold and officious. Andrews was in a quandary. What should he do now?

He thus described the critical hours: 'That night we talked till 1 a.m. Finally, an alternative phrase occurred to me. The difference seemed to be very slight, but Gandhi found it acceptable. 'If General Smuts will accept your phrase', he said as we went to bed, 'then everything is finished.' In the morning, saying nothing to Gandhi, I went to Smuts and at eight o'clock found him alone. I told him Gandhi's personal anxiety, and showed him the suggested wording. 'I don't mind a bit', he said, 'it makes no difference as far as I am concerned.' 'Would you make the change and sign it on the spot?' 'Certainly'.'[22] The newly inserted phrase vindicated Gandhi's honour.

---

19 *Collected Works*, 12, pp.609-11.

20 Cf. Tendulkar, *op.cit.*, p.181.

21 Guha, *op.cit.*, p. 505.

22 'Unpublished Reminiscences', cited in Chaturvedi, Banarsidas, and Marjorie Sykes, *Charles Freer Andrews: A Narrative*, p. 109; cf. also, *Collected Works*, 12, p. 611.

On January 21, 1914, the deal was duly signed, the task accomplished! Just as they were about to start on their journey back, a second telegram arrived from Phoenix to inform them that Kasturba was better. Latent malaria seized Andrews on the train; and when they reached Durban amid scenes of jubilation, Willie Pearson handed the weary Andrews a letter informing him of his mother's serious illness owing to a chill caught at Christmas. The news of her death the next day was a most painful blow; but he was comforted by Kasturba and the other ladies, who said, 'we will be your mothers now.' Andrews wrote to Tagore that his mother's love and devotion played a unique part 'in quickening my love for India herself... Her spirit will shine out at me through Indian eyes and Indian mothers' faces.'[23]

Andrews also wrote to Gokhale about Gandhi: "His work in South Africa is done – and nobly done...He must go, both for his own sake and the community's...for if he stays, he will dwarf everyone else...Let him go to India and be with you...'[24]

Gandhi had indeed been under staggering strain. The ebb and flow of the *satyāgraha*, the limitless worries of its organization and direction, his imprisonment, Kasturba's alarming illness, differences between the father and the eldest son heading towards estrangement, and the suspense of Gandhi's negotiations with Smuts, were all taking their toll!

Meanwhile, the passive resisters were released in batches, including the wife of Sheikh Mehtab and her mother; Mrs. Thambi Naidoo and the other Tamil women. Their heroic sacrifices were praised in songs sung by Sheikh Mehtab; and in speeches delivered by the Polaks and Sonja Schlesin.[25]

Andrews accompanied Gandhi and Kasturba to Cape Town, where on February 12, he gave a lecture on the life and work of Tagore at the town Hall. Lord Gladstone, the Governor-General, presided. He apprised his audience, which included many members of Parliament, of the loftiness of Indian thought and ideals mirrored in the poetry and writings of Tagore; and felt later that this lecture 'marked the turning of the tide of public

---

23 'To Rabindranath Tagore,' 27th January, 1914, cited in *ibid.*, p. 109.
24 Cf. Guha, *op.cit.*, p. 106.
25 Cf. Guha, *op.cit.*, p. 507.

opinion in favour of the Indian cause.'[26] Tagore's universalism visualized the union of the East and West in the higher phases of life and thought. Even a single voice of truth, transcending the discordant divisions of race, colour, creed, commerce and politics, could herald the 'downfall of ancient tyrannies and the coming in of new world forces which make for peace.'[27]

At a farewell party given for Andrews by the Indians of Cape Town, W.P. Schreiner, MP, hailed him as an emissary of 'the entire brotherhood of humanity.' So was Schreiner himself, in a land riven by racism! Andrews praised the 'chivalrous attitude' of Gandhi, and the 'great considerateness' of Smuts' in the solution of the *satyāgraha*. Any reference to his own healing touch was precluded by his modesty!

On February 21, Andrews set sail for England. And five days later, he sent Gandhi a letter full of love and regard for his new friend. Both were earnest seekers of the Truth and God. Both persevered to bridge the gulf between the East and West; between the white and coloured races; between the followers of various faiths negotiating numerous ways to God. They became life-long friends!

Report of Solomon Commission

On March 7, 1914, the Solomon Commission submitted its report to the Government. The virtual boycott of the Commission had shortened and accelerated its work. Expeditiously published in the last week of March, the report recommended the concession of Indians' main demands.

On March 9, 1914, Gandhi's eldest brother Lakshmidas passed away at Porbandar. He gave expression to his great grief in a touching letter to Kallenbach: '…I was hurrying everything on so that I could go to India with the quickest despatch and fall down at his feet and nurse him. But it was not to be. Now I must go to a family of widows with my poor self as the head…'[28] His other brother, Karsandas, had died in June, 1913. He had to provide for five family widows, including his sister and two sisters-in-law. But his own life was now in danger. He heard that irate Muslims in Johannesburg wanted to murder him, as he was unable to get Muslim polygamy recognized. They accused him of betraying them and

---

26 Chaturvedi, Banarsidas, and Marjorie Sykes, *op. cit.*, p. 112.

27 Cited in Guha, *op.cit.*, pp. 508, 626, n.22

28 Cf. Chadha, *op.cit.*, p. 190.

their religion. 'That would indeed be welcome and a fit end to my work,' he wrote to Chhaganlal, with instructions for the family. He wanted them to live like farmers on the land. If he was murdered, they could approach Pranjivan Mehta for monetary aid to support the widows. Harilal had to take care of Kasturba.[29]

On March 22, 1914, a meeting of the Transvaal Muslims in the Hamidiya Hall resolved that 'the recognition of one wife only and her children ... will molest and violate the principle of our sacred religion.' They also declared that Gandhi, Polak and their associates did not represent the Muslim community.[30]

Gandhi wrote to Gokhale in praise of Andrews and Pearson; but said he was disappointed with Benjamin Robertson, who was weak, insincere and divisive. If there was a settlement in March, he hoped to leave South Africa with his family in April. About 20 men, women and children from the Phoenix school would also go to reside with him in India. He wanted to learn at Gokhale's feet and 'gain the necessary experience.' He assured Gokhale that he would 'scrupulously observe' the promise of silence for a year in relation to Indian affairs after his arrival back home. He wanted to nurse Gokhale and attend on him; to take orders from someone 'whom I love and look up to.'[31]

Kasturba fell gravely ill in Cape Town. She could not eat any solids; and survived only on grapes and orange juice. He made her fast; and fed her *neem* leaves in water. Her health improved; and she could sit up and eat again. It was due, he said, to his methods of nature-cure, and faith in God.

Indians' Relief Act

On March 11, 1914, Smuts said in a speech in the Senate that Gandhi was allowed to function freely, as he did in South Africa, 'because he never advocated methods of violence to overthrow the state.'[32] On March 23, Smuts announced in the Assembly that the Government was considering the Report of the Commission. In May and June, the Assembly and the

---

29 *Collected Works*, 12, 'Letter to Chhaganlal Gandhi,' pp.380-383.

30 Cf. Guha, *op.cit.*, p. 513.

31 'Letter to G.K.Gokhale', February 27, 1914, *Collected Works*, 12, pp. 360-61.

32 *Collected Works*, 12, p. 665.

Senate of the South African Parliament passed the Indians' Relief Act, or Act 22 of 1914.

All monogamous Indian marriages solemnized in accordance with Hindu, Muslim and Parsi rites were recognized as valid. The £3 tax was abolished; and arrears were cancelled. A domicile certificate with the holder's thumbprint was deemed sufficient proof of the right to enter the Union. The rights of all *bona fide* former residents were assured. The right of 'specially exempted' educated Indians to enter South Africa was conceded; and Smuts agreed that all existing laws would be 'administered in a just manner and with due regard to vested rights.'[33]

In his last letter to General Smuts, Gandhi pointed out that 'some day or other these matters will require further and sympathetic consideration by the Government'. He emphasized that 'complete satisfaction cannot be expected until full civic rights have been conceded to the resident Indian population.'[34] The *satyāgraha*, which began in 1906, finally came to an end![35]

Indian press noted the closure of the *satyāgraha* with pride and satisfaction, giving their due credit to the passive resisters. *Sadhva*, a Kannada weekly cited by Guha, gave high praise to Gandhi's distinctive political strategy: 'Not a sword was drawn, not a gun fired...He performed, so to speak, the obsequies of unrighteousness. History has its heroes in men of the type of Alexander the Great whose fame is measured by the havoc and the devastation they caused, but heroism of the type displayed by Mr. Gandhi in making iniquity's defeat its own end is without a parallel.'[36]

Phoenix and Another Fast

Gandhi and Kasturba returned to Phoenix in early May. Her health improved steadily, defying Gandhi's dark forebodings; and he wrote to Gokhale that they could meet him in London, where he was spending the summer, before they went to India.

---

33 *Satyagraha in South Africa*, p. 304; Gandhi, Rajmohan, *op.cit.*, p. 170.
34 *Satyagraha in South Africa, Collected Works,* Vol. 29, p.267.
35 *Ibid.*
36 *Sadhva*, 24 July, 1914; Guha, *op.cit.*, p.514.

Rumours of sexual transgressions once again rocked the even tenor of life at Phoenix. Kasturba told Gandhi that Jeki Mehta still had a romantic interest in Manilal. Gandhi accused his wife of undue prejudice against Jeki; and Kasturba in turn accused him of shielding her. They had a frightful quarrel, the worst in their thirty years of marriage. Gandhi poured himself out in a letter to Kallenbach: 'Immediately she began to howl. I had made her leave all the good food in order to kill her. I was tired of her, I wished her to die, I was a hooded snake...The more I spoke the more vicious she became...She is quite normal today. But yesterday was one of the richest lessons of my life. All the charges she brought against me she undoubtedly means...Yes, a man who wishes to work with detachment must not marry. I cannot complain of her being a particularly bad wife...no other woman would probably have stood the changes in her husband's life as she has. On the whole she has not thwarted me and has been most exemplary...My point is that you cannot attach yourself to a particular woman and yet live for humanity. The two do not harmonize....'[37]

Marriage and family were expendable in pursuit of what he construed as his higher duty. Even though private, this letter to his friend is inexcusable for its breach of privacy in a husband-wife exchange; for its use of words that would have hurt Kasturba if she could read them! The advice not to attach oneself to a particular woman may be misinterpreted. Not everyone wants to be celibate. Attachment to a partner does not in any way militate against social service. If anything, it makes one mentally and emotionally stable, more rational, more patient, more understanding, more forgiving, and more focussed on one's task without the distraction of other attractions. The only thing needed is the will to serve!

Kasturba blamed Jeki for trying to seduce her son. Gandhi blamed Jeki, as well as Manilal, whom he had exhorted to work hard to be 'esteemed in India as a *brahmachari* of a high order.'[38] Gandhi found it hard to cope with Manilal's failure to live up to the ideals of his father. He had also written harshly to Harilal, disapproving of his obsessive love for his wife.

The letter to Kallenbach reveals Gandhi's impatience with his wife, and a certain lack of understanding; but it also takes note of her discontent and dissatisfaction arising out of the choices made by him, to which he

---

37 Gandhi to Kallenbach, 12 April 1914, *Collected Works*, Vol. 96, pp.181-2.
38 Letter to Manilal Gandhi, *Collected Works*, 12, p. 395.

subjected her. Neither he, nor she could foresee their fateful future at the time of their marriage!

Two weeks after their quarrel, Jeki Mehta was making sexual advances to another man. Gandhi was angry. He felt hurt. She had betrayed him, her father and her people. He decided to send her back to her husband in Fiji. Her lapse commanded Gandhi's atonement for his imperfect supervision. He would fast for two weeks. Kasturba entreated him to desist. It would wreck his health. But the fanatical, obstinate disciplinarian was not open to any dissuasion. By the end of the fast, he wrote to Kallenbach, he was 'near death's door': 'Mrs. Gandhi was divine. Immediately she realized that there was no turning me back, she set about making my path smooth. She forgot her own sorrows and became my ministering angel.'[39] He was an impossible husband married to a goddess of forbearance and compassion!

---

39 Gandhi to Kallenbach, 18 May 1914, *Collected Works*, 96, p.190.; Guha, *op.cit.*, p.516.

Chapter 71

Farewell Meetings

On June 27, 1914, a meeting of the Europeans and Indians celebrated the passage of the Indians' Relief Bill. Gandhi thanked the many European friends whose sympathy and help significantly contributed to the success of the Indian struggle. He had tried to see the question with European eyes. The bill was a 'settlement of present difficulties'. Indians sought neither equality with the governing race, nor the franchise. These things were for the future, but beyond current practical politics. All he wanted was that, 'on the basis of the rights now conceded to them, they should be suffered to live with dignity and honour on the soil of South Africa.'[1]

Gandhi wrote to Gokhale that he and Kasturba would go to London. Kallenbach would accompany them, and go on to India with them. The bill was duly gazetted; and they made their bookings for July 18, 1914. They left Cape Town on July 1 for Kimberley, where Gandhi spoke at a reception on July 2. He was only 'a soldier in the army of voluntary sufferers,' who were entitled to the 'real honours'. Their sufferings had melted the hearts of the Europeans. Kallenbach, Polak and other European friends deserved the gratitude of Indians for all their help. He thanked Botha, who threatened to resign if the bill was not passed. He thanked the Viceroy of India, Lord Hardinge, and Mr. Gokhale, whose statements and active efforts brought about the settlement.[2]

On July 8, Gandhi and Kasturba were given a fond farewell in the Durban

---

1   Speech at Congratulatory Meeting, Cape Town, June 27,1914, *Collected Works*, 12. pp.436-438.
2   *Collected Works*, 12, pp. 440-1.

Farewell Meetings

Town Hall. W. Holmes, the Mayor, presided. This was the very place where the whites had talked of lynching him at angry meetings held against him in the past. Indians and Europeans now met there in a spirit of peace and goodwill. Addresses on behalf of a number of organizations all over South Africa were read. Indian and European admirers spoke in glowing terms. He modestly told them that neither he nor his wife deserved the praise lavished on them. He thanked the Europeans for all their help and kindness; F.A. Laughton who 'stood by him against the mob' in 1897; and Mrs. Alexander, who 'protected him with her umbrella from the missiles thrown by the excited crowd.' He told them that passive resistance was a weapon of the purest type; it was not the weapon of the weak. It needed far greater courage. 'It was the courage of a Jesus, a Daniel, a Cranmer, a Latimer and a Ridley who could go calmly to suffering and death, and the courage of a Tolstoy who dared to defy the Czars of Russia, that stood out as the greatest.'

Gandhi thanked Botha for his statesmanship when he said that his government would stand or fall by this measure. He thanked Lord Hardinge and Gokhale; Kallenbach and Polak. He had received love and sympathy from the Europeans; and he would leave South Africa with 'no ill-will against a single European.'[3]

On July 9, he was congratulated by the Gujaratis of Durban. He asked them to cultivate Gujarati, their mother tongue, and study the history and traditions of their Motherland. He also urged them to extend their hospitality to the other communities; to cultivate respect for Hindus and Muslims alike, which would undoubtedly help their progress in South Africa.[4]

He had two more engagements on the 9th of July. He attended a Sports Day for children. The trophy was presented by Rustomji, who, Gandhi said in his speech, would 'die for them, live for them'.[5]

The second function was a reception given by the Dheds, untouchables who discharged sanitary duties. He called them 'our own brethren, and to regard them with the slightest disrespect not only argues our own

---

3   *Collected Works*, 12, pp.445-447.

4   *Ibid.*, pp. 454-456.

5   *Ibid.*, pp.456-458.

unworthiness but is morally wrong, for it is contrary to the teaching of the *Bhagavad Gītā*.'[6]

Gandhi deserves praise for his bold stand against untouchability. He was no doubt a pioneer among reformers. But to say that they should be treated as 'brethren' in obedience to the precept of the *Gītā* is also to presume that, in the absence of such a recommendation or command, people could do otherwise. It is morally imperative to treat them as equals, with respect, as brethren, irrespective of what the *Gītā* or any other text says! We know the notorious passages of Manu against women and the *Śūdras*, the erstwhile untouchables and other service classes. If so-called scriptures violate basic morality in their prescriptions or dispensations, we owe it to ourselves as rational human beings to reject them with all the emphasis at our command!

Europeans of Durban hosted a banquet for Gandhi on July 11, 1914. In his speech, Gandhi observed that the struggle had 'quickened the conscience of South Africa – and…there was a different tone prevailing today.' The Commission and the Act had solved a few problems; but 'it was not a complete settlement. It was not a charter of civil liberties.' He asked for 'a sense of justice' in the administration of laws.

There was another party for them at Phoenix on the 11th of July, 1914. Gandhi spoke briefly, followed by West, who also referred to their friendship that had gone from strength to strength in eleven years, and its effect on their lives and the Phoenix Settlement. Some English and Gujarati hymns brought a fitting closure to the function. West had played a pivotal part in sustaining Phoenix and helping the *Satyāgraha*. Parsi Rustomji was the other principal supporter of Gandhi in Natal.

Gandhi then went into the interior, and spoke to a large audience of indentured labourers at Verulam. 'A visit to this place was like going on a pilgrimage, for the Indian friends here played a great part in the recent strike.' They had 'done something really great.' He advised them to never re-indenture. On completion of their current contracts they did not have to pay the £3 tax any more to stay as free men; and if they remained in South Africa for the next three years, they would be treated as domiciled there. They could then go to India at their own expense, and return. Those who resolved to go to India not to return, could claim their travelling expenses

---

6   *Ibid.*, p. 459.

from the Government.

He expressed his unhappiness at the fact that some indentured workers had raised their hands in retaliation against excessive cruelty. If he had been with them, he would have had his head broken rather than allowing them to do what they did. Should they ever have to strike in future, they would have to put up with every atrocity including shooting and hanging, without raising their hands in violent retaliation; and 'even the stoniest heart will melt. Such is the power of satyāgraha.' Gandhi told them: 'You are under indenture with one person for five years, but I am under indenture with 300 million for a life-time.'[7]

Gandhi spoke to the indentured labourers and other Indians at a meeting held on the Football Club Ground in Durban on July 12, 1914. He told them that South Africa was the motherland for the Indians born there; and 'their future' was 'bound up with that of this country.' He pleaded with them not to waste the money saved with the abolition of the £3 tax on alcohol or gold. He exhorted them to desist from drinking, and picket the wine and liquor shops to discourage and dissuade their friends and fellows from intoxication.[8]

In his parting message to the Indian residents of Durban on the eve of his departure, Gandhi reminded them that they had to 'work unitedly as Indians', whether they were 'Hindus or Muslims, Parsis or Christians.' Their newly acquired prestige would certainly depend on their unity and capacity to 'work together.'[9]

He left Durban for Johannesburg on July 12. He had met some of his dearest and closest European and Indian friends there. His philosophy of *Satyāgraha* took shape in Johannesburg. And it was tried and tested in relation to life and its problems in Johannesburg.

A farewell banquet was given in the Masonic Hall on July 14, in honour of Gandhi, Kasturba and Kallenbach. Addresses on behalf of the British Indian Association, the Chinese Association, the Tamil Benefit Society, the Transvaal Indian Women's Association, the Gujarati, the Mahomedan and the Parsi communities, were presented. A. M. Cachalia and Thambi

---

7   *Collected Works*, 12, pp. 465-467.

8   *Ibid.*, pp. 471-2.

9   *Ibid.*, p.472.

Naidoo, the first to sign the Address of the British Indian Association, were Gandhi's leading colleagues in the movement. Cachalia was a Gujarati. Thambi Naidoo, a Tamil, said to Gandhi: 'On behalf of myself and my wife, I have the honour to present these four boys [his sons] to be servants of India.'

Gandhi, in his speech, praised and thanked his European and Indian friends for their love, kindness and courage in standing shoulder-to-shoulder with him in his struggle for justice and fair play. He and his wife Kasturba dedicated the adulation heaped on them to the 'Divine Essence, which pervaded everyone and everything in the Universe'. They gratefully accepted the precious gift of Thambi Naidoo's sons, and hoped that they would be able to live up to their responsibility.

It was in Johannesburg that he with his friends laid the foundation of the Passive Resistance Movement in 1906. That was where he met the late Mr. Doke, his friend, philosopher, guide and biographer. That was where Mrs. Doke nursed him back to health after a murderous assault on him by one of his own misguided countrymen. That was where he met Kallenbach, Polak and Sonja Schlesin. That was where the European Committee under the Presidentship of Hosken was formed to help lift Indians from the depths of darkness and despair. Johannesburg gave to the *Satyāgraha* the young girl Valliamma, 'who had died in the cause of truth.' And it was Johannesburg that gave two more young martyrs to the cause, Nagappen and Narayansamy.

Gandhi also paid tribute to the memory of Harbatsingh, the seventy-five years old ex-indentured labourer, whom he met in jail, and who died in jail for the abolition of the iniquitous three-pound tax, which he himself did not even have to pay any more.[10]

In an interview to *The Transvaal Leader* on July 14, 1914, Gandhi said he was going to India for good, 'with the intention of never returning.' He thanked Botha, Smuts and the 'Opposition' for conceding to the Indians 'entirely what they had been fighting for and suffering for during the last eight years. They had never asked for political equality. He had never asked for the vote. But he had insisted on the 'removal of racial distinctions.' He recalled 'the little acts of kindness that were done by obscure individuals.' He remembered 'the station master who brought him a glass of milk

---

10 *Golden Number, Indian Opinion*, 1914; *Collected Works*, 12, pp.473-78.

and a couple of boiled eggs', which he could not take owing to his self-imposed discipline. He recalled the proprietor of a hotel, who offered him a room when he saw him shivering. He remembered a 'woman who ran a small store'. She placed everything she had at the disposal of the passive resisters. Her 'British sense of sympathy' touched their hearts. The whole community in Charlestown and Newcastle came to their help.

The representative of *The Transvaal Leader* added his own estimate of Gandhi to the report: '...the most arresting figure in the Indian community in South Africa today is to say good-bye to a country in which he has spent many years crowded with experience and exertion, his work on behalf of his countrymen at last crowned with success....he has moved steadily on over obstacles that might daunt the bravest, to the goal on which his eye has been fixed...In the qualities of the heart and of the soul, you may believe the best of Gandhi, but you would wonder, did you see him, that so frail a figure could house so vigorous a character.'[11]

Gandhi thanked Lord Hardinge, the Viceroy of India, for the pressure he brought to bear on the final settlement; and praised Charles F. Andrews for the spirit of justice and accommodation that he awakened in the hearts of the statesmen. He requested his European friends to continue with their kind help to Indians through the European Committee and other channels. South Africa, he told them, would be second only to India in his love for their land.[12]

Gandhi wrote a brief message for Indians on the eve of his departure from South Africa. He exhorted them to rise above meaningless religious rivalries and provincial differences, and 'all ideas of high and low which divide men into Brahmins, Kshatriyas, Vaishyas and Shudras.' They were all subject to the same laws; disunity would disable them.

He gave the main credit for the glorious *Satyāgraha* to 'the sacrifices of Indians born in this country.' He told them without mincing words that their habits of living were 'very dirty', 'pathetic indeed'; and they had to mend their ways to command the respect that they craved. And he also warned them against consumption of, and addiction to alcohol.

He was conscious of the difficulties presented by the Dealers Licences

---

11   *Collected Works*, 12, pp. 479-481, n.1.

12   *Ibid.*, pp. 473-478.

Act. He called upon them to 'demand complete freedom of trade'; and said that they 'ought to get it.' It was not possible to secure anything more 'on the issue of marriages'. 'There is no better law elsewhere…'

If they were united, truthful and courageous, they could realize in the next fifteen years complete freedom of trade, full rights of land-ownership in all provinces, and freedom of movement from one province to another.[13]

On July 15, Gandhi spoke at the ceremonial unveiling of memorial tablets in honour of Nagappen and Valliamma[14]; and attended three more meetings. At the meeting of the Transvaal Indian Women's Association to bid him farewell, he praised them for their courage and sacrifices; and exhorted them to stay united. The martyrdom of Valliamma would always inspire them to stand up and be counted whenever an occasion or situation so demanded.

At the Muslim meeting in the familiar Hamidiya Hall, he was criticized by Essop Mian, his comrade-in-arms in the earlier *satyāgrahas*, for his inability to secure recognition of Muslim polygamy in the new marriage laws. What had they gained from the settlement? Gandhi said that they had gained everything they asked for. They had gained everything in the list of demands sent to the Government through Cachalia's letter. The merchants had gained most of all. 'The Indian community had raised its status in the estimation of Europeans throughout South Africa. They could no longer be classed as coolies by General Botha and the others. The term had been removed as a term of reproach, silently but effectively. If they had not fought for the past eight years, no trace would have been left here of Indians as a self-respecting community.'

Not a single Hindu said that he was not satisfied with the marriage question. Polygamy had been an unresolved question for fifty years. The only question that arose was concerned with the validity of monogamous marriages. What was asked for, was granted. They could practise polygamy; but it was not legalized. 'All he expected the South African Government to do was to become tolerant of polygamy, but not to legalize it.'[15]

The meeting of the Tamil community was attended by both Indians and

---

13 *Ibid.*, pp.481-486.

14 *Ibid.*, p.486.

15 *Ibid.*, pp. 489-493.

Europeans, including Kasturba, Sonja Schlesin, and a number of ladies. Thambi Naidoo presided. Gandhi lauded the Tamils' faith in God and Truth; their courage of conviction; and the participation of their brave men and women in the *Satyāgraha*. Some of them gave their lives for the cause. Some of them sacrificed whatever they had on the altar of duty. Some of them were deported. No sacrifice for the larger community was too big! The majority of women who went to jail were Tamil. And Tamil women were mainly instrumental in bringing out the miners and plantation workers on strike. He did not even speak their language; and yet they hearkened to his call. Thanks to their courage and capacity for suffering and sacrifice, the crushing £3 tax was now a thing of the past; and their marriages and their families were at once sacred as well as legal.

He wanted to say something more, something vitally important! 'He felt they would have come to South Africa in vain if they were to carry those caste prejudices with them. The caste system had its uses, but that was an abuse.' If they persisted in calling each other high and low, they would ruin themselves. There was no high caste or low caste. The only thing to remember was that they were 'all Indians, all Tamils'.[16]

On July 16, 1914, Gandhi was in Pretoria at 8 a.m., to receive an address presented to him at the Indian Location. Vere Stent presided over the meeting, which was also attended by Chamney. Stent, Chamney and Haji Habeeb were warm in their praise for Gandhi, who thanked them all; and mentioned the compliment Chamney paid him when he went to arrest Gandhi at the head of 2,000 marchers with only one policeman to assist him. It was a clear demonstration of Chamney's faith in Gandhi's passive resistance. He spoke with feeling of the sympathy and support received from his European friends. And he urged his Indian friends 'to exercise patience and cultivate European opinion' to get the remaining wrongs redressed.

Gandhi returned to Johannesburg the same day to attend a farewell given by the Gujarati community. He thanked them for all their help in the past; but chided them for holding back in the last *Satyāgraha*. They did not do as much for the cause as the Tamils did. They had to learn a thing or two from the Tamils. Even though he could not talk to the Tamils in their language, they still made the greatest contribution to the struggle. And

---

16 *Indian Opinion*, 5-8-1914; *Collected Works*, 12, pp.493-5.

even though Gandhi could easily explain his aims and objectives to the Gujaratis in their common language, money still mattered more to them than the call of duty. He also warned them against gold-smuggling and alcoholic addiction. If they listened to his advice, his seeming harshness would ultimately 'prove wholesome'. He was going back to India; but he would always remember their affection.

Gandhi, Kasturba and Kallenbach then took a train to Cape Town. A procession of carriages, with a band marching in front, took them from the station to the city. They stayed at the house of Morris and Ruth Alexander, Jewish friends of Kallenbach. Morris was a lawyer and member of Parliament. Ruth came from a family of learned rabbis. Gandhi did not use the master-bedroom offered; and slept on the floor. The disarming simplicity of the guests impressed the hosts. Ruth classed Gandhi with her father, and Olive Schreiner.[17]

On July 18, the party proceeded to the docks, where addresses by the Madras Indian Association and by the Port Elizabeth Indians were presented to him. Gandhi also received a gold watch as a present; and Kallenbach was given a pair of binoculars. Dr. J. H. Gool for the Indians, and Dr. Abdurahman for the Coloureds, heaped praise on Gandhi, who was humble in his response. 'If he had done anything for his countrymen in South Africa, that in itself was sufficient reward for him.' They had given him costly gifts, 'an indication' of their love, sympathy and support; but not consistent with the life he tried to lead. He had come to South Africa 21 years ago, as a total stranger. 'One need not fear or despair of a land which had produced an Olive Schreiner, W. P. Schreiner, and a John X. Merriman…a land which had produced these noble men and women was a land that had a great future.'

He turned, placed his hand on Kallenbach's shoulder, and said: 'Why, I carry away with me not my blood brother, but my European brother. Is that not sufficient earnest of what South Africa has given to me, and is it possible for me to forget South Africa for a single moment?'

The future lay entirely in the people's hands. They would deserve by their conduct whatever might be in store for them. He appealed to his European friends to take a humanitarian and imperial view of the Indian question. He hoped that this Empire was 'not founded on material, but on spiritual

---

17   Cf. Lev, Shimon, *op. cit.*, p.102; Guha, *op.cit.*, p. 526.

foundations.' His loyalty arose from his devotion to the 'ideals of the British Constitution'. He wanted both Britons and Indians to make sure that 'those ideals of the British Constitution always remained a sacred treasure.'[18]

Gandhis and Kallenbach then boarded the SS *Kinfaus Castle*; and were on their way to England! They were travelling in third class! The Polaks, away in England, could not participate in the farewell functions in South Africa.

Hundreds of telegrams from a very wide cross-section of the South African population awaited their arrival on board. Gandhi relayed a message of thanks on July 18 itself, for the love and sympathy received, expressing the hope that 'the goodwill shown to us personally by so many European friends will be transferred to those to whose cause our lives in South Africa were dedicated.'[19] 132 telegrams of these farewells are now preserved in the National Archives of India; and a fair number are from Muslims.[20]

In contrast, Jan Christian Smuts could not hide his sense of relief when he wrote to Sir Benjamin Robertson: '…the saint has left our shores – I sincerely hope for ever.'

---

18 Farewell Speech at Cape Town, July 18, 1914, *Collected Works*, 12, pp. 503-505.

19 *Collected Works*, 12, p. 506.

20 Cf. Guha, *op.cit.*, p. 528.

Chapter 72

Gandhi, the Africans and the British

Gandhi came to believe in *Brahman* or Divinity residing in all living beings, and hence in the oneness and equality of all humankind. Yet, the new lawyer on the threshold of life in South Africa, trying to make ends meet, to make a success of his chosen profession, to realize his dream of first class travel and first class living in nice houses in prestigious neighbourhoods in an unknown country already riven apart by naked racism, did not know himself how to rise above it; how to come to terms with the African world and the African race with its strange earthy ways! There was a dread of the unknown, which inhibited his thinking, his anxieties and his apprehensions. As time passed, he looked around and saw the reality; admired the strength and majesty of the African race; and gradually realized that it was their land; the Europeans and the Indians were later arrivals. But the reality being what it was, and the whites being in a position of unassailable, dictatorial primacy, they were to be placated and converted first. And when a couple of opportunities allowed him to speak, he showed his expanding vision of racial equality, of the Africans in the fullness of time coming into their own!

Even though Gandhi expressed sympathy for the rights of Africans, he could not do much more. Had he tried, the white reaction would have been utterly ruthless and devastating. His campaign, however, taught the South African blacks that they could also stand up in protest against injustice. His *Satyāgraha* inspired the African national cause, the cause of justice above race. It appealed to the Indians, as it did to the black Africans. A campaign like his would attract European support. Infusion of a moral purpose and spiritual significance into the racial struggle would strike sympathetic chords in human hearts. The African National Congress and

Nelson Mandela used that lesson to telling advantage against the inhuman policies and practices of apartheid. The inculcation of that awareness was Gandhi's priceless gift to the South Africans. Mandela himself acknowledged that the non-violent campaign of Gandhi in 1913 provided the model for campaigns involving the masses in his youth. Gandhi was no doubt the first man in history 'to extend the principle of non-violence from the individual to the social and political plane.'[1]

He knew that in the country in which he found himself, in the circumstances he encountered, he and the other Indians, like the native Africans, were entirely at the mercy of the whites. And the whites could be roused to a sense of what was right, proper and fair, just and desirable, only in the light of their own religious commandments; through persuasion; through loving but determined non-violent protest; and through self-suffering. Their conscience had to be stirred. But he also knew that they would not give up their advantages, forswear their supremacy, and desist from exploitation of the Indians and Africans. Such self-denial is neither ordered, nor easily achieved. Immediate equality was beyond the bounds of current possibilities. But he told the Europeans of Durban in his farewell speech that they could not for ever postpone the day when the coloured races would enjoy equality and liberty side by side with them all in South Africa.

South Africa of the first decade of the 20th century presented a spectacle of stark inequality. Races and classes led separate lives, apart from one another. To Gandhi, the country presented a venue for forging the unity and togetherness first of the Indians, and then of entire humanity.

He had come from a small regional backwater of a princely state of Kathiawar, where his world was peopled only by Indians, and a distant British Resident. He had spent three years in England, and soon after his return, found himself on his way to South Africa. He had not seen or known any Africans at close range before; and was certainly not above a feeling of racial and cultural superiority over them. He had little knowledge of their culture or heritage conditioned by their geography; and his derogatory references to them as Kaffirs, as the others called them, were shaped by his surroundings. He protested at bracketing the Indians with them, which we can understand in terms of the necessity for a docile,

---

1 Cf. Radhakrishnan, S., 'Introduction' to *All Men Are Brothers: Life And Thoughts Of Mahatma Gandhi As Told In His Own Words*, Unesco, Melbourne University Press, 1959, p. xiv.

vulnerable community to safeguard its future and economic progress from the twin dangers of native resentment and white rejection.

It slowly but surely dawned on Gandhi that the blacks were the true masters of the land; and deserved better in the land of their origin and birth. He wrote in *Indian Opinion* in 1904-5 about the laws and practices that discriminated heavily against the Africans. His awareness was increasing, as he communicated the reality of their hopelessness through his paper. He decried their deprivation and called their dispossession of land unjust and unfair. He sympathized with their distress; and he was aghast at their suppression in the Zulu war. He pleaded for justice for the Africans, who were human, and felt hurt and slighted as the others did; and silently resented and rejected their subordination and servitude. They were gradually getting educated; and waking up to a sense of their cruel dispossession and social disablement.[2]

Gandhi published an appreciative account of 'a very impressive speech' by Dube, his neighbour near Phoenix, in which the latter spoke of the Africans working hard to improve their lot; and asked for sympathy and assistance. Gandhi's summary of the speech clearly implies his endorsement of its contents, despite the use of the term 'Kaffirs'.

In 1908, he projected a vision of the commingling of races in South Africa; and prescribed a strategy for the Africans to overcome their ills and disablement. He knew that change was yet distant; and the African hopes of freedom and equality in their own homeland were just amorphous dreams in the context of the current reality. However, his faith in British justice, painfully slow, yet certain in the fullness of time to improve and correct things, appeared steadfast. One may wonder at that optimism at loggerheads with the economic and political interests of the Empire and its ruling race! But it is there for us to see.

Gandhi's busy life with all its trials and tribulations gave him little respite to cultivate the Africans in a world of sharp divisions, in which he did not visualize immediate equality; or for that matter, even in the near future! He saw it only as a distant goal, but nevertheless attainable and inevitable in the fullness of time. He laboured alongside South Africans on the Tolstoy Farm; and acknowledged their industry and physical superiority. He commended the discharge of the Zulu Chief Dinizulu on

---

2   Cf. *Collected Works*, 4, p. 444; *Indian Opinion*, 22-4-1905.

the occasion of the South African Union's inauguration; and hoped that it would 'naturally fire the imagination of the natives.' When the authorities did not allow Africans to sit with the whites at the 1910 High School Examinations in Pretoria, as the Town-Hall had prohibited the entry of African and coloured persons into the building, Gandhi asked why? He wrote that the white attitude necessitated and triggered the fight in the Transvaal 'to put an end to this state of affairs'; and pointed out that 'the fight against a people with deep prejudice should take a long time' to bear fruit.[3]

He knew Dube, and respected him. When Gokhale visited South Africa, Gandhi took him to Dube's Industrial School, where the two talked to the African leader to apprise themselves of his thoughts and dreams, and of the problems of the Africans. Pixley Seme, one of the prime movers of the nascent native political consciousness, came to Tolstoy farm to confer with Gandhi before the foundation of the African Nationl Congress. The Natal Indian Congress founded by Gandhi would certainly have been a source of inspiration; and Gandhi might even have suggested the name of Dube for their first President. *Indian Opinion* conveyed its congratulations to Dube on his election as President; and published two paragraphs from his 'excellent' message to his people. Charles Andrews describes a typical scene at Phoenix: 'The strain of a long day of unwearied ministry among the poor was over. In the still after-glow of twilight, Mahatma Gandhi was seated under the open sky. He nursed a sick child on his lap, a little Muslim boy, and next to him was a Christian Zulu girl from the mission across the hill. He read us some Gujerati verses about the love of God... Then these Gujerati verses were sung by the children's voices. He asked me to sing "Lead, Kindly Light" as the darkness grew deeper, and in the silence which followed its close repeated the last lines...'[4]

Gandhi was trying to get close to the Africans, but would not force the pace. He was a gradualist; a cautious crusader! It was beyond all bounds of possibility for him to do anything for the Africans. Even for the Indians, he was not asking for too much more than the barest of justice and fair play, to make it possible for them to make ends meet, and eke out a sufferable existence without disabling, destabilizing persecution through racial restrictions and unbearable taxation. He showed the blacks how they

---

3   Cf. *Collected Works*, 10, p. 113.
4   Cf. Chatrurvedi, Banarsidas, and Marjorie Sykes, *op. cit.*, p. 111.

could also stand up for themselves and use non-violent non-cooperation to press their demands on the Government. The *Mahatma* was in the making. The young lawyer was waking up to the realities of South African politics and racial oppression. His hands were full with the issues faced by the Indians; the difficulties they encountered; and the *Satyāgraha* and its consequences. On the eve of his departure for India, he wrote against the white land-grab in South Africa and the wilful dispossession of the blacks, which was indeed the most pressing problem, beside which all other problems including those of Indians paled into comparative insignificance.

It would need another life-time to struggle for the emancipation of the blacks, and the restoration of their pride and place in the land of their ancestors. He showed the way, and later, from India, encouraged all oppressed peoples to resort to *satyāgraha* with *ahiṁsā* to achieve their goals without any hatred in their hearts for their oppressors. Their suffering would move the authors of tyranny towards compassion and self-correction!

The young lawyer changed into the Great Soul, who winced at the raw reality, and called for justice and fair play without any insidious racial discrimination. Equality without exceptions was to be Gandhi's final statement of faith!

The sudden propaganda erupting in Africa against the 'racist' Gandhi is entirely misconceived and misdirected. In a new book, *The South African Gandhi: Stretcher-Bearer of Empire,* Ashwin Desai and Goolam Vahed charge Gandhi with keeping the Indian struggle 'separate from that of Africans and coloureds even though the latter were denied political rights on the basis of colour and could also lay claim to being British subjects.' They forget that Gandhi was not demanding any political rights for the Indians. He did not ask for the vote. He did not seek equality. His modest demands talked only of civic rights. He asked for very basic relief to make life bearable; for repeal of the three-pound tax which wrecked people's lives and crushed their hopes of freedom. And even for the realization of these infinitesimal demands, they had to suffer and sacrifice beyond endurance. Could he have any hope at all that widening the struggle would be tolerated by the contemptuous and violent whites? The freedom of movement and trade that he sought for the Indians was also not unlimited!

He did not 'cut Indians off from Africans.' That was the reality he had to confront when he came to South Africa in 1893. He was not the *Mahatma* he became at the end of the story. The young man had hardly ever set eyes on Africans before he came to South Africa. A certain prejudice was inevitable in the prevailing state of affairs; and in his utter ignorance of the Africans and their culture.

It is not right to say that he was indifferent to the plight of the indentured. It was only gradually that a lawyer called to South Africa by merchants to look after their interests would find his feet in the country, and then look around at the stark realities of the unequal society he found himself in. Once he had established himself, he certainly began to help them; and never deserted them. He was a cautious planner, always preoccupied with the bounds of current possibilities; always quietly asking for change, until at last *satyāgraha* came to the fore.

He did not believe that state power should remain in the hands of the whites. But he saw the ineluctable reality of their entrenched, unassailable power and predominance. He knew that he could not dislodge or force or coerce them; or persuade them to cede their power to the blacks and the coloureds. It took almost a century to defeat the dictatorship of colour. It was, for him, beyond all bounds of possibility; and any attempt on his part to challenge the might of the whites and ask for equal political and social rights would have been ruthlessly crushed. He would have been deported; or even killed. The use of the term *Kaffir* by him was borrowed from current practice; and as I have already said, he was not above colour prejudice on his arrival; and for a few years after his stay in the country.

Writing to the Natal Parliament in 1893 to combat or refute the view that the Indians were just a little better than the 'savages or the natives of Africa', no doubt betrayed his prejudice and sense of superiority. But that was 1893. What did he know of Africa and the Africans? Calling him an advocate of 'Aryan brotherhood' is an entirely erroneous interpretation of his attempt to tell the whites that Indians came from the Indo-European stock, and were legatees of a civilization second to none in the scope and scale of its achievements. Any disparagement of the Africans did not form part of that exercise!

If in 1904, Gandhi wrote against the mixing of the Kaffirs with the Indians, he was also then a believer in caste and its constraints. He detested alcohol, whether consumed by the blacks or Indians. When Durban was hit by the outbreak of plague in 1905, he wrote against herding the Indians and Africans 'together indiscriminately at the hospital', because it made controlling the disease more difficult. There were varying standards of cleanliness and hygiene. There were cultural differences. There was the fear of the unknown. He did not yet know the Africans very well. But his attitude was slowly and steadily changing. He was becoming conscious of their position; their right to the land of their birth; and of their dispossession and disabilities.

He was twenty-four years old when he arrived in South Africa. He was not perfect; but he was an honest, earnest seeker of perfection; and gradually became 'more radical and progressive than most of his contemporaries.' He certainly did not want to be a 'junior partner' in the exercise of power. No one wanted to make him one. No one thought of it. No Indian in the two decades of Gandhi's stay in South Africa dreamt of it.

Desai seems to know better than Mandela, who gave due credit to Gandhi for his contribution to the great South African struggle for equality and justice. Desai's intemperate prose fails to dent Gandhi's image as a bridge-builder and visionary of the equality of all races in an ideal world, including South Africa. Desai and Vahed also admit that Gandhi 'did raise universal demands for equality and dignity.' Do we really have to re-write history to curry favour with our current masters?[5] Damaging, defacing or removing his statues from where they were thoughtfully installed, as a mark of respect for his suffering and service to entire humanity, is an exercise in incomprehension, deliberate or engineered!

Gandhi and the British

We have talked of Gandhi's love of, and admiration for the British. But he decried and strenuously objected to any kind of colour prejudice, or colour bar. He tried to understand and explain British apathy or non-action in terms of British conservatism, which it was not easy to overcome. He had faith in British justice and fair play despite the patent reality of British prejudice in relation to colour; the exploitation of Indians and others by the British; the exclusion of Indians from places and professions and positions in administration and commerce. The abject acceptance of a subordinate secondary position is implicit or explicit in many of his

---

5   Cf. Soutik Biswas, Delhi Correspondent, 17 September 2015, From the sectionIndia, http://www.bbc.com/news/world-asia-india-34265882

writings, speeches and positional postures. He cites the speech of Lord Curzon at the Guildhall in London, in which the latter talks of treating Indians with absolute equality and justice to endear the Empire to their hearts and minds. But Gandhi sees it all as a distant goal in the context of the South African reality.

When the protracted talks and negotiations with the authorities did not yield the desired results, and official intransigence stayed unmoved, when the custodians of imperial interests remained impervious to pleas for reason and justice, and their myopia deterred the vision of a more fruitful, harmonious future, Gandhi's optimism remained undiminished. His persistence stayed unfazed; and his suasive endeavour continued without a trace of bitterness; without any expression of wrath in word or deed; without any sense of despair. His faith in the capacity of the British to see reason, to do the just thing even to their own pecuniary and political detriment, did not easily forsake him. It took heavy blows of repression to remind him that the task was not easy, if not impossible. Self-denial on the part of exploiting nations and their representatives is the stuff of an idealist's dreams. It is contrary to ordinary human nature to give up great advantages in obedience to dictates of morality, or calls for justice!

Chapter 73

Ahiṁsā, Satya and Brahmacarya

Gandhi's non-violence arose from an age-long legacy of *ahiṁsā* preached by the Hindus, Jainas and Buddhists alike, transformed into an active, corrective force by the powerful influence of Tolstoy. The Kapiṣṭhala-Kaṭha Saṁhitā uses the term *ahiṁsā* in a moral sense concerned with the non-killing of animals.[1] The monosyllabic Upaniṣadic command *da* asking us to practise *dayā* (compassion), *dāna* (charity) and *dama* (self-control) is nothing but the translation of *ahiṁsā* into meaningful action. The *Chāndogya Upaniṣad* calls *ahiṁsā* our principal duty, and extends it to the welfare of all living beings.[2] Patañjali, the father of *rāja-yoga*, categorically labels *hiṁsā* (violence) as incompatible with spiritual progress and self-realization. And we are told that *ahiṁsā* means absence of oppression (*anabhidroha*) towards all beings, in all respects, at all times.[3] Even though the Buddha decried extreme self-mortification and advocated the middle-path (*majjhimā paṭipadā*) to achieve inner peace and *nirvāṇa*, *ahiṁsā*, not to hurt, not to harm, not to kill, was central to his creed. The *Bodhisattva* suffered for the redemption of others; took upon himself the sins of others; gave his life to save those of others. Jainism has penance and total self-abnegation at the core of its precepts in the practice of *ahiṁsā* stretched to the limits of possibility. Gandhi imbibed all these influences consciously as well as unconsciously, as his part of the collective Indian psyche. Penance for the sins of others took the karmic consequence to a willing Gandhi.

---

1   31.11

2   3.17.4

3   *Yoga Sūtra*, 2.30; cf. Unto Tähtinen, *Ahiṁsā: Non-violence in Indian Tradition*, Navajivan Publishing House, Ahmedabad, 1976, pp.2-3

'It is no non-violence if we merely love those that love us. It is non-violence only when we love those that hate us. I know how difficult it is to follow this grand law of love. But are not all great and good things difficult to do?'[4] Gandhi tells us that he made tireless appeals to reason till the year 1906 in the hope of convincing those in power to redress genuine grievances, but to no avail! At a critical juncture, when disappointment and despair might have led to ugly violence, he realized that degrading laws should be deliberately disobeyed; and submission to any punishment including jail would be preferable to acquiescence in tyranny. 'Thus came into being the moral equivalent of war.'[5]

The goodness and nobility of his goals notwithstanding, his fasts clearly expressed his will to coerce, if he could not otherwise persuade his opponents to accept some kind of compromise. Coercion was an undeniable part of the exercise. Gandhi was aware of it; and his opponents accused him of emotional blackmail. Coercion of any kind may at times be construed as just another form of violence! It is important, and indeed imperative, to move the hearts of those who are otherwise impervious to reason. 'The penetration of the heart comes from suffering. It opens up the inner understanding in man. Suffering is the badge of the human race, not the sword.'[6] Exploitation in any form is incompatible with non-violence. Love is the strongest, yet the humblest force in the world. 'The hardest heart and the grossest ignorance must disappear before the rising sun of suffering without anger and without malice.'[7] Gandhi's non-violence poses a challenge and active 'moral opposition to immoralities'. 'The resistance of the soul' to the tyrant would finally force his recognition without subjecting him to any humiliation, helping only to uplift him.[8] We should never hate our adversary, even if we find it hard to love him. There is no room for rancour. And there is no room for cowardice. *Ahiṁsā* is the death-defying weapon of the brave! *Ahiṁsā* is the means. Truth is the end.

Gandhi's love and solicitude for all humankind transcended his concerns for his immediate family. That is understandable in the context of his public

---

4 Gandhi, *All Men Are Brothers*, p. 86.

5 *Ibid.*, p. 90.

6 *Ibid.*, p. 91.

7 *Ibid.*, p. 93.

8 *Ibid.*, p. 93.

life, but not if it led to total disregard for an ageing elder brother in need of help! An inexorable, implacable imposition of his will on his wife and sons cannot be easily viewed as an exercise of *ahiṁsā* in thought, word and deed. They were coerced into accepting his dictates. Harilal, the eldest son, finally rebelled, though the other members of the family complied. Gandhi's causes were great and unexceptionable; his determination was unwavering; but his methods and attitude towards his followers could at times be emotionally cruel and dictatorial.

Gandhi and Satya (Truth)

I have already discussed Gandhi's love of Truth and steadfast devotion to Truth in my *Introduction*. He chided Lord Curzon for claiming Truth as primarily a western virtue as opposed to the duplicity of the Orient. He highlighted Curzon's ignorance of the emphasis on truth and truthfulness in India's religious and social tradition.[9]

He quotes from the *Sāma Veda*: '...conquer wrath with peace; untruth with truth.' He quotes the *Muṇḍaka Upaniṣad*: 'truth alone prevails and not untruth...it is by this path that the sages...have obtained salvation in Him who is the infinite ocean of Truth[10]. He quotes the *Taittirīya Upaniṣad*[11]: 'Speak the Truth, observe duty, do not swerve from Truth.' He quotes the same *Upaniṣad* again: 'Brahma is Truth eternal, intelligence immeasurable.'[12] He quotes the *Mahānārāyaṇa Upaniṣad*[13]: 'Speech rests on Truth; everything rests on Truth.' He quotes the *Mahābhārata*: 'there is no duty greater than truth and no sin more heinous than untruth.' He quotes Rāma in the *Rāmāyaṇa*:'Truth and mercy are immemorial characteristics of a king's conduct ...The man who speaks truth in this world attains the highest imperishable state... It is called the basis of everything...All things are founded on truth; nothing is higher than it...'

He quotes Bhīṣma: 'Truth is eternal Brahman... Everything rests on Truth'[14]. He cites many other authorities and goes on to say that according

---

9   Cf. *Indian Opinion*,1.4.1905; *Collected Works*, Vol. 4, pp. 392-394.

10   III.I.6

11   I-II-I

12   II.I.I

13   27.1

14   Śānti Parva, CLXII, 5.

to Hinduism, God himself is Truth.[15] The importance of Truth to the Indian mind is easily conveyed in proper personal names given to Indians by their parents. To list just a few, we have Satyendra, Satyavān, Satyavatī, Satyavrata, Satyapāla, Satyaloka, Satyavāhana, Satyabhāmā, Satyamvadā. Satya is the name of God Viṣṇu, exemplifying truth. The truthfulness of Indians has been spoken of by outsiders from very ancient times. Magasthenes (c.302BC) declared that no Indian was ever convicted of lying, and that witnesses and seals were regarded as unnecessary in the signing of contracts. Hiuen-Tsang (630 AD) was impressed by the honesty of Indians and their love of truth. Marco Polo (1293 AD) applauded the honesty of the Hindus, who would not resort to lying 'for anything on earth'. Sir William Sleeman in the nineteenth century said of the Hindu farmers: 'I have had before me hundreds of cases in which a man's property, liberty and life depended upon his telling a lie, and he has refused to tell it.'[16]

When Gandhi chose the word *Satyāgraha* (Truth-force or Soul-force) for his movement, he began to understand and identify God with Truth. One who served the Truth would never suffer defeat. Sacrifice was synonymous with the divine law; and one who waged his struggle with an equable mind for the sake of God and duty, would not incur any sin. Identification of *Satyāgraha* with soul-force invested it with divine purpose and activity. The development of perfect soul-force would unfailingly attain one's objective.

Truth and goodness go together in Hindu thought. The Sanskrit word *Sat* refers to the ultimate reality of the cosmos. The word *Satya* (Truth) comes from *Sat*, and like it, encompasses the reality of the world around, and its integrity. That would make it easier for one to comprehend the identification of God with Truth, and of Truth with God. As the *Ṛgveda* tells us: *ekaṁ sat viprāḥ bahudhā vadanti*: the Reality is one, but is variously described by the wise. *Ekaṁ santaṁ kavayaḥ bahudhā kalpayanti*: that which is one

---

15 We may easily multiply the quotes from Indian texts in which truth is spoken of as the greatest of all virtues. *Nāsti satyāt paraṁ tapaḥ*: there is no austerity higher than truth and truthfulness; *satyaṁ svargasya sādhanaṁ*: truth is the means to attain heaven; *satyena dhāryate lokaḥ*: by truth is the world supported; *satyād devo varṣati*: by truth we gain the bounty of God, the rains to slake the earth's thirst; *nānṛtāt pātakaṁ paraṁ*: there is no greater sin than untruth.

16 Cf. Benjamin Walker, *Hindu World*, Vol. 2, George Allen & Unwin, London, 1968, p. 524.

is described in different ways by the seers.

That reality inhering the universe became the Truth for Gandhi. And that Truth expressed itself in Gandhi's insistence upon social and political justice in his campaign, which thus became a true *Satyāgraha*, a realization of the self, and of one's rightful place in the scheme of things. The same divinity is immanent in us all[17]; and *Satyāgraha* is meant to awaken us all to a true sense of our being, and of our indivisibility.

'To me personally', Gandhi tells us, 'there is no distinction between a brahmin and a bhangi'.[18] He repeats: 'To my mind, there is no distinction between a Hindu and a Muslim or Christian…I maintain that the Hindu religion teaches us to look upon all with an equal eye without making distinctions between Hindu and Muslim, Brahmin and *bhangi*, and that is the religion I follow.'[19]

Gandhi emphasizes the need to overcome anger, love and hate in order to know the Truth.[20] Freedom from passions is a prerequisite. It is not enough to constantly talk of the truth, or tell the truth as one sees it, or knows it, or feels it. It is important to act in accordance with the Truth. One's thought and action should transcend any consideration of 'love and hate, happiness and misery'. What should that action then express? What should it seek to achieve? The only objective we can think of is justice and fair play. Truth would otherwise be as ethereal and incomprehensible as it would be indefinable. The validation of this Truth would only be its corrective, ameliorative efficacy and relevance. Even so, it would not be, and should not be devoid of love, which is the fount of compassion and any altruistic activity. To be human is to be concerned, to be solicitous about not only one's own, but the world's welfare. Gandhi seeks to identify this Truth with God. We always pray to God for protection from dangers and calamities, many of which are the consequence of our own folly. Gandhi is a firm believer in God, whom both the believer and the unbeliever can identify with the primal cause of creation. But the total extinction of human emotions and passions would in fact hinder rather than help the understanding of the order of nature, the purpose of creation,

---

17 *samaṁ sarveṣu bhūteṣu*, *Gītā*, XIII. 28.

18 *Collected Works*, Vol.4, p.430

19 *Collected Works*, Vol.4, p. 431; *Indian Opinion*, 20.5.1905.

20 *Autobiography*, p. 254.

and the function of the Creator or the primal cause of being and becoming. Why should it be necessary to divest ourselves of all our natural human impulses and emotions to understand the Truth, to commune with the Truth, to correspond with the Truth, to act according to the Truth? To do so would be tantamount to a wilful destruction or denial of the links with life as it arises and has its being. Life without emotions, without passions, is the negation of life itself, and a total contradiction in terms.

Prepossession with Brahmacarya

His insistence on *brahmacarya* or celibacy by his followers, the inmates of his *ashram*, was also an act of emotional cruelty, and sadistic denial of an emotional and physical need for loving fulfilment. *Brahmacarya* in India is at odds with life's reality. It is a chimerical ideal totally ignored by the gods and goddesses of the Hindu mythology, the sages of the great Epics, and men and women strutting across the stage of real life. The Hindu *Tantra* and the Buddhist *Vajrayāna* equate *mokṣa* or *nirvāṇa* with release through sublime sex. The gods and goddesses are depicted in icons that delete their duality in their sexual union. Even otherwise, they are almost always depicted in the close company of their consorts, like Viṣṇu and Lakṣmī, Śiva and Pārvatī, Rāma and Sītā, Kṛṣṇa and Rādhā, the Buddhas, Bodhisattvas and their Tārās. The temples of India glorify sex as equally divine and human, as the source of life and its consummation.

Gandhi's obsession with sexual abstinence was diametrically opposed to India's popular legacy, and amounted to a wilful negation of life. The enjoyment of life and the acceptance of its physical imperatives is by no means antithetical to social commitment and social service. It is a category of violence to preclude sex between wedded partners, not to speak of willing adults outside matrimony. If approached by a woman in her *ṛtu* (season), refusal of sex by a man in ancient India was considered equal to the destruction of a foetus (*bhrūṇa-hatyā*). *Brahmacarya* in Indian life and legend has been the stuff of myth at variance with life's realities. *Kāma* (sexual love) is one of life's ordained *puruṣārthas* (activities).

Chapter 74

Steps to Sainthood: Uneasy Birth of a Mahatma

Made as we are, predisposed as we are, we do not give unqualified praise; we cannot express unquestioning appreciation. Nothing is perfect. Even the moon has its blemishes, including the foot marks left by men on its surface! Every human being must have some shortcomings; otherwise, he or she would either be less or more than a human being; an oddity; an aberration; an incredible apparition! When we write of someone, we must drag him down to the level of quotidian human concerns or human failings. If we do not, we are not critical; we are less than perceptive; we are mere hagiographers. To be authentic, to be true to reality, we have to highlight the questionable more than the adorable aspects of our subject's personality. We have to pull down the 'great' to the level of our existence, to the tenor of our experience. If we do not, we have no critical acumen; we are hero-worshippers! It is difficult, if not impossible, to strike a golden mean between adulation and critical appraisal sometimes verging on iconoclastic demolition. We almost unconsciously judge people and their achievements against the yardstick that we apply to ourselves. How and why can they exceed the limits and constraints that confine and condition our sense of duty, service and sacrifice? More often than not, we view people and the reality with suspicion, with distrust, with an in-built reluctance to believe what others can do, if we cannot do so ourselves! I am no exception to the rule. But if I criticize Gandhi, as I do in many contexts, I also applaud his unique contribution to the history of humanity! Rilke wrote that fame is the sum of misunderstandings attached to a name. But Gandhi's cruel, uncompromising candour and devotion to truth leaves little room for any! Whatever criticism we may level at or against him is made possible by his disconcerting openness and disarming honesty. He bares himself to his skin to enable us to see him in his totality. We may like what we see, or else disapprove. He is impervious to praise or disapproval!

> *Nindantu nītinipuṇāḥ yadivāstuvantu....*
>
> *nyāyyāt pathaḥ pravicalanti padaṁ na dhīrāḥ.* (Bhartṛhari)

'The worldly-wise may give praise or abuse; but those possessed of patience do not swerve from the path of justice.'

The invitation to South Africa provided the opportunity and the venue for Gandhi's development and self-expression, which made the world rise from its apathy and take notice. Naked white discrimination transformed the lawyer into an activist. The professional lawyer became a social philosopher. The presence of Indians from different parts of India in South Africa made him confront and comprehend the reality of the linguistic and religious diversity of India. It helped make him an authentic Indian.

He began his life in South Africa as legal adviser to a rich Indian Muslim merchant; but his clientele steadily expanded to include the rich and the poor alike; and from £105 a year, he rose to be a top lawyer making five to six thousand pounds a year. His conscious, heart-felt identification with the poorest of them all was realized during the painful progress of the struggle to find for Indians living room under the South African sun, where they could breathe with a measure of dignity, justice and freedom, without which life becomes a biting curse; and existence loses its purpose. South Africa made Gandhi!

Very few act on what they learn; but Gandhi translated his lessons into practical reality, literally living the truths that he came to believe. He learned to live in peace with the followers of different faiths. He learned to respect their faiths. He learned to embrace their universal truths. He learned to cherish and practise their charity and compassion. He learned to live with the Westerners and join their search for spiritual truth and the meaning of life. They learned from him; and shared his vision of truth and justice; of human equality; of irreducible common human dignity. South Africa brought him into contact with like-minded people, who had a streak of non-conformism and eccentricity, and of idealism, such as Ritch, Polak, Kallenbach, West, Sonja Schlesin and many more. Living in close contact with unorthodox Jews and Christians would have been out of the bounds of probability in India. Muslims were his clients, close friends and comrades in his campaigns in South Africa. He learned, as he always emphasized, the need for freedom of conscience, freedom of faith, freedom of assembly and organization, and freedom of speech, without ever impinging on the freedom of others.

He realized the need for loving co-existence with different religions. He realized the need to listen and learn, to embrace good ideas wherever they came from, and to translate them into reality by right action. He did not want to convert anyone to a new faith; he saw truth in all religions; and he clearly saw the possibility of happiness and peace with others in them all. As he saw the immanence of the Divine in all living beings, he could hate no one; he could only love them all!

He spoke against invidious social divisions and distinctions; against the pernicious prejudices of caste; identified himself with the *bhangī* or the scavenger; and upheld the dignity of every vocation. Life embraced them all. Life needed them all. Any idea of high and low was wrong and reprehensible. All Indians were Indians. All Tamils were Tamils. The taint of caste and untouchability had to be erased, and any divisiveness eradicated! His followers came from a wide cross-section of humanity; from varying backgrounds, including Muslims, Christians, Jews, Parsis and Hindus, North Indians and South Indians, merchants and bankers, priests and indentured workers, farmers and hawkers. He nurtured a moral and political community, who were taught the correlation between means and ends; and the overriding importance of right means to the achievement of right ends. Questionable means would always result in questionable ends! The astounding devotion of his friends and followers assumed forms of abiding reverence. They would not hesitate to embrace poverty and suffering at his command; and would gladly go to jail at his bidding. They knew that he was right ahead of them, leading by example! His austerity, industry and courage won their admiration and wholehearted allegiance.

The merchants chased wealth; but he chose a sparse and simple life of hard manual labour. He had no quarrel with them; but wanted them to hold their wealth in trust for the welfare of the community. He retained the respect of educated Hindus and Muslims who did not always subscribe to his spartan way of life, but still supported the causes dear to his heart.

He founded a new political party in South Africa, the Natal Indian Congress, which showed his foresight and sagacity, to counter the hostility of the European rulers and officials; to provide an organized forum for the helpless Indian merchants and labourers in face of the unceasing onslaught on their dignity and livelihood. South Africa made him rise to the need of the hour; and assume charge of their welfare and protection from injustice. Situations and circumstances evoke the latent qualities and inner strength of a man. With a new self-assurance in his new surroundings, he wrote to Dadabhai Naoroji: 'I am the only available person who can handle the question.'

He was only twenty-five years old. But he felt compelled to do what he could, to assist his countrymen against legislative and executive attacks on their very existence and economic well-being. As the author and founder of a political party, he could disseminate and pursue his ideals without let or hindrance from any entrenched leadership. He was tilling virgin soil. Precedents and professionals were non-existent. His ideas developed as he went along; and practice led to theoretical formulation. He established a clear connection between truth, vows and politics. There were no great prizes to chase. There was professional antipathy. Even during the first days of his arrival in the country, he had been thrown out of a railway compartment, and manhandled by a coach-conductor. And then, later, there was the attempt to lynch him. His forbearance and forgiveness came to the fore, side by side with his determination to challenge inequity!

He adopted very original, novel modes of action against oppression and injustice. A new philosophy of social concern and correction through persuasion, conviction and conversion, always with love and without rancour, with non-violent non-cooperation as the instrument of action, went into operation. Acquiescence in injustice is tantamount to complicity in tyranny. It becomes one's duty to stand up and be counted; to protest, to denounce and decry dictatorship and folly; to do so loudly without mincing words, but also without intemperance, abuse and anger. Correction through non-violent non-acceptance and non-cooperation, through self-subjection to suffering inflicted by those in power, without any malice towards them, will take place when their hearts are touched, and they rise above naked self-service at the expense of others. Gandhi's faith in non-violence knew no bounds! *Satya* is synonymous with justice, decency, humanity and fair play; and *āgraha* is insistence upon it with one's soul in direct communion with the Divine Will and purpose expressed in truthful action. God and Truth become identical in the attempt at defeating hatred, exploitation and violence, enthroning love and solicitude for the eradication of colour prejudice; for an end to the exploitation of man by man. The uncomplaining capacity for self-suffering for the sake of fairness in human relationships will finally win over the selfish folly of those operating the levers of power. Listen to your inner voice; do not flinch from the performance of your duty to yourself and others as dictated by necessity. Do not submerge yourself in the submissive compliance around you, which is a sad consequence of fear and insecurity! *Satyāgraha* expresses the anguish of a soul at the perpetration of a great wrong; and its non-violent attempt to redress it. It is an exercise in self-discipline before self-expression in speech and action. 'Love', as Gandhi said, 'does not burn others, it burns itself.'

Satyāgraha arose out of the frustration and failure of petitions and memorials that moved no one; failed to make the authors of injustice uneasy; and were contemptuously ignored and put aside. Gandhi propounded the theory, laid down the discipline, and led by personal example. He planned his campaigns with meticulous care and painful attention to detail; spelled out the far-ranging significance of the *satyāgrahas*; their moral content and objectives; and the political implications. That non-violent *satyāgraha* was nobler and more effective than violent struggle involving bloodshed, loss of lives and widely ramifying misery, was assiduously explained in letters, speeches, articles, editorials, and in the book that jolted its readers, *Hind Swaraj*! He explained indefatigably! *Satyāgraha* he thought, was 'perhaps the mightiest instrument on earth.' He would use it for the achievement of national goals; he would use it in his fight against poverty. He waged a painful, principled struggle for India's independence based on non-violent civil disobedience and non-cooperation; willingly and unhesitatingly accepted the punishments repeatedly imposed on him; and became a shining symbol of self-sacrifice for the good of both his people and their opponents. Utter unconcern for personal interests or welfare, and the deliberate rejection of any self-defence kept attention riveted on the pursuit of equal justice for all. His *satyāgraha* made him a sentinel of hope; a bastion of non-cooperation with oppression!

Marxism, with its gore and gulags, was not for him! Brands of socialism marred by cruelty, violence and war, oppression and imprisonments, muzzling of free expression, free movement, free association, freedom of conscience, made him recoil with pain. Imposition of uniformity by force was unacceptable!

He blossomed into a fine, forceful writer and editor. He had begun early, in London while yet a student, writing for *The Vegetarian*. He wrote so many letters to the newspapers in Natal, and petitions to the Government. And in 1903, he started the *Indian Opinion* to advocate and advance the interests of Indians in South Africa. He wrote in Gujarati and English; supervised its production; and kept it financially afloat. Practice makes one perfect! He became a skilful writer, a powerful editor. He was not an orator in the classical mould, and spoke in a low, measured voice. Yet they avidly listened to his words dripping with truth and honesty; words that carried conviction! His exemplary life and selfless conduct inspired great devotion.

As his politics assumed its form and ideological lineaments, Gandhi the man, the thinker, the social worker came to the fore. His religious streak was visible even in his early years in India and England. But in South Africa he made a serious study of comparative religion. His spiritual advancement mattered more than anything else! His deep interest in Christianity and its serious study did not lead to his conversion. His spiritual mentor Raychandbhai encouraged him to look for truth in all the major religions of the world without any need for conversion from one faith to another. He was born a Hindu. He died a Hindu. He studied Islam and other major religions, including Hinduism. Jainism gave him the ideas of *aparigraha*, non-possession, and *anekāntavāda*, the many-sidedness of Reality; and the *Gītā* reinforced *aparigraha* with the goal of *niṣkāma-karma*, selfless performance of duty. Both widened his outlook; fortified his religious tolerance; gave him immeasurable strength and stamina to work for public welfare; and steeled his faith in the propriety of his involvement in public life.

Few men were so deeply influenced by the books they read. Ruskin's *Unto This Last* led to the foundation of the Phoenix Farm; and admiration for dignity of manual labour. The farmer's is the most praiseworthy and the most respectable calling, in tune with nature, in harmony with the elements, protective of the environment, supportive of life. Honest hard physical work produces the food that feeds life. That is true bread-labour lauded by Tolstoy, inspired by Bondareff, and sanctified by Gandhi's derivation of this commandment from the *Gītā*. Sacrifice is equated with bread-labour; and he who does not work with his hands is a thief who is not entitled to the food he eats. Manual work is the noblest mode of existential exertion, leading to an authentic experience of fulfilment! Gandhi's life of voluntary poverty was the translation of an ideal into reality. He stood for the primacy of man over machine! Productive, meaningful human employment is the only basis of human happiness! And we must realize that the earth's finite resources will not be able to withstand the onslaught of infinite human demand!

Gandhi found echoes of his ideas and ideals in Tolstoy. Like Tolstoy, he recoiled in horror at the sight of state violence. Like Tolstoy, he upheld the citizens' right to civil disobedience. On subjects such as modern civilization and industrialization, sex, and education in schools, his ideals ran fairly close to those of Tolstoy. They wrote to each other. Young Gandhi expressed his admiration and devotion; and the old man, assailed by intimations of mortality, was happy to endorse Gandhi's practical application of his ideas to current human situations.

Hind Swaraj, influenced by both Ruskin and Tolstoy, fired two salvoes, one aimed at the practitioners of violence and terror to rid India of the British yoke; and the other at the modern civilization of the West, including its imperial hegemony.

Gandhi's single-minded preoccupation in South Africa was the welfare of Indians; defence of their rights; and the demand for basic civil liberties. The opposition of the whites, and the fury of the white mob in Durban failed to dent his fortitude or curb his pride in the principles he espoused and fought for. It only helped to steel his purpose; shaped his ideas and his view of the world; and deepened his understanding of people's insecurities, fears and prejudices. The attacks, physical and political, some from the prejudiced pen of an Indian, P.S. Aiyar, added to his awareness and understanding of reality.

Alfred Milner and Jan Smuts treated his demands with undisguised contempt. If either of them had been empathetic and obliging, posterity might not have heard of any Gandhi. Oblivion might have engulfed the lawyer; the struggle might not have transpired; civil disobedience might not have come about; the *satyāgraha* might not have rocked the smooth course of white supremacy; and might not have been put to use in India to challenge the repressive might of the Raj. These are the teasing 'ifs' and 'buts' of history; of human nature and its responses to given situations; of its ability or otherwise to see right and curb its prejudice and selfishness to make room, even if ever so slight, for others' accommodation in bearable conditions of existence! The tug of war between the racist Smuts and the advocate of idealized British Imperialism produced the leader who went on to become a *Mahatma*. And if his white adversaries gave shape to his world-view, the murderous Pathans brought out his forgiveness and aspiration for Hindu-Muslim unity! There had been no one like him. There would perhaps be no one like him!

Gandhi awakened the poor, illiterate workers to a sense of their own worth and dignity; to the need for action to ameliorate their lot and mend their lives. He put them centre-stage in the theatre of political action to challenge the authors of remorseless exploitation and glaring injustice. His call galvanized the sleepy Tamils into a new awareness, into a new cycle of self-suffering to force their masters and the rulers of South Africa to realize the need for corrective action. They and the indentured workers from North India made him a leader of the poor; a leader of the masses. They made him one of their own in his dress and way of life. The labourers of Natal showed him what he could achieve by harnessing the power of the masses to rock the juggernaut of imperial oppression. They taught him, even as he taught them! The injection of the multitude into the social and political struggle made him the hero he was; the *Mahatma* he was! Their brave, stoic acceptance of loss of almost everything they had, and of punishment including jail and whipping and shooting, convinced him of their capacity, as of the masses in India, to wage an unflagging struggle for their honour, for their freedom, for their country. The idea of induction of the masses into the national conflict came from the successful participation of the indentured workers in the South African struggle. The cooperation and camaraderie of the Hindus and Muslims in South Africa fostered his faith in the possibility of Hindu-Muslim unity.

Class, caste, kin, religion and language created hurdles that impeded and discouraged dialogue and inter-mixture. Gandhi crossed all those barriers and fraternized specially with the classes that were discriminated against, and disadvantaged. The residents of Phoenix and Tolstoy farms came from all creeds and castes. Under his inspiration, owing to his exhortation, they bonded together in an all-inclusive social movement. Other forces and factors in a foreign land also militated against these divisions, blurring the lines of distinction. Gandhi's advice and example moved them all towards unity. In Natal, in the Transvaal, in the great strikes and the epic march of 1913, Indians of every religion, every class and caste, every province of the north, west and south, labourers, merchants and priests ate together, talked together, walked together, struggled together, and suffered together.

Not only that, Gandhi was the first man in history to bring Indian women to the forefront of social and political movements. He made them active participants in the *satyāgraha* as equal partners of men. They were always there right beside their men, to support, encourage and cheer them on; and to go to jail with them. Gandhi's contacts and close association with Western women like the articulate Millie Polak, and the intrepid Sonja Schlesin, convinced him that Indian women could also hold their own against men in the rough and tumble of social and political action. He could count many women among his friends.

He had seen the suffragettes at work in 1906 and 1911. That was no doubt an object lesson in passive resistance; in dour pertinacity; in courage and action! The Tamil women proved the truth of what he had seen in England by their resolution; by their freedom from fear; by their forthright support; by their tireless march and powers of persuasion to move the miners and plantation workers to join the struggle.

During the *satyāgrahas* in the Transvaal in 1907-10, almost 3000 Indians courted arrest and imprisonment. They were about 35% of the Indians residing in the colony. The most astonishing aspect of the struggle was the sight of merchants, the Gujaratis in particular, throwing caution to the winds, taking great political risks, defying authority, going to jail! Far away from their homeland, with no one to fall back upon, they cast their timidity aside to march into jail. Street hawkers, workers and professionals joined the *satyāgraha* regardless of the consequences; of the uncertainty about success! Why did they do it? How did they muster the courage to brave the lion in his den? They derived their strength from their leader, who was right beside them; and would lay down his life for them. Two attempts on his life had left him undaunted; and secured beyond any questioning his leadership credentials! He had progressed from self to the others. He had prepared himself to live for the Indian people, for their happiness and welfare, with which he identified his own. He was a true *Bodhisattva* in the sense that he would strive to march with them all to the promised millennium! Salvation would be a common achievement, equally shared.

There would indeed be no happiness, no arrival in isolation!

Gandhi's relations with the Chinese were revelatory in their vision. He brought them alongside; and made them march together with the Indians in pursuit of justice and fairness. They were present beside him in the Empire Theatre on September 11, 1906. They burnt their registration certificates together with the Indians. They courted arrest right beside them. When the passive resisters signed a pact with the Transvaal Government in January, 1908, there were three signatories, Gandhi, Thambi Naidoo, and Leung Quinn, the leader of the Chinese. Leung Quinn was even ahead of Gandhi when he said in a speech in Madras that the *Satyāgraha* was for 'the honour of Asia.'[1]

Gandhi became a matchless practitioner of patience and forbearance. He did not have a magic wand to cast a spell on the world and change it in an instant. He knew that change and improvement was always inevitably gradual, never immediate. It would necessarily be a saga of one step following another in the steady march towards the goal of racial equality. He lived with Europeans in his own house in South Africa to set for the whites an example of inter-racial living in love and harmony. He had great affection for his Indian and European friends, whose enthusiastic support for his causes made a difference! Ahmed Cachalia, Thambi Naidoo, Parsi Rustomji, Doke, Polak, Ritch, Kallenbach, West and Sonja Schlesin played pivotal roles in his campaigns; and the participation of his European friends in the *satyāgrahas* demonstrated the capacity of many whites to rise above the bigotry of race.

He brought his whole family in South Africa, including his wife, children and nephews, into the struggle as participants in the *satyāgraha*, subordinated like himself to the pursuit of his goals. It was a long-drawn-out exercise in self-control, self-suffering and self-sacrifice. It took two full decades to burnish his techniques and apply them with purposeful determination to finally achieve a measure of success, a sense of realization, an awareness of the power of non-violent protest and refusal to acquiesce in tyranny. But we must also recognize the vagaries of human nature. We may not hate anyone. We may not hurt anyone through our speech and action. We may truly love everyone. Yet, it may not lead to the desired goal of attracting their love, their acceptance, and their support. Gandhi,

---

1   Cf. Guha, *op.cit.*, p.539.

though, would never lose hope. He would never cease striving. He would never relinquish faith in human capacity to rise above self and selfishness to share equally the world and its resources for the happiness of entire humanity. Never say die! Never give up! Tenacious hope defies defeat; and tireless optimism induces right action, regardless of consequence! *Karma* only is your duty!!

His marriage survived owing to the forbearance, love and devotion of Kasturba, who was ever so often at the receiving end of his ire. Some would say it did, owing to her helplessness, as there was no viable alternative; no socially permissible course of action. But he, too, loved her, and was, after all, only human! She certainly helped make him the saint he became, the *Mahatma* the world worshipped. His *brahmacarya* was an aberration, an obsession, side by side with his concupiscence,[2] which he ceaselessly tried to smother and lull into deep slumber. All his pronouncements on its virtues and value violate the law of life and nature; and are definitely detrimental to mental composure! The prescription of celibacy for one and all including married couples is totally unacceptable, as it is depletive of equanimity, and of the free flow of love and life. The belief that celibacy leads to the acquisition of supernatural powers can only be sustained by superstitious faith not supported by any scientific proof, whatsoever!

He loved his sons, in his own way. He was harsh with the eldest, and strict with the others. He wanted them to be like him; to be his clones. He imposed his values on them; and gave them little choice. He denied them broad-based education; and taught them only what he considered worthwhile. They learned from him; and accidentally from the people and the world around them. They were normal young men gifted with intelligence and curiosity; animated by dreams and ambition; but held in check by his overbearing ideological dictation. There was not much non-violence in that attitude, not in a physical sense, but certainly in a psychological sense, in an ideological sense! It may also be seen as an attempt at deliberate mental conditioning, against which Harilal, the eldest son, finally rebelled. He courted arrest and imprisonment as many as six

---

2   Jad Adams tells us: 'When Gandhi was tormented by sexual thoughts, perhaps his impacted colon was pressing on his prostate gland and stimulating him sexually. This would explain why some diets, by reducing his constipation, would help him feel less sexual.' We do not know! See his *Gandhi: Naked Ambition*, p.92.

times as an active participant in the *satyāgraha*; but failed to please his father. The two came to differ in their values and view of life. Manilal and Ramdas also went to jail in the campaign. The younger sons succumbed to the father's beneficent despotism; and grew up to be responsible citizens of the world. Manilal gave his entire life to the cause of Indians in South Africa; and joined hands with the Africans to work for the liberation of both from white tyranny. He also ran the *Indian Opinion.* Devadas, the youngest, became Editor of a premier Indian daily, *The Hindustan times.*

Gandhi did injustice to Mehtab, the friend of his boyhood days, in his *Autobiography.* He mentions only his moral lapses, but not his participation in the Indian struggle in South Africa. His name is suppressed, supposedly so that his family might not be embarrassed. But it was immediately discovered and published by the reviewers and readers of the book. Despite his unique greatness, Gandhi was unable to forget and forgive!

He never intended to stay in South Africa for ever. He went back to India in 1901; and wanted to do so later. Circumstances held him back, as new challenges roused him to action. Made of common clay, he fashioned himself into the extraordinary human being that the world beheld. He forsook legal work for money; and handed over his lucrative practice to Ritch and Polak. He divested himself of all his property and belongings. He practised and preached simplicity; cut his needs and adopted an ascetic mode of hard-working life. Leisure and pleasure were deliberately discarded, as sugar, salt and spices, meat and alcohol were religiously cut out of his food and drinks. But he paid obsessive attention to his body by continually chopping, changing and regulating his diet, even though he regarded it as an impediment to God-realization. He practised and preached eating sparingly; distrusted modern medicine, and relied more on traditional and natural methods of treatment. He respected the environment, and stressed the need to conserve the earth's resources by containing and curtailing the ever increasing wants of humankind. He practised and preached patience in the pursuit of his objectives, only gradually pushing forward the bounds of possibility. *Satya* (truth), *ahiṁsā* (non-violence), and *satyāgraha* (soul-force insisting upon truth) became his instruments for deliverance from injustice and inequity! He devoted and dedicated his entire self to the cause of the oppressed Indians of Natal and the Transvaal. He did not matter. His family did not matter. They were all expendable in the struggle to improve the lot of his people in South Africa!

Gandhi's work in South Africa did not solve the country's problems for the foreseeable future; did not resolve the Indian question; and provided only partial relief from their many disabilities. And all that evaporated with the arrival and enthronement of the evils of apartheid. A new species of racial tyranny, utterly remorseless and ruthless, engulfed the vast majority of the country's population, blacks as well as coloureds. But Gandhi showed the way. He demonstrated the possibilities. His success, even though partial, and fleeting in the scale of time, nevertheless proved that the entrenched, standardized, systematized, enforced racial oppression could be challenged, and certainly made to bend!

Gandhi realized the limits of his ambition to remake the world. He said so in a letter he wrote to his friend Pranjivan Mehta from South Africa. He always knew it, with intense grief during his last days, before his assassination! That was the inescapable tragedy of his great life, as it would be of any other. But he never quietly sat down only to envision; he stood up, walked and worked to realize his ideals, as they took shape in the course of a life of breathless action. The splendour of his idealism arose out of his involvement in life and his unceasing struggle for justice. 'There always are in the world a few inspired men', said Plato, 'whose acquaintance is beyond price.'

Humankind did not exactly forsake their prejudices, hatred, cruelty and violence! But his example and his sacrifices did rouse many from their cold unconcern; and made the world a somewhat better place than the one he was born in. His goals are our goals. We must never give up. To do so is to discard the best of our human heritage, deny our duty, and diminish our humanity! Despair would defeat us. Undying hope, repeatedly reiterated in words, policies and action will help heal the wounds inflicted by human hatred and folly. Love must deliver!

No two individuals are ever identical in thought and belief. Difference is the essence of reality, the ineluctable truth of life. If we want to live in peace and harmony, we have no option but to be respectful, and accepting of difference, so long as the difference does not threaten our own autonomy to lead our lives according to our lights. Difference and dissent are always at centre-stage. We must learn to cope. Uniformity of thought and belief is a mirage we love to chase, but fail to find, establish or impose on others. Indeed, it is not even desirable, as it will make our lives insufferably dull! We must, therefore, live and let live. We must overcome mindless aversion; we must exorcise the poison of the past; we must unite the Hindu, Buddhist, Muslim, Sikh, Christian and the Jew in love, and live for one another without impinging on our respective religious practices. Different religions must co-exist in peace with one another; different races must live together in common accord, if humankind hanker for a future with a meaning, devoid of the acerbities and atrocities of the past! That is what Gandhi lived for. That was the burden of his life's song in South Africa! Truth in its entirety cannot be contained in a single formulation. It is dynamic; it evolves; it expands; and the Divine Voice cannot ever fall silent. Truth is the story of our spiritual evolution that knows no bounds and brooks no cessation! We cannot silence the voices that will go on expressing this Truth. Any prohibitions on free, exploratory and constructive speech detract from the scope of our certitude!

The man who said good-bye to South Africa had no resemblance with the young lawyer who had come to the country in 1893. The immaculately dressed man of the world was no longer there. The resident in houses of prestigious suburbs of Durban and Johannesburg was no longer there. The successful lawyer making money was no longer there. Replacing him was a very different person!

Gandhi had cast aside his formal western clothes, and wore a *kurta* and *lungi*, which identified him with the poorest of the poor indentured labourers. He had no money. Even his fares had been paid from the donations collected and sent by Gokhale. He was travelling third class with his wife Kasturba, and friend Kallenbach. He had no possessions to speak of. He had come to South Africa to make money. He did make money. He did acquire property. But he gave it all away!

When he came to South Africa, he was unknown, an obscure young man from an obscure corner of the world. But now he was known all over the world, lauded up to the sky in the country of his birth. His philosophy and his methods were already subjects of serious study both in the East and West. First mentioned as a *Mahatma* in addresses presented to him at Verulam, and in a letter that Pranjivan Mehta wrote to Gokhale, he had truly become one, but how? What made him a *Mahatma*? Not his birth, not his family heritage, not his legal credentials, but his capacity to identify himself with the poorest of the poor, the most oppressed of the oppressed! He did so in letter and spirit; in precept and practice; in his food and clothes; in his way of life marked by simplicity and austerity of his own choosing. He did so by his readiness to stand beside them; and suffer for and with them. He did so by his full-throated condemnation of the so-called custodians of class and caste, and of untouchability. Campaigning for human equality, and embracing self-suffering to awaken the dormant humanity of his opponents made him a *Mahatma*. The absence of any anger and bitterness towards his oppressors made him a *Mahatma*. His invincible optimism and faith in human perfectibility made him a *Mahatma*!

He sought to teach India's imperial masters the virtue of self-denial in their rule over India; to give primacy to India's welfare instead of their personal and national interests; and to rise above the concerns of British aggrandizement at the limitless expense of India. He sought to attempt and achieve the impossible, but never despaired; and refused to tire! The story of that epic endeavour will form the burden of the second volume of this loving undertaking.

Chapter 75

Postscript: Relevance of Gandhi

There is an inessential Gandhi, a subject of interest and curiosity for his idiosyncrasies and eccentricities, that often endear him to us, but also quite as often exasperate. And there is an essential Gandhi, who is as relevant today as he was in his day! If you believe in the brotherhood and sisterhood of humankind, if you believe in human equality, Gandhi is relevant; his life is relevant; his example is relevant; his precept is relevant. If you stand against discrimination based on race and colour, Gandhi is relevant. If you stand against class and caste, Gandhi is relevant. His contribution to the removal of untouchability in India and the equality of castes and classes was instrumental in the inclusion of these principles in the Constitution and laws of India. Affirmative discrimination in favour of the disadvantaged classes to right the wrongs of the past was due to his lead and inspiration.

If you stand for the equality of the sexes, Gandhi is relevant. He was the first man to bring Indian women to the forefront of the social and political fray. He campaigned against child marriages; for the education of women, and their participation in India's national life.

If you stand against the oppression of man by man, Gandhi is relevant. If you stand against the oppression and exploitation of one nation by another, Gandhi is your man. If you stand against violence and war, Gandhi is your man.

If you believe in religious tolerance, if you respect all religions, if you respect an individual's right to dissent, if you believe in loving, peaceful co-existence despite doctrinal differences, Gandhi is supremely relevant. He built bridges and promoted friendships between different religious communities; and had close Christian, Jewish and Muslim friends. From day one of his public life, he worked for establishing Hindu-Muslim unity; for the acceptance and celebration of religious diversity; for tolerance and respectful understanding; for fruitful, affectionate co-existence. That India is not a Hindu Pakistan is due not a little to his precept and practice; to his great suffering and sacrifice for the establishment of the principle that religion and the state would stay apart; and there would be no discrimination in favour of one against the other on grounds of religion. He gave his life for Hindu-Muslim unity; and we owe it to him never to tire in our pursuit of that goal.

He was a social reformer, reconciler of religions, and a promoter of inter-religious and inter-racial harmony through dialogue, as emperors Aśoka and Akbar had been in the past. He was also a freedom fighter. He did it all with the weapons of love and non-violence, with willing self-suffering to convince and convert the perpetrators of wrong. His life illustrated his role as a prophet of love, non-violence and peace.

He initiated non-violent resistance to injustice and social and state oppression. He rose and inspired his followers to rise with him against unjust laws and dictatorial regimes. In a world racked and riven by insensate violence, which is a travesty of our common humanity, and of all our religions, he became the great exemplar of *ahiṁsā* in all his campaigns. His freedom from fear, his forgiveness, and his infinite capacity for self-sacrifice should always inspire us! He believed in the same Divinity inhering all life, and hence the cultivation of the capacity to share all our joys and sorrows. Our destinies are intertwined. We cannot be happy in isolation!

He respected and promoted the languages of India; and insisted on the use of Indian languages in order to find and give expression to the heart and soul of India. That is a challenge and invitation to which India has yet to respond in full measure!

He stood for decency and decorum, courtesy and honesty in public debate. He wanted public life to be totally free from the taints of dishonesty and deceit. He wanted truth to be practised, rather than only spoken of!

He wanted to ensure work for the masses that would preserve their dignity and provide for their needs. He wanted to ensure the primacy of man over machine. He wanted everyone to work hard to earn his bread. He wanted to make sure that economic growth would not destroy the earth and its environment! If, therefore, you respect mother earth, and stand against conspicuous consumption regardless of consequences, the message of Gandhi is most relevant. It behoves us to protect the earth and her finite resources; limit our exploitation of her bounty; conserve her environment by cutting our needs and desisting from activity that threatens the future of the planet and all those who live on it. We owe it to ourselves, and all other living beings whose existence is threatened by our improvidence. Gandhi cut his needs and embraced austerity; and showed his respect for mother earth and the tiller of the soil by adopting his vocation to grow food for himself and others.

Human intelligence knows no limits; and human inventiveness continually explores new horizons. Automation advances apace; and artificial intelligence poses unknown threats to human autonomy. We cannot possibly put a brake on the progress of technology; but would do well to be mindful of the advice of Gandhi to preserve the primacy of man over machine! We cannot forget Gandhi. We shall do so at our own peril!

Glossary of Indian Words

Ahiṁsā	non-violence.
Ahmadiya	a Muslim sect; a person belonging to the sect.
Anekānta-vāda	many-sidedness of reality.
Aparigraha	non-posession.
Arya Samaj	a Hindu organization.
Ashram	retreat or centre established for the pursuit of spiritual and temporal goals.
Āśrama	stage of life. There are four stages specified.
Avatāra	incarnation of Divinity.
Āyurveda	Indian science of medicine.
Āyurvedic	belonging to Āyurveda.
Ba	mother in Gujarati. Ba was added to the name of Gandhi's wife Kastur.
Bania	a trading Hindu caste.
Bapu	father. Gandhi is often called Bapu.
Bhai	brother.
Bhajan	devotional songs.
Bhakti	devotional worship.
Bhangi	scavenger. They were treated as untouchables.

Brahma	Ultimate Reality.
Brāhmaṇa	the priestly class in ancient Indian social classification.
Brahmacarya	celibacy. First stage of life.
Brahmin	the priestly caste. Popular spelling.
Caraka	an ancient authority on Indian medicine.
Chaturmās	four months of the rainy season.
Caitra	month of Hindu calendar. Coincides with the beginning of Spring.
Daal	lentils.
Darshan	view of a deity or person conferring merit.
Dhamma	duty; code of conduct.
Dharma	duty, code of conduct, religion.
Dharmaśālā	charitable inn built for pilgrims and travellers.
Dashehrā	a Hindu festival celebrating the victory of good over evil.
Diwan	prime-minister.
Durbar	court.
Gṛhastha	household, householder. The second stage of life.
Hakīm	*doctor.*
Harṭāl	strike, signifying suspension of work.
Haveli	a substantial building. The word is often used for temples in Gujarat.
Iṣṭa-devatā	personally preferred name of God.
Jaina, Jain	follower of the Jaina religion; pertaining to the Jaina religion.

Glossary of Indian Words

Jāti	caste.
Kṣatriya	the warrior class in ancient Indian social classification.
Kurta	tunic.
Kula-devatā	family deity.
Mahatma	great soul.
Moha	attachment.
Mokṣa	salvation.
Mung	lentils.
Munshi	clerk.
Niyoga	union of man and woman for the limited purpose of procreation.
Paṇḍā	priest.
Purda	seclusion of women
Praṇāmī	a Hindu sect.
Ṛṣi	sage.
Sādhu	hermit.
Saṁnyāsa/Sannyāsa	the fourth stage of life signifying renunciation of worldly pursuits.
Saṁsāra	transmigration. Process of reincarnation.
Sarvodaya	welfare of all, as opposed to the greatest good of the greatest number.
Śāstra	sacred text.
Satya	truth.
Satyāgraha	insistence upon truth; soul-force.

Sheth	a wealthy person or merchant.
Śikhā	a knot of hair at the top of the head.
Śūdra	the fourth class in ancient Indian social classification.
Swadeshī	home-made.
Swāmī	a recluse.
Swarāj	self-rule.
Vaidya	doctor.
Vaishnava	of God Viṣṇu.
Vakil	lawyer.
Varṇa	a class in social classification. There are four *varṇas: Brāhmaṇa, Kṣatriya, Vaiśya* and *Śūdra*.

Note: We have retained the common spellings of many words in popular use.

Select Bibliography

Adams, Jad, *Gandhi: Naked Ambition,* Quercus, London, 2010

Andrews, C.F., *Mahatma Gandhi's Ideas,* Allen and Unwin, London, 1931

Anonymous, *M.K. Gandhi: A Sketch of His Life and Work,* G.A. Natesan & Co., Madras, 1910

Ashe, Geoffrey, *Gandhi A Study in Revolution,* Heinemann, London, 1968

Bhana, Surendra, and Joy Brain, *Setting Down Roots: Indian Migrants in South Africa, 1860- 1911,* Witwatersrand University Press, Johannesburg, 1990

Bhana, S., and G.Vahed, *The Making of Political Reformer Gandhi in South Africa 1893-1914,* Manohar, New Delhi, 2005

Bhandarkar, D.R., *Aśoka,* Calcutta University, Calcutta, 1955

The Bhagavad Gītā according to Gandhi, translated by Mahadev Desai, Important Books, USA, 2013

Bondurant, Joan V., *Conquest of Violence: The Gandhian Philosophy of Conflict,* University of California Press, Berkeley, 1971

Brown, Judith M., *Gandhi: Prisoner of Hope,* Yale University Press, New Haven and London, 1989

Brown, Judith M., and Anthony Parel, *The Cambridge Companion to Gandhi,* Cambridge University Press, Cambridge, 2011

Chadha, Yogesh, *Rediscovering Gandhi,* Century, London, 1997

Chatterjee, Margaret, *Gandhi and His Jewish Friends,* Macmillan, London, 1992

Chaturvedi, Banarasi Das, and Marjorie Sykes, *Charles Freer Andrews; A Narrative,* Allen and Unwin, London, 1949. Printed in India by Publications Division, Government of India, Delhi, 1982

Collins, Larry, and Dominique Lapierre, *Freedom at Midnight,* Collins, London, 1975

de Waal, Frans, *The Bonobo and the Atheist: In Search of Humanism Among the Primates*, Norton, New York, 2013

    Are We Smart Enough to know How Smart Other Animals Are? Granta Books, London, 2016

    Good Natured, Harvard University Press, Harvard, 1997

    Primates and Philosophers, Princeton University Press, Princeton, 2009

Desai, Ashwin, and Goolam Vahed, *Inside Indenture: A South African Story, 1860-1914,* Madiba Publishers, Durban, 2007

Desai, Mahadev, *The Diary of Mahadev Desai,* Vol.1, translated by V.G. Desai, Navajivan, Ahmedabad, 1953

Dhupelia-Mesthrie, Uma, *Gandhi's Prisoner? The Life of Gandhi's Son Manilal,* Kwela Books, Cape Town, 2004

Erikson, Erik H., *Gandhi's Truth: On the Origins of Militant Nonviolence,* W.W. Norton &Co, New York, 1969

Fischer, Louis, *The Life of Mahatma Gandhi,* Harper and Brothers, New York, 1950

    Gandhi: His Life and Message for the World, A Mentor Book, New American Library, New York, 1954

    The Essential Gandhi, An Anthology: His Life, Work and Ideas, Vintage Books, New York, 1962

Gandhi, M.K., 'The Foods of India', originally published in the *Vegetarian Messenger*, 1 May 1891; *Collected Works*, Vol.1

    Guide to London, Collected Works, Vol. 1

Select Bibliography

India of My Dreams, Rajpal, New Delhi, 2009

Hind Swaraj or Indian Home Rule, Navajivan, Ahmedabad, 1990

An Autobiography or The Story of My Experiments with Truth. Translated from the original in Gujarati by Mahadev Desai, Navajivan Trust, 1927, Reprint, 1959

Speeches and Writings of M.K. Gandhi: with an *Introduction* by C.F. Andrews, a *Tribute* by G.A. Natesan, a *Biographical Sketch* by Mr H.S.L. Polak, G.A. Natesan & Co., Madras, 1918

Collected Works of Mahatma Gandhi, 100 Volumes, The Publications Division, Ministry of Information and Broadcasting, Government of India, 1958 onwards.

Vol.1, 1958

Vol.2, 1959

Vol.3, 1960

Vol.4, 1960

Vol.5, 1961

Vol.6, 1961

Vol.7, 1962

Vol.8, 1962

Vol.9, 1963

Vol.10, 1963

Vol.11, 1964

Vol.12, 1964

Vol.29, 1968

Satyagraha in South Africa, Translated from Gujarati by Valji Govindji Desai, S. Ganesan, Madras, 1928. Third Edition, Navajivan, Ahmedabad, 1961, reproduced in Collected Works,

Vol. 29, 1968

All Men are Brothers: Life and Thoughts of Mahatma Gandhi in His Own Words, Unesco, Melbourne University Press, Melbourne, 1959

Gandhi, Rajmohan, *The Good Boatman: A portrait of Gandhi*, Viking, New Delhi, 1995

Gandhi The Man, His People and the Empire, Haus Books, London, 2007

Gandhi, Prabhudas, *My Childhood with Gandhiji*, Navajivan, Ahmedabad, 1957

Gokhale, Gopal Krishna, *Speeches and Writings of Gopal Krishna Gokhale*, G A Natesan & Co., Third Edition, Madras (after 1916?)

Gora, *An Atheist with Gandhi*, Navajivan, Ahmedabad, 1951

Guha, Ramachandra, *Gandhi Before India*, Allen Lane, Penguin Books, London, 2013

Henning, C.G., *The Indentured Indian in Natal 1860-1917*, Promilla & Co., New Delhi, 1993

Holms, Bob, 'The Making of Morality', *New Scientist*, 18 May 2013

Holmes, John, *My Gandhi*, Harper and Brothers, New York, 1953

Hughes, Heather, *First President: A Life of John L. Dube, Founding Father of the ANC.*, Jacana, Auckland Park, South Africa, 2011

Hunt, James D., *Gandhi in London*, Revised Edition, Promilla & Co., New Delhi, 1993

Gandhi and the Nonconformists in South Africa, Promilla & Co., New Delhi, 1986

Iyer, Raghavan N., *The Moral and Political Thought of Mahatma Gandhi*, OUP, New York, 1973

Jack, Homer A., (ed.), *The Wit and Wisdom of Gandhi*, The Beacon Press, Boston, 1951 (ed.), *The Gandhi Reader: A Source Book of His Life and Writings,* Dennis Dobson, London, 1958

Laidlaw, James, *Riches and Renunciation: Religion, Economy and Society among the Jains,* Clarendon Press, Oxford, 1955

Lelyveld, Joseph, *Great Soul: Mahatma Gandhi and His Struggle with India,* Alfred A. Knopf, New York, 2011

Lev, Shimon, *Soulmates: The Story of Mahatma Gandhi and Hermann Kallenbach,* Orient BlackSwan, New Delhi, 2012

Malabari, Behrami M., *The Indian Eye on English Life,* London, 1893

Mehta, Mansukhlal, R., (ed.), *Shrimad Rajchandra,* a Gujarati book, 1914

Mehta, P.J., *M.K. Gandhi and the South African Indian Problem,* G.A. Natesan and Co., Madras, 1912

Morton, Eleanor, *Women Behind Mahatma Gandhi,* Max Reinhardt, London, 1954

Mukherjee, R., (ed.), *The Penguin Gandhi Reader,* Penguin Books India, 1993

Nanda, B.R., *Mahatma Gandhi: A Biography,* OUP, Oxford, 1958. Reprinted, Allen and Unwin, London, 1965

O'Connor, Daniel, *Gospel, Raj and Swaraj: The Missionary Years of C.F. Andrews (1904-14),* Peter Lang, Frankfurt, 1990

Oldfield, Josiah, 'My Friend Gandhi', in Chandra Shankar Shukla, (ed.), *Reminiscences of Gandhiji,* Vora & Co., Bombay, 1951

Parikh, Nilam, *Gandhiji's Lost Jewel: Harilal Gandhi,* National Gandhi Museum, New Delhi, 2001

Polak, H.S.L., *The Indians of South Africa: Helots Within the Empire and How They are Treated,* G.A. Natesan & Co., Madras, 1909

Polaks, H.S.L. and M.G., 'Mohandas Karamchand Gandhi: Greatest Figure in Modern India', in Rushbrook Williams (ed.), *Great Men of India,* The Home Library Club, The Times of India, The Statesman Associated Papers of Ceylon Ltd., Bombay, 1939

Polak, H.S.L., H.N. Brailsford and Lord Pethick-Lawrence, *Mahatma Gandhi*, Oldhams Press Ltd., London, 1949

Polak, Millie Graham, *Mr. Gandhi: The Man*, Allen & Unwin, London, 1931

Pyarelal, *Mahatma Gandhi*, Vol. 1, *The Early Phase*, Navajivan Publishing House, Ahmedabad, 1986

Rajagopalachari, C., (ed.), *Mr. Gandhi's Jail Experiences: Told by Himself*, T. Adinarayana Cetti, Salem, 1913

Ray, S., (ed.), *Gandhi, India and the World*, Nachiketa Publishing Ltd., Bombay, 1970

Rolland, Romain, *Mahatma Gandhi*, Allen & Unwin, London, 1924

Sarid, Isa, and Christian Bartolf, *Hermann Kallenbach: Mahatma Gandhi's Friend in South Africa*, Gandhi Informations Zentrum, Berlin, 1997

Sheean, Vincent, *Lead Kindly Light*, Random House, New York, 1949

Shirer, William, *Gandhi A Memoir*, Simon and Schuster, New York, 1979

Singh, Sarva Daman, *Polyandry in Ancient India*, Motilal Banarsidass, Delhi, 1988

'Terracottas from Manwā Ḍīh (Sitapur)', in *Journal of the U.P. Historical Society*, Vol. XVIII (N.S.), Parts 1-2, Lucknow, 1970, pp.1-5.

Singh, Sarva Daman, and Mahavir Singh, (ed.), *Indians Abroad*, Published by Maulana Abul Kalam Azad Institute of Asian Studies, Kolkata, Hope India Publications/ Greenwich Millennium, Gurgaon and London, 2003

Tähtinen, Unto, *Ahiṁsā: Non-violence in Indian Tradition*, Navajivan, Ahmedabad, 1983

Tendulkar, D.G., *Mahatma: Life of Mohandas Karamchand Gandhi*, in Eight Volumes.

Volume One 1869-1920., Published by V.K. Jhaveri & D.G. Tendulkar, Bombay, 1951

Tidrick, Kathryn, *Gandhi: A Political and Spiritual Life,* I.B. Taurus, London, 2006

Upadhyaya, J.M., *Mahatma Gandhi as a Student,* Publications Division, Government of India, New Delhi, 1965

Mahatma Gandhi: A Teacher's Discovery, Sardar Patel University, Vallabh Vidyanagar, 1969

Woodcock, George, *Gandhi,* Fontana/ Collins, London, 1974

Wyllie, John, *India at the Parting of the Ways,* Lincoln Williams, London, 1934

Index

A

Aafreedi, Navras J. xi

Abdul Gani, Sheth 92

Abdulla Haji Adam 147

Abdulla Sheth 89, 91, 110, 213. *See also* Dada Abdulla

Abdurahman, Dr. 468, 496

Act of 1885, amended in 1886 100

Adam, Sheth Abdul Karim Haji 147

Adams, Jad 27, 28, 108, 196, 522, 535

Adams, James Matthew 135

Africans x, 88, 132, 138, 275, 297, 325, 380, 452, 463, 498, 499, 500, 501, 502, 503, 504, 523

Aga Khan 371

Agra 182

Ahiṁsā 8, 15, 16, 17, 27, 30, 32, 39, 79, 84, 107, 133, 140, 157, 158, 161, 191, 238, 250, 347, 366, 367, 370, 402, 468, 473, 502, 506, 508, 523, 528

Ahmedabad 4, 17, 24, 43, 79, 85, 159, 242, 349, 399, 401, 506, 536, 537, 538, 540

Aiyar, P.S., Durban journalist 397, 411, 421, 430, 454

Ajīva 107

Alam, Mir 289, 290, 309, 330

Alcohol 22, 35, 70, 130, 292, 294, 364, 365, 491, 493, 503, 523

Alexander, Mrs 149, 151, 489

Alexander, R.C., 207

Alexandra Tea Room 208

Allinson, Thomas 58, 63

Ally, Haji Ojer 274

Ambulance Corps 163, 164, 165, 179, 208, 248, 249, 252

Ameer Ali 274

Ampthill, Lord 325, 331, 332, 333, 338, 395, 433, 461, 479

Amrit Bazar Patrika 143

Andhra 378

Andrews, C.F. 372, 469, 476, 537, 539

Anekāntavāda, many-sidedness of reality 39, 517

Anglia, M.C. 326, 449

Anglo-Boer war 179

Anjuman-e-Islam, later called the Pan-Islamic Society 70

Annie Besant, Mrs 65, 66, 70, 182, 343, 392

Aparigraha, non-possession 18, 194, 195, 197, 517

Ape-ancestors 365

Apramāda, diligence 209

Arabic 86

Arabs 87, 100

Ārya Samāj 201, 202

Āsavas 364

Ashe, Geoffrey 23, 57

Asiatic Department 187, 188, 190, 191

Asiatic peril 243

Aśoka 14, 16, 66, 201, 528, 535

Aśoka's *dhamma* 14

Aswat, Ebrahim Ismail 298

Atharva Veda 20

Atheists 69

Ātman, the soul 201, 262

Australia xii, 321, 377, 413

Avoca 463

Azad, Maulana Abul Kalam Azad 19, 540

B

Baby Christ 25

Badri 198, 213

Bai Fatima 448

Baker, A. W., Attorney 94

Balasundaram 122, 123, 124, 125, 143, 443

Balfour 460

Bambatha, Zulu Leader 248, 363

Banaras viii, 177, 180, 181, 182, 337, 343

Banerji, Kalicharan 178

Banerji, Surendranath 143, 280

Bangabasi 143

Bania 50, 531

Bannerji, W.C. 70

Bannerman, Sir Henry 276

Bapoo 458

Bapu 336, 368, 531

Bartolf, Christian 461, 540

Basutoland Star 287

Bazaars 240

Beach Grove 119, 132

Becharji Swami, a Jaina Monk 50

Belur math 179

Bengal 179, 200, 343, 348, 370, 429

Bengal Club 143

Bengal's partition 348

Bhai 17, 39, 389, 460, 531

INDEX

Bhajan 531

Bhakti 531

Bhana, S 293, 409, 442, 535

Bhandarkar, D.R. 201, 535

Bhandarkar, R.G. 142

Bhaṅgī, untouchable scavenger 514

Bharata 198

Bharati, Agehananda 201

Bhartṛhari 257, 360, 513

Bhatt, Shamal 66

Bhavnagar 49

Bhav Singh Ji 80

Bhīṣma 261, 508

Bhownaggree, Sir M. 242, 274, 276, 315, 332, 339

Bible 42, 66, 95, 107, 108, 287, 326

Bipin Chandra Pal 316, 337

Birdwood, Sir George 275

Bishop of Madras 469

Blavatsky, Madame 65, 70, 108

Blount 363

Bodhisattva 31, 506

Boers 163, 164, 187, 188, 240, 275, 277, 288, 321

Bohras 87

Bombay 90, 131, 137, 141, 174, 183, 234, 276

Booth, Dr. 162, 249, 443

Botha, Louis 277, 278, 285, 288, 310, 324, 371, 412, 418, 419, 430, 465, 488, 489, 492, 494

Bradlaugh, Charles 65, 69

Brahmacārī 12, 254, 255

Brahmacarya viii, ix, x, 168, 251, 252, 258, 320, 506, 511, 532

Brāhmaṇa, class 532, 534

Brahman, ultimate reality 253, 254, 498, 508

Brahmin, caste 5, 42, 50, 181, 510, 532

Brailsford, H.N. 419, 540

Brain, Joy 442, 535

Bṛhaspati 260

British Indian Association 266, 271, 279, 308, 314, 327, 328, 431, 441, 491, 492

British Parliament 70, 114, 115, 241, 242, 349, 366

British rule over India due to Divine Will 246

Broom, Herbert 56

Brown, Judith 409, 535

Buddha 7, 65, 66, 92, 201, 209, 295, 506

Buddhism 13, 40, 201, 293

Burma 179

C

Cachalia, A.M. 316, 326, 327, 328, 431, 441, 447, 460, 491, 492, 494, 521

Caitra, name of a month 41, 532

Calcutta viii, 136, 137, 143, 144, 174, 175, 177, 178, 179, 180, 201, 343, 411, 535

Cama, Nadeshir 328

Canada 321, 338, 345, 377

Cape Colony 88, 163, 321, 374

Cape Town 188, 329, 369, 371, 414, 415, 437, 482, 483, 484, 488, 496, 497, 536

Carlyle 17, 67, 131, 287, 326

Carpenter, Edward 60, 345

Carpenter, Mary 70

Cartwright, Albert 287, 298, 307, 310

Caxton Hall 315

Ceylon 164, 187, 188, 395, 539

Ceylon Civil Service 188

Chadha, Yogesh 272, 535

Chamberlain, Joseph 115, 150, 153, 154, 186, 187, 188

Chamney, Montford 271, 281, 283, 290, 297, 298, 299, 302, 303, 309, 458, 495

Chanchal, wife of Harilal 267, 323, 403, 437

Charlestown 91, 454, 455, 456, 457, 493

Chatterjee, Margaret 210, 535

Chaturmas 38

Chaturvedi, Banarsidas 476, 477, 478, 481, 483

Chesney, Editor of Pioneer 137

Chesterton, G.K. 66, 344, 347

Chettiar, V.A. 328

Chirol, Sir Valentine 469

Christ 7, 23, 25, 96, 106, 107, 108, 151, 178, 244, 285, 287, 288, 367, 469, 480

Christian 16, 25, 45, 62, 65, 66, 71, 95, 96, 106, 107, 108, 109, 112, 131, 139, 156, 159, 178, 194, 208, 235, 284, 285, 286, 314, 339, 367, 379, 381, 386, 392, 395, 427, 445, 461, 497, 501, 510, 525, 528, 540

Christian convention 106

Christianity vii, 14, 16, 45, 57, 60, 65, 73, 95, 96, 97, 106, 108, 109, 134, 288, 293, 385, 416, 428, 480, 517

Churchgate 185

Churchill, Winston 276, 331

Coach journey 91

Coates, Michael 95, 109, 207

Collins, Larry 24, 536

Colonial-Born Indian Educational Association 121

Congress, Indian National 70, 120, 174, 200, 279, 280, 331, 348,

INDEX

370, 406, 411, 429, 476

Congress, Natal Indian 121, 122, 127, 128, 134, 155

Coolie barrister 88

Coolie Locations viii, 212

Coolie merchants 88

Coolies 126

Coomaraswamy, Ananda 316

Coovadia, E.S. 265

Cotton, Sir Henry 274

Courier Mail 13

Cow protection 351

Cox, Harold 274

Crossing of the Natal border into Transvaal 457

Curzon, Lord 177, 242, 324, 332, 505, 508

D

Dada Abdulla 81, 86, 91, 102, 104, 107, 117, 125, 135, 145, 146. *See also* Abdulla Sheth

Dada Abdulla & Co 81, 125

Dadabhai Naoroji 53, 70, 71, 114, 115, 154, 241, 274, 276, 341, 348, 363, 421, 515

Daily News 55

Daily Telegraph 55, 143

Dalal, Chandulal Bhagubhai 399

Dallow, Edward 398

Dama, Self control 506

Dannhauser 452, 453

Darśana, perception 5, 329

Dashehra, festival 455

Das, Taraknath 345

Datta, V.N. 332

Dave, Kevalram 183

Dawkins, Richard 3

Dayal, Bhawani 313, 451

Dealers' Licences Act 152

Death of Lakshmidas, Gandhi's brother 483

Delagoa Bay 210, 377, 393, 400

Desai, Ashwin 445, 448, 465, 536

Desai, Mahadev 13, 17, 23, 182, 535, 536

Desai, Pragji 381, 400, 401

Desai, Purushottamdas 314

Deshpande, M.S. 18

Despard, Charlotte French Mrs. 335

Devadas, Gandhi's son 410

de Waal, Frans 536

Dharmaśālā, a house of charity 445

Dharmavicāra 131

Dhingra, Madanlal 331, 332, 345, 357

Dick, Miss 190, 209

Dilke, Sir Charles 275

Dinizulu, Zulu Chief 377, 500

Dīrghatamas 260

DiSalvo, Charles 30, 65, 78, 104, 113, 116, 119, 125, 126, 127, 135, 136, 138, 153, 154, 163, 164, 165, 191, 240, 241, 243, 244, 266, 270, 271, 273, 278, 281, 282, 284, 285, 289, 290, 301, 311, 312, 354, 394

Diwan, prime minister 35, 36, 44, 50, 532

Doctors 20, 184, 204, 234, 254, 277, 320, 349, 350, 354, 355, 362

Doke, Joseph J. Rev. 213, 250, 286, 322, 327, 338, 347, 440

Doke's Biography of Gandhi 366

Doke's death 440

Droṇācārya, teacher in *Mahabharata* 360

Dube, John L., Zulu Leader 232, 246, 286, 406, 407, 418, 452, 467, 500, 501, 538

Duncan, Patrick 270, 271

Dundee 417, 452, 454, 459, 460

Durban 86, 89, 108, 418, 442, 447, 451, 467, 471, 477, 488, 491, 518

Dutt, R. C. 361, 363

Dvivedi, M.N. 194

E

Earth and Water Cures viii, 203

Education of Sons 236

Edwards, William Douglas 56

Ekalavya, rejected pupil of Droṇācārya 360

Elgin, Lord 128, 129, 274, 276, 277

Emerson 17, 326

Erikson, Erik 24, 25, 48, 72, 250, 386, 536

Escombe, Harry 119, 146, 147, 148, 150, 152, 155

Esoteric Christian Union 71

Esselen, Edward 471

Essop Mia 279, 280, 494

European Friends viii

Evidence Act 77

Experiments with Truth 4, 36, 85, 537

F

Fabian Society 60, 70

Failure of Diplomacy 336

Faith in Human Equality viii, 192

Fasting 208, 234, 254, 255, 295, 388, 389, 390, 438

Fischer, Abraham, Minister of the Interior 431

Fischer, Louis 14, 23, 536

Fitzpatrick, Sir Percy 310

G

Gaekwar 358, 469

INDEX

Gandhi, Chhaganlal 400, 413, 444, 484

Gandhi, Karamchand, called Kaba, Gandhi's father 35

Gandhi, Maganlal 186, 232, 261, 324, 368, 380, 396, 400, 401, 444, 446, 468, 469

Gandhi, Mohandas Karamchand, Mahatma 51

    Born on October 2, 1869 37

    Married at 13 46

    Passed the Matriculation Examination 49

    Three oaths, not to touch meat, wine and women abroad 50

    Set sail for Great Britain 51

    Three definitions of meat in England 61

    Called to the bar 71

    Left for South Africa 186

    Asked to take off his turban 124

    Pushed out of a train 90

    Assaulted by coach conductor 93

    Kicked into the street by policeman 100

    Resolution of Abdulla's case 104

    True practice of law 104

    Spiritual Quickening 106

    Persuaded to stay on 111

    Founded Natal Indian Congress 120

    Rescue of Balasundaram 125, 443

    Wrote *The Green Pamphlet* 138

    Pelted with 'stones, brickbats and rotten eggs' 149

    As a Householder 156

    As the father 161

    Faith in Human Equality 192

    Launched *Indian Opinion* 199

    Established Phoenix 232

    Gandhi and the British 504

    Organised an ambulance corps 248

    Mass meeting on Sep. 11, 1906 134

    Beginning of passive resistance 18, 261, 279, 280, 300, 310, 313, 323, 329, 338, 343, 344, 348, 357, 358, 366, 370, 395, 397, 398, 399, 406, 408, 420, 426, 428, 431, 432, 433, 434, 441, 447, 448, 449, 452, 454, 461, 465, 468, 481, 489, 495, 520

    Went to jail, January 10, 1908 286

    Attacked by Mir Alam 290

    Attacked once more 296

    Speech at Johannesburg YMCA 297

    Burning of certificates 312

Jailed on October 14, 1908 315

   Jailed on February 25, 1909 324

   Wrote Hind Swaraj between Nov. 13 and 22, 1909 344

   Established Tolstoy farm 378

   Led Great March of 1913 210

   In the garb of an indentured worker on Dec 22, 1913 123, 443, 464

   Deal with Smuts 304

   Left South Africa on Jul 18, 1914 213

Gandhi, Prabhudas 327, 438, 538

Gandhi, Rajmohan 26, 27, 28, 49, 108, 186, 199, 210, 276, 280, 296, 315, 327, 348, 367, 380, 403, 416, 418, 445, 449, 456, 458, 464, 472, 477, 485, 538

Gandhi, Uttamchand, Gandhi's grandfather, known as Ota Bapa 35

Ganges 143

Gani, Sheth Abdul 93

General strike 465, 479

Ghose, Aurobindo 343

Ghoshal, Janakinath 176

Ghosh, Rash Behari 280

Gibson, J.C. 373

Girmit, agreement of indenture 87

Girmitiyas, indentured workers 87

Gītā, Bhagavad 194

Gladstone, Lord, Governor-General 419, 433, 479, 480, 482

Gladstone, Mr. 169

Gladstone, Mrs. 169

God 181, 183, 185, 195, 201, 206, 235, 253, 262, 289, 331, 351, 391, 419, 455, 495

Godfrey, William 275

Gokhale, G.K. ix, 76, 101, 142, 143, 166, 171, 176, 177, 178, 179, 180, 183, 185, 200, 209, 280, 341, 342, 343, 348, 369, 370, 371, 372, 374, 375, 376, 392, 400, 403, 414, 415, 416, 417, 418, 419, 420, 421, 422, 423, 430, 431, 433, 434, 446, 449, 453, 457, 459, 461, 462, 463, 467, 468, 469, 474, 476, 478, 481, 482, 484, 485, 488, 489, 501, 525, 538

Golden Pagoda, Rangoon 179

Gondal 469

Goodeve, Louis A. 56

Govindji, Jayshanker 326

Gregorowski, R. 270

Gregson, F.S.K. 479

Greylingstaad 458, 460

Gṛhastha, Householder viii, 156, 258, 532

Griffin, Sir Lepel 274, 276

Guha, Ramachandra 30, 31, 38, 44, 49, 60, 69, 71, 79, 87, 88, 132, 133, 145, 146, 151, 152, 154, 155, 163, 170, 175, 179, 208,

240, 242, 261, 268, 270, 271, 273, 274, 277, 280, 283, 286, 287, 293, 294, 298, 304, 307, 310, 313, 317, 321, 325, 326, 329, 330, 339, 340, 341, 343, 366, 369, 371, 372, 392, 393, 397, 398, 400, 402, 406, 415, 418, 419, 422, 429, 430, 431, 433, 435, 436, 437, 442, 448, 453, 454, 455, 458, 459, 461, 462, 467, 468, 469, 470, 474, 477, 479, 481, 482, 483, 484, 485, 487, 496, 497, 521, 538

Gujarat 35, 39, 87, 342, 378, 401, 532

Gujarati 43, 57, 64, 103, 107, 159, 161, 199, 203, 231, 237, 239, 246, 247, 269, 313, 314, 324, 325, 326, 330, 333, 337, 346, 366, 382, 387, 391, 399, 401, 403, 413, 418, 425, 448, 473, 474, 489, 490, 491, 492, 495, 517, 531, 537, 539

Gustave Eiffel's Iron Tower 67

H

Habib, Haji 272, 328, 329

Hajee Amod Johari 413

Hamidiya Islamic Society 271, 285

Hammik, Sir Murray 469

Hancock, F. D. 469

Hanifabai 449

Hanna Lazar 292, 408

Hardinge, Lord 177, 470, 474, 488, 489, 493

Harijan 7, 9, 13

Harilal ix, 234, 236, 267, 268, 296, 305, 306, 311, 323, 324, 325, 337, 359, 399, 400, 401, 402, 403, 404, 437, 438, 447, 478, 484, 486, 508, 522, 539

Hariścandra 42

Harṭāl, strike, withdrawal of support and services 274, 282

Hattingspruit 451, 454

Haveli 38, 532

Hay, Stephen 40

Het Volk, the Boer Party 277, 468

Hey Ram, an exclamation 30

High Court, Bombay 77, 79, 104, 185, 186

Himalaya 143

Hindi, India's national language 25, 199, 237, 326, 360, 382, 387, 424, 451, 474

Hind Swaraj ix, 19, 338, 347, 348, 349, 353, 354, 356, 358, 360, 363, 365, 366, 367, 368, 381, 403, 516, 518, 537

Hinduism 13, 14, 16, 40, 42, 44, 45, 65, 73, 95, 107, 131, 179, 200, 201, 257, 293, 385, 509, 517

Hindu Law 77

Hindu-Muslim unity in India 280

Hindus 10, 15, 43, 45, 69, 87, 98, 112, 156, 192, 212, 279, 291, 314, 324, 326, 341, 342, 346, 350, 351, 352, 353, 364, 378, 385, 393, 405, 415, 489, 491, 506, 509, 514, 519

Hindustani 137, 271

Hiuen-Tsang 509

Hobhouse, Emily 474

Holmes, John 23, 538

Hosken, William 278, 283, 307, 310, 322, 398, 416, 471

Hotel Cecil 276

House of Commons 69, 115, 335

Hughes, Heather 467, 538

Humanitarian League 60

Hunter, W.W. 114

Hunt, James D. 273, 275

Hurbatsingh 473

Huxley 287, 359

Hygiene 138, 380

I

Illustrated London News 344

Immigration Restriction Act 152, 153

Imperial Legislative Council of India 374

Indenture 87, 123, 128, 129, 138, 374, 375, 411, 448, 454, 466, 473, 490, 491

Indermaur, John 56

India Club 175, 177

Indian Ambulance Corps 163, 179, 208, 248, 249

Indian Marriages 426

Indian Opinion viii, 140, 199, 200, 203, 209, 210, 213, 231, 232, 233, 241, 243, 244, 245, 246, 249, 261, 266, 270, 273, 274, 279, 280, 282, 283, 285, 290, 296, 301, 306, 314, 322, 326, 328, 330, 332, 337, 344, 367, 369, 371, 372, 378, 379, 391, 392, 393, 398, 405, 406, 407, 413, 415, 417, 418, 425, 426, 427, 428, 429, 430, 432, 433, 438, 440, 443, 445, 449, 450, 452, 455, 456, 461, 462, 466, 468, 470, 473, 474, 476, 477, 492, 495, 500, 501, 508, 510, 517, 523

Indians 485, 488, 491, 493, 494, 496, 501, 503, 514

Indians' Relief Act 484, 485

Inner Temple 55

Insurance policy, Gandhi's 195, 196

Irving, Washington 131

Isaacs, Gabriel 210, 322

Islam 19, 70, 86, 107, 201, 385, 387, 517

Īśopaniṣad 13

Iṣṭa-devatā, personally favoured name of God 42

Iyer, Raghavan N. 14, 26, 538

J

Jaina 39, 50, 107, 201, 262, 294, 347, 532

Jainism 13, 39, 40, 201, 257, 506, 517

Jains 44, 170, 539

INDEX

Jaipur 182

Jamnagar 183

Jeki (Jayakunvar), daughter of Pranjivan Mehta 436, 437, 438, 444, 486, 487

Jesus 58, 95, 96, 106, 109, 137, 178, 196, 285, 286, 367, 489

Jews 192, 209, 210, 212, 275, 294, 413, 424, 462, 513, 514

Jhaveri, Abdul Karim 81

Jinnah, M.A. 18, 19, 24, 31, 152, 341, 376

Jīva 107

Johannesburg viii, ix, 91, 92, 110, 189, 190, 191, 194, 198, 200, 203, 207, 208, 209, 211, 212, 213, 233, 235, 236, 248, 249, 265, 267, 269, 274, 277, 278, 285, 286, 288, 292, 294, 297, 300, 302, 306, 313, 315, 318, 320, 323, 327, 329, 330, 371, 372, 378, 379, 380, 381, 392, 398, 399, 400, 401, 405, 406, 408, 415, 416, 420, 423, 424, 431, 434, 436, 440, 442, 444, 445, 447, 455, 458, 467, 471, 483, 491, 492, 495, 525, 535

Johannesburg Star 278, 300

Johnson, Samuel 287

Jones, Stanley 23

Joosab, Haji Muhammad Haji, Sheth 98

Jorissen, Justice 104

Journal of the London Vegetarian Society 80

Just, Adolf 203, 208

K

Kaffirs 380, 397, 499, 500, 503

Kali 350

Kallenbach Archive in Haifa, Israel 292

Kallenbach, Hermann 133, 207, 208, 292, 326, 436, 445, 461, 539, 540

Kāma 64, 511

Karamchand 36

Karma 9, 33, 39, 107, 182, 201, 206, 517

Karmayogin 343

Karsandas, elder brother of Gandhi 36, 45, 46, 483

Kashi, wife of Chhaganlal 444

Kasturba, wife of Gandhi 444

Kathiawar 19, 35, 38, 45, 81, 82, 130, 339, 499

Khan, P.R. 208

Kharpade 316

Kheda 204

Kimberley 415, 488

Kingsford, Anna 58, 66, 108, 130

Kitchin, Herbert 293

Koran 38, 86, 107, 287

Kraal 292, 379

Krause, Dr. 100

Krishnavarma, Shyamji 275, 280, 344, 367

Krodha 64

Kṛṣṇa 38, 39, 40, 42, 69, 264, 455, 511

Krugersdorp 415

Kṣatriya 533, 534

Kuhne 184, 198, 203, 208, 235, 438

Kula-devatā, family deity 36

Kutiyana, native village of the Gandhis 35

L

Labour politics 70

Laidlaw, James 170

Lajpat Rai, Lala 18, 316, 400

Lakshmidas, elder brother of Gandhi 36, 49, 50, 54, 75, 77, 80, 81, 196, 197, 198, 267, 268, 483

Lakṣmaṇa 198

Lalitavistara, an account of Buddha's life 66

Lapierre, Dominique 24, 536

Laughton, F.A. 148, 149, 151, 165, 207, 393, 418, 468, 489

Lavator 71

Law Society of Natal 118

Lawyers 311, 353

Lazarus, D.M. 445

Leavitt, Keith 13

Lely, Frederic 56

Lelyveld, Joseph 28, 29, 30, 111, 139, 250, 310, 434, 450, 452, 464, 472, 539

Leonard, J.W. 103

Lev, Shimon 208, 292, 314, 408, 424, 459, 461, 462, 496, 539

Lingaṁ 10

Linlithgow, Lord 363

Literary and Debating Society 327

Livingstone, John 103, 104

Loane, Mark, Dr. xi

Lobha 64

Lomu 85

London 154, 162, 179, 196, 207, 241, 270, 280, 315, 320, 328, 334, 341, 346, 357, 369, 395, 406, 433, 488, 505, 517

London India Society 369

London Vegetarian Society 59

Love of the British 139

M

MacDonald, Ramsay 469

Machinery evil 361

Macintyre, William J. 265

Madras 143, 250, 332, 339, 342, 371, 392, 393, 405, 469, 496, 521, 535, 537, 538, 539

Madrasis 98

Mahābhārata 10, 38, 69, 209, 261, 360, 508

Mahānārāyaṇa Upaniṣad 508

Maharajas 177, 392

Mahatma iii, x, xi, 1, 6, 14, 19, 23, 24, 26, 28, 29, 30, 33, 34, 35, 36, 44, 65, 78, 83, 124, 182, 193, 208, 209, 250, 260, 276, 280, 289, 291, 292, 294, 310, 342, 343, 366, 419, 461, 468, 499, 501, 502, 503, 512, 519, 522, 525, 526, 533, 535, 536, 537, 538, 539, 540, 541

Mahomet (Muhammad) 131

Maine, Sir H. S. 114

Maitland, Edward 108, 109

Malabari, Behrami M. 58, 539

Malaviya, Madan Mohan 177, 370, 371

Manchester 361

Mandela, Nelson 499, 504

Manilal, son of Gandhi 82, 183, 184, 262, 317, 327, 336, 368, 371, 372, 378, 402, 424, 436, 437, 438, 447, 478, 486, 523, 536

Maṇiratnamālā 109

Manning, Cardinal 69

Manning, Elizabeth 70

Mann, Sergeant W. 453

Mantra, hymn 38, 477

Manusmṛti 42, 258, 326

Marco Polo 509

Maritzburg 444

Marx, Karl 31, 70

Matthew 15, 135, 196

Mauritius 174, 437

Mazmudar, Tryambakrai 52

Mazzini 363

Mehtab, Sheikh 45, 132, 145, 326, 393, 448, 477, 482

Mehta, Mansukhlal, R. 539

Mehta, Sir Pherozeshah 141, 174, 186, 451, 470

Memons 87

Merriman, J.X. 415, 496

Meyer, F.B., Rev. 339

Milner, Alfred, Lord 240, 242, 518

Mir Alam, a Pathan, attacked Gandhi 289

Modh Banias 79

Modi, Narendra 20

Moha 64, 533

Mohamed, Dawad 449

Mohan, Gandhi's first name 37, 38, 39, 43, 44, 50, 77, 478

Mokṣa ix, 13, 262, 263, 533

Molteno, Betty, Miss 477, 478

Mombasa 85

Monia, childhood nickname of Gandhi 37, 41

Morley, John 276

Morton, Eleanor 23, 539

Motan, Habib 243

Mother Mary 25

Mountain View 292, 379, 417, 424, 434, 444

Mount Edgecomb 464

Mozambique 86, 369

Muhammad Tyeb Haji Khan 89, 98

Müller, Max 114

Mumukṣu Prakaraṇa of Yogavāśiṣṭha 109

Muslim League 31, 339

Muslims 15, 19, 27, 31, 35, 43, 44, 45, 69, 87, 89, 98, 112, 136, 212, 279, 280, 307, 314, 324, 326, 341, 342, 350, 351, 352, 353, 364, 378, 379, 385, 390, 393, 415, 449, 483, 484, 489, 491, 497, 514, 519

Mysore 113

N

Naidoo, Mrs. P.K. 450, 451

Naidoo, N. Gopal 328

Naidoo, Thambi 288, 290, 304, 305, 323, 326, 372, 378, 434, 444, 449, 450, 451, 454, 455, 482, 491, 492, 495, 521

Nanda, B.R. 539

Nanji, Dr. 318

Naoroji, Dadabhai 53, 70, 71, 114, 115, 154, 241, 274, 276, 341, 348, 363, 421, 515

Narmad 47

Narmadashankar 131

Natal vii, ix, 86, 87, 88, 108, 110, 114, 115, 116, 117, 118, 119, 120, 121, 122, 124, 125, 126, 127, 128, 132, 134, 135, 136, 138, 140, 145, 146, 147, 148, 150, 151, 152, 153, 154, 155, 163, 172, 183, 185, 187, 188, 189, 231, 247, 248, 250, 279, 281, 284, 286, 287, 302, 306, 311, 312, 313, 314, 315, 324, 371, 372, 373, 374, 375, 376, 392, 393, 395, 398, 406, 411, 412, 413, 417, 419, 426, 430, 431, 434, 442, 443, 444, 445, 446, 448, 449, 451, 452, 453, 455, 457, 458, 459, 460, 462, 463, 464, 465, 467, 468, 470, 472, 473, 477, 479, 490, 501, 503, 515, 517, 519, 520, 523, 538

Natal Government Railway 126

Natal Mercury 87, 88, 108, 127, 135, 136, 140, 151, 287, 314, 315, 445, 452, 477

Natal Witness 118, 119, 153, 445

Natesan, G.A. 339, 342, 371, 405, 468, 469, 535, 537, 538, 539

Nature cure 21

Nawab of Junagarh 35

Nazar, Mansukhlal 199

Nehru, Motilal 339

Newcastle 417, 443, 445, 449, 450, 451, 452, 453, 454, 460, 493

New Testament 66, 338, 424

Nichol, Dr. 55

Nivedita, Sister 179

Niyoga 10, 533

Nizam 371, 469

Nordau, Max 17, 363

Notting Hill 65, 70

O

O'Connor, Daniel 476, 539

Ohlange Industrial School 418

Old Bailey 331

Oldfield, Josiah 59, 62, 68, 108, 207, 275, 293, 539

Old Testament 66

Orange Free State 88, 99, 110, 163, 396, 416, 430, 431, 442

Original sin 178

P

Padshah, Pestonji 142

Palanpur 182

Palestine 424

Pall Mall Gazette 55

Palmford 457

Pancīkaraṇa 109

Paṇḍā, priest 181

Pankhurst, Emmaline, Mrs 335

Parāśara 260

Parekh, Devchand 185

Paris 59, 67, 179

Parsi coats and trousers 144

Parsi Rustomji 136, 162, 313, 325, 326, 372, 413, 448, 490, 521

Parsis 43, 45, 79, 87, 89, 98, 192, 212, 323, 341, 351, 364, 378, 390, 415, 491, 514

Parsi saree 144

Parsi style 144

Partition of Bengal 200

Pārvatī 25, 511

Passive Resistance Association 279

Passive Resistance Relief Fund 371

Passive Resistance, soul force 278, 279, 287, 327, 371, 372, 392, 406, 440, 451, 492

Patañjali Yoga Darśana 326

Patel, S.K. 455

Pathans 289, 290, 294, 296, 304, 324, 519

Pearson, W.W. 476

Pembroke 476

Persians 87, 344

Pethick-Lawrence, H.N., Lord 419, 540

Petit, Sir Jehangir 341

Phillips, Charles 322, 373

Phoenix viii, x, 12, 210, 231, 232, 233, 236, 245, 246, 249, 252, 267, 286, 293, 314, 317, 318, 319, 323, 325, 369, 371, 379, 393, 400, 406, 407, 412, 413, 423, 424, 434, 436, 437, 444, 446, 451, 463, 464, 468, 478, 482, 484, 485, 486, 490, 500, 501, 517, 519

Pietermaritzburg 89, 90, 91, 451, 467, 472

Pillay, C.M. 275

Pillay, Mrs. T. 450

Pincutt, Frederick 71

Plague viii, 138, 212

Plato 287, 363, 524

Plymouth Brothers 137

Polak, Henry, S.L. ix, 207, 208, 213, 275, 287, 311, 314, 325, 328, 329, 331, 337, 341, 347, 371, 398, 432, 445, 477

Polak, Millie 235, 267, 293, 429, 437, 450, 520

Pollock, David 283, 284, 325, 398

Poll tax of £3 100, 128

Porbandar 35, 36, 37, 38, 44, 46, 50, 56, 80, 81, 339, 469, 483

Porridge Bowl 58

Praṇāmīs 38, 42

Prāṇa Nāth 38

Pranjivan Mehta, Dr. 53, 179, 294, 331, 339, 342, 345, 347, 369, 400, 405, 436, 444, 484, 524, 525

Pretoria vii, 89, 92, 93, 94, 98, 99, 101, 102, 103, 110, 115, 131, 165, 166, 187, 207, 270, 278, 285, 288, 325, 327, 418, 419, 474, 478, 479, 495, 501

Prince Ranjitsinhji 53

Privy Council 154

Protector of Immigrants 122, 123, 126, 127, 375

Public Service viii, 134, 162

Punarjanma, rebirth 194

Punjabis 98

Purificatory rite 76

Putli Ba, Gandhi's mother 36, 37, 38, 50

Pyarelal 3, 23, 36, 37, 38, 41, 45, 48, 51, 59, 90, 540

Pythagoras 58

Q

Qaid-e-Azam 19

Quarantine Act 152, 153

Quinn, Leung, Newton 288, 308, 310, 395, 416, 521

R

Radhakrishnan, S. 499

Rahim Karim Khan 162

Raj 143, 366, 470, 476, 518, 539

Rajagopalachari, C. 469, 540

Rajas 177

Rājayoga 194

Rajkot 36, 44, 46, 77, 80, 81, 90, 138, 140, 169, 174, 182, 183

Raliat, sister of Gandhi 37

Rāma-carita-mānasa, Tulasī's *Rāmāyaṇa* 25, 42

Rāma-nāma, repetition of Rāma's name 41

Ramdas, son of Gandhi 159, 234, 368, 444, 478, 523

Ram Sundar Pandit 281, 303

Ranade, Mahadev Govind 141, 166

Rana Khimoji 35

Rana Pratap 400

Rand Daily Mail 243, 271, 394, 431, 462

Rangoon 179, 342, 343, 369

Raychandbhai, or Rajchandra, poet and religious scholar 107, 109, 131, 158, 169, 170, 262, 391, 403, 517

Ray, P. C. 178

Ray, S. 540

Rees, John D. 274

Resolution of Dada Abdulla's case, a lawyer's true function 104

Reuters 138, 145, 150, 452

Ṛgveda 25, 509

Rhodes, Cecil 70

Richards, Samuel 134

Right means 365

Ripon College 175

Ripon, Lord 115, 154

Ritch, L.W. 190, 194, 207, 208, 210, 233, 276, 331, 377, 378, 398, 405, 413, 421, 431, 448, 455, 462, 472, 513, 521, 523

RMS *Saxon* 414

Roberts, John Lutchman 134

Robertson, Sir Benjamin 474, 481, 497

Rolland, Romain 23, 540

Rose-Innes, James, Chief Justice 243

Roux, Edward 406

Royeppen, Joseph 371, 377

Ṛṣis 10, 260

Ṛta 25

Runciman, Mr. 415

Rupali Ba, Queen Regent 35

Ruskin 17, 60, 231, 232, 233, 235, 238, 287, 294, 363, 379, 391, 413, 517, 518

Russian Orthodox Church 293

S

Sadāgraha 261

Ṣaḍdarśana Samuccaya of HaribhadraSūrī 109

Sadhavā 318

Salt, Henry 58, 59, 63, 207

Salt-Tax 71, 349

Samabhāva, equability 194

Samaldas College 49

Sāma Veda 508

Sanātanī 5, 40

Sandars, Thomas Collett 56

Sanitation and hygiene 20, 32, 139, 167, 235, 256, 413, 456

Sankey, John 337

Santa Cruz 185

Śānti Parva 508

Santok, wife of Maganlal 444

Sarid, Isa 461, 540

Sarvodaya, welfare of all 31, 231, 533

Śāstras, scriptures 253, 255

Śāstric, scriptural 139

Sat 509

Satyāgraha ix, 8, 32, 84, 92, 118, 133, 155, 178, 191, 200, 209, 210, 213, 241, 245, 261, 279, 295, 296, 299, 300, 301, 302, 304, 306, 311, 313, 323, 324, 328, 330, 337, 342, 362, 363, 369, 372, 377, 378, 388, 389, 392, 393, 396, 407, 429, 433, 473, 495, 502, 509, 510, 516, 521, 533

Satyāgrahīs 159, 210, 306, 307, 323, 325, 326, 330, 371, 377, 378, 379, 399, 402, 404, 429, 443, 444, 445, 451, 452, 454, 455, 468, 472, 480

Satya-Hariścandra, name of a play 42

Saubhāgyavatī 318

Saunders 143, 144

Savarkar, V.D. 276, 316, 331, 338, 345

Schlesin, Sonja 209, 314, 372, 398, 420, 432, 462, 482, 492, 495, 513, 520, 521

Schreiner, Olive 321, 322, 329, 415, 496

Schreiner, W. P. 321, 414, 431, 496

Schwann, Sir Charles 275

Scott, Walter 287

Searle judgement 428, 430, 432, 445

Segaon 366

Selborne, Lord 274, 283, 321, 325

Seme, Pixley 406, 501

Sen, Keshav Chandra 179

Sermon on the Mount 338

Servants of India Society 341

Shaw, Bernard 66

Sheean, Vincent 23, 540

Shelley 60

Sherard 363

Sheurmann, Max 125

Shirer, William 24, 540

Shivaji 400

Shri Ramakrishna 400

Shukla, Chandrashekhar 400

Shukla, Dalpatram 53

Śikhā, tuft of hair on top of the head 534

Sindhis 98

Singh, Sarva Daman iii, iv, xii, 87, 257, 540

Sir Edwin Arnold 62, 65

Sir William Sleeman 509

Śiva 25, 511

Smuts, J. C. 277, 278, 279, 283, 285, 287, 288, 289, 290, 295, 296, 297, 298, 299, 300, 301, 302, 303, 304, 307, 308, 309, 310, 311, 312, 324, 325, 328, 332, 333, 334, 395, 396, 397, 413, 415, 419, 423, 426, 434, 435, 441, 443, 448, 453, 456, 457, 458, 459, 462, 465, 470, 471, 472, 474, 478, 479, 480, 481, 482, 483, 484, 485, 492, 497, 518, 519

Snell, Edmund 57

Socrates 287

Solomon, William 470, 471

Soma 22, 364

Sorabji Shapurji 302, 326, 411

Sotheby's 292

South Africa vii, viii, ix, xi, 8, 12, 16, 17, 18, 21, 28, 30, 41, 56, 63, 66, 69, 78, 81, 82, 83, 84, 85, 86, 87, 89, 90, 92, 95, 99, 101, 102, 110, 111, 112, 117, 118, 121, 122, 129, 130, 132, 133, 134, 136, 137, 138, 140, 141, 142, 143, 144, 145, 148, 150, 152, 155, 159, 160, 161, 165, 166, 167, 169, 172, 175, 176, 177, 179, 186, 187, 192, 194, 195, 196, 197, 198, 199, 200, 207, 208, 210, 212, 213, 232, 234, 235, 238, 242, 245, 246, 247, 267, 268, 269, 270, 273, 276, 277, 278, 280, 281, 284, 286, 288, 291, 292, 293, 297, 304, 310, 316, 320, 321, 322, 324, 328, 330, 332, 333, 338, 339, 341, 342, 343, 344, 346, 347, 348, 353, 354, 368, 370, 371, 372, 374, 375, 377, 382, 392, 393, 394, 395, 400, 402, 404, 405, 406, 408, 411, 412, 414, 415, 416, 417, 420, 421, 425, 427, 428, 429, 430, 432, 433, 434, 440, 441, 442, 443, 445, 446, 447, 449, 451, 456, 461, 462, 467, 469, 470, 471, 472, 473, 476, 480, 482, 484, 485, 488, 489, 490, 491, 493, 494, 495, 496, 497, 498, 499, 500, 501, 502, 503, 504, 513, 514, 515, 517, 518, 519, 521, 523, 524, 525, 535, 537, 538, 539, 540

South Africa General Mission 95

South African jails 136

South African Native National Congress 406

Southampton 53, 274, 331

Spiritual Striving viii, 194

Spiritual Training 383

Śravaṇa 40, 42

SS *Clyde* 51

S.S. *Courland* 135

SS *Kenilworth Castle* 329

SS *Kildonan Castle* 348

SS *Kinfaus Castle* 497

SS *Naderi* 145, 146

Stanley, Lord Edward Lyulph 274

Star 278, 287, 300, 398, 431, 434

Śūdras 490

Suffragettes 335, 429, 520

Suhāgin 318

Surā 22, 364

Surtis 98

Swadeshi 200, 429

Swami Dayananda Saraswati 400

Swan, Maureen 116, 463

Swaraj ix, 19, 338, 347, 348, 349, 353, 354, 356, 358, 360, 362, 363, 365, 366, 367, 368, 381, 403, 476, 516, 518, 537, 539

Sydney, Olivier 60

Sykes, Marjorie 476, 477, 478, 481, 483, 501, 536

T

Tagore, Rabindranath 6, 179, 343, 359, 469, 476, 477, 480, 482, 483

Tähtinen, Unto 506, 540

Taittirīya Upaniṣad 508

Taj Mahal 416

Tāmasika food 79

Tamil, language 122, 136, 143, 175, 199, 275, 304, 326, 328, 360, 371, 372, 382, 397, 418, 421, 429, 435, 443, 445, 449, 451, 453, 474, 482, 491, 492, 494, 495, 520

Tamilnadu 378

Tamils 87, 136, 137, 156, 304, 313, 323, 326, 372, 444, 495, 514, 519

Tapascharyā, austerities 473

Tata, Ratanji Jamshedji 228, 369, 371, 378, 392, 412

Taylor 363

Tea, cocoa 314

Teakworth 458

Telugus 87, 137

Tendulkar, D. G. 3, 14, 23, 280, 289, 291, 309, 310, 313, 326, 327, 328, 331, 341, 369, 370, 371, 372, 379, 396, 411, 413, 415,

417, 419, 420, 421, 427, 444, 445, 447, 454, 456, 457, 459, 462, 469, 479, 481, 540, 541

Thakore, ruler 44, 469

The Boer War 162, 208, 321

The Central, Vegetarian restaurant 58, 59

The Englishman 58, 80, 93, 143

The Friend, a journal 283

The Great March 210

The Light of Asia 65, 66

The Natal Advertiser 115, 140

Theosophical Lodge 194, 200, 207

Theosophical Society 71, 131

Theosophy 57, 65, 66, 73

The Pioneer 137, 138

The Song Celestial, by Sir Edwin Arnold 65

The Statesman 143, 164, 539

The Times of India 115, 164, 539

The Times of London 322

The Vegetarian, a journal 57, 63, 536

Third class, railway travel 92, 93, 180, 380, 447, 497, 525

Thoreau, Henry David 17, 60, 273, 280, 323, 326, 363

Thornton, Thomas 275

Tidrick, Kathryn 248, 326, 472

Tilak, B. G. 142, 175, 400

Tinker, Hugh 476

Tolstoy Farm ix, 210, 293, 378, 379, 381, 385, 386, 389, 390, 391, 395, 396, 397, 405, 406, 407, 412, 417, 424, 444, 456, 472, 500

Tolstoy, Leo 17, 60, 108, 345, 346, 363, 366, 391, 399, 506

Town Councils 153, 154

Trafalgar Square 53

Tram cars 178

Transvaal ix, 86, 88, 92, 98, 99, 100, 146, 148, 163, 165, 187, 188, 189, 190, 208, 240, 241, 242, 269, 270, 271, 272, 274, 275, 276, 277, 280, 281, 284, 285, 286, 287, 288, 289, 298, 299, 300, 302, 303, 304, 308, 309, 310, 311, 312, 313, 314, 315, 316, 322, 324, 330, 331, 341, 342, 343, 346, 362, 367, 369, 370, 371, 372, 373, 374, 375, 376, 377, 378, 393, 395, 397, 407, 411, 412, 416, 418, 419, 420, 423, 426, 430, 431, 432, 434, 441, 442, 443, 444, 446, 447, 448, 449, 450, 451, 452, 455, 456, 457, 458, 459, 460, 462, 468, 472, 484, 491, 492, 493, 494, 501, 520, 521, 523

Transvaal Critic 208

Transvaal Leader 241, 284, 287, 372, 416, 447, 448, 458, 462, 468, 493

Transvaal Supreme Court 188, 298

Trine, Ralph Waldo 326

Tripathi, Govardhanram 47, 401

Trustee 195

Tudor, Owen 57

Tulasī Dāsa 25, 32

Tulasī's *Rāmāyaṇa* 36, 41, 403

Tulsidas, Gandhi's uncle 44

Turban, Gandhi asked to take his off 86

Tyāga, sacrifice 209

U

Uka, name of a scavenger 43

Uma Dhupelia-Mesthrie 437

Uncovenanted Indians Act 152, 153

Untouchability 5, 6, 32, 43, 107, 175, 176, 202, 490, 514, 526, 527

Untouchables 6, 12, 24, 139, 156, 166, 212, 489, 490, 531

Upadhyaya, J.M. 541

Upaniṣadic 25, 506

Upaniṣads 40, 131, 326, 348

Urdu 136, 382, 448

Uttamchand, Gandhi's grandfather, popularly known as Ota Bapa 35

V

Vahed, Goolam xi, 445, 448, 460, 465, 502, 536

Vaidyas, Ayurvedic doctors 204, 254

Vaishnava temple, Haveli 38

Vaiṣṇava Jana, devotional song 42

Vakil, lawyer 534

Vallabhācārya 36

Valliamma 472, 492, 494

Vālmīki 10, 38

Vankaner 36

Vasudhaiva kuṭumbakaṁ, the whole earth is one family 29

Vedas 107, 201, 359

Vegetarianism 21, 53, 58, 62, 71, 72, 130, 319

Vegetarian Society 57, 59, 62, 63, 71, 78, 80, 170, 207

Verulam 490, 525

Viceroy 128, 143, 148, 242, 274, 324, 332, 363, 465, 468, 470, 474, 488, 493

Victoria Hotel 53

Vijaya-daśamī, Dashehra 338

Vikmatji, Rana 35

Virchand 78

Vivekananda, Swami 179, 194

Vocational training 382

Vogl, William 398

Volksrust 315, 317, 324, 325, 444, 445, 447, 449, 457, 458, 459, 462

Vora, Haridas 267

Vyavaharik, Madanjit 199

W

Wacha, Dinshaw 141

Walker, Benjamin 509

Walk-outs, from plantations and sugar refineries 463

Wedderburn, Sir William 348, 433

Wellington 106

Went to jail, January 10, 1908 286

West, Albert 207, 208, 213, 314, 317, 325, 412, 468, 476

Westminster Palace Hotel, London 331

White, Frederick 57

White Leaguers 240

Whitman 60

Wiener, Leo 261

Williams, Howard 58

Williams, Joshua 56

Wragg, Sir Walter 125

Wrangham, Richard 21

Wylie, Lt. Col. 471

Wyllie, Sir Curzon 331

Y

Yeravda jail 136, 326

Yogasūtras of Patañjali 194

Yoni 10

Z

Zanzibar 85, 369

Zionists 424

Zoroastrians 44

Zulu Rebellion ix, 248

Author

PROFESSOR SARVA DAMAN SINGH, B.A.(HONS.), M.A., PH.D. (UNIVERSITY OF LONDON), PH.D. (UNIVERSITY OF QUEENSLAND, AUSTRALIA), F.R.A.S., was born at Angai, in District Mathura of Uttar Pradesh, India; and migrated to Australia in 1974. He won many awards and five gold medals during the course of a distinguished educational career at the universities of Lucknow and London. He has taught at the University of Lucknow; National Academy of Administration, Government of India, Mussoorie; Vikram University, Ujjain; and the University of Queensland, Australia; and held chairs of Indian History, Culture and Archaeology. He is at present Director of the Institute of Asian Studies, Brisbane.

He has travelled widely, and lectured at universities and institutions in India, Sri Lanka, U.K., France, Germany, the U.S.A., South Korea, Fiji, New Zealand and Australia.

Apart from his contributions to numerous books, his publications include *Ancient Indian Warfare with Special Reference to the Vedic Period*, E.J. Brill, Leiden, with later editions brought out by Motilal Banarasidas, Delhi; *The Archaeology of the Lucknow Region*, Paritosh Prakashan, Lucknow; *Polyandry in Ancient India*, Vikas, and Motilal Banarasidas, Delhi; *Culture through the Ages*, (B.N. Puri Felicitation Volume), Agam, Delhi; *The Art of Pir Tareen-Evocation of Beauty in Life and Nature*, published by the Institute of Asian Studies, Brisbane; and *Indians Abroad*, Hope India Publications and Greenwich Millennium Press Ltd, Gurgaon and London.

As Honorary Consul of India in Queensland from 2003 till 2011, he addressed numerous forums, always stressing the indivisibility of humanity, and its cultural diversity as a natural expression of its floriferous creativity.

www.ingramcontent.com/pod-product-compliance
Lightning Source LLC
Chambersburg PA
CBHW031152020526
44117CB00042B/238